Up and Running
with
Autodesk Navisworks 2016

Deepak Maini
Head of Technical, Manufacturing Solutions
Cadgroup Australia

Copy Editor
Pragya Katariya, Owner and Lead Editor, Ocean Blue Communications
www.oceanbluecommunications.com

Technical Editor
Dhanjeet Sah, BIM Consultant, Cadgroup Australia Pty Ltd
Bruce Trevena, Plant Solutions Engineer, Cadgroup Australia Pty Ltd
Drishti Maini, Founder and Owner, DDM Designs, Sydney Australia

Cover Designer
Dushyant Chauhan, DDM Designs Australia

Cover Illustration of the Building Model
Dushyant Chauhan, DDM Designs Australia.

Autodesk and Autodesk Navisworks are registered trademarks or trademarks of Autodesk, Inc., and/or its subsidiaries and/or affiliates in the USA and/or other countries.

Autodesk screen shots reprinted with the permission of Autodesk, Inc.

ISBN-13: 978-1511679091
ISBN-10: 1511679093

Dedication

To all engineers and designers who create innovative products and make this world a better place to live

To my mum and dad who have always supported me unconditionally in my endeavors

To my wife Drishti and my son Vansh whose motivation, support, and inspiration made this textbook possible

Foreword

Autodesk Navisworks allows users to collaborate various aspects of the design and provides a detailed view of how the project will look on completion even before a single piece of equipment is installed on the actual site.

This textbook covers Autodesk Navisworks in detail and empowers users to reap full benefits of the software. The users can create the project in a virtual environment to understand and resolve any problems that may arise before executing the project in the realtime environment.

Scott Gibbs
Senior Subsea Designer, Technip Oceania Pty Ltd

Acknowledgments

I would like to thank the following people for allowing me to use their models in this textbook:

Bruce Trevena
Plant Solutions Engineer, Cadgroup Australia Pty Ltd

Scott Gibbs
Senior Subsea Designer, Technip Oceania Pty Ltd

Samuel Macalister
Samuel Macalister, Senior Technical Sales Specialist - BIM, Autodesk Inc.

Ryan McKinley
Senior Civil Drafter, Engineering and Operations, Tenix

Ankur Mathur
Founder & CEO, SANRACHNA: *BIM & Virtual Construction Consultants*

I would also like to thank the following people for helping me at various stages of this project:

John Ayre, Managing Director, Cadgroup Australia
Matthias Kunz, kubit GmbH
David Nesbit, Discipline Lead – Design, Technip Oceania Pty Ltd
Richard Parker, Sr. Product Manager, Autodesk Navisworks, Autodesk, Inc.
Joan E. Allen, Sr. Product Manager, Autodesk BIM 360™, Autodesk, Inc.
Anthony Governanti, Sales and Technical Enablement, Construction, Autodesk Inc.
Ryan McMahon, Sr. Product Manager, Factory Design Suite, Autodesk, Inc.
Mitko Vidanovski, Project Manager - Reality Solutions Group
Tomislav Golubovic, Senior Technical Sales Specialist – Plant & Infrastructure, Autodesk
Ian Matthew, Technical Marketing Manager - Natural Resources, Autodesk Inc.

About the Author

Deepak Maini (Sydney, Australia) is a qualified Mechanical Engineer with more than 17 years of experience in working with various CAD software. He has been teaching various CAD software for more than 16 years. Deepak's experience of Autodesk Navisworks goes back to the days when this software was still Navisworks JetStream. More details about him can be found on his website **http://www.deepakmaini.com**

Deepak is also a Guest Lecturer at the University of Technology Sydney (UTS) and the University of New South Wales (UNSW), two of the leading universities in Australia. In addition, he is one of the lead presenters at various events showcasing the latest Autodesk technology all around Australia and is regularly invited to present Autodesk Navisworks and Autodesk BIM 360 Glue at various User Group events around the country.

Deepak is a regular speaker at Autodesk University in Las Vegas and was awarded the "Top Rated" speaker ranking at Autodesk University 2014.

Deepak is currently working as the Head of Technical, Manufacturing Solutions with Cadgroup Australia, the first Platinum Autodesk Partner in the southern hemisphere.

Deepak's Contact Details

Email: deepak@deepakmaini.com
Website: http://www.deepakmaini.com

Accessing Tutorial Files

The author has provided all the files required to complete the tutorials in this textbook. To download these files:

1. Visit http://www.deepakmaini.com/Navisworks/Navisworks.htm

2. Click on **Up and Running with Autodesk Navisworks 2016**.

3. On the top right of the page, click on **ACCESSING TOC/TUTORIAL FILES**.

4. Click on the **Tutorial Files** link.

Free Teaching Resources for Faculty

The author has provided the following free teaching resources for the faculty:

1. Video of every tutorial in the textbook.
2. PowerPoint Slides of all chapters in the textbook.
3. Teacher's Guide with answers to the end of chapter **Class Test Questions**.
4. Help in designing the course curriculum.

To access these resources, please contact the author at **deepak@deepakmaini.com**.

Accessing Videos of the Tutorials in this Textbook

The author provides complimentary access to the videos of all tutorials in this textbook. To access these videos, please email your proof of purchase to the author at the following email address:

      deepak@deepakmaini.com.

Preface

Welcome to the first edition of Up and Running with Autodesk Navisworks 2016.

This textbook consists of ten chapters for the plant and Building Information Modeling (BIM) industry, a project-based chapter for the Autodesk Factory Design Suite users, and a project-based chapter on Autodesk BIM360 Glue integration with Autodesk Navisworks.

The first ten chapters start with the detailed description of the Autodesk Navisworks tools and concepts. These are then followed by the detailed plant and BIM tutorials. Every section of the tutorials starts with a brief description of what you will be doing in that section. This will help you to understand why and not just how you have to do certain things.

Real-world plant and BIM models have been carefully selected to discuss the tools and concepts in the tutorials of every chapter. You will be able to find various similarities between the models used in this textbook and your current projects. This will allow you to apply the concepts learned in this textbook to your day-to-day work.

*I have also added the "**What I Do**" sections in most chapters. In these sections, I have discussed the approach I take while working with Autodesk Navisworks. You will also find a number of notes and tips that discuss additional utilities of various concepts.*

*The chapter for the **Autodesk Factory Design Suite** users is written with project-based approach. This approach will allow you to learn Autodesk Navisworks as it is used in the Autodesk Factory Design Suite workflow.*

*The chapter on the **BIM Data Collaboration with Autodesk BIM 360 Glue** discusses the Autodesk BIM 360 Glue integration with Autodesk Navisworks. This chapter shows you how to use the Autodesk BIM 360 Glue desktop application and iPad app to access and review BIM data.*

I hope you find learning the software using this textbook an enriching experience and are able to apply the concepts in real life situations.

If you have any feedback about this textbook, please feel free to write to me at the following email address:

deepak@deepakmaini.com

TABLE OF CONTENTS

Chapter 1 - Introduction to Autodesk Navisworks

Chapter 2 - Selecting and Manipulating Objects in the Scene

Chapter 3 - Viewpoints, Animations, and Measurements

Chapter 4 - Reviewing and Sectioning the Design

Chapter 5 - Autodesk Navisworks Productivity Tools

Chapter 6 - Working with the Autodesk Rendering Module

Chapter 7 - Working with the Animator and Scripter Modules

Chapter 8 - Creating Construction Simulations Using the TimeLiner Module

Chapter 9 - Introduction to the Quantification Module

Chapter 10 - Working with the Clash Detective Module

Chapter 11 - Autodesk Navisworks for Autodesk Factory Design Suite

Chapter 12 - BIM Data Collaboration with Autodesk BIM 360 Glue

Chapter 1 – Introduction to Autodesk Navisworks

The objectives of this chapter are to:

√   *Introduce you to Autodesk Navisworks.*
√   *Familiarize you with Autodesk Navisworks interface.*
√   *Explain various Autodesk Navisworks file types.*
√   *Teach you various means of collaborating designs in Autodesk Navisworks.*
√   *Teach you to publish a password-protected file that can be opened in the free Autodesk Navisworks viewer.*
√   *Teach you various navigation tools available in Autodesk Navisworks.*

AUTODESK NAVISWORKS

Autodesk Navisworks is a 3D design collaboration tool that lets you import models from various design platforms to create an aggregated design for visualization and review. The resulting design is a virtual model in which you can navigate in realtime and create walkthroughs that allow better understanding of the design intent. This virtual model can be shared with various teams to find and fix problems, thus allowing for a more effective management and coordination of the project.

Figure 1 shows a virtual building created in Autodesk Navisworks. This figure also shows the **Selection Tree** showing various components of this building.

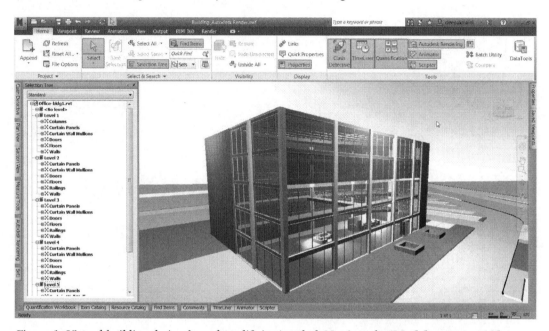

*Figure 1 Virtual building design brought to life in Autodesk Navisworks (**Model courtesy Ankur Mathur, Founder and CEO, SANRACHNA:BIM and Virtual Construction Consultants**)*

Figure 2 shows a virtual plant model aggregated in Autodesk Navisworks. The **Selection Tree** shows various components of this plant model.

AUTODESK NAVISWORKS PRODUCTS

Autodesk Navisworks has been bundled in various Autodesk Suites in recent years. But in terms of product offerings, Autodesk Navisworks offers the following three flavors:

Autodesk Navisworks Simulate

This is the base level of the two Autodesk Navisworks products. It includes the following modules:

♦ **Publisher**: *To publish NWD files that can be viewed in a free viewer called Autodesk Navisworks Freedom.*

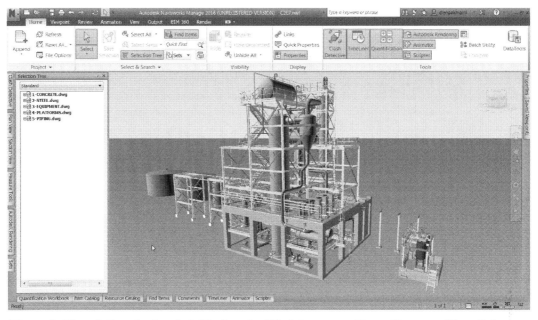

*Figure 2 Virtual plant in Autodesk Navisworks (**Model courtesy Bruce Trevena, Plant Solutions Engineer, Cadgroup Australia Pty Ltd**)*

- **Autodesk Rendering**: *To create high quality photorealistic visualizations of the Autodesk Navisworks scene.*
- **TimeLiner**: *To create simulation of construction schedules.*
- **Animator and Scripter**: *To create movement of objects in the scene.*
- **Quantification**: *To perform quantity takeoff from the Autodesk Navisworks scene. This module was introduced in Release 2014.*

Autodesk Navisworks Manage

This is the top level of the two Autodesk Navisworks products. It includes the following module in addition to all the modules included in Autodesk Navisworks Simulate:

- **Clash Detective**: *To perform and report interferences between different components of the Autodesk Navisworks scene.*

 Note: *All the modules of Autodesk Navisworks will be discussed in detail in the later chapters of this book.*

Autodesk Navisworks Freedom

This is the free viewer that can be used to view the published Autodesk Navisworks model. This tool is generally used by various stakeholders to analyze, interrogate, and communicate the design intent at various stages of the design process. It can be downloaded from the Autodesk Navisworks Web site http://www.autodesk.com/products/navisworks/autodesk-navisworks-freedom.

AUTODESK NAVISWORKS INTERFACE

Figure 3 shows various components of the Autodesk Navisworks interface.

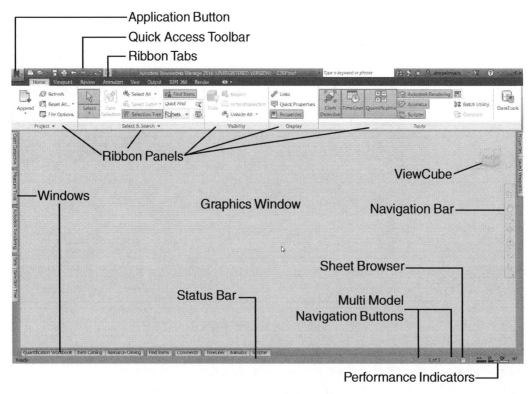

Figure 3 *The Autodesk Navisworks interface*

Autodesk Navisworks Interface Components

The following are the various components of Autodesk Navisworks interface:

Application Button

This button is used to display the application menu, which is divided into two areas, as shown in Figure 4. The area on the left shows standard tools such as **Save**, **Save As** etc. The area on the right shows the recent files that you opened in Autodesk Navisworks. The buttons on the bottom right of this area can be used to change Autodesk Navisworks global options and to close this program.

Quick Access Toolbar

This toolbar has the buttons that you often use, such as **Open**, **New**, **Save**, **Undo**, **Redo** etc. The down arrow (called flyout) on the right of this toolbar has an option to display the toolbar below the ribbons.

Ribbon Tabs

These are a collection of ribbon panels that logically group Autodesk Navisworks tool buttons.

Figure 4 The Application Button

Ribbon Panels
These are logical groups of Autodesk Navisworks tool buttons. Some ribbon panels have a down arrow at the bottom that is used to expand the panel and show additional tool buttons.

Graphics Window
This is the area where the design is displayed and manipulated.

ViewCube
This is a visualization tool used to display the static views of the model from various directions. You can click on one of the faces or the edges of the ViewCube to display the model from that particular direction. You can also click on one of the corners of the ViewCube to display the 3D view of the model from that direction. This visualization tool is discussed in detail later in this chapter.

Navigation Bar
Various drawing display tools available in Autodesk Navisworks are located on this toolbar.

Status Bar
This bar runs through the bottom of the Autodesk Navisworks window. The left side of this bar shows a prompt sequence related to some tools in Autodesk Navisworks. The right side of this bar has performance indicators that are discussed below.

Sheet Browser
This button is used to turn on the **Sheet Browser** palette.

Multi Model Navigation Buttons

If you have loaded multiple models in the **Sheet Browser**, you can use these buttons to switch between them.

Performance Indicators

The right side of the status bar hosts performance indicators, which are discussed next.

Pencil Indicator Bar

Generally, when you are zooming, panning or walking in a large design, depending on your machine performance, the entre view is not loaded for every frame. This bar shows how much of the view is currently loaded. In other words, it indicates that there are objects dropped from the current display.

Disk Indicator Bar

This is the second indicator bar and is used to show how much of the current model is loaded from the disc into the memory.

Web Server Indicator Bar

This indictor bar is used only when you are opening a model from a web server, a URL, or BIM 360 Glue. It indicates how much of the model is downloaded from the web into the memory. If the model is not opened from a web server, this indicator bar will remain white.

Memory Indicator

This indictor shows how much memory, in Megabytes, is being currently used by Autodesk Navisworks.

Autodesk Navisworks Windows

For the ease of performing various tasks, Autodesk Navisworks provides a number of windows that can be turned on or off, depending on their requirements. The following are some important windows that you will need while working with Autodesk Navisworks.

Selection Tree

The **Selection Tree** can be turned on or off using its button on the **Select & Search** panel of the **Home** ribbon tab. This tree is used to select the components in the current design. There are three displays of this tree; **Standard**, **Compact**, and **Properties**.

In the **Standard** display, which is also the default display, this tree shows the hierarchical structure of the way the model was created in the native CAD program. For example, if the model was created in a program like AutoCAD Plant 3D, it will show the DWG files, the layers, and the components on that particular layer, as shown in Figure 5. Similarly, if the model was created in Autodesk Revit, it will show various levels of the building and the components of those levels, as shown in Figure 6.

In the **Compact** display, this tree by default shows only the layer names under the file. This can be customized using Autodesk Navisworks global options, which will be discussed later in this chapter.

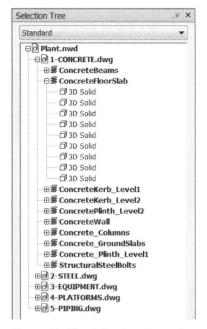

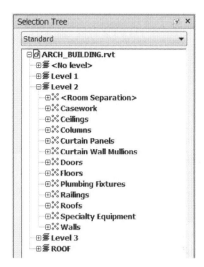

Figure 5 *The **Selection Tree** of an AutoCAD Plant 3D model*

Figure 6 *The **Selection Tree** of an Autodesk Revit model*

In the **Properties** display, this tree shows various properties of the components in your design.

Properties Window

The **Properties** window shows the properties associated with the selected object. These properties are categorized under various tabs. By default, this window appears blank. It will be populated only when you make a selection from the **Selection Tree** or from the graphics window. The properties listed in this window are the Autodesk Navisworks item properties and also the properties that are carried over from the native CAD program.

Saved Viewpoints Window

To turn this window on, click on the **View** ribbon tab and then expand the **Windows** flyout from the **Workspace** ribbon panel. This window shows the viewpoints that are imported from the native CAD program and the ones that are created inside Autodesk Navisworks. This window also shows the animations that are available in the model, see Figure 7.

 Note: The rest of the windows will be discussed in later chapters of this textbook.

AUTODESK NAVISWORKS WORKSPACES

Turning various windows on and off on regular basis is a tedious job. As a result, Autodesk Navisworks has a really smart concept of workspaces, which controls the visibility and location of various windows on the screen. You can turn on the visibility of the windows that you often use

Figure 7 *The* **Saved Viewpoints** *window showing viewpoints and animations*

and then save the screen display as a workspace. As a result, if any window is turned off by mistake, you can reload your workspace to restore the visibility and location of the windows. By default, Autodesk Navisworks installation comes with four workspaces. The buttons to load these workspaces or to create a new one are available on the **View** ribbon tab under the **Workspace** ribbon panel, as shown in Figure 8.

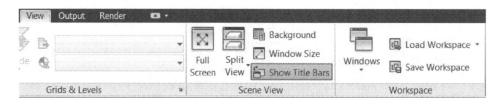

Figure 8 *The* **Workspace** *ribbon panel on the* **View** *ribbon tab*

To load the default workspaces, click on the **Load Workspace** flyout. The four default workspaces are discussed next.

Safe Mode

This workspace loads the **Selection Tree** and **Plan View** windows docked on the left of the screen, the **Comments** window docked at the bottom of the screen, and the **Tilt Bar**, **Properties**, and **Saved Viewpoints** windows docked on the right of the screen.

Navisworks Minimal

This is the default workspace and has no window loaded on the screen.

Navisworks Standard

This workspace loads windows such as the **Clash Detective**, **Selection Tree**, **Sets**, **Find Items**, **Comments**, **Properties** etc. docked in the auto-hide mode around the graphics window.

Navisworks Extended

This workspace is similar to the **Safe Mode** workspace but has additional windows such as **Clash Detective**, **Sets**, and **Measure Tool** windows docked to the left in the auto-hide mode. In the auto-hide mode, the window slides out when you move the cursor over it. In addition, this workspace also has more windows, such as **Find Items**, **Comments**, **TimeLiner**, **Animator**, **Scripter**, and so on docked at the bottom of the screen in the auto-hide mode. Figure 9 shows the Autodesk Navisworks screen in this workspace.

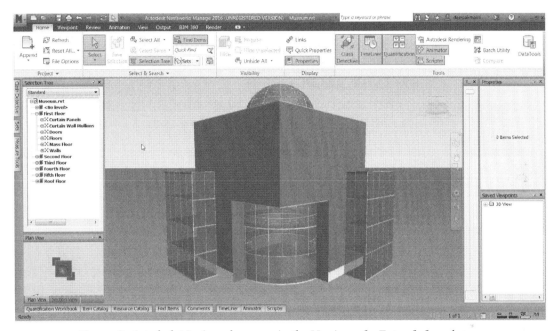

*Figure 9 Autodesk Navisworks screen in the **Navisworks Extended** workspace*

 Tip: *To switch a window to auto-hide mode, click on the push-pin icon on the top right of that particular window.*

Creating a User-Defined Workspace

To create your own workspace, simply turn on the visibility of the windows that you need from the **Home** ribbon tab or from the **View** ribbon tab > **Workspace** ribbon panel > **Windows** flyout. Alternatively, you can activate the **Navisworks Extended** workspace and then turn off the windows you do not need. Once the Autodesk Navisworks interface looks like what you need, click the **View** ribbon tab > **Workspace** ribbon panel > **Save Workspace** button; the **Save Workspace** dialog box will be displayed. By default, the workspace is saved inside your roaming profile folder. Specify the workspace name and then click on the **Save** button; the workspace will be saved as a .XML file. This workspace will now be listed in the **Load Workspace** flyout.

Tip: *If you want multiple people in your team to use the same workspace, save the custom workspace on a network drive and have all the users load the workspace from there.*

NATIVE FILE SUPPORT

To allow seamless working on a project, Autodesk Navisworks allows you to directly work with a large number of popular 3D CAD files. This allows you to work with live models and if the design changes in the native CAD program, you simply need to refresh the Autodesk Navisworks model by clicking the **Refresh** button on the **Quick Access Toolbar**. The following table shows the file formats that can be directly opened in Autodesk Navisworks.

CAD/Laser Files	File Format	Supported Versions
3DS Max	.3ds, .prj	Releases 8 to 2016
ASCII Laser File	.asc, .txt	N/A
AutoCAD	.dwg, .dxf	Up to Release 2016
Autodesk Inventor	.ipt, .iam, .ipj	Up to Release 2016
Autodesk Revit	.rvt, .rfa, .rte	Release 2011 to 2016
Catia	.model, .session, .exp, .dlv3 .CATPart .CATProduct, .cgr	v4, v5
CIS/2	.stp	Structural Frame Schema
DWF	.dwf, .dwfx	All versions
Faro	.fls, .fws, .iQscan, .iQmod, .iQwsp	FARO SDK 4.8
FBX	.fbx	FBX SDK 2011.3.1
IFC	.IFC	IFC2X PLATFORM, IFC2X FINAL, IFC2X2 FINAL, IFC2X3
IGES	.igs, .iges	All versions
Informatix MAN	.man, .cv7	v10
JT Open	.jt	Up to 10.0.
Leica	.pts, .ptx	N/A
Microstation	.dgn	v8 - v8.5, XM (8.9)
NX	.prt	Version 3 – 8.0
PDS Design Review	.dri	Legacy file format. Support up to 2007.
Parasolids	.x_b	Up to schema 16

CAD/Laser Files	File Format	Supported Versions
Pro/ENGINEER	.prt, .asm, .g, .neu	Up to Wildfire 5.0 and Creo 3.0
Riegl	.3dd	Version 3.5 or high
RVM	.rvm	Up to 12.0 SP5
SketchUp	.skp	Up to 2014
Solidworks	.prt, .sldprt, .sldasm	2003-2015
STEP	.stp, .step	AP214, AP203E2
STL	.stl	Binary only
VRML	.wrl, .wrz	VRML1, VRML2
Z+F	.zfc, .zfs	SDK version 2.2.1.0

Autodesk Navisworks NWC File Export Utility

For programs that do not have the native file support in Autodesk Navisworks, there is an export utility made available to the customers by Autodesk. This utility allows you to install a plug-in that lets you export the native file as a Navisworks Cache file (.NWC) that can be opened or appended in the Autodesk Navisworks scene. You can visit the Autodesk Navisworks web page to download and install this utility.

 Note: Some programs that are installed on AutoCAD as the third party add-ins, such as ProSteel or CADWorx, will need their object enablers installed on the machine that hosts Autodesk Navisworks. Alternatively, these files can be exported from the native programs as a NWC format file, which can be opened in Autodesk Navisworks.

AUTODESK NAVISWORKS FILE FORMATS

Autodesk Navisworks has three native file formats: NWC, NWF, and NWD. These file formats are explained below.

NWC Files

This is the cache file format and is a smart technology inside Autodesk Navisworks that lets you open unchanged designs very quickly. This file is automatically created when you load a native file such as an AutoCAD, Autodesk Revit, Microstation etc. The NWC file is saved with the same name and in the same folder that has the native file. During the next loading process, Autodesk Navisworks compares the NWC file with the native file. If the NWC file is newer, the model is loaded quickly using the cached file. However, if the native file is newer than the NWC file, which shows the model has changed, the NWC file is recreated.

NWF Files

This is the file set format that only has links to the native files through NWC files or Autodesk ReCap files and Autodesk Navisworks related information, such as viewpoints, redline markups, timeliner data, clash test information and so on. When you save your Autodesk Navisworks design for the first time, this is the default file format that is selected in the **Save As** dialog box.

This file does not have any design geometry information, and so it is a very small file. This file is typically used when the current project is ongoing and you expect changes in the native files. If the native file is deleted or moved to a different location, and you open the NWF file, the **Resolve** dialog box will be displayed, as shown in Figure 10, informing you about the missing file. You can point it to a new location or decide to ignore the missing file and load the rest of the model.

*Figure 10 The **Resolve** dialog box informing about the missing native file*

NWD Files

This file format contains the entire design geometry information and the Autodesk Navisworks related information in a single file. It does not have any link to any other native file, and so this file is not updated if there are any changes in the native files. The NWD files are generally created to take a snapshot of the design in time, which can be shared with the people within or outside your organization. The files can be created by using the **Save As** tool or the **Publish** tool. Both these tools are available in the **Application Button**. While publishing the NWD files using the **Publish** tool, you can also specify a password and an expiry date after which the file cannot be opened. This is a good way to safeguard your intellectual property.

COLLABORATING DESIGNS IN AUTODESK NAVISWORKS

When starting the collaboration process from scratch, the first file is opened using the **Open** tool and the remaining files are aggregated using the **Append** tool. Both these tools are discussed below.

Opening Files

> **Quick Access Toolbar > Open**
> **Application Button > Open**

When you invoke the **Open** tool, the **Open** dialog box will be displayed, as shown in Figure 11. You can select the type of file that you want to open using the **Files of type** list, refer to the same figure. Using the **Look in** list or the shortcuts available on the left of this dialog box, browse to the folder where the files are saved. You can double-click on the file to open or select the name of the file and then click on the **Open** button. Figure 12 shows the first file opened in the Autodesk Navisworks scene. This is an AutoCAD Plant 3D file showing the structural steel layout of the plant. The **Selection Tree** shows the DWG file and the layers in that file.

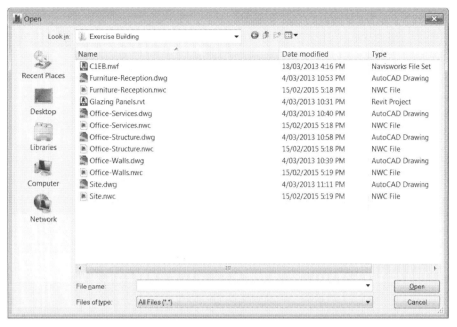

Figure 11 The **Open** dialog box to open the first file

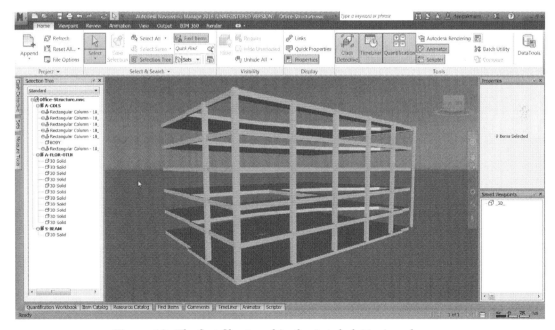

Figure 12 The first file opened in the Autodesk Navisworks scene

 Tip: Autodesk Navisworks does not support previewing files before opening. If you want to preview files, you can use the **Sheet Browser** window discussed later in this chapter.

Note: *The most important thing to remember while aggregating files in Autodesk Navisworks is that the files will be placed at the coordinate location on which they were modeled in the native program. Because this is generally not the case, there is a special exercise in this chapter that shows you how to change the location of the inserted files.*

Opening from Web Server

Application Button > Open Flyout > Open URL

The **Open URL** tool lets you open a file from a web server or a URL location. When you invoke this tool, the **Open URL** dialog box will be displayed, as shown in Figure 13. Enter the location of the file in this dialog box. The drop-down list also shows you some recent locations that you used to open the files.

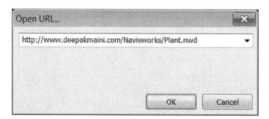

Figure 13 *Opening files from a web server*

While opening the file using this method, the **Web Server Indicator Bar** on the lower right of the screen will show you the progress of the file load.

 Note: *When you open a file from the web server and save it as an NWF file, Autodesk Navisworks will look for the same web server location when you open this file the next time. Therefore, you need to be connected to the Internet to be able to open the file. If not, the **Resolve** dialog box will be displayed informing you about this missing file.*

Appending Files

Quick Access Toolbar > Open Flyout > Append Home Ribbon Tab > Project Ribbon Panel > Append

Once the first file is opened, the remaining files can be brought into the design using the **Append** tool. When you invoke this tool, the **Append** dialog box will be displayed, which looks very similar to the **Open** dialog box shown earlier. You can select one or multiple files to append at the same time. Figure 14 shows additional files appended to the first file.

You will notice that once you start appending files in your Autodesk Navisworks scene, the title bar at the top of the window will show **Untitled**, suggesting that this file needs to be saved.

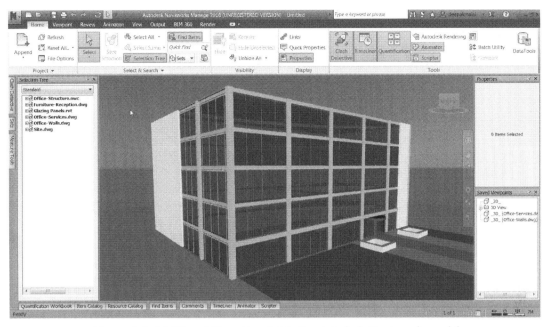

Figure 14 *Additional files appended to the Autodesk Navisworks model*

Merging Files

> **Quick Access Toolbar > Open Flyout > Merge**
> **Home Ribbon Tab > Project Ribbon Panel > Append Flyout > Merge**

Merging is a smart concept in Autodesk Navisworks that lets you import only the Autodesk Navisworks related information from an NWF file into your existing file without copying the model geometry. Consider a case where a project manager sends an NWD file to the following three teams:

Team A: For design review and redline markup
Team B: For creating walkthrough animations and viewpoints
Team C: For performing clash tests

If all these three teams send their NWD file back to the project manager, who then appends these files into the original file, there will be three overlapping copies of the geometry information in the model. To avoid this, after the three teams finish their work, they need to save their files in the NWF format using the **Save As** tool and then send this file back to the project manager. The project manager at his end needs to use the **Merge** tool to load the NWF file from the individual teams. While merging the files from the teams, the **Resolve** dialog box will be displayed, informing the project manager about the missing NWD file. This time, this error can be ignored and all the Autodesk Navisworks related information will be brought to the original NWD file.

SCENE STATISTICS

Home Ribbon Tab > Project Ribbon Panel > Scene Statistic

Sometimes you will notice when you open or append a native file, instead of showing the geometry of that file, Autodesk Navisworks scene only shows proxy objects, such as wireframes of the original design. This is generally caused by the missing object enablers. For example, if you are opening or appending an AutoCAD Plant 3D file in Autodesk Navisworks on a machine that does not have the native AutoCAD Plant 3D installed, you will only see proxy objects. The easiest way to find out which object enabler is missing is using the **Scene Statistics** tool, which is available when you expand the **Project** ribbon panel on the **Home** ribbon tab, as shown in Figure 15.

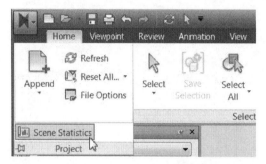

Figure 15 *Invoking the* **Scene Statistics** *tool from the* **Project** *ribbon panel*

When you invoke this tool, the **Scene Statistics** window will be displayed, as shown in Figure 16, listing the files that are affected by the missing object enabler. The application name whose object enabler is missing will also be listed, along with the product description, the company details, and in a lot of cases, even the company Web site. This window will also show the details of any issues with the Autodesk Navisworks scene.

SHEET BROWSER

Status Bar> Sheet Browser
View Ribbon Bar > Workspace Ribbon Panel > Windows Flyout

Autodesk Navisworks does not support multiple files being opened in the same session. As a result, if you want to preview a file before opening it or appending it in the current scene, you will have to open another session of Autodesk Navisworks. Instead of doing this, you can use the

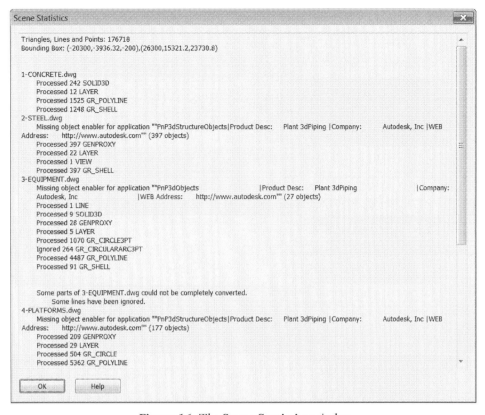

*Figure 16 The **Scene Statistics** window*

Sheet Browser window to open and preview a file before appending in the current scene. Note that to open a file in the **Sheet Browser**, you need to first open a file in the Autodesk Navisworks window. Once the first file is opened, you can click the **Sheet Browser** button on the lower right of the status bar or click the **View** ribbon tab > **Workspace** ribbon panel > **Windows** flyout. Figure 17 shows the **Sheet Browser** window invoked after opening the **Office-Structure.dwg** file. This window can display the content in the list view or thumbnail view, which can be set using the buttons available close to the top right of this window.

To preview a model before appending or merging it in the current Autodesk Navisworks scene, click the **Import Sheets & Models** button from the top right corner of the **Sheet Browser** window; the **Insert From File** dialog box will be displayed. Select the desired file or multiple files to open in the **Sheet Browser**. While opening the files, if they are not prepared for use in Autodesk Navisworks, a blue and red arrow symbol will be displayed on the files. Select all the files that are not prepared, right-click to display a shortcut menu and select **Prepare All Sheets/Models**.

Once the files are prepared, you can double-click on them to open them in the Autodesk Navisworks window. Note that in this case, the original file will not be closed. You can at any time double-click on the name of the original file to change the scene to that file. If you want to append or merge the file from the **Sheet Browser** to the original scene, double-click on the original file to make that as

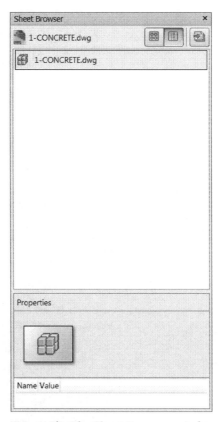

Figure 17 *The Sheet Browser window*

the current scene. Now, right-click on the files that you opened in the **Sheet Browser** and select **Append to Current Model/Merge to Current Model**; the **Selection Tree** will show you all the files.

 *Note: After you have appended or merged the files, it is recommended to right-click on those files in the **Sheet Browser** and delete them. The files will only be removed from the **Sheet Browser** window and not from the Autodesk Navisworks scene where they are appended.*

SAVING YOUR WORK

It is important to regularly save your work to avoid any unexpected loss of data because of machine problems. Autodesk Navisworks provides you three tools for manually saving your work as well as an option to auto-save the files. All these options are discussed next.

Save Tool

> **Quick Access Toolbar > Save**
> **Application Button > Save**

This tool is used to save the Autodesk Navisworks file for the first time and also for all the subsequent saves on the same file. When you invoke this tool for the first time, the **Save As** dialog box will be displayed, as shown in Figure 18. This dialog box lets you specify the name and the location of the file you are saving.

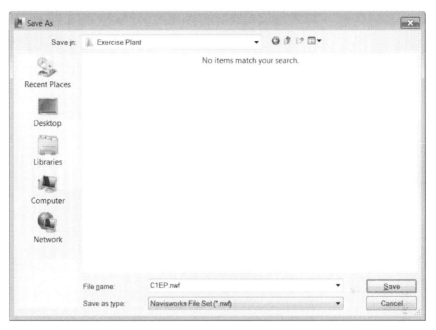

*Figure 18 The **Save As** dialog box*

By default, the file type is set as **Navisworks File Set (*.nwf)**. As mentioned earlier, this is the format that you use when the work is in progress so that the link is maintained with the native files. You can also change the file type to a previous version NWF or NWD file.

Save As Tool

> **Application Button > Save As**

This tool is used to save a copy of the current file with some other name but at a different location or to save the current file in different format. This tool can also be used to save the files in an older version file. When you invoke this tool, the **Save As** dialog box will be displayed, similar to the one shown in Figure 18. You can specify the name, the file type, and the location in this dialog box to create a copy of the original file.

Note: Using the **Save** or **Save As** tool to save an NWD file is not recommended. Instead, you should use the **Publish** tool, which provides you the option of password protecting your file and also specifying an expiry date for the file. This tool is discussed in the following section.

Publish Tool

> **Application Button > Publish**
> **Output Ribbon Tab > Publish Ribbon Panel > NWD**

This tool is specifically designed to publish the NWD files. As mentioned earlier, this file format contains the entire design geometry information, along with the Autodesk Navisworks related information, in a single file. It has no link to the native CAD files. When you invoke this tool, the **Publish** dialog box will be displayed, as shown in Figure 19. The options in this dialog box are discussed next.

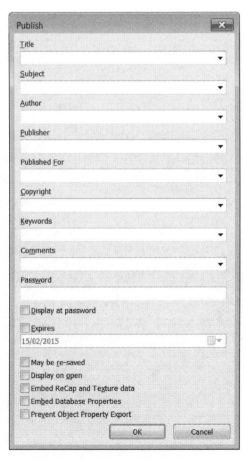

Figure 19 The **Publish** dialog box

Title
This text box is used to specify the title of the published NWD file.

Subject
This text box is used to specify the subject of the published NWD file.

Author
The author of the published NWD file is specified in this text box. You can specify your name here.

Publisher
This text box is used to specify the publisher of the NWD file. You can specify your company name here.

Published For
The client for whom you are publishing the NWD file is entered in this text box.

Copyright
This text box is used to specify who has the copyright for the current design.

Keywords
If you want to search the published NWD file based on some keywords, enter them in this text box.

Comments
Any additional comments about the published NWD file are entered in this text box.

Password
If you want to password protect the published NWD file, enter the password here. This is a really smart way of keeping your intellectual property safe. If a password is specified here, when you click **OK** in this dialog box, you will be prompted to confirm the password.

Display at password
If this tick box is selected, the **Publish** dialog box will be displayed to the user who is opening the published NWD file. The user will also be able to view all the information entered in the above-mentioned text boxes.

Expires
This tick box is selected if you want the file to expire at a certain date. This is generally used in cases where you publish a new NWD file regularly and you do not want the stake holders to view an old file. When you select this tick box, the calendar list will be activated from where you can select the date of expiry.

May be re-saved

This tick box is selected to allow the user to save changes such as a new viewpoint, hiding or unhiding the objects, and so on in the published NWD file. If this tick box is not selected, the changes in the published NWD file can only be saved as an NWF file with a link to the NWD file.

Display on open

If this tick box is selected, the **Publish** dialog box, with all the information entered in it, will be displayed to the user opening the published NWD file.

Embed ReCap and Texture data

This tick box is selected to embed all the externally referenced files, such as Autodesk ReCap point cloud files and the texture data files, in the NWD file. If this tick box is not selected while publishing an NWD file with Autodesk ReCap point cloud data, and the NWD file is opened on a different machine, the **Resolve** dialog box will be displayed informing you that the external reference cannot be resolved. You will have to manually click on the **Browse** button in this dialog box to select the point cloud data from the current machine.

 Note: The file size of an NWD file with embedded point cloud data is significantly larger than the one without the embedded point cloud.

Embed Database Properties

If the Autodesk Navisworks scene has external database properties linked, selecting this tick box will embed all those properties in the published NWD file.

Prevent Object Property Export

Selecting this tick box will not publish any object properties that were imported into Autodesk Navisworks from the native CAD program.

After specifying all the information in the **Publish** dialog box, click **OK**. If you specified a password for the file, you will be prompted to confirm the password. On confirming the password, the **Save As** dialog box will be displayed that lets you specify the name and the location of the file. Note that in the **Save as type** list, only the **Navisworks (*.nwd)** option is available.

What I do

*I generally password-protect my files and also specify their expiry date. This not only helps me to keep my files safe but also ensures that they are not accessible to anyone after the set period. This also avoids any blame game if anything goes wrong during the construction stage of the design. In case the textures that I am using are not standard Autodesk Navisworks textures, I make sure to embed them. I also make sure to select the **Display on open** tick box so that while opening my files, the users can see who owns the copyrights of the file.*

Auto-Save

Shortcut Key F12
Right-click Shortcut Menu > Global Options

To prevent any unexpected loss of data, Autodesk Navisworks automatically saves your work at regular intervals. By default, this is done every fifteen minutes. You can use the **Auto-Save** option of the **General** category of the **Options Editor** dialog box, as shown in Figure 20, to make any changes to these settings. These options are discussed next.

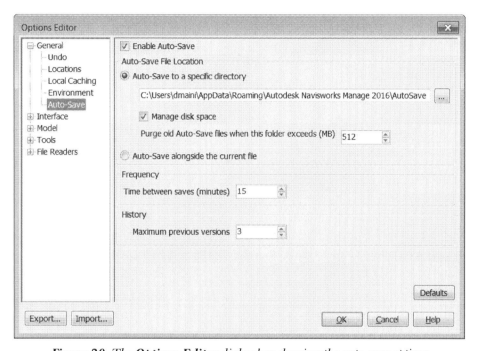

*Figure 20 The **Options Editor** dialog box showing the auto-save options*

Enable Auto-Save
This tick box is selected to turn on the auto-save option. This is turned on by default.

Auto-Save to a specific directory
This box lets you specify the location of the auto-save file. You can select the browse button on the right of this box to browse and select the desired folder.

Manage disk space
If this tick box is selected, you will be allowed to enter the minimum size of the auto-save folder after which the old auto-save files will be purged.

Auto-Save alongside the current file

This radio button is selected to auto-save the file in the same folder where you select to save the original file.

Time between saves (minutes)

This spinner is used to specify the interval between subsequent auto-saves.

Maximum previous versions

This spinner lets you specify how many previous versions of the auto-save files are retained. The oldest auto-save file will be deleted if the number of files exceed the value in this spinner.

DELETING FILES FROM THE SCENE

Autodesk Navisworks allows you to delete one or more files from the current scene if the file is not yet saved or it has been saved as an NWF file. Note that the files cannot be deleted from the NWD files. To delete a file, right-click on its name in the **Selection Tree** and click **Delete** from the shortcut menu, as shown in Figure 21.

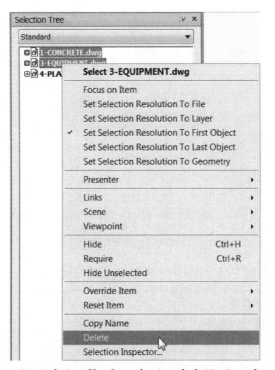

Figure 21 Deleting files from the Autodesk Navisworks scene

NAVIGATING THROUGH THE MODEL

Autodesk Navisworks provides various navigation tools to help you navigate through the model.

These tools are available on the **Navigation Bar** on the right side of the graphics window or on the **Viewpoint** ribbon tab > **Navigate** ribbon panel, as shown in Figure 22. These tools are discussed next.

*Figure 22 The **Navigate** ribbon panel*

 Tip: It is easier to invoke the navigation tools from the **Navigation Bar** instead of changing to the **Viewpoint** ribbon tab and then using the **Navigate** ribbon panel.

Steering Wheels

```
Navigation Bar > Steering Wheels
Viewpoint Ribbon Tab > Navigate Ribbon Panel > Full Navigation Wheel
```

Steering wheel is a smart tool that gives you access to various navigation tools at one single location. This tool comes in three display modes: **View Object**, **Tour Building**, and **Full Navigation**. All these modes are discussed next.

View Object Display

This display mode of the steering wheel is divided into four areas called wedges, as shown in Figure 23. These four wedges provide you access to the **Orbit**, **Rewind**, **Zoom**, and **Center** tools. All these tools are discussed next.

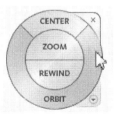

*Figure 23 The steering wheel in the **View Object** display*

Orbit
By pressing and holding down the left mouse button on the **Orbit** wedge, you can dynamically orbit around a pivot point on the model. This pivot point is called center point. You can drag the mouse in various directions to see how the view changes dynamically. This tool comes in handy if you wish to dynamically view the model from various directions.

Center

While orbiting large models, the pivot point around which the model orbits is important. To change the default pivot point, press and hold the left mouse button down on the **Center** wedge in the steering wheel and then drag and drop it on one of the vertices of the model that you want to use as the pivot. The model will shift, bringing the selected vertex at the center of the screen. Now if you orbit the model, you will notice that the model orbits around the new pivot.

Rewind

This tool is used to rewind to the previous view that was active in the scene. When you invoke this tool, the navigation history bar is displayed, as shown in Figure 24. You can select a view from this bar to activate it.

Figure 24 *The navigation history bar*

Zoom

This tool is used to zoom in or out of the scene in realtime using the default center point or the center defined using the **Center** tool. To zoom in, press and hold down the left mouse button on this wedge and drag the mouse forward. To zoom out, press and hold down the left mouse button on this wedge and drag the mouse back.

 Note: *While working with any navigation tool, you can move the cursor over the ViewCube and click on the **Home** icon on the upper left of the ViewCube to change the current view to the default home view.*

Tour Building Display

To invoke this display, click on the **Steering Wheels** flyout and select the **Basic Tour Building** option. The steering wheel in this display mode is shown in Figure 25. This wheel provides you the wedges to access the **Forward**, **Look**, **Rewind**, and **Up/Down** tools. All these tools are discussed next.

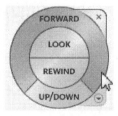

Figure 25 *The steering wheel in the **Tour Building** display*

Forward

This tool is used to zoom in and out of the center point of the scene by pressing and holding down the left mouse button on this wedge and dragging the mouse forward or back.

Look

This tool is used to look around the model, similar to standing still and turning your head in various directions. While holding the left mouse button down on this tool, you can also press the arrow keys on the keyboard to move forward, back, left, and right. This tool can also work as the **Look At** tool if you hold down the SHIFT key before activating this tool. The **Look At** tool lets you display the scene from a direction normal to the flat face of a selected object. Also, the pivot point will be moved on the selected face. The **Look** and **Look At** tools can also be invoked using the **Look Around** flyout on the **Navigate** ribbon panel.

Up/Down

You can use this tool to move up and down the various levels of your design while maintaining the current magnification. For example, while viewing the first level of the building, you decide to navigate to the second level. To do this, press and hold down the left mouse button on this tool and drag the mouse up.

 Note: *The up and down directions of the steering wheel are linked to the top view of the ViewCube. If the model is oriented at 90-degrees in the scene, the **Up/Down** tool will act as forward back tool.*

 Tip: *You can toggle on or off the **Steering Wheel** tool by clicking anywhere in the graphics window and then pressing the SHIFT+W key.*

Full Navigation Display

To invoke this display, click on the **Steering Wheels** flyout and select the **Full Navigation** option. This display shows all the tools of the previous two displays and also the wedge to invoke the **Pan** tool, refer to Figure 26. The **Pan** tool is discussed next.

Figure 26 *The steering wheel in the **Full Navigation** display*

Pan

This tool is used to scroll the view, without changing the magnification of the current display.

Tip: *You can press and hold the wheel button of the mouse and drag it at any time to pan the scene.*

Zoom Tools

> **Navigation Bar > Zoom Flyout**
> **Viewpoint Ribbon Tab > Navigate Ribbon Panel > Zoom Flyout**

The **Zoom** flyout provides four tools to change the magnification factory of your current scene: **Zoom Window**, **Zoom**, **Zoom Selected**, and **Zoom All**. All these tools are discussed next.

Zoom Window

This tool allows you to define a window by dragging the mouse and specifying two corners. The part of the scene that is within that window will be displayed to the extents of the graphics window.

Zoom

This tool lets you interactively zoom in and out of the current scene using the current pivot point. When you invoke this tool, the cursor changes to the magnifying glass. Press and hold down the left mouse button and drag the mouse up to zoom in and down to zoom out. If you want to zoom around a different pivot point, press and hold the left mouse button on that vertex of the scene and drag the mouse.

Zoom Selected

This tool lets you zoom the current scene such that the selected object is displayed to the extents of the graphics window. You can select the object before or after invoking this tool.

Zoom All

This tool zooms to the extents of the Autodesk Navisworks model.

Orbit Tools

> **Navigation Bar > Orbit Flyout**
> **Viewpoint Ribbon Tab > Navigate Ribbon Panel > Orbit Flyout**

The **Orbit** tools also allow you to dynamically view the model by orbiting it around its pivot point. The flyout provides three tools: **Orbit**, **Free Orbit**, and **Constrained Orbit**. All these tools are discussed next.

Orbit

This tool allows you to dynamically orbit around the pivot point of the model without allowing the camera to roll.

Free Orbit

This tool allows the unrestricted orbiting around the pivot point of the model. Remember that because orbit is unrestricted, the camera can be rolled in any direction.

Constrained Orbit

This tool allows only a turntable orbiting around the pivot point, maintaining the up direction of the current scene.

 Tip: *To change the pivot point of the scene, move the cursor over a vertex of the model and scroll the wheel button of the mouse once. This new pivot point will now be used to orbit the model.*

> ### *What I do*
> *I generally do not use the **Steering Wheel** or **Orbit** commands. I use the wheel button of the mouse to navigate around the model. To zoom in or out, simply scroll the wheel button of the mouse forward or back. To pan, press and hold the wheel button and drag the mouse. To orbit, press and hold down the SHIFT key and the wheel button of the mouse and drag. This behavior is similar to the **Orbit** tool with the difference that it does not allow the camera roll. To change the pivot point, move the cursor over the desired vertex and then scroll the wheel button of the mouse once.*

Focus Tool

> **Navigation Bar > Look Around Flyout > Focus**
> **Viewpoint Ribbon Tab > Navigate Ribbon Panel > Look Around Flyout > Focus**

The **Focus** tool allows you to select a vertex on the model. The selected vertex is brought to the center of the graphics window and is also used as the pivot point for the orbit tools.

 Note: *The other tools in this ribbon panel will be discussed in the later chapters.*

CHANGING THE CAMERA OPTIONS

The **Viewpoint** ribbon tab > **Camera** ribbon panel provides you with the options of changing the camera of your current Autodesk Navisworks scene. Figure 27 shows the expanded **Camera** ribbon panel. These options are discussed next.

Field of View (F.O.V.) Slider

> **Viewpoint Ribbon Tab > Camera Ribbon Panel > F.O.V.**

This slider bar is used to increase or reduce the view of the scene that can be viewed by the current camera.

Figure 27 *The **Camera** ribbon panel*

Perspective Flyout

> **Viewpoint Ribbon Tab > Camera Ribbon Panel > Perspective Flyout**

This flyout is used to change the current view to the perspective view or the orthographic view. The perspective view gives a more realistic display of the model.

 Note: *Certain tools such as **Walk** will automatically change the current view to perspective, if it was not already set.*

Align Camera Flyout

> **Viewpoint Ribbon Tab > Camera Ribbon Panel > Align Camera**

This flyout provides you the options that are used to align the camera along the X, Y, or Z direction of the current scene. To find out the X, Y, and Z directions of the current scene, click the **View** ribbon tab > **Navigation Aids** ribbon panel > **HUD** flyout > **XYZ Axes**. The **Straighten** option aligns the camera to one of the axes if the current view is off by a maximum of 13-degrees.

Show Tilt Bar

> **Viewpoint Ribbon Tab > Camera Ribbon Panel > Show Tilt Bar**

This button displays the **Tilt Bar** docked on the right side of the graphics window. This bar allows you to rotate the current camera up or down.

Position Entry Boxes

> **Viewpoint Ribbon Tab > Camera Ribbon Panel > Position**

These boxes show the X, Y, and Z coordinates of the position of the current camera based on the current linear display units. You can change the values in these boxes based on your requirements.

Look At Entry Boxes

Viewpoint Ribbon Tab > Camera Ribbon Panel > Look At

These boxes shows the X, Y, and Z coordinates of the focus point of the current camera based on the current linear display units.

Roll Spinner

Viewpoint Ribbon Tab > Camera Ribbon Panel > Roll

This spinner allows you to specify the left or right rolling of the camera around the axis normal to the graphics window.

CHANGING THE RENDER STYLE OPTIONS

The **Viewpoint** ribbon tab > **Render Style** ribbon panel provides you with the options of changing the lighting and render mode of the scene. There are also the options to specify what type of objects are displayed on the screen, as shown in Figure 28. These options are discussed next.

Figure 28 *The **Render Style** ribbon panel*

Lighting Flyout

Viewpoint Ribbon Tab > Render Style Ribbon Panel > Lighting Flyout

This flyout provides the following four options of lighting the model:

Full Lights
This mode uses the lights specified in the **Presenter/Autodesk Rendering** modules of Autodesk Navisworks.

Scene Lights
This mode uses the lights specified in native CAD program for the current file. If the lights are not specified in the native CAD program, two default opposing lights will be used to display the model.

Head Light

This mode uses a single source of light located at the camera pointing at the camera focus point. However, the model lit using this lighting style does not look realistic.

No Lights

This mode turns off all lights in the scene, thereby displaying the model with a flat shading, based on the color of the model.

Render Mode Flyout

Viewpoint Ribbon Tab > Render Style Ribbon Panel > Render Mode Flyout

This flyout provides the following four options to render the scene:

Full Render

This mode displays a fully rendered view of the model by applying the material and textures to the objects.

Shaded

This mode displays the model as shaded with no material or textures applied.

Wireframe

This mode displays the model as wireframe with all visible and hidden edges turned on. It is very hard to clearly identify the objects in the current scene in this display mode.

Hidden Line

This mode displays the model as wireframe but with the hidden lines turned off.

Surfaces

Viewpoint Ribbon Tab > Render Style Ribbon Panel > Surfaces Button

This button toggles on or off the display of native CAD surfaces in the current scene. Note that Autodesk Navisworks will convert the solid objects from the native CAD model into surfaces to make the files compact. As a result, if you toggle this button off, no solid face will be displayed in the current scene.

Lines

Viewpoint Ribbon Tab > Render Style Ribbon Panel > Lines Button

This button toggles on or off the display of lines that were created in the native CAD program. Note that this button will be grayed out if there are no line objects in the native CAD file.

Points

| Viewpoint Ribbon Tab > Render Style Ribbon Panel > Points Button |

This button toggles on or off the display of the points created in the native CAD program.

 Note: *The work points or sketched point created in Autodesk Inventor will not be brought into Autodesk Navisworks.*

Snap Points

| Viewpoint Ribbon Tab > Render Style Ribbon Panel > Snap Points Button |

This button toggles on or off the snap points of the objects, such as the endpoints and midpoints of lines, center points, and quadrant points of a circle etc.

Text

| Viewpoint Ribbon Tab > Render Style Ribbon Panel > Snap Points Button |

This button toggles on or off the display of the text in the current scene. Note that this button will be grayed out if there was no text written in the native CAD file.

VIEWCUBE

The ViewCube is displayed on the top right corner of the graphics window. As mentioned earlier, it is a visualization tool used to display the static views of the model from various directions. By default, it appears faded, which is the inactive state. But when you move the cursor over it, the ViewCube becomes active, highlighting the face, edge, or corner on which you move your cursor.

You can click on one of the faces or the edges of the ViewCube to display the model from the direction normal to that face or edge. You can also click on one of the corners of the ViewCube to display the 3D view of the model from that direction. When you move the cursor over the ViewCube, the **Home** icon appears that lets you change the current view of the model to the default 3D view. If you right-click on the ViewCube, a shortcut menu appears, as shown in Figure 29. The options in this shortcut menu are discussed next.

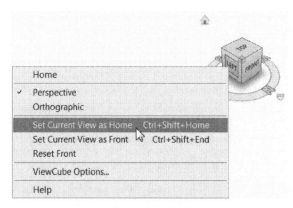

Figure 29 *The ViewCube shortcut menu*

Home

This option changes the current view to the home view.

Perspective/Orthographic

These options are used to set the current scene to perspective or orthographic display. The **Perspective** option is selected by default.

 Note: *If the **Sun** button is turned on in the **Autodesk Rendering** window, the **Orthographic** option will not be available in the ViewCube shortcut menu.*

Set Current View as Home

This option is used to set the current view as the home view for future use. You can use any navigation tool to set the camera to any view and then use this option to set that view as the home view. As a result, next time whenever you click on the **Home** icon, you will be taken to the new home view that you set.

Set Current View as Front

Sometimes when you start aggregating the models in Autodesk Navisworks, the default front view of the ViewCube does not show the desired front view of the model. This option is used to change the front view to any desired direction by clicking that face or edge of the ViewCube and then selecting this option from the shortcut menu.

Reset Front

This option is used to reset the default front view of the ViewCube.

ViewCube Options

Selecting this option displays the **Options Editor** dialog box showing the **ViewCube** options in the **Interface** category. These options are used to specify the settings related to ViewCube, such as size, inactivity opacity, showing the compass below the ViewCube etc.

HANDS-ON EXERCISES

You will now work on hands-on exercises using the concepts learned in this chapter.

Hands-on Exercise (Plant)	*In this exercise, you will complete the following tasks:*
	1. Open an AutoCAD Plant 3D file and change the render styles.
	2. Create a user-defined workspace.
	3. Append additional files to create an Autodesk Navisworks scene, as shown in Figure 30.
	4. Use various navigation tools to navigate around the model.
	5. Publish a password-protected NWD file.
	6. Open a file from a web server.

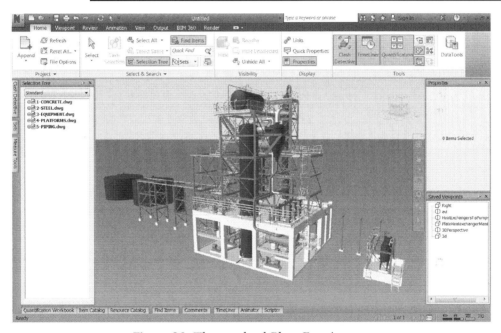

Figure 30 The completed Plant Exercise scene

Section 1: Opening the File and Changing Render Styles

In this section, you will open the first file of the plant model. You will then change the render and lighting styles of the scene.

1. Start Autodesk Navisworks by double-clicking its desktop icon or by clicking **Start > All Programs > Autodesk > Navisworks Manage 2016/Simulate 2016 > Manage 2016/ Simulate 2016**.

 Note: *If you are using one of the suites that has a dashboard, such as the Product Design Suite or the Factory Design Suite, you can also use the **Applications** tab of the dashboard to start Autodesk Navisworks.*

2. Click **Quick Access Toolbar > Open** to display the **Open** dialog box.

3. Browse to the **Chapter 1 > Exercise Plant** folder of the exercise files. Change the file type from the **Files of type** list to **Autodesk DWG/DXF file (*.dwg, *.dxf)**.

4. Double-click on the **1-CONCRETE.dwg** file to open it; the model opens in the Autodesk Navisworks window, as shown in Figure 31.

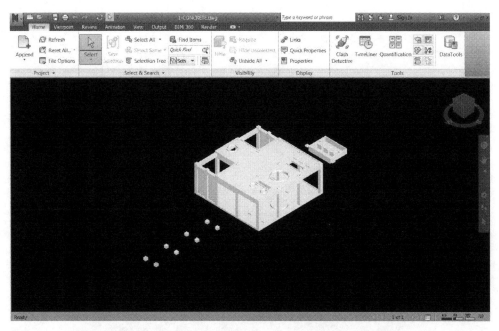

Figure 31 *The Autodesk Navisworks window with the first file opened*

You will notice that the model in the current lighting does not look realistic. So it is better to change the lighting and render style.

5. Click the **Viewpoint** ribbon tab > **Render Style** ribbon panel > **Lighting** flyout and select **Full Lights**; the model is displayed in full lighting.

6. From the same ribbon panel, click on the **Mode** flyout and select **Shaded** to display the model in full render mode.

Section 2: Creating a User-Defined Workspace

By default, Autodesk Navisworks opens in the workspace in which all the required windows are not opened. As a result, you need to change the workspace. It is recommended that you create your own workspace with the visibility turned on for the windows that you often use. You can then restore this workspace at any point of time.

1. Click **View** ribbon tab > **Workspace** ribbon panel > **Load Workspace** flyout > **Navisworks Standard**; Autodesk Navisworks resets to display the model in this workspace.

You will notice that in this workspace, some windows are displayed in the auto-hide mode around the graphics window.

2. Move the cursor over the **Selection Tree** window; notice that the window slides out showing you the 1-CONCRETE.dwg file.

3. Move the cursor back on the graphics window and the **Selection Tree** window slides in and hides again.

4. Click **View** ribbon tab > **Workspace** ribbon panel > **Load Workspace** flyout > **Navisworks Extended**; Autodesk Navisworks resets to display this workspace.

    In this workspace, you will see some windows docked on the screen and some in the auto-hide mode. Next, you will create your own workspace by closing some of the windows.

5. Click on the **Close** button [X] on the top right of the **Plan View**, **Section View**, and **Tilt Bar** windows to close them.

6. Click **View** ribbon tab > **Workspace** ribbon panel > **Save Workspace** to display the **Save Current Workspace** dialog box.

7. Browse to the folder of the exercise files and save the current workspace with the name **Training**. The file will be saved with the .XML extension.

    Next time when you start Autodesk Navisworks, it will open in this user-defined workspace.

8. Click **View** ribbon tab > **Workspace** ribbon panel > **Load Workspace** flyout and you will notice that the workspace you created is not listed here. This is because you did not save the workspace in the default directory.

    To ensure the workspace you created is listed in the **Load Workspace** flyout, save its copy in the default workspace directory.

9. Click **View** ribbon tab > **Workspace** ribbon panel > **Save Workspace** to redisplay the **Save Current Workspace** dialog box. This dialog box takes you to the default directory.

10. Save the workspace here with the name **Training**.

11. Click **View** ribbon tab > **Workspace** ribbon panel > **Load Workspace** flyout and you will notice that the workspace you created is now listed here.

12. Press the ESC key to cancel the flyout and return to the Autodesk Navisworks window.

Section 3: Appending Additional Files to Complete the Scene

In this section, you will append the remaining files of the plant to complete the scene. For this project, the files are provided in the AutoCAD Plant 3D format. You will append all these files to create the final scene.

1. Click **Home** ribbon tab > **Project** ribbon panel > **Append** to open the **Append** dialog box.

2. Browse to the **Chapter 1 > Exercise Plant** folder, if it is not listed in the dialog box. Double-click the **2-STEEL.dwg** file to append to the current scene.

3. Expand the **Project** ribbon panel on the **Home** ribbon tab and click **Scene Statistics** to display the **Scene Statistics** dialog box.

4. If the **Scene Statistics** dialog box displays any information about any missing object enablers, make a note of it and close the dialog box. Close the current file without saving. Next, go to the folder of Exercise 1 and delete all the **1-CONCRETE.nwc** and **2-STEEL.nwc** files. Now, download and install the missing object enablers.

   If there are no missing object enablers, go directly to step 6.

5. Repeat the process of opening the **1-CONCRETE.dwg** file, changing the render styles and appending the **2-STEEL.dwg** file.

   Next, you will append the additional files to complete the scene. Autodesk Navisworks does not provide the preview of the files being aggregated in the scene. As a result, you need to use the **Sheet Browser** to preview the models before appending.

6. Click the **Sheet Browser** button on the right side of the status bar, which is located at the bottom Autodesk Navisworks window.

7. Click the **Import Sheets & Models** button on the top right of the **Sheet Browser** to display the **Insert From File** dialog box.

8. Hold down the SHIFT key and select the **3-EQUIPMENT.dwg**, **4-PLATFORMS.dwg**, and **5-PIPING.dwg** files. Click **Open** in the dialog box; the three files are listed in the **Sheet Browser**, along with the original **1-CONCRETE.dwg** file.

9. Click the **List View** button near the top right of the **Sheet Browser** window to change the view to the list view, if it is not already set to this view.

10. Move the **Sheet Browser** to the right of the window. Double-click on the **3-EQUIPMENT.dwg** file to preview this file in the Autodesk Navisworks window.

11. Press and hold down the SHIFT key and the wheel button of the mouse and drag the cursor to orbit around this equipment file.

12. Double-click on the **4-PLATFORMS.dwg** file to activate it in the Autodesk Navisworks window.

13. Press and hold down the SHIFT key and the wheel button of the mouse and drag the cursor to orbit around this file.

14. Double-click **1-CONCRETE.dwg** in the **Sheet Browser** to restore the view to this file.

   Note that although this file is listed as **1-CONCRETE.dwg** in the **Sheet Browser**, the **Selection Tree** also shows the **2-STEEL.dwg** file appended in the scene.

15. Select the **3-EQUIPMENT.dwg** in the **Sheet Browser**. Now, hold down the SHIFT key and select **4-PLATFORMS.dwg** and **5-PIPING.dwg files**. Right-click on any of these files and then select **Append to Current Model**.

    You will notice that these files are now listed in the **Selection Tree**.

16. With the three files still selected in the **Sheet Browser**, right-click on any of these files and then select **Delete** from the shortcut menu.

17. Close the **Sheet Browser**.

    By default, the background color of the Autodesk Navisworks scene is set to Black. Next, you will change the background color.

18. Right-click in the blank area of the graphics window and select **Background** from the shortcut menu; the **Background Settings** dialog box is displayed.

19. From the **Mode** list, click **Horizon**, as shown in Figure 32. Click **OK** to close the dialog box.

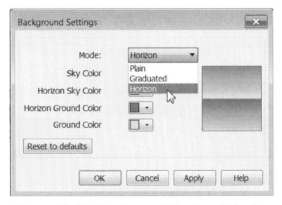

*Figure 32 The **Background Settings** dialog box*

 Note: *The background settings are saved with the file. If you start a new file, it will have the default Black background.*

Section 4: Navigating Around the Model

In this section, you will navigate around the model using various navigation tools.

1. Move the cursor over the ViewCube on the top right of the graphics window and select the **Home** icon to change the current view to the default home view.

2. Click on the **Orbit** button from the **Navigation Bar** on the right side of the graphics window to invoke this tool; the cursor changes to the orbit cursor.

3. Move the orbit cursor anywhere outside the model. Now, press and hold down the left mouse button and drag the mouse upward so you can see the sky, see Figure 33.

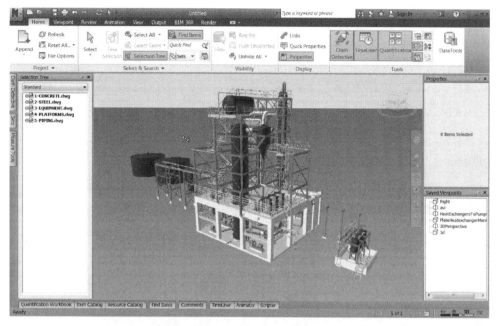

Figure 33 *Orbiting around the model*

4. Next, press and hold down the left mouse button and drag the mouse toward the right to orbit horizontally around the model.

5. Change the current view to the Home view. Click the **Full Navigation Wheel** button from the **Navigation Bar** to invoke this tool.

6. Move the wheel outside the model. Press and hold down the left mouse button on the **Orbit** wedge and drag the cursor in various directions.

    You will notice that while orbiting using the **Orbit** tool and the steering wheel, the model orbits around a default pivot point. You will now change this pivot point.

7. Change the current view to the Home view. Press and hold down the left mouse button on the **Center** wedge and drop it on top of any of the steel columns on the extreme left of the model. Release the left mouse button when the screen shows the Green pivot point; the model shifts such that the new pivot point moves to the center of the graphics window.

8. Press and hold down the left mouse button on the **Orbit** wedge and drag the mouse; the model orbits around the new pivot point.

9. Click anywhere in the graphics window and press the SHIFT+W key to exit the steering wheel; you will return to the **Orbit** tool, which was active before you invoked the steering wheel.

10. Press and hold the left mouse button and drag the mouse; you will notice that the model still orbits around the new pivot point.

11. Change the current view to the Home view. Click on the **Select** button on the **Quick Access Toolbar** to exit the **Orbit** tool.

    Next, you will use the wheel mouse button to navigate through the model.

12. Press and hold down the wheel button of the mouse and pan the view to bring the model to the center of the graphics window.

13. Next, press and hold down the SHIFT key and then press and hold down the wheel button and drag the mouse; the model orbits around the pivot point specified earlier.

14. Change the current view to the Home view.

15. Move the cursor over the top of the concrete closest to you. Scroll the wheel button of the mouse forward and back once; you will notice that the corner of the concrete is now set as the pivot point.

16. Press and hold down the SHIFT key and the wheel button and drag the mouse; the model orbits around the new pivot point.

17. Change the view to the Home view and then invoke the **Full Navigation Wheel** tool from the **Navigation Bar**.

18. Hold the SHIFT key down and then press and hold down the left mouse button inside the **Look** wedge; this tool will now act as the **Look At** tool. Move the cursor over the front face of any one of the left concrete columns and release the SHIFT key and the left mouse button; the model will be displayed from the direction normal to the selected face. Also, the pivot point will be moved on the selected face.

19. Click anywhere in the blank area of the graphics window. Now, press the SHIFT+W key to exit the steering wheel.

20. Press and hold down the SHIFT key and the wheel button to orbit the model around the pivot point on the face selected in the previous step.

21. Release the SHIFT key and only hold the wheel button down to pan the model to the center of the graphics window.

22. Scroll the wheel button on any vertex of the model to make it the current pivot point. Now, orbit again by holding down the SHIFT key and wheel button around the new pivot.

    You will notice that orbiting, zooming and panning using the wheel button is a lot easier than using the individual navigation tools.

23. Change the current view to the Home view.

Section 5: Saving the File

In this section, you will save the file as an NWF file.

1. Click the **Save** button on the **Quick Access Toolbar** to invoke the **Save As** dialog box.

2. Browse to the **Chapter 1 > Exercise Plant** folder, if it is not already listed in the dialog box.

3. Specify the name of the file as **C1EP**. The format is set to NWF, which is what you want. This format will have the link to the native AutoCAD Plant 3D files. So if any of these files change, the Autodesk Navisworks scene will only need a refresh to display the updated model.

4. Click **Save** to save the **C1EP.nwf** file; the title bar of the Autodesk Navisworks window shows you the name of the file.

Section 6: Publishing the NWD File

The NWF file saved in the previous section is only used within your organization by the people who have access to the associated Plant files. However, if you want to send the model to someone outside your organization, you will have to publish the NWD file. The following steps show you how to do this.

1. Click the **Application Button** on the top left corner of the Autodesk Navisworks window and then select **Publish**; the **Publish** dialog box will be displayed.

2. Enter Plant Exercise 1 in the **Title** and **Subject** boxes.

3. Enter your name in the **Author** box.

4. Enter Deepak Maini in the **Copyright** box.

5. Enter **1234** as the password in the **Password** box.

6. Select the **Display at password** tick box.

7. Select the **Expires** tick box and pick a date one month from today.

8. Select the **Display on open** tick box.

9. Click **OK** in the **Publish** dialog box; the **Password** dialog box will be displayed.

10. Enter **1234** in the **Password** dialog box and click **OK**; the **Save As** dialog box is displayed.

11. Browse to the **Chapter 1 > Exercise Plant** folder, if it is not already listed. Enter the name of the file as **Plant Exercise 1**. Click **Save**.

Section 7: Opening the Published NWD File

In this section, you will open the NWD file you published in the previous section.

1. Click the **Open** button on the **Quick Access Toolbar** to display the **Open** dialog box.

2. Browse to the **Chapter 1 > Exercise Plant** folder, if it is not already listed. Change the file type from the **Files of type** list to **Navisworks (*.nwd)**; the published file is displayed.

3. Double-click on the published **Plant Exercise 1.nwd** file; the **Publish** dialog box is displayed, prompting you for the password.

4. Enter **1234** as the password and click **OK**; the file is opened.

   Notice that in the **Selection Tree**, the name of the published file is displayed at the top, followed by all the files that you appended in it. Also notice that because this is a published file, you are not allowed to delete any of the files from it.

 Note: If you opened a password-protected published file by typing in the correct password, when you open this file again in the same session of Autodesk Navisworks, you will not be prompted to type in the password again. However, if you close Autodesk Navisworks and start again, you will be prompted for the password.

 Tip: Anyone who does not have access to Autodesk Navisworks can also open an NWD file in the free Autodesk Navisworks Freedom viewer. This viewer can be downloaded from the Autodesk Navisworks Web site http://www.autodesk.com/products/navisworks/ autodesk-navisworks-freedom.

Section 8: Opening a File from the Web Server

As mentioned earlier, Autodesk Navisworks allows you to directly open a file from the Web server. In this section, you will open the file located at the Web site of the author of this textbook, Deepak Maini.

1. Click **Application Button > Open > Open URL** to display the **Open URL** dialog box.

2. Enter the following path in the file to open and click **OK**:

   http://www.deepakmaini.com/Navisworks/Plant.nwd

   The file starts to load from the server. Notice how the **Web Server Indicator Bar** changes during the load process.

3. Navigate around the model using the SHIFT key and wheel mouse button or by using various navigation tools.

4. Click the **Save** button on the **Quick Access Toolbar**; you will be prompted to save this file as an NWF file because the file on the Web server is a locked file.

5. Cancel the dialog box and click the **New** button on the **Quick Access Toolbar** to close the file.

Hands-on Exercise (BIM)	*In this exercise, you will complete the following tasks:* 1. Open a building structure file and change the render styles. 2. Create a user-defined workspace. 3. Append additional building files to create an Autodesk Navisworks scene, as shown in Figure 34. 4. Use various navigation tools to navigate around the model. 5. Publish a password-protected NWD file. 6. Open a file from Web server.

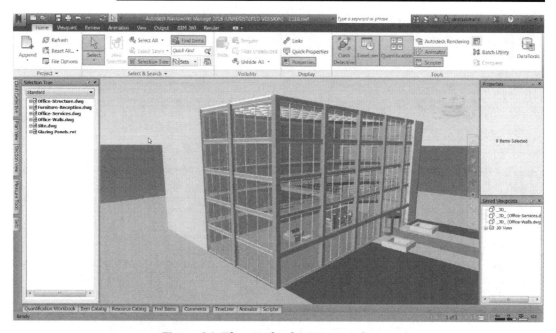

Figure 34 *The completed BIM tutorial scene*

Section 1: Opening the File and Changing Render Styles

In this section, you will open the first file of the building model. You will then change the render and lighting styles of the scene.

1. Start Autodesk Navisworks by double-clicking its desktop icon or by clicking **Start > All Programs > Autodesk > Navisworks Manage 2016/Simulate 2016 > Manage 2016/Simulate 2016**.

 Note: *If you are using one of the suites that has a dashboard, such as the Product Design Suite or the Factory Design Suite, you can also use the **Applications** tab of the dashboard to start Autodesk Navisworks.*

2. Click **Quick Access Toolbar > Open** to display the **Open** dialog box.

3. Browse to the **Chapter 1 > Exercise Building** folder. Change the file type from the **Files of type** list to **Autodesk DWG/DXF file (*.dwg, *.dxf)**.

4. Double-click on the **Office-Structure.dwg** file to open it; the model opens in the Autodesk Navisworks scene.

5. Move the cursor over the ViewCube on the top right corner of the graphics window and then click on the **Home** icon; the model changes to the home view, as shown in Figure 35.

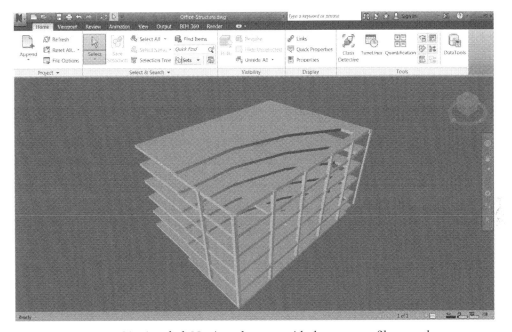

Figure 35 Autodesk Navisworks scene with the structure file opened

You will notice that the model in the current lighting does not look realistic. So it is better to change the lighting and render style.

6. Click the **Viewpoint** ribbon tab > **Render Style** ribbon panel > **Lighting** flyout and select **Full Lights**; the model will be displayed in full lighting.

7. From the same ribbon panel, click on the **Mode** flyout and select **Shaded** to display the model in shaded mode.

Section 2: Creating a User-Defined Workspace

By default, Autodesk Navisworks opens in the workspace in which all the required windows are not opened. As a result, you need to change the workspace. It is recommended that you create your own workspace with the visibility turned on for the windows that you often use. You can then restore this workspace at any point of time.

1. Click **View** ribbon tab > **Workspace** ribbon panel > **Load Workspace** flyout > **Navisworks Standard** to activate this workspace.

You will notice that in this workspace, some windows are displayed in the auto-hide mode around the graphics window.

2. Move the cursor over the **Selection Tree** window; notice that the window slides out showing you the content of the structure file.

3. Move the cursor back on the graphics window and the **Selection Tree** window will slide in and hide again.

4. Click **View** ribbon tab > **Workspace** ribbon panel > **Load Workspace** flyout > **Navisworks Extended** to activate this workspace.

   In this workspace, you will see some windows docked on the screen and some in the auto-hide mode. Next, you will create your own workspace by closing some of the windows.

5. Click on the **Close** button [X] on the top right of the **Plan View**, **Section View**, and **Tilt Bar** windows to close them.

6. Click **View** ribbon tab > **Workspace** ribbon panel > **Save Workspace** to display the **Save Current Workspace** dialog box.

7. Browse to the folder of the exercise files and save the current workspace with the name **Training**. The file will be saved with the .XML extension.

   Next time when you start Autodesk Navisworks, it will open in this user-defined workspace.

8. Click **View** ribbon tab > **Workspace** ribbon panel > **Load Workspace** flyout and you will notice that the workspace you created is not listed here. This is because you did not save the workspace in the default directory.

   To ensure the workspace you created is listed in the **Load Workspace** flyout, save its copy in the default workspace directory.

9. Click **View** ribbon tab > **Workspace** ribbon panel > **Save Workspace** to redisplay the **Save Current Workspace** dialog box. This dialog box takes you to the default directory.

10. Save the workspace here with the name **Training**.

11. Click **View** ribbon tab > **Workspace** ribbon panel > **Load Workspace** flyout and you will notice that the workspace you created is now listed here.

12. Press ESC to cancel the flyout and return to the Autodesk Navisworks window.

Section 3: Appending Additional Files to Complete the Scene

In this section, you will append the remaining files of the building to complete the scene. For this project, some files are provided in the AutoCAD format and there is also a file provided in the Autodesk Revit format. You will append all these files to create the final scene.

1. Click **Home** ribbon tab > **Project** ribbon panel > **Append** to open the **Append** dialog box.

2. Browse to the **Chapter 1 > Exercise Building** folder, if it is not already listed in the dialog box. Hold down the CTRL key and select all the .DWG files except the **Office-Structure.dwg** as it is already opened. Click **Open**.

   All these files are appended in the current scene and are listed in the **Selection Tree**.

   Next, you will use the **Sheet Browser** to preview the glazing file before appending it.

3. Click the **Sheet Browser** button on the right side of the status bar, which is located at the bottom Autodesk Navisworks window.

4. Click the **Import Sheets & Models** button on the top right of the **Sheet Browser** to display the **Insert From File** dialog box.

5. Click on the **Files of type** list and select **Revit (*.rvt, *.rfa, *.rte)**.

6. Select the **Glazing Panels.rvt** file. Click **Open** in the dialog box; the file will be listed in the **Sheet Browser** along with the first file you opened.

7. In the **Sheet Browser** window, double-click on the **Glazing Panels.rvt** file to preview this file in the Autodesk Navisworks window.

8. Scroll the wheel mouse button on any object in this file to move the pivot point there. Now, press and hold down the SHIFT key and the wheel button of the mouse and drag the cursor to orbit around this glazing panels file.

9. Double-click the **Office-Structure.dwg** file to restore the view to this file.

10. Right-click on the **Glazing Panels.rvt** file in the **Sheet Browser** and then select **Append to Current Model**.

    You will notice that this file is now listed in the **Selection Tree**.

    Next, you will delete the **Glazing Panels.rvt** file from the **Sheet Browser**.

11. Right-click on the **Glazing Panels.rvt** file in the **Sheet Browser** and then select **Delete**.

12. Close the **Sheet Browser**.

    By default, the background color of the Autodesk Navisworks scene is set to Black. Next, you will change the background color.

13. Right-click in the blank area of the graphics window and select **Background** from the shortcut menu; the **Background Settings** dialog box will be displayed.

14. From the **Mode** list, click **Horizon**, as shown in Figure 36. Click **OK** to close the dialog box.

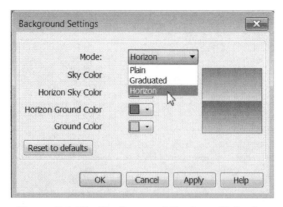

Figure 36 The **Background Settings** *dialog box*

Section 4: Navigating Around the Model

In this section, you will navigate around the model using various navigation tools.

1. Click the **Orbit** button from the **Navigation Bar** on the right side of the graphics window to invoke this tool; the cursor changes to the orbit cursor.

2. Move the orbit cursor anywhere outside the model. Now, press and hold down the left mouse button and drag the mouse upward so you can see the sky, as shown in Figure 37.

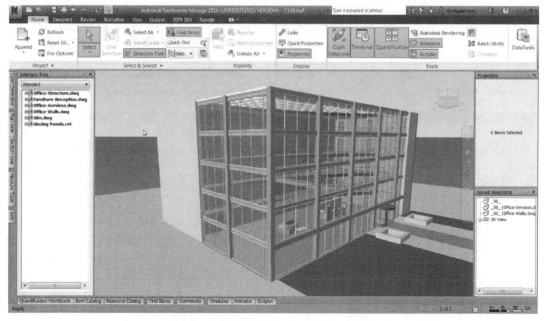

Figure 37 Orbiting around the model

3. Next, press and hold down the left mouse button and drag the mouse toward the right to orbit horizontally around the model.

4. Change the current view to the **Home** view. Click on the **Full Navigation Wheel** button from the **Navigation Bar** to invoke this tool.

5. Move the wheel outside the model. Press and hold down the left mouse button on the **Orbit** wedge and drag the mouse in various directions.

    You will notice that while orbiting using the **Orbit** tool and the steering wheel, the model orbits around a default pivot point. You will now change this pivot point.

6. Change the current view to the **Home** view. Press and hold down the left mouse button on the **Center** wedge and drag it on the top left corner of the roof slab. Release the left mouse button when the screen shows the Green pivot point; the model shifts such that the new pivot point moves to the center of the graphics window.

7. Press and hold down the left mouse button on the **Orbit** wedge and drag the mouse; the model orbits around the new pivot point.

8. Click anywhere in the graphics window and press the SHIFT+W key to exit the steering wheel; you will return back to the **Orbit** tool, which was active before you invoked the steering wheel.

9. Press and hold the left mouse button and drag the mouse; you will notice that the model still orbits around the new pivot point.

10. Change the current view to the Home view. Click the **Select** button on the **Quick Access Toolbar** to exit the **Orbit** tool.

    Next, you will use the wheel button of the mouse to navigate through the model.

11. Press and hold down the wheel button of the mouse and pan the view to bring the model at the center of the graphics window.

12. Next, press and hold down the SHIFT key and then press and hold the wheel button and drag the mouse; the model orbits around the pivot point specified earlier.

13. Release the SHIFT key and then move the cursor on the corner at the top of the building.

14. Scroll the wheel button of the mouse forward and back once; you will notice that the corner of the building is now set as the pivot point.

15. Press and hold down the SHIFT key and the wheel button and drag the mouse; the model orbits around the new pivot point.

16. Change the view to the Home view and then invoke the **Full Navigation Wheel** tool from the **Navigation Bar**.

17. Hold the SHIFT key down and then press and hold the left mouse button inside the **Look** wedge; this tool will now act as the **Look At** tool. Move the cursor over one of the glass panels above the main entrance and release the SHIFT key and the left mouse button; the model will be displayed from the direction normal to the selected face. Also, the pivot point will be moved on the selected face.

18. Click anywhere in the blank area of the graphics window and then press the SHIFT+W key to exit the steering wheel. Now, press and hold the SHIFT key and wheel button to orbit the model around the pivot point on the face selected in the previous step.

19. Release the SHIFT key and only hold down the wheel button to pan the model to the center of the graphics window.

20. Scroll the wheel button on any of the vertices of the model to make it the current pivot point. Now, orbit again by holding the SHIFT key and wheel button around the new pivot.

    You will notice that orbiting, zooming and panning using the wheel button is a lot easier than using the individual navigation tools.

Section 5: Saving the File

In this section, you will save the file as an NWF format file.

1. Change the current view to the **Home** view. Click the **Save** button on the **Quick Access Toolbar** to invoke the **Save As** dialog box.

2. Browse to the **Chapter 1 > Exercise Building** folder, if it is not already listed in the dialog box.

3. Specify the name of the file as **C1EB**. The format is set to NWF, which is what you want. This format will have the link to the native building files. So if any of these files change, the Autodesk Navisworks scene will only need a refresh to display the updated scene.

4. Click **Save** to save the **C1EB.nwf** file; the title bar of the Autodesk Navisworks window will show you the name of the file.

Section 6: Publishing the NWD File

The NWF file saved in the previous section is only used within your organization by the people who have access to the associated building files. However, if you want to send the model to someone outside your organization, you will have to publish the NWD file. The following steps show you how to do this.

1. Click the **Application Button** on the top left corner of the Autodesk Navisworks window and then select **Publish**; the **Publish** dialog box will be displayed.

2. Enter Building Exercise 1 in the **Title** and **Subject** boxes.

3. Enter your name in the **Author** box.

4. Enter Deepak Maini in the **Copyright** box.

5. Enter **1234** as the password in the **Password** box.

6. Select the **Display at password** tick box.

7. Select the **Expires** tick box and pick a date one month from today.

8. Select the **Display on open** tick box.

9. Click **OK** in the **Publish** dialog box; the **Password** dialog box will be displayed.

10. Enter **1234** in the **Password** dialog box and click **OK**; the **Save As** dialog box will be displayed.

11. Browse to the **Chapter 1 > Exercise Building** folder, if it is not already listed. Enter the name of the file as Building Exercise 1. Click **Save**.

Section 7: Opening the Published NWD File

In this section, you will open the NWD file you published in the previous section.

1. Click the **Open** button on the **Quick Access Toolbar** to display the **Open** dialog box.

2. Browse to the **Chapter 1 > Exercise Building** folder, if it is not already listed. Change the file type from the **Files of type** list to **Navisworks (*.nwd)**; the published file will be displayed.

3. Double-click on the published **Building Exercise 1.nwd** file; the **Publish** dialog box will be displayed, prompting you for the password.

4. Enter **1234** as the password and click **OK**; the file will be opened.

    Notice that in the **Selection Tree**, the name of the published file is displayed at the top, followed by all the files that you appended in it. Also notice that because this is a published file, you are not allowed to delete any of the files from it.

  Note: If you opened a password-protected published file by typing in the correct password, when you open this file again in the same session of Autodesk Navisworks, you will not be prompted to type in the password again. However, if you close Autodesk Navisworks and start again, you will be prompted for the password.

  Tip: Anyone who does not have access to Autodesk Navisworks can still open an NWD file in the free Autodesk Navisworks Freedom viewer. This viewer can be downloaded from the Autodesk Navisworks Web site http://www.autodesk.com/products/navisworks/ autodesk-navisworks-freedom.

Section 8: Opening a File from the Web Server

As mentioned earlier, Autodesk Navisworks allows you to directly open a file from the Web server. In this section, you will open the file located at the Web site of the author of this textbook, Deepak Maini.

1. Click **Application Button > Open > Open URL** to display the **Open URL** dialog box.

2. Enter the following path in the file to open and click **OK**:

    http://www.deepakmaini.com/Navisworks/Building.nwd

    The file starts to load. Notice how the **Web Server Indicator Bar** changes during the load process.

3. Navigate around the model by holding down the SHIFT key and wheel mouse button or by using various navigation tools.

4. Click the **Save** button on the **Quick Access Toolbar**; you will be prompted to save this file as an NWF file because the file on the web server is a locked file.

5. Cancel out of the dialog box and click the **New** button on the **Quick Access Toolbar** to close the file.

Skill Evaluation

Evaluate your skills to see how many questions you can answer correctly. The answers to these questions are given at the end of the book.

1. Autodesk Navisworks Simulate does not include the **TimeLiner** module. (True/False)

2. The **Quantification** module is only available in Autodesk Navisworks Manage. (True/False)

3. Autodesk Navisworks allows you to create a user-defined workspace. (True/False)

4. You can use the wheel button on the mouse to activate various navigation tools. (True/False)

5. The NWD file can also be opened in Autodesk Navisworks Freedom viewer. (True/False)

6. Which one is not an Autodesk Navisworks product?

   (A) Autodesk Navisworks Manage   (B) Autodesk Navisworks Simulate
   (C) Autodesk Navisworks Preview   (D) Autodesk Navisworks Freedom

7. Which one is not an Autodesk Navisworks file type?

   (A) NWB   (B) NWC
   (C) NWD   (D) NWF

8. Which one is not an option in the **Orbit** flyout?

   (A) **Orbit**   (B) **Full Orbit**
   (C) **Free Orbit**   (D) **Constrained Orbit**

9. Which tool is used to create a password protected Autodesk Navisworks file?

   (A) **Publish**   (B) **Save**
   (C) **Output**   (D) **Save As**

10. What is the default frequency of the auto-save?

    (A) 10 minutes   (B) 15 minutes
    (C) 20 minutes   (D) 5 minutes

Class Test Questions

Answer the following questions:

1. Which module is only available in Autodesk Navisworks Manage?

2. Which tool is used to create the NWD file that expires after a certain period of time?

3. What key and mouse button combination is used to orbit the model?

4. Which format file is automatically created when you open a native CAD/Laser scanner file?

5. Which Autodesk Navisworks format file does not let you delete the files from the **Selection Tree**?

Chapter 2 – Selecting and Manipulating Objects in the Scene

The objectives of this chapter are to:

√   *Familiarize you with various selection resolutions.*
√   *Explain various methods of selecting objects.*
√   *Teach you how to control the visibility of the objects in the scene.*
√   *Explain the use of various item tools.*
√   *Teach you how to override or restore the object appearance.*
√   *Explain how to change the units, location, and orientation of a CAD file.*
√   *Teach you how to create selection sets and search sets.*
√   *Explain how to view native object properties and create custom object properties.*
√   *Teach you how to display quick object properties of the model in the graphics window.*

OBJECT SELECTION

Selecting objects is an important part of any design collaboration process. Autodesk Navisworks provides you various tools to effectively select objects. These tools are available on the **Home** ribbon tab > **Select & Search** ribbon panel. Figure 1 shows this panel in the expanded form.

Figure 1 *The **Select & Search** ribbon panel in the expanded form*

Before you start selecting the objects, it is important for you to understand the various types of selection resolutions. These are discussed next.

 Note: *The properties displayed in the **Properties** window are dependent on the selection resolution.*

Selection Resolution

The selection resolution controls what gets selected when you try to make a selection. Autodesk Navisworks provides you various selection resolutions that can be changed from the **Selection Resolution** flyout in the **Select & Search** ribbon panel, as shown in Figure 2, or by right-clicking in the **Selection Tree**, as shown in Figure 3. All these selection resolutions are discussed next.

Figure 2 *The **Selection Resolution** flyout*

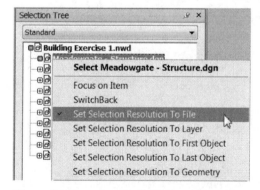

Figure 3 *Changing the **Selection Resolution** from the **Selection Tree***

File

If the selection resolution is set to **File**, the entire file will be selected when you select any object in that file. Note that if you are working with the NWF file, and this selection resolution is set, only the native CAD file will be selected when you select any object in that file. However, if you are working with the NWD file, and this selection resolution is set, everything in the entire scene will be selected when you select any object.

Layer

If the selection resolution is set and you select an object, all other objects on the layer of the selected object will be selected. Figure 4 shows Autodesk Navisworks scene with the entire StructuralSteel_Columns layer selected upon selecting a single column from the graphics window.

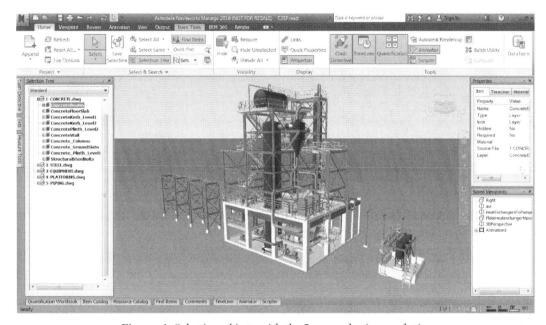

*Figure 4 Selecting objects with the **Layer** selection resolution*

First Object

If this selection resolution is set, the first branch of objects under the layer are selected. However, for the designs that do not have layers, such as Autodesk Inventor assembly, this selection resolution will select the first level subassembly or part inside the main assembly.

Last Unique

This selection resolution can only be set using the **Selection Resolution** flyout. If this is the current selection resolution, the last unique branch of object in the **Selection Tree** will be selected.

Last Object

This selection resolution drills down to the last branch of object in the **Selection Tree**.

Geometry

This selection resolution allows selection of the objects in the geometry branch.

Select Flyout

This flyout provides two selections tools, as shown in Figure 5. These tools are discussed next.

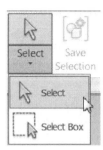

Figure 5 *The **Select** flyout*

Select

This is the default selection tool and is used to select only the object on which you click, either in the graphics window or in the **Selection Tree**. You can hold the CTRL key down to select multiple objects by clicking on them. The selection will be made based on the current selection resolution. This means that if the selection resolution is set to **File**, clicking on any object will select all the objects in that particular file. This selection tool is also available in the **Quick Access Toolbar**.

 Note: *Holding down the SHIFT key and selecting any object will select everything in the Autodesk Navisworks scene. Repeating this process will cycle through various selection resolutions.*

 Tip: *Holding down the CTRL key and clicking on an object will allow you to add or remove it from the current selection.*

Select Box

This option lets you select objects by pressing and holding the left mouse button down and dragging a box around them. Note that for the objects to be selected, they need to be fully inside the box. It is important to understand that the selection will be made based on the current selection resolution. This means that if the selection resolution is set to **Layer**, having any one object fully enclosed inside the selection box will select all the objects on the layer of that object.

 Tip: *Pressing and holding down the SHIFT and SPACEBAR keys will change the **Select** tool to **Select Box** tool.*

*Our technical support team gets this question once in a while from the Autodesk Navisworks users that they cannot select an object by clicking on it. In most cases, the selection type is by mistake set to **Select Box**. As a result, clicking on the object does not work.*

 Note: *The buttons in most Autodesk Navisworks flyouts are sticky buttons. This means that the button of the tool that was clicked last will be the current button displayed in the flyout. For example, in case the **Select Box** tool was selected last from the flyout, this tool button will be displayed in the **Select & Search** ribbon panel.*

Select All Flyout

This flyout provides three tools, as shown in Figure 6. These tools are discussed next.

Figure 6 *The Select All flyout*

Select All

Clicking this tool selects everything in the Autodesk Navisworks scene.

Select None

This tool deselects everything in the Autodesk Navisworks scene. You can press the ESC key or click anywhere in the blank area of the screen to deselect everything.

Invert Selection

Clicking this tool deselects everything that is currently selected and selects everything that was not selected.

Select Same Flyout

This flyout will only be active if you have made a selection. The options in this flyout will vary depending on the type of file you are working with and the type of object selected. Figure 7 shows the options that are available when you select an object from an AutoCAD Plant 3D file that has material assigned in Autodesk Navisworks. Figure 8 show the options available in this flyout when you select an Autodesk Revit object. These options are discussed next.

 Note: If you have multiple objects selected, the options in the *Select Same* flyout will select additional objects matching the criteria of any of the selected objects.

Select Multiple Instances

This option selects all the other instances of the selected object, such as multiple instances of a nut or a bolt in an Autodesk Inventor assembly. Note that this option will only be active if there are multiple copies available of the selected object.

Same Name

This option selects all the objects that have the same name as the object currently selected.

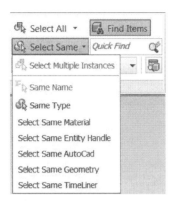

Figure 7 *The* ***Select Same*** *flyout for an AutoCAD Plant 3D object*

Figure 8 *The* ***Select Same*** *flyout for an Autodesk Revit object*

Same Type

This option selects all the objects that are of the same type as the object currently selected. For example, in an AutoCAD Plant 3D model, if you select a structural member and then click **Same Type**, all the structural members from the Autodesk Navisworks scene will be selected.

Select Same Material

This option selects all the objects that are assigned the same material as the object currently selected.

Select Same Geometry

This option selects all the objects that have the same geometry as the object currently selected.

Select Same TimeLiner

This option selects all the objects that are assigned to the same **TimeLiner** task as the currently selected object.

Select Same <Property>

These options depend on the file and the object selected. For example, **Select Same Summary** for an Autodesk Inventor file or **Select Same Revit Material** for an Autodesk Revit file. These options are used to select all the objects that match the same property as that of the currently selected object.

Selection Tree

This button is used to toggle on or off the visibility of the **Selection Tree** window.

Note: *The remaining tools on the* ***Select & Search*** *ribbon panel will be discussed later in this chapter.*

CONTROLLING VISIBILITY OF OBJECTS

Autodesk Navisworks provides you various tools to turn on or off the visibility of the selected objects. This can be done using the **Visibility** ribbon panel on the **Home** ribbon tab, as shown in Figure 9.

*Figure 9 The **Visibility** ribbon panel*

 Note: *Some of these tools are also available on the **Item Tools** ribbon tab > **Visibility** ribbon panel, which is only made available when you make a selection.*

The tools on the **Home** ribbon tab > **Visibility** ribbon panel are discussed next.

Hide

This tool will only be active if there are some objects currently selected in the graphics window or in the **Selection Tree**. This tool works as a toggle to hide or unhide the current selection. You can also select one or multiple objects in the **Selection Tree** and use the right-click shortcut menu to hide or unhide the selected objects, as shown in Figure 10. Once the objects are hidden, they will be displayed grayed out in the **Selection Tree**. If you right-click on the hidden objects in the **Selection Tree**, a tick mark will be displayed on the **Hide** option, informing you that the objects are currently hidden.

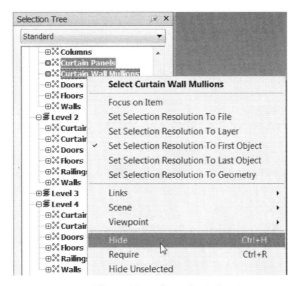

*Figure 10 Hiding objects from the **Selection Tree***

Require

The **Require** tool will also be available only when there are some objects selected. This tool is used to control the visibility of important objects when you are navigating around a large model. By default, during the navigation process, Autodesk Navisworks makes an intelligent decision of dropping certain objects temporarily until the current frame is rebuilt. This is evident from the **Pencil Indicator Bar** on the lower right corner of the Autodesk Navisworks window. During this process, if the objects important to you are also dropped from the scene, you can select them and make them required by clicking the **Require** button or by right-clicking on them in the **Selection Tree**. This will ensure they are not dropped from the frames during navigation. The objects that are made required are displayed in Red in the **Selection Tree**.

 Tip: CTRL + H is the shortcut key to hide or unhide objects. CTRL + R is the shortcut key to make objects required or not required.

Hide Unselected

This tool will be available only when there are some objects selected. It is used to hide the objects that are not selected. This can also be done by right-clicking on the objects you want to keep visible in the **Selection Tree** and selecting **Hide Unselected** from the shortcut menu.

Unhide All

This tool is used to unhide all the objects in the Autodesk Navisworks scene.

Unrequire All

This tool is available in the **Unhide All** flyout and is used to unrequire all the objects that were made required.

What I do

*While working with large Autodesk Navisworks models, there are times when I have to unhide everything and then return to the current visibility at a later stage. Instead of keeping track of which objects are hidden, I simply create a new viewpoint by right-clicking in the **Saved Viewpoint** window. Then I right-click on the new viewpoint and select **Edit** to display the **Edit Viewpoint** dialog box. In this dialog box, I select the **Hide/Required** tick box on the lower left corner to save the visibility of the objects in my current viewpoint. Now, I can unhide all objects without any hesitation. To restore the previous visibility, I simply click on the viewpoint that I created. Creating and editing viewpoints will be discussed in later chapters.*

ITEM TOOLS

As mentioned earlier, the **Item Tools** ribbon tab is displayed only when you select one or more objects. Various panels are available in this ribbon tab that can be used to control visibility, transformation, appearance etc. of the model. Figure 11 shows this ribbon tab with the **Transform** and **Appearance** ribbon panel. The tools in these panels are discussed next. The tools in the remaining panels were either discussed earlier or will be discussed in later chapters.

Figure 11 *The* **Transform** *and* **Appearance** *ribbon panel of the* **Item Tools** *ribbon tab*

Transform Ribbon Panel

The tools in this ribbon panel are used to transform the selected objects. These tools are discussed next.

Move

This tool is used to move the selected objects. When you invoke this tool, the move gizmo is displayed. If there is only one object selected, this gizmo is displayed at the center of that object. If there are multiple objects displayed, this gizmo is displayed at the transformation center of all objects combined, see Figure 12.

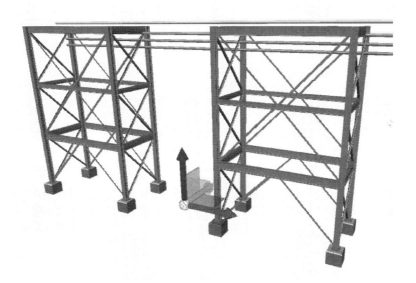

Figure 12 *The* **Move** *gizmo to move multiple objects*

This gizmo represents the X, Y, and Z axis of the Autodesk Navisworks scene in Red, Green, and Blue. When you move the cursor over any of these axes, it is highlighted and the cursor changes to the hand cursor. This indicates that you can drag the mouse to move the selected objects along the selected axis direction. Alternatively, you can move the cursor over any of the planes in the gizmo and drag to move the selected objects in that plane.

Dragging the sphere at the origin of the gizmo lets you move the objects by snapping the transformation center to an edge or a vertex of the model.

If you want to move the objects by specifying the exact values, expand the **Transform** ribbon panel and enter the values in the **Position X**, **Y**, and **Z** boxes. You can also change the location of the transformation center using the **Transformation Center X**, **Y**, and **Z** boxes. Note that these values are based on the current display units.

 *Tip: To change the location of the transformation center dynamically, hold the CTRL key down and drag the sphere at the origin of the **Move** gizmo to the desired edge or vertex. You cannot drop it at a blank location on the screen using this method.*

What I do

*If I have to move objects by specifying accurate values, I right-click on the selected objects and select **Override Item > Override Transform** from the shortcut menu. This displays the **Override Transform** dialog box that lets me type in the exact X, Y, and Z values based on the current display units.*

---

 *Note: You can also move the selected objects using the **Measure** tool. This tool will be discussed in later chapters.*

Rotate

This tool is used to rotate the selected objects. When you invoke this tool, the rotate gizmo is displayed at the transformation center of the selected objects. To dynamically rotate the object, move the cursor over the arc representing the plane between the axis; the cursor changes to the hand cursor. Now, press and drag the mouse to rotate the objects around the transformation center. Note that if you drag one of the axes, only the gizmo moves, changing the location of the transformation center.

If you want to rotate the objects by an accurate angle, expand the **Transform** ribbon panel and enter the rotation angle value in the **Rotation X**, **Y**, or **Z** boxes.

What I do

*After using the **Move** or **Rotate** tool, every time a selection is made, the **Move** or **Rotate** gizmo is displayed. This is really annoying if I do not want to move or rotate the objects. To stop this from happening, I simply select any object and then from the **Item Tool** ribbon tab, clear the **Move** or **Rotate** tool. These gizmos are no longer displayed on every object selection unless I click on these tools again.*

Scale

This tool is used to scale the selected objects around the origin of the **Scale** gizmo. When you invoke this tool, the scale gizmo will be displayed. You can drag one of the axes of the scale gizmo to scale the object only in that direction or drag one of the triangles to scale the object in that plane. If you drag the sphere at the origin of the gizmo, the selected objects will be scaled uniformly in all directions.

You can also specify exact scale values by expanding the **Transform** ribbon panel and entering the scale factors in the **Scale X, Y**, or **Z** boxes.

 Tip: *Because the objects are scaled around the origin of the **Scale** gizmo, it is not recommended to scale multiple objects at the same time. On doing so, they will move away from their original location.*

Reset Transform

This tool is used to restore the original shape, location, and orientation of the selected objects. It cancels any move, rotate, or scale operations performed on the selected object. This tool is also available on the **Home** ribbon tab > **Project** ribbon panel > **Reset All** flyout.

Appearance Ribbon Panel

The tools in this ribbon panel are used to change the transparency and color of the selected objects. These tools are discussed next.

Transparency

This slider bar is used to set the transparency of the selected objects. Setting this value to 100% will make the objects disappear. However, you will still be able to select them by clicking on them. Figure 13 shows the Autodesk Revit building with the transparency of the glazed panels set to 0%. Figure 14 shows the same building with the transparency of the glazed panels set to 90%.

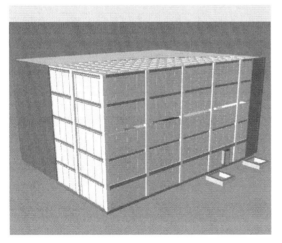

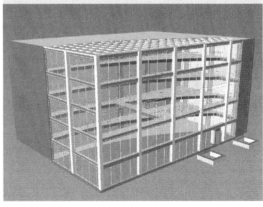

Figure 13 Building showing the glazed panels with 0% transparency

Figure 14 Building showing the glazed panels with 90% transparency

Color

This list is used to change the color of the selected objects. Clicking on **More Colors** from this list will display the **Color** dialog box with more color options. Clicking on the **Define Custom Colors >>** button in the **Color** dialog box will expand this dialog box. In the expanded area, you can define your own custom color by specifying the hue, saturation, and luminance values or the Red, Green, and Blue values. You can click on the **Add to Custom Colors** button to add the new color to the custom box for future use.

Reset Appearance

The **Reset Appearance** tool is used to reset the color and transparency of the selected objects to the original settings. This tool is also available on the **Home** ribbon tab > **Project** ribbon panel > **Reset All** flyout.

MODIFYING UNITS, SIZE, AND LOCATION OF A CAD FILE

As mentioned in the earlier chapter, Autodesk Navisworks lets you aggregate models from different CAD platforms and design teams. During this process, you will face scenarios where the files were created in different units and with different coordinates. As a result, when you start appending the files, they will not sit at the location where they are supposed to. In this case, it is recommended to ask the design team to fix the original file. However, sometimes it is not possible to do that. For those cases, Autodesk Navisworks provides you with the **Units and Transform** tool that lets you change the units, location and orientation of an entire file. This tool is available when you right-click on a file in the **Selection Tree**, as shown in Figure 15. When you invoke this tool, the **Units and Transform** dialog box will be displayed, as shown in Figure 16. The options in this dialog box are discussed next.

Units

This list displays the units of the selected file. You can click on this list to change the units; the model in the file will be scaled to match the new units. For example, if the object was drawn in the CAD file in Inches and the value of the dimension was originally 500", changing the units of that file to Millimeter will scale the file down such that the dimension will now become 500 mm.

Origin

If you want to move the selected file to a different location, enter the coordinates in the **Origin** boxes. Keep in mind that the file moved using this method cannot be restored to the original location using the **Reset Transform** tool discussed in the previous section. If you want to do that, you will have to go back to the **Units and Transform** dialog box. This dialog box remembers the value you typed in the **Origin** boxes to move the object. You can change these values back to zero to restore the original location of the file.

Reflected Transform

This tick box is selected if you want to use the mirrored scale for the transformation.

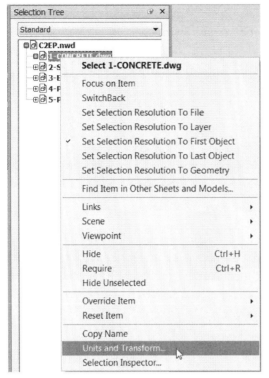

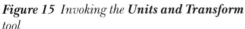

Figure 15 Invoking the **Units and Transform** tool

Figure 16 The **Units and Transform** dialog box

Rotation

This options in this area are used to rotate the file. The value of the rotation angle is specified in the **about** box. The rotation axis is defined by setting the value of that axis to 1 and the remaining two axes to 0 in the boxes below the **about** box. For example, if you want to rotate the file by 90-degrees around the Z axis, enter **90** in the **about** box and **0, 0, 1** in the boxes below.

Scale

The boxes in this area are used to specify the scale factor along the X, Y, and Z axes.

SELECTION SETS AND SEARCH SETS

Selecting objects is a task performed frequently in Autodesk Navisworks. However, selecting multiple objects becomes a tedious job, especially if you have to regularly select a large number of objects. To simplify this process, Autodesk Navisworks lets you group the objects that you regularly select in a set so that next time when you are required to select the same objects, you can simply click on the set. If you have large number of sets in the Autodesk Navisworks scene, you can organize them in folders for ease of use. There are two types of sets available, selection sets and search sets. Both these are discussed next.

Selection Sets

These sets are created by selecting the objects first and then saving them in a set with a name. The selection sets can be modified at any time to add or remove objects. The following sections explain the procedures for creating and modifying the selection sets.

Procedure for Creating Selection Sets

The following steps explain the procedure for creating a selection set.

a. Turn on the visibility of the **Sets** window and dock it on the left of the screen by clicking on the **Auto-Hide** button on the top right of this window. If you are going to use the **Selection Tree** for the selection purpose, you can dock it on top of the **Sets** window.

b. Select the required objects from the **Selection Tree** or the graphics window. You can use various combinations of the selection resolution and the **Select Same** tools to select the required objects.

c. Click the **Save Selection** button from the toolbar on top of the **Sets** window; a new item is added in this window with the default name as Selection Set. Change the name to the required name.

d. Click anywhere in the blank area of the graphics window to deselect everything. Now, click on the selection set that you just created to reselect all the previous objects again in one click.

e. If you want to place this set in a folder, click on the **New Folder** button from the **Sets** window; a new folder is added with the name Folder.

f. Change the name of the folder to any required name. Now, drag and drop the selection set created previously in this folder.

g. To create a new set that is placed automatically in this folder, select the required objects and then right-click on the folder. Click **Save Selection** from the shortcut menu to save the new set in this folder. Figure 17 shows a couple of selection sets created and organized inside a folder.

Figure 17 Selection sets organized in a folder

Procedure for Modifying Selection Sets

As mentioned earlier, you can add or remove objects from the selection sets at any time. The following steps explain the process.

a. From the **Sets** window, click on the name of the selection set to modify; all the objects under that set will be selected.

b. Hold down the CTRL key. Now, from the graphics window or the **Selection Tree**, deselect the objects that you want to remove.

c. Right-click on the selection set in the **Sets** window to display the shortcut menu.

d. Click **Update** from the shortcut menu to remove the deselected objects from the set.

e. Click anywhere in the blank area of the graphics window to deselect everything. Now, click on the name of the selection set again in the **Sets** window; you will notice that the set does not select the objects that you removed.

f. To add additional objects to the set, click on the name of the set to make sure it is selected. Now, hold down the CTRL key and select additional objects from the graphics window or the **Selection Tree**.

g. Right-click on the name of the set in the **Sets** window and click **Update** from the shortcut menu; the new objects will be added to the set.

h. To copy a selection set, click on the name of the selection set and then click the **Duplicate** button from the **Sets** window; a new set will be added with the same name and the suffix (1).

i. Right-click on the new set and click **Rename** to rename the new set. Add or remove objects from it, as required, and then update the set.

 Tip: You can right-click on a selection set and click **Hide/Show** to hide or show all the objects in the current selection set.

Search Sets

This is a very handy tool that lets you search and select object based on their properties and then save them as a set for future selection. For example, in an Autodesk Revit file, you can search all the items with the name "Curtain Wall Mullions" and then save the search as a set. The common searches can also be exported and then imported in another file with similar objects.

If you want to search objects based on their basic criteria, such as layer names, you can use the **Quick Find** box available on the **Home** ribbon tab > **Select & Search** ribbon panel. However, if you want to perform complex searches, such as the search based on the value of an object property, you can use the **Find Items** window that can be turned on using the **Find Items** button on the **Home** ribbon tab > **Select & Search** ribbon panel. Figure 18 shows a floating **Find Items** window. This window has two panes; the left pane shows the selection tree of the current file and the right pane shows various options to perform a search. The options in these two panes are discussed next.

 Note: If you are using the **Training** workspace created in the previous chapter, the **Find Items** window will be available on the lower left corner in the auto-hide mode.

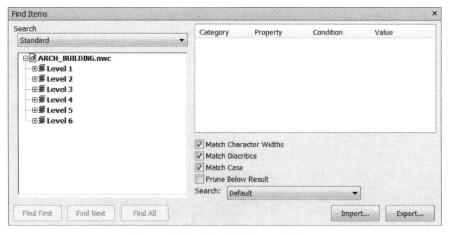

Figure 18   *The* **Find Items** *window*

Search

This list is available on the top left of the **Find Items** window. It lets you specify whether the components in the selection tree listed below this list should be displayed as standard, compact, or as properties tree. If your current model has some sets created, this list will also show the options to display those sets. If nothing is selected in the tree below this list, the search will be performed on everything in the scene. If you want to restrict the search only to certain branches of the tree, select them from this area.

Search Statement Area

This is the area on the right side of the **Find Items** window and is used to create one or more search statements. The search statements that you create are based on the four columns available in this area. These columns are discussed next.

Category

This column lets you select the category on which you want to base your search. When you click on this column of the first row, all the categories available in the current Autodesk Navisworks scene will be displayed in a drop-down list, as shown in Figure 19. Note that these categories change, depending on the original CAD model you are working with.

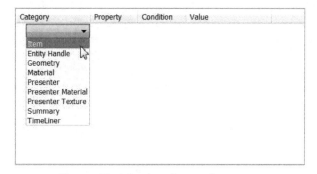

Figure 19   *Selecting the search category*

Property
This column is used to select the property that you want to search for based on the category that you selected earlier.

 Tip*: You can drag the column to resize them if you cannot see the full information inside that particular column.*

Condition
This column is used to select the condition operator for the category and property selected earlier.

 Tip*: You can use the **Wildcard** condition to search for objects if you are not sure about the value of the property.*

Value
This column is used to select the value of the property selected earlier. When you click on this column, only the value of the property that you selected will be displayed.

 Note*: You can right-click on a search statement row and select **Negate Condition** from the shortcut menu. This will search for the objects that do not match the search criteria that you defined in the row.*

You can also add another row of search statement. By default, the new row will work as an "And" condition. This means that only those objects will be displayed as the search result that meets the criteria in both the rows. You can right-click on the additional rows and click **Or Condition** to make them "Or" condition. This means the search results will show all the objects that meet the criteria in the first or second row.

Match Character Width
Selecting this tick box will ensure only those objects that match the search character width are selected as the search results.

Match Diacritics
Selecting this tick box will ensure only those objects that match special pronunciation of the words are selected as the search result.

Match Case
Select this tick box if you want to only search for objects matching the case of your search value.

Prune Below Result
This tick box is used when you have selected the branches you want to restrict your search on from the left pane of the **Find Items** window. If this tick box is selected, the search will stop as soon as the first object matching the search criteria is found.

Search Drop-down List
This drop-down list has the following three options:

Default

This option searches for all the objects in and below the tree branch selected in the left pane of the **Find Items** window.

Below Selected Paths

This option searches for all the objects below the tree branch selected in the left pane of the **Find Items** window.

Selected Paths Only

This option searches for all the objects only in the tree branch selected in the left pane of the **Find Items** window.

Export

As mentioned earlier, the common search criteria can be saved and used in other files as well. This button is used to export the current search criteria as a .XML file. You can save it on a network to make the search criteria available to others in your team.

Import

This button is used to import the .XML file of the search criteria that was saved earlier.

Find First

This button is used to find and select the first object matching the search criteria.

Find Next

This button is used to find and select the next object matching the search criteria.

Find All

This button is used to find and select all the objects in the current Autodesk Navisworks scene that match the search criteria.

Once the search results are selected, you can save them as search sets by clicking on the **Save Search** button on the **Sets** window.

Procedure for Creating Search Sets

The following steps show you how to perform various types of searches and save them as sets.

a.   In the **Find Items** window, click on the first row under the **Category** column; a list displaying various categories will be displayed. Select the required category from this list.

You can drag the column heading partition to increase the width of the column.

b.   Click on the first row under the **Property** column and select the required property for the item you selected in the previous column.

c.   Click on the first row under the **Condition** column and select the required condition. Selecting **Wildcard** will let you use special characters, such as asterisk (*), in your searches.

d. Click on the first row under the **Value** column and select the required value; a second row is automatically added.

e. If you want to filter down your search further, specify the information in the second row. By default, this row will act as the "And" condition. This means that only the objects matching the criteria in both the rows will be selected as the search result. If required, right-click on the second row and select **Or Condition** from the shortcut menu. This means that any object that matches the search criteria in the first row or the second row will be selected as the search result.

f. Click on the **Find All** button to find and select all the items matching the search criteria.

g. Display the **Sets** window and dock it on the screen by clicking the **Auto-Hide** button on the top right of this window.

h. Click the **Save Search** button from the toolbar on the top of the **Sets** window; a new set is added with the default name as **Search Set**.

i. Rename the search set by right-clicking on the name of the search set and selecting **Rename** from the shortcut menu.

Procedure for Exporting and Importing Search Sets

The following steps show you how to export and import search sets.

a. From the **Sets** window, click on the **Import/Export** flyout on the right corner of the toolbar on top of the **Sets** window.

b. From the flyout, select the **Export Search Sets** option to display the **Export** dialog box.

c. Browse to the folder where you want to save the search set and then enter the name of the search set. Click the **Save** button to save this set; the file will be saved with the .XML extension.

d. Open the file that has objects similar to the objects listed in the search criteria that you saved.

e. From the **Sets** window, click on the **Import/Export** flyout on the right corner of the toolbar and select the **Import Search Sets** option.

f. Browse to the folder where you saved the search and double-click on the name of the search set file; the search criteria will now be listed as a search set in the **Sets** window.

g. Click on the name of the search set; all the objects matching the search criteria will be selected in this file.

 *Note: The icon of the search set that is displayed in the **Sets** window is different from that of the selection set. This helps you understand that only the sets with the search icon will be exported.*

VIEWING OBJECT PROPERTIES

Autodesk Navisworks engine is able to import the native object properties from most of the CAD programs. These properties let you better understand the design intent and requirements. These properties will be displayed in the **Properties** window when you select an object. Depending on the object selected, there will be various tabs available in the **Properties** window representing various categories and the properties related to those categories. Note that the properties displayed are dependent on the selection resolution. As a result, if the selection resolution is set to **File**, only the file properties will be displayed and not the properties of any object inside that file.

Figure 20 shows the floating **Properties** window displaying the element properties of an Autodesk Revit wall. Figure 21 shows the same window showing the AutoCAD properties of an AutoCAD Plant 3D pipe.

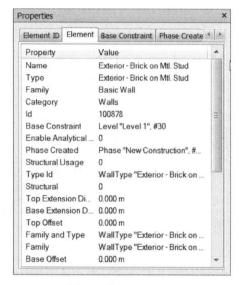

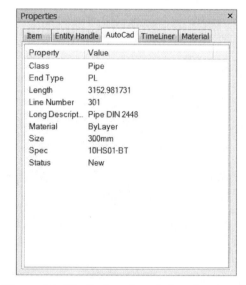

Figure 20 *The **Properties** window showing the element properties of an Autodesk Revit wall*

Figure 21 *The **Properties** window showing the AutoCAD properties of an AutoCAD Plant 3D pipe*

Creating Custom Properties

Autodesk Navisworks allows you to add custom tabs to the **Properties** window for the selected objects where you can create your own custom properties. However, remember that these properties will be dependent on the selection resolution. This means that if the selection resolution was set to **Layer** when you selected the objects and created the custom tab and properties, they will only be displayed when you select that layer again. If you select an object in that layer, the custom tab and properties will not be displayed.

To create a new custom tab and property, select the required object and then right-click inside any tab of the **Properties** window; the shortcut menu will be displayed. Click the **Add New User Data Tab** option; a new user tab with the default name **User Data** is added and is made current.

Now, right-click inside the new tab to display the shortcut menu. Select the **Rename Tab** option from the shortcut menu and rename the tab to the desired name.

To create custom properties, right-click in the new tab and move the cursor over the **Insert New Property** option in the shortcut menu. You are allowed to create a new property based on the following four types:

String
Use this option when the custom property you want to create is text, special characters, numbers or any combination of these.

Boolean
Use this option when the custom property you want to create can only have its value as **Yes** or **No**.

Float
Use this option when the custom property you want to create can only have its value as a decimal number such as 1234.5678.

Integer
Use this option when the custom property you want to create can only have its value as a positive whole number, a negative whole number, or zero.

Once you select any of these options, a row under the **Property** column in the new tab is activated that lets you enter the name of the property. To specify or edit the value of the property, double-click on the **Value** column of that property; the **Autodesk Navisworks Manage/Simulate 2016** dialog box will be displayed that lets you enter or edit the value. Note that if you enter a value that does not comply with the property type, a dialog box will be displayed informing you that it is an invalid value for the property type.

 Note: Right-clicking on a custom property displays a shortcut menu that provides you options to copy the property value, copy the entire row, delete the property, add or delete the custom tab, insert new property, and so on.

DYNAMICALLY DISPLAYING OBJECT PROPERTIES ON THE MODEL

Autodesk Navisworks allows you to dynamically display some of the object properties by simply moving the cursor over the model in the graphics window. These are called quick properties. To display quick properties on the model, turn them on by clicking the **Quick Properties** button on the **Home** ribbon tab > **Display** ribbon panel. When the quick properties are on, move the cursor over any object in the graphics window. By default, the **Item Name** and **Item Type** properties are dynamically displayed.

To specify which properties are displayed when you turn on the quick properties, right-click on the blank area of the screen and select **Global Options** from the shortcut menu; the **Options Editor** dialog box will be displayed. You can also press the F12 key to invoke this dialog box. Expand the **Interface** category from the left and then expand the **Quick Properties** subcategory. Click on **Definitions**; the right side of the dialog box will display the two default quick properties, as shown in Figure 22.

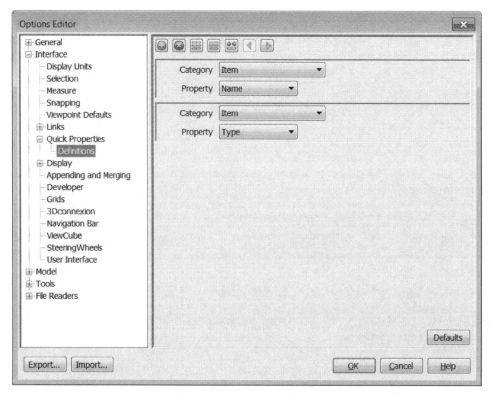

*Figure 22 The **Options Editor** dialog box showing the default quick properties*

To add an additional property to be displayed as a quick property, click on the **Add element** button, which is the Green button with the + symbol; a new item name property is added at the top. Click on the **Category** list of the top item and change it to the required category. Next, click on the **Property** list of the top item and change it to the required property. Similarly, you can add as many quick properties as you want. To delete a quick property, click on the **Remove element** button, which is the Red button with the X symbol. Note that the property on the top of the list will be removed.

Figure 23 shows an Autodesk Revit model showing some quick properties of a wall.

*Note: By default, the quick property definition elements are displayed as the list view in the right pane of the **Options Editor**. You can change the display to the grid view or the record view by clicking on their respective buttons in the right pane of the **Options Editor**.*

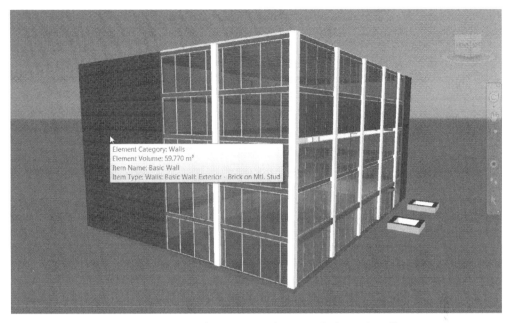

Figure 23 *Quick properties of an Autodesk Revit wall*

 Tip: *You can hide the visibility of category names in the quick properties that are displayed in the graphics window. To do this, invoke the **Options Editor** by pressing the F12 key or by right-clicking in the blank area of the screen and selecting **Options Editor** from the shortcut menu. From the left pane of the dialog box, expand **Interface** and then click on **Quick Properties**. Now, from the right pane, select the **Hide Category** tick box.*

SELECTION INSPECTOR

Home Ribbon Tab > Select & Search Ribbon Panel > Selection Inspector
View Ribbon Tab > Workspace Ribbon Panel > Windows Flyout > Selection Inspector

The **Selection Inspector** window lists the objects currently selected and all their configured quick properties. You can select one or multiple objects from the graphics window or the **Selection Tree**. The number of objects currently selected are displayed near the top left corner of this window. The selected objects can be saved as a selection set from this window. You can also export a CSV file of all the objects listed in this window. Figure 24 shows the **Selection Inspector** window showing various objects selected and their respective quick properties. The options in this window are discussed next.

Quick Property Definition

Clicking this button displays the **Options Editor** dialog box with the **Quick Properties >
Definitions** page active so that you can configure what quick properties you want to be displayed in the **Selection Inspector** window and also in the Autodesk Navisworks scene.

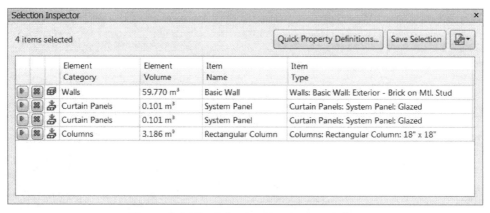

Figure 24 *The Selection Inspector window*

Save Selection

Clicking this button saves the objects listed in the **Selection Inspector** window as a selection set with the default name of **Selection Set**. You can use the **Sets** window to rename this set.

Export Flyout

Clicking this flyout displays the **Export CSV** option that lets you save the current selection as a CSV file using the **Export to CSV** dialog box. You can browse to the location where you want to save the CSV file and then enter the name. All the selected objects, along with the configured quick properties, will be saved in this file.

Show Item

This is the button with the Green play symbol displayed on the left of the selection row. Clicking this button zooms the selected object to the extents of the graphics screen.

Deselect

This is the button with the Red X symbol displayed on the left of the selection row. Clicking this button deselects the objects in that row and removes them from the **Selection Inspector** window.

APPEARANCE PROFILER

Home Ribbon Tab > Tools Ribbon Panel > Appearance Profiler
View Ribbon Tab > Workspace Ribbon Panel > Windows Flyout > Appearance Profiler

This is a really smart tool in Autodesk Navisworks that lets you select objects and then assign color and transparency to them for ease of identification. You can select objects based on their properties or use a selection set or a search set already created in the current scene. The common appearances can also be exported and then imported in multiple files.

Figure 25 shows the **Appearance Profiler** window displaying appearances assigned to some selected objects and sets.

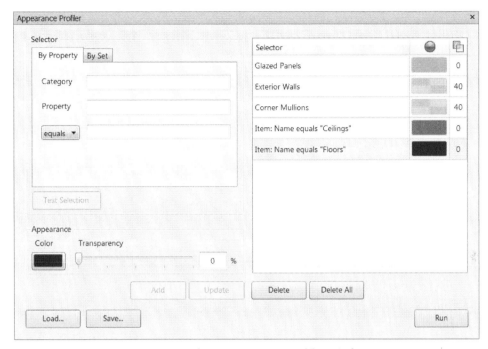

*Figure 25 The **Appearance Profiler** window*

The options in this window are discussed next.

Selector Area

The options available in this area are discussed next.

By Property Tab

This tab is used to select objects based on their property values. You can define the categories and their properties in their in their respective text boxes. The value of the property is entered in the box below the **Property** box. The **equals/does not equal** conditions can be used to specify whether to search for the objects with the property value equal to or not equal to the one entered in this tab.

By Set Tab

This tab lists all the selection and search sets available in the current file. The **Refresh** button is used to synchronize any changes that are made to the sets. Clicking this button also ensures that the new sets created in the **Sets** window are also displayed in the **By Sets** tab of the **Appearance Profiler** window.

Test Selection

This button is used to select objects based on the criteria specified in the **By Property** tab or the objects that comply with the properties of the set selected in the **By Set** tab.

Appearance Area

The options available are used to assign color and transparency overrides to the objects selected using the **Test Selection** button. Note that these overrides will only be applied when you click the **Add** button.

Selector List

The list displays various objects or sets selected and their respective color and transparency overrides. You can select any item in this list and then click the **Test Selection** button to select the objects again.

Add Button

This button is used to assign the color and transparency overrides to the selected objects and add them to the **Selector** list.

Update Button

If the item selected in the **Selector** list is changed, this button is used to update the item with those changes. The changes include the selection criteria or the appearance overrides.

Delete Button

This button is used to delete the item selected in the **Selector** list.

Delete All Button

This button is used to delete all the items in the **Selector** list.

Save Button

This button is used to export the current appearance profile for use in other files. When you click this button, the **Save As** dialog box will be displayed that lets you specify the location and name of the file to be saved. This file will be saved in the DAT format.

Load Button

This button is used to import the DAT files of the appearance profiles. When you click this button, the **Load** dialog box will be displayed that lets you select the appearance profile file that you want to import to the current Autodesk Navisworks scene.

What I do

In most consulting projects I work on, there are BIM standards that we have to follow to assign colors to objects such as rectangular ducts, flexible ducts, pumps, mechanical equipment, and so on. To avoid the hassle of manually selecting these objects and changing their properties in all the files, I prefer creating an appearance profile based on search sets and saving it as a template. This allows me to load the appearance profile and run it to assign the required colors to the objects in every new file I get.

HANDS-ON EXERCISES

Next, you will work on hands-on exercises by using the concepts learned in this chapter.

Hands-on Exercise (Plant)	*In this exercise, you will complete the following tasks:* 1. *Open the **C2EP.nwf** file and select objects based on various selection tools and resolutions.* 2. *Turn on and off the visibility of the objects in the scene.* 3. *Override the appearance and transformation of objects in the scene.* 4. *Create selection and search sets.* 5. *Export search sets from one file and import to the other.* 6. *View object properties and create custom properties for certain objects.* 7. *Turn on the visibility of quick properties and customize them.* 8. *Open AutoCAD pressure vessels and change the file units.*

Section 1: Opening the File and Selecting Objects

In this section, you will open the required file and select objects using various selection resolutions. You will also use the **Select**, **Select All**, and **Select Same** flyouts to make selections.

1. Start Autodesk Navisworks, if it is not already running.

2. Click the **Open** button on the **Quick Access Toolbar**; the **Open** dialog box is displayed.

3. Browse to the **Chapter 2 > Exercise Plant** folder. Change the file type from the **Files of type** list to **Navisworks File Set (*.nwf)** and double-click on the **C2EP.nwf** file to open it. This file is similar to the one you saved in the previous chapter.

4. On the **Home** ribbon tab, expand the **Select & Search** ribbon panel and click on the pin icon on the left of the expanded ribbon panel to pin it on the screen.

5. From the **Selection Resolution** list, click **File**; this sets the selection resolution to file.

6. Click on any steel member in the graphics window; you will notice that the **2-STEEL.dwg** file is highlighted in the **Selection Tree** and all the structural steel objects are selected in the graphics window.

7. Click on any pipe object from the graphics window; the **5-PIPING.dwg** file is highlighted in the **Selection Tree** and all the pipe objects are selected in the graphics window.

8. From the expanded **Select & Search** ribbon panel, click on the **Selection Resolution** list and select **Layer**; this sets the selection resolution to layer.

9. Click on any of the concrete columns from the graphics window; the **1-CONCRETE.dwg** file is expanded in the **Selection Tree** and the **Concrete_Columns** layer is highlighted. Also, all the concrete columns are selected in the graphics window.

10. From the graphics window, click on one of the vessels on the right side of the plant; the **3-EQUIPMENT.dwg** file is expanded in the **Selection Tree** and the **Vessels** layer is highlighted. Also, all the vessels are selected in the graphics window.

11. From the expanded **Select & Search** ribbon panel, click on the **Selection Resolution** list and select **First Object**; this sets the selection resolution to the first branch under layers in the **Selection Tree**.

12. Click on any of the vertical steel columns; the **2-STEEL.dwg** file and the **StructuralSteel_Columns** layer inside it is expanded and one of the **3D Solid** objects is highlighted in the **Selection Tree**.

13. In the expanded **Select & Search** ribbon panel, click on the **Select Same** flyout and click **Select Same Geometry**; all the objects matching the geometry of the originally selected object are selected in the graphics window. All these objects are also highlighted in the **Selection Tree**. Figure 26 shows the highlighted objects in the graphics window and also in the **Selection Tree**.

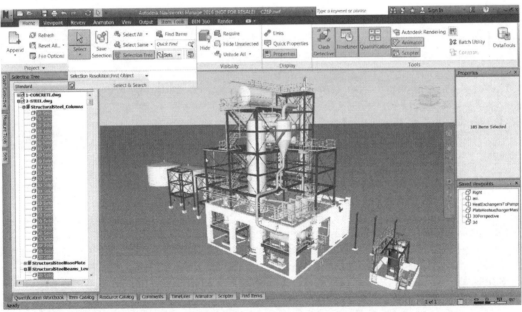

*Figure 26 Structural steel objects selected using the **Select Same** flyout*

14. In the **Select & Search** ribbon panel, click on the **Select All** flyout and click **Select None**; everything is deselected.

 Tip: *As mentioned earlier, you can also press the ESC key or click anywhere in the blank area of the graphics window to deselect everything.*

15. Unpin the **Select & Search** ribbon panel by clicking on the pin icon on the left.

Section 2: Controlling the Visibility of Selected Objects

In this section, you will hide and unhide the objects in the current scene. You will use the **First Object** selection resolution that was set in the previous section to select objects.

1. Click on one of the concrete columns in the graphics window. Now, in the **Select & Search** ribbon panel, click on the **Select Same** flyout and click **Select Same Geometry**; all the concrete objects in the current scene are selected.

2. In the **Visibility** ribbon panel, click **Hide** to hide the selected concrete objects in the scene. If the information dialog box is displayed informing you about hiding all the instances of the objects, Click **OK**.

3. Press ESC to deselect everything.

4. Hold down the SHIFT key and middle mouse button and drag the mouse to orbit the model. Notice that the concrete objects are no longer displayed.

5. In the **Visibility** panel, click **Unhide All**; all the concrete objects are redisplayed in the scene.

6. Hold down the SHIFT key and middle mouse button and drag the mouse to orbit the model. Notice that there are no objects hidden in the scene.

7. Orbit the model to a view similar to the start view of the file.

8. In the **Selection Tree**, click on the **5-PIPING.dwg** file. Hold down the CTRL key and select the **2-STEEL.dwg** file also.

9. In the **Select & Search** ribbon panel, click on the **Select None** flyout and click **Invert Selection**; the two files you selected are deselected and the remaining files are selected.

10. In the **Visibility** panel, click **Hide**; the selected files are hidden. Click anywhere in the blank area of the graphics window and notice how the hidden files are displayed in gray in the **Selection Tree**.

11. In the **Visibility** panel, click **Unhide All**; all the objects are made visible in the scene.

Section 3: Overriding the Appearance and Transformation of Objects

In this section, you will use the tools in the **Item Tools** ribbon tab to move the concrete columns. You will change the color and transparency of the structural steel members in the scene.

1. Click on the **1-CONCRETE.dwg** file from the **Selection Tree**. Now, in the **Navigation Bar** on the right side of the graphics window, click the **Zoom Window** flyout and select **Zoom Selected**; the view zooms to the extents of the selected file.

2. Click anywhere in the blank area of the graphics window to deselect everything.

Next, you will use the SHIFT key to cycle through various selection resolutions while selecting objects.

3. Click on one of the concrete columns to select it.

4. Hold down the SHIFT key and click on the same column again; the **1-CONCRETE.dwg** file is selected.

5. With the SHIFT key still held down, click on the same column again; the selection resolution changes to **Layer** and the **Concrete_Columns** layer is selected in the **1-CONCRETE.dwg** file.

   When an object is selected, the **Item Tools** ribbon tab is displayed. You will use this ribbon tab to move the selected columns.

6. Click on the **Item Tools** ribbon tab. Expand the **Transform** ribbon panel and pin it on the screen using the pin icon on the left of this ribbon panel.

7. In the expanded **Transform** ribbon panel, click the **Move** tool; the move gizmo is displayed at the transformation center of the concrete columns.

8. Move the cursor over the Red axis; it turns Yellow and the cursor changes to the hand cursor.

9. Press and hold down the left mouse button and drag the columns to the right; all the columns move to the right.

10. In the expanded **Transform** ribbon panel, click on the **Reset Transform** tool; all the columns are moved back to their original location.

11. With the concrete columns still selected, in the **Position Y** box of the expanded **Transform** ribbon panel, enter **-50** if the units are in Inches. If the units are in Meters, enter **-2**; the columns move through the specified distance in the negative Y direction.

12. In the expanded **Transform** ribbon panel, click on the **Reset Transform** tool; all the columns are moved back to their original location.

13. Click the **Move** tool again to close this tool and turn off the visibility of the move gizmo.

14. Click anywhere in the graphics window to deselect everything.

15. Click on one of the vertical steel columns. Now, hold the SHIFT key down and click on the same column again; the **2-STEEL.dwg** file is selected.

16. Click on the **Item Tools** tab. From the **Appearance** ribbon panel, click on the **Color** flyout and select the Yellow color.

17. Press the ESC key; all the structural steel members are changed to Yellow.

18. Click the **Save** button on the **Quick Access Toolbar** to save the changes in the file.

 Tip: *If you regularly change the color and transparency of walls or any other common objects, you can use the **Appearance Profiler** window discussed earlier in this chapter to create an appearance profile and export it for use in other files.*

Section 4: Creating Selection Sets

In this section, you will create various selection sets. To create these, the **Sets** window will be used. It is assumed that you are using the **Training** workspace created in the previous chapter. As a result, the **Sets** window is displayed in the auto-hide mode in the left of the **Selection Tree**. If not, refer to the Hands-on exercise of the previous chapter to see how to create and save a workspace.

1. Click **Sets** from the left of the **Selection Tree** to display the **Sets** window.

2. Click on the pin icon on the top right of this window to dock it on the screen below the **Selection Tree**.

3. In the graphics window, click on one of the steel columns.

4. From the **Home** ribbon tab > **Select & Search** ribbon panel, click the **Select Same** flyout and then click **Select Same Geometry**; all the steel beams and columns are selected. Note that none of the cross-bracing members are selected.

5. From the toolbar on the top of the **Sets** window, click the **Save Selection** button; a new selection set is added.

6. Rename the set to **Steel Beams & Columns**.

7. In the graphics window, click on one of the handrailing members.

8. From the **Select & Search** ribbon panel, click the **Select Same** flyout and then click **Select Same Geometry**; most of the handrailing members are selected.

 Note: *There are some handrailing members that are not selected. This is because they were created as different member type objects in the original CAD application.*

9. From the toolbar on the top of the **Sets** window, click the **Save Selection** button; a new selection set is added.

10. Rename the set to **Handrailing**. Click anywhere in the blank area of the graphics window to deselect everything.

11. In the **Sets** window, click on the **Steel Beams & Columns** set; all the objects in this set are selected.

12. Hold down the CTRL key and click on the **Handrailing** set; all the objects in this set are also selected.

13. Right-click on any of these sets in the **Sets** window and select **Hide** from the shortcut menu; all the objects in both the sets are hidden.

14. On the **Home** ribbon tab > **Visibility** ribbon panel, click **Unhide All** to redisplay the objects of the two sets.

15. Click anywhere in the blank area of the graphics window to deselect everything.

16. From the **Quick Access** toolbar, click the **Save** button to save the current file.

Section 5: Creating Search Sets

In this section, you will use the **Find Items** window to search and select objects in the C2WP.nwd file. You will then save the search results as search sets.

1. From the **Quick Access** toolbar, invoke the **Open** tool; the **Open** dialog box is displayed.

2. Change the **Files of type** to **Navisworks (*.nwd)** and then double-click on **C2EP.nwd**.

3. Move the cursor over **Find Items** below the graphics window; the **Find Items** window is displayed.

4. Dock this window at the bottom of the graphics window by clicking the **Auto-Hide** button on the top right corner of this window.

 *Tip: With various windows docked on the screen, the graphics window area reduces. You can auto-hide the windows that you do not require immediately and redisplay them whenever needed. For example, in this case, you can auto-hide the **Properties** and **Saved Viewpoints** window by clicking on the **Auto-Hide** button on the top right of these windows.*

5. In the right pane of the **Find Items** window, drag the partitions of all the columns to make them wider.

6. Click on the first row under the **Category** column and select **AutoCad** from the list.

7. From the list displayed under the **Property** column, select **Line Number**.

8. From the list displayed under the **Condition** column, select =.

9. From the list displayed under the **Value** column, select **105**; a new row is added.

10. From the second row list under the **Category** column, select **AutoCad**.

11. From the list displayed under the **Property** column, select **Class**.

12. From the list displayed under the **Condition** column, select =.

13. From the list displayed under the **Value** column, select **Pipe**.

Remember that the second row will act as the "And" condition.

14. Click on the **Find All** button; all the pipes with the line number 105 are selected.

15. From the toolbar on the top of the **Sets** window, click on the **Save Search**; a new search set is added.

16. Rename the search set to **Line 105 Pipes** by right-clicking on the new search set and selecting the **Rename** option.

17. Click anywhere in the blank area of the graphics window to deselect everything.

18. With the two rows still available in the **Find Items** window, click on the list in the first row of the **Property** column and select **Schedule**.

19. Click on the list in the first row of the **Condition** column and select =.

20. Click on the list in the first row of the **Value** column and select **SCH10S**.

21. Click on the second row list displayed under the **Property** column and select **Class**.

22. From the list displayed under the **Condition** column, select =.

23. From the list displayed under the **Value** column, select **Pipe**.

24. Click the **Find All** button; all the schedule SCH10S pipes are selected.

25. From the toolbar on the top of the **Sets** window, click **Save Search**; a new search set is added.

26. Rename the search set to **SCH10S Pipes** by right-clicking on the new search set and selecting the **Rename** option.

Section 6: Exporting and Importing Search Sets

In this section, you will export the search sets created in the previous section and then import them to the file opened from the web server.

1. From the toolbar in the **Sets** window, click on the **Import/Export** flyout and select the **Export Search Sets** option to display the **Export** dialog box.

2. Browse to the **Chapter 2 > Exercise Plant** folder and enter the name of the file as **Plant**.

3. Click the **Save** button to save the two search sets; the file is saved with the .XML extension.

4. Click the **Application Button** and then click **Open > Open URL** to display the **Open URL** dialog box.

5. If you are prompted to save the file, click **No**.

6. Enter the following path in the dialog box and click **OK**:

    http://www.deepakmaini.com/Navisworks/Plant.nwd

    The model is opened from the web server.

7. From the toolbar in the **Sets** window, click on the **Import/Export** flyout and select the **Import Search Sets** option to display the **Import** dialog box.

8. Browse to the **Chapter 2 > Exercise Plant** folder, if it is not already listed in the dialog box.

9. Double-click on the **Plant.xml** file; the two search sets are loaded in the current file and are displayed in the **Sets** window.

10. Click on the **Line 105 Pipes** search set in the **Sets** window; the two search conditions are displayed in the **Find Items** window. Also, all the objects matching this search criteria are selected.

11. Click on the **SCH10S Pipes** search set in the **Sets** window; the two search conditions are displayed in the **Find Items** window. Also, all the objects matching this search criteria are selected.

    This shows that the searches that are common to your project can be exported and imported in various files.

12. Click the **New** button on the **Quick Access Toolbar** and click **No** in the dialog box to close the current file without saving.

Section 7: Viewing Object Properties

In this section, you will select various objects and view their properties in the **Properties** window. To make sure that only the required windows are displayed on the screen, you will first restore the **Training** workspace created in the previous chapter.

1. Click the **View** ribbon tab > **Workspace** ribbon panel > **Load Workspace** flyout and click **Training**; Autodesk Navisworks resets to open this workspace.

2. Click on the **Application Button** and from the **Recent Documents** area, click **C2EP.nwd** to open this recently used file.

3. Move the cursor over the left edge of the **Properties** window available on the right of the graphics window. When the double-sided arrow is displayed, press and hold the left mouse button down and drag it to the left to widen this window.

4. Click on one of the steel columns; the **Properties** window displays the properties in the **Item** tab by default.

5. In the **Properties** window, scroll to the right and click on the **AutoCad** tab to display the AutoCAD Plant 3D properties of the selected object, see Figure 27.

6. Hold the SHIFT key down and click on the same steel column two times; the **2-STEEL.dwg** file is selected and the **Properties** window now displays the properties of the file. Click on the **Item** tab to see the properties in this tab, as shown in Figure 28.

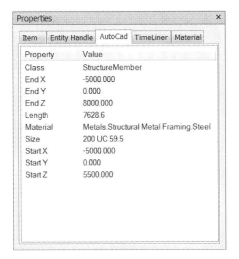

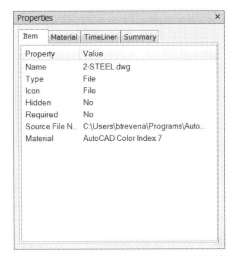

*Figure 27 The **Properties** window showing the properties of an object in the **AutoCad** tab*

*Figure 28 The **Properties** window showing the properties of a file in the **Item** tab*

Tip: Similarly, selected objects based on the **Layer** selection resolution show the layer properties.

7. In the **Selection Tree**, expand the **3-EQUIPMENT.dwg** file and then expand the **Vessels** layer; all the vessels in this layer are displayed in the tree.

8. Click on the first vessel in the list.

9. If the **AutoCad** tab is not already displayed, use the right arrow key on the top right of the **Properties** window to scroll right to the **AutoCad** tab. Once displayed, click on this tab; the AutoCAD Plant 3D properties of the vessel are displayed.

10. One by one, click on the remaining vessels in the **Vessels** layer to view the AutoCAD Plant 3D properties of all the vessels.

11. Click anywhere in the blank area of the graphics window to deselect everything. Change the view to the **Home** view, if it is not already set to that.

Section 8: Creating Custom Object Properties

In this section, you will create custom properties for the selected objects. You will use various selection resolutions to select objects for this purpose.

1. Click on one of the Green pumps located on the ground level of the plant. Hold down the SHIFT key and continue clicking on the pump until the **Pumps** layer is highlighted in the **Selection Tree**.

2. Once the **Pumps** layer is highlighted, right-click in the blank area of the **Properties** window and select **Add New User Data Tab**; a new custom tab is added with the default name of **User Data**.

3. If required, use the arrow keys on the top right of the **Properties** window to scroll to the new tab. Once displayed, click on it to make it the current tab.

4. Right-click anywhere inside the new tab and select **Rename Tab** from the shortcut menu.

5. In the dialog box that is displayed, enter **Pump Details** as the name of the tab and click **OK**.

6. Right-click anywhere inside this tab again and select **Insert New Property > String** from the shortcut menu; a new row is added under the **Property** column.

7. Type **Flow Rate** as the property name and press ENTER.

8. Double-click on the first row under the **Value** column; a dialog box is displayed to enter the value of this custom property,

9. Enter **145 L/min** as the property value and click **OK** in the dialog box.

10. Right-click inside the tab again and select **Insert New Property > Boolean** from the shortcut menu; a new row is added under the **Property** column with a default value as **No**.

11. Type **In Warehouse** as the property name and press ENTER.

12. Double-click on **No** under the **Value** column of the second row, the value changes to **Yes**. Figure 29 shows the **Properties** window with the **Pump Details** tab and the properties in it.

13. Click anywhere in the blank area of the graphics window to deselect everything.

14. Right-click on the **Pumps** layer in the **Selection Tree** and select **Set Selection Resolution To First Object** from the shortcut menu, if it is not already ticked.

15. Click on any one of the pumps again in the graphics window.

    Notice that the **Properties** window does not have the **Pump Details** tab. This is because this tab was created for the layer selection.

16. Click on the **Pumps** layer from the **Selection Tree**; the **Pump Details** tab is displayed in the **Properties** window. You may need to use the arrow keys on the top right of this window to scroll to this tab.

17. Click anywhere in the blank area of the graphics window to deselect everything.

Section 9: Turning on and Customizing Quick Properties

In this section, you will turn on the visibility of the quick properties. You will change the selection resolution to display the quick properties for that particular resolution. You will

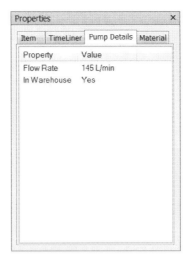

Figure 29 The **Pump Details** *tab*

also customize the quick properties to dynamically display the properties created in the previous section.

1. On the **Home** ribbon tab > **Display** ribbon panel, click the **Quick Properties** button; this turns on the display of quick properties.

2. Move the cursor over one of the concrete columns; the item name and item type properties of the concrete column are dynamically displayed on the model.

3. Move the cursor over one of the steel members; the item name and item type properties of the steel member are dynamically displayed on the model.

4. Right-click on any file in the **Selection Tree** and select **Set Selection Resolution To Layer** from the shortcut menu.

5. Move the cursor over one of the concrete columns; the item name property remains the same but the item type now displays **Layer**. This is because of the selection resolution set to **Layer**.

   Next, you will modify the display of quick properties using the **Options Editor** dialog box.

6. Press the F12 key to display the **Options Editor** dialog box.

7. From the left pane, expand **Interface > Quick Properties** and select **Definitions**; the right pane displays the two default elements.

 Note: If there were additional quick properties added earlier in Autodesk Navisworks, they will also be displayed. This is because these settings are stored with the software.

8. Click the **Add element** button from the right pane of the dialog box; a new property element is added at the top of the previous two elements.

9. From the **Category** list of the first element, click **AutoCad**.

10. From the **Property** list of the first element, click **Pressure Class**.

11. Click on the **Add element** button again; a new element is added at the top of the previous three elements.

12. From the **Category** list of the first element, click **Pump Details**.

13. From the **Property** list of the first element, click **Flow Rate**.

14. Click **OK** to close the **Options Editor** dialog box.

15. Right-click on any file in the **Selection Tree** and select **Set Selection Resolution To First Object** from the shortcut menu.

16. Move the cursor over one of the heat exchanger object; notice that the AutoCad Pressure Class property is also shown in the quick properties now, see Figure 30.

Figure 30　The quick properties of a heat exchanger

In this case, the Pump Details properties are not displayed. This is because these properties are for the **Pump** layer objects.

17. Move the cursor over one of the structural steel members; notice that only the two default properties are displayed. This is because these objects do not have any AutoCad Pressure Class or Pump Details properties assigned.

18. Move the cursor over one of the Green pumps; all four properties are displayed, as shown in Figure 31.

Figure 31 *The quick properties of a pump*

19. Click **New** on the **Quick Access Toolbar** to start a new file. When prompted to save changes to the current file, click **No**.

Section 10: Opening AutoCAD Pressure Vessels and Changing File Units

In this section, you will open two pressure vessels created in AutoCAD. One of them was created with Millimeter as the units and the other one with Inches as the units. You will change the units of the second pressure vessel to Millimeters and also move the first pressure vessel closer to the second one.

But first, you will also change the global option to smoothen the facets of the objects in the AutoCAD file using the **Options Editor**.

1. Press the F12 key to open the **Options Editor** dialog box.

2. From the left pane, expand **File Readers** and then click **DWG/DXF**; the related options will appear in the right pane of the dialog box.

3. In the right pane, for the **Faceting Factor** box at the top, enter **8** as the value.

   This will smoothen the faces of the curved objects in the AutoCAD file that you open. Note that bigger the value, larger will be the file size of the Autodesk Navisworks file that you create.

4. From the left pane, expand **Interface** and then click on **Display Units**. From the area on the right, change the display units to Inches.

5. Click **OK** to close the **Options Editor** dialog box.

6. Click **Open** on the **Quick Access Toolbar** to display the **Open** dialog box.

7. Click on **Files of type** list and change it to **Autodesk DWG/DXF file (*.dwg, *.dxf)**, if it is not already set to that.

8. Browse to the **Chapter 2 > Exercise Plant** folder, if it is not already listed in the dialog box.

9. Double-click on the **Left-pressure-vessel.dwg** file to open it.

10. From the **Home** ribbon tab > **Project** ribbon panel, click **Append** to display the **Append** dialog box.

11. Double-click on the **Right-pressure-vessel.dwg** file to append it to the current file.

12. From the **Viewpoint** ribbon tab > **Render Style** ribbon panel, change the lighting to **Full Lights** and mode to **Full Render**.

13. Change the current view to the **Home** view; notice that the pressure vessel away from you looks tiny, see Figure 32.

   Next, you will investigate the reason why one of the pressure vessels appears tiny.

14. From the **Selection Tree**, right-click on the **Left-pressure-vessel.dwg** file and select **Units and Transform** from the shortcut menu; the **Units and Transform** dialog box is displayed.

15. Notice that the units of this file are in Millimeters. Close the dialog box by clicking **OK**.

16. From the **Selection Tree**, right-click on the **Right-pressure-vessel.dwg** file and select **Units and Transform** from the shortcut menu to display the **Units and Transform** dialog box.

   Notice that the units of this file are in Inches. This is the reason why this pressure vessel appears huge with respect to the first one. Next, you will change its units.

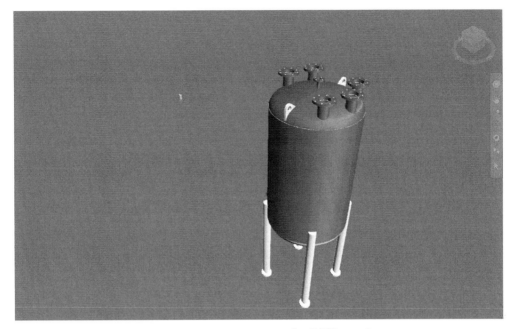

Figure 32 *Two pressure vessels of different sizes*

17. From the **Units** list, select **Millimeters** and click **OK**; the file scales down 25.4 times as there are 25.4 Millimeters in an Inch. As a result, the size of this pressure vessel appears similar to that of the other pressure vessel.

18. Change the current view to the **Home** view.

    Next, you will move the first pressure vessel closer to the second one. However, without any indicator of the X, Y, and Z directions, it is not possible to figure out which direction to move the file in. So you will turn on the visibility of the XYZ axes first.

19. From the **View** ribbon tab > **Navigation Aids** ribbon panel, click the **HUD** flyout and select **XYZ Axes**.

    The XYZ indicator icon appears at the lower left corner of the graphics window. This indicates that the pressure vessel needs to be moved in the X axis direction.

20. From the **Selection Tree**, right-click on the **Left-pressure-vessel.dwg** file and select **Units and Transform** from the shortcut menu.

    Because the current units are set to Inches, the value for the movement needs to be entered in Inches as well. This is indicated by **(in)** shown next to **Origin** in the dialog box.

21. In the first box under the **Origin** area, enter **15** as the value and click **OK** in the dialog box; the first pressure moves 15 Inches closer to the second one.

22. Scroll the wheel button on top of one of the legs of the left pressure vessel to move the orbit pivot point there.

23. Hold down the SHIFT key and the wheel mouse button and drag to orbit the scene. Notice that the two pressure vessels look similar.

24. Change the current view to **Home** view.

25. Click the **View** ribbon tab > **Navigation Aids** ribbon panel > **HUD** flyout and clear the **XYZ Axes** tick box to turn it off.

26. Click the **Save** button on the **Quick Access Toolbar** to invoke the **Save As** dialog box.

27. Enter **Vessels** as the file name and click **Save** in the dialog box; the file is saved with NWF extension.

28. Click **New** on the **Quick Access Toolbar** to close this file.

Hands-on Exercise (BIM)	In this exercise, you will complete the following tasks: 1. Open an Autodesk Revit file and select objects based on various selection tools and resolutions. 2. Turn on and off the visibility of the objects in the scene. 3. Override the appearance and transformation of objects in the scene. 4. Create selection and search sets. 5. Export search sets from one file and import to the other. 6. View object properties and create custom properties for certain objects. 7. Turn on the visibility of quick properties and customize them. 8. Change the file units and transform it.

Section 1: Opening the File and Selecting Objects

In this section, you will open and work with an Autodesk Revit file. When you open an Autodesk Revit file, by default, the grids are turned on. So you will first turn off the grids in the scene. You will then select objects using various selection resolutions in this file. You will also use the **Select**, **Select All**, and **Select Same** flyouts to make selections.

1. Start Autodesk Navisworks, if it is not already running.

2. Click the **Open** button on the **Quick Access Toolbar**; the **Open** dialog box is displayed.

3. Browse to the **Chapter 2 > Exercise Building** folder. Click on the **Files of type** list and select **Revit (*.rvt, *.rfa, *.rte)**.

4. Double-click on the **ARCH_BUILDING.rvt** file to open it.

   Autodesk Revit model will start to load in Autodesk Navisworks. Because it is the first time you are opening this file, the content takes time to load.

5. Change the current view to the Home view.

   If the grids and levels for Autodesk Revit file were turned on earlier on this computer, you need to turn these off for this exercise. If the grids and levels are not visible, go to step 7.

6. Click the **View** ribbon tab > **Grids & Levels** ribbon panel and then click the **Show Grid** button to turn the grids off.

7. Hold down the SHIFT key and the wheel mouse button and orbit the model up so that it appears similar to the one shown in Figure 33.

8. On the **Home** ribbon tab, expand the **Select & Search** ribbon panel and click on the pin icon on the left of the expanded ribbon panel to pin it on the screen.

9. From the **Selection Resolution** list, click **File**; this sets the selection resolution to file.

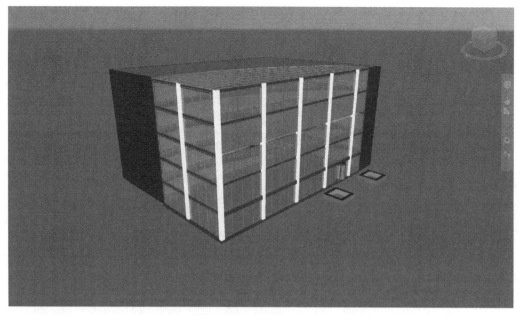

Figure 33 *The Autodesk Revit building*

10. Click on any glass panel of the building in the graphics window; the entire file is highlighted in the **Selection Tree** and all the objects are selected in the graphics window.

11. Click anywhere in the blank area of the screen to deselect everything. From the expanded **Select & Search** ribbon panel, click on the **Selection Resolution** list and select **Layer**; this sets the selection resolution to layer.

12. Click on any of the glass panels above the main entrance of the building; the file is expanded in the **Selection Tree** and the **Level 2** layer is highlighted. Also, all the objects in this layer are selected in the graphics window.

13. From the expanded **Select & Search** ribbon panel, click on the **Selection Resolution** list and select **First Object**.

14. Click on the left exterior wall of the building; the branches in the **Selection Tree** are expanded and in the **Exterior - Brick on Mtl. Stud** category, one of the **Basic Wall** object is highlighted.

15. In the expanded **Select & Search** ribbon panel, click on the **Select Same** flyout and click **Same Type**; all the **Basic Wall** objects under the **Exterior - Brick on Mtl. Stud** category are highlighted in the **Selection Tree**. All the walls are also selected in the graphics window, as shown in Figure 34.

16. In the **Select & Search** ribbon panel, click on the **Select All** flyout and click **Select None**; everything is deselected.

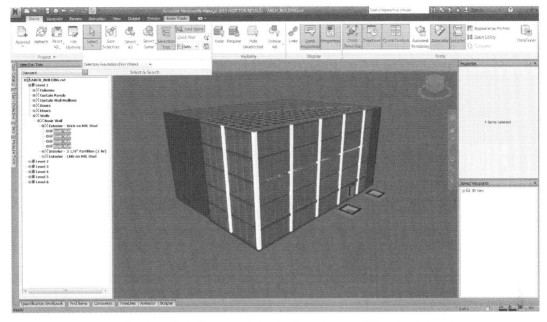

Figure 34 *Selecting all the basic walls in the* **Exterior - Brick on Mtl. Stud** *category*

 Tip: *As mentioned earlier, you can also press the ESC key or click anywhere in the blank area of the graphics window to deselect everything.*

17. Unpin the **Select & Search** ribbon panel by clicking on the pin icon on the left.

Section 2: Controlling the Visibility of Selected Objects

In this section, you will hide and unhide the selected objects in the current scene. You will use the **First Object** selection resolution that was set in the previous section to select objects.

1. From the graphics window, click on the left wall of the building.

2. In the **Select & Search** ribbon panel, click on the **Select Same** flyout and click **Select Same Revit Type**; all the exterior basic walls in the scene are selected.

3. In the **Visibility** ribbon panel, click **Hide** to hide the selected walls from the scene.

4. Click anywhere in the graphics window to deselect everything.

5. Hold down the SHIFT key and middle mouse button and drag the mouse to orbit the model. Notice that the exterior walls are no longer displayed.

6. In the **Visibility** panel, click **Unhide All**; all the walls are redisplayed in the scene.

7. Hold down the SHIFT key and middle mouse button and drag the mouse to orbit the model. Notice that all the walls are displayed in the scene.

8. Orbit the model to a view similar to the start view of the file.

9. In the **Selection Tree**, expand **ARCH_BUILDING.rvt** and click on the **Level 1** layer.

10. In the **Select & Search** ribbon panel, click on the **Select None** flyout and click **Invert Selection**; the layer you selected is deselected and the remaining layers are selected.

11. In the **Visibility** panel, click **Hide**; the objects on the selected layers are hidden. Click in the blank area and notice how the hidden layers are displayed in gray in the **Selection Tree**.

12. In the **Visibility** panel, click **Unhide All**; all the objects are made visible in the scene.

Section 3: Overriding the Appearance and Transformation of Objects

In this section, you will use the tools in the **Item Tools** ribbon tab to move the exterior walls. You will also change the color and transparency of the exterior walls in the scene.

1. In the graphics window, click on the brick wall on the front of the building.

2. Hold down the SHIFT key and click on the same wall again; the next branch in the **Selection Tree** is highlighted.

3. With the SHIFT key still held down, keep clicking on the same wall; notice how the selection resolution changes to select various objects.

4. Click in the blank area of the graphics window to deselect everything.

5. Click on one of the vertical columns on the front face of the building.

6. From the **Select & Search** ribbon panel, click the **Select Same** flyout and click **Same Type**; all the columns are selected.

    When you select objects, the **Item Tools** ribbon tab is displayed. You will use this ribbon tab to move the selected columns.

7. Click on the **Item Tools** ribbon tab. Expand the **Transform** ribbon panel and pin it on the screen using the pin icon on the left of this ribbon panel.

8. In the expanded **Transform** ribbon panel, click the **Move** tool; the move gizmo is displayed at the transformation center of the walls.

9. Move the cursor over the Green axis; it turns Yellow and the cursor changes to the hand cursor. Now, press and hold down the left mouse button and drag to the right; all the columns move to the right.

10. In the expanded **Transform** ribbon panel, click on the **Reset Transform** tool; all the columns are moved back to their original location.

11. With the columns still selected, in the **Position Y** box of the expanded **Transform** ribbon panel, enter **1000** if the units are displayed in Inches. If the units are displayed in Meters, enter **25**; the walls move through the specified distance in the Y direction.

12. In the expanded **Transform** ribbon panel, click on the **Reset Transform** tool; all the columns are moved back to their original location.

13. Click the **Move** tool again to close this tool and turn off the visibility of the move gizmo.

14. From the **Appearance** ribbon panel, click on the **Color** flyout and select the MediumOrchid color, which is the second last color in the palette; all the selected columns are changed to this color.

15. Drag the **Transparency** slider to **40%** to make these columns transparent.

16. Click anywhere in the blank area of the graphics window to deselect everything. The Autodesk Navisworks scene with these changes is shown in Figure 35.

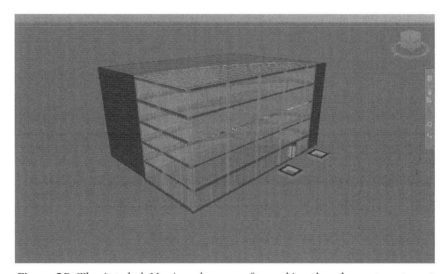

Figure 35 The Autodesk Navisworks scene after making the columns transparent

 Tip: *If you regularly change the color and transparency of walls or any other common objects, you can use the* ***Appearance Profiler*** *window discussed earlier in this chapter to create an appearance profile and export it for use in other files.*

17. Click the **Save** button on the **Quick Access Toolbar** to display the **Save As** dialog box.

18. Browse to **Chapter 2 > Exercise Building** folder.

19. Enter **C2EB** as the name of the file and click **Save**; the file is saved with NWF extension.

Section 4: Creating Selection Sets

In this section, you will create various selection sets. To create these, the **Sets** window will be used. It is assumed that you are using the **Training** workspace created in the previous chapter. As a result, the **Sets** window is displayed in the auto-hide mode in the left of the **Selection Tree**. If not, refer to the Hands-on exercise of the previous chapter to see how to create and save a workspace.

1. Click **Sets** from the left of the **Selection Tree** to display the **Sets** window.

2. Click on the pin icon on the top right of this window to dock it on the screen below the **Selection Tree**.

3. In the graphics window, click on one of the glass panels above the main entrance of the building.

4. From the **Home** ribbon tab > **Select & Search** ribbon panel, click the **Select Same** flyout and then click **Select Same Revit Type**; all the glass panels in the building are selected.

5. From the toolbar on the top of the **Sets** window, click the **Save Selection** button; a new selection set is added.

6. Rename the set to **Glazed Panels**.

7. In the graphics window, click on the left wall of the building.

8. From the **Select & Search** ribbon panel, click the **Select Same** flyout and then click **Same Name**; all the walls named **Basic Wall** are selected.

9. From the toolbar on the top of the **Sets** window, click the **Save Selection** button; a new selection set is added.

10. Rename the set to **Basic Walls**. Click anywhere in the blank area of the graphics window to deselect everything.

11. In the **Sets** window, click on the **Glazed Panels** set; all the objects in this set are selected.

12. Hold the CTRL key down and click on the **Basic Walls** set; all the objects in this set are also selected.

13. Right-click on any of these sets in the **Sets** window and select **Hide** from the shortcut menu; all the objects in both the sets are hidden.

14. On the **Home** ribbon tab > **Visibility** ribbon panel, click on **Unhide All** to redisplay the objects of the two sets.

15. Click anywhere in the blank area of the graphics window to deselect everything.

Section 5: Creating Search Sets

In this section, you will use the **Find Items** window to search and select objects, You will then save the search results as search sets.

1. Move the cursor over **Find Items** below the graphics window; the **Find Items** window is displayed.

2. Dock this window at the bottom of the screen by clicking on the **Auto-Hide** button on the top right corner of this window.

 *Tip: With various windows docked on the screen, the graphics window area reduces. You can auto-hide the windows that you do not require immediately and redisplay them whenever needed. For example, in this case, you can auto-hide the **Properties** and **Saved Viewpoints** window by clicking on the **Auto-Hide** button on the top right of these windows.*

3. In the right pane of the **Find Items** window, drag the partitions of all the columns to make them wider.

4. Click on the first row under the **Category** column and select **Revit Type** from the list.

5. From the list displayed under the **Property** column, select **Corner Mullion**.

6. From the list displayed under the **Condition** column, select =.

7. From the list displayed under the **Value** column, type **0** and press ENTER; a new row is added below the first row.

8. Click on the second row under the **Category** column and select **Revit Type** from the list.

9. From the list displayed under the **Property** column, select **Corner Mullion**.

10. From the list displayed under the **Condition** column, select =.

11. In the list displayed under the **Value** column, type **1**.

    Remember that the second row will act as the "And" condition.

12. Click on the **Find All** button; a dialog box will appear informing you no objects were found. Click **OK** in the dialog box.

    The reason there were no objects selected is because the two search statements are looking for corner mullions that have values of 0 and 1. There are no such objects in the model. Therefore, you need to change the second search statement to "Or" condition.

13. Right-click on the second search statement and click **Or Condition** from the shortcut menu; a + symbol will be displayed on the left of the search statement.

14. Now, click **Find All**; all the corner mullions with the value of 0 or 1 are selected.

15. From the toolbar on the top of the **Sets** window, click on the **Save Search**; a new search set is added.

16. Rename the search set to **Corner Mullions** by right-clicking on the new search set and selecting the **Rename** option.

17. Click anywhere in the blank area of the graphics window to deselect everything.

    Next, you will perform search based on wildcards.

18. Right-click on any one of the search rows and click **Delete All Conditions** from the shortcut menu.

19. Click on the first row under the **Category** column and select **Item** from the list.

20. Click on the list in the first row of the **Property** column and select **Type**.

21. Click on the list in the first row of the **Condition** column and select **Wildcard**.

22. Click on the list in the first row of the **Value** column and type ***Exterior***.

23. Click on the second row under the **Category** column and select **Item** from the list.

24. Click on the list in the second row of the **Property** column and select **Type**.

25. Click on the list in the second row of the **Condition** column and select **Wildcard**.

26. Click on the list in the first row of the **Value** column and type ***Walls***.

27. Click the **Find All** button; all the exterior walls are selected.

28. From the toolbar on the top of the **Sets** window, click on the **Save Search**; a new search set is added.

29. Rename the search set to **Exterior Walls** by right-clicking on the new search set and selecting the **Rename** option.

Section 6: Exporting and Importing Search Sets

In this section, you will export the search sets created in the previous section and then import them to the file opened from the web server.

1. From the toolbar in the **Sets** window, click on the **Import/Export** flyout and select the **Export Search Sets** option to display the **Export** dialog box.

2. Browse to the **Chapter 2 > Exercise Building** folder and enter the name of the search file as **Building**.

3. Click the **Save** button to save the two search sets; the file is saved with the .XML extension.

4. Click the **Save** button on the **Quick Access Toolbar** to save the current file.

5. Click the **Open** button on the **Quick Access Toolbar**; the **Open** dialog box is displayed.

6. In the dialog box, click on the **Files of type** and change it to **Revit (*.rvt, *.rfa, *.rte)**.

7. Browse to **Chapter 2 > Exercise Building** folder and double-click on the **Museum.rvt** file; the Autodesk Revit file of the Museum is opened.

8. Press and hold down the SHIFT key and the wheel mouse button and drag to change the view to a view similar to the one shown in Figure 36.

9. From the toolbar in the **Sets** window, click on the **Import/Export** flyout and select the **Import Search Sets** option to display the **Import** dialog box.

10. Browse to the **Chapter 2 > Exercise Building** folder, if it is not already listed in the dialog box.

11. Double-click on the **Building.xml** file; the two search sets are loaded in the current file and are displayed in the **Sets** window.

12. Click on the **Corner Mullions** search set in the **Sets** window; the two search conditions are displayed in the **Find Items** window. Also, all the objects matching this search criteria are selected.

13. Click on the **Exterior Walls** search set in the **Sets** window; the two search conditions are displayed in the **Find Items** window. Also, all the objects matching this search criteria are selected, as shown in Figure 36.

   This shows that the searches that are common to your project can be exported and imported in various files.

14. Click the **New** button on the **Quick Access Toolbar** and click **No** in the dialog box to close the current file without saving.

Section 7: Viewing Object Properties

In this section, you will select various objects and view their properties in the **Properties** window. To make sure only the required windows are displayed on the screen, you will first restore the **Training** workspace created in the previous chapter.

1. Click the **View** ribbon tab > **Workspace** ribbon panel > **Load Workspace** flyout and click **Training**; Autodesk Navisworks resets to open this workspace.

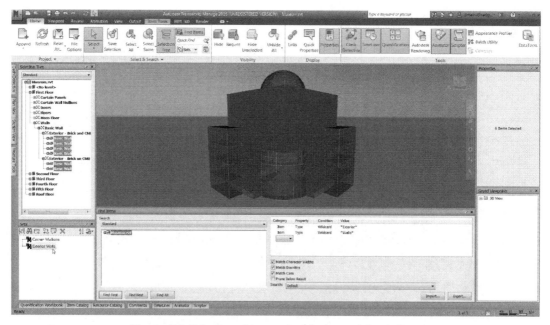

Figure 36 *Selecting objects using the imported search set*

2. Click on the **Application Button** and from the **Recent Documents** area, click **C2EB.nwf** to open this recently used file.

3. Move the cursor over the left edge of the **Properties** window available on the right of the graphics window. When the double-sided arrow is displayed, press and hold the left mouse button down and drag it to the left to widen this window.

4. Click on one of the glass panels; the **Properties** window displays the properties in the **Item** tab by default.

5. Click on the **Element** tab from the **Properties** window to display the element properties of the selected object, see Figure 37. Note that your values may be different as you may have selected a different panel.

6. Click on the brick wall on the front face of the building; the element properties of the wall are shown in the **Element** tab of the **Properties** window. Scroll up in this tab and the properties will be similar to those shown in Figure 38.

 Tip: You can use the arrow keys on the top right of the **Properties** window to scroll to the other tabs to view the properties.

7. In the **Selection Tree**, expand the **Level 1 > Doors > Single-Flush > 36" x 84"** and click one of the **Single-Flush** doors.

8. Use the arrow keys on the top right of the **Properties** window to scroll to the **Revit Type** tab. Once displayed, click on this tab; the Revit Type properties of the selected object are displayed.

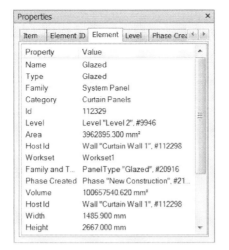

Figure 37 The **Properties** *window showing the element properties of a glass panel*

Figure 38 The **Properties** *window showing the element properties of a wall*

9. Click anywhere in the blank area of the graphics window to deselect everything. Change the view to the Home view, if it is not already set to that.

Section 8: Creating Custom Object Properties

In this section, you will create custom properties for curtain panels on levels 1, 2, and 3. However, Autodesk Navisworks does not allow you to view properties of objects in different layers or categories. As a result, if you select the curtain panels on all the layers, the **Properties** window will be grayed out. So you will have to create the custom properties of curtain panels of one layer at a time.

1. From the **Selection Tree**, expand **Level 1** and then click **Curtain Panels**; all the curtain panels on level 1 are selected.

2. Right-click in the blank area of the **Properties** window and select **Add New User Data Tab**; a new custom tab is added with the default name of **User Data**.

3. If need be, use the arrow keys on the top right of the **Properties** window to scroll to the new tab. Once displayed, click on it to make it the current tab.

4. Right-click in the blank area of the new tab and select **Rename Tab** from the shortcut menu.

5. In the dialog box that is displayed, enter **Panel Details** as the name of the tab and click **OK**.

6. Right-click anywhere in the blank area of the **Panel Details** tab and select **Insert New Property > String** from the shortcut menu; a new row is added under the **Property** column.

7. Type **Glass Type** as the property name and press ENTER.

8. Double-click on the first row under the **Value** column and type **Tint Toughened** as the property value in the dialog box. Click **OK** to close the dialog box.

9. Right-click inside the tab again and select **Insert New Property > Boolean** from the shortcut menu; a new row is added under the **Property** column with a default value as **No**.

10. Type **Tinting Required** as the property name and press ENTER. Figure 39 shows the **Properties** window with the **Panel Details** tab and the properties in it.

Figure 39   The **Properties** *window with the custom tab*

11. Click anywhere in the blank area of the graphics window to deselect everything.

12. Click on one of the bottom glass panels on the facade of the building.

Notice that the **Properties** window does not have the **Panel Details** tab. This is because this tab was created for the **Curtain Panels** category and will only appear when this category is selected from the **Selection Tree**.

13. Click on the **Curtain Panels** category from the **Selection Tree**; the **Panel Details** tab is displayed in the **Properties** window.

14. Click anywhere in the blank area of the graphics window to deselect everything.

15. Click the **Save** button on the **Quick Access Toolbar** to save the current file.

Section 9: Turning on and Customizing the Quick Properties

In this section, you will turn on the visibility of the quick properties. You will change the selection resolution to display the quick properties for that particular resolution. You will also customize the quick properties to dynamically display the properties created in the previous section.

1. On the **Home** ribbon tab > **Display** ribbon panel, click the **Quick Properties** button; this turns on the display of quick properties.

2. Move the cursor over the brick wall on the front face of the building; the item name and item type properties of the wall are dynamically displayed on the model.

3. Move the cursor over one of the glass panels; the item name and item type properties of the panel are dynamically displayed on the model.

4. Right-click on any object in the **Selection Tree** and select **Set Selection Resolution To Geometry** from the shortcut menu.

5. Move the cursor over the same wall of the building; the item name and item type properties of the geometry are displayed now.

   Next, you will modify the display of quick properties using the **Options Editor** dialog box.

6. Press the F12 key to display the **Options Editor** dialog box.

7. From the left pane, expand **Interface** > **Quick Properties** and select **Definitions**; the right pane displays the two default elements.

 Note: *If there were additional quick properties added earlier in Autodesk Navisworks, they will be displayed as well. This is because these settings are stored in the software.*

8. Click the **Add element** button from the right pane of the dialog box; a new property element is added at the top of the previous two elements.

9. From the **Category** list of the first element, click **Panel Details**.

10. From the **Property** list of the first element, click **Glass Type**.

11. Click on the **Add element** button again; a new property element is added at the top of the previous three elements.

12. From the **Category** list of the first element, click **Element**.

13. From the **Property** list of the first element, click **Volume**.

14. Click **OK** to close the **Options Editor** dialog box.

15. Move the cursor over the wall on the front face of the building; notice that the quick properties now show the Element Volume property as well, see Figure 40.

   In this case, the Panel Details properties are not displayed because these properties are for the **Curtain Panel** objects.

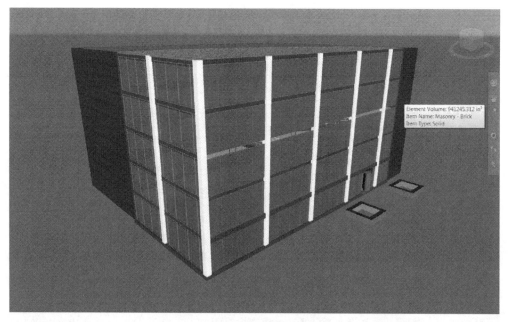

Figure 40 *The element volume quick property displayed on the wall in addition to the default quick properties*

16. Move the cursor over one of glass panels on level 1; the four properties associated to this selection are displayed, as shown in Figure 41. Remember that if you move the cursor over the glass panels on any other level, the **Panel Details** property will not be displayed.

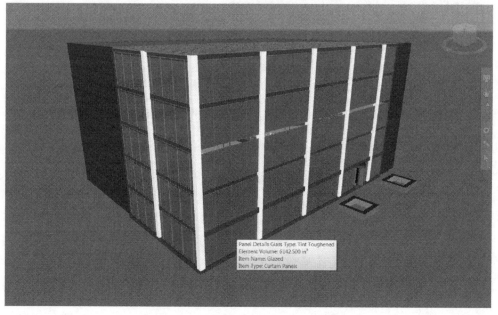

Figure 41 *Customized quick properties displayed on the glass panel in addition to the default quick properties*

17. Click **Save** on the **Quick Access Toolbar** to save the file and then click **New** to close the current file.

Section 10: Opening AutoCAD Files and Changing Units

In this section, you will open the structural model of a building and append the architectural model. The structural model was created with Millimeters as the units and the architectural model was created with Inches as the units. As a result, the two models will not match. So you will change the units of the structural model to Inches to match the size of the architectural model.

But first, you will also change the global option to smoothen the facets of the objects in the AutoCAD file using the **Options Editor**.

1. Press the F12 key to open the **Options Editor** dialog box.

2. From the left pane, expand **File Readers** and then click **DWG/DXF**; the related options will appear in the right pane of the dialog box.

3. In the right pane, for the **Faceting Factor** box at the top, enter **8** as the value.

   This will smoothen the faces of the curved objects in the AutoCAD file that you will open. Note that bigger the value, larger will be the file size of the Autodesk Navisworks file that you will create.

4. From the left pane, expand **Interface** and then click on **Display Units**. From the area on the right, change the display units to Inches.

5. Click **OK** to close the **Options Editor** dialog box.

6. Click **Open** on the **Quick Access Toolbar** to display the **Open** dialog box.

7. Click on **Files of type** list and change it to **Autodesk DWG/DXF file (*.dwg, *.dxf)**, if it is not already set to that.

8. Browse to the **Chapter 2 > Exercise Building** folder, if it is not already listed in the dialog box.

9. Double-click on the **Structure.dwg** file to open it.

10. From the **Home** ribbon tab > **Project** ribbon panel, click **Append** to display the **Append** dialog box.

11. Double-click on the **Architecture.dwg** file to append it to the current file.

12. From the **Viewpoint** ribbon tab > **Render Style** ribbon panel, change the lighting to **Full Lights** and mode to **Full Render**.

13. From the **Navigation Bar**, click the **Zoom Window** flyout and then click **Zoom All**; notice that the structural model looks tiny compared to the architectural model, as shown in Figure 42.

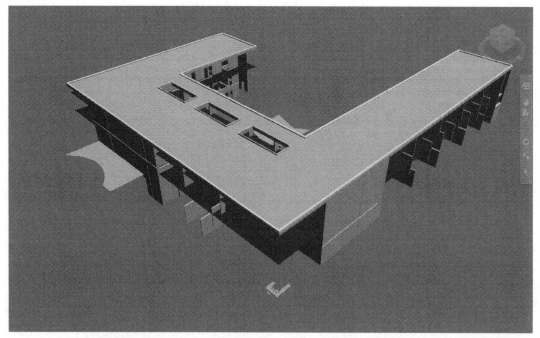

Figure 42 *Autodesk Navisworks scene after appending the architectural model with the structural model*

Next, you will investigate the reason why the structural model appears tiny.

14. From the **Selection Tree**, right-click on the **Architecture.dwg** file and select **Units and Transform** from the shortcut menu; the **Units and Transform** dialog box is displayed.

15. Note that the units of this file are in Inches. Close the dialog box by clicking **OK**.

16. From the **Selection Tree**, right-click on the **Structure.dwg** file and select **Units and Transform** from the shortcut menu to display the **Units and Transform** dialog box.

    Notice that the units of this file are in Millimeters. This is the reason this file appears tiny in the scene. Next, you will change its units.

17. From the **Units** list, select **Inches** and click **OK**; the file scales up 25.4 times as there are 25.4 Millimeters in an Inch. As a result, the size of this file matches that of the architectural file.

18. From the **Navigation Bar**, click **Zoom All**; notice that the architectural model size now matches the structural model size.

19. Press and hold the SHIFT key and the wheel mouse button down and drag the cursor to orbit around the model.

20. Orbit the model to a view similar to the one shown in Figure 43.

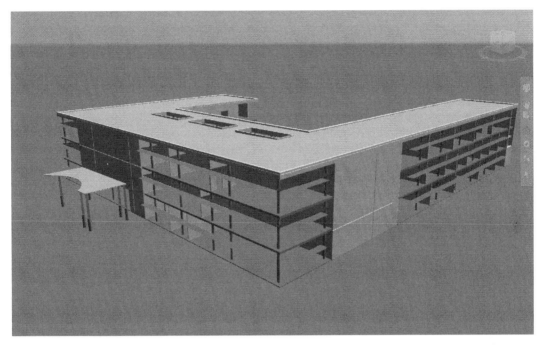

Figure 43 *Autodesk Navisworks scene after changing the units of the structural model*

21. Click the **Save** button on the **Quick Access Toolbar** to invoke the **Save As** dialog box.

22. Enter **Building** as the file name and click **Save** in the dialog box; the file is saved with NWF extension.

23. Click **New** on the **Quick Access Toolbar** to close this file.

Skill Evaluation

Evaluate your skills to see how many questions you can answer correctly. The answers to these questions are given at the end of the book.

1. Select Previous is a type of selection resolution. (True/False)

2. Autodesk Navisworks does not allow you to select objects by dragging a box around them. (True/False)

3. By default, the additional search conditions are "And" conditions. (True/False)

4. The **Item Tools** ribbon tab is only displayed when you select an object. (True/False)

5. The objects that you regularly select can be saved as a set for future use. (True/False)

6. Which two are not a type of sets that can be saved in the **Sets** window?

    (A) Selection Set   (B) Object Set
    (C) Search Sets   (D) Transformation Set

7. Which tool is used to toggle on or off the visibility of quick properties in the scene?

    (A) **Quick Properties**   (B) **Properties**
    (C) **Select Next**   (D) **Dynamic Properties**

8. Which of the following items are included when you export search sets?

    (A) All Selection Sets   (B) All Search Sets
    (C) Selected Selection Sets   (D) You will be prompted to select sets

9. By default, which two quick properties are displayed?

    (A) Item Source   (B) Item Type
    (C) Item Category   (D) Item Name

10. Which window is used to search objects based on their properties?

    (A) **Find Items**   (B) **Look Up Items**
    (C) **Search Items**   (D) **Search Properties**

Class Test Questions

Answer the following questions:

1. Selection sets once created cannot be modified?

2. Which window is used to create custom properties for the selected objects?

3. How do you change a search statement in the **Find Items** window to make it behave as an "Or" condition?

4. What are the four types of custom properties that you can create for the selected objects?

5. Which tool is used to move the objects back to their original location?

Chapter 3 – Viewpoints, Animations, and Measurements

The objectives of this chapter are to:

√ *Show you how to walk and fly in a scene.*
√ *Teach you how to reduce the object drop outs during navigation.*
√ *Familiarize you with the process of creating viewpoints.*
√ *Teach you how to add realism to your navigation.*
√ *Teach you how to create walkthrough animations.*
√ *Teach you how to create animations using viewpoints.*
√ *Show you how to export animations.*
√ *Explain how to measure objects in the scene.*
√ *Show you how to move selected objects by the measured distance value.*

REALTIME NAVIGATION IN THE DESIGN

As mentioned in the previous chapters, Autodesk Navisworks lets you create virtual models in which you can navigate in realtime by walking or flying around your design. This gives you a realistic experience of the model before even a single brick is laid on the construction site. The realtime walkthroughs and flythroughs can also be recorded and played again in future. The realtime navigation tools are discussed next.

Walk Tool

> **Navigation Bar > Walk**
> **Viewpoint Ribbon Tab > Navigate Ribbon Panel > Walk**

This tool is used to walk in the design in realtime. The walk can also be recorded to create a walkthrough animation. When you invoke this tool, the current view is changed to the perspective view and the cursor changes to human feet. You can now press and hold the left mouse button down and drag the mouse to start walking. You will walk in the direction in which the mouse is getting dragged. For example, dragging the cursor forward will let you walk forward. Similarly, dragging the cursor to the right will let you walk to the right.

With this tool active, you can also use the arrow keys on the keyboard to walk forward, back, left and, right. These keys create a much smoother walk compared to using the mouse drag.

> ### What I do
> *While using the **Walk** tool, I use the wheel mouse button extensively. With this tool active, I can view up and down the scene by scrolling the mouse. Its like standing still and tilting my head up and down. When this tool is active, I can also go from one level to the other by holding down the wheel mouse button and dragging up or down. Similarly, I can also pan sideways by holding the wheel mouse button down when this tool active.*

Steering Wheel > Walk

> **Navigation Bar > Steering Wheel**
> **Viewpoint Ribbon Tab > Navigate Ribbon Panel > Steering Wheel**

The **Walk** wedge of the steering wheel can also be used to walk around the design. When you press and hold the left mouse button down on the **Walk** wedge, a circle is displayed close to the bottom of the graphics window and the cursor changes to the walk arrow cursor. You can drag the cursor in any direction to start walking in that direction. While walking using this method, pressing the Up or Down arrow key will change the height of the level on which you are walking. While dragging the mouse, you can also hold the SHIFT key down to go up or down in the current view.

While walking using this tool, you can press and hold the + key to increase the speed of the walk. If you want to permanently change the walk speed, press the F12 key to display the **Options Editor** dialog box. Expand **Interface** from the left pane and then click **SteeringWheels** to display its options in the right pane. The **Walk Tool** area displays the options related to the **Walk** tool of the steering wheel, as shown in Figure 1. These options are discussed next.

*Figure 1   The **Walk Tool** area to change walk settings*

Constrain Walk angle

Selecting this tick box ensures that the top view of the current scene is respected while walking. This options is turned on by default. You will generally turn this option off if the top view of your model does not match with the top view of the ViewCube.

Use Viewpoint Linear Speed

This tick box is used when you start walking from a particular saved viewpoint. If this tick box is selected, the linear walk speed specified in the saved viewpoint will be used for walking. The value set in the **Walk Speed** slider will be used as a multiplier for the viewpoint linear speed. If this tick box is cleared, the speed set in the **Walk Speed** slider will be used for walking.

Walk Speed Slider

This slider is used to set the global walk speed. This value will be used in all the files opened henceforth in Autodesk Navisworks.

 Tip: *Autodesk Navisworks provides you the option to make the **Walk** tool behave as the **Walk** option of the steering wheel. To do this, invoke the **Options Editor** dialog box by pressing the F12 key. From the left pane, expand **Interface** and then click **Navigation Bar**. From the right pane, clear the **Use classic Walk** tick box.*

Fly Tool

Navigation Bar > Walk Flyout > Fly
Viewpoint Ribbon Tab > Navigate Ribbon Panel > Walk Flyout > Fly

This tool lets you fly around the design as if you were in an aircraft. When you invoke this tool, the cursor changes to an airplane icon. Press and hold the left mouse button down and drag the mouse to fly around the design.

CONTROLLING THE OBJECT DROP OUTS DURING NAVIGATION

When navigating through large models, similar to the one shown in Figure 2, there are always some object drop outs. Although these objects are redisplayed after you pause or end the navigation, but in some cases, it is not acceptable. Especially, if the objects important to you are getting dropped out.

As mentioned in Chapter 1, you can stop the important objects from getting dropped out by making them required. To do this, select the objects from the **Selection Tree** or the graphics window and click the **Require** button on the **Home** ribbon tab > **Visibility** ribbon panel. The selected objects will appear in Red in the **Selection Tree**, indicating they are made required.

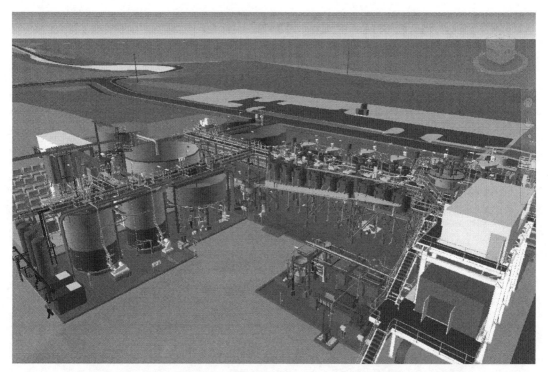

*Figure 2 A large plant model (**Model Courtesy Calder Maloney Pty Ltd**)*

In addition to making objects required, Autodesk Navisworks provides a couple of other options that help you reduce or stop dropping out of all the objects during navigation. However, you need to remember that if the object drop out is reduced, the navigation becomes jerky. These two options of reducing or stopping the object drop outs are discussed next.

Reducing the Object Drop Outs Using the File Options

The **Speed** tab of the **File Options** dialog box can be used to reduce the object drop outs during navigation. To display this dialog box, right-click in the blank area of the graphics window and select **File Options** from the shortcut menu to display the **File Options** dialog box. Holding down the SHIFT + F11 keys also displays this dialog box. In the dialog box, click the **Speed** tab. The **Frame Rate** spinner in this tab lets you define the frame rate for navigation. The default value is 6. This value corresponds to how many frames to be rendered per second during the navigation. More the value of this spinner, smoother will be the animation, but more will be the objects drop out.

To reduce the object drop out, specify a smaller value, such as 2. This will reduce the object drop outs during navigation using tools such as **Orbit**, **Walk**, **Fly**, and so on. The drawback is that the navigation will be jerky.

Stopping Object Drop Outs Using the Options Editor

If you do not want any object to be dropped out during navigation, you can prevent it using the **Options Editor** dialog box. Similar to the previous option, the drawback in using this option is also that the navigation will be jerky as the frames will be skipped during navigation. The following steps show you how to stop all objects from getting dropped out during the navigation:

a. Press F12 to display the **Options Editor** dialog box.

b. From the left pane, expand **Interface** and then click on **Display**.

c. From the right pane, clear the **Guarantee Frame Rate** tick box in the **Detail** area, as shown in Figure 3. This will ensure that none of the objects are dropped out during the navigation. However, this will also mean that the frame rate specified for the file will not be guaranteed and the navigation will be jerky.

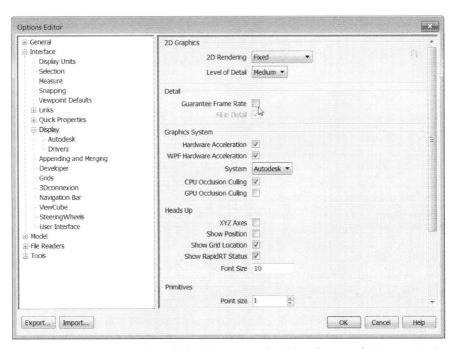

Figure 3 *The **Options Editor** dialog box to stop the object drop out during navigation*

VIEWPOINTS

Autodesk Navisworks lets you save a still shot of the current scene by saving the camera location and camera target. These still shots are called viewpoints. The viewpoints are created and saved in the **Saved Viewpoints** window. In addition to saving the camera-related information, viewpoints also allow you to save the visibility and appearance of the objects in the current scene as well as the design review information such as markups and comments. The viewpoints that are regularly used in your project can also be exported from one file and then imported to other files.

Keep in mind that the viewpoints also remember the navigation tool that was active while creating the viewpoint and will restore the same tool when you activate that viewpoint.

While opening a native CAD file, if there were some camera views created and saved in that file, they are by default automatically converted into Autodesk Navisworks viewpoints and are displayed in the **Saved Viewpoints** window. Figure 4 shows the **Saved Viewpoints** window displaying the viewpoints created automatically from an AutoCAD file. Figure 5 shows the same window displaying the viewpoints created from an Autodesk Revit file.

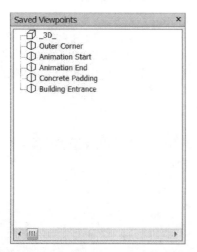

Figure 4 *The **Saved Viewpoint** window showing viewpoints imported with an AutoCAD file*

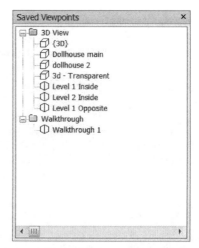

Figure 5 *The **Saved Viewpoint** window showing viewpoints imported with an Autodesk Revit file*

You can decide to continue using these viewpoints or delete them by right-clicking on them in the **Saved Viewpoints** window and clicking **Delete** from the shortcut menu. You can also create your own viewpoints within Autodesk Navisworks. This process is discussed next.

 Note: *It is assumed that you are using the **Training** workspace created in Chapter 1 and the **Saved Viewpoints** window is docked below the **Properties** window. If not, click on the **View** ribbon tab > **Workspace** ribbon panel > **Windows** flyout and select **Saved Viewpoints** to turn on the visibility of this window.*

Creating Viewpoints

The following steps show you how to create and save viewpoints in Autodesk Navisworks.

a. Using the navigation tools on the **Navigation Bar** or using the SHIFT key and the wheel mouse button, orient the model in the view that you want to save.

b. Right-click in the **Saved Viewpoints** window and click **Save Viewpoint** from the shortcut menu; a new viewpoint is added with **View** as the default name.

c. Rename the viewpoint to the required name.

VIEWPOINT SHORTCUT MENU

Once a viewpoint is created and saved in the **Saved Viewpoints** window, if you right-click on it, a shortcut menu is displayed, as shown in Figure 6. Some of these options are discussed next. The remaining options will be discussed later in this chapter.

*Figure 6 The **Viewpoint** shortcut menu*

Save Viewpoint
This option is used to save the current scene as a new viewpoint.

New Folder
If your Autodesk Navisworks scene has a large number of viewpoints and animations, it is better to organize them in folders. This option is used to add a new folder to do that.

Add Copy
This option is used to create a copy of the selected viewpoint. The copied viewpoints have the same name with an increment number inside the parenthesis as the suffix.

Edit

If you want to change the camera or target of a saved viewpoint, or you want to control the visibility and appearance of the objects in that viewpoint, you can right-click on that viewpoint in the **Saved Viewpoints** window and select **Edit** from the shortcut menu; the **Edit Viewpoint** dialog box will be displayed, as shown in Figure 7. The options in this dialog box are discussed next.

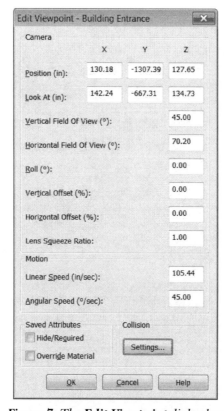

*Figure 7 The **Edit Viewpoint** dialog box*

Camera Area

This area provides you with the options to change camera settings such as the camera location, target, field of view, and so on. These options are discussed next.

Position

The **Position** boxes are used to change the X, Y, and Z coordinates of the current camera location.

Look At

The **Look At** boxes are used to change the X, Y, and Z coordinates of the current camera target.

Vertical Field Of View

The edit box is used to change the angle of the vertical field of view of the camera.

Horizontal Field Of View

The edit box is used to change the angle of the horizontal field of view of the camera. This value is the same as that defined in the **F.O.V.** slider in the **Viewpoint** ribbon tab **Camera** ribbon panel.

Roll

The edit box is used to rotate the current view around an axis normal to the screen.

Vertical Offset

The edit box is used to enter the value by which you want to vertically offset the camera from its current position. This value is defined in percentage.

Horizontal Offset

The edit box is used to enter the value by which you want to horizontally offset the camera from its current position. This value is defined in percentage.

Lens Squeeze Ratio

The edit box is used to squeeze the lens horizontally or vertically. A value of less than 1 will squeeze the lens vertically. As a result, all the objects will appear squeezed vertically. A value of more than 1 will squeeze the lens horizontally. As a result, all the objects will appear squeezed horizontally. Value of 1 will show the object without any squeeze. This is the default value.

What I do

*If I have to change the camera settings of a viewpoint, I generally go back to the graphics window and use the navigation tools to orient the model to the required view. Next, I right-click on the viewpoint that I need to change and click **Update** from the shortcut menu. This updates the viewpoint to the new camera settings.*

Motion Area

The options in this area are used when you create an animation based on the viewpoints. These options are discussed next.

Linear Speed

This box lets you enter the straight-line speed of the motion from this viewpoint to the next in the animation.

Angular Speed

This box lets you enter the angular speed of turning the camera from this viewpoint to the next in the animation.

Saved Attributes Area

The options in this area are used to control the visibility and appearance of the objects in the viewpoint. These options are discussed next.

Hide/Required

Selecting the **Hide/Required** tick box will ensure that any objects that were hidden or made required when this viewpoint was created will be again hidden or made required when you click on this viewpoint next time.

Override Appearance

Selecting this tick box will save the appearance overrides with the viewpoint.

 *Tip: You can permanently turn on the options to save the object visibility and appearance overrides using the **Options Editor**. From the left pane, expand **Interface** and click on **Viewpoint Defaults**. From the right pane, select the **Save Hide/Required Attributes** and **Override Appearance** tick boxes. Henceforth, whenever you create a viewpoint in any file, these two options will be turned on.*

Collision Area

This area provides the **Settings** button that is used to display the **Collision** dialog box, as shown in Figure 8. This dialog box is used to control the collision, gravity, crouching, and third person settings for the current viewpoint. These are discussed next.

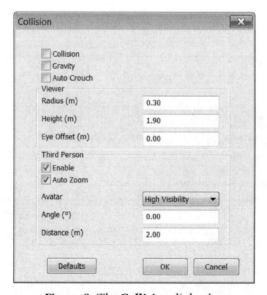

Figure 8 *The Collision dialog box*

Collision

This tick box is used to turn the collision on for the current viewpoint. Collision is discussed in detail later in this chapter.

Gravity

This tick box is used to turn the gravity on for the current viewpoint. Gravity is discussed in detail later in this chapter.

Auto Crouch

This tick box is used to turn the crouching on for the current viewpoint. It is discussed in detail later in this chapter.

Radius

This edit box is used to enter the radius of the collision volume or the third person avatar that will be displayed in the scene.

Height

This edit box is used to enter the height of the collision volume or the third person avatar that will be displayed in the scene.

Eye Offset

This edit box is used to enter the location of the camera with respect to the top of the avatar. A vault of 0.0 will look at the top of the avatar head. A value of 10 Inches will move the camera 10 Inches below the top of the avatar head.

Enable

This tick box is used to turn on the visibility of the avatar in the current viewpoint.

Auto Zoom

This tick box is used when the camera behind the third person collides with an object in the scene. In that case, if this tick box is turned on, the view will automatically be changed from the third person's view to the avatar's view.

Avatar

This list is used to select the required avatar.

Angle

This edit box is used to specify the angle at which the camera will look at the avatar.

 ***Tip**: If you are using the **Walk** tool, you can scroll the wheel mouse button to change the angle at which the camera looks at the avatar.*

Distance

This edit box is used to specify the distance between the camera and the avatar.

Update

This option of the viewpoint shortcut menu is used to update the selected viewpoint to reflect the current Autodesk Navisworks scene. This is generally used when you have changed the camera or object visibility and appearance and want to override an existing viewpoint with those changes.

Transform

Selecting this option displays the **Transform** dialog box that lets you move the camera by specifying the X, Y, and Z distances.

Delete

This option is used to delete one or more selected viewpoints.

Rename

This option is used to rename the selected viewpoint.

Copy Name

This option is used to copy the name of the selected viewpoint.

Sort

This option is used to alphabetically sort the viewpoints and animations in the **Saved Viewpoints** window.

The remaining options of the viewpoint shortcut menu will be discussed later in this chapter.

ADDING REALISM TO THE NAVIGATION

Autodesk Navisworks lets you add realism to the navigation by adding a third person, turning on the gravity and collision, and also letting the third person crouch under certain objects. All these tools are discussed next.

Third Person

Navigation Bar > Walk Flyout > Third Person
Viewpoint Ribbon Tab > Navigate Ribbon Panel > Third Person
Shortcut Key = CTRL + T

Turning on the third person will display an avatar in the scene and the Autodesk Navisworks model will be viewed from that third person's perspective. There are a number of different avatars that you can use. Figure 9 shows a plant model in which the default construction worker is displayed. Figure 10 shows the office female avatar at the entrance of a building.

 Note: *Our technical support team gets this question quite often from the customers that they have changed the avatar from **Global Options**, but when they turn the third person on, they still see the old avatar. To answer this question, a special topic is added next that shows how to change the avatar.*

Figure 9 *The default construction worker avatar looking at the plant model*

Figure 10 *The office female avatar at the entrance of a building*

Changing Third Person Avatar

Depending on your requirements, you will have to regularly change the third person avatar. But changing the avatar from the global options does not display the new avatar when you turn it on next. This is because the global options are to configure the default settings for the viewpoints. The following steps show how to permanently change the avatar.

a.   Open the file in which you want to display the avatar.

b.   Right-click in the **Saved Viewpoints** window and add a viewpoint. Change the name to any name you want.

c.   Right-click on the viewpoint and click **Edit** from the shortcut menu to display the **Edit Viewpoint** dialog box.

d.   Click **Settings** from the **Collision** area to display the **Collision** dialog box.

e.   Click the **Enable** tick box to turn the third person on, if it is not already turned on.

f.   Click on the **Avatar** list and select the desired avatar.

g.   Depending on the avatar selected, enter the **Radius**, **Height**, and **Distance** edit boxes. The following table shows common settings that generally work for the avatars.

	Radius	Height	Distance
Female Avatar	11 Inches 0.3 Meters	68 Inches 1.72 Meters	150 Inches 3.8 Meters
Male Avatar	11 Inches 0.3 Meters	72 Inches 1.9 Meters	170 Inches 4 Meters

h.   Click **OK** in the **Collision** dialog box and then click **OK** in the **Edit Viewpoint** dialog box.

i.   Sometimes, the avatar may still not be displayed or it may be displayed with an incorrect size. In that case, click on the **Walk** tool and walk a little. The avatar will be displayed correctly.

j.   Turn off the third person by pressing the CTRL + T key. This is the shortcut to toggle on or off the visibility of the third person.

k.   Using the SHIFT key and the wheel mouse button, orbit the model. Now, press the CTRL + T key again; the avatar that you set up in the viewpoint will be displayed although you are not in that viewpoint.

l.   Repeat steps b to j to change the avatar to something else.

Later in this chapter, you will learn how to change the default avatar for all new files.

Tip*: The avatar configured for the viewpoint that you selected last will be displayed next time whenever you turn the third person on anywhere in the scene.*

Gravity

Navigation Bar > Walk Flyout > Third Person > Gravity
Viewpoint Ribbon Tab > Navigate Ribbon Panel > Third Person > Gravity
Shortcut Key = CTRL + G

This option will only be available when you invoke the **Walk** tool or turn on the **Steering Wheel** tool to navigate around the model. The gravity will ensure that you always walk on a physical ground plane instead of floating in the air during navigation. This allows a realistic navigation in the model and lets you feel the bumps, if any, during your walk. This is also a very handy option when you want to go up and down the stairs. Note that if the gravity is turned on and you are walking in the area with no physical ground or floor, the gravity will keep dragging you down to no where in the model. In that case, you need to turn off the gravity.

> ### What I do
> *I use the CTRL + G key quite often to turn the gravity on and off. The reason is that in most cases I need to start walking in my model from the area where there is no physical floor. So I turn off the gravity by pressing the CTRL + G key. Once I am in the area that has a physical floor, I turn on the gravity using the same shortcut key. This way I do not have to stop walking and then use the flyouts to turn the gravity on or off.*

Collision

Navigation Bar > Walk Flyout > Third Person > Collision
Viewpoint Ribbon Tab > Navigate Ribbon Panel > Third Person > Collision
Shortcut Key = CTRL + D

This option will be automatically turned on when you turn the gravity on. With this option turned on, you will not be allowed to walk or fly past any solid object in your path. For example, if you come to a door that is closed, you will not be allowed to walk or fly past it. You will be represented by a volume defined using the **Radius** and **Height** values specified in the **Collision** dialog box.

Crouching

Navigation Bar > Walk Flyout > Third Person > Crouching
Viewpoint Ribbon Tab > Navigate Ribbon Panel > Third Person > Crouching

This option works in conjunction with the collision. When you turn this option on, the collision will also be turned on, if it is not already on. Crouching allows you to crouch under the objects that you cannot go past with the current standing height. Figure 11 shows an avatar crouching under a pipe.

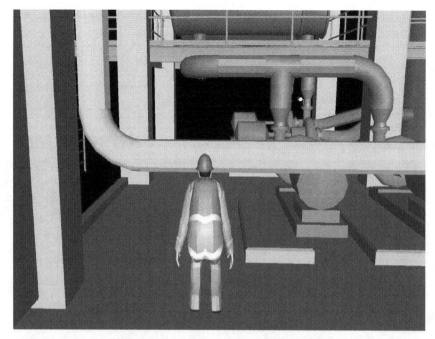

Figure 11 *Avatar crouching under a pipe*

 Note: *While walking with the collision turned on, sometimes the avatar turns transparent. This means that the camera behind the avatar is colliding with something in the scene.*

GLOBAL VIEWPOINT DEFAULT SETTINGS

Autodesk Navisworks lets you specify the global settings for the viewpoints. As a result, every new file that you open, the viewpoints will follow those settings. The following steps show you how to do this.

a. Press the F12 key to display the **Options Editor** dialog box.

b. From the left pane, expand **Interface** and click on **Viewpoint Default**; the right pane displays the viewpoint settings.

c. If you want, you can select the **Save Hide/Required Attributes** and **Override Appearance** tick boxes. This will ensure that all your new viewpoints will by default remember the object visibility and the appearance override information.

d. Click **Settings** from the **Collision** area to display the **Default Collision** dialog box. Define the collision and avatar settings that you want to be the default for all new files and their viewpoints. Note that if you open an existing Autodesk Navisworks file, it will still use the viewpoint and avatar settings defined in that particular file.

 Note: *In a new file, the Autodesk Navisworks viewpoints created upon opening or appending a native CAD file with predefined views will automatically be assigned the settings defined in the above-mentioned steps.*

CREATING WALKTHROUGH ANIMATIONS

Autodesk Navisworks lets you create walkthrough animations by recording the walk or by using the viewpoints. Both these methods are discussed next.

Recording the Walk

Animation Ribbon Tab > Create Ribbon Panel > Record

The **Record** tool lets you record your navigation through the model as frames. The animation name and the frames of the animation will be listed in the **Saved Viewpoints** window. Remember that using this method, all your navigation will be recorded as part of the animation. This means that if you zoom or pan the view, it will also be recorded as a part of the animation. Also, if you pause anywhere during the navigation, the pause will be recorded as stationary frames. If you really need to create a pause in your animation, click on the **Pause** button from the **Recording** ribbon panel that is displayed when you start recording the navigation. This will add a cut between the animation frames. You can expand the animation in the **Saved Viewpoints** window and right-click on the cut to change the pause duration.

Once you finish the recording, you can click on the **Record** button again to stop recording or click on the **Stop** button in the **Recording** panel. The recorded animation will be displayed in the **Saved Viewpoints** window with the default name as Animation1. If you right-click on the recorded animation and select **Edit** from the shortcut menu, the **Edit Animation** dialog box will be displayed. Using this dialog box, you can change the duration of the animation. You can also use the options in this dialog box to play the animation in a continuous loop and synchronize angular and linear speeds of the animation.

If the pause was not added while creating the animation, it can be added later also. To do this, expand the animation in the **Saved Viewpoints** window. Right-click on the frame before which you want to add the pause and select **Add Cut** from the shortcut menu. This will add a new cut above the selected frame. Right-click on the cut and click **Edit** from the shortcut menu to display the **Edit Animation Cut** dialog box in which you can change the pause duration.

The following steps show how to record a walkthrough animation.

a. Using various navigation tools or the SHIFT key and wheel mouse button, navigate to the view from where you want to start the walkthrough animation.

b. Invoke the **Walk** tool. If required, turn on the visibility of the third person and turn gravity, collision, and crouching on.

c. Click the **Animation** ribbon tab and then click **Record** from the **Create** ribbon panel.

d. Press and hold the left mouse button down and start walking in the model.

e. Once you have finished walking, press the **Record** button again to stop recording; a new animation is added in the **Saved Viewpoints** window with the default name of **Animation1**. The name is highlighted and you can change it to any desired name.

f.   Expand the animation in the **Saved Viewpoints** window; all the frames in this animation are listed. If there are any undesired frames, they can be deleted by right-clicking on them and selecting **Delete** from the shortcut menu.

g.   To add a pause in the animation, scroll half way through the animation frames and then right-click on one of the frames to display the shortcut menu.

h.   Click **Add Cut** from the shortcut menu and then press ENTER to accept the default name.

i.   Right-click on the cut and select **Edit** from the shortcut menu.

j,   Enter the duration of the pause in the **Edit Animation Cut** edit box and click **OK** to close it.

k.   Right-click on the name of the animation in the **Saved Viewpoints** window and select **Edit**.

l.   In the **Edit Animation** dialog box, enter the duration that you want this animation to play for.

Creating Viewpoint Animation

Autodesk Navisworks lets you create a blank animation in which you can drag and drop as many number of still viewpoints from the **Saved Viewpoints** window. When played, this animation will show a motion transitioning through all the viewpoints in the same order in which they appear in the animation. This is a really handy way to create complex animations. You can also control the visibility and color overrides of the objects in this type of animation.

The following steps show how to create this type of animation.

a.   Using the **Saved Viewpoints** window, create the viewpoints that you want to transition through in your animation. Make sure they appear in the same sequence in which you want to transition through them.

b.   Turn off the visibility and override the material of some objects in the viewpoints. Because the object visibility and material override options were turned on globally earlier in this chapter, the new viewpoints that you create will automatically have these options turned on.

c.   Right-click in the **Saved Viewpoints** window and click **Add Animation** from the shortcut menu; a new animation is added with the default name as **Animation**.

d.   Rename it to any desired name.

e.   In the **Saved Viewpoints** window, select all the viewpoints that you want to add to the animation.

f.   Drag and drop the selected viewpoints in the blank animation that you added.

Tip: You can drag the viewpoints in the animation to change their sequences. You can also drag a viewpoint from the animation and drop it outside in the blank area of the **Saved Viewpoints** *window to remove it from the animation. Similarly, you can drag a viewpoint from the* **Saved Viewpoints** *window and drop it on the name of an existing animation to add it to the animation.*

g.   In the **Saved Viewpoints** window, right-click on the animation and click **Edit** from the shortcut menu to display the **Edit Animation** dialog box.

h.   Enter the duration that you want to play this animation for in the **Duration** edit box and click **OK** to close the dialog box.

 Tip: If you want the animation to transition a bit slower than the usual speed between certain views, you can right-click on a viewpoint and click **Edit** *from the shortcut menu. In the* **Edit Viewpoint** *dialog box, reduce the speed in the* **Linear Speed** *edit box. This will ensure that the transition from this view to the next is slower compared to the usual animation speed.*

i.   To add a pause in this animation, right-click on the viewpoint above which you want the pause and select **Add Cut** from the shortcut menu.

j.   Right-click on the cut and select **Edit** from the shortcut menu to change the pause duration.

What I do
When saving viewpoints that I want to add to an animation, I prefer using the **Walk** *tool rather than the* **Orbit** *or* **Zoom** *tool to go from one view to the other to save it as a viewpoint. While playing the resulting animation, the transitioning from one viewpoint to the other is a lot smoother this way.*

Playing the Animations

> **Animation Ribbon Tab > Playback Ribbon Panel > Play**

To playback the animation that you saved, click on that animation in the **Saved Viewpoints** window and then click on the **Play** button on the **Animate** ribbon tab > **Playback** ribbon panel. You can pause, rewind and replay the animation using the other buttons available in this ribbon panel. While playing the animation, the frames or the viewpoints of the animations will be highlighted, if the animation is expanded in the **Saved Viewpoints** window.

Combining Multiple Animations
Similar to dragging and dropping viewpoints in a blank animation, Autodesk Navisworks also lets you drag and drop existing animations in a new blank animation. The existing animations could be a recorded one or a viewpoint based. To do this, right-click in the **Saved Viewpoints** window and click **Add Animation** from the shortcut menu to add a blank animation. Now, drag and drop

the existing animations in this. They will be played in the same sequence in which they appear in the new animation. You can change the duration of the new combined animation by right-clicking on it and selecting **Edit** from the shortcut menu. Figure 12 shows the **Saved Viewpoints** window showing an animation created by combining a viewpoint-based animation and a recorded animation.

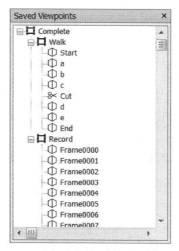

Figure 12 The Saved Viewpoints window showing a combined animation

Exporting Animations

Animation Ribbon Tab > Export Ribbon Panel > Export Animation

---

The animations created and saved in the current scene can be exported as .AVI files to be opened on a machine that does not have Autodesk Navisworks. To do this, click the animation you want to export from the **Saved Viewpoints** window and then click **Animation** ribbon tab > **Export** ribbon panel > **Export Animation**; the **Animation Export** dialog box will be displayed, as shown in Figure 13.

From the **Format** list, select **Windows AVI** and then click on the **Options** button on the right of this list to display the **Video Compression** dialog box. Click **Full Frames (Uncompressed)** from the **Compressor** list and click **OK** in the dialog box.

From the **Type** list in the **Size** area, select **Use Aspect Ratio**. Enter **800** in the **Width** edit box; the value in the **Height** edit box will change automatically.

In the **FPS** spinner in the **Options** area, enter **12** as the value of frames per second. Remember that bigger the value of frames per second, smoother the animation, but larger will be the resulting AVI file size.

Click **OK** in the **Animation Export** dialog box; the **Save As** dialog box will be displayed that lets you specify the name and location of the AVI file.

Figure 13 *The **Animation Export** dialog box*

What I do

I avoid exporting the animation from the Autodesk Navisworks scene unless it is to be embedded in a document. The reason is that the exported AVI files have really large sizes. As a result, they are difficult to manage and share with the stakeholders. I prefer publishing the NWD file, which also contains the animations. The NWD file can be opened in the free Autodesk Navisworks Freedom viewer so the person viewing the file does not need a license of Autodesk Navisworks. In Autodesk Navisworks Freedom, they can play the animation similar to the way it is done in Autodesk Navisworks. Because the NWD files are a lot smaller in size compared to the AVI files, they are easy to manage and share.

EXPORTING AND IMPORTING VIEWPOINTS

Autodesk Navisworks allows you to export all the saved viewpoints along with the viewpoint animations and then import them to another file. All the information about the avatar visibility and the camera location and target will also be included with the exported viewpoints and viewpoint animations and will be restored when you import them in another file.

The following steps show you how to export and import viewpoints and viewpoint animations.

a. Open the file from which you want to export the viewpoints and viewpoint animations.

b. Right-click in the **Saved Viewpoint** window to display the shortcut menu.

c. Click **Export Viewpoints** from the shortcut menu to display the **Export** dialog box.

d.   Using the **Export** dialog box, specify the location and the name of the XML file that will store all the information about the viewpoints and viewpoint animations.

e.   Open the file in which you want to import the viewpoints and viewpoint animations.

f.   Right-click in the **Saved Viewpoints** window to display the shortcut menu.

g.   From the shortcut menu, click **Import Viewpoint**; the **Import** dialog box will be displayed.

h.   Browse to the location where you saved the exported XML file and double-click on it; all the viewpoints and viewpoint animations will be imported to the current file.

MEASURING OBJECTS

Autodesk Navisworks allows you to measure distances, angles, and areas of the objects in the scene. You can also move the selected objects by the measured distance value. All this is done using the tools available in the **Review** ribbon tab > **Measure** ribbon panel > **Measure** flyout, shown in Figure 14. The coordinates of the selected points and the measured values are displayed in the graphics window as well as in the **Measure Tools** window, as shown in Figure 15.

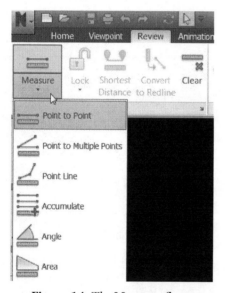

*Figure 14 The **Measure** flyout*

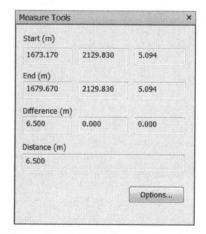

*Figure 15 The **Measure Tools** window*

The measurement values will be displayed in the current display units. To change the units, press F12 to display the **Options Editor**. From the left pane, expand **Interface** and click **Display Units**. From the right pane, click the **Linear Units** list and select the desired units.

All the measurement tools are discussed next.

Tip*: For accuracy of measurements, it is important to make sure that object snapping is turned on. To do this, press the F12 key. In the **Options Editor** dialog box, expand **Interface** from the left pane and then click **Snapping**. From the right pane, make sure **Snap to Vertex**, **Snap to Edge**, and **Snap to Line Vertex** tick boxes are turned on. The value in the **Tolerance** edit box defines how close you need to be to the object before the cursor snaps to it.*

Measuring Point to Point Distance

Review Ribbon Tab > Measure Ribbon Panel > Measure Flyout > Point to Point

This tool lets you measure the distance between two selected points, which can be on faces, edges, vertices, or any combination of these. When you invoke this tool, the cursor changes to crosshairs. If you move the crosshairs over a face, a rectangle will be displayed aligned to that face, informing you that the cursor has snapped to a face. If you move the crosshairs on an edge or a sketched line, a line will be displayed over it, informing you that the cursor has snapped to an edge or a line. If you move the cursor over a point or a vertex, a cross will be displayed, informing you that the cursor has snapped to a vertex or a point.

When you select the first point, its X, Y, and Z coordinates are displayed in the **Start** display boxes in the **Measure Tools** window. When you select the second point, its coordinates, along with the difference in coordinate values, are displayed in the **End** and **Difference** display boxes, respectively. The measured distance is displayed in the **Distance** display box and in the graphics window. Figure 16 shows an Autodesk Navisworks scene showing the measured distance. This figure also shows the **Measure Tools** window showing various values.

You can perform any number of measurements using this method, however, only the last measurement will be displayed in the graphics window and the **Measure Tools** window.

 Note*: Before learning about the other measure tools, you need to learn to clear the current measurements. This is discussed next.*

Clearing Measurement

Review Ribbon Tab > Measure Ribbon Panel > Clear

This tool is used to clear the current measurements from the graphics window as well as the **Measure Tools** window. By default, the measured value remains on the model after you exit the measurement tool. Even when you change the view or navigate through the model, this value remains in the graphics window. If you do not want this value to be displayed, use the **Clear** tool.

 Tip*: While measuring objects, you can press the right mouse button at any time to clear the current measurement. This, however, will not clear the shortest distance measurement, which is discussed later in this chapter.*

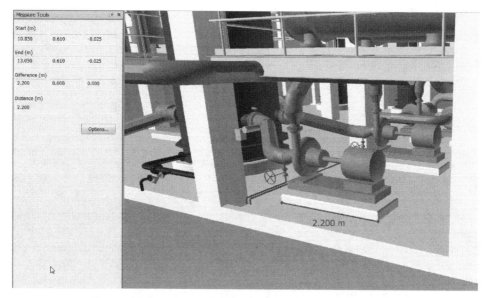

*Figure 16 Measuring distance using the **Point to Point** tool*

Measuring Point to Multiple Points

Review Ribbon Tab > **Measure Ribbon Panel** > **Measure Flyout** >
Point to Multiple Points

This tool lets you measure the distance between the first selected point and multiple other points. The points can be on faces, edges, vertices, or any combination of these. The first point that you select remains selected and you can continuously pick any number of points as the second point. Note that only the last measurement will be displayed in the graphics window and in the **Measure Tools** window. Figure 17 shows a plant model in which the first measurement is made between the two bottom vertices of the concrete and the crosshairs picking another vertex to measure distance to that.

Measuring Point Line

Review Ribbon Tab > **Measure Ribbon Panel** > **Measure Flyout** > **Point Line**

This tool lets you measure the cumulative distance between multiple points. You can keep clicking as many number of points and the cumulative value will be displayed in the graphics window and in the **Measure Tools** window. Figure 18 shows cumulative distance between the three vertices of the front face of concrete in a plant model.

Figure 17 Point to multiple point measurement

Figure 18 Point line measurement

Measuring Accumulated Distances

> **Review Ribbon Tab > Measure Ribbon Panel > Measure Flyout > Accumulate**

This tool works similar to the **Point Line** tool, with the difference that instead of selecting continuous points, you need to select points in pairs. This means that after selecting the first two points, you will have to select the previous point again as the first point for the next measurement.

Measuring Angles

> **Review Ribbon Tab > Measure Ribbon Panel > Measure Flyout > Angle**

This tool lets you measure the angle between three selected points. Note that the second point will be used as the angle vertex point. Figure 19 shows the angle measured between three points. In this case, the top corner vertex was selected as the second point.

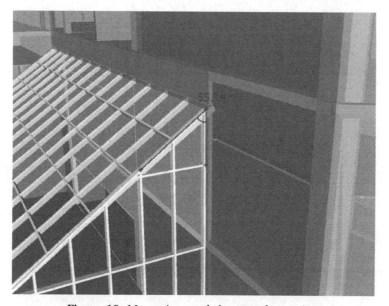

Figure 19 *Measuring angle between three points*

 *Tip: To measure the coordinates of a point, use any measurement tool and click on that point; its coordinates will be displayed in the **Start** display boxes in the **Measure Tools** window.*

Measuring Area

> **Review Ribbon Tab > Measure Ribbon Panel > Measure Flyout > Area**

This tool lets you measure the area of a region defined by the selected points. You can select as many number of points to measure the area. As soon as you select the third point, the area of the triangle formed by the first three points will be displayed. You can keep selecting points and the area will keep updating. Figure 20 shows the area displayed between the first three points selected on the front face of the concrete and the cursor ready to select the fourth point.

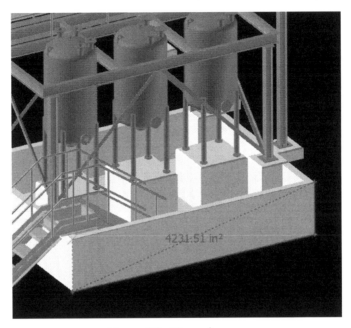

Figure 20 *Measuring area*

Measuring Shortest Distance Between Two Objects

Review Ribbon Tab > Measure Ribbon Panel > Shortest Distance

This tool lets you measure the shortest distance between two selected objects. For this tool to be active, you need to first select two objects. This tool is really handy when you want to measure the shortest distance between two round or curved objects such as pipes or vessels. Figure 21 shows the shortest distance measured between the flanges of two vessels.

Transforming Objects

Review Ribbon Tab > Expanded Measure Ribbon Panel > Transform Selected Items

This tool lets you transform the selected object by the value equal to the measured distance or angle. For this tool to be active, you need to have an object selected and a distance or angle measured. These two could be in any sequence. This means that you can select the objects first and them perform the measurement or you can perform the measurement first and then select the object as the measurement is displayed. Remember that the selected object will be transformed in the vector direction of the first point to the second point.

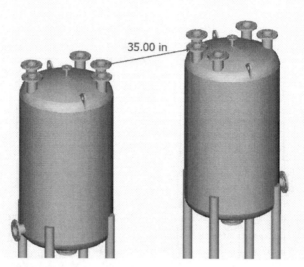

Figure 21 *Shortest distance between two selected objects*

What I do

*I have faced a number of situations when I had to append multiple files from different contractors with different coordinates that did not match when appended together. In such situations, I measure the distance between any two points that are supposed to match in the scene. Then I select one of the files from the **Selection Tree** and use the **Transform Objects** tool to move the selected file by the measured distance.*

Converting Measurements to Redline

Review Ribbon Tab > Measure Ribbon Panel > Convert to Redline

This tool lets you convert the measurement into a redline markup. For this tool to be active, a measured value has to be visible in the graphics window. When you click this tool, a new viewpoint is created in the **Saved Viewpoints** window with the name **View**. This viewpoint saves the camera orientation and the measurement value. Once converted into a redline markup, the measurement will disappear from the graphics window when you change the view or navigate through the model. However, this value will reappear as soon as you click on the saved viewpoint.

 Note: *Clicking the **Clear** button does not clear the measurement value that is converted into a redline markup. But as soon as you change the view by using any navigation tool, this value will disappear.*

Locking Measurements

Review Ribbon Tab > Measure Ribbon Panel > Lock Flyout

Autodesk Navisworks allows you to lock the X, Y, or Z direction or the parallel or perpendicular direction from the start point of the measurement. If you lock the X, Y, or Z direction, the measurement in only that particular direction will be shown. If you lock parallel or perpendicular direction, the measurement will only be shown parallel or perpendicular to the face of the start point.

For the ease of understanding, the locked measurements are color-coded. The measurements locked in the X direction will be displayed in Red, the measurements locked in the Y direction will be displayed in Green, and the measurements locked in the Z direction will be displayed in Blue. Similarly, the measurements locked parallel to the face of the start point will be displayed in Magenta and the measurements locked perpendicular to the face of the start point will be displayed in Yellow.

Changing the Display of Measurements

Clicking the **Options** button in the **Measure Tools** window displays the **Options Editor** dialog box with **Interface** > **Measure** selected from the left pane. The options in the right pane are discussed next.

Line Thickness

```
Measure Tools Window > Options
```

This spinner is used to specify the thickness value of the measurement that will be displayed in the graphics window.

Color

This list is used to change the color of the measurements.

In 3D

If this tick box is selected, any part of the measurement line that is inside an object in the scene will be hidden. By default, this tick box is cleared. As a result, the measurement lines will not be hidden by the objects in the scene.

Show measurement values in Scene view

If this tick box is selected, the measurement value will also be displayed in the graphics window. Clearing this tick box will only display the value in the **Measure Tools** window and not on the graphics screen. However, the measurement lines will still be displayed in the graphics window.

Use center lines

Selecting this tick box ensures that while measuring the shortest distance between two parametric cylindrical parts, the value will be from the center lines and not the outside faces. Note that the center lines are only supported in the parametric cylindrical parts created in the software such as MicroStation (DGN) and PDMS Review (RVM).

HANDS-ON EXERCISES

You will now work on hands-on exercises by using the concepts learned in this chapter.

Hands-on Exercise (Plant)	*In this exercise, you will complete the following tasks:*
	1. *Open an Autodesk Navisworks NWF file.*
	2. *Create and save various viewpoints in the model.*
	3. *Use the **Walk** tool to walk in the model.*
	4. *Record a walkthrough animation.*
	5. *Create viewpoint-based animation.*
	6. *Measure various objects in the scene.*
	7. *Transform objects using the measured distance value.*

Section 1: Opening the File and Creating Viewpoints

In this exercise, you will open an NWF file, which is created using a DWFx file. In this file, you will create various viewpoints looking at different parts of the plant. It is assumed that you are using the **Training** workspace created in Chapter 1. Therefore, the **Saved Viewpoints** window is available on the right side of the graphics window, docked below the **Properties** window. If not, refer to the Plant Exercise of that chapter to create a workspace.

1. Start Autodesk Navisworks, if it is not already opened on your machine.

2. Invoke the **Open** dialog box and change the file type to **Navisworks File Set (*.nwf)**.

3. Browse to the **Chapter 3 > Exercise Plant** folder and then double-click on the **Plant-GA.nwf** file.

   Before proceeding further, you will change the display units to your required units.

4. Press F12 to display the **Options Editor** dialog box. From the left pane, expand **Interface** and select **Display Units**. From the right pane, select the desired units from the **Linear Units** list. Close the dialog box by clicking **OK**.

5. Assign the horizon background to the file by right-clicking in the blank area of the graphics window and selecting the **Background** option from the shortcut menu.

   Next, you will create five viewpoints. Four viewpoints will be to view the model from four corners and the fifth will be at the start of the Yellow concrete frame.

6. Using the wheel mouse button or various navigation tools, zoom and orbit the view to display the model similar to the one shown in Figure 22.

7. Right-click in the **Saved Viewpoints** window and select **Save Viewpoint** from the shortcut menu. Rename the viewpoint to **Overview 1**.

8. Using the wheel mouse button or various navigation tools, zoom and orbit the view to display the model similar to the one shown in Figure 23.

Figure 22 *The Autodesk Navisworks scene for the first viewpoint*

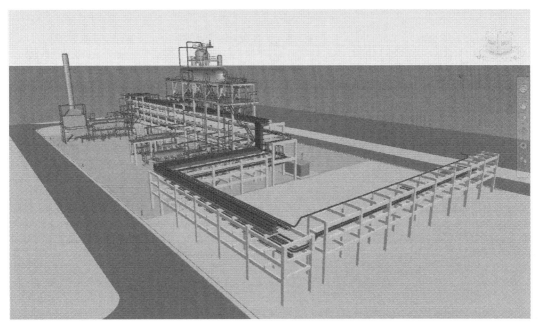

Figure 23 *The Autodesk Navisworks scene for the second viewpoint*

9. Right-click in the **Saved Viewpoints** window and select **Save Viewpoint** from the shortcut menu. Rename the viewpoint to **Overview 2**.

10. Similarly, create the **Overview 3** and **Overview 4** viewpoints looking at the model from the two other corners.

11. In the **Saved Viewpoints** window, click on the **Overview 1** viewpoint to activate it.

    Next, you will create a viewpoint at the start of the Yellow concrete structure. This is to the left of the Green vessel displayed toward the left side looking at the model from the current view.

12. Using the wheel mouse button or various navigation tools, zoom and orbit the view to display the model similar to the one shown in Figure 24. If the model looks twisted, click on the **Viewpoint** ribbon tab > **Camera** ribbon panel > **Align Camera** flyout and select **Straighten**.

*Figure 24 The **Walk Start** viewpoint showing the model*

13. Right-click in the **Saved Viewpoints** window and select **Save Viewpoint** from the shortcut menu. Rename the viewpoint to **Walk Start**.

Section 2: Walking in the Model

Next, you will walk in the model using the **Walk** tool. The walk will start from the viewpoint last saved in the previous section. But before you start walking, you will edit the last viewpoint to turn on the visibility of a third person.

1. In the **Saved Viewpoints** window, right-click on the **Walk Start** viewpoint and click **Edit** from the shortcut menu; the **Edit Viewpoint - Walk Start** dialog box is displayed.

2. From the **Collision** area, click **Settings** to display the **Collision** dialog box.

3. Click the **Enable** tick box in the **Third Person** area to turn on the third person.

4. From the **Avatar** list, select **High Visibility**.

5. Enter the following values in their respective boxes. Use the values suitable to your display units.

Radius:	**11 Inches**
	0.3 Meters
Height:	**72 Inches**
	1.9 Meters
Distance:	**170 Inches**
	4 Meters

6. Make sure the rest of the values are set to 0. Click **OK** in the **Collision** dialog box and then click **OK** in the **Edit Viewpoint - Walk Start** dialog box; an avatar appears in high visibility clothing.

7. If the avatar appears to be crouching, press and hold the wheel mouse button down and drag it a little; the avatar stands upright, as shown in Figure 25.

*Figure 25 The **Walk Start** viewpoint showing the avatar*

8. From the **Navigation Bar** on the right side of the graphics window, click the **Walk** tool; the cursor changes to human feet cursor.

9. Press and hold the left mouse button down and drag the mouse forward; the avatar starts moving forward slowly.

Tip*: If the avatar appears to be inside the floor, press and hold down the wheel mouse button and drag the mouse up to bring it out of the floor.*

10. Once the avatar is just past the manhole at the start of the concrete structure, press the CTRL + G key to turn on the gravity and collision.

11. Press and hold down the left mouse button and drag the mouse forward to restart the walk; if the avatar was floating in the air, it will come back to the ground level.

 Tip*: While walking, you can press and hold down the wheel mouse button and drag it sideways to pan the view and line up the avatar with the objects in the scene.*

12. Continue walking to the end of this section of the Yellow structure and then turn to the right to walk toward the right. Make sure you stay on the Pink floor.

13. Similarly, at the end of the Yellow structure, turn right again. Walk close to the section shown in Figure 26.

Figure 26 *Walking in the scene*

In the section of the plant shown in the figure above, there is a steel beam at a height lower than the height of the avatar. With the collision turned on, you will not be allowed to walk through that steel. To do that, you need to turn the crouching on. It is better to create a viewpoint at this stage so if something goes wrong in your walk, you can come back to this view.

14. In the **Saved Viewpoints** window, right-click to display the shortcut menu and click **Save Viewpoint**. Enter **Crouch** as the name of the viewpoint.

15. Right-click on this new viewpoint and click **Edit** from the shortcut menu.

16. In the **Edit Viewpoint - Crouch** dialog box, click **Settings** from the **Collision** area.

17. From the **Collision** dialog box, select the **Auto Crouch** tick box; this turns the crouching on for this viewpoint. Click **OK** in both the dialog boxes to close them.

18. Press and hold the left mouse button down and continue to walk. As soon as you come close to the steel, the avatar will crouch under the steel. At this point, it will also become transparent. This indicates that the camera behind the avatar is interfering with some object in the scene.

19. Continue walking forward and the avatar will appear again. Once the avatar goes past the light Blue vessel, turn right.

    Be careful about the ditch past the Pink floor. With the gravity turned on, if you go past the Pink floor, the avatar will fall in the ditch. In that case, restart from the **Crouch** viewpoint.

20. Walk close to the back of the Green vessel, as shown in Figure 27.

Figure 27 *Ending the walk*

21. In the **Saved Viewpoints** window, right-click and click **Save Viewpoint** from the shortcut menu. Enter **Walk End** as the name of the viewpoint.

Section 3: Recording the Walk

You will now record the walk going through the same sections of the plant as in the previous section. As mentioned earlier in this chapter, if you do not do anything on the screen after clicking the **Record** tool, it will also be recorded in the animation as stationary frames. So it is important that you are ready to start recording the walk before you invoke this tool.

1. From the **Saved Viewpoints** window, click on the **Walk Start** viewpoint.

2. Invoke the **Walk** tool from the **Navigation Bar**. Press and hold down the left mouse button and start walking forward. Stop when the avatar is just past the first set of Yellow columns.

3. Press CTRL + G key to turn the gravity and collision on.

4. In the **Navigation Bar**, click the **Walk** flyout and click **Crouch** to turn the crouching on.

5. Press and hold down the left mouse button down and walk forward a little to make sure the avatar is on the ground.

   Next, you will start recording your walk. At any point during the recording, you can click the **Pause** button on the **Recording** ribbon panel to pause the recording and read the exercise steps.

6. From the **Animation** ribbon tab > **Create** ribbon panel, click **Record**.

7. Press and hold down the left mouse button and start walking. Follow the same path as mentioned in the previous section.

8. Once you come to the view similar to the **Walk End** viewpoint, click the **Record** button again to stop recording; a new animation is added in the **Saved Viewpoints** window.

9. Rename the animation to **Walkthrough**.

10. Save the current file.

    Next, you will edit and play the animation you just saved.

11. In the **Saved Viewpoints** window, right-click the on **Walkthrough** animation and click **Edit** from the shortcut menu; the **Edit Animation: Walkthrough** dialog box is displayed.

12. Enter **50** as the value in the **Duration** edit box. Click **OK** to close the dialog box.

13. In the **Saved Viewpoints** window, click the **Walkthrough** animation again and then click the **Play** button from the **Animation** ribbon tab > **Playback** ribbon panel.

 *Tip: If there are any unwanted pauses or delays in the animation, you can expand the animation in the **Saved Viewpoints** window and delete those frames.*

Section 4: Creating Animation Based on the Viewpoints

In this section, you will create an animation based on the viewpoints. You will create copies of the **Walk Start**, **Crouch**, and the **Walk End** viewpoints and use them for this animation. You will also add more intermediate viewpoints to create a smooth walk.

 Note: The realism of gravity, collision, and crouching is not considered in the viewpoint animations. However, gravity helps to create viewpoints in which you are always on the ground and not floating in the air.

1. From the **Saved Viewpoints** window, select the **Walk Start** viewpoint. Then hold the CTRL key down and select the **Crouch** and **Walk End** viewpoints as well.

2. Right-click on any of the selected viewpoints and click **Add Copy** from the shortcut menu; a copy of each of the selected viewpoints is added with a suffix (1) in the name.

3. Rename the **Walk Start (1)** viewpoint to **Start**, **Crouch (1)** viewpoint to **6**, and **Walk End (1)** viewpoint to **End**.

4. Click on the **Start** viewpoint to go to the start of the walk. Now, invoke the **Walk** tool from the **Navigation Bar** and press and hold down the left mouse button to start walking forward.

5. Once the avatar is inside the Yellow frame, press the CTRL + G key to turn on the gravity. Although the gravity is not respected in the animation, it helps you create the next viewpoint at the ground level.

6. Right-click on the **Start** viewpoint and click **Update** from the shortcut menu.

7. Press and hold down the left mouse button and start walking forward; the avatar comes to the ground if it was floating in the air.

    As mentioned earlier, you can press and hold down the wheel mouse button to pan the avatar sideways or up and down. This helps to line it up with the objects in the scene.

8. Walk to the end of this frame section and stop just before turning right.

9. Right-click in the blank area of the **Saved Viewpoints** window and click **Save Viewpoint** from the shortcut menu; a new viewpoint is added. Name this viewpoint as **2**.

    Next, you will create a viewpoint just after turning right. If you do not create this viewpoint, the avatar will cut across the concrete structure in the animation.

10. Slowly turn right and walk forward a little, just to the point where the avatar is in line with the first column in this section.

11. Right-click in the blank area of the **Saved Viewpoints** window and click **Save Viewpoint** from the shortcut menu; a new viewpoint is added. Name this viewpoint as **3**.

12. Press and hold down the left mouse button and walk forward to the end of this section. Stop just before the last concrete column.

13. Right-click in the blank area of the **Saved Viewpoints** window and click **Save Viewpoint** from the shortcut menu; a new viewpoint is added. Name this viewpoint as **4**.

14. Slowly turn right and walk forward a little to the point where the avatar is just past the Yellow concrete beam, as shown in Figure 28. You can press and hold down the wheel mouse button and drag sideways to line it correctly.

15. Right-click in the blank area of the **Saved Viewpoints** window and click **Save Viewpoint** from the shortcut menu; a new viewpoint is added. Name this viewpoint as **5**.

Figure 28 *View for creating viewpoint 5*

16. In the **Saved Viewpoints** window, click on the **6** viewpoint. Press and hold down the left mouse button and start walking; the avatar crouches under the steel and the stairs. Note that this crouching will not be shown in the animation.

17. Stop when the avatar is in line the Blue vessel on the right.

 Note: *While walking forward from the **6** viewpoint, if the avatar falls in the ditch past the Blue vessel, start again from the **6** viewpoint. You can also press CTRL + G key to turn off the gravity if you are having trouble with the previous step.*

18. Right-click in the blank area of the **Saved Viewpoints** window and click **Save Viewpoint** from the shortcut menu; a new viewpoint is added. Name this viewpoint as **7**.

19. Press and hold down the left mouse button, walk forward a little and then turn right to a view similar to the one shown in Figure 29.

20. Right-click in the blank area of the **Saved Viewpoints** window and click **Save Viewpoint** from the shortcut menu; a new viewpoint is added. Name this viewpoint as **8**.

    This completes all the viewpoints that you need for the viewpoint walk. Next, you will insert a blank animation and drag and drop these viewpoints in it.

21. Right-click in the blank area of the **Saved Viewpoints** window and click **Add Animation** from the shortcut menu. Name this animation **Viewpoint Walk**.

22. In the **Saved Viewpoints** window, click on the **Start** viewpoint. Next, hold the CTRL key down and select viewpoints **2**, **3**, **4**, and **5**. Release the CTRL key.

    You now need to drag and drop these viewpoints in the **Viewpoint Walk** animation. It is recommended that this is done by holding down the left mouse button on the icon of one of

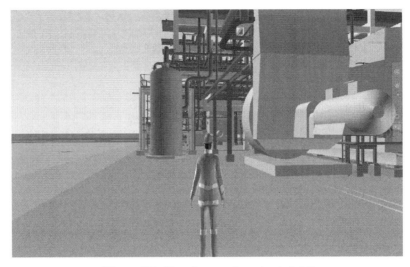

Figure 29 *View for creating viewpoint 8*

the viewpoints. If you try to drag the name of the viewpoint, some times it will go into the rename mode.

23. Press and hold down the left mouse button on the icon of one of the selected viewpoints and drop them on the name of the **Viewpoint Walk** animation; this will add these viewpoints in the correct sequence to the animation.

24. Click on the **6** viewpoint. Next, hold the CTRL key down and select viewpoints **7** and **8**. Release the CTRL key.

25. Press and hold down the left mouse button on the icon of one of the selected viewpoints and drop them on the name of the **Viewpoint Walk** animation; this will add these viewpoints in the correct sequence to the animation.

26. Press and hold down the left mouse button on the **End** viewpoint and drop it on the name of the **Viewpoint Walk** animation; this will add the viewpoint at the end of the animation.

    Next, you will edit the duration of the viewpoint animation.

27. In the **Saved Viewpoints** window, right-click on the **Viewpoint Walk** animation and click **Edit** from the shortcut menu; the **Edit Animation: Viewpoint Walk** dialog box is displayed.

28. Enter **50** as the duration value and click **OK** in the dialog box; you are automatically taken to the start of this animation.

29. With this animation still selected in the **Saved Viewpoints** window, click the **Play** button on the **Animation** ribbon tab > **Playback** ribbon panel; the animation starts to play.

30. After the animation ends, click the **Stop** button and save the current file.

Section 5: Organizing Viewpoints and Animations in Folders

In this section, organize the **Saved Viewpoints** window by creating separate folders for the viewpoints and animations.

1. Click in the blank area of the **Saved Viewpoints** window to deselect the animation.

2. In the **Saved Viewpoints** window, right-click in the blank area on the right of one of the overview viewpoints and click **New Folder** from the shortcut menu. Name this folder as **Viewpoints**.

 Note: *If the animation is selected and you add a folder, it gets added inside the animation. This is the reason you need to first deselect the animation.*

3. Click in the blank area of the **Saved Viewpoints** window to deselect the folder. Now, repeat step 2 and name the new folder as **Animations**.

4. Click on the **Overview 1** viewpoint. Press and hold down the SHIFT key and select the **Walk End** viewpoint; all the viewpoints in between are also selected.

    If you try to drag the viewpoint by holding its name, it may go into the rename mode. Therefore, it is important for you to click on the icon of the viewpoints while dragging them.

5. Holding down the icon of one of the selected viewpoints, drag and drop them in the **Viewpoints** folder.

6. Click the **Walkthrough** animation and then hold down the CTRL key and click on the **Viewpoint Walk** animation.

7. Holding down the icon of one of the selected animation, drag and drop them in the **Animations** folder. The **Saved Viewpoints** window should look similar to the one shown in Figure 30.

Figure 30 Viewpoints and animations organized in folders

Section 6: Measuring the Objects in the Model

In this section, you will perform various measurements on the objects in the model. To view various measurements, you will dock the **Measure Tools** window on the screen. You will use various viewpoints saved earlier to go to the view to measure objects. But first, you will change the color and the thickness of the measurements.

1. Click on **Measure Tools** from the left side of the **Selection Tree** and dock the window on the screen by clicking the **Auto-Hide** button on the top right of this window.

2. Click the **Options** button in the **Measure Tools** window to display the **Options Editor** dialog box.

3. In the right pane of the dialog box, enter **2** as the value in the **Line Thickness** spinner.

4. From the **Color** list, select the **Red** color.

5. From the left pane, click **Snapping**.

6. From the right pane, select the **Snap to Vertex**, **Snap to Edge**, and **Snap to Line Vertex** tick boxes, if they are not selected already.

7. Click **OK** in the dialog box to return back to the graphics window.

   You will start with measuring the length of the concrete beam at the start of the concrete structure section. You will use the **Walk Start** viewpoint and walk forward a little to measure this beam.

8. From the **Saved Viewpoints** window, expand the **Viewpoints** folder, if not already expanded, and select the **Walk Start** viewpoint.

9. Press the CTRL + T key to turn off the avatar. If need be, use the **Walk** tool to walk closer to the start section of the concrete structure.

   Because you need to measure two distances, you will use the **Point to Multiple Points** tool.

10. From the **Review** ribbon tab > **Measure** ribbon panel > **Measure** flyout, invoke the **Point to Multiple Points** tool.

11. Move the cursor over the bottom left vertex of the Yellow beam. When the cursor snaps to the vertex, a cross appears. At this point, click to select the vertex; the X, Y, and Z coordinates of the selected vertex are displayed in the **Start** display boxes of the **Measure Tools** window.

12. Move the cursor across to the bottom right vertex of the beam and click when the cross appears; the length of the beam is displayed on the screen in the units that you have selected as your display units. Figure 31 shows this measurement in Inches. This value is also displayed in the **Measure Tools** window, along with the coordinates of the second vertex and the difference in the start and end coordinates.

   Next, you will measure the width of the beam. Because you used the **Point to Multiple Points** tool, the lower left vertex of the beam is still selected as the first point.

Figure 31 *Measuring the length of the beam*

13. Move the cursor over the top left vertex of the beam and click when the cross is displayed; the measurement of the width of the beam is displayed on the screen and the values are also displayed in the **Measure Tools** window.

    Next, you will measure the area of the front face of the same beam.

14. From **Review** ribbon tab > **Measure** ribbon panel > **Measure** flyout, invoke the **Area** tool.

15. One by one, click on the four vertices of the front face of the beam. Make sure you click only when the cross is displayed. Once you click the fourth point, the area of the face is displayed in the graphics window and in the **Measure Tools** window.

16. Right-click anywhere in the graphics window to clear all the measurements.

    Next, you will measure the shortest distance between two pipes. For this, you will use the **Crouch** viewpoint.

17. From the **Saved Viewpoints** window, click on the **Crouch** viewpoint; the avatar is displayed and the **Walk** tool is active.

18. Press the CTRL + T key to turn off the avatar and the third person view.

19. Press and hold down the left mouse button and walk a little to the right and then back to display the view similar to the one shown in Figure 32.

Figure 32 *View to measure the shortest distance between pipes*

20. Click the **Select** tool from the **Quick Access Toolbar**.

    Next, you will select two pipes to measure the distance between those. But first, you need to make sure the correct selection resolution is turned on.

21. Right-click on any object in the **Selection Tree** and click **Select Selection Resolution To Geometry** from the shortcut menu, if not already clicked.

22. Click any vertical Brown pipe in the view and then hold the CTRL key down and click any other vertical Brown pipe.

23. From the **Review** ribbon tab > **Measure** ribbon panel, click the **Shortest Distance** tool; the shortest distance between the two selected pipes is displayed.

24. Click the **Clear** button from the **Measure** ribbon panel to clear the measurement.

    Next, you will measure the shortest distance between a vessel and a pipe displayed in the **Walk End** viewpoint.

25. From the **Saved Viewpoints** window, click the **Walk End** viewpoint; the avatar is displayed and the **Walk** tool is active.

26. Press the CTRL + T key to turn off the avatar and the third person view. If need be, use the **Walk** tool and walk back a little so you can view the Green vessel on the left and a Brown pipe on the right.

27. Click the **Select** tool from the **Quick Access Toolbar**.

28. Click on the Green vessel and then hold down the CTRL key and click on any Brown pipe.

29. From the **Review** ribbon tab > **Measure** ribbon panel, click the **Shortest Distance** tool; the shortest distance between the two selected objects is displayed.

30. Click the **Clear** button from the **Measure** ribbon panel and then press the ESC key to deselect everything.

31. From the **Saved Viewpoints** window, select the **Overview 1** viewpoint.

32. Save the current file.

Section 7: Transforming Objects Using the Measured Distance Value

A very common problem that you will face while working on projects is when you append multiple files, they do not match because they are created with different coordinates. In this section, you will resolve that problem by measuring the distance between two points and then moving one of the files using the measured distance value.

1. Invoke the **Open** dialog box and then change the file types to **Autodesk DWG/DXF (*.dwg,*.dxf)**. Browse to the **Chapter 3 > Exercise Plant** folder and double-click on the **CONCRETE.dwg** file.

2. In the **Viewpoint** ribbon tab > **Render Style** ribbon panel, change the lighting to **Scene Lights** and mode to **Shaded**. The concrete objects on your screen will be displayed in Yellow. They are changed to a different color in the figures here for clarity.

3. Invoke the **Append** dialog box and double-click on the **STEEL.dwg** file; the file is appended.

4. Change the view to the **Home** view.

   Orbit the model and you will notice that the structural steel objects do not match with the concrete objects. This is because in the native CAD programs, these files were created with different coordinates. Normally, in this case you will ask the design team to fix this problem. But some times, you do not have access to the design team. As a result, this problem has to be resolved within Autodesk Navisworks. This is done next. But because these files were created with Millimeters as the units, you will first change the display units to Millimeters.

5. Press F12 and from the left pane of the **Options Editor** dialog box, expand **Interface** and then click **Display Units**. From the right pane, select **Millimeters** from the **Linear Units** list. Click **OK** to close the dialog box.

   Next, you will measure the distance between the bottom left corner of the bottom face of the steel plate shown in Figure 33 and the bottom left point of the top face of the concrete block shown in the same figure.

6. Zoom closer to the concrete block shown inside the smaller ellipse in Figure 33.

7. From the **Review** ribbon tab > **Measure** ribbon panel > **Measure** flyout, invoke the **Point to Point** tool.

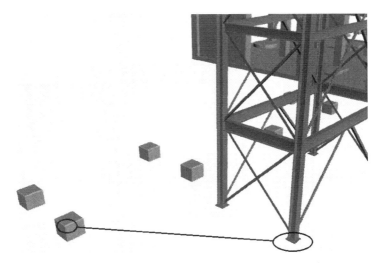

Figure 33 Objects between which you need to measure distance

8. Move the cursor over the lower left vertex of the top face of the concrete block and when the cross appears, click that vertex; its coordinates are displayed in the **Start** display boxes of the **Measure Tools** window as **-23546.78, 5334.39, 248.60**.

9. Zoom to the steel plate shown in the bigger ellipse in Figure 33.

10. Move the cursor over the lower left vertex of the bottom face of the steel plate and when the cross appears, click that vertex; its coordinates are displayed in the **End** display boxes of the **Measure Tools** window as **-20150.00, -150.00, 500.00**.

11. From the **Selection Tree** window, select the **CONCRETE.dwg** file.

12. Expand the **Measure** ribbon panel and click the **Transform Selected Items** button.

    The concrete file moves such that the two points that were selected to measure the distance now match. However, this is not the correct position of the concrete file. It needs to be moved again so make it sit at its correct position. To find out how much the file needs to move, you will measure the length and width of the concrete block and the steel plate.

13. From the **Measure** flyout, invoke the **Point to Multiple Points** tool.

14. Move the cursor over the lower left corner of the top face of the concrete block and click when the cross appears.

15. Now, move the cursor over the right corner of the same face and click when the cross appears; the distance is displayed as **550**.

16. With the lower left corner still selected, move the cursor over the upper left corner of the same face; the distance value displayed is again **550**.

17. Right-click to clear this measurement.

18. Repeat the same process to measure the length and width of the steel plate. Notice that it is a square of 300X300 size. Right-click to clear all measurements.

    So the concrete needs to move further 125X125. To find out the direction of move, you need to turn on the XYZ axes.

19. From the **View** ribbon tab > **Navigation Aids** ribbon panel > **HUD** flyout, click **XYZ Axes**.

    According to the axes, the concrete file needs to move -125 in X and Y directions.

20. In the **Selection Tree**, click on the **CONCRETE.dwg** file if it is not already selected.

21. Click the **Item Tools** ribbon tab and then expand and pin the **Transform** ribbon panel.

22. Click the **Move** tool and enter **-125** in the **Position X** box; the file moves -125 in the X direction.

    In some cases, you may need to refresh the **Move** tool to be able to enter the value again.

23. Click on the **Move** tool to exit out of it and then click on this tool again to reinvoke it. Enter **-125** in the **Position Y** box; the file moves -125 in the Y direction; the concrete is aligned with the steel. Orbit the model to see the entire plant, as shown in Figure 34.

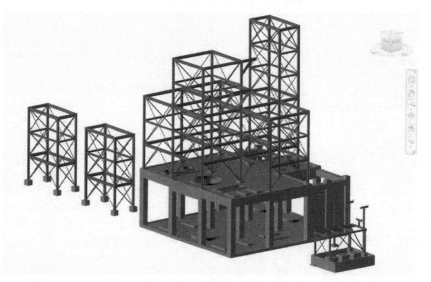

Figure 34 Plant after moving the concrete to match with the steel

24. Click on the **Move** tool to exit it and then press the ESC key to deselect everything.

25. From the **View** ribbon tab > **Navigation Aids** ribbon panel > **HUD** flyout, click **XYZ Axes** to turn it off.

26. Undock the **Measure Tools** window and then save the current file as **MOVE.nwf**.

Hands-on Exercise (BIM)	In this exercise, you will complete the following tasks: 1. Open an Autodesk Navisworks NWD file. 2. Create and save various viewpoints in the model. 3. Use the **Walk** tool to walk in the model. 4. Record a walkthrough animation. 5. Create viewpoint-based animation. 6. Measure various objects in the scene. 7. Transform objects using the measured distance value.

Section 1: Opening the File and Creating Viewpoints

In this section, you will open an NWD file and create various viewpoints looking at different parts of the model. It is assumed that you are using the **Training** workspace created in Chapter 1. Therefore, the **Saved Viewpoints** window is available on the right side of the graphics window, docked below the **Properties** window. If not, refer to the Building Exercise of that chapter to create a workspace.

1. Start Autodesk Navisworks, if it is not already opened on your machine.

2. Invoke the **Open** dialog box and change the file type to **Navisworks (*.nwd)**, if it is not already set to this.

3. Browse to the **Chapter 3 > Exercise Building** folder and then double-click on the **C03-Building.nwd** file.

    Before proceeding further, you will change the display units to your required units.

4. Press F12 to display the **Options Editor** dialog box. From the left pane, expand **Interface** and select **Display Units**. From the right pane, select the desired units from the **Linear Units** list. Close the dialog box by clicking **OK**.

5. From the **Viewpoint** ribbon tab, change the current lighting to **Full Lights** and render style to **Shaded**.

6. Assign the horizon background to the file by right-clicking in the blank area of the graphics window and selecting the **Background** option from the shortcut menu.

    Next, you will create five viewpoints. Four viewpoints will be to view the model from four corners and the fifth will be at the start of the Green walk way.

7. Using the SHIFT key and the wheel mouse button or other navigation tools, zoom and orbit the view to display the model similar to the one shown in Figure 35.

8. Right-click in the **Saved Viewpoints** window and select **Save Viewpoint** from the shortcut menu. Rename the viewpoint to **Overview 1**.

9. Using the wheel mouse button or various navigation tools, zoom and orbit the view to display the model similar to the one shown in Figure 36.

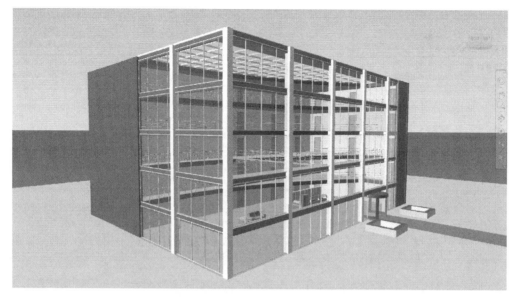

Figure 35 *Model oriented for the first viewpoint*

Figure 36 *Model oriented for the second viewpoint*

10. Right-click in the **Saved Viewpoints** window and select **Save Viewpoint** from the shortcut menu. Rename the viewpoint to **Overview 2**.

Tip: As mentioned in the earlier chapters, you can scroll the wheel mouse button once anywhere on the model to move the pivot point there and then use the SHIFT key and wheel mouse button to orbit the model.

11. Similarly, create the **Overview 3** and **Overview 4** viewpoints looking at the model from the two other corners.

12. In the **Saved Viewpoints** window, click on the **Overview 1** viewpoint to activate it.

    Next, you will create a viewpoint at the start of the Green walk way in front of the building. This viewpoint will later be used to create a walkthrough in the scene.

13. Using the wheel mouse button or various navigation tools, zoom and orbit the view to display the model similar to the one shown in Figure 37. If the model looks twisted, click on the **Viewpoint** ribbon tab > **Camera** ribbon panel > **Align Camera** flyout and select **Straighten**.

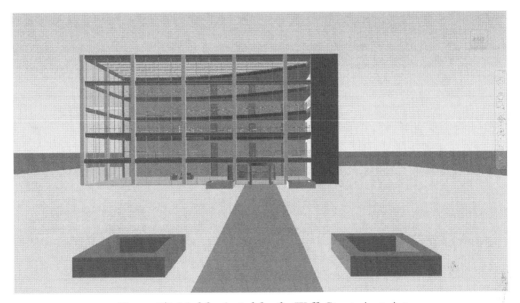

*Figure 37 Model oriented for the **Walk Start** viewpoint*

14. Right-click in the **Saved Viewpoints** window and select **Save Viewpoint** from the shortcut menu. Rename the viewpoint to **Walk Start**.

Section 2: Walking in the Model

Next, you will walk in the model using the **Walk** tool. The walk will start from the viewpoint last saved in the previous section. But before you start walking, you will edit the last viewpoint to turn on the visibility of a third person.

1. In the **Saved Viewpoints** window, right-click on the **Walk Start** viewpoint and click **Edit** from the shortcut menu; the **Edit Viewpoint - Walk Start** dialog box is displayed.

2. From the **Collision** area, click **Settings** to display the **Collision** dialog box.

3. Click the **Enable** tick box in the **Third Person** area to turn on the third person.

4. From the **Avatar** list, select **Office Female**, if not already selected.

5. Enter the following values in their respective boxes. Use the values suitable to your display units.

    Radius: 11 Inches
                     0.3 Meters

    Height: 68 Inches
                     1.72 Meters

    Distance: 80 Inches
                     2 Meters

6. Click **OK** in the **Collision** dialog box and then click **OK** in the **Edit Viewpoint - Walk Start** dialog box; the office female avatar appears.

7. If the avatar appears to be crouching, press and hold the wheel mouse button down and drag it a little; the avatar stands upright, as shown in Figure 38.

Figure 38 Viewpoint with the avatar turned on

8. From the **Navigation Bar** on the right side of the graphics window, click the **Walk** tool; the cursor changes to human feet cursor.

9. Press and hold down the left mouse button and drag the mouse forward; the avatar starts moving forward slowly.

    If the avatar appears to be inside the floor, press and hold down the wheel mouse button and drag the mouse up to bring it out of the floor.

10. Once the avatar has gone past the two Brown objects, press the CTRL + G key to turn on the gravity and collision.

11. Press and hold down the left mouse button and drag the mouse forward to restart the walk; if the avatar was floating in the air, it will come back to the ground level.

 Tip: *While walking, you can press and hold down the wheel mouse button and drag it sideways to pan the view and line up the avatar with the objects in the scene.*

12. Continue walking to the entrance door.

    With the collision turned on, you will not be able to walk through the solid entrance door. Therefore, you need to turn off the collision.

13. Press the CTRL + D key to turn off the collision.

14. Press and hold down the left mouse button and continue walking; you will be able to walk through the revolving glass doors. Stop in front of the reception.

15. Press and hold down the left mouse button and drag it to the left; the avatar turns left. The view looks similar to the one shown in Figure 39.

Figure 39 Avatar looking at the reception

16. Press and hold down the left mouse button and drag it to the left; the avatar turns around and you are able to view the revolving door behind it.

17. Press and hold down the mouse button and drag it to the right so that the avatar is looking at the view similar to the one shown in the previous figure.

    Because it is an important section of the building, it is better to create a viewpoint here so you can come back to this area whenever you want.

18. In the **Saved Viewpoints** window, right-click to display the shortcut menu and click **Save Viewpoint**. Enter **Reception** as the name of the viewpoint.

For the **Reception** viewpoint, you will now make changes to the avatar settings.

19. In the **Saved Viewpoints** window, right-click on the **Reception** viewpoint and click **Edit** from the shortcut menu; the **Edit Viewpoint - Reception** dialog box is displayed.

20. Click **Settings** from the **Collision** area; the **Collision** dialog box is displayed.

21. Depending on the display units you are using, in the **Distance** edit box, enter **1.25 Meters** or **50 Inches** as the value. Click **OK** to close the **Collision** dialog box and then click **OK** to close the **Edit Viewpoint - Reception** dialog box.

    You will notice that the camera is very close to the avatar and you cannot see its full form. This is acceptable for this section of the exercise.

22. Continue walking towards the sofa and turn right when the avatar is in front of the sofa, as shown in Figure 40.

Figure 40 *The avatar looking at the sofa*

23. In the **Saved Viewpoints** window, right-click to display the shortcut menu and click **Save Viewpoint**. Enter **Sofa** as the name of the viewpoint.

24. Press and hold down the left mouse button and drag it to the left to turn the avatar to the left.

25. Walk to the left corner of the building, as shown in Figure 41.

26. In the **Saved Viewpoints** window, right-click and click **Save Viewpoint** from the shortcut menu. Enter **Building Corner** as the name of the viewpoint.

27. Save the file.

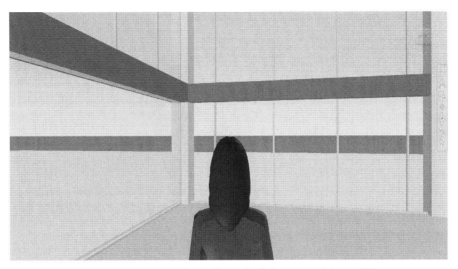

Figure 41 *Stopping the walk at the left corner of the building*

Section 3: Recording the Walk

In this section, you will create a new viewpoint and change its settings. You will then record the walk up to the reception, view the area around the reception, walk towards the left, past the sofa, then turn around and walk back to the reception.

1. From the **Saved Viewpoints** window, click on the **Walk Start** viewpoint.

2. Invoke the **Walk** tool from the **Navigation Bar**. Press and hold down the left mouse button and start walking forward. Stop when the avatar walks past the Brown objects.

3. Press CTRL + G key to turn the gravity and collision on.

4. Press and hold down the left mouse button and walk forward a little to make sure the avatar is on the ground.

   At this point, you will create a new viewpoint and edit the camera settings for the avatar.

5. In the **Saved Viewpoints** window, right-click and click **Save Viewpoint** from the shortcut menu. Enter **Walk Recording** as the name of the viewpoint.

6. Right-click on the viewpoint and click **Edit** from the shortcut menu; the **Edit Viewpoint - Walk Recording** dialog box is displayed.

7. Click **Settings** from the **Collision** area; the **Collision** dialog box is displayed.

8. In the **Viewer** area, depending on the display units you are using, enter **6 Inches** or **0.15 Meters** as the value in the **Eye Offset** edit box.

9. From the **Third Person** area, enter **15** as the value in the **Angle** edit box and **50 Inches** or **1.25 Meters** as the value in the **Distance** edit box.

10. Click **OK** in both the dialog boxes to close them. The viewpoint should look similar to the one shown in Figure 42.

Figure 42 *View for the* **Walk Recording** *viewpoint*

Next, you will start recording your walk. As mentioned earlier in this chapter, if you do not do anything on the screen after clicking the **Record** tool, it will also be recorded in the animation as stationary frames. So it is important that you are ready to start recording the walk before you invoke this tool. It is important to mention here that you can **Pause** the animation during the recording if you want to read the exercise steps.

11. Click the **Animation** ribbon tab and from the **Create** ribbon panel, click **Record**.

12. Press and hold down the left mouse button and start walking. Once you come close to the entrance door, stop walking and press the CTRL + D key to turn off the collision and gravity. This allows you to walk through the solid door.

13. Once you are in front of the reception area, press and hold down the left mouse button and drag it to the right to view the area on the right of the avatar.

14. Keep holding down the left mouse button and drag to the left to turn left and view the sofa.

15. Turn to the left so the avatar is viewing the far end of the wall of the building, past the sofa.

16. Start walking ahead, Once the avatar is in front of the sofa, turn right and look at the sofa. Then turn left and walk towards the left corner of the building.

17. Once you are at the end of this section of the building, drag the mouse to the right so that the avatar turns around.

18. Walk straight back to the reception.

19. Press the **Record** button to stop the recording; a new animation is added in the **Saved Viewpoints** window.

20. Rename the animation to **Walkthrough**.

    In the part of the animation where you paused the walk to turn off the collision, a cut is added. You can delete this cut and also some frames under that to remove the pause from the animation.

21. In the **Saved Viewpoints** window, expand the **Walkthrough** animation.

22. Scroll down the frames of the animation and select **Cut0**. Hold down the SHIFT key and select 10 frames under the cut.

23. Right-click on the selected frames and click **Delete** from the shortcut menu.

24. Scroll up and collapse the **Walkthrough** animation by clicking on the - sign on the left of its name.

    Next, you will edit and play the animation you just saved.

25. In the **Saved Viewpoints** window, right-click on the **Walkthrough** animation and click **Edit** from the shortcut menu; the **Edit Animation: Walkthrough** dialog box is displayed.

26. Enter **40** as the value in the **Duration** edit box. Click **OK** to close the dialog box.

27. With the animation selected, click the **Stop** button if it is highlighted in the **Playback** ribbon panel. Now, click the **Play** button; the animation plays for the specified duration.

28. After the animation ends, click the **Stop** button in the **Playback** ribbon panel; you are taken to the start view of the animation.

29. Save the file.

Section 4: Creating Viewpoints-based Animation

In this section, you will create an animation based on the viewpoints. You will create copies of some of the existing viewpoints and use them for this animation. You will also add more intermediate viewpoints to create a smooth walk.

 Note: The realism of gravity, collision, and crouching is not considered in the viewpoint animations. However, gravity helps to create viewpoints in which you are always on the ground and not floating in the air.

1. From the **Saved Viewpoints** window, select the **Walk Start** viewpoint. Then hold the CTRL key down and select the **Reception**, **Sofa**, and **Building Corner** viewpoints.

2. Right-click on any of the selected viewpoints and click **Add Copy** from the shortcut menu; a copy of each of the selected viewpoints is added with a suffix (1) in the name.

3. Rename the **Walk Start (1)** viewpoint to **Start**, **Reception (1)** viewpoint to **4**, **Sofa (1)** viewpoint to **6** and **Building Corner (1)** viewpoint to **End**.

4. Click on the **Start** viewpoint to go to the start of the walk. Now, invoke the **Walk** tool from the **Navigation Bar** and press and hold down the left mouse button to start walking forward.

5. Once the avatar is past the Brown objects, press the CTRL + G key to turn the gravity on.

   Although the gravity is not respected in the animation, it helps you create the next viewpoint at the ground level.

6. Press and hold down the left mouse button and start walking forward; the avatar comes to the ground if it was floating in the air.

   As mentioned earlier, you can press and hold down the wheel mouse button to pan the avatar sideways or up and down. This helps to line it up with the objects in the scene.

7. Walk to the front of the entrance door and stop there.

8. Right-click in the blank area of the **Saved Viewpoints** window and click **Save Viewpoint** from the shortcut menu; a new viewpoint is added. Name this viewpoint as **2**.

   Next, you will create a viewpoint just after entering the building.

9. Press the CTRL + D key to turn off the gravity and collision. Walk past the door and stop once the avatar enters the building.

10. Right-click in the blank area of the **Saved Viewpoints** window and click **Save Viewpoint** from the shortcut menu; a new viewpoint is added. Name this viewpoint as **3**.

11. In the **Saved Viewpoints** window, click on the **4** viewpoint.

12. Press and hold down the left mouse button and start walking towards the end of the reception, as shown in Figure 43.

13. Right-click in the blank area of the **Saved Viewpoints** window and click **Save Viewpoint** from the shortcut menu; a new viewpoint is added. Name this viewpoint as **5**.

   This completes all the viewpoints that you need for the viewpoint walk. Next, you will insert a blank animation and drag and drop these viewpoints in it.

14. Right-click in the blank area of the **Saved Viewpoints** window and click **Add Animation** from the shortcut menu; a new blank animation is added. Name this animation as **Viewpoint Walk**.

15. In the **Saved Viewpoints** window, click on the **Start** viewpoint. Next, hold the CTRL key down and select viewpoints **2** and **3**. Release the CTRL key.

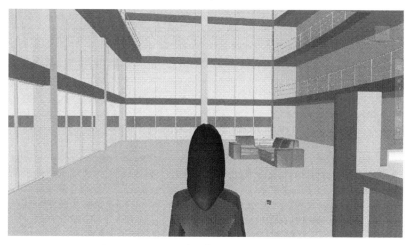

Figure 43 *View for the viewpoint named* **5**

16. Press and hold down the left mouse button on one of the selected viewpoints and drop them on the name of the **Viewpoint Walk** animation; this will add these viewpoints in the right sequence in the animation.

17. Click on the **4** viewpoint. Next, hold the CTRL key down and select viewpoint **5**. Release the CTRL key.

18. Press and hold down the left mouse button on one of the selected viewpoints and drop them on the name of the **Viewpoint Walk** animation; this will add these viewpoints in the right sequence in the animation.

19. Click on the **6** viewpoint. Next, hold the CTRL key down and select the **End** viewpoint. Drag and drop them on the name of the **Viewpoint Walk** animation; this will add the viewpoints at the end of the animation.

    Next, you will edit the duration of the viewpoint animation.

20. In the **Saved Viewpoints** window, right-click on the **Viewpoint Walk** animation and click **Edit** from the shortcut menu; the **Edit Animation: Viewpoint Walk** dialog box is displayed.

21. Enter **30** as the duration value and click **OK** in the dialog box; you are automatically taken to the start of this animation.

22. With this animation still selected in the **Saved Viewpoints** window, click the **Play** button on the **Animation** ribbon tab > **Playback** ribbon panel; the animation starts to play.

23. Click the **Stop** button after the animation stops and then save the current file.

Section 5: Organizing Viewpoints and Animations in Folders

In this section, organize the **Saved Viewpoints** window by creating separate folders for the viewpoints and animations.

1. Click in the blank area of the **Saved Viewpoints** window to deselect the animation.

2. In the **Saved Viewpoints** window, right-click in the blank area on the right of one of the overview viewpoints and click **New Folder** from the shortcut menu. Name this folder as **Viewpoints**.

 Note: *If the animation is selected and you add a folder, it gets added inside the animation. This is the reason you need to first deselect the animation.*

3. Click in the blank area of the **Saved Viewpoints** window to deselect the folder. Now, repeat step 2 and name the new folder as **Animations**.

4. Click on the **Overview 1** viewpoint. Press and hold down the SHIFT key and select the **Walk Recording** viewpoint; all the viewpoints in between are also selected.

 Note*: If you try to drag the animation by holding its name, it will go into the rename animation mode. Therefore, it is important for you to click on the icon of the animations while dragging them.*

5. Holding down the icon of one of the viewpoints, drag and drop them in the **Viewpoints** folder.

6. Click the **Walkthrough** animation and then hold down the CTRL key and click on the **Viewpoint Walk** animation.

7. Holding down the icon of one of the animations, drag and drop them in the **Animations** folder. The **Saved Viewpoints** window should look similar to the one shown in Figure 44.

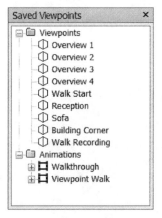

Figure 44 *The **Saved Viewpoints** window with the viewpoints and animations organized in folders*

8. Save the current file.

Section 6: Measuring the Objects in the Model

In this section, you will perform various measurements on the objects in the model. To view various measurement values, you will dock the **Measure Tools** window on the screen. You will use various viewpoints saved earlier to go to the view to measure objects. But first, you will change the color and the thickness of the measurements.

1. Click on **Measure Tools** from the left side of the **Selection Tree** and dock it on the screen by clicking the **Auto-Hide** button on the top right of this window.

2. Click the **Options** button in the **Measure Tools** window to display the **Options Editor** dialog box.

3. In the right pane of the dialog box, enter **2** as the value in the **Line Thickness** spinner, if not already set to this value.

4. From the **Color** list, select the **Red** color, if not already selected.

5. From the left pane, click **Snapping**.

6. From the right pane, select the **Snap to Vertex**, **Snap to Edge**, and **Snap to Line Vertex** tick boxes, if they are not selected already.

7. Click **OK** in the dialog box to return back to the graphics window.

   You will start with measuring the width and height of the revolving door frame. You will use the **2** viewpoint.

8. From the **Saved Viewpoints** window, expand the **Animations** folder and then expand the **Viewpoint Walk** animation. Select the **2** viewpoint.

9. Press the CTRL + T key to turn off the avatar. If need be, use the **Walk** tool to walk back or forward to view the complete revolving door.

   Because you need to measure two distances, you will use the **Point to Multiple Points** tool.

10. From the **Review** ribbon tab > **Measure** ribbon panel > **Measure** flyout, invoke the **Point to Multiple Points** tool.

11. Move the cursor over the top left vertex of the inside of the door frame, refer to Figure 45. When the cursor snaps to the vertex, a cross appears. At this point, click to select the vertex; the X, Y, and Z coordinates of the selected vertex are displayed in the **Start** display boxes of the **Measure Tools** window.

12. Move the cursor down to the bottom vertex, refer to Figure 45, and click when the cross appears; the height of the frame is displayed on the screen. This value is also displayed in the **Measure Tools** window, along with the coordinates of the second vertex and the difference in the start and end coordinates. Figure 45 shows a zoomed in view of this measurement.

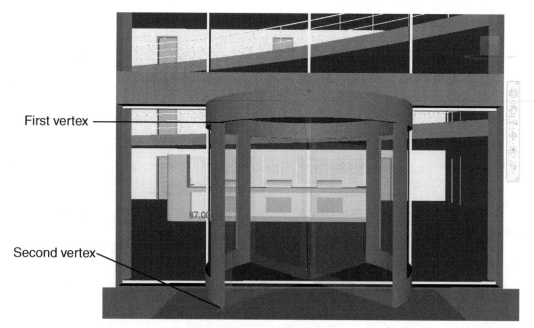

First vertex

Second vertex

87.00

Figure 45 Measuring the height of the door frame

Next, you will measure the width of the opening of the door. Because you used the **Point to Multiple Points** tool, the top left vertex of the door frame is still selected as the first point.

13. Move the cursor across to the right vertex of the revolving door and click when the cross is displayed; the measurement of the width of the frame is displayed on the screen and the values are also displayed in the **Measure Tools** window.

    Next, you will measure the area of the inside frame of one of the glass panels above the revolving door.

14. Pan the view down so that you can see the glass panels above the revolving door. Now, from the **Review** ribbon tab > **Measure** ribbon panel > **Measure** flyout, invoke the **Area** tool.

15. One by one, click on the four vertices of the inside frame of one of the glass panels. Make sure you click only when the cross is displayed.

    Once you click the fourth point, the area of the glass panel is displayed in the graphics window and in the **Measure Tools** window.

16. Click the **Clear** button from the **Measure** ribbon panel to clear all the measurements.

    Next, you will measure the shortest distance between the walls behind the sofa and the glass wall in front of the sofa. For this, you will use the **5** viewpoint.

17. From the expanded **Viewpoint Walk** animation in the **Saved Viewpoints** window, click on the **5** viewpoint; the avatar is displayed and the **Walk** tool is active.

18. Press the CTRL + T key to turn off the avatar and the third person view.

19. Press and hold down the left mouse button and walk forward towards the sofa to the view similar to the one shown in Figure 46.

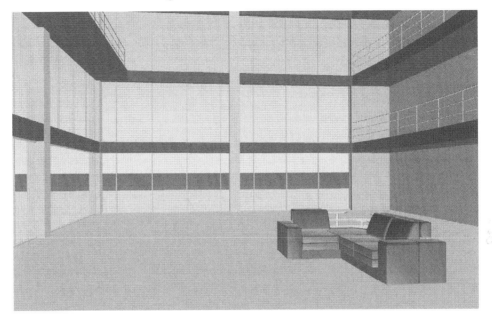

Figure 46 *View to measure the shortest distance between two walls*

20. Click the **Select** tool from the **Quick Access Toolbar**.

    Next, you will select the two items to measure the shortest distance. But first, you need to make sure the correct selection resolution is turned on.

21. Right-click on any object in the **Selection Tree** and click **Select Selection Resolution To Geometry** from the shortcut menu, if not already clicked.

22. Select the wall behind the sofa and then hold the CTRL key down and select one of the glass panels in front of the sofa.

23. From the **Measure** ribbon panel, invoke the **Shortest Distance** tool; the shortest distance between the two selected walls is displayed.

24. Activate the viewpoint **5** again and notice the measurement of the shortest distance.

25. Press the ESC key to deselect the two objects and then click the **Clear** button from the **Measure** ribbon panel; the measurement will be cleared from the graphics window.

26. From the **Saved Viewpoints** window, select the **Overview 1** viewpoint.

27. Save the current file and then start a new file to close the current file.

Section 7: Transforming Objects Using the Measured Distance Value

A very common problem that you will face while working on projects is when you append multiple files, they do not match because they are created with different coordinates. In this section, you will resolve that problem by measuring the distance between two vertices and then moving one of the files using the measured distance value.

1. Invoke the **Open** dialog box and change the file type to **Autodesk DWG.DXF (*.dwg,*.dxf)**.

2. Browse to the **Chapter 3 > Exercise Building** folder and double-click on the **Structure.dwg** file.

3. From the **Viewpoint** ribbon tab, change the lighting to **Scene Lights** and the render mode to **Shaded**.

4. Right-click in the graphics window and using the **Background** option, set the background color to a light color.

5. Invoke the **Append** dialog box and double-click on the **Walls.dwg** file; this file is appended in the scene.

6. Change the current view to the **Home** view. The scene appears as shown in Figure 47.

Figure 47 Scene after appending the walls file with the structure file

As you can see, the walls do not match with the structure. To make these objects match, you will measure the distance between the vertex of the wall and the vertex of the structure shown inside the ellipses in Figures 48 and 49, and move the walls by that distance.

7. Zoom to the vertex of the **Walls.dwg** file displayed inside the ellipse in Figure 48.

8. Invoke the **Point to Point** tool from the **Review** ribbon tab > **Measure** ribbon panel > **Measure** flyout.

9. Move the cursor over the vertex shown in the ellipse in Figure 48. When the cross appears, select the vertex.

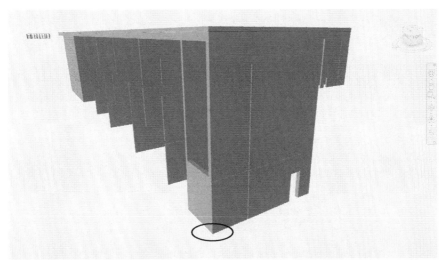

Figure 48 The first vertex for measurement

If you are using Inches as the display units, the coordinates of the selected vertex are displayed as **38739.22, -448.23, 0.00** in the **Start** boxes of the **Measure Tools** window. If you are using Meters as the display units, the coordinates are **983.98, -11.39, 0.00**.

10. Change the view to the **Home** view. Using the wheel mouse button, zoom to the area shown in the ellipse in Figure 49.

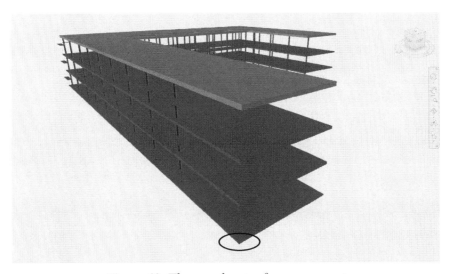

Figure 49 The second vertex for measurement

11. With the **Point to Point** tool still active and the first point already selected, move the cursor over the vertex of the top face of the slab shown inside the ellipse in Figure 49.

12. When the cross appears, select the vertex as the second point of measurement.

    If you are using Inches as the display units, the coordinates are displayed as **2606.66, -6.00, 0.00** in the **End** boxes of the **Measure Tools** window. If you are using Meters as the display units, the coordinates are displayed as **66.21, -0.15, 0.00**.

13. From the **Selection Tree**, select the **Walls.dwg** file.

14. From the **Review** ribbon tab, expand the **Measure** flyout and click the **Transform Selected Items** button; the walls move on top of the structure.

15. Press the ESC key to deselect everything.

16. Undock the **Measure Tools** window.

17. Orbit the model to a view similar to the one shown in Figure 50.

Figure 50   *Scene after moving the walls*

18. Save this file as **MOVE.nwf** in the **Chapter 3 > Exercise Building** folder.

Skill Evaluation

Evaluate your skills to see how many questions you can answer correctly. The answers to these questions are given at the end of the book.

1. Viewpoints once saved cannot be edited. (True/False)

2. The avatars can be changed for all saved viewpoints. (True/False)

3. The animation recorded in Autodesk Navisworks cannot be exported. (True/False)

4. Autodesk Navisworks allows you to measure shortest distance between two selected objects. (True/False)

5. You can combine multiple animations in a single animation. (True/False)

6. Which tool allows you to measure the distance from one point to multiple other points?

   (A) **Point to Point**   (B) **Multiple Points**
   (C) **Measure Points**   (D) **Point to Multiple Points**

7. Which tool lets you record a walkthrough animation?

   (A) **Video**   (B) **Record**
   (C) **Record Animation**   (D) None

8. Which tool allows you to convert a measured dimension into a redline markup?

   (A) **Convert to Redline**   (B) **Redline**
   (C) **Convert Measurement**   (D) None

9. Which realism type stops you from walking through solid objects in the scene?

   (A) **Collision**   (B) **Walk**
   (C) **Third Person**   (D) **Avatar**

10. What is the shortcut key to turn on the third person?

    (A) **CTRL + P**   (B) **CTRL + SHIFT + T**
    (C) **CTRL + T**   (D) **CTRL + SHIFT + P**

Class Test Questions

Answer the following questions:

1. How will you measure the XYZ coordinates of a selected point?

2. How will you change the avatar of a selected viewpoint?

3. How many minimum points do you need to measure an area?

4. How do you edit the duration of an animation?

5. Can the viewpoints and animations be organized in folders?

Chapter 4 – Reviewing and Sectioning the Design

The objectives of this chapter are to:

√ Familiarize you with the process of reviewing the designs in Autodesk Navisworks.
√ Show you how to add redline markups.
√ Familiarize you with the process of creating and reviewing comments in the design.
√ Familiarize you with the process of creating and reviewing tags in the design.
√ Show you how to find specific comments in the design.
√ Teach you how to section the models using one or more section planes.
√ Show you how to link section planes.
√ Teach you how to section the models using a section box.

DESIGN REVIEW IN AUTODESK NAVISWORKS

Autodesk Navisworks provides you various tools to review your design. These include redline markups, comments, and tags. It is important to mention here that while adding redline markups, if the viewpoint is not already saved, it is automatically created and saved as a part of the process. The design review components added to the model and published in the NWD file can also be viewed in the Autodesk Navisworks Freedom viewer. The following sections explain all these design review tools in detail.

Redline Markups

The **Redline** ribbon panel on the **Review** ribbon tab provides you the tools to add redline markups, refer to Figure 1.

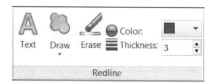

*Figure 1 The **Redline** ribbon panel*

After you finish adding a redline markup, a new viewpoint is automatically added. If you change the view or orbit the model, the redline information will disappear from the scene. This information will be restored when you click on the viewpoint in which the redline information was added.

The tools available in the **Redline** ribbon panel are discussed next.

Text

Review Ribbon Tab > Redline Ribbon Panel > Text

This tool allows you to add redline text in the current viewpoint. You can write the text by activating an existing viewpoint. If you do not have a viewpoint already saved, a new viewpoint with the default name **View** will be automatically created at the end of the process of writing text. When you invoke this tool, the cursor will change to a pencil cursor. Click at the location in the scene where you want to add the redline text. On doing so, the **Autodesk Navisworks Manage/Simulate 2016** dialog box will be displayed that allows you to enter the redline text, as shown in Figure 2.

Figure 2 The dialog box to enter the redline text

Figure 3 shows the redline text written in the dialog box and Figure 4 shows how this text appears in the Autodesk Navisworks scene.

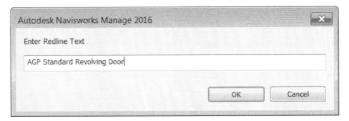

Figure 3 *The redline markup text to be displayed in the Autodesk Navisworks scene*

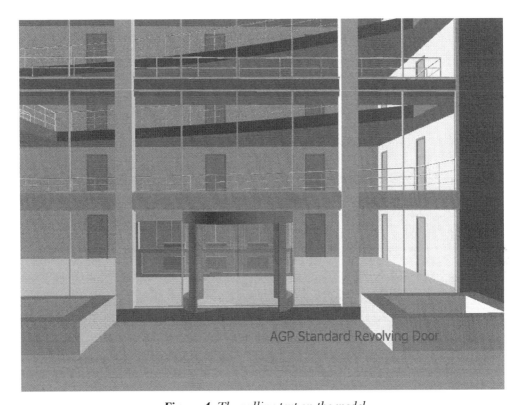

Figure 4 *The redline text on the model*

Moving a Redline Text

Autodesk Navisworks allows you to move a redline text written in a saved viewpoint. The following steps show you how to do it.

a.　Activate the viewpoint in which the redline text was written.

b. Right-click on the redline text to display the shortcut menu.

c. From the shortcut menu, click **Move**.

d. Click on the new location point; the text will move such that the lower left corner of the first line of text will be aligned with the new point that you specified.

Editing a Redline Text

Autodesk Navisworks also allows you to edit a redline text written in a saved viewpoint. The following steps show you how to do it.

a. Activate the viewpoint in which the redline text was written.

b. Right-click on the redline text to display the shortcut menu.

c. From the shortcut menu, click **Edit**; the **Autodesk Navisworks Manage/Simulate 2016** dialog box will be displayed with the current text.

d. Edit the text in the dialog box and click **OK**.

Draw Flyout

Review Ribbon Tab > Redline Ribbon Panel > Draw Flyout

The **Draw** flyout provides you various tools to draw shapes around the area about which you are writing the redline text, see Figure 5. Remember that starting Autodesk Navisworks 2016, you do not need to activate an existing viewpoint to add any of these shapes. A new viewpoint with the default name of **View** will be automatically added once you finish drawing the object. The tools available in this flyout are discussed next.

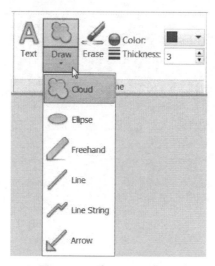

*Figure 5 The **Draw** flyout*

Cloud

This tool lets you draw a cloud in the current viewpoint. Generally, it is used to enclose the part of the design about which you want to write a redline text. When you invoke this tool, the cursor changes to a pencil cursor. To start drawing a cloud, click anywhere in the graphics window. Clicking additional points in the clockwise direction will create the cloud and clicking the additional points in the counterclockwise direction will create a reverse cloud. To close the cloud, right-click anywhere in the graphics window. The size of the cloud arc will depend on how far you click from the previous point. In Figure 6, the cloud on the left is created by clicking on the points in the clockwise direction and the cloud on the right is created by clicking the points in the counterclockwise direction.

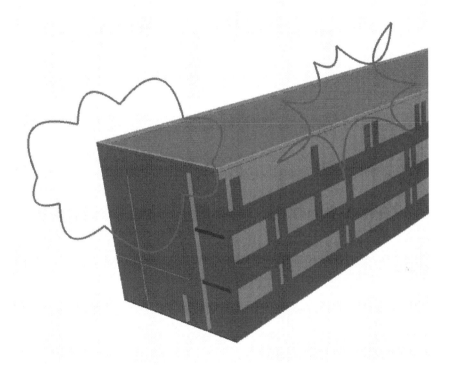

Figure 6   *Clouds created by clicking in the clockwise and counterclockwise directions*

Ellipse

This tool lets you draw an ellipse in the current viewpoint to enclose an area. When you invoke this tool, the cursor changes to a pencil cursor. To draw the ellipse, press and hold down the left mouse button and drag to define the two opposite corners. The ellipse will be created inside the box defined by those two corners. Figure 7 shows a redline ellipse created in the current viewpoint.

Freehand

This tool lets you draw a freehand shape in the current viewpoint. When you invoke this tool, the cursor changes to a pencil cursor. To start drawing a freehand shape, press and hold

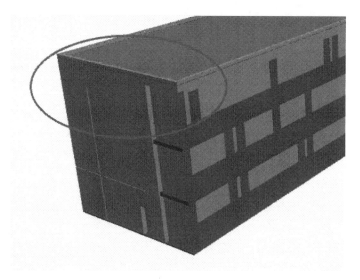

Figure 7 *The redline ellipse*

down the left mouse button and drag the cursor. You can draw any type of shape by dragging the cursor around.

Line

This tool is used to draw a straight line by clicking two points in the graphics window. Generally, the lines are drawn to associate a redline text with a redline shape. When you invoke this tool, the cursor changes to a pencil cursor. To draw a line, click two points in the graphics window. Figure 8 shows a redline text associated with a redline cloud using a line.

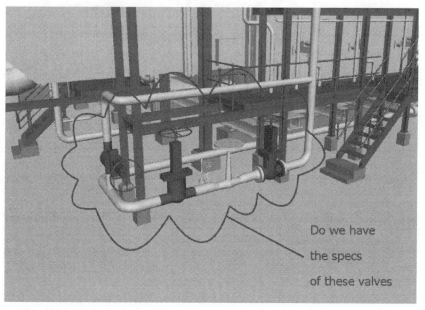

Do we have
the specs
of these valves

Figure 8 *A redline text associated with a redline cloud using a line*

Line String

This tool is used to draw continuous end-connected lines in the current viewpoint. When you invoke this tool, the cursor changes to a pencil cursor. To start drawing the lines, click anywhere in the graphics window. Note that unlike the **Cloud** tool, in this case right-clicking will not close the loop. You will have to manually click on the start point to close the loop. With the **Line String** tool active, right-clicking will end the continuous lines and you will be allowed to specify the first point to start a new line string.

Arrow

This tool is used to draw arrows that can be used to associate redline text to the objects in the scene. When you invoke this tool, the cursor changes to the pencil cursor. The arrow is created by specifying two points. The first point is the start point of the arrow line and the second point is where the arrowhead will be located. Figure 9 shows two arrows drawn in the current viewpoint.

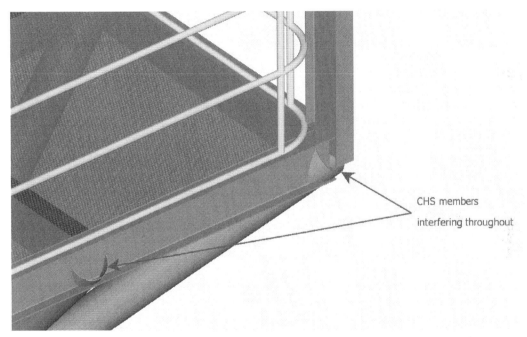

Figure 9 Two redline arrows created in the scene to associate redline text to objects in the scene

Erase

Review Ribbon Tab > Redline Ribbon Panel > Erase

This tool is used to erase the redline markups from the current viewpoint by dragging a box around them. Remember that to be able to erase an object, it has to be fully enclosed inside the erase box. For line string, only the lines that are fully enclosed inside the erase box will be deleted. To delete an ellipse or cloud, you need to enclose the entire object inside the erase box. To delete text written in multiple lines, you need to enclose all the lines of text in the erase box.

*Tip: In case of a redline text, it is easier to erase it by right-clicking on the first line of text and clicking **Delete Redline** from the shortcut menu.*

Color

> **Review Ribbon Tab > Redline Ribbon Panel > Color**

This list is used to specify the color for the redline markups. The default color is Red. Clicking on this list and selecting **More Colors** will display the **Color** dialog box with additional basic colors. You can also expand the dialog box by clicking the **Define Custom Color** button and create your own colors based on the Hue, Saturation, and Luminance values or the Red, Green, and Blue values.

Thickness

> **Review Ribbon Tab > Redline Ribbon Panel > Thickness**

This spinner is used to specify the thickness of the redline markups. This value can range between 1 and 9.

 Note: *One of the biggest drawbacks of adding redline markups on the graphics window is that you cannot search for the text. If you want to write a text that you can search for, you can use the **Comments** tool that is discussed next.*

Comments

Autodesk Navisworks lets you write comments associated with viewpoints, animations, and sets using the tools available in the **Comments** ribbon panel. The comments added in the design are displayed in the **Comments** window. This window not only stores the text information, but also the date and time when it was added, the author who added it, a specific identification number, and also the status of the text.

The main advantage of using comments is that you can search for them at any stage based on any of this information. Figure 10 shows the **Comments** window displaying a comment added to an animation.

Figure 11 shows the **Comments** ribbon panel. The tools available on this ribbon panel are discussed next.

View Comments

> **Review Ribbon Tab > Comments Ribbon Panel > View Comments**

This tool is used to toggle on or off the display of the **Comments** window. This window is divided in two halves. The upper half is used to add, edit, view, and delete comments. The lower half is used to display the selected comment in detail. The columns displayed in the upper half of this window are discussed next.

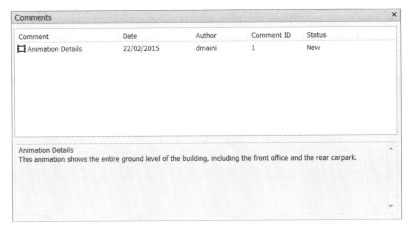

Figure 10 The **Comments** *window showing the comments added to an animation*

Figure 11 The **Comments** *ribbon panel*

Comment
This column displays the first line of the comment text. The detailed comment text is displayed in the lower half of the **Comments** window.

Date
This column displays the date and time when the comment was added. The date and time will be displayed based on the **Region and Language** settings of your computer.

Author
This column displays the name of the author who added the comments.

Comment ID
This column displays the identification number assigned to the comment when it was added.

Status
This column displays the status of the comment. By default, when you add a comment, its status is set to **New**. This can be changed after the person for whom the comment was meant has read it. This will be discussed later in this chapter.

The following sections explain how to add comments to viewpoints, viewpoint animations, and sets.

Adding Comments to a Saved Viewpoint

The following steps show how to add comments to a saved viewpoint:

a. From the **Review** ribbon tab > **Comments** ribbon panel, click the **View Comments** tool; the **Comments** window will be docked at the bottom of the graphics window.

b. From the **Saved Viewpoints** window, click the viewpoint to which you want to add comments; the model will be reoriented based on the selected viewpoint. If the viewpoint does not exist, you can create it.

c. From the **Saved Viewpoints** window, right-click on the current viewpoint and click **Add Comment** from the shortcut menu; the **Add Comment** dialog box will be displayed, as shown in Figure 12.

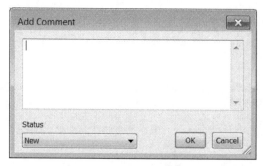

*Figure 12 The **Add Comment** dialog box*

d. In the first line, enter the comment heading. The text added in this line will be displayed under the **Comments** column of the **Comments** window.

e. Press and hold down the CTRL key and press ENTER; the cursor will go to the second line to add comment.

f. Enter the comment text in the second line. You can also copy a paragraph text and paste it here. The lower half of the **Comments** window will show the entire comment text that you write here.

g. Set the comment status by clicking on the **Status** list. By default, for a new comment it is set to **New**. The other options in this list are **Active**, **Approved**, and **Resolved**.

h. Click **OK** in the **Add Comment** dialog box; the added comment will be displayed in the **Comments** window.

 *Note: You can also activate a saved viewpoint and then right-click in the upper half of the **Comments** window and click **Add Comment** from the shortcut menu. This will display the **Add Comment** dialog box in which you can enter the comment. When you make the viewpoint active, the comment and its details will be displayed in the **Comments** window.*

Adding Comments to a Saved Viewpoint Animation

The following steps show how to add comments to a saved viewpoint animation:

a. If the **Comments** window is not displayed, from the **Review** ribbon tab > **Comments** ribbon panel, click the **View Comments** tool; the **Comments** window will be docked at the bottom of the graphics window.

b. From the **Saved Viewpoints** window, click the animation to which you want to add comments; the view changes to the animation camera view.

c. Right-click on the animation and click **Add Comment** from the shortcut menu; the **Add Comment** dialog box will be displayed. Alternatively, right-click in the upper half of the **Comments** window and click **Add Comment** from the shortcut menu.

d. In the first line, enter the comment heading. The text added in this line will be displayed under the **Comments** column of the **Comments** window.

e. Press and hold down the CTRL key and press ENTER; the cursor will go to the second line to add comment.

f. Enter the comment text in the second line. You can also copy a paragraph text and paste it here. The lower half of the **Comments** window will show the entire comment text that you write here.

g. Set the comment status by clicking on the **Status** list. By default, for a new comment it is set to **New**.

h. Click **OK** in the **Add Comment** dialog box; the added comment will be displayed in the **Comments** window. Note that in step c, if you right-clicked on an animation to add the comment, it will only be displayed in the **Comments** window when you click on the animation from the **Saved Viewpoints** window.

Adding Comments to a Selection Set or a Search Set

The following steps show how to add comments to a selection set or a search set:

a. If the **Comments** window is not displayed, from the **Review** ribbon tab > **Comments** ribbon panel, click the **View Comments** tool; the **Comments** window will be docked at the bottom of the graphics window.

b. From the **Sets** window, click the set to which you want to add comments; the objects included in that set will be highlighted in the graphics window.

c. Right-click on the set and click **Add Comment** from the shortcut menu; the **Add Comment** dialog box will be displayed. Alternatively, right-click in the upper half of the **Comments** window and click **Add Comment** from the shortcut menu.

d. In the first line, enter the comment heading. The text added in this line will be displayed under the **Comments** column of the **Comments** window.

e. Press and hold down the CTRL key and press ENTER; the cursor will go to the second line to add comment.

f. Enter the comment text in the second line. You can also copy a paragraph text and paste it here. The lower half of the **Comments** window will show the entire comment text that you write here.

g. Set the comment status by clicking on the **Status** list. By default, for a new comment it is set to **New**.

h. Click **OK** in the **Add Comment** dialog box; the added comment will be displayed in the **Comments** window. Note that in step c, if you right-clicked on a set to add the comment, it will only be displayed in the **Comments** window when you click on the set from the **Sets** window.

*Note: You can also add multiple comments to the same viewpoint, viewpoint animation, and sets. When you click on these, all the comments associated with them will be listed in the **Comments** window.*

Finding Comments

Review Ribbon Tab > Comments Ribbon Panel > Find Comments

As mentioned earlier, one of the advantages of adding comments is that you can search for them in the current scene. This is done using the **Find Comments** tool. When you invoke this tool, the **Find Comments** window will be displayed, as shown in Figure 13.

This window is divided into two halves. The upper half displays the options that you can use to define the criteria based on which you want to search the comments. The lower half displays the comments that are found based on the criteria defined. The options available in the upper half of this window are discussed next.

Comments Tab

This tab allows you to search the comments based on the text string in it, its author, its identification number, and the status, refer to Figure 13. You can use wildcards such as asterisk (*) in your searches. You can also select the tick boxes to only search the comments that match the case, diacritics, and character widths defined in this tab. After specifying the information in this tab, click the **Find** button; all the comments matching the search criteria will be displayed in the lower half of this dialog box.

Date Modified

This tab lets you search for the comments based on the date when the comments were added, see Figure 14. Selecting the **All comments** radio button and clicking the **Find** button will display all comments regardless of when they were added. Selecting the **between** radio

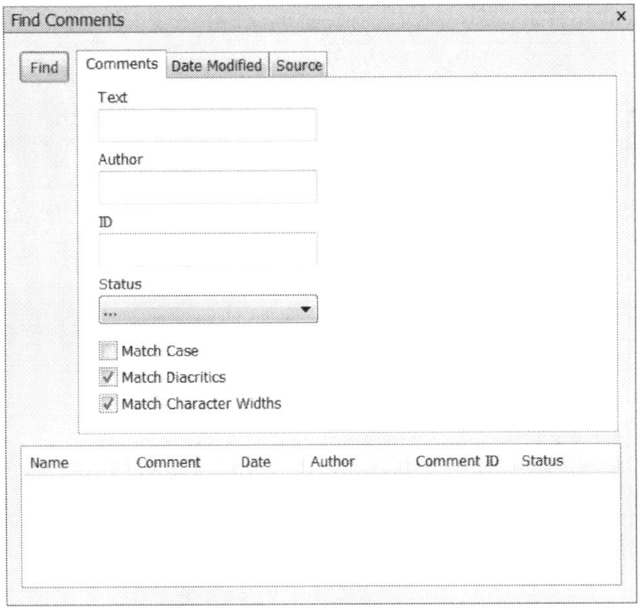

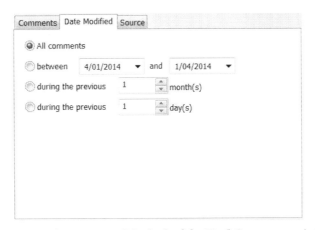

Figure 13 The **Find Comments** window

Figure 14 The **Date Modified** tab of the **Find Comments** window

button allows you to search for comments written between a start and an end date. You can also select the radio buttons to search for comments written within the previous specified months or day.

Source
This tab lets you specify the source of the comments search, see Figure 15. After specifying the search criteria, click the **Find** button in the **Find Comments** window; all the comments matching the search criteria will be displayed in the lower half of this window.

What I do

*One of the very common questions that I am asked is how to export a report of all the markups, comments, and tags from Autodesk Navisworks. Unfortunately, there is no such facility available yet. However, the workaround that I use is that I export the viewpoint report by right-clicking in the **Saved Viewpoints** window. The report is written in the HTML format that not only includes all the viewpoints, but also the redline markups, comments, and tags associated with those viewpoints.*

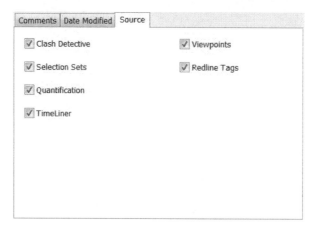

*Figure 15 The **Source** tab of the **Find Comments** window*

Figure 16 shows various comments found using this window.

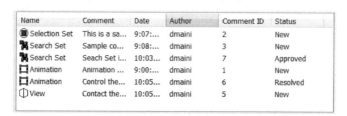

*Figure 16 Comments found using the **Find Comments** window*

 Note: As shown in Figure 16, the icon of the comment source is displayed on the left of the comment name. This helps you identify the source of the comment.

Quick Find Comments

Review Ribbon Tab > Comments Ribbon Panel > Quick Find Comments

Autodesk Navisworks also lets you perform a quick search for comments by typing any information related to the comments in the **Quick Find Comments** text box. You can enter a part of the text string, the author information, and so on. You can also use the wildcards while searching for comments in this box.

When you type the search information in this text box and press ENTER, the **Find Comments** window will be displayed with the comments matching the quick search criteria listed in the lower half of this window.

Editing Comments

Once the comments are viewed by the concerned people, they can then edit or add more information to the comments. If need be, the comment status can also be changed. The following steps show you how to do this:

a. If the **Comments** window is not displayed, from the **Review** ribbon tab > **Comments** ribbon panel, click the **View Comments** tool.

b. Dock this window at the bottom of the graphics window using the **Auto-Hide** button on the top right corner of this window.

c. Click on the comment source or search for the comment using the **Find Comments** window and click on the comment; it will be displayed in the **Comments** window.

d. Right-click on the comment in the **Comments** window and click **Edit Comment** from the shortcut menu; the **Edit Comment** dialog box will be displayed, as shown in Figure 17.

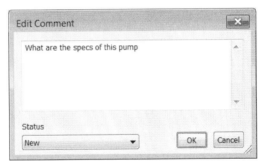

Figure 17 The **Edit Comment** *dialog box*

e. Select the text that you want to edit and enter the new text. If you want to add text in the next line, click at the end of the first line of text. Now, press and hold the CTRL key down and press ENTER; the cursor will go to the next line. You can enter the text here.

f. To change the status of the comment, click on the **Status** list and select the required status.

g. Click **OK** in the **Edit Comment** dialog box; the edited comment will be displayed in the **Comments** window. Also, the date and time will be changed to the current date and time.

 Note: In later chapters, you will learn to add comments to timeliner tasks and clash results.

Renumbering Comment IDs

> **Review Ribbon Tab > Expanded Comments Ribbon Panel > Renumber Comment IDs**

As mentioned earlier, every comment that you add is assigned a specific identification number. If you are creating a scene by appending or merging various Autodesk Navisworks files with comments in them, there are chances that the comment identification numbers will be duplicated. The Renumber Comments IDs tool renumbers the comments such that each comment has a unique identification number.

Tags

Adding tags to the design is a sophisticated way of writing comments that are directly related to a viewpoint. While adding tags, you are allowed to specify the location of the tag identification number in the Autodesk Navisworks scene. A viewpoint will automatically be created if it is not already active, and you will be allowed to write comments associated with that tag in the **Add Comment** dialog box. These tag comments will also be listed in the **Comments** window and you will be able to search for them at any stage.

Figure 18 shows the **Tags** ribbon panel. The tools available in this panel are discussed next.

*Figure 18 The **Tags** ribbon panel*

Add Tags

> **Review Ribbon Tab > Tags Ribbon Panel > Add Tags**

This tool is used to add tags in the scene. After you invoke this tool, click on the object with which you want to associate the tag and the comment. Next, click on a location where you want the tag identification number to be located. As soon as you specify the second point, a balloon will be added between the two points showing the tag number. Also, a new viewpoint will be added with the default name of **Tag View** with the current tag number as the suffix and the **Add Comment** dialog box will be displayed. You can add comment to be associated with the tag and specify the status of the comment in this dialog box. As mentioned earlier, you can hold down the CTRL key and press ENTER to write the text in the next line of the **Add Comment** dialog box. If the **Comments** window is docked on the screen, the comment associated with the tag will be displayed in this window.

Figure 19 shows an Autodesk Navisworks scene with a tag added to it. The comment associated with the tag is displayed in the **Comments** window and the viewpoint that was created for this tag is displayed in the **Saved Viewpoints** window.

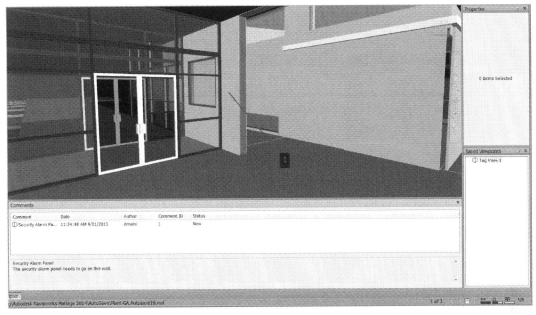

Figure 19 *Tag added in the Autodesk Navisworks scene*

Searching Tag IDs

Review Ribbon Tab > Tags Ribbon Panel > Tag ID

The **Tag ID** spinner in the **Tags** ribbon panel is used to search the tags based on their identification numbers. This spinner is available on the right of the **Add Tag** button. After entering the tag ID number in this spinner, click the **Go to Tag** button on the right. The view will be oriented to the tag viewpoint and the comment associated with the tag will be displayed in the **Comments** window, if it is docked on the screen.

Renumbering Tag IDs

Review Ribbon Tab > Expanded Tags Ribbon Panel > Renumber Tag IDs

Similar to renumbering comment IDs, you may also need to renumber the tag IDs if you are collaborating multiple Autodesk Navisworks files with tags in them. This is to remove the duplicate tag ID numbers. To do this, expand the **Tags** ribbon panel and click the **Renumber Tag IDs** tool.

SECTIONING THE MODEL

Autodesk Navisworks allows you to section the model and view the inside of the design. The model can be sectioned using one or more section planes or using a section box. Figure 20 shows the partial view of a building with its front part sectioned.

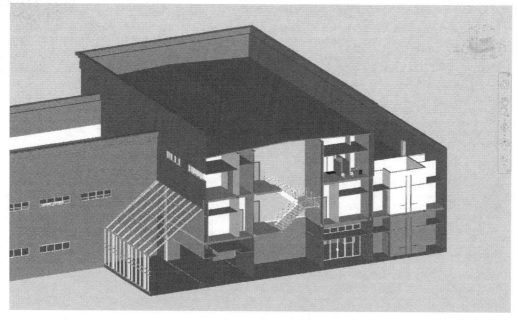

Figure 20 The building with the front part sectioned

By default, the sectioning is disabled. To enable the sectioning, click **Viewpoint** ribbon tab > **Sectioning** ribbon panel > **Enable Sectioning**; the **Sectioning Tools** ribbon tab will be displayed, as shown in Figure 21.

*Figure 21 The **Sectioning Tools** ribbon tab*

The following sections explain how to section the model using one or more section planes or using a section box.

Sectioning a Model Using a Single Section Plane

This method allows you to section a model using one section plane. The following steps show you how to section a model using this method.

a.   If the sectioning is not already enabled, enable it by clicking **Viewpoint** ribbon tab > **Sectioning** ribbon panel > **Enable Sectioning**; the **Sectioning Tools** ribbon panel will be displayed.

b.   By default, the model appears sectioned using a plane parallel to the Front view of the

ViewCube. If not, in the **Planes Settings** ribbon panel, click on the **Current: Plane 1** list and click on the light globe icon on the left of **Plane 1** to activate this plane; the light globe icon will turn Yellow.

c. In the same ribbon panel, click on the **Alignment** list and select one of the other standard views to align the section plane to. These standard views correspond to the faces of the ViewCube. Selecting the **Align To View** option aligns the section plane parallel to the screen. The model will be sectioned similar to the one shown in Figure 22. Selecting the **Align To Surface** option lets you align the section plane to a face of an object in the model. Selecting the **Align To Line** option lets you align the section plane normal to a sketched line in the model at the point where you click.

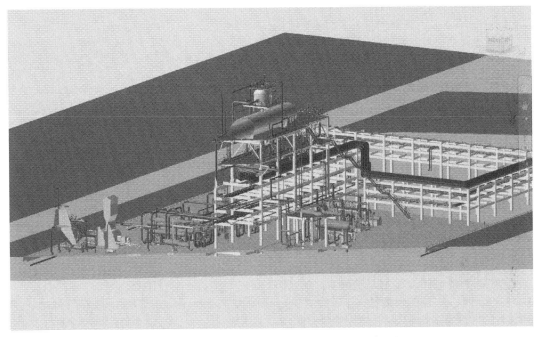

Figure 22 A model being sectioned normal to the view

d. From the **Transform** ribbon panel, click the **Move** tool; a section plane will be displayed in the scene with the move gizmo. Move the cursor over one of the axes of this gizmo and drag the section plane to the required location. Alternatively, you can expand the **Transform** ribbon panel and enter the X, Y, and, Z coordinate values of the section plane in their respective edit boxes. The part of the model on one side of the plane will be sectioned. You can also use the **Rotate** tool from the **Transform** ribbon panel to rotate the section plane using the gizmo or by entering the values. Clicking the **Fit Selection** button will position the section plane at the edge or face of the selected object closest to the section plane alignment face.

  Note: *The axes of the move or rotate gizmo are color-coded. The Red color represents X-axis, Green color represents Y-axis, and Blue color represents Z-axis. This allows you to enter the value in the correct box in the expanded **Transform** ribbon panel.*

e. After moving or rotating the section plane, click on the **Move** or **Rotate** tool again to turn off the visibility of the section plane.

Figure 23 shows a plant model sectioned using a plane aligned to the front face of the model. In this view, the section plane is also visible with the move gizmo.

Figure 23 A model sectioned using the plane aligned to the front view of the model

Sectioning a Model Using Multiple Section Planes

This method allows you to section a model using multiple section planes. This method of sectioning is similar to the previous method, with the difference that you also select additional section planes and align and transform them. You can select up to six section planes to section the model. The following steps show you how to section a model using this method.

a. If the sectioning is not already enabled, enable it by clicking **Viewpoint** ribbon tab > **Sectioning** ribbon panel > **Enable Sectioning**; the **Sectioning Tools** ribbon panel will be displayed.

b. In the **Planes Settings** ribbon panel, click on the **Current: Plane 1** list and click on the light globe icon on the left of **Plane 1** to activate this plane; the light globe icon will turn Yellow.

c. In the same ribbon panel, click on the **Alignment** list and select one of the standard views to align the section plane to. Alternatively, use the current view, a face of the object in the model, or a line to align the section plane to.

d. From the **Transform** ribbon panel, click the **Move** or **Rotate** tool and transform the section plane using the gizmo. You can also expand the **Transform** ribbon panel and enter the transformation values in their respective boxes.

e. In the **Planes Settings** ribbon panel, click on the **Current: Plane 1** list and click on **Plane 2** to activate this plane; the light globe icon on the left of this plane will turn Yellow.

f. In the same ribbon panel, click on the **Alignment** list and select one of the standard views to align the section plane to. Alternatively, use the current view, a face of the object in the model, or a line to align the section plane to.

g. From the **Transform** ribbon panel, click the **Move** or **Rotate** tool and transform the section plane using the gizmo. You can also expand the **Transform** ribbon panel and enter the transformation values in their respective boxes.

h. Similarly, you can repeat steps e to h to add as many number of planes to section the model.

i. After moving or rotating the section plane, click on the **Move** or **Rotate** tool again to turn off the visibility of the section plane.

 *Tip: At any point of time, you can select the section plane from the **Current: Plane** list in the **Planes Settings** ribbon panel and edit the transformation of that plane using the **Move** or **Rotate** tool.*

Figure 24 shows a plant model sectioned using two planes. One of the planes is aligned to the front face of the model and the other one is aligned to the left face. The visibility of the section planes is turned off in this view by exiting the **Move** tool.

Figure 24 A plant model sectioned using two section planes

Sectioning a Model using Linked Section Planes

While sectioning a model using multiple section planes, Autodesk Navisworks lets you link them in order to view a slice of the model. The linked section planes are transformed together, thus showing you the model in slices. Generally, it is done with two section planes aligned to the opposite faces of the model. The following steps show you how to do this.

a.   If the sectioning is not already enabled, enable it by clicking **Viewpoint** ribbon tab > **Sectioning** ribbon panel > **Enable Sectioning**; the **Sectioning Tools** ribbon panel will be displayed.

b.   In the **Planes Settings** ribbon panel, click on the **Current: Plane 1** list and click on the light globe icon on the left of **Plane 1** to activate this plane; the light globe icon will turn Yellow.

c.   In the same ribbon panel, click on the **Alignment** list and select one of the standard views to align the section plane to. Alternatively, use the current view, a face of the object in the model, or a line to align the section plane to.

d.   From the **Transform** ribbon panel, click the **Move** or **Rotate** tool and transform the section plane using the gizmo. You can also expand the **Transform** ribbon panel and enter the transformation values in their respective boxes.

e.   In the **Planes Settings** ribbon panel, click on the **Current: Plane 1** list and click on **Plane 2** to activate this plane; the light globe icon on the left of this plane will turn Yellow.

f.   In the same ribbon panel, click on the **Alignment** list and select the alignment opposite to the one you selected for the previous plane. For example, if you selected the **Top** alignment for the previous plane, select the **Bottom** alignment in this case.

   Tip: If you have selected a custom alignment for the first plane using a face of a line, you can select the same alignment again and rotate the plane 180-degrees to flip the side of the model to be sectioned.

g.   From the **Transform** ribbon panel, click the **Move** or **Rotate** tool and transform the section plane using the gizmo. You can also expand the **Transform** ribbon panel and enter the transformation values in their respective boxes.

h.   After the two planes are in the right position and you can see the slice of the model, click the **Link Section Planes** button in the **Planes Settings** ribbon panel to link the two planes.

i.   If you use the move gizmo now, you will notice that only the current section plane is visible. However, when you move this plane, the other section plane also moves, thus maintaining the thickness of the original slice.

Figure 25 shows a slice of the building model sectioned using two linked section planes. In this case, the upper plane was aligned to the top view and the lower plane was aligned to the bottom view of the ViewCube.

Figure 25   *A building model sectioned using two aligned planes*

Sectioning a Model using a Section Box

This method of sectioning lets you define a section box. The part of the model inside the box is retained and the part outside this box will be sectioned. Figure 26 shows a building model section using a box. This figure also shows the section box with the move gizmo. The following steps explain how to section a model using this method.

a.   If the sectioning is not already enabled, enable it by clicking **Viewpoint** ribbon tab > **Sectioning** ribbon panel > **Enable Sectioning**; the **Sectioning Tools** ribbon panel will be displayed.

b.   In the **Mode** ribbon panel, click the **Planes** flyout and select the **Box** tool; a section box will be displayed on the model.

c.   From the **Transform** ribbon panel, click the **Scale** tool; the scale gizmo will be displayed in the section box.

d.   Press and hold down the left mouse button and drag one of the axes or the triangular plane to scale the section box in that direction. Alternatively, drag the sphere at the center of the gizmo to scale it uniformly in all directions. You can also expand the **Transform** ribbon panel and enter the length, width, and height of the section box in the **Scale** edit boxes.

e.   Click the **Move** or **Rotate** tool and transform the section box using the gizmo or by entering the transformation values in the expanded **Transform** ribbon panel.

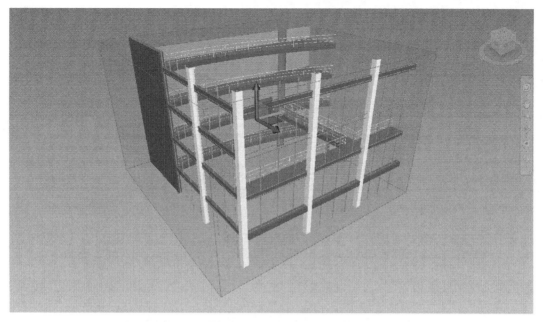

Figure 26 *A building model sectioned using a section box*

f.   Click the **Fit Selection** tool to resize the section box and enclose the selected object inside it.

Saving a Sectioned View

Sectioning Tools Ribbon Tab > Save Ribbon Panel > Save Viewpoint

The **Save Viewpoint** tool allows you to save the current viewpoint with the sectioned model. The viewpoint will not only store the camera information but also the sectioned model, the visibility of the section planes or section box, and the section tool that was last active. If the sectioning is disabled and you are in a different view, clicking a section view will display the sectioned model and also enable the sectioning.

HANDS-ON EXERCISES

You will now work on hands-on exercises using the concepts learned in this chapter.

Hands-on Exercise (Plant)	In this exercise, you will complete the following tasks: 1. Add redline markups to the viewpoints and animation in the scene. 2. Add comments to various viewpoints, animations, and sets. 3. Add tags to the objects in the scene. 4. Perform searches for comments and tags. 5. Section the Autodesk Navisworks model using section planes. 6. Section the Autodesk Navisworks model using section box. 7. Merge the information from the current file into another file.

Section 1: Opening a File and Adding Redline Markups

In this section, you will open the NWF file of a plant structure model created in Autodesk Inventor. This model already has some viewpoints and sets created. You will activate these viewpoints and then add redline markups in those viewpoints.

1. Open the **C04-Vessel-Assm.nwf** file from the **Chapter 4 > Exercise Plant** folder; the file opens with a plant structure model in it, as shown in Figure 27.

Figure 27 The model for the exercise

You will now use the **Platform** viewpoint to add redline markups about the platform. However, as mentioned earlier, if you do not have a viewpoint saved, it is automatically saved when you finish adding the redline markup.

2. Activate the **Platform** viewpoint from the **Saved Viewpoints** window.

3. Click the **Review** ribbon tab to display the various redline tools.

4. On the **Redline** ribbon panel, enter **3** as the value in the **Thickness** spinner, if it is not already set to that; the redline markups that you create now will appear thicker.

5. From the **Redline** ribbon panel, invoke the **Text** tool; the cursor changes to the pencil cursor.

6. Click anywhere in the blank area of the graphics window on the right of the Yellow beam to specify the start point of the text, refer to Figure 28; the **Autodesk Navisworks Manage/ Simulate 2016** dialog box is displayed prompting you to enter the redline text.

7. Type the following text and press **OK** in the dialog box (note the incorrect spelling of Steel):

Use Webforge Steet Grating Pattern A or B

In this text, the text Steel is misspelled as Steet to show you how to edit the text later.

8. From the **Redline** ribbon panel > **Draw** flyout, click the **Arrow** tool and draw an arrow from the middle left alignment point of the text to anywhere on the platform, as shown in Figure 28.

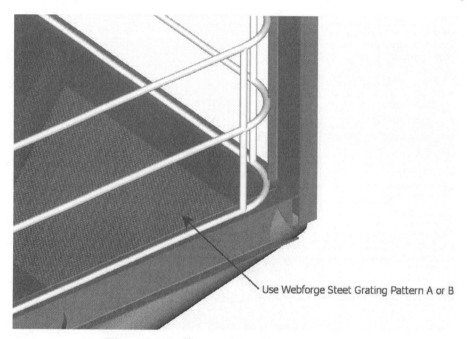

Figure 28 *Redline markup added to the platform*

As mentioned earlier, there is a spelling mistake in the text. You will now fix that.

9. Right-click on the redline text you added in step 7 and click **Edit** from the shortcut menu; the **Autodesk Navisworks Manage/Simulate 2016** dialog box is displayed with the text in it.

10. Change the spelling of the text **Steet** to **Steel** and click **OK** in the dialog box.

Next, you will add redline markup to the **Stairs** viewpoint.

11. Activate the **Stairs** viewpoint from the **Saved Viewpoints** window.

12. Invoke the **Text** tool from the **Redline** ribbon panel and click anywhere in the blank area of the graphics window on the right of the stairs, refer to Figure 29; you will be prompted to enter the redline text in the dialog box.

13. Type the following text and press **OK** in the dialog box:

All Treads Welded, Abrasive Nosing Type T5

14. From the **Redline** ribbon panel > **Draw** flyout, click the **Arrow** tool and draw two arrows from the left of the **WELDED** text to any two treads of the stair, as shown in Figure 29.

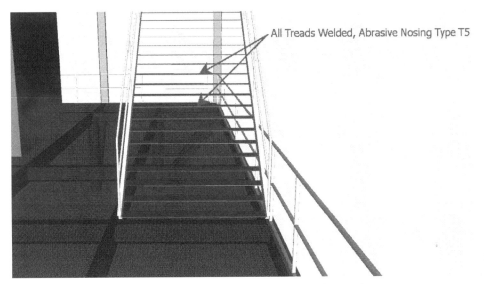

Figure 29 *Redline markup added to the tread*

15. Save the file.

Section 2: Adding Comments to Viewpoints and Sets

As mentioned earlier in this chapter, one of the drawbacks of adding redline text is that you cannot later search for this text. As a result, it is better to add comments so that they appear in the searches. In this section, you will add comments to the viewpoints and sets.

1. Activate the **Interferences** viewpoint.

You will now create a cloud similar to the one shown in Figure 30. It is important that you pick points in the clockwise direction to get the cloud looking like it. Also, note that you can close the cloud by right-clicking close to the start point.

2. From the **Redline** ribbon panel > **Draw** flyout, click the **Cloud** tool.

3. Create a cloud similar to the one shown in Figure 30 by clicking the points in the clockwise direction. Remember that clicking the next point close to the previous point will create smaller arcs and that you can close the cloud by right-clicking close to the start point.

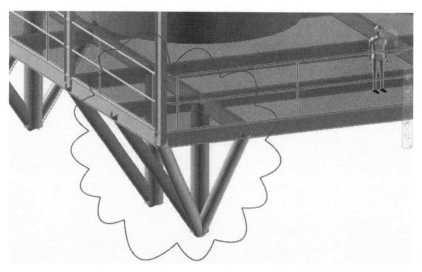

Figure 30 *The cloud created for the comment*

4. From the bottom left of the Autodesk Navisworks window, click **Comments** to display the **Comments** window. Dock this window below the graphics window using the **Auto-Hide** button. If need be, resize the window.

5. In the **Saved Viewpoints** window, right-click on the **Interferences** viewpoint and click **Add Comment** from the shortcut menu; the **Add Comment** dialog box is displayed.

6. Type **Interferences** as the first line of text. This is the text that will be displayed under the **Comment** column in the upper half of the **Comments** window.

7. Press and hold down the CTRL key and press ENTER.

8. Release the CTRL key and enter the following text in the second line:

   Steel members interfering throughout the structure. This needs fixing before the meeting with the Project Director.

9. The **Status** is by default set to **New**. Click **OK** in the dialog box; the **Comments** window appears similar to the one shown in Figure 31.

   Next, you will add a comment to the **Stairs** selection set. The text of the comment will be the same as the one you wrote for the **Stairs** viewpoint. This will make sure that this comment appears while searching for the text.

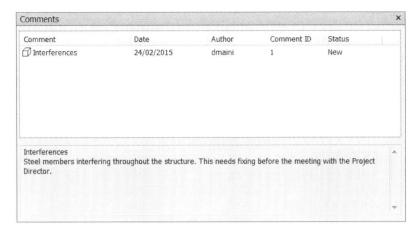

*Figure 31 The **Comments** window showing the comment added to the viewpoint*

10. Dock the **Sets** window below the **Selection Tree**, if it is not already there.

11. From the **Sets** window, right-click on the **Stairs** selection set and click **Add Comment**; the **Add Comment** dialog box is displayed.

12. Type **Tread Details** as the first line of text. This is the text that will be displayed under the **Comment** column in the upper half of the **Comments** window.

13. Press and hold down the CTRL key and press ENTER.

14. Release the CTRL key and enter the following text in the second line:

    All Treads WELDED Fixing, Banded Ends, Abrasive Nosing - Type T5

15. Click **OK** in the dialog box; the comment does not appear in the **Comments** window.

    The reason this comment does not appear in the **Comments** window is because the **Stairs** set is not selected.

16. From the **Sets** window, select the **Stairs** set; the comment added to this set is displayed in the **Comments** window. Note that these types of comments are not dependent on the viewpoint.

    Next, you will add a comment to the **Platforms** search set.

17. From the **Sets** window, right-click on the **Platforms** search set and click **Add Comment**; the **Add Comment** dialog box is displayed.

18. Type **Platform Details** as the first line of text. This is the text that will be displayed under the **Comment** column in the upper half of the **Comments** window.

19. Press and hold down the CTRL key and press ENTER.

20. Release the CTRL key and enter the following text in the second line:

    Use Webforge Steel Grating Pattern A or B

21. Click **OK** in the dialog box. Select the **Platforms** set again from the **Sets** window; the comment added to this set is displayed in the **Comments** window.

    Next, you will add a comment to the **Walkthrough** animation.

22. Press ESC to deselect everything.

23. From the **Saved Viewpoints** window, right-click on the **Walkthrough** animation and click **Add Comment** from the shortcut menu.

24. Type **Gravity in Animation** as the first line of text.

25. Press and hold down the CTRL key and press ENTER to go to the second line and enter the following text in the second line:

    This walkthrough animation uses gravity and so you can get realistic experience of avatar going up the stairs.

26. Click **OK** to close the dialog box and then select this animation to view the comment.

27. Save the file.

Section 3: Adding Tags to the Objects in the Viewpoints

Although adding comments is better than redline markups, the drawback of the comments is that they do not have any reference to the objects in the scene. So it is hard to realize there are comments added in the current file unless you search for them. For this reason, adding tags is the best option. They not only relate to the objects in the scene but also include comments that can be searched for. In this section, you will add tags to the objects in the **Bottom View** viewpoint. If the viewpoint was not created, a viewpoint is automatically created while adding a tag.

1. Activate the **Bottom View** viewpoint.

2. From the **Tags** ribbon panel, invoke the **Add Tag** tool.

   A tag is added by clicking two points in the graphics window. The first point is on the object to which the tag and the comment are to be associated and the second point is where you want the tag balloon to be located.

3. Click anywhere on the left cylindrical member to specify the start point of the tag line, refer to Figure 32.

4. Click anywhere in the blank area of the graphics window on the left of the circular member you picked in the previous step, refer to Figure 32.

As soon as you specify the second point of the tag, the **Add Comment** window is displayed.

5. Type **Missing Support Members** as the first line of text.

6. Press and hold down the CTRL key and press ENTER to go to the second line and enter the following text in the second line:

   Support members missing around this circular member.

7. Click **OK** in the dialog box. Figure 32 shows the viewpoint with the tag and also the comment in the **Comments** window.

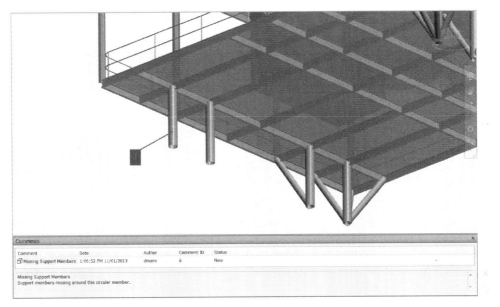

*Figure 32 The tag and comment added to the circular member in the **Bottom View** viewpoint*

Next, you will create a similar tag with the same comment for the circular member next to the previous one.

8. With the **Add Tag** tool still active, click anywhere on the circular member on the right of the previous member, refer to Figure 33.

9. For the second point, click anywhere below the balloon of the previous tag, refer to Figure 33; the **Add Comment** dialog box is displayed.

10. Type **Missing Support Members** as the first line of text.

11. Press and hold down the CTRL key and press ENTER to go to the second line and enter the following text in the second line:

    Support members missing around this circular member.

12. Click **OK** in the dialog box. Figure 33 shows both the tags and also the two comments in the resized **Comments** window.

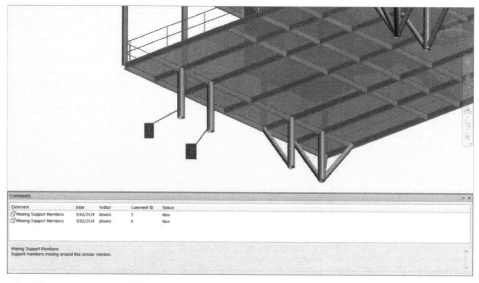

Figure 33 *The tags added to the two circular members in the **Bottom View** viewpoint*

13. Activate the **Overview** viewpoint.

Section 4: Searching and Editing Comments

In this section, you will search for the comments added in the previous sections of this exercise.

1. Click the **Find Comments** button from the **Comments** ribbon panel; the **Find Comments** dialog box is displayed.

2. With nothing entered, click the **Find** button in the dialog box; all the comments added in the current file will be displayed in the lower half of the dialog box, as shown in Figure 34.

   This is the method for searching all the comments added in your current file. Notice the icon on the left of the names in the **Name** column. These icons help you identify the source of the comment.

3. Under the **Comments** tab of the dialog box, type ***Webforge*** in the **Text** box and then click the **Find** button; the lower half of the dialog box displays the comment that was added to the **Platforms** search set. This comment has the text Webforge in it.

4. Under the **Comments** tab of the dialog box, type ***welded*** in the **Text** box and then click the **Find** button; the lower half of the dialog box displays the comment that was added to the **Stairs** selection set.

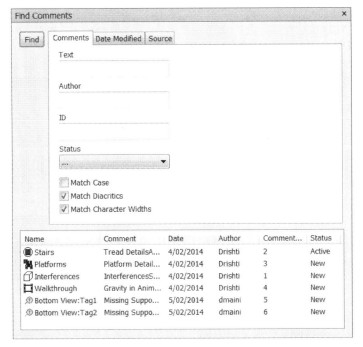

Figure 34 The **Find Comments** *dialog box showing all the comments*

5. Click on the searched comment under the **Name** column in the lower half of the **Find Comments** dialog box; the comment is now listed in the **Comments** window as well.

6. Close the **Find Comments** dialog box.

7. Right-click on the comment in the **Comments** window and click **Edit Comment** from the shortcut menu; the **Edit Comment** dialog box is displayed.

8. Click at the end of the last line of text in the dialog box. Press and hold down the CTRL key and press ENTER twice.

9. Release the CTRL key and type the following text:

   Type T5 not available, Type T6 is used.

10. Click on the **Status** list and select **Active**.

11. Click **OK** in the dialog box; the updated comment is reflected in the **Comments** window.

12. Activate the **Overview** viewpoint.

Section 5: Viewing and Editing Tags

In this section, you will activate the viewpoints in which the tags were added using the tag identification numbers.

1. In the **Tags** ribbon panel, the **Tag ID** spinner shows **1** as the current number. Click the **Go to Tag** button on the right of this spinner; the **Bottom View** viewpoint is restored and the two tags added to this viewpoint are displayed. Also, the **Comments** window shows the comments of the two tags.

2. Right-click on the first comment in the **Comments** window and click **Edit Comment** from the shortcut menu.

3. Click at the end of the second line of text in the dialog box. Press and hold down the CTRL key and press ENTER twice.

4. Release the CTRL key and type the following text:

    This has been fixed in the latest model. When you receive the NWC file of the model next week, refresh this NWF file to view the changes.

5. Click on the **Status** list and select **Resolved**.

6. Click **OK** in the dialog box; the first comment is updated in the **Comments** window and the status now shows **Resolved**.

7. Right-click on the second comment in the **Comments** window and click **Edit Comment** from the shortcut menu.

8. Click at the end of the second line of text in the dialog box. Press and hold down the CTRL key and press ENTER twice.

9. Release the CTRL key and type the following text:

    This has been fixed in the latest model. When you receive the NWC file of the model next week, refresh this NWF file to view the changes.

10. Click on the **Status** list and select **Resolved**.

11. Click **OK** in the dialog box; the second comment is also updated in the **Comments** window and the status now shows **Resolved**.

12. Orbit the model to change the current view.

13. In the **Tags** ribbon panel, type **2** in the **Tag ID** spinner.

14. Click the **Go to Tag** button on the right of this spinner; the **Bottom View** viewpoint is restored and the tags and comments are displayed again.

15. Close the **Comments** window and activate the **Overview** viewpoint.

16. Save the file.

Section 6: Sectioning the Model Using Section Planes

In this section, you will section the model using section planes and then save the sectioned views as viewpoints so that they could be restored later. But because you will move section planes by entering the move values in this section, you first need to set the display units.

1. Press F12 to display the **Options Editor** dialog box. From the left pane, click **Interface > Display Units**. From the right pane, select the display units to Meters or Inches.

2. From the **Viewpoint** ribbon tab > **Sectioning** ribbon panel, click **Enable Sectioning**; the **Sectioning Tools** ribbon tab is displayed.

3. From the **Planes Settings** ribbon panel, click **Current: Plane 1** list. If the light globe of **Plane 1** is Yellow, click on it to turn it off. Now, click on **Plane 3**.

This plane is aligned with the front view of the ViewCube. As a result, it sections the model using a plane parallel to the front view of the model, as shown in Figure 35. Also, as you can see in this figure, the move gizmo will be displayed on the section plane.

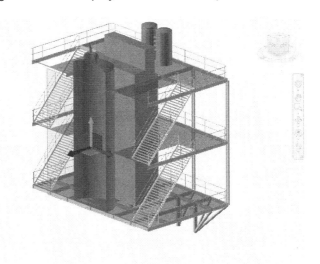

Figure 35 The model with the front half sectioned

4. Click on the **Move** tool in the **Transform** ribbon panel to exit this tool and to turn off the visibility of the section plane and the move gizmo.

It is better to save this viewpoint so you can restore it whenever you want.

5. From the **Save** ribbon panel, click the **Save Viewpoint** tool; a new viewpoint is added.

6. Rename the new viewpoint to **Front Section**.

Next, you will section the model using two section planes and will then link these planes. But first, you need to turn off the sectioning using the current plane.

7. From the **Planes Settings** ribbon panel, click **Current: Plane 3** list and then click on the Yellow light globe on the left of **Plane 3**; the sectioning using this plane is turned off.

8. From the same list, click on **Plane 1** to turn on the sectioning using this plane. Next, click the **Alignment** list and select **Top** to make sure this plane is aligned to the top face of the ViewCube.

9. If the section plane and move gizmo are not displayed, click the **Move** tool to display them.

10. Expand the **Transform** ribbon panel and enter **600 Inches** or **15.25 Meters** as the value in the **Position Z** edit box; the top part of the model is sectioned, refer to the top sectioning in Figure 36.

 *Tip: Sometimes when you try to enter the value in the expanded **Transform** ribbon panel, the value is not accepted. In this case, click on the transform tool button once to exit the tool and then click again to reinvoke it. You can also move the cursor on the axis of the move gizmo and then drag it when the axis turns Yellow to dynamically move the section plane.*

11. From the **Planes Settings** ribbon panel, click **Current: Plane 1** list and then click on **Plane 2**.

   This plane is aligned with the bottom face of the ViewCube. As a result, the lower part of the model is sectioned.

12. Expand the **Transform** ribbon panel and enter **300 Inches** or **7.62 Meters** as the value in the **Position Z** edit box; the lower part of the model is sectioned, refer to Figure 36.

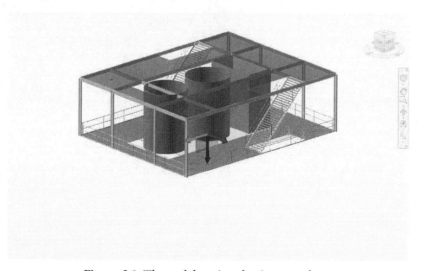

Figure 36 The model sectioned using two planes

13. From the **Planes Settings** ribbon panel, click **Link Section Planes**; the two section planes are linked and will move together now.

Before proceeding further, it is better to save this viewpoint.

14. From the **Save** ribbon panel, click the **Save Viewpoint** tool and rename the viewpoint to **Slice Section**.

15 Move the cursor over the Blue axis of the move gizmo that appears on the lower section plane and drag it down; you will notice that the upper plane also moves with it.

16. Drag the move gizmo up and notice how both the planes move together.

17. Activate the **Overview** viewpoint; the complete model is displayed without sectioning.

18. Save the file.

Section 7: Sectioning the Model Using Section Box

In this section, you will section the model using the section box. You will also save the sectioned view of the model as viewpoints so they could be restored later.

1. From the **Viewpoint** ribbon tab > **Sectioning** ribbon panel, click **Enable Sectioning**; the **Sectioning Tools** ribbon tab is displayed.

2. From the **Mode** ribbon panel, click the **Planes** flyout and click **Box**; the model is sectioned using a box of a default size.

3. From the **Transform** ribbon panel, click the **Scale** tool.

4. Expand the **Transform** ribbon panel and enter **590 Inches** or **15 Meters** as the values in the **Size X, Y, Z** edit boxes.

5. Click on the **Scale** tool again to exit; the model appears similar to the one shown in Figure 37.

6. From the **Save** ribbon panel, click the **Save Viewpoint** tool and rename the new viewpoint to **Section Box**.

7. From the **Transform** ribbon panel, click the **Move** tool and move the section box using the move gizmo. Notice how the model is still sectioned in a box shape.

8. Activate the **Overview** viewpoint.

9. From the **Selection Tree**, expand **Vessel-Assem.nwc** and then click **Equipment:1**; the large equipments are highlighted in the graphics window.

10. From the **Viewpoint** ribbon tab > **Sectioning** ribbon panel, click **Enable Sectioning**; the **Sectioning Tools** ribbon tab is displayed.

11. From the **Mode** ribbon panel, click the **Planes** flyout and click **Box**; the model is sectioned using a box of a default size.

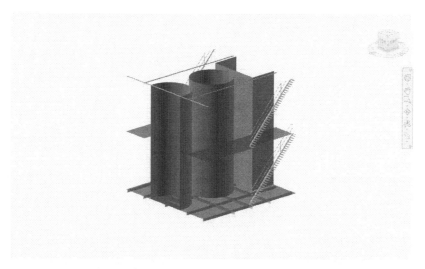

Figure 37 *Model sectioned using the section box*

12. From the **Transform** ribbon panel, click **Fit Selection**; the section box resizes to fit the selected equipments in the box.

13. Press the ESC key to deselect the equipments.

14. Click on the **Move** button again to deselect this tool. The model looks similar to the one shown in Figure 38.

Figure 38 *Section box resized to fit the equipment*

15. From the **Save** ribbon panel, click the **Save Viewpoint** tool and rename the viewpoint to **Section Equipment**.

16. Click the **Overview** viewpoint and save the model.

Section 8: Merging Models

In this section, you will use the **Merge** tool to merge the file you worked on in the earlier sections with another Autodesk Navisworks file of the same model. As mentioned in the previous chapters, the advantage of merging files is that the geometry information is not duplicated. Only the Autodesk Navisworks objects such as viewpoints, redline markups, tags, and so on are copied.

1. Open the **Platform-V1.nwf** file from the **Chapter 4 > Exercise Plant** folder.

    This model looks similar to the one you have been working on. However, the redline markups and tags in this model are different from those in the file you worked on earlier. Also, it does not have any section viewpoints you created in the previous file.

2. Activate the **Platform** viewpoint and notice that the redline markup here is about the handrailing.

3. Activate the **Bottom View** viewpoint and notice the tag and the associated comment in the **Comments** window.

    Next, you will merge the **C04-Vessel-Assem.nwf** file with this one.

4. Activate the **Overview** viewpoint.

5. From the **Home** ribbon tab > **Project** ribbon panel, expand the **Append** flyout and click **Merge**; the **Merge** dialog box is displayed.

6. Double-click on the **C04-Vessel-Assem.nwf** file; it is merged with the current file.

    Notice how the additional viewpoints are displayed in the **Saved Viewpoints** window.

7. From the bottom left of the Autodesk Navisworks window, click **Comments** and dock the **Comments** window below the graphics window.

8. From the **Sets** window, click on the **Stairs** selection set; the comment that was added to this set in the **C04-Vessel-Assem.nwf** file is now displayed in the **Comments** window.

9. Similarly, from the **Sets** window, select the **Platforms** search set; the comment that was added to this in the **C04-Vessel-Assem.nwf** file is displayed in the **Comments** window.

10. Press the ESC key to deselect everything.

11. Activate the **Front Section** viewpoint and notice how this model is displayed as sectioned.

    In this file, there was a tag numbered 1. In the **C04-Vessel-Assem.nwf** file also, there were two tags numbered 1 and 2. This will cause confusion so it is important to renumber the tags.

12. From the **Review** ribbon tab, expand the **Tags** ribbon panel and click **Renumber Tag IDs**; the tags will be renumbered.

13. With **1** listed in the **Tag ID** spinner in the **Tags** ribbon panel, click the **Go to Tag** button on the right of this spinner; the viewpoint changes to display tag 1.

14. Type **2** in the **Tag ID** spinner in the **Tags** ribbon panel and then click the **Go to Tag** button; tags 2 and 3 are now displayed as they were added in the same viewpoint.

15. Restore the **Training** workspace from the **View** ribbon tab > **Workspace** ribbon panel > **Load Workspace** flyout.

Section 9: Exporting Viewpoints Report

As mentioned earlier, Autodesk Navisworks does not have the facility to export a report of all the redline markups, comments, and tags. However, it allows you to export the viewpoints report, which also in turn, exports these items. In this section, you will export the viewpoints report. But before doing that, you need to edit the size of the images in the viewpoint report. This is done by opening the **Options Editor** dialog box in the administrator mode.

1. Hold down the SHIFT key and then right-click and select **Global Options** from the shortcut menu; the **Options Editor** opens in the administrator mode.

2. From the left pane, expand **Interface** and select **Viewpoint Defaults**; the right pane shows the **Viewpoints Report** area below the other options. This area is not displayed if you invoke the **Options Editor** dialog box in the normal mode.

3. Change the **Image Height** to **600** and **Image Width** to **800** and then close the dialog box.

4. From the **Saved Viewpoints** window, delete the **Walkthrough** animation.

5. Right-click in the blank area of the **Saved Viewpoints** window and select **Export Viewpoints Report**; the **Export** dialog box is displayed.

6. Browse to the **Chapter 4 > Exercise Plant** folder and create a subfolder there called **Report**.

7. Activate the **Report** folder and save the current file with the name **Review-Report**; the report is saved in the HTML format.

8. Using Windows Explorer, browse to the **Chapter 4 > Exercise Plant > Report folder**; notice the HTML file there and also the images for all the viewpoints as well as the animation frames.

9. Double-click on the **Review-Report.html** file to open the report.

You will notice that the redline text appears below the **Camera Position** information. However, all the tag comments are displayed in their own boxes with status, user, and time information.

10. Close this file and return to the Autodesk Navisworks window.

11. Save the file and start a new file.

Hands-on Exercise (BIM)	In this exercise, you will complete the following tasks:
	1. Add redline markups to the viewpoints and animation in the scene.
	2. Add comments to various viewpoints, animations, and sets.
	3. Add tags to the objects in the scene.
	4. Perform searches for comments and tags.
	5. Section the Autodesk Navisworks model using section planes.
	6. Section the Autodesk Navisworks model using section box.
	7. Merge the information from the current file into another file.

Section 1: Opening a File and Adding Redline Markups

In this section, you will open the Autodesk Navisworks file of a building model. This model already has some viewpoints and sets created. You will activate these viewpoints and then add redline markups in those viewpoints.

1. Open the **C04-Building.nwf** file from the **Chapter 4 > Exercise Building** folder; the file opens with a building model in it, as shown in Figure 39. The building model for this exercise is **courtesy Ankur Mathur, Founder and CEO, SANRACHNA:BIM and Virtual Construction Consultants**.

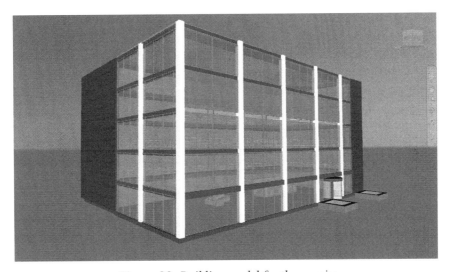

Figure 39 *Building model for the exercise*

You will now use the **Main Entrance** viewpoint to add redline markups about the platform. However, as mentioned earlier, if you do not have a viewpoint saved, it is automatically saved when you finish adding the redline markup.

2. Activate the **Main Entrance** viewpoint from the **Saved Viewpoints** window.

3. Click the **Review** ribbon tab to display the various redline tools.

4. On the **Redline** ribbon panel, enter **3** as the value in the **Thickness** spinner, if it is not already set to that; the redline markups that you create will now appear thicker.

5. From the **Redline** ribbon panel, invoke the **Text** tool; the cursor changes to the pencil cursor.

6. Click anywhere on the lower right side of the entrance door to specify the start point of the text, refer to Figure 40; the **Autodesk Navisworks Manage/Simulate 2016** dialog box is displayed prompting you to enter the redline text.

7. Type the following text and press **OK** in the dialog box (note the incorrect spelling of Revolving):

    AGP Duotour Series Revolivng Door

    In this text, the text **Revolving** is misspelled as **Revolivng** so that you can be shown how to edit the text later.

8. From the **Redline** ribbon panel > **Draw** flyout, click the **Arrow** tool and draw an arrow from the middle left alignment point of the text to anywhere on the revolving door, as shown in Figure 40.

*Figure 40 Redline markup added to the **Main Entrance** viewpoint*

As mentioned earlier, there is a spelling mistake in the text. You will now fix that.

9. Right-click on the first line of the redline text you added in step 7 and click **Edit** from the shortcut menu; the **Autodesk Navisworks Manage/Simulate 2016** dialog box is displayed with the text in it.

10. Change the spelling of the text **Revolivng** to **Revolving** and click **OK** in the dialog box.

    Next, you will add redline markup to the **Office Entrances** viewpoint.

11. Activate the **Office Entrances** viewpoint from the **Saved Viewpoints** window.

12. Invoke the **Text** tool from the **Redline** ribbon panel and click anywhere between the two doors displayed in this viewpoint; you will be prompted to enter the redline text in the dialog box.

13. Type the following text and press **OK** in the dialog box:

    Proximity card door locks required

14. From the **Redline** ribbon panel > **Draw** flyout, click the **Arrow** tool and draw two arrows from the text to the two doors, as shown in Figure 41.

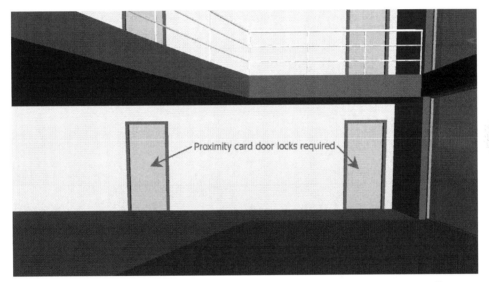

*Figure 41   Redline markup added to the **Office Entrance** viewpoint*

15. Save the file.

Section 2: Adding Comments to Viewpoints and Sets

As mentioned earlier in this chapter, one of the drawbacks of adding redline text is that you cannot search for this text. As a result, it is better to add comments so that they appear in the searches. In this section, you will add comments to the viewpoints and sets.

1. Activate the **Sofa** viewpoint.

   You will now create a cloud similar to the one shown in Figure 42. It is important that you pick points in the clockwise direction to get the cloud looking like it. Also, note that you can close the cloud by right-clicking near the start point of the cloud.

2. From the **Redline** ribbon panel > **Draw** flyout, click the **Cloud** tool.

3. Create a cloud similar to the one shown in Figure 42 by clicking the points in the clockwise direction. Remember that clicking the next point close to the previous point will create smaller arcs and that you can close the cloud by right-clicking near the start point of the cloud.

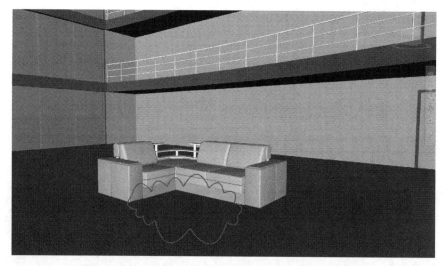

Figure 42 *A redline cloud drawn in the* **Sofa** *viewpoint*

4. From the **Comments** ribbon panel, click the **View Comments** tool; the **Comments** window is displayed. Dock this window below the graphics window using the **Auto-Hide** button.

5. Right-click in the upper half of the **Comments** window and click **Add Comment** from the shortcut menu; the **Add Comment** dialog box is displayed.

6. Type **Glass Table** as the first line of text. This is the text that will be displayed under the **Comment** column in the upper half of the **Comments** window.

7. Press and hold down the CTRL key and press ENTER.

8. Release the CTRL key and enter the following text in the second line:

    Place a glass table here and also a couple of decoration pieces.

9. The **Status** is by default set to **New**. Click **OK** in the dialog box; the **Comments** window appears similar to the one shown in Figure 43.

    Next, you will add a comment to the **Revolving Door** selection set. The comment will be the same as the one you added as the redline text in the previous section. This will make sure that this comment appears while searching for the text.

10. Dock the **Sets** window below the **Selection Tree**, if it is not already there.

11. From the **Sets** window, right-click on the **Revolving Door** selection set and click **Add Comment**; the **Add Comment** dialog box is displayed.

12. Type **Door Details** as the first line of text. This is the text that will be displayed under the **Comment** column in the upper half of the **Comments** window.

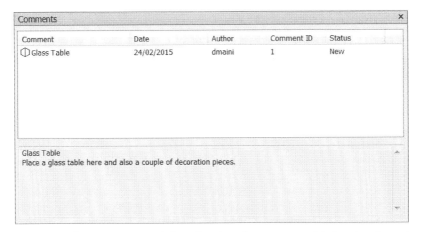

Figure 43 *The* **Comments** *window showing the comment added to the viewpoint*

13. Press and hold down the CTRL key and press ENTER.

14. Release the CTRL key and enter the following text in the second line:

AGP Duotour Series Revolving Door

15. Click **OK** in the dialog box; the comment does not appear in the **Comments** window.

    The reason this comment does not appear in the **Comments** window is because the **Revolving Door** set is not selected.

16. From the **Sets** window, select the **Revolving Door** set; the comment added to this set is displayed in the **Comments** window. Note that these types of comments are not dependent on the viewpoint.

    Next, you will add a comment to the **Glazed Panels** search set.

17. From the **Sets** window, right-click on the **Glazed Panels** search set and click **Add Comment**; the **Add Comment** dialog box is displayed.

18. Type **Glazing Details** as the first line of text. This is the text that will be displayed under the **Comment** column in the upper half of the **Comments** window.

19. Press and hold down the CTRL key and press ENTER.

20. Release the CTRL key and enter the following text in the second line:

Cantilevered Glass Fins to be used for Glazing

21. Click **OK** in the dialog box and then select this set again from the **Sets** window; the comment added to this set is displayed in the **Comments** window.

22. Press the ESC key to deselect everything.

    Next, you will add a comment to the **Walkthrough** animation.

23. From the **Saved Viewpoints** window, right-click on the **Walkthrough** animation and click **Add Comment** from the shortcut menu.

24. Type **Walk Inside** as the first line of text.

25. Press and hold down the CTRL key and press ENTER to go to the second line and enter the following text in the second line:

    This walkthrough animation takes you from the main entrance to the inside.

26. Click **OK** to close the dialog box and then click on the animation to view its comments.

27. Save the file.

Section 3: Adding Tags to the Objects in the Viewpoints

Although adding comments is better than redline markups, the drawback of the comments is that they do not have any reference to the objects or viewpoints. So it is hard to realize there are comments added in the current file unless you search for them. For this reason, adding tags is the best option. They not only relate to the objects in the viewpoints, they also include comments that can be searched for. In this section, you will add a tag to the wall in the **Alarm Panel** viewpoint. If the viewpoint was not created, a viewpoint is automatically created while adding a tag.

1. Activate the **Alarm Panel** viewpoint.

2. From the **Tags** ribbon panel, invoke the **Add Tag** tool.

   A tag is added by clicking two points in the graphics window. The first point is on the object to which the tag and comment are to be associated and the second point is where you want the tag balloon to be located.

3. Click anywhere on the column on the right of the revolving door to specify the start point of the tag line, refer to Figure 44.

4. Click anywhere on the left of the column you picked in the previous step, refer to Figure 44.

   As soon as you specify the second point of the tag, the **Add Comment** window is displayed.

5. Type **Alarm Panel** as the first line of text.

6. Press and hold down the CTRL key and press ENTER to go to the second line and enter the following text in the second line:

   Security Alarm Panel to be installed here.

7. Click **OK** in the dialog box. Figure 44 shows the viewpoint with the tag and the **Comments** window showing the associated comment.

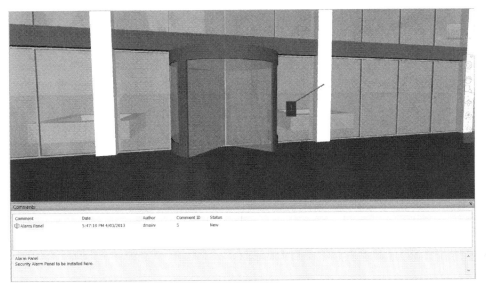

Figure 44 *The tag added to the **Alarm Panel** viewpoint*

Next, you will add another comment to the **Alarm Sensor** viewpoint.

8. Activate the **Alarm Sensor** viewpoint.

9. From the **Tags** ribbon panel, invoke the **Add Tag** tool.

10. Click close to the top left of the glass frame to specify the start point of the tag line, refer to Figure 45.

11. Click diagonally left of the point you picked in the previous step, refer to Figure 45.

    As soon as you specify the second point of the tag, the **Add Comment** window is displayed.

12. Type **Alarm Sensor** as the first line of text.

13. Press and hold down the CTRL key and press ENTER to go to the second line and enter the following text in the second line and then click **OK** in the dialog box:

    An Alarm sensor to be installed here as well. Make it zone 2.

    Figure 45 shows the graphics window with the tag and also the **Comments** window with the comments.

14. Activate the **Overview** viewpoint.

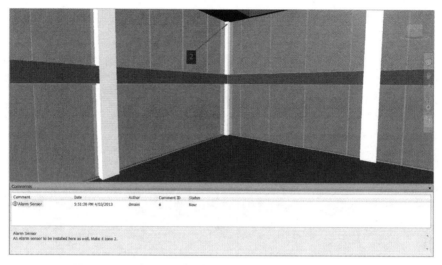

Figure 45 *The tag added to the **Alarm Sensor** viewpoint*

Section 4: Searching and Editing Comments

In this section, you will search for the comments added in the previous sections of this exercise.

1. Click the **Find Comments** button from the **Comments** ribbon panel; the **Find Comments** dialog box is displayed.

2. With nothing entered, click the **Find** button in the dialog box; all the comments added in the current file will be displayed in the lower half of the dialog box, as shown in Figure 46.

    This is the method for searching all the comments added in your current file. Notice the icon on the left of the names in the **Name** column. These icons help you identify the source of the comment.

3. Under the **Comments** tab of the dialog box, type ***Door*** in the **Text** box and then click the **Find** button; the lower half of the dialog box displays the comment that was added to the **Revolving Door** selection set. This comment has the text Door in it.

4. Under the **Comments** tab of the dialog box, type ***table*** in the **Text** box and then click the **Find** button; the lower half of the dialog box displays the comment that was added to the **Sofa** viewpoint.

5. Click on the searched comment under the **Name** column in the lower half of the **Find Comments** dialog box; the comment is now listed in the **Comments** window as well and the **Sofa** viewpoint is activated.

6. Close the **Find Comments** dialog box.

7. Right-click on the comment in the **Comments** window and click **Edit Comment** from the shortcut menu; the **Edit Comment** dialog box is displayed.

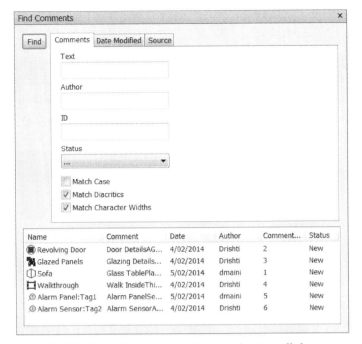

*Figure 46 The **Find Comments** dialog box showing all the comments*

8. Click at the end of the last line of text in the dialog box. Press and hold down the CTRL key and press ENTER twice.

9. Release the CTRL key and type the following text:

   Is there any preference of the shape of the table?

10. Click on the **Status** list and select **Active**.

11. Click **OK** in the dialog box; the updated comment is reflected in the **Comments** window.

12. Activate the **Overview** viewpoint and then save the file.

Section 5: Viewing and Editing Tags

In this section, you will activate the viewpoints in which the tags were added using the tag identification numbers.

1. In the **Tags** ribbon panel > **Tag ID** spinner, enter **1** as the current number, if not already set to this value. Click the **Go to Tag** button on the right of this spinner; the **Alarm Panel** viewpoint is restored and the tag added to this viewpoint is displayed. Also, the **Comments** window shows the comment of the tag.

2. Right-click on the comment in the **Comments** window and click **Edit Comment** from the shortcut menu.

3. Click at the end of the second line of text in the dialog box. Press and hold down the CTRL key and press ENTER twice.

4. Release the CTRL key and type the following text:

    How many total zones do we need? The supplier can include up to 8 zones in the original quote.

5. Click on the **Status** list and select **Active**.

6. Click **OK** in the dialog box; the first comment is updated in the **Comments** window and the status now shows **Active**.

7. In the **Tags** ribbon panel, type **2** in the **Tag ID** spinner.

8. Click the **Go to Tag** button on the right of this spinner; the viewpoint related to this tag number is activated and the tag and comment are displayed.

9. Close the **Comments** window and save the file.

Section 6: Sectioning the Model Using Section Planes

In this section, you will section the model using section planes. You will also save the sectioned views of the model as viewpoints so those viewpoints could be restored later. But because you will move section planes by entering the move values in this section, you need to set the display units.

1. Press F12 to display the **Options Editor** dialog box. From the left pane, click **Interface > Display Units**. From the right pane, select Meters or Inches as the display units.

2. Activate the **Section** viewpoint.

3. From the **Viewpoint** ribbon tab > **Sectioning** ribbon panel, click **Enable Sectioning**; the **Sectioning Tools** ribbon tab is displayed.

4. From the **Planes Settings** ribbon panel, click **Current: Plane 1** list and turn off the Yellow light globe of **Plane 1**. Next, click on **Plane 6**; a section plane is displayed in the graphics window. This plane is aligned with the right face of the ViewCube.

5. Move the cursor over the Blue axis of the move gizmo on the section plane; the cursor changes to the hand cursor.

6. Drag the move gizmo back and stop just in front of the reception area, as shown in Figure 47.

7. Click on the **Move** tool in the **Transform** ribbon panel to exit this tool and to turn off the visibility of the section plane and the move gizmo.

    It is better to save this viewpoint so you can restore it whenever you want.

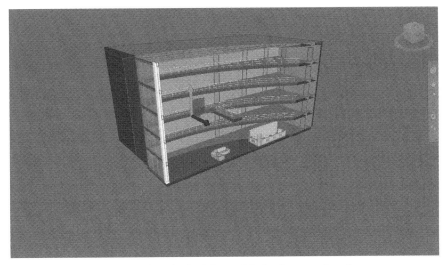

Figure 47 *The building with the front sectioned*

8. From the **Save** ribbon panel, click the **Save Viewpoint** tool; a new viewpoint is added.

9. Rename the new viewpoint to **Front Section**.

    Next, you will section the model using two section planes and will then link these planes. But first, you need to turn off the sectioning using the current plane.

10. From the **Planes Settings** ribbon panel, click on **Current: Plane 6** list and then click on the Yellow light globe on the left of **Plane 6** to turn off the sectioning using this plane.

    The first plane that you need to select for sectioning is **Plane 1** as this plane is aligned to the top face of the ViewCube.

11. From the same list, click on **Plane 1** to turn on the sectioning using this plane. Next, from the **Alignment** list, select **Top**.

    Next, you will invoke the **Move** tool and then move the section plane by specifying its location in the expanded **Transform** ribbon panel.

 *Tip: Sometimes when you try to enter the value in the expanded **Transform** ribbon panel, the value is not accepted. In this case, click on the transform tool button once to exit the tool and then click again to reinvoke it.*

12. Click the **Move** tool and then expand the **Transform** ribbon panel. Enter **485 Inches** or **12.3 Meters** as the value in the **Position Z** edit box; the top part of the model is sectioned, refer to the top sectioning in Figure 48.

 Tip: You can also move the cursor on the Blue axis of the move gizmo and then drag it when the axis turns Yellow to dynamically move the section plane.

13. From the **Planes Settings** ribbon panel, click **Current: Plane 1** list and then click on **Plane 2**.

   This plane is aligned with the bottom face of the ViewCube. As a result, the lower part of the model is sectioned.

14. Expand the **Transform** ribbon panel and enter **350 Inches** or **8.85 Meters** as the value in the **Position Z** edit box; the lower part of the model is sectioned, refer to Figure 48.

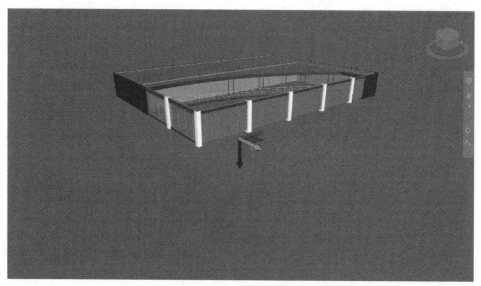

Figure 48   *The model sectioned using two planes*

15. From the **Planes Settings** ribbon panel, click **Link Section Planes**; the two section planes are linked and will move together now.

   Before proceeding further, it is better to save this viewpoint.

16. From the **Save** ribbon panel, click the **Save Viewpoint** tool and rename the viewpoint to **Slice Section**.

17. Move the cursor over the Blue axis of the move gizmo that appears on the lower section plane and drag it down; you will notice that the upper plane also moves with it.

18. Drag the move gizmo up and notice how both the planes move together.

19. Activate the **Section** viewpoint; the complete model is displayed without sectioning.

20. Save the file.

Section 7: Sectioning the Model Using Section Box

In this section, you will section the model using the section box. You will also save the sectioned view of the model as viewpoints so they could be restored later.

1. From the **Viewpoint** ribbon tab > **Sectioning** ribbon panel, click **Enable Sectioning**; the **Sectioning Tools** ribbon tab is displayed.

2. From the **Mode** ribbon panel, click the **Planes** flyout and click **Box**; the model is sectioned using a box of a default size.

3. From the **Transform** ribbon panel, click the **Scale** tool and then expand and pin the **Transform** ribbon panel.

4. Move the cursor over the sphere in the scale gizmo; the cursor changes to the hand cursor and the sphere turns Yellow.

5. Press and hold down the left mouse button down and drag the mouse up. Stop when the values in the **Size** boxes are close to **890** Inches or **22.5** Meters.

6. Clear the pin on the **Transform** ribbon panel and then click on the **Scale** tool again to exit; the model appears similar to the one shown in Figure 49.

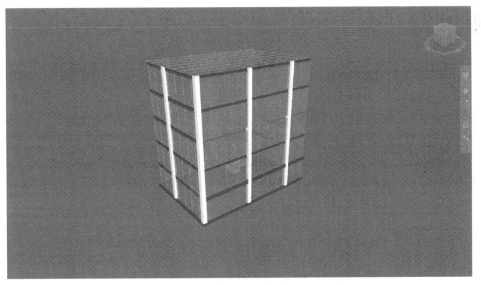

Figure 49 The model sectioned using the section box

7. From the **Save** ribbon panel, click the **Save Viewpoint** tool and rename the new viewpoint to **Section Box**.

8. From the **Transform** ribbon panel, click the **Move** tool and move the section box using the move gizmo. Notice how the model is still sectioned in a box shape.

9. Activate the **Section** viewpoint.

10. From the **Selection Tree**, expand **Office_Building.nwc** and then click **Level 2**; all the objects on Level 2 are selected.

11. From the **Viewpoint** ribbon tab > **Sectioning** ribbon panel, click **Enable Sectioning**; the **Sectioning Tools** ribbon tab is displayed.

12. From the **Mode** ribbon panel, click the **Planes** flyout and click **Box**; the model is sectioned using a box of a default size.

13. From the **Transform** ribbon panel, click **Fit Selection**; the section box resizes to fit Level 2 objects in the box.

14. Press the ESC key to deselect the objects and then exit the **Move** tool. The model looks similar to the one shown in Figure 50.

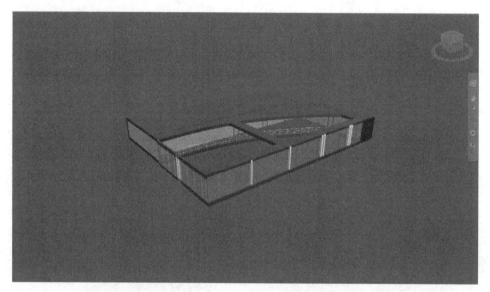

*Figure 50 The model sectioned using the **Fit Selection** option*

15. From the **Save** ribbon panel, click the **Save Viewpoint** tool and rename the viewpoint to **Section Level 2**.

16. Click the **Overview** viewpoint and save the model.

Section 8: Merging Models

In this section, you will use the **Merge** tool to merge the file you worked on in the previous sections with another Autodesk Navisworks file of the same model. As mentioned in the previous chapters, the advantage of merging files is that the geometry information is not duplicated. Only the Autodesk Navisworks objects such as viewpoints, redline markups, tags, and so on are copied.

1. Click the **Sheet Browser** button on the status bar near the lower right corner of the Autodesk Navisworks window; the **Sheet Browser** window is displayed.

2. Using the **Import Sheets & Models** button, open the **Building-V1.nwf** file from the **Chapter 4 > Exercise Building** folder.

3. Double-click on its name **Office_Building.nwc (Building-V1.nwf)** in the **Sheet Browser**.

   This model looks similar to the one you have been working on. However, the redline markups and tags in this model are different from those in the file you worked on earlier. Also, it does not have any section viewpoints you created in the previous file.

4. From the **Review** ribbon tab > **Comments** ribbon panel, click **View Comments** to dock the **Comments** window below the graphics window.

5. Activate the **Office Entrances** viewpoint and notice that a tag is added to this viewpoint. Also, the comment of the tag is displayed in the **Comments** window.

   You will now merge this file with the **C04-Building.nwd** file that you were working on earlier.

6. In the **Sheet Browser** window, double-click on **Office_Building.nwc** to switch back to the original file.

7. Again in the **Sheet Browser** window, right-click on the **Office_Building.nwc (Building-V1.nwf)** file and select **Merge into Current Model**; the two files are merged together.

   Notice how the additional viewpoints are displayed in the **Saved Viewpoints** window.

8. In the **Sheet Browser** window, right-click on the **Office_Building.nwc (Building-V1.nwf)** file and select **Delete**; the file is removed from the **Sheet Browser**.

9. Close the **Sheet Browser** window.

10. From the **Sets** window, click on the **Revolving Door** selection set; the comment that was added to this set in the **C04-Building.nwf** file is now displayed in the **Comments** window.

11. Similarly, from the **Sets** window, select the **Glazed Panels** search set; the comment that was added to this in the **C04-Building.nwf** file is displayed the **Comments** window.

12. Press ESC to deselect everything.

13. Activate the **Front Section** viewpoint and notice how this model is displayed as sectioned.

    In this file, there was a tag numbered 1. In the **C04-Building.nwf** file also, there were two tags numbered 1 and 2. This will cause confusion, so it is important to renumber the tags.

14. Expand the **Tags** ribbon panel and click **Renumber Tag IDs**; the tags will be renumbered.

15. With **1** listed in the **Tag ID** spinner in the **Tags** ribbon panel, click the **Go to Tag** button on the right of this spinner; the viewpoint changes to display tag 1, which was the tag added to the current file.

16. Type **2** in the **Tag ID** spinner in the **Tags** ribbon panel and then click the **Go to Tag** button; tag 2 is displayed in the **Alarm Sensor** viewpoint.

17. Activate the **Overview** viewpoint and then close the **Comments** window.

18. Restore the **Training** workspace from the **View** ribbon tab > **Workspace** ribbon panel > **Load Workspace** flyout.

19. Save the file.

Section 9: Exporting Viewpoints Report

As mentioned earlier, Autodesk Navisworks does not have the facility to export a report of all the redline markups, comments, and tags. However, it allows you to export the viewpoints report, which also in turn, exports these items. In this section, you will export the viewpoints report. But before doing that, you need to edit the size of the images in the viewpoint report. This is done by opening the **Options Editor** dialog box in the administrator mode.

1. Hold down the SHIFT key and then right-click and select **Global Options** from the shortcut menu; the **Options Editor** opens in the administrator mode.

2. From the left pane, expand **Interface** and select **Viewpoint Defaults**; the right pane shows the **Viewpoints Report** area below the other options. This area is not displayed if you invoke the **Options Editor** dialog box in the normal mode.

3. Change the **Image Height** to **600** and **Image Width** to **800** and then close the dialog box.

4. From the **Saved Viewpoints** window, delete the **Walkthrough** animation.

5. Right-click in the blank area of the **Saved Viewpoints** window and select **Export Viewpoints Report**; the **Export** dialog box is displayed.

6. Browse to the **Chapter 4 > Exercise Building** folder and create a subfolder there called **Report**.

7. Activate the **Report** folder and save the current file with the name **Review-Report**; the report is saved in the HTML format.

8. Using Windows Explorer, browse to the **Chapter 4 > Exercise Building > Report** folder; notice the HTML file there and also the images for all the viewpoints as well as the animation frames.

9. Double-click on the **Review-Report.html** file to open the report.

   You will notice that the redline text appears below the **Camera Position** information. However, all the tag comments are displayed in their own boxes with status, user, and time information.

10. Close this file and return to the Autodesk Navisworks window.

11. Save the file and start a new file.

Skill Evaluation

Evaluate your skills to see how many questions you can answer correctly. The answers to these questions are given at the end of the book.

1. Redline markups require a saved viewpoint to be created first. (True/False)

2. A redline text once added cannot be edited. (True/False)

3. Autodesk Navisworks allows you to add comments to a selected viewpoint animation. (True/False)

4. You can only section a model using one section plane. (True/False)

5. Section box size cannot be changed. (True/False)

6. Which tool allows you to add a balloon to an object in the current viewpoint and add text associated with it?

   (A) **Balloon**   (B) **Comments**
   (C) **Add Tag**   (D) None

7. Which tool is used to search for the comments in the current model?

   (A) **Find Comments**   (B) **Search Comments**
   (C) **Add Comments**   (D) None

8. Which of the following tools is used to draw an arrow markup?

   (A) **Leader**   (B) **Arrow**
   (C) **Redline Arrow**   (D) None

9. Which tool allows you to fit the section box around the selected objects?

   (A) **Fit**   (B) **Box Selection**
   (C) **Box**   (D) **Fit Selection**

10. What tool is used to link section planes?

    (A) **Link Plane**   (B) **Link Section**
    (C) **Link Section Plane**   (D) **Section Plane**

Class Test Questions

Answer the following questions:

1. How can you edit the redline text written in multiple lines?

2. Which section plane is by default aligned to the front face of the ViewCube?

3. In the **Add Comment** dialog box, which key allows you to write the text in the second line?

4. How do you add comments to the search sets?

5. How do you change the thickness of the redline markup?

Chapter 5 – Autodesk Navisworks Productivity Tools

The objectives of this chapter are to:

√   *Introduce you to grids and levels in the Autodesk Revit files.*
√   *Show you how to add links to the objects in Autodesk Navisworks scene.*
√   *Show you how to compare two versions of the models to find differences.*
√   *Teach you how to link external databases to Autodesk Navisworks objects.*
√   *Explain how to use the **Batch Utility** tool.*
√   *Teach you how to split the Autodesk Navisworks window.*
√   *Teach you how to work with full screen mode.*

DISPLAYING GRIDS AND LEVELS IN AN AUTODESK REVIT FILE

When you open or append a native Autodesk Revit (*.RVT) file or a .NWC file exported from Autodesk Revit, the grids and levels from that file can be viewed in Autodesk Navisworks. You are also allowed to turn off these grids and levels in the Autodesk Navisworks scene. This is done using the **Grids & Levels** ribbon panel available on the **View** ribbon tab, refer to Figure 1. Note that the options in this ribbon panel are grayed out if you open a non-Autodesk Revit file.

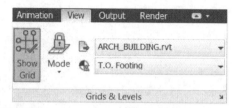

Figure 1 The Grids & Levels ribbon panel

The various options in this ribbon panel are discussed next.

 Tip: *When you open a native Autodesk Revit file, the **HUD** flyout in the **View** ribbon tab > **Navigation Aids** ribbon panel shows an addition option called **Grid Location**. Turning this option on will show the camera location based on the current grid and level.*

Show Grid

This button is used to toggle on or off the display of the grids in the model.

Mode Flyout

This flyout is used to specify how the grids will be displayed in the model. Note that most options in this flyout will only be available if the current view is shown in the perspective display. The options available in this flyout are discussed next.

Above and Below

This option displays the grids of the levels above and below the level on which the current camera is located. By default, the grids of the level below are shown in Green and the grids of the level above are shown in Red. Figure 2 shows the front of a building showing the grids using this method. This figure also shows the grid location readout on the lower left corner of the graphics window.

Above

This option displays the grids of the level above the current camera location.

Below

This options displays the grids of the level below the current camera location.

Figure 2 *The grids of the levels above and below displayed in the model*

All

This option displays the grids of all the levels of the building. Note that although the grids are turned on for all the levels, the grid labels will only be displayed on the level above and below the current camera location. For the rest of the levels, only the grid lines will be displayed.

Fixed

This option displays the grids of only the level that you specify. The level to display the grid can be selected from the **Display Level** list located on the right of this flyout. Note that this list will only be available when you select the **Fixed** grid mode.

Active Grid List

This list is used when you have multiple grids available from various Autodesk Revit files appended in the current scene. This list lets you select the grids of the file to be displayed in the scene.

Display Level List

As mentioned earlier, this list is used to select the level for which the grids will be displayed in the scene. This list will only be available when you select the **Fixed** option from the **Mode** flyout.

Changing the Grids and Levels Settings

Autodesk Navisworks allows you to change colors, label heights, and the display mode settings of grids and levels. To do this, click the **Grids Dialog Launcher** button, which is a little arrow button, on the lower right corner of the **Grids & Levels** ribbon panel. When you click this button, the **Options Editor** dialog box will be displayed with the **Grids** settings in the right pane, as shown in Figure 3. These options are discussed next.

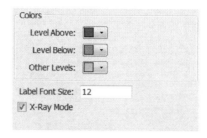

*Figure 3 The **Grids** settings*

Colors Area

The **Color** area lets you select the color of the grids on the levels above and below. The color of the other level will be used to display the grids when **All** is selected from the **Mode** list.

Label Font Size

The edit box lets you specify the height of the label text.

X-Ray Mode

If this tick box is selected, the grid lines hidden behind certain objects in the scene will be displayed with dashed lines. If this tick box is cleared, the part of the grid lines hidden behind the objects will not be displayed.

LINKING FILES AND URLs TO THE OBJECTS IN THE SCENE

Autodesk Navisworks allows you to link external files or URLs to the objects in the scene. These links are really useful to provide information such as specification sheets, service schedules, Web site addresses, and so on with the model. Consider a case where a pump in the desalination plant develops a fault. To find the details of the pump, the project manager can navigate to that pump in the Autodesk Navisworks model and click on the link associated with the pump to get all its specifications and also the supplier's Web site to order it.

Similarly, consider a building model where additional zones are to be added to the ducted air-conditioning system. The project manager can navigate to the existing ductwork in the Autodesk Navisworks model and click on the links associated with it to find how the ducts are currently configured, the details of the company, and the sales person to contact.

You can toggle on or off the visibility of the links in the Autodesk Navisworks scene. These links can also be edited at any time. However, note that if you have linked external files such as a Microsoft Word document or a PDF file, these files will also need to be provided with the Autodesk Navisworks model. You can add one or more links to the same object. If you select objects that have links added to them, the **Properties** window will show a tab called **Hyperlinks** that will show the details of the links.

Figure 4 shows an Autodesk Navisworks scene in which links are added to the platform and the handrailing. These links are enclosed in ellipses to highlight where they are located.

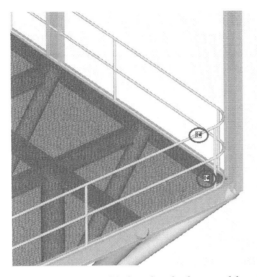

Figure 4 Links added to the platform and handrailing

The following sections show you how to add, edit, and delete links to the objects in the scene.

Adding Links to the Objects in the Scene

The following steps show you how to add links to the objects in the scene.

a. In the graphics window or the **Selection Tree**, select the objects to which the link has to be added.

b. Right-click and select **Links > Add Link** from the shortcut menu; the **Add Link** dialog box will be displayed, as shown in Figure 5.

*Figure 5 The **Add Link** dialog box*

c. Enter the name of the link in the **Name** text box. This name will be displayed whenever you move the cursor over this link icon in the graphics window.

d. If you are adding the link to an external URL, copy it from the web browser and paste it in the **Link to file or URL** text box. If you are adding the link to a file, click the **Browse** button on the right of this text box to display the **Choose Link** dialog box, as shown in Figure 6. This dialog box lets you select the file that you want to link. The **Files of type** list allows you to select files such as audio, video, Autodesk Navisworks, HTML, documents, and so on. Click **OK** in this dialog box after selecting the desired file.

Figure 6 *The **Choose Link** dialog box to link a file*

e. From the **Category** list in the **Add Link** dialog box, select the desired category. By default, there are two categories: **Hyperlink** and **Label**. By default, selecting **Hyperlink** will display an icon of the link on the model. However, selecting **Label** will display the text that you enter in the **Name** text box. If you want the link to be in a different category, enter its name in the **Category** list. For custom categories, by default, the icons are displayed in the graphics window.

 Note: *Autodesk Navisworks allows you to configure whether you want to display link as icons or text. This is discussed in detail later in this chapter.*

f. Click the **Add** button under the **Attachment Points** area and specify the location of the link icon on the object. Note that this point has to be on the object that you originally selected to add the link to. It cannot be placed in the blank area of the graphics window. If you want to edit the location of the attachment point, click the **Clear All** button and redefine the location of the attachment point using the **Add** button.

g.   Click **OK** in the dialog box to add the link.

Figure 7 shows an Autodesk Navisworks scene displaying three links of various categories. These links are enclosed in ellipses to highlight their location.

*Figure 7 Model showing various types of links (**Model courtesy Ryan McKinley, Senior Civil Drafter, Engineering and Operations, Tenix**)*

 Tip: *If you select an object that has been assigned links, the **Properties** window will show an additional tab called **Hyperlink** that shows the name, URL, and category of the link assigned to the object.*

Turning On the Visibility of the Links in the Scene

```
Home Ribbon Tab > Display Ribbon Panel > Links
```

By default, the visibility of the links is turned off in the scene. As a result, if you have added links, you will not be able to see their icons or text in the graphics window. To turn on the visibility of links, click the **Links** button on the **Home** ribbon tab > **Display** ribbon panel.

Controlling the Global Display of Links

When you turn on the visibility of links in the scene, by default, Autodesk Navisworks not only displays the text and icons of links but also the icons of viewpoints, redline tags, timeliner, quantifications, clashes, and so on. With all these icons turned on, the screen looks cluttered. To reduce this cluttering, you can use the **Options Editor** dialog box and turn off the visibility of the unwanted icons. The following steps show you how to do this.

a.   Press F12 to display the **Options Editor** dialog box.

b. From the left pane, expand **Interface > Links** and click on **Standard Categories**; the right pane will display all the standard categories for which the link visibility is turned on.

c. From the right pane, turn off the visibility of all the icons, except those of hyperlink and label.

d. Using the **Icon Type** list, you can decide whether to display the icon or the text of the link in the graphics window for these categories.

e. From the left pane, click **User-Defined Categories**; the right pane shows the categories that you have created. If need be, turn off the visibility of any of these category icons.

f. Click **OK** in the dialog box.

Editing the Links Assigned to the Objects

The links, once added, can also be edited at any stage. The editing includes changing the name of the link, the linked file or URL, the attachment point, and so on. The following steps show you how to do this.

a. In the graphics window, right-click on the link icon or text; a shortcut menu will be displayed, as shown in Figure 8.

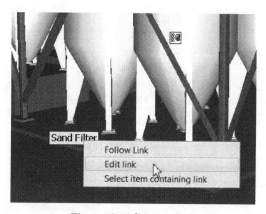

Figure 8 Editing a link

b. From this shortcut menu, click **Edit Link**; the **Edit Links** dialog box will be displayed, as shown in Figure 9.

 *Tip: The **Edit Links** dialog box shown in Figure 9 can also be used to add additional links or delete existing links.*

c. Click on the name of the link under the **Name** column and then click the **Edit** button from the right side of the dialog box; the **Edit Link** dialog box will be displayed. This dialog box is similar to the **Add Link** dialog box. You can edit the name, the linked file or URL, the category, or the attachment point of the link using this dialog box.

d. Exit the dialog boxes to return back to the graphics window.

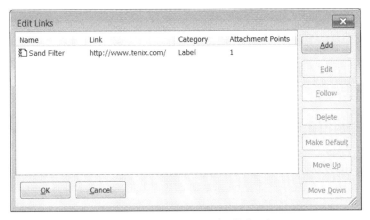

Figure 9 *The* **Edit Links** *dialog box*

 Note: *You can assign multiple links to the same objects. All the assigned links will be displayed in the graphics window if they are turned on. When you edit one of the links of that object, all the links assigned to it will be displayed in the* **Edit Links** *dialog box.*

Following the Links Assigned to the Objects

The links assigned to the object can be opened at any time by selecting the link or the object and using the right-click shortcut menu. The following steps show you how to do this.

a. In the graphics window, right-click on the link icon or text and click **Follow Link** from the shortcut menu; the linked file or URL will be opened.

b. Alternatively, right-click on the object to which the link is assigned and move the cursor over **Links** in the shortcut menu; all the links assigned to the object are displayed, as shown in Figure 10.

c. From the cascading shortcut menu, click on the link that you want to open.

 Tip: *You can also select the object to which the link is assigned and right-click in the* **Hyperlink** *tab of the* **Properties** *window to follow a link. But in this case, you can only follow the default link, which is the first link assigned to the object. You can change the order of the links using the* **Edit Links** *dialog box shown in the earlier sections. Alternatively, you can click on a link in this dialog box and then click the* **Make Default** *button to make the selected link as the default link.*

COMPARING MODELS OR OBJECTS IN THE SCENE

> **Home Ribbon Tab > Tools Ribbon Panel > Compare**

While working on a large project, you will regularly get updated models from various teams. Some times, it will be hard for you to understand the differences between the previous version of the model and the latest version that you are given. To overcome this problem, Autodesk Navisworks provides the **Compare** tool. This tool allows you to compare two versions of the files

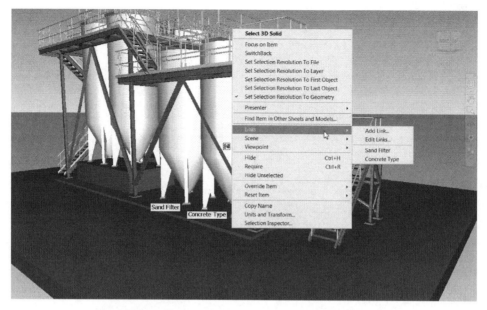

Figure 10 *Following the link by right-clicking on the object*

by appending them in a scene. It also allows you to compare two selected objects in the scene. Note that this tool will only be available when you select two files or objects in the scene.

When you invoke this tool, the **Compare** dialog box will be displayed, as shown in Figure 11.

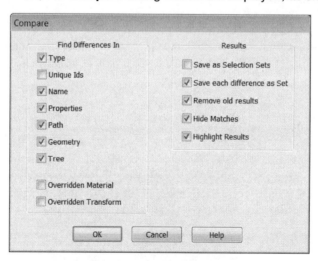

Figure 11 *The **Compare** dialog box*

The options available in this dialog box are discussed next.

Find Differences In Area

This area allows you to select the object properties that you want to compare to find the differences in. If you have moved or changed the appearance of the models in Autodesk Navisworks, make sure you clear the **Overridden Material** and **Overridden Transform** tick boxes. This will ensure that the material and location overrides of the objects in the model are not compared.

Results Area
This area allows you to specify how you want to display the comparison results. The options in this area are discussed next.

Save as Selection Sets
Selecting this tick box allows you to create selection sets of the objects that are matched, objects that are unmatched, and the objects that are different in each of the files. The **Comments** window displays the comments about all of these sets.

Save each difference as Set
Selecting this tick box will ensure that the differences of the objects selected to compare are saved as sets. This will allow you to click on the sets to view the differences in the graphics window. If the **Comments** window is docked on the screen, the comments about the comparison result of the selected set will also be displayed in this window.

Remove old results
Selecting this tick box will delete the sets created as part of any old comparison.

Hide Matches
Selecting this tick box will hide the objects that are matching. This allows only the visibility of the non-matching objects and so it will be easier for you to view the differences.

Highlight Results
Selecting this tick box allows you to highlight the results of the comparison in the graphics window.

Procedure to Compare the Models
The following steps show you how to compare two different models.

a. Start a new file in Autodesk Navisworks and append the two versions of the model.

b. Create a viewpoint and rename it as **Original View**. Turn on the option save hide/required objects by editing this view. This is to return back to the original view after comparing the two models.

c. From the **Selection Tree**, select both the files.

d. From the **Home** ribbon tab > **Tools** ribbon pane, invoke the **Compare** tool; the **Compare** dialog box will be displayed.

e. Select the required options in the dialog box and click **OK**; the comparison result will be displayed in the graphics window.

f.   Activate the **Sets** window and click on the sets, if created, to view the differences between the two models.

LINKING EXTERNAL DATABASES TO THE AUTODESK NAVISWORKS OBJECTS

Depending on how the model was created in the native program, when you create an Autodesk Navisworks scene using those models, the objects may not have all the required properties associated with them. Also, if the models from the native program are exported in formats such as DWG, to be made available on a supplier's Web site, most of the associated properties will be lost. As a result, when you click on these models, they will only have basic properties associated with them. As mentioned in the earlier chapters, you can select such objects and manually create their custom properties. However, if there is a large amount of property data to be associated with the objects, it is not feasible to do it manually. Also, if the properties that you need to assign are available in the external databases, it is recommended to link the database itself, rather than adding the properties manually.

For example, consider a case where you need to assign the specifications written in a database to all the pumps, heat exchangers, and the valves in the plant model shown in Figure 12. In this case, you can link the properties in the external databases directly to the objects in the Autodesk Navisworks scene using the **DataTools**.

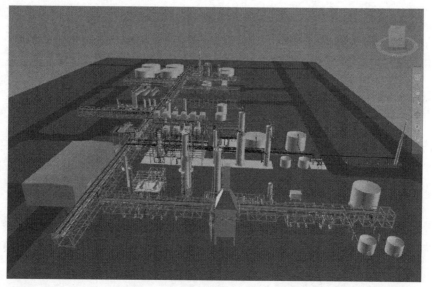

*Figure 12 A large plant model to assign database properties (**Model courtesy Tomislav Golubovic and Ian Matthew, Autodesk Inc.**)*

The **DataTools** use the ODBC drivers to assign the properties from the external databases to the objects in the current Autodesk Navisworks scene. It is important to mention here that if you are using a 32-BIT computer that has a database program such as Microsoft Excel, Microsoft Access, and so on installed, the 32-BIT ODBC drivers will work with the **DataTools** in Autodesk Navisworks on that computer without any problem. However, on a 64-BIT computer, the 32-BIT

ODBC drivers will not work by default. To make the ODBC drivers on a 64-BIT computer work with the **DataTools** in Autodesk Navisworks, you will have to make some changes on that computer. The following section explains the changes that have to be made on these machines.

Getting a 64-BIT Computer Ready to Use DataTools

To be able to get a 64-BIT computer ready to use the **DataTools**, you will have to uninstall and later reinstall 32-BIT Microsoft Office on your computer. To make sure it goes ahead smoothly, it is important that you have the installer media of Microsoft Office and related product codes handy. Also, you will need the administrative rights on your computer to uninstall and install the software. If need be, get your IT helpdesk involved in this process.

The following is what you need to do:

a.   Go to the following Web page:

http://www.microsoft.com/en-us/download/details.aspx?id=13255

b.   Click on the **Download** button and download the **AccessDatabaseEngine_x64.exe** file.

c.   Uninstall Microsoft Office and all the other 32-BIT Microsoft Office software that are installed on your computer.

d   Uninstall Microsoft Access Database Engine 2010 Redistributable 32-BIT, if it is installed on your computer.

e.   Install Microsoft Access Database Engine 2010 Redistributable 64-BIT that you downloaded in step b.

f.   Reinstall Microsoft Office and all the other Microsoft Office software that you uninstalled.

This will ensure that your computer is able to use the ODBC drivers to link external databases to the objects in Autodesk Navisworks.

Linking Database Properties

In Autodesk Navisworks, you can link the database to a particular file or to the Autodesk Navisworks application. If the database is linked to the file, it will only be available for use in that particular file. However, if you link the database to the application, it will be available for use in any file that you work with. The following sections explain how to link database to a file and to the application.

Linking Database to an Autodesk Navisworks File

This method is used when you want to link the database to a particular file. The following is what you need to do:

a.   Open the file that has objects to which you want to link the database properties.

b.   Right-click in the blank area of the graphics window and click **File Options** from the shortcut menu; the **File Options** dialog box will be displayed.

c. Click the **DataTools** tab, which is the last tab in the dialog box. If there are databases already assigned to this file, they will be listed here.

d. Click the **New** button to display the **New Link** dialog box, as shown in Figure 13.

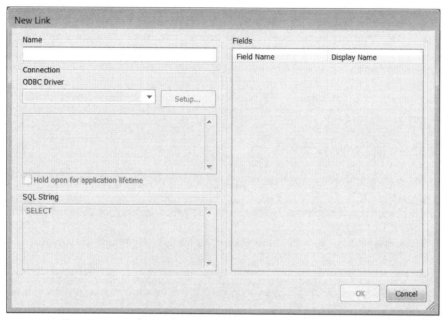

*Figure 13 The **New Link** dialog box to link an external database*

e. Enter the name of this link in the **Name** edit box. This name will also be assigned to the tab that will appear in the **Properties** window when you select the objects to which the database is linked.

f. Select the ODBC driver you want to use from the **ODBC Driver** list.

g. Click the **Setup** button on the right of **ODBC Driver** list to select the database file that you want to link.

   *Tip: If clicking the **Setup** button does not display any dialog box, this means that the ODBC drivers are not working. If you have already performed the steps to get your 64-BIT computer ready to use the **DataTools** discussed on the previous page, you will have to get the assistance of the IT helpdesk to get it working.*

h. In the **SQL String** area, enter the SQL query to link the information in the database to the objects in the Autodesk Navisworks scene. There are some sample queries discussed after the next section.

i. In the **Fields** area on the right side of the **New Link** dialog box, double-click in the first row under the **Field Name** column and enter the name of the column that you are linking from the external database. Note that the name here should be entered exactly the way the name of the column appears in the database.

j.   Double-click on the first row under **Display Name** and enter how you want the database column name to be displayed in the Autodesk Navisworks **Properties** window.

k.   Click **OK** in the **New Link** dialog box to return to the **File Options** dialog box; the database link that you created will now be listed here.

Linking Database to the Autodesk Navisworks Application

This method is used when you want to link the database that is available in all the files that you work on in future. The following is what you need to do:

a.   From the **Home** ribbon tab > **Tools** ribbon panel, click **DataTools**; the **DataTools** dialog box will be displayed. This dialog box already has some database link templates available, as shown in Figure 14.

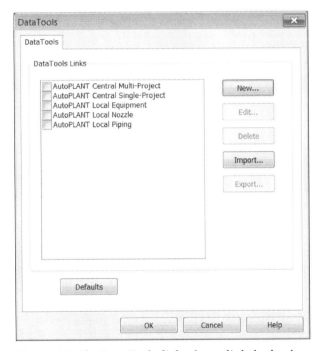

*Figure 14 The **DataTools** dialog box to link the database to the Autodesk Navisworks application*

b.   Click the **New** button to display the **New Link** dialog box. This is the name of the tab that will appear in the **Properties** window when you select the objects to which the database is linked.

c.   Enter the name of this link in the **Name** edit box.

d.   Select the ODBC driver you want to use from the **ODBC Driver** list.

e.   Click the **Setup** button on the right of **ODBC Driver** list to select the database file that you want to link.

 Tip: *If clicking the **Setup** button does not display any dialog box, this means that the ODBC drivers are not working. If you have already performed the steps to get your 64-BIT computer ready to use the **DataTools** discussed on the previous page, you will have to seek the assistance of the IT helpdesk to get it working.*

f.   In the **SQL String** area, enter the SQL query to link the information in the database to the objects in the Autodesk Navisworks scene. There are some sample queries discussed after the next section.

g.   In the **Fields** area on the right side of the **New Link** dialog box, double-click in the first row under the **Field Name** column and enter the name of the column that you are linking from the external database. Note that the name here should be entered exactly the way the name of the column appears in the database.

h.   Double-click in the first row under **Display Name** and enter how you want the database column name to be displayed in Autodesk Navisworks **Properties** window.

i.   Click **OK** in the **New Link** dialog box to return to the **DataTools** dialog box; the database link that you created will now be listed here.

SQL Query Strings

The SQL query string that you add to link the table has to be in a specific format. It needs to include the name of the database that you are linking and the name of the column to be linked. You also need to specify the matching object property to which the column in the database is to be linked. If you want to link all the columns from the database, you can use asterisk (*) for the column names. Also, make sure that the spaces are only added between the required words. For example, there is no space after %prop in the examples below.

The following examples illustrate sample SQL queries and their descriptions.

Example 1:

   SELECT DETAILS From PlantDetails Where CLASS = %prop("AutoCad","Class")

   In this query, you are opening a database table called **PlantDetails**. This database has two columns, **CLASS** and **DETAILS**, as shown in Figure 15. The **DataTools** will search for the Autodesk Navisworks objects that have the **AutoCad** category property called **Class** and the value matching with the values in the **CLASS** column shown below. Once found, they will be assigned the properties in the **DETAILS** column of the database.

Example 2:

   SELECT * FROM ProjectInfo WHERE REVITTYPE = %prop("Revit Type","Name")

1	2
CLASS ▾	**DETAILS** ▾
HeatExchanger	MOC SS Duplex + Ti Cladded
Pump	250m³/h; 1100USgpm
Valve	BS 5163, 150 microns
Reducer	MAX W/B Ratio = 0.5

Figure 15 The database sample

In this query, you are opening a database table called **ProjectInfo**, shown in Figure 16. You want to assign the properties in all the columns in this database, therefore, you have used asterisk (*) in the query. The **DataTools** will search for the Autodesk Navisworks objects that have the **Revit Type** category property called **Name** and the value matching with those in the **REVITTYPE** column. Once found, they will be assigned the properties in all the columns of the database.

1	2	3	4
REVITTYPE ▾	**SUPPLIER** ▾	**AUTHORIZED BY** ▾	**WEBSITE** ▾
Clear Glazing	Viridian	Project Engineer	http://www.viridianglass.com.au/
Interior Glazing	AU Glass	Project Engineer	http://www.australianglassgroup.com.au/
No Vision Glazing	AU Glass	Project Engineer	http://www.australianglassgroup.com.au/
Baby Changing Station	Kaola Kare	Interior Designer	http://www.babychangestations.com.au
Hand Dryer	Dyson	Interior Designer	http://www.dyson.com.au/dryers/

Figure 16 The database sample

WORKING WITH THE BATCH UTILITY TOOL

```
Home Ribbon Tab > Tools Ribbon Panel > Batch Utility
```

The **Batch Utility** tool allows you to schedule the process of appending files from a certain location and outputting them as a .NWD or a .NWF file. Consider a case where various contractors working on a project upload files on a network location every Wednesday night. So instead of the project manager coming in on Thursday morning and manually appending all the files to create an Autodesk Navisworks scene, they can schedule the **Batch Utility** tool to do it automatically. This tool will select all the defined file types from a specified folder and then append them together to create an Autodesk Navisworks scene. This scene can then be saved as a single or multiple .NWD file or .NWF files, depending on your requirements.

When you invoke this tool, the **Navisworks Batch Utility** dialog box will be displayed, as shown in Figure 17. The options available in this area are discussed next.

Input Area

The options in this area are used to specify the information about the input files. Click on the list at the top of this area to select the disk drive from which you want to input the files. The area below this list allows you to select a particular folder on the selected drive where the input files are saved or will be copied for scheduling. The list below this area allows you to select the files of type that you want to select for inputting.

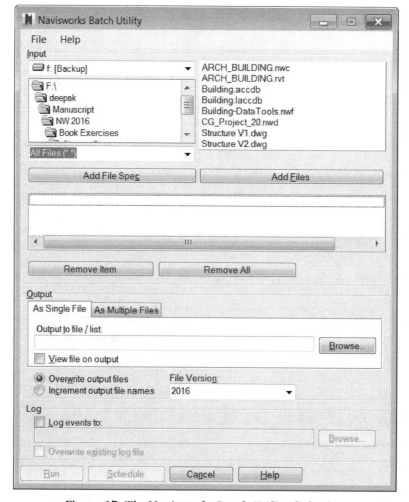

Figure 17 *The **Navisworks Batch Utility** dialog box*

When you select the file type, all the files of that type available inside the specified folder will be listed in the area on the right. You can select the files to be added from this area and then click the **Add Files** button. Alternatively, you can click the **Add File Spec** button to select all the files of that type. This button is also used when you are scheduling the appending of files that are not available in that folder yet. The **Remove Item** is used to remove the selected files or file spec from being used.

Figure 18 shows the **Input** area showing various types of files to be selected for appending from the **Navisworks Project** folder on the **I: (Backup)** drive.

 Note: *If you select the .NWD file as the input file, you will have to ensure that this file was originally published with **May be re-saved** tick box selected in the **Publish** dialog box.*

Output Area

The options in this area are used to specify the location and format of the output file. By default,

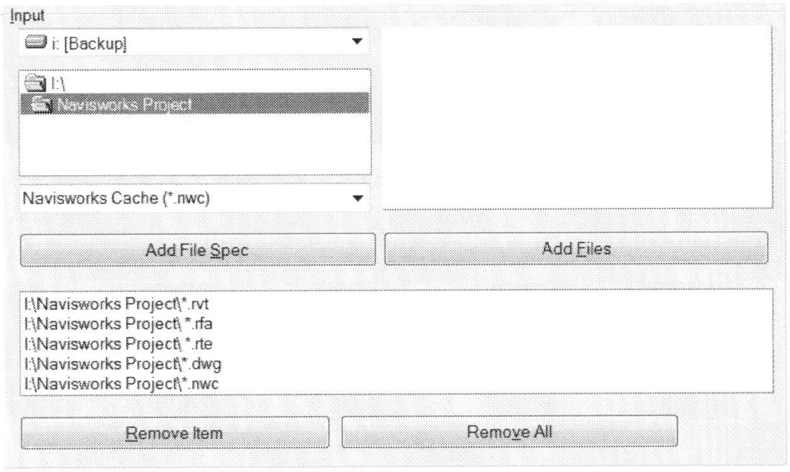

Figure 18 *The **Input** area showing the file types to be selected for appending*

the **As Single File** tab is active. This tab is used to save the Autodesk Navisworks scene as a single file. Click the **Browse** button on the right side of the **Out to file / list** box; the **Save output as** dialog box will be displayed. This dialog box allows you to specify the location of the output file. You can also click on the **Save as type** list in this dialog box to specify whether you want to save the output file as a .NWD file or a .NWF file. The **View file on output** tick box will open the output file as soon as it is created.

If you want to save multiple output files, activate the **As Multiple Files** tab. Note that in this case, the output files can only be saved as .NWD files and not as .NWF files. Using the options in this tab, you can decide to save the output files in the same location as the input files or you can specify the location where you want to save the output files using the **Browse** button.

If there are files with the same name as the output files in the folder that you select to save the output files, you can decide to overwrite them by selecting the **Overwrite output files** radio button. Alternatively, you can select the **Increment output file names** radio button to retain the existing files and increment the output file names with a four digit number, starting with 0001.

Figure 19 shows the **Output** area showing the options to output a single NWD file.

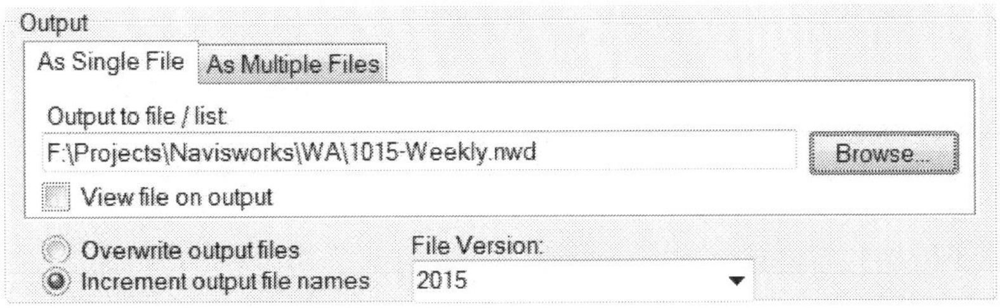

Figure 19 *The **Output** area showing the options to output a single NWD file*

Log Area

If something goes wrong while creating the output file, it is important for you to know. This can be done by writing a log file that can be viewed for any error at a later stage. To do this, click the **Log events to** tick box in the **Log** area and specify the location and the name of the log file using the **Browse** button. Selecting the **Overwrite existing log file** tick box allows you to overwrite any existing log file with the latest information.

Run

This button is used to run the **Batch Utility** tool straight away to create the output file.

Schedule

This button is used to schedule the creation of the output file for a later time. This is done by creating a schedule task file. When you click this button, the **Save task file as** dialog box will be displayed. This dialog box allows you to specify the location of the schedule task file. This file is saved as a .TXT file. After you specify the location of this file, and click **Save** in the **Save task file as** dialog box, the **Schedule Task** dialog box will be displayed. This dialog box allows you to enter the credentials of the user account that will be used to create the output file, see Figure 20.

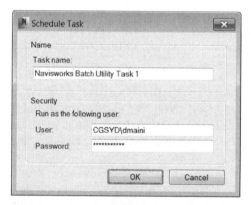

*Figure 20 The **Schedule Task** dialog box*

Specify the user account information in this dialog box and then click **OK**; the **Navisworks Batch Utility** dialog box will be displayed. This dialog box has three tabs. These tabs are discussed next.

Task Tab

This tab shows you the information that you specified to create the scheduled task and the login account that will be used to run the task.

Schedule Tab

This tab allows you to schedule when you want to run the **Batch Utility** tool. By default, this tab will show **<Task not scheduled>** as there are no tasks scheduled. To schedule a task, click the **New** button; the lower half of the dialog box will be activated and will show you the options to schedule the task. Using these options, you can specify how often you want to run this task and also start day and time. Figure 21 shows this tab with a task scheduled to run at 4:00 AM every Thursday.

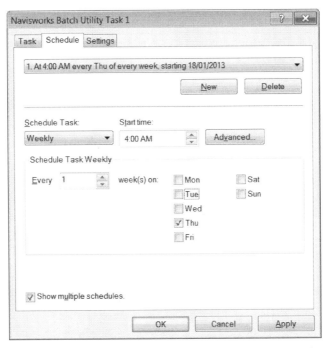

*Figure 21 Specifying the schedule to run the **Batch Utility** tool weekly*

Settings Tab

This tab is used to specify what happens after the completion of the task. It also provides the options related to the idle time of the computer and power management.

SPLITTING THE AUTODESK NAVISWORKS VIEW

View Ribbon Tab > Scene View Ribbon Panel > Split View Flyout

Autodesk Navisworks allows you to split the graphics window horizontally or vertically to view the same model in multiple windows. This allows you to zoom into an area to view the details in one window and still display the entire model in the other window. Using the **Split View** flyout, you can split the window horizontally or vertically. You can click on any of the split windows to make it active. The active split window can further be split using the same way. Note that performing operations such as selecting, hiding, etc. on the objects in one window will also be reflected in other windows. However, performing operations such as sectioning in one window will not be reflected in the other window. So you will be able to view the sectioned model in one window and the complete model in the other window.

The secondary window will have the **Close** button on the top right. You can use this button to turn off this window and end the splitting.

Figure 22 shows the Autodesk Navisworks window split vertically into two. The left window shows the model sectioned, whereas the right window shows the complete model.

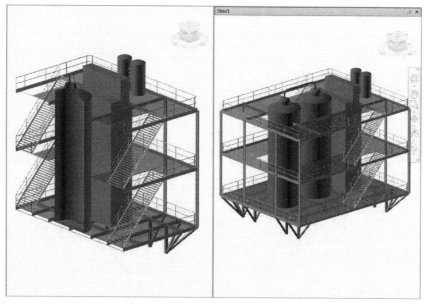

Figure 22 Autodesk Navisworks window split vertically with the left window showing sectioned model

WORKING WITH THE FULL SCREEN DISPLAY

View Ribbon Tab > Scene View Ribbon Panel > Full Screen
Shortcut Key: F11

While presenting your Autodesk Navisworks design to the customer or the stakeholders, you can view the model in full screen display also. This display mode only displays the content of the graphics window and turns off all the other windows and ribbons from the screen. This is a handy feature, especially while playing animations. This can be done using the **Full Screen** tool on the **View** ribbon tab > **Scene View** ribbon panel or using the F11 shortcut key.

Note that once you are in the full screen mode, pressing the ESC key will not restore the normal Autodesk Navisworks window. You will have to press the F11 shortcut key to exit out of the full screen model. Alternatively, you can right-click and then select **Viewpoint > Full Screen** from the shortcut menu.

THE SWITCHBACK FUNCTIONALITY

Autodesk Navisworks provides you with a very smart functionality called switchback, which allows you to switch back to the native CAD software from the NWF or NWD files, if you are working with the native files. This is a very useful functionality to modify the CAD model in the native CAD software. However, for this functionality to work, you need to have the CAD software installed on the same computer as Autodesk Navisworks and also get it ready for switchback.

The following procedures show how to use the switchback functionality with various CAD software.

Using the Switchback Functionality with AutoCAD or AutoCAD-Based Software

Remember that the switchback functionality is only available with AutoCAD 2004 or later versions. The following steps show you how to use the switchback functionality with AutoCAD or AutoCAD-based software such as AutoCAD Plant 3D, AutoCAD Mechanical, and so on.

a. Start AutoCAD or AutoCAD-based program.

b. Type a command **NWLOAD** and press ENTER; the command line will show **Navisworks ready**.

*Note: If you regularly work with the switchback functionality, you can add the option to automatically load the Autodesk Navisworks exporter plug-in in AutoCAD. This can be done by adding the required version of the Autodesk Navisworks exporter in the **Startup Suite** of the **Load/Unload Applications** dialog box displayed using the **APPLOAD** command in AutoCAD. The exporter is generally available in the **<Install Drive>:\Program Files\Common Files\Autodesk Shared\Navisworks\2016\nwexport20XX** folder where XX is the release number.*

*Tip: When you type the **NWLOAD** command and get an error about the unknown command, it means that Autodesk Navisworks was installed before installing AutoCAD or AutoCAD-based software. This can be resolved by loading the Autodesk Navisworks exporter utility using the **APPLOAD** command. As mentioned earlier, the exporter is generally available in the **<Install Drive>:\Program Files\Common Files\Autodesk Shared\Navisworks\2016\nwexport20XX** folder where XX is the release number.*

c. Return to the Autodesk Navisworks window. Right-click on the DWG file in the **Selection Tree** or any object of the DWG file in the graphics window and click **SwitchBack** from the shortcut menu; the model will be opened in AutoCAD or the AutoCAD-based software zoomed to the same view as that in Autodesk Navisworks.

d. Make the modification in the model, as required, and then save the file.

e. Return to the Autodesk Navisworks window and then click the **Refresh** button on the **Quick Access Toolbar**; the changes you made in the DWG file will be reflected in the Autodesk Navisworks scene.

Using the Switchback Functionality with Microstation V7/V8 or Software Based on Them

The following steps show you how to use the switchback functionality with Microstation V7/V8 or the software based on them.

a. Start Microstation V7/V8 or the program based on them.

b. Click **Utilities > Key In** to display the **Key-In** dialog box.

c. In the dialog box, type **MDL LOAD NWEXPORT10** and exit the dialog box.

 Note: If you regularly work with the switchback functionality with Microstation, it is better to add NWEXPORT10 to the MDL plug-ins.

d. Return to the Autodesk Navisworks window. Right-click on the Microstation file in the **Selection Tree** or any object of that file in the graphics window and click **SwitchBack** from the shortcut menu; the model will be loaded in Microstation.

e. Make the required changes in the model in Microstation and save the file.

f. Return to the Autodesk Navisworks window and then click the **Refresh** button on the **Quick Access Toolbar**; the changes you made in the Microstation will be reflected in the Autodesk Navisworks scene.

Using the Switchback Functionality with Autodesk Revit

Remember that the switchback functionality only works with Autodesk Revit 2012 or later. The following steps show you how to use the switchback functionality to resolve clashes in Autodesk Revit.

a. Start Autodesk Revit and then start a new project or open an existing project.

b. Click the **Add-Ins** ribbon tab.

c. From the **External** ribbon panel, click **External Tools** flyout > **Navisworks Switchback 2016**.

d. Return to the Autodesk Navisworks window. Right-click on the Autodesk Revit file in the **Selection Tree** or any object of that file in the graphics window and select **SwitchBack** from the shortcut menu; the model will be loaded in Autodesk Revit.

e. Make the required changes in the model in Autodesk Revit and save the file.

f. Return to the Autodesk Navisworks window and then click the **Refresh** button on the **Quick Access Toolbar**; the changes you made in the Autodesk Revit will be reflected in the Autodesk Navisworks scene.

Using the Switchback Functionality with Autodesk Inventor

Autodesk Inventor does not need any special setup to get it ready for switchback. It just needs to be started alongside Autodesk Navisworks. However, it is recommended that the project is changed to the project of the design you are working on in Autodesk Navisworks. The following steps show how to use the switchback functionality with Autodesk Inventor.

a. Start Autodesk Inventor and change the project to the project of the file opened in Autodesk Navisworks.

b. Return to the Autodesk Navisworks window. Right-click on the Autodesk Inventor file in the **Selection Tree** or any object of the that file in the graphics window and select **SwitchBack** from the shortcut menu; the model will be loaded in Autodesk Inventor.

c. Make the required changes in the model in Autodesk Inventor and save the file.

d. Return to the Autodesk Navisworks window and then click the **Refresh** button on the **Quick Access Toolbar**; the changes you made in the Autodesk Inventor will be reflected in the Autodesk Navisworks scene.

HANDS-ON EXERCISES

You will now work on some hands-on exercises using the concepts learned in this chapter.

Hands-on Exercise (Plant)	*In this exercise, you will complete the following tasks:* 1. *Open the **Sand Filters.nwd** file and turn on the visibility of links.* 2. *Activate various viewpoints and add links to the objects in the scene.* 3. *Edit links that you have added to the objects in the model.* 4. *Open two different versions of a design and compare the two models.* 5. *Open the Equipments.nwd file and attach an external database to the objects in this file.* 6. *Use the **Batch Utility** tool to schedule the process of creating Autodesk Navisworks files by appending various files.*

Section 1: Opening the NWD File and Turning On the Visibility of Links

In this section, you will open the **Sand Filters.nwd** file **(courtesy Ryan McKinley, Senior Civil Drafter, Engineering and Operations, Tenix)**. You will use various viewpoints in this file to add links. But to make sure that these links can be seen in the graphics window, you will first turn on the visibility of links.

1. From the **Chapter 5 > Exercise Plant** folder, open the **Sand Filters.nwd** file.

   For the better visibility of the model, you first need to change the lighting style.

2. From the **Viewpoint** ribbon tab > **Render Style** ribbon panel > **Lighting** flyout, click **Scene Lights**; the lighting in the scene becomes brighter.

3. Click the **Home** ribbon tab. Figure 23 shows the scene in this file.

Figure 23 *The scene in the **Sand Filters.nwd** file (**Model courtesy Ryan McKinley, Senior Civil Drafter, Engineering and Operations, Tenix**)*

Next, you will turn on the visibility of links in the scene.

4. From the **Home** ribbon tab > **Display** ribbon panel, click the **Links** button to turn on the visibility of links.

    You will notice that there are some link icons displayed on the model. This is because by default, when you turn on the visibility of links, the icons of the saved viewpoints and sets are also displayed in the graphics window. You need to turn these off using the **Options Editor** dialog box.

5. Press the F12 key to display the **Options Editor** dialog box.

6. From the left pane, expand **Interface > Links** and then click **Standard Categories**; the right pane displays the categories for which the links are visible.

7. From the right pane, turn off the visibility of all the links except hyperlink and label and then click **OK** in the dialog box to exit.

Section 2: Adding Links

As mentioned earlier, you will use various saved viewpoints to add links to the objects in the scene.

1. Activate the **Access Foundation** viewpoint.

2. Select the foundation platform on which the oxidation filters are mounted, refer to Figure 24.

3. Right-click on the selected platform and select **Links > Add Link** from the shortcut menu; the **Add Link** dialog box is displayed.

4. Enter the name of the link as **Sand Filter Platform** in the **Name** text box.

5. In the **Link to file or URL** text box, type **http://www.tenix.com/**.

6. From the **Category** list, select **Label**.

7. From the **Attachment Points** area, click the **Add** button and pick a point where it shows **Sand Filter Platform** in Figure 24.

8. Click **OK** in the dialog box; the link is added and is displayed as label in the graphics window, as shown in Figure 24.

    Next, you will add another link to the same platform.

9. Right-click on the same foundation platform and select **Links > Add Link** from the shortcut menu; the **Add Link** dialog box is displayed.

10. Enter the name of the link as **Concrete Type** in the **Name** text box.

11. In the **Link to file or URL** text box, type **http://boral.com.au/**.

12. From the **Category** list, select **Label**.

13. From the **Attachment Points** area, click the **Add** button and pick a point where it shows **Concrete Type** in Figure 24.

14. Click **OK** in the dialog box; the link is added and is displayed as label in the graphics window, as shown in Figure 24.

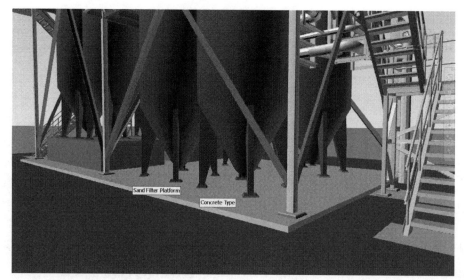

Figure 24 The scene showing the two links added to the foundation platform

Next, you will add the link to one of the oxidation filters by activating the **Oxidation Filter** viewpoint.

15. Activate the **Oxidation Filter** viewpoint.

16. Right-click on the oxidation filter nearest to you (the Red cylindrical vessel) and select **Links > Add Link** from the shortcut menu; the **Add Link** dialog box is displayed.

17. Enter the name of the link as **Oxidation Filter** in the **Name** text box.

18. In the **Link to file or URL** text box, type **http://www.tenix.com/**.

19. From the **Category** list, select **Hyperlink**.

20. From the **Attachment Points** area, click the **Add** button and pick a point anywhere on the oxidation filter, refer to Figure 25.

21. Click **OK** in the dialog box; the link is added and is displayed as an icon in the graphics window. For your convenience, the link is encircled in an ellipse in Figure 25.

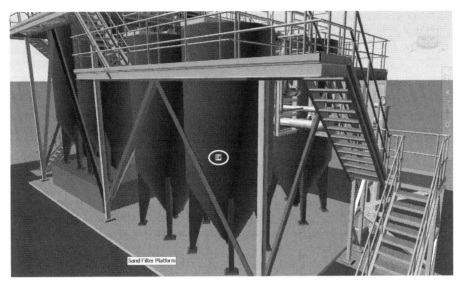

Figure 25 *The scene showing the link added to the oxidation filter*

Next, you will add the link to one of the handrails by activating the **Handrailing** viewpoint.

22. Activate the **Handrailing** viewpoint.

23. Right-click on one of the handrails in this viewpoint and select **Links > Add Link** from the shortcut menu; the **Add Link** dialog box is displayed.

24. Enter the name of the link as **Handrailing** in the **Name** text box.

25. In the **Link to file or URL** text box, type **Webforge Handrailing**.

26. From the **Category** list, select **Label**.

27. From the **Attachment Points** area, click the **Add** button and pick a point anywhere on the handrails that you selected, refer to Figure 26.

28. Click **OK** in the dialog box and then press ESC to deselect the handrails; the link is added and is displayed as a label in the graphics window, as shown inside the ellipse in Figure 26.

Section 3: Following and Editing Links

The main reason of adding links to the objects in the scene is that you can use those links to display the related information. This can be done by following the links, which is what you will do in this section.

1. Activate the **Access Foundation** viewpoint.

2. Click on the **Sand Filter Platform** link; a Web browser is opened that takes you to the Tenix Web site. This is because you specified this Web site as the URL for this link.

Figure 26 *The scene showing the link added to the handrails*

3. Return back to the Autodesk Navisworks window.

4. Click on the **Concrete Type** link; a Web browser is opened that takes you to the Boral Web site. This is because you specified this Web site as the URL for this link.

5. Return back to the Autodesk Navisworks window and activate the **Handrailing** viewpoint.

6. Click on the **Handrailing** link; an error dialog box is displayed informing you that it failed to resolve the link. This is because there was no URL or file associated with the link.

   You will now edit this link to add a URL.

7. Right-click on the **Handrailing** link and click **Edit Link** from the shortcut menu; the **Edit Links** dialog box is displayed, as shown in Figure 27.

8. In the dialog box, right-click on **Handrailing** under the **Name** column and click **Edit** from the shortcut menu; the **Edit Link** dialog box is displayed.

9. In the **Link to file or URL** text box, type **http://www.webforge.com.au/** and click **OK** in the dialog box.

10. Click **OK** in the **Edit Links** dialog box.

11. Click on the **Handrailing** link; a Web browser is opened that takes you to the Webforge Web site. This is because you specified this Web site as the URL for this link.

12. Close the Web browser and return to the Autodesk Navisworks window.

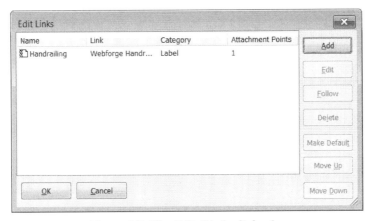

Figure 27 *The **Edit Links** dialog box*

13. From the **Home** ribbon tab > **Display** ribbon panel, click the **Links** button to turn off the visibility of links.

14. Save the file.

Section 4: Comparing Two Versions of a Model

As mentioned earlier, while working on a large project, you will regularly get updated models from various contractors. In this section, you will learn to find the differences between two versions of the same model by comparing them.

1. Start a new file and then append the **Vessel-Assem V1.nwc** and **Vessel-Assem V2.nwc** files from the **Chapter 5 > Exercise Plant** folder.

2. Change the view to the **Home** view and then dock the **Comments** window at the bottom of the graphics window.

   Next, you will save the current viewpoint so that you can restore the visibility of the objects after comparing the two models.

3. Save the current viewpoint with the name **Initial View**. Edit this viewpoint and turn on the **Hide/Required** and **Override Appearance** options.

4. From the **Selection Tree** select both the files.

5. From the **Home** ribbon tab > **Tools** ribbon panel, click the **Compare** button; the **Compare** dialog box is displayed.

6. Select the options in this dialog box, as shown in Figure 28.

7. Click **OK** in the dialog box.

8. Dock the **Sets** window below the **Selection Tree**; the sets created during the comparison of the two models are displayed in the **Sets** window.

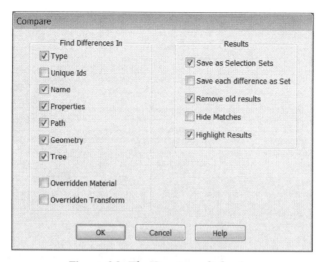

Figure 28 *The* ***Compare*** *dialog box*

9. Resize the **Sets** window so that you can see full names of the sets. Then click on the first set named **Compare:Matched:Vessel-Assem V1.nwc**; the **Comments** window shows 371 objects in this file matched with the other file.

10. Click on the second set named **Compare:Matched:Vessel-Assem V2.nwc** and you will see that the **Comments** window shows the same comment.

    This is to inform you that 371 objects matched in both the files.

11. Click on the set named **Compare:Differences:Vessel-Assem V1.nwc**; the **Comments** window shows 5 objects have differences. Also, the objects that have differences are highlighted, see Figure 29.

What I do

Depending on the content in the models that I am comparing, I generally turn off the ***Hide Matches*** *tick box in the* ***Compare*** *dialog box. This ensures that the matching objects in the model are not turned off. This helps me look at the comparison between the model in the overall context of the model. For example, in this exercise, when you click on the* ***Compare:Differences:Vessel-Assem V1.nwc*** *set, you can see that the central openings in the level 2 and 3 platforms have square corners whereas the platforms in the other file have rounded corners, refer to Figure 29.*

---

12. Orbit the scene to view the bottom view of the model and then click on the **Compare:Unmatched:Vessel-Assem V2.nwc** set; the **Comments** window shows that there are 7 objects that are unmatched. Also, the unmatched objects are highlighted. This means that the 7 objects that are highlighted are only available in version 2 of the model.

13. Hide the unselected objects and orbit the model to see the unmatched objects.

14. Deselect everything and then activate the **Initial View** viewpoint.

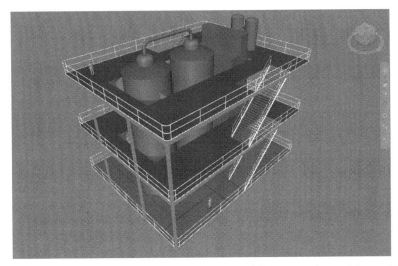

Figure 29 *The scene showing the comparison of the two versions of the model*

15. Save the file with the name **Compare.NWF** in the **Chapter 5 > Exercise Plant** folder.

16. Activate the **Training** workspace that you created in Chapter 1.

Section 5: Linking an External Database to the Objects

In this section, you will open the **Equipments.nwd** file and then use the **DataTools** to link the information in the Microsoft Access database file to the objects in the scene.

1. If you are using a 64-BIT computer, make sure you perform the steps given in the section **Getting a 64-BIT Computer Ready to Use DataTools** on page 5-13.

2. Open the **Equipments.nwd** file from the **Chapter 5 > Exercise Plant** folder.

   This file has some search sets created to show you how many objects of each type are in this file. Normally, you do not need these sets to be created first. To view these sets, you first need to turn on the **Sets** window.

3. Dock the **Sets** window below the **Selection Tree** and then select the **Pumps** set; the **Properties** window shows that 28 items are selected. This shows that there are 28 pumps in the current file.

4. Dock the **Find Items** window below the graphics screen. With the set still selected, notice that the right pane of the **Find Items** window shows that this set is created by searching a category called **AutoCad** that has a property called **Class** with the value equal to **Pump**.

5. Select the **Tanks** set from the **Sets** window; the **Properties** window shows that there are 17 tanks selected. Notice the search criteria that was used to create this search set.

   Assigning properties to each of these selected objects is a tedious process. Therefore, you will use the **DataTools** to assign properties together to all the objects in these sets. The search criteria that was used to create the search sets will be used to link the external database to these objects.

6. Undock the **Sets** and **Find Items** windows and then deselect everything.

7. Right-click anywhere in the graphics window and select **File Options** from the shortcut menu; the **File Options** dialog box is displayed.

8. Click the **DataTools** tab in the dialog box and then click the **New** button in this tab.

9. In the **New Link** dialog box, type **Specifications** as the name in the **Name** text box.

10. From the **ODBC Driver** list, select **Microsoft Access Driver (*.mdb,*.accdb)**.

11. Click the **Setup** button on the right of the **ODBC Driver** list; the **ODBC Microsoft Access Setup** dialog box is displayed.

12. From the **Database** area, click the **Select** button; the **Select Database** dialog box is displayed.

13. Using this dialog box, browse to the **Chapter 5 > Exercise Plant** folder and double-click **Class.accdb** file. This file has a table called **PlantDetails** that has five columns, as shown in Figure 30.

PlantDetails				
ID ▾	Supplier ▾	Specifications ▾	CLASS ▾	Technical Docs ▾
1	Versa-Matic	FLOW RATE (Adjustable) 0-30 gpm (125lpm)	Pump	www.deepakmaini.com
5	PetroStar	MOC SS Duplex + Ti Cladded	HeatExchanger	www.deepakmaini.com
8	Davey	Maximum operating pressure 1600kPa (232 psi)	Tank	www.deepakmaini.com
10	Brisbane Tank	Agitators top entry Carbon Steel Pressure Vessels	Vessel	www.deepakmaini.com

Figure 30 The database to be linked

14. Click **OK** in the **ODBC Microsoft Access Setup** dialog box.

15. In the **SQL String** area, enter the following text in bold. Because SELECT is already written in the text box, you can start with a space after SELECT. Make sure you type in spaces and double quotes correctly. Notice that there is no space after %.

SELECT * From PlantDetails Where CLASS = %prop("AutoCad","Class")

Explanation of the SQL string:

*In this query, you are opening a database table called **PlantDetails** shown in Figure 30. You want to assign the properties in all the columns in this database, therefore, you have used asterisk (*) in the query. The **DataTools** will search for the Autodesk Navisworks objects that have the **AutoCad** category property called **Class** and the value matching with those in the **CLASS** column of the database. Once found, they will be assigned the properties in all the columns of the database. Note that the **ID** column is a Microsoft Access default column and will not be assigned.*

16. On the right side of the **New Link** dialog box, double-click in the first row under **Field Name** and type **Supplier**.

17. Double-click below the row you have added and type **Specifications**.

18. Double-click below the row you have added and type **Technical Docs**. The **New Link** dialog box, after entering the name of the three rows, is shown in Figure 31.

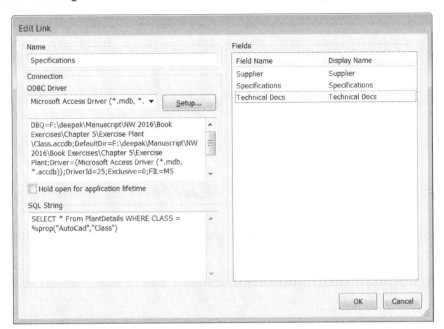

*Figure 31 The **New Link** dialog box to link the external database*

19. Click **OK** in the dialog box to return to the **DataTools** tab of the **File Options** dialog box; the **DataTools Links** area shows the **Specifications** link that you created.

20. Make sure there is a tick mark on the left of **Specifications**. Click **OK** in the **File Options** dialog box.

 *Tip: If the error dialog box is displayed informing you that it is unable to set one or more links to active, this means that there is an error in the SQL string that you have added or the way the rows were added in the **Fields** area. Make sure you correct these.*

Once the external database is linked, the associated information will be displayed in the **Properties** window when you select any of the objects to which the database was linked. To test it, you will activate the saved viewpoints.

21. Activate the **Pump1** viewpoint and select any pump displayed in the scene.

22. Using the right arrow key on the top right of the **Properties** window, scroll to the right to the **Specifications** tab; the columns that were available in the external database are displayed

with the associated information as rows in this tab. Figure 32 shows the resized **Properties** window showing the tab and the information from the external database.

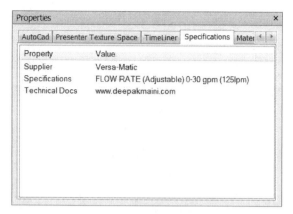

Figure 32 *The **Properties** window showing the tab and information from the external database*

23. Activate the **HeatExchangers** viewpoint and select one of the red heat exchangers from the graphics window; the **Properties** window shows the **Specifications** tab with the associated external database information.

24. Similarly, activate the **Tanks** and **Vessels** viewpoints and select the objects to view the properties that are assigned to them using the external database.

What I do

*I prefer linking databases using the **File Options** dialog box instead of **DataTools** from the **Home** ribbon tab > **Tools** ribbon panel. This way the database is only linked to the current file instead of being available globally in all the files that I open.*

---

25. Save the file and start a new file.

Section 6: Splitting the Autodesk Navisworks Window and Using the Full Screen Mode

In this section, you will split the Autodesk Navisworks window and view different parts of the design in the two windows. You will also use the full screen mode to view the model.

1. Open the **SBR Treatment Plant.nwd** file. Change the lighting style to **Scene Lights**. The model appears as shown in Figure 33.

2. From the **View** ribbon tab > **Scene View** ribbon panel > **Split View** flyout, select **Split Vertical**; the view is split vertically and the model is now displayed in the two windows.

3. Click on the sky in the left window to make it current and then activate the **Overview** viewpoint.

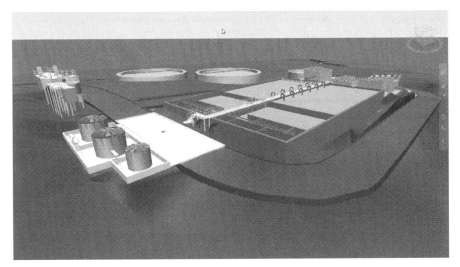

Figure 33 *The SBR treatment plant (**Model courtesy Ryan McKinley, Senior Civil Drafter, Engineering and Operations, Tenix**)*

4. Click on the sky in the right window to make it current and then activate the **View5** viewpoint. Figure 34 shows the model in the two windows.

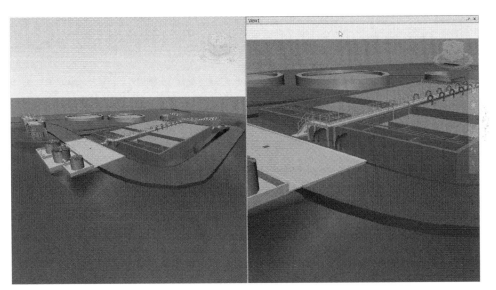

Figure 34 *The SBR treatment plant shown in two windows*

5. Close the right view window by clicking on the **X** button on the top right of this window.

Next, you will view the animation in the full screen mode. But because you cannot click the **Play** button in the full screen mode, you will have to first play the animation and then activate the full screen mode.

6. Click on the **Walkthrough** animation in the **Saved Viewpoints** window to activate this animation.

7. From the **Animation** ribbon tab > **Playback** ribbon panel, click the **Play** button and then press the F11 key to activate the full screen mode; the animation will play in the full screen mode.

8. After the animation stops, press the F11 key again to return to the normal display.

9. Start a new file and if prompted, do not save changes in the current file.

Section 7: Using the Batch Utility to Schedule Creation of a .NWD File

In this section, you will use the **Batch Utility** tool to schedule the creation of a .NWD file by appending the files available in the folder.

1. From the **Home** ribbon tab > **Tools** ribbon panel, click **Batch Utility**; the **Navisworks Batch Utility** dialog box is displayed.

2. From the **Input** area, browse to the **Chapter 5 > Exercise Plant > Batch Utility** folder.

3. From the list above the **Add File Spec** button, select **Autodesk DWG/DXF file (*.dwg,*.dxf)**; three files are displayed on the right side of the **Input** area.

4. Click the **Add File Spec** button; two new specification rows are added that will select all the Autodesk .DWG and .DXF files from the selected folder.

5. From the **Output** area of the dialog box, in the **As Single File** tab, select the **Browse** button; the **Save output as** dialog box is displayed.

6. Browse to the **Chapter 5 > Exercise Plant** folder and then type **Scheduled** as the name of the file. Make sure **Navisworks document (*.nwd)** is selected from the **Save as type** list of the dialog box.

7. Click **Save** in the dialog box to return to the **Navisworks Batch Utility** dialog box.

8. Select the **Overwrite output files** radio button. This will ensure that if there is any existing file with the name **Scheduled** in the output folder, it will be overwritten with the new file.

9. In the **Log** area, select the **Log events to** tick box and then click the **Browse** button to display the **Save log as** dialog box.

10. Browse to the **Chapter 5 > Exercise Plant** folder to save the log file. Enter **Batch.log** as the name of the log file.

    This will ensure that if something goes wrong during the batch process, the errors will be written in the log file.

11. Select the **Overwrite existing log file** tick box.

12. Click the **Schedule Command** button; the **Save task file as** dialog box is displayed.

13. Enter the task file name as **Schedule** and click **Save** in the dialog box; the **Schedule Task** dialog box is displayed.

14. Enter your windows login username and password in the **Security** area and click **OK** in the dialog box; the **Navisworks Batch Utility Task 1** dialog box is displayed.

15. Click the **Schedule** tab and then click the **New** button; the options in the lower half of this dialog box are activated.

16. From the **Schedule Task** list, select **Once**.

17. In the **Start Time** area, set the time five minutes after the current local time.

18. Click **OK** in the **Navisworks Batch Utility Task 1** dialog box. If the **Set Account Information** dialog box is displayed, enter your windows login and password.

19. Close the **Navisworks Batch Utility** dialog box.

 *Note: After five minutes, when the batch utility will create the Autodesk Navisworks file, the **taskeng.exe** command window will be displayed for a few seconds.*

20. After five minutes, go to the **Chapter 5 > Exercise Plant** folder and then open the **Scheduled.nwd** file.

Hands-on Exercise (BIM)	In this exercise, you will complete the following tasks:
	1. Open the **CG_Project_20.nwd** file and turn on the visibility of grids and levels in the view.
	2. Activate various viewpoints and add links to the objects in the scene.
	3. Edit links that you have added to the objects in the model.
	4. Open two different versions of a design and compare the two models.
	5. Open the **Building-DataTools.nwf** file and attach an external database to the objects in this file.
	6. Use the **Batch Utility** tool to schedule the process of creating Autodesk Navisworks files by appending various files.

Section 1: Opening the NWD file and Turning on the Visibility of Grids and Levels

As mentioned earlier in this chapter, if you are working with an Autodesk Revit file, you can turn on the visibility of grids and levels in that model. However, note that the grids and levels must be created in the model in Autodesk Revit. In this section, you will open the **CG_Project_20.nwd** file **(courtesy Samuel Macalister, Senior Technical Sales Specialist – BIM, Autodesk Inc.)**, which is created from an Autodesk Revit.

1. From the **Chapter 5 > Exercise Building** folder, open the **CG_Project_20.nwd** file.

   This file has materials and textures assigned to the objects in Autodesk Revit. Those materials and textures are directly imported in Autodesk Navisworks.

   Before proceeding further, it is important to make sure the rendering and lighting style is set correctly.

2. On the **Viewpoint** ribbon tab > **Render Style** ribbon panel > **Mode** flyout, make sure **Full Render** is selected.

3. From the **Render Style** ribbon panel > **Lighting** flyout, make sure **Scene Lights** is selected. The model looks similar to the one shown in Figure 35.

4. Activate the **Front** viewpoint.

5. On the **View** ribbon tab > **Grids & Levels** ribbon panel, click the **Show Grid** button to turn the grids on, if they are not already turned on.

6. On the same ribbon panel, from the **Mode** flyout, select **Above and Below**; the grids of the level above and below are displayed.

   Figure 36 shows the model in the **Front** viewpoint with the grids of the level above and below turned on.

7. Activate the **Overview** viewpoint.

Figure 35 *The scene with the textures turned on* **(Model courtesy Samuel Macalister, Senior Technical Sales Specialist – BIM, Autodesk Inc.)**

Figure 36 *The model with the grids of the level above and below turned on*

8. From the **Mode** flyout, select **All**. Notice the grids of the level above the camera are displayed in Red, the level immediately below the camera are displayed in Green, and the rest of the grids are displayed in Gray.

9. Activate the **Kitchen** viewpoint. Notice how some grid lines are displayed in dashed. This is because by default, the X-ray mode of grid display is turned on in the global options.

10. Activate the **Front** viewpoint.

11. From the **Mode** flyout, select **Fixed**; the **Display Level** list is activated on the right of the **Mode** flyout.

12. From the **Display Level** list, one by one, select **Level 1**, **Ceiling**, **Top of Parapet**, and **Roof Level** and notice how the grids change.

13. Click the **Show Grid** button to turn off the visibility of grids.

14. Activate the **Overview** viewpoint.

Section 2: Turning On the Visibility of Links and Customizing their Display

In this section, you will use various viewpoints in this file to add links. But to make sure that these links can be seen in the graphics window, you will first turn on the visibility of links.

1. From the **Home** ribbon tab > **Display** ribbon panel, click the **Links** button to turn on the visibility of links.

   You will notice a number of link icons displayed on the model. This is because by default, when you turn on the visibility of links, the icons of the saved viewpoints and sets are also displayed. You need to turn this off using the **Options Editor** dialog box.

2. Press the F12 key to display the **Options Editor** dialog box.

3. From the left pane, expand **Interface > Links** and then click **Standard Categories**; the right pane displays the categories for which the links are visible.

4. From the right pane, turn off the visibility of all the categories except hyperlink and label and then click **OK** in the dialog box to exit.

Section 3: Adding Links

As mentioned earlier, you will use various saved viewpoints to add links to the objects in the scene.

1. Activate the **Kitchen** viewpoint.

2. Right-click on the left kitchen cabinet and select **Links > Add Link** from the shortcut menu.

3. Enter the name of the link as **Kitchen Installer** in the **Name** text box.

4. In the **Link to file or URL** text box, type **http://www.nobbykitchens.com.au/**.

5. From the **Category** list, select **Label**.

6. From the **Attachment Points** area, click the **Add** button and pick a point anywhere on the selected cabinet.

7. Click **OK** in the dialog box; the link is added and is displayed as a label in the graphics window, as shown in Figure 37.

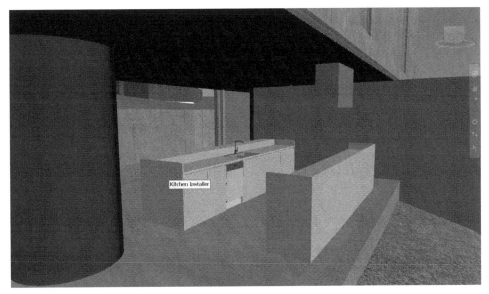

Figure 37 Link added to the kitchen cabinet

Next, you will add a link to the dishwasher in the **Dishwasher** viewpoint.

8. Activate the **Dishwasher** viewpoint.

9. Right-click on the dishwasher and select **Links > Add Link** from the shortcut menu; the **Add Link** dialog box is displayed.

10. Enter the name of the link as **Dishwasher** in the **Name** text box.

11. In the **Link to file or URL** text box, type **Miele**.

12. From the **Category** list, select **Label**.

13. From the **Attachment Points** area, click the **Add** button and pick a point anywhere on the dishwasher.

14. Click **OK** in the dialog box; the link is added and is displayed as label in the graphics window, as shown in Figure 38.

Next, you will add the link to the bathtub in the **Bathtub** viewpoint.

15. Activate the **Bathtub** viewpoint.

16. Right-click on the bathtub and select **Links > Add Link** from the shortcut menu; the **Add Link** dialog box is displayed.

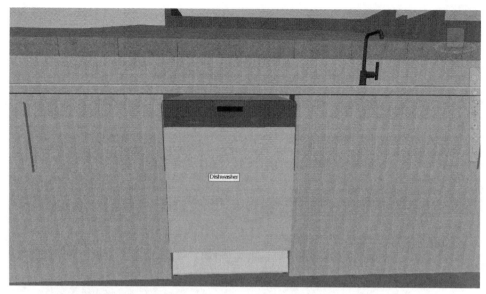

Figure 38 *The scene showing a link added to the dishwasher*

17. Enter the name of the link as **TOTO-Nexus** in the **Name** text box.

18. In the **Link to file or URL** text box, type **http://www.totousa.com/**.

19. From the **Category** list, select **Hyperlink**.

20. From the **Attachment Points** area, click the **Add** button and pick a point anywhere on the bathtub.

21. Click **OK** in the dialog box; the link is displayed as an icon in the graphics window.

Section 4: Following and Editing Links

The main reason of adding links to the objects in the scene is that you can then use those links to display related information. This can be done by following the links, which is what you will do in this section.

1. Activate the **Kitchen** viewpoint.

2. Click on the **Kitchen Installer** link; a Web browser is opened that takes you to the Nobby Kitchen Web site. This is because you specified this Web site as the URL for this link.

3. Return back to the Autodesk Navisworks window.

4. Activate the **Bathtub** viewpoint.

5. Click on the **TOTO-Nexus** link; a Web browser is opened that takes you to the TOTO Web site. This is because you specified this Web site as the URL for this link.

6. Activate the **Dishwasher** viewpoint.

7. Click on the **Dishwasher** link; an error dialog box is displayed informing you that it failed to resolve the link. This is because there was no URL or file associated with the link.

    You will now edit this link to add a URL.

8. Right-click on the **Dishwasher** link and click **Edit Link** from the shortcut menu; the **Edit Links** dialog box is displayed, as shown in Figure 39.

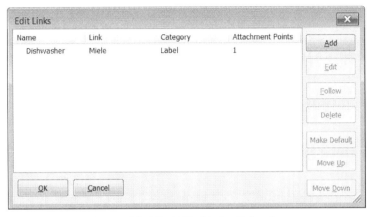

Figure 39 The **Edit Links** *dialog box*

9. In the dialog box, right-click on **Dishwasher** under the **Name** column and click **Edit** from the shortcut menu; the **Edit Link** dialog box is displayed.

10. In the **Link to file or URL** text box, type **http://www.mieleusa.com/**.

11. Click **OK** in the **Edit Link** dialog box and then click **OK** in the **Edit Links** dialog box.

12. Click on the **Dishwasher** link; a Web browser is opened that takes you to the Miele USA Web site. This is because you specified this Web site as the URL for this link.

13. From the **Home** ribbon tab > **Display** ribbon panel, click the **Links** button to turn off the visibility of links.

14. Activate the **Overview** viewpoint and then save the file.

Section 5: Comparing Two Versions of a Model

As mentioned earlier, while working on a large project, you will regularly get updated models from the contractor. In this section, you will learn to find the differences between two versions of the same model by comparing them.

1. Start a new file and then append the **Structure V1.dwg** and **Structure V2.dwg** files from the **Chapter 5 > Exercise Building** folder.

2.   Change the view to the **Home** view and then dock the **Comments** window at the bottom of the graphics window.

Next, you will save the current viewpoint so that you can restore the visibility of the objects after comparing the two models.

3.   Save the current viewpoint with the name **Initial View** and then edit it to turn on the **Hide/ Required** and **Override Appearance** options.

4.   From the **Selection Tree** select both the files.

5.   From the **Home** ribbon tab > **Tools** ribbon panel, click the **Compare** button; the **Compare** dialog box is displayed.

6.   Select the options in this dialog box, as shown in Figure 40.

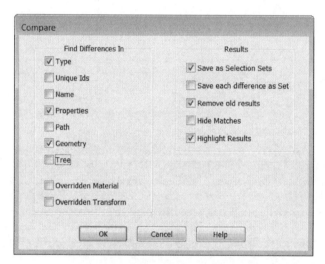

Figure 40 The **Compare** *dialog box*

7.   Click **OK** in the dialog box.

8.   Dock the **Sets** window below the **Selection Tree**; the sets created during the comparison of the two models are displayed in this window.

9.   Resize the **Sets** window so that you can see full names of the sets.

10. Click on the first set named **Compare:Differences:Structure V1.dwg**; the **Comments** window shows 259 objects have differences.

11. Click on the second set named **Compare:Differences:Structure V2.dwg** and you will see that the **Comments** window shows the same comment.

This comment informs you that 259 objects had differences in the two files. Note that these differences also include the difference in the properties, which is not the true reflection of the difference in the physical model. You will later compare the two models again by clearing the options to compare the properties as well.

12. Click on the set named **Compare:Unmatched:Structure V2.dwg**; the **Comments** window shows that there are 140 objects that are unmatched. Also, the unmatched objects are highlighted. This means that the 140 objects that are highlighted are only available in version 2 of the model.

13. With the **Compare:Unmatched:Structure V2.dwg** set still selected, hide the unselected objects from the scene.

    Orbit the model to view the objects that are only available in version 2 of the model.

14. Deselect everything by clicking in the blank area of the graphics window.

15. Activate the **Initial View** viewpoint.

16. Select both the files again from the **Selection Tree**.

17. From the **Home** ribbon tab > **Tools** ribbon panel, click the **Compare** button; the **Compare** dialog box is displayed.

18. From the **Find Differences In** area, clear the **Properties** tick box and click **OK** in the dialog box; the sets created during the comparison of the two models are displayed in the **Sets** window.

    Notice that the first two sets now show matched objects.

19. Click on the set named **Compare:Matched:Structure V1.dwg**; the **Comments** window shows that there are 243 objects that matched.

20. Click on the set named **Compare:Unmatched:Structure V2.dwg**; the **Comments** window still shows that there are 140 objects that are unmatched.

    As shown in the previous steps, you can easily compare and view the differences between various versions of the files that you receive from the contractors.

21. Activate the **Training** workspace that you created in Chapter 1.

22. Save the model with the name **Compare.nwf** in the **Chapter 5 > Exercise Building** folder.

Section 6: Linking an External Database to the Objects

In this section, you will open the **Building-DataTools.nwf** file and then use the **DataTools** to link the information in the Microsoft Access database file to the objects in the scene.

1. If you are using a 64-BIT computer, make sure you perform the steps given in the section **Getting a 64-BIT Computer Ready to Use DataTools** on page 5-13.

2. Open the **Building-DataTools.nwf** file from the **Chapter 5 > Exercise Building** folder.

    This file has some search sets created to show you how many objects of each type are in this file. Normally, you do not need these sets to be created first. To view these sets, you first need to turn on the **Sets** window.

3. Dock the **Sets** window below the **Selection Tree** and then select the **Glazed Panels** set; the **Properties** window shows that 283 items are selected. This shows that there are 283 glazed panel objects in the current file.

4. Dock the **Find Items** window below the graphics screen. With the set still selected, notice that the right pane of the **Find Items** window shows that this set is created by searching a category called **Item** that has a property called **Name** with the value equal to **Glazed**.

5. Select the **Handrailing** set from the **Sets** window; the **Properties** window shows that there are 22 handrailings selected. Notice the search criteria that was used to create this search set.

    Assigning properties to each of these selected objects is a tedious process. Therefore, you will use the **DataTools** to assign properties together to all the objects in these sets. The search criteria that was used to create the search sets will be used to link the external database to these objects.

6. Undock the **Find Items** window and then deselect everything.

7. Right-click anywhere in the graphics window and select **File Options** from the shortcut menu; the **File Options** dialog box is displayed.

8. Click the **DataTools** tab in the dialog box and then click the **New** button in this tab.

9. In the **New Link** dialog box, type **Specifications** as the name in the **Name** text box.

10. From the **ODBC Driver** list, select **Microsoft Access Driver (*.mdb,*.accdb)**.

11. Click the **Setup** button on the right of the **ODBC Driver** list; the **ODBC Microsoft Access Setup** dialog box is displayed.

12. From the **Database** area, click the **Select** button; the **Select Database** dialog box is displayed.

13. Using this dialog box, browse to the **Chapter 5 > Exercise Building** folder and double-click **Building.accdb** file. This file has a table called **BuildingDetails** that has five columns, as shown in Figure 41.

ID	Supplier	Authorized By	Type	Website
1	AU Glass	Project Engineer	Glazed	http://www.australianglassgroup.com.au/
5	Webforge	Project Engineer	Handrail - Pipe	http://www.webforge.com.au/access_prod
8	AU Glass	Project Engineer	1.5" x 2.5" rectangular	http://www.australianglassgroup.com.au/
10	Stegbar	Interior Designer	Door - Panel	http://www.stegbar.com.au/products/wind

Figure 41   The database to be linked

14. Click **OK** in the **ODBC Microsoft Access Setup** dialog box to return to the **New Link** dialog box.

15. In the **SQL String** area, enter the following text in bold. Make sure you type in spaces and double quotes correctly. Notice that there is no space after %prop.

    SELECT * From BuildingDetails Where Type = %prop("Item","Name")

Explanation of the SQL string:

*In this query, you are opening a database table called **BuildingDetails** shown in Figure 41. You want to assign the properties in all the columns in this database, therefore, you have used asterisk (*) in the query. The **DataTools** will search for the Autodesk Navisworks objects that have the **Item** category property called **Name** and the value matching with those in the **Type** column of the database. Once found, they will be assigned the properties in all the columns of the database. Note that the **ID** column is a Microsoft Access default column and will not be assigned.*

16. On the right side of the **New Link** dialog box, double-click in the first row under **Field Name** and type **Supplier**.

17. Double-click below the row you have added and type **Authorized By**.

18. Double-click below the row you have added and type **Website**. The **New Link** dialog box, after entering the name of the three rows, is shown in Figure 42.

19. Click **OK** in the dialog box to return to the **DataTools** tab of the **File Options** dialog box; the **DataTools Links** area shows the **Specifications** link that you created.

20. Make sure there is a tick mark on the left of **Specifications**. Click **OK** in the **File Options** dialog box.

 *Tip: If the error dialog box is displayed informing you that it is unable to set one or more links to active, this means that there is an error in the SQL string that you have added or the way the rows were added in the **Fields** area. Make sure you correct these.*

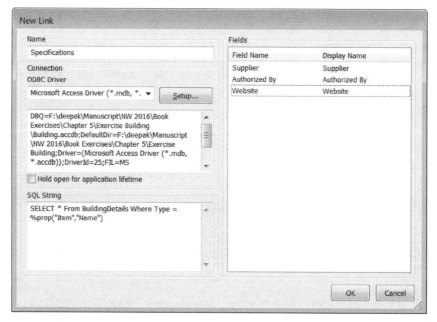

Figure 42 *The New Link dialog box to link the external database*

Once the external database is linked, the associated information will be displayed in the **Properties** window when you select any of the objects to which the database was linked. To test it, you will select one of the objects in the sets.

21. From the **Sets** window, select the **Glazed Panels** set; all the objects in this set are highlighted in the **Selection Tree** and in the graphics window.

22. From the **Selection Tree**, select one of the highlighted **Glazed** objects.

23. Using the right arrow key on the top right of the **Properties** window, scroll to the right to the **Specifications** tab; the columns that were available in the external database are displayed with the associated information as rows in this tab. Figure 43 shows the resized **Properties** window showing the tab and the information from the external database.

24. Select the **Mullions** set and select one of the highlighted **1.5" x 2.5" rectangular** objects from the **Selection Tree**; the **Properties** window shows the **Specifications** tab with the associated external database information.

25. Select the **Handrailing** set and select one of the **Handrail - Pipe** objects from the **Selection Tree**; the **Properties** window shows the **Specifications** tab with the associated external database information.

26. Similarly, select the **Door Panels** set and select any one **Door - Panel** object to view the properties that are assigned to it using the external database.

27. Save the file.

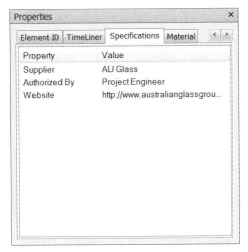

*Figure 43 The **Properties** window showing the tab
and information from the external database*

What I do

*I prefer linking databases using the **File Options** dialog box instead of **DataTools** from the **Home** ribbon tab > **Tools** ribbon panel. This way the database is only linked to the current file instead of being available globally in all the files that I open.*

Section 7: Splitting the Autodesk Navisworks Window and Using the Full Screen Mode

In this section, you will split the Autodesk Navisworks window and view different parts of the design in the two windows. You will also use the full screen mode to view the model.

1. Activate the **Overview** viewpoint.

2. From the **View** ribbon tab > **Scene View** ribbon panel, click the **Split View** flyout and select **Split Vertical**; the view is split vertically and the model is now displayed in the two windows.

3. Click inside the left view window to make it current and then activate the **Overview** viewpoint.

4. Click inside the right window to make it current and then activate the **Door Panels** viewpoint. Figure 44 shows the model in the two windows.

5. Close the right window by clicking on the **X** button on the top right of this window.

   Next, you will view the animation in the full screen mode. But because you cannot click the **Play** button in the full screen mode, you will have to first play the animation and then activate the full screen mode.

6. Click on the **Walkthrough** animation in the **Saved Viewpoints** window to make it current.

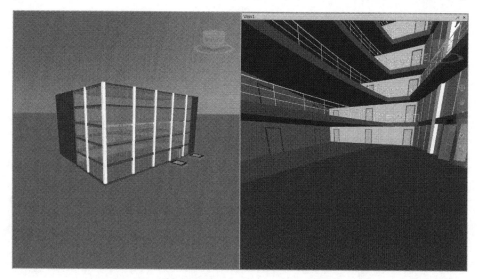

Figure 44 *The building model shown in two windows*

7. From then **Animation** ribbon tab > **Playback** ribbon panel, click the **Play** button and then press the F11 key; the animation will play in the full screen mode.

8. After the animation stops, press the F11 key again to return to the normal display.

9. Save this file and then start a new file.

Section 8: Using the Batch Utility to Schedule Creation of a .NWD File

In this section, you will use the **Batch Utility** tool to schedule the creation of a .NWD file by appending the files available in the folder.

1. From the **Home** ribbon tab > **Tools** ribbon panel, click **Batch Utility**; the **Navisworks Batch Utility** dialog box is displayed.

2. From the **Input** area, browse to the **Chapter 5 > Exercise Building > Batch Utility** folder.

3. From the list above the **Add File Spec** button, select **Autodesk DWG/DXF file (*.dwg,*.dxf)**; a .DWG displayed on the right side of the **Input** area.

4. Click the **Add File Spec** button; two new specification rows are added that will select all the Autodesk .DWG and .DXF files from the selected folder.

5. From the same list, select **MicroStation Design (*.dgn,*.prp,*.prw)**; a .DGN file is displayed on the right side of the **Input** area.

6. Click the **Add File Spec** button; three new specification rows are added that will select all the Microstation files from the selected folder.

7. From the **Output** area of the dialog box, in the **As Single File** tab, select the **Browse** button; the **Save output as** dialog box is displayed.

8. Browse to the **Chapter 5 > Exercise Building** folder and then type **Scheduled** as the name of the file. Make sure **Navisworks document (*.nwd)** is selected from the **Save as type** list of the dialog box.

9. Click **Save** in the dialog box to return to the **Navisworks Batch Utility** dialog box.

10. Select the **Overwrite output files** radio button. This will ensure that if there is any existing file with the name **Scheduled** in the output folder, it will be overwritten with the new file.

11. In the **Log** area, select the **Log events to** tick box and then click the **Browse** button to display the **Save log as** dialog box.

12. Browse to the **Chapter 5 > Exercise Building** folder to save the log file. Enter **Batch.log** as the name of the log file.

    This will ensure that if something goes wrong during the batch process, the errors will be written in the log file.

13. Select the **Overwrite existing log file** tick box.

14. Click the **Schedule Command** button; the **Save task file as** dialog box is displayed.

15. Enter the task file name as **Schedule** and click **Save** in the dialog box; the **Schedule Task** dialog box is displayed.

16. Enter your windows login username and password in the **Security** area and click **OK** in the dialog box; the **Navisworks Batch Utility Task 1** dialog box is displayed.

17. Click the **Schedule** tab and then click the **New** button; the options in the lower half of this dialog box are activated.

18. From the **Schedule Task** list, select **Once**.

19. In the **Start Time** area, set the time five minutes after the current local time.

20. Click **OK** in the **Navisworks Batch Utility Task 1** dialog box. If the **Set Account Information** dialog box is displayed, enter your windows login and password.

21. Close the **Navisworks Batch Utility** dialog box.

 *Note: After five minutes, when the batch utility will create the Autodesk Navisworks file, the **taskeng.exe** command window will be displayed for a few seconds.*

22. After five minutes, go to the **Chapter 5 > Exercise Building** folder and then open the **Scheduled.nwd** file.

Skill Evaluation

Evaluate your skills to see how many questions you can answer correctly. The answers to these questions are given at the end of the book.

1. Grids and levels can be displayed in an AutoCAD Plant 3D file. (True/False)

2. A PDF document cannot be linked to the objects in the scene. (True/False)

3. Autodesk Navisworks allows you to compare two versions of the same model. (True/False)

4. Autodesk Navisworks does not allow you to link Microsoft Access files as an external database to the objects in the model. (True/False)

5. Autodesk Navisworks allows you to switch back to some native CAD software to make changes to the design if you are working with native files. (True/False)

6. Which dialog box allows you to add an external database only to the current file?

    (A) **File Options**   (B) **Data Options**
    (C) **Global Options**   (D) None

7. What is the shortcut key to toggle on or off the display of the full screen mode?

    (A) F8   (B) F9
    (C) F10   (D) F11

8. While splitting the Autodesk Navisworks screen, which options are available?

    (A) **Split Vertical**   (B) **Split Horizontal**
    (C) Both   (D) None

9. Which tool allows you to compare two different versions of the model?

    (A) **Compare**   (B) **Check**
    (C) **Test**   (D) **Find**

10. What are the two default link categories available while adding links to the model?

    (A) Label, Hypername   (B) Label, Hyperlink
    (C) Label, Link   (D) Name, Link

Class Test Questions

Answer the following questions:

1. Explain the following SQL query:

   SELECT * From Details Where Name = %prop("Item","Name")

2. How will you turn off the visibility of the link icons of the viewpoint?

3. Which tool will you use to schedule the creation of a .NWD file by appending existing files?

4. How will you open a Web site address linked to an object using the **Link** tool?

5. How many models can you compare at a time?

Chapter 6 – Working with the Autodesk Rendering Module

The objectives of this chapter are to:

√   Introduce you to the **Autodesk Rendering** module of Autodesk Navisworks.
√   Explain how to apply materials to the objects in the scene.
√   Explain how to apply lighting to the scene.
√   Teach you how to create a photorealistic rendering of the scene.
√   Teach you how to export a photorealistic image of the scene.
√   Teach you how to render your designs using the Autodesk 360 cloud services.
√   Show you how to preview the renderings using the Autodesk 360 render gallery.

CREATING PHOTOREALISTIC RENDERINGS

Render Ribbon Tab > System Ribbon Panel > Autodesk Rendering

Autodesk Navisworks allows you to create a high quality rendered image or animation of the scene using the **Autodesk Rendering** module. These rendered images or animations can be used in the upstream or downstream departments for creating marketing material, presentations, technical documents, and so on. Figure 1 shows the **Render** ribbon tab with various ribbon panels and tools to create high quality rendered images.

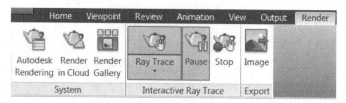

Figure 1 *The **Render** ribbon tab*

The **Autodesk Rendering** module works on the concept of a unified material library across all Autodesk products. As a result, if you open a model created in a native Autodesk product such as Autodesk Revit, Autodesk Inventor, AutoCAD, and so on, all the materials assigned to the objects in those products will be imported in Autodesk Navisworks. As a result, you do not have to assign the materials again to the objects in Autodesk Navisworks. Using this module, you can also create a library of custom materials that you often use and then load that library in any Autodesk Navisworks file whenever needed.

Autodesk Navisworks provides you the option to render your designs locally on your computer or in the cloud. The advantage of cloud rendering is that it offloads all the rendering process on to the Autodesk 360 cloud rendering services, allowing your computer resources to be used for other processes.

 Note: *The cloud credits charged for rendering the designs in the cloud are dependent on the size, quality, and type of rendering. It is recommended that you check with your local Autodesk reseller to know more about this.*

THE AUTODESK RENDERING WINDOW

The **Autodesk Rendering** window is used to assign material, create lights, and define environments for the photorealistic rendering. The various tabs in this window are discussed next.

Materials Tab

The **Materials** tab of the **Autodesk Rendering** window shown in Figure 2 is used to assign materials to the objects in the scene. This tab is divided in two halves. The upper half shows the materials that were assigned to the model in the native Autodesk product. For example, Figure 2 shows the materials that were assigned to the objects in Autodesk Inventor. These materials are classified as the document material. You

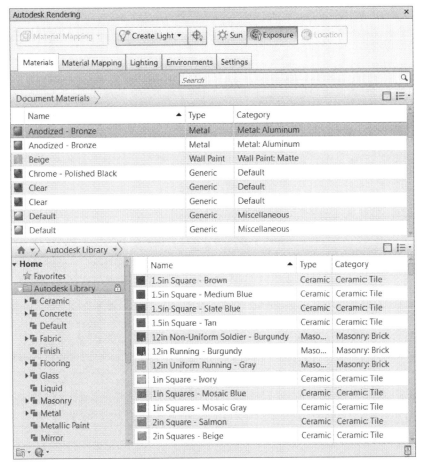

Figure 2 The Autodesk Rendering window showing the Materials tab

can right-click on any document material and click **Select Objects Applied To** to select all the objects to which that particular document material is applied.

The lower half of the **Materials** tab is divided into two panes. The left pane shows the **Favorites** library, **Autodesk Library**, and **Autodesk Advanced Library** of materials. The **Autodesk Library** shows materials logically organized in various categories, such as **Ceramic**, **Concrete**, **Metal**, **Glass** and so on. The **Autodesk Advanced Library** shows advanced categories of materials that are available in the **Autodesk Library**. The **Favorites** library is by default blank and is generally used to add materials that you often use. You can right-click on any material from the **Autodesk Library** or **Autodesk Advanced Library** and add it to the **Favorites** library so that next time you can directly select it from this library rather than browsing through the other two libraries. The right pane shows the materials available under the material library or the category that you have selected. You can drag and drop the material from this pane directly on the object to assign the material. Alternatively, you can right-click on any material from the right pane and assign to the selection using the shortcut menu. Using the same shortcut menu, you can also add the material to the **Favorites** library or the **Document Materials**. Note that the **Rename** and **Delete** options are only available for the materials available in the **Favorites** library.

Procedure for Assigning Materials Using the Autodesk Rendering Window

The following steps show how to use the **Materials** tab of the **Autodesk Rendering** window to assign material to the objects in the scene.

a.   Activate the **Materials** tab of the **Autodesk Rendering** window, if not already active.

b.   Select the objects or the set of objects to which you need to assign the material.

c.   From the **Document Materials** area in the upper half of the **Materials** tab or from one of the libraries in the lower half, select the material you want to assign. Alternatively, you can use the **Search** box in the upper half of the dialog box to search for a material.

d.   Right-click on the selected material and from the shortcut menu, select **Assign to Selection**; the material will be assigned to the selected objects and will also be added to the **Document Materials** area. Alternatively, you can drag and drop the material on the object to which you want to assign the material.

 *Note: To see the realistic effects of the materials assigned, you need to render the scene using the **Render** ribbon tab > **Interactive Ray Trace** ribbon panel > **Ray Trace** tool.*

Procedure for Adding Materials to the Favorites Library

As mentioned earlier, the materials that you commonly use can be added to the **Favorites** library. These materials are then available for use in all the files that you open henceforth. The following steps show how to add materials to the **Favorites** library.

a.   Select the material from the **Document Materials** area or the Autodesk libraries and then right-click on it to display the shortcut menu.

b.   From the shortcut menu, click **Add to > Favorites**.

c.   You can also right-click on the **Favorites** library and create categories in it. This way, the materials can directly be added to that category of the **Favorites** library.

Figure 3 shows the lower half of the **Materials** tab of the **Autodesk Rendering** window showing the **Favorites** library with various categories and materials added to those categories.

Material Mapping Tab

When you assign materials to the objects, you need to make sure the materials are mapped correctly on the objects. This is done using the **Material Mapping** tab. This tab by default is blank and will only show options when you select the geometry object from the graphics window or the **Selection Tree**. Depending on the object to which you have assigned the material, the Autodesk Navisworks will decide the best mapping based on planar, box, cylindrical, and spherical mappings. To change the mapping type, click on the **Box** flyout on the top left corner of the **Autodesk Rendering** window. Based on the mapping selected, the options will change in the **Material Mapping** tab. Figure 4 shows this tab with the box mapping options.

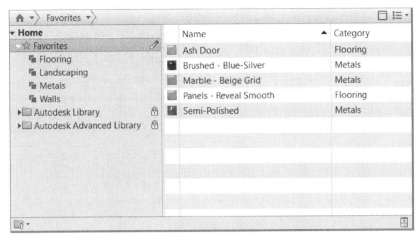

*Figure 3 Categories and materials added to the **Favorites** library*

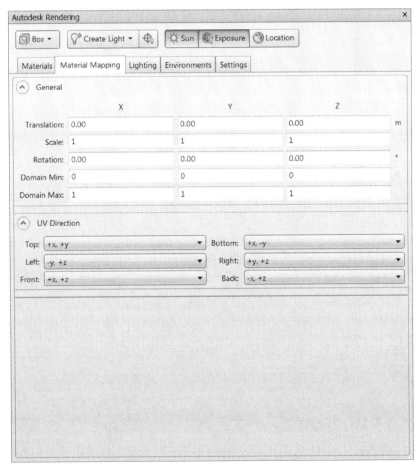

*Figure 4 The **Autodesk Rendering** window with the **Material Mapping** tab*

Procedure for Changing the Material Mapping Type

The following steps show how to change the material mapping type specified for the selected object.

a.   Select the object whose mapping type you want to change. Note that if you are selecting the object from the graphics window, you will need to change the selection resolution to geometry.

b.   From the **Autodesk Rendering** window, click the **Box** flyout on the top left corner and select the required mapping type.

Procedure for Changing the Material Mapping Options

The following steps show how to change the material mapping options for the selected object.

a.   Set the object whose mapping options you want to change. Note that if you are selecting the object from the graphics window, you will need to change the selection resolution to geometry.

b.   From the **Autodesk Rendering** window, click the **Material Mapping** tab; the mapping options related to the mapping type will be displayed.

c.   From the **General** area, change the general settings such as scaling and rotation.

d.   For the **Box** mapping type, the **UV Direction** area will be displayed, refer to Figure 4. Use the options in this area to change the UV directions of all six faces of the box mapping.

e.   For the **Cylindrical** mapping type, the **Cap** area will be displayed that allows you to change the threshold and UV settings for the cylindrical cap.

Lighting Tab

The **Lighting** tab displays the lights that have been added to the current Autodesk Navisworks scene. You can click on any light and its properties will be displayed in the right pane of this tab, as shown in Figure 5.

These lights are created using the **Create Light** flyout located in the toolbar above the tabs in the **Autodesk Rendering** window. Using this flyout, you can create the following four types of lights:

Point Lights: Point lights are similar to light globes that have a location and light the area in all directions.

Spot Lights: Spot lights are targeted lights that originate from a particular location and only light a target area of the scene.

Distance Lights: Distant lights are used to light a particular area of the scene along a beam of light defined by the source and target of the light.

Web Lights: Web lights are photometric lights that use nonuniform light distribution information provided by the light manufacturers in .IES format.

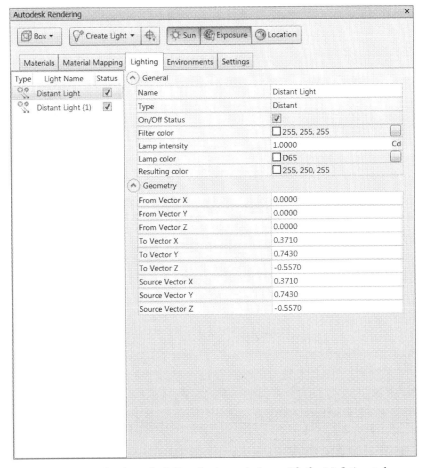

Figure 5 *The **Autodesk Rendering** window with the **Lighting** tab*

The following are the procedures to add all these lights to the scene.

Procedure for Adding a Point Light to the Scene
The following steps show how to add a point light to the scene.

a. From the **Create Light** flyout, click **Point Light**; if you cursor is currently on an object in the scene, the point light glyph will be displayed so that you can specify the location of the light. However, if the cursor is in the blank area of the scene, it will change to the hand cursor. It is recommended that you place the point lights on certain objects in the scene, such as ceilings, walls, and so on.

b. Move the cursor over the face of the object (generally ceilings) and click to specify the location of the point light; the light will be added to the scene and the move gizmo will be displayed on the light glyph in the graphics window. Also, the light information will be displayed in the **Lighting** tab of the **Autodesk Rendering** window.

Tip: *If you do not want a light to be located on the face of an object, you can initially pick the face while placing the light and then use the move gizmo to move the light to another location.*

c. If need be, use the move gizmo on the light glyph to change the location of the light.

d. In the light properties on the **Lighting** tab, click on the **Lamp intensity** swatch to display the **Light Intensity** dialog box in which you can change the light intensity.

e. Click on the **Lamp color** swatch to display the **Lamp Color** dialog box. Select one of the standard lamp colors from the **Standard color** list or click on the **Kelvin colors** radio button and enter a value.

f. Click in the blank area below the lights in the left pane of the **Lighting** tab to turn off the visibility of the move gizmo on the light glyph.

Figure 6 shows the reception area of the building with a point light of intensity 200 and Figure 7 shows the same area with the point light of intensity 1000. In both cases, the light is located in the ceiling above the reception.

Figure 6 *The reception area lit with a point light of intensity 200*

 Tip: *You can use the **Light Glyphs** button on the right of the **Create Light** flyout to turn off the visibility of the light glyph from the graphics window.*

Figure 7 *The reception area lit with a point light of intensity 1000*

Procedure for Adding a Spot Light to the Scene

The spot light needs a position and a target to be defined. The following steps explain how to add a spot light to the scene.

a. From the **Create Light** flyout, click **Spot Light**; if your cursor is currently on an object in the scene, the spot light glyph will be displayed with a location cursor so that you can specify the location of the light. However, if the cursor is in the blank area of the scene, it will change to the hand cursor. It is recommended that you place these lights on a certain object in the scene.

b. Move the cursor over the face of the object (generally ceilings) and click to specify the location of the spot light; the light position will be defined.

c. Move the cursor over the object on which you want to target the spot light and click on it; the spot light will be added to the scene and the move gizmo will be displayed on the position of the light glyph in the graphics window. Also, the light information will be displayed in the **Lighting** tab of the **Autodesk Rendering** window.

d. If need be, use the move gizmo on the light glyph to change the location of the light.

e. Click on the sphere displayed at the target location; the move gizmo will be displayed at the target. If need be, use the move gizmo at the target location to change the target.

f. In the light properties on the **Lighting** tab, modify the hotspot and falloff angles, if need be.

g. Click on the **Lamp intensity** swatch to display the **Light Intensity** dialog box in which you can change the light intensity.

h. Click on the **Lamp color** swatch to display the **Lamp Color** dialog box. Select one of the standard lamp colors from the **Standard color** list or click on the **Kelvin colors** radio button and enter a value.

i. Click in the blank area below the lights in the left pane of the **Lighting** tab to turn off the visibility of the move gizmo on the light glyph.

Figure 8 shows a scene lit using the spot light. This figure also shows the light glyph and the move gizmo at the source location.

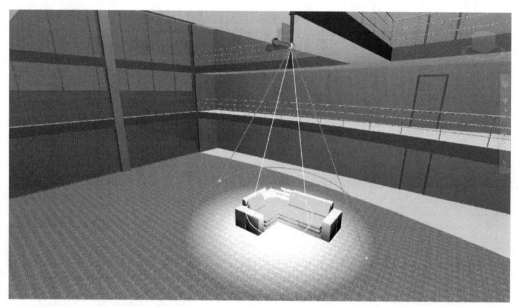

Figure 8 A scene lit with a spot light and the move gizmo at the target of the spot light

Procedure for Adding a Distant Light to the Scene
The following steps show how to add a distant light to the scene.

a. From the **Create Light** flyout, click **Distant Light**; if you cursor is currently on an object in the scene, the distant light glyph will be displayed so that you can specify the location of the light. However, if the cursor is in the blank area of the scene, it will change to the hand cursor. This is because the distant lights cannot be located in the blank area. You need to place them on certain objects in the scene.

b. Move the cursor over the face of the object and click to specify the location of the distant light; the light position will be defined.

c. Move the cursor over the object on which you want to target the distant light and click on it; the distant light will be added to the scene and the move gizmo will be displayed on the position of the light glyph in the graphics window. Also, the light information will be displayed in the **Lighting** tab of the **Autodesk Rendering** window.

d. If need be, use the move gizmo on the light glyph to change the location of the light.

e. Click on the sphere displayed at the target location; the move gizmo will be displayed at the target. If need be, use the move gizmo at the target location to change the target.

f. Click on the **Lamp intensity** edit box to change the light intensity.

g. Click on the **Lamp color** swatch to display the **Lamp Color** dialog box. Select one of the standard lamp colors from the **Standard color** list or click on the **Kelvin colors** radio button and enter a value.

h. Click in the blank area below the lights in the left pane of the **Lighting** tab to turn off the visibility of the move gizmo on the light glyph.

Procedure for Adding a Web Light to the Scene

The following steps show how to add a web light to the scene.

a. From the **Create Light** flyout, click **Web Light**; if you cursor is currently on an object in the scene, the web light glyph will be displayed so that you can specify the location of the light. However, if the cursor is in the blank area of the scene, it will change to the hand cursor. This is because the web lights cannot be located in the blank area. You need to place them on certain objects in the scene.

b. Move the cursor over the face of the object and click to specify the location of the web light; the light position will be defined.

c. Move the cursor over the object on which you want to target the web light and click on it; the web light will be added to the scene and the move gizmo will be displayed on the position of the light glyph in the graphics window. Also, the light information will be displayed in the **Lighting** tab of the **Autodesk Rendering** window.

d. If need be, use the move gizmo on the light glyph to change the location of the light.

e. Click on the sphere displayed at the target location; the move gizmo will be displayed at the target. If need be, use the move gizmo at the target location to change the target.

f. Click on the **Lamp intensity** edit box to change the light intensity.

g. Click on the **Lamp color** swatch to display the **Lamp Color** dialog box. Select one of the standard lamp colors from the **Standard color** list or click on the **Kelvin colors** radio button and enter a value.

h. If you have the .IES format file of the light distribution information provided by the light manufacturer, click the **Web file** swatch; the **Open** dialog box will be displayed. Browse and select the file and click **Open** in the dialog box.

i. Click in the blank area below the lights in the left pane of the **Lighting** tab to turn off the visibility of the move gizmo on the light glyph.

Environments Tab

The **Environments** tab is used to control the display and settings of the sun light, sky and exposure in the scene, as shown in Figure 9. The three areas displayed in this tab are discussed next.

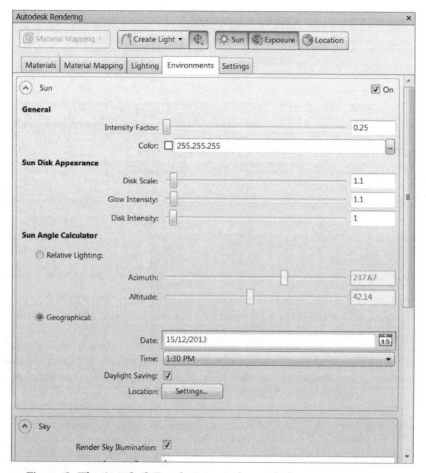

*Figure 9 The **Autodesk Rendering** window with the **Environments** tab*

Sun Area

This area is used to control the settings related to the sun light. Clicking the **On** tick box turns the sun light on. You can also use the **Sun** button on the toolbar above the tabs to turn the sun light on or off. Using the **General** options, you can control the intensity and color of the sun light. The **Sun Disk Appearance** settings are used to specify how the sun disk will appear in the sky of the current scene. The **Sun Angle Calculator** is used to specify the date, time, and daylight saving related information.

Note: If you have turned the sun light on, the model can only be viewed in the perspective display. You cannot change it to orthographic display with the sun light turned on.

Sky Area

This area is used to control the settings related to the sky. Note that the options in this area will only be available if the sun light is turned on. In this area, you can control the options such as sky illumination, intensity factor, haze, blur, night and ground color, and horizon height.

Exposure Area

This area is used to control the exposure related settings. You can also use the **Exposure** button above the tabs to toggle the exposure on or off.

Figure 10 shows a scene lit with the sun turned off. In this scene, there are some web lights, point lights, distant lights and a spot light turned on.

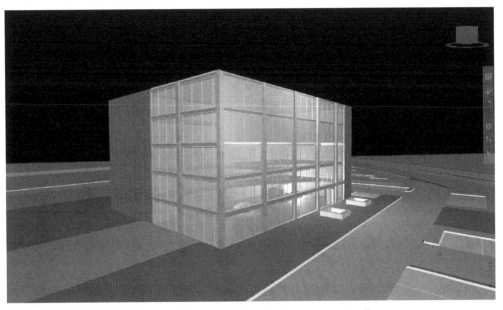

Figure 10 *A scene lit with the sun turned off*

Figure 11 shows the same scene with the sun turned on, along with the other lights. Because the sun light is turned on in this figure, you can also see the sky in the background.

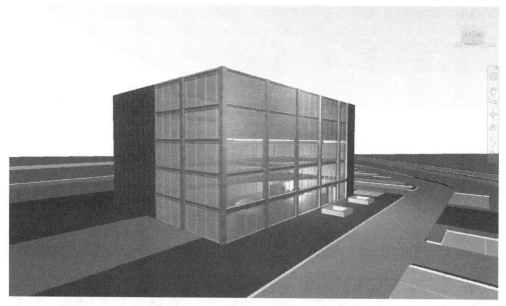

Figure 11 *A scene lit with the sun turned on*

Settings Tab

This tab, shown in Figure 12, is used to control the render style presets that are available in the **Ray Trace** flyout in the **Render** ribbon tab > **Interactive Ray Trace** ribbon panel. The various options available in the tab are discussed next.

Current Render Preset: List

All the available render presets are available in this list. Select the preset that you want to edit. The settings that you define for the preset here will be used when you select this preset while rendering using the **Ray Trace** flyout in the **Render** ribbon tab.

Basic Area

This area is used to control the quality of the rendering for the selected preset using the render level or the time that will be used for rendering. The rendering level value can be set between 1 to 50, with the quality of rendering increasing with the higher value. However, the rendering time will also increase if you increase the level of rendering.

Advanced Area

This area is used to control the complexity of the lighting calculation and the numeric precision.

Location Settings

The **Location** button located above the tabs in the **Autodesk Rendering** window allows you to specify the geographic location of your project. When you click this button, the **Geographic Location** dialog box will be displayed, as shown in Figure 13. You can specify the latitude, longitude, time zone, and the North direction using the options in this dialog box. This allows you to apply realistic sun light exposure to your project in the Autodesk Navisworks scene.

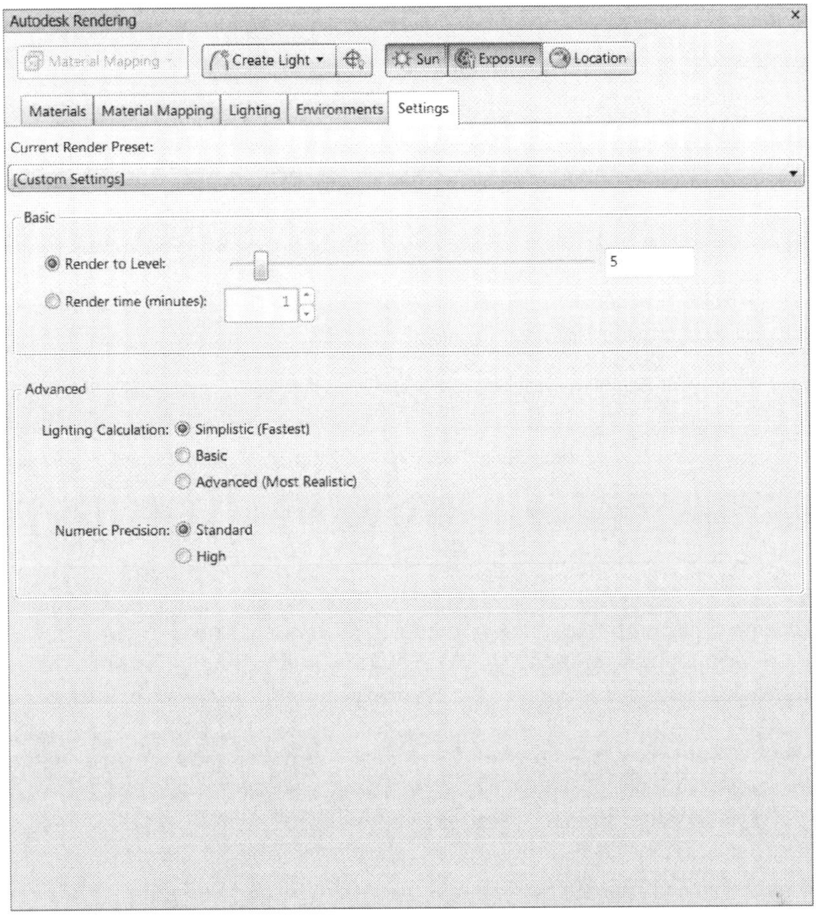

Figure 12 The **Autodesk Rendering** *window with the* **Settings** *tab*

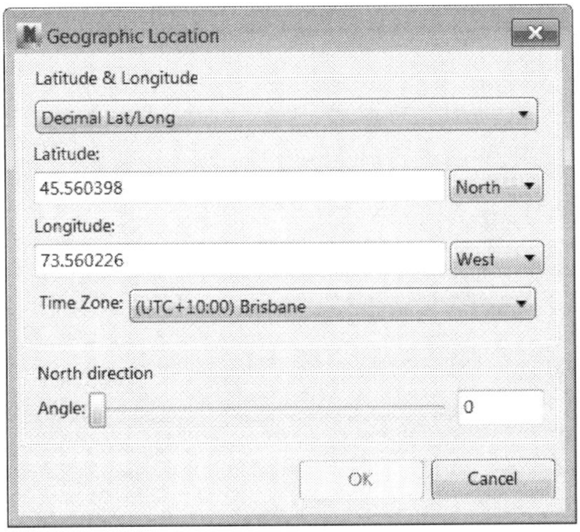

Figure 13 The **Geographic Location** *dialog box*

RAY TRACE RENDERING OF THE AUTODESK NAVISWORKS SCENE

Render Ribbon Tab > Interactive Ray Trace Ribbon Panel > Ray Trace Flyout

The **Ray Trace** flyout allows you to interactively render your Autodesk Navisworks scene based on one of the render presets. The following are the various presets available in this flyout to render the scene.

Low Quality: This rendering is used when you want to quickly check how the scene looks with the current material and lighting. This preset renders the scene to level 5 with the lighting calculation set to fastest and the numeric precision set to standard in the **Settings** tab of the **Autodesk Rendering** window.

Medium Quality: This rendering is used to preview the final rendering. This preset renders the scene to level 10 with the lighting calculation set to basic and the numeric precision set to standard in the **Settings** tab of the **Autodesk Rendering** window.

High Quality: This rendering is used to create high quality rendered images of your scene. This preset renders the scene to level 20 with the lighting calculation set to most realistic and the numeric precision set to high in the **Settings** tab of the **Autodesk Rendering** window.

Coffee Break Rendering: This preset is similar to **Low Quality** preset, with the difference being the render time in this preset is set to 10 minutes so the rendering can be completed over the coffee break.

Lunch Break Rendering: This preset is similar to **Medium Quality** preset, with the difference being the render time in this preset is set to 60 minutes so the rendering can be completed over the lunch break.

Overnight Rendering: This preset is similar to **High Quality** preset, with the difference being the render time in this preset is set to 720 minutes. This allows the scene to be rendered overnight and create the best quality rendered image.

Custom Settings: This option will display the **Settings** tab of the **Autodesk Rendering** window to configure the custom rendering settings. These settings will then be used when you click the **Ray Trace** button to render the scene.

Figure 14 shows a scene rendered using a high quality ray trace option.

Pausing/Stopping Interactive Rendering

Render Ribbon Tab > Interactive Ray Trace Ribbon Panel > Pause/Stop

Once you have started rendering a scene, you can pause or stop it using the **Pause** and **Stop** tools available on the **Interactive Ray Trace** ribbon panel. The paused rendering can be resumed

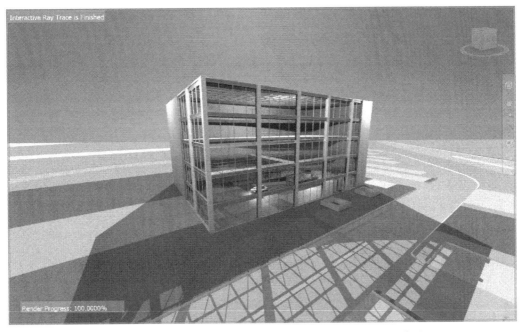

Figure 14 A scene rendered using high quality ray trace rendering

by clearing the **Pause** button. However, if you stop a rendering, you will have to start the entire rendering from start again using the **Ray Trace** tool.

SAVING RENDERED IMAGES

Render Ribbon Tab > Export Ribbon Panel > Image

Autodesk Navisworks allows you to save the rendered Autodesk Navisworks scene in various image formats. This is done using the **Image** tool. Note that this tool will only be available once the ray trace rendering of the scene is completed. When you choose this button, the **Save As** dialog box will be displayed that allows you to specify the name and location of the rendered image. You can select the required image format type from the **Save as type** list in this dialog box.

RENDERING IN CLOUD

Render Ribbon Tab > System Ribbon Panel > Render in Cloud

Rendering in cloud allows you to offload the rendering process to Autodesk 360 cloud rendering services, ensuring your computer resources remain free for other tasks. It is important to remember that this is an Autodesk Subscription service and is only available to the customers who have active subscription with Autodesk software.

Note; *While rendering in cloud, only the* **Exterior: Sun only** *or the* **Interior: Sun only** *lighting scheme will be used.*

To access this service, you will have to sign in using your Autodesk subscription credentials. As mentioned earlier, depending on the type of rendering you require, there will be cloud credits used from your Autodesk Subscription account. To know more about cloud credits, please get in touch with your local Autodesk reseller.

The following steps show how to render your design in cloud:

a. Assign all the materials and material mapping to the model you want to render.

b. Click the **Render in Cloud** button from the **Render** ribbon tab > **System** ribbon panel.

c. If you are not already logged in using your Autodesk Subscription account, the **Autodesk - Sign In** dialog box will be displayed and you will be prompted to sign in, as shown in Figure 15.

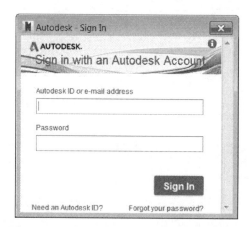

*Figure 15 The **Autodesk - Sign In** dialog box*

d. Enter your Autodesk Subscription credentials and click **Sign In**.

e. Once you sign in, the **Render in Cloud** dialog box will be displayed, as shown in Figure 16.

f. Select the view to render, output type, render quality, image size, exposure, and file format from this dialog box.

g. The cloud credit that are required for current rendering, the total cloud credits available, and the total cloud credits remaining after this rendering are listed in the area above the **Start Rendering** button. Also, the estimated wait time is shown below this area. Figure 16 shows the settings that will render your design without using any cloud credits and the estimated wait time for this rendering is 1 hour.

 Tip: *Select the* **Interactive Panorama** *option from the* **Output Type** *list creates a panoramic rendered image that you can drag to explore the rendered scene.*

Figure 16 *The **Render in Cloud** dialog box*

h. Select the **Email me when complete** tick box. This will ensure that an email is sent to the email address associated with your Autodesk Subscription credentials once the rendering is completed.

i. Click the **Start Rendering** button; the **Render in Cloud** dialog box will be displayed that will show the progress of uploading the model to the cloud. Once the model is uploaded, you can continue using Autodesk Navisworks and your computer for other tasks.

j. Once the rendering is completed, you will get an email similar to the one shown in Figure 17 informing that the rendering is completed and you can download the rendered image.

The next section explains how to preview and download the rendered images from the Autodesk 360 cloud render gallery.

Previewing and Downloading Rendered Images from the Autodesk 360 Cloud Render Gallery

Render Ribbon Tab > System Ribbon Panel > Render Gallery

Once the cloud rendering is completed, you can preview the rendered images and download them using the **Render Gallery** button. If you are not already signed in using your Autodesk Subscription credentials, you will be prompted to do that when you invoke this tool. Upon signing

Dear Deepak Maini!

The Building_Autodesk Render.nwf image you rendered using Autodesk®
360 is ready.
Login to your Autodesk® 360 account to view images in the render gallery.

> Sign In

Tip of the day:

- When using the lighting scheme option, rendering in Autodesk®
  360 creates the same result when you select 'Exterior: Sun only'
  or 'Interior: Sun only'.

Have you tried this feature? How are you using rendering in Autodesk®
360? Share your story

Figure 17   Email informing about the completion of cloud rendering

in, the Web browser window will be opened with your **Autodesk 360 Rendering** gallery, as shown in Figure 18. On this page, you will also be shown all the renderings that are completed and the ones that are in-progress.

The following procedure shows you how to download an image from the Autodesk 360 Rendering gallery.

a. Click the **Render Gallery** button from the **Render** ribbon tab > **System** ribbon panel; the Web browser window will be opened with your **Autodesk 360 Rendering** page.

b. Expand the name of the file that you rendered in cloud; the thumbnails of all the rendered images of that file will be displayed. Figure 18 shows the **Building_Autodesk Render.nwf** expanded. You can see that the panorama image is in the queue for rendering and the still image is already rendered.

c. Click the arrow displayed on the lower right corner of the thumbnail image.

d. From the shortcut menu, click **Download Image**; the image will start to download in the default download folder of your Web browser.

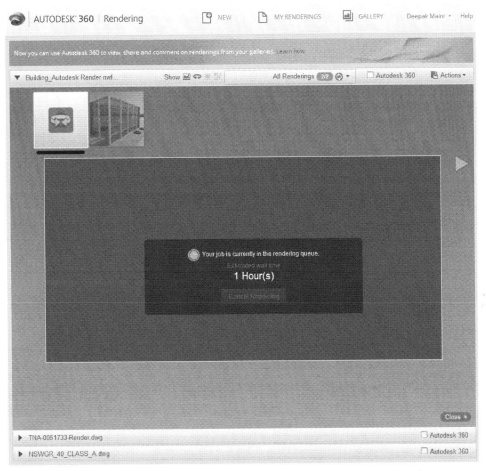

*Figure 18 The **Autodesk 360 Rendering Gallery** showing all the completed and in-progress renderings*

 Note: *When downloading the panoramic image, you have an option of downloading it as HTML viewer or image strip. If you download it as HTML viewer, you will be able to drag the view to explore the rendered scene.*

HANDS-ON EXERCISES

You will now work on hands-on exercises by using the concepts learned in this chapter.

Hands-on Exercise (Plant)	*In this exercise, you will complete the following tasks:* *1. Open an Autodesk Navisworks file and assign materials to the objects in it using the* ***Autodesk Rendering*** *module.* *2. Add lights to the scene.* *3. Render it using the ray trace rendering.* *4. Save the rendered image.* *5. Render the same scene in cloud (optional).*

Section 1: Opening a File and Assigning Materials to the Objects in the Scene

In this section, you will open the **Sand Filters.nwd** file and assign materials to the objects in the scene.

1. From **Chapter 6 > Exercise Plant** folder, open the **Sand Filters.nwd** file. The model for the exercise looks similar to the one shown in Figure 19.

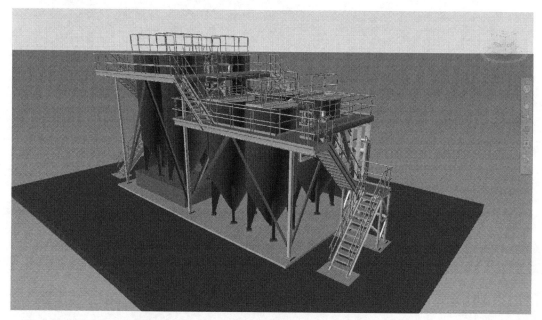

*Figure 19 The model for the exercise (**Model courtesy Ryan McKinley, Senior Civil Drafter, Engineering and Operations, Tenix**)*

2. From the **Render** ribbon tab > **System** ribbon panel, click **Autodesk Rendering**; the **Autodesk Rendering** window is displayed.

3. Dock this window on the left of the graphics window.

4. Hide the **Selection Tree**, **Properties**, and **Saved Viewpoints** windows to make more space for the graphics window.

    For the ease of selection, there are sets created that you can select to assign the materials.

5. Dock the **Sets** window on the left of the graphics window and select the **Site** set.

6. In the lower half of the **Materials** tab of the **Autodesk Rendering** window, expand **Autodesk Library** in the left pane and then select **Concrete**; all the available concrete materials are displayed in the right pane.

7. From the right pane, right-click on the **Exposed Aggregate - Medium** material and select **Assign to Selection** from the shortcut menu; the material is assigned to the site slab.

 Note: *As you assign the materials to the objects, they are also added to the **Document Materials** area in the upper half of the **Materials** tab.*

8. Press ESC and then zoom closer to the site object to see the effect of the material.

9. From the **Sets** window, select the **Foundation** set.

10. In the right pane of the **Autodesk Rendering** window, scroll down to the **Panels - Reveal Smooth** material. Now, right-click on it and select **Assign to Selection** from the shortcut menu; the material is assigned to the foundation.

11. From the **Sets** window, select the **Oxidation & Denitrification Filters** set.

12. In the left pane, expand **Metal** and then select **Steel**; all the available steel materials are displayed in the right pane.

13. From the right pane, scroll down to the **Stainless - Brushed** material. Right-click on it and select **Assign to Selection** from the shortcut menu; the material is assigned to the filters.

14. From the **Sets** window, select the **OXIDATION FILTER FEED PIPEWORK** set.

15. Hold down the CTRL key and select the **OXIDATION TO DENITRIFICATION FILTER FEED PIPEWORK**, **DENITRIFICATION FILTER OUTLET PIPEWORK**, and **BACKWASH PIPEWORK** sets.

16. In the right pane, scroll to the **Semi-Polished** material.

17. Right-click on this material and select **Assign to Selection** from the shortcut menu; the material is assigned to the set.

    Next, you will add the **Steel** material to the document materials and then modify it to make it appear Yellow. This material will then be assigned to the **Structure**, **Pipe Supports**, and **Railing** sets.

18. From the right pane, scroll down to the **Steel** material. Right-click on it and select **Add to > Document Materials** from the shortcut menu; the material is added to the document materials and is listed in the upper half of the dialog box.

19. In the upper half of the dialog box, double-click on the **Steel** material; the **Material Editor** dialog box is displayed.

20. From the expanded **Generic** area, click on **RGB 224 223 219** on the right of the **Color** text; the **Color** dialog box is displayed.

21. Click on the **Yellow** color from the second row of colors and then click **OK** in the **Color** dialog box; the color displayed on the right of the **Color** text is **RGB 255 255 0** in the **Material Editor** dialog box.

22. Click the **Information** tab and in the **Name** box, change the name of the material to **Steel - Yellow**.

23. Close the dialog box; the name of the color changes in the **Document Materials** area to **Steel - Yellow**.

24. From the **Sets** window, select the **Structure** set.

25. Hold down the CTRL key and select the **Pipe Supports** and **Railing** sets.

26. From the **Document Materials** area in the upper half of the **Autodesk Rendering** window, right-click on the **Steel - Yellow** material and select **Assign to Selection** from the shortcut menu; the material is assigned to the selected sets.

27. Press ESC to deselect everything. Notice the **Steel - Yellow** material assigned to the objects in the sets you selected above.

    Next, you need to assign a mesh material to the **Grating** set. For this, you will search for all the mesh materials using the **Search** box on the top right of the **Document Materials**.

28. In the **Search** box on the top right of the **Document Materials** area, type **Mesh**; all the available mesh materials are listed in the lower half of the dialog box.

 Note: If you search for a material and it is not available as a document material, the Document Material area is displayed as blank. All the other materials you added earlier will be hidden. Once you delete the text from the Search box, all the document materials will be redisplayed.

29. In the lower half of the dialog box, right-click on **Plate - Mesh** and select **Add to > Document Materials** from the shortcut menu; the material is added to the document materials and is listed in the upper half of the dialog box.

30. From the **Sets** window, select the **Grating** set.

31. From the **Document Materials** area in the upper half of the **Autodesk Rendering** window, right-click on the **Plate - Mesh** material and select **Assign to Selection** from the shortcut menu; the material is assigned to the selected set.

32. Zoom close to one of the grating plates and notice the grating pattern of the material applied.

33. Activate the **Overview** viewpoint. The Autodesk Navisworks scene, after assigning all the materials, will look similar to the one shown in Figure 20.

Figure 20 The Autodesk Navisworks scene after assigning materials

Section 2: Adding Lights to the Scene

In this section, you will add various lights to the scene. There are two default distant lights added to the scene. Once you have created all the required lights, you will delete these two distant lights.

1. Click on the **Create Light** flyout at the top in the **Autodesk Rendering** window and select **Point**.

2. Move the cursor to the blank area of the graphics window; the cursor changes to the hand cursor and the point light glyph is attached to it.

3. Move the cursor over the corner of the handrailing shown in the ellipse in Figure 21. When the hand cursor changes to the circular cursor, click on that location; a new point light is added and the scene is lit using that light. Also, the move gizmo is displayed on the light.

   You will now move this light up using the Blue axis of the move gizmo. When a new light is added, its position is displayed in the **Geometry** area of the **Lighting** tab of the **Autodesk Rendering** window.

Figure 21 *The ellipse showing the location of the point light*

4.　Drag the Blue axis of the move gizmo on the new point light to a location whose **Position Z** value is displayed close to **39300** in the **Geometry** area of the **Lighting** tab of the **Autodesk Rendering** window.

　　Tip: *If you click in the blank area of the graphics window, the move gizmo on the light disappears. In this case, click on the light in the graphics window again to display the move gizmo.*

5.　Click on the **Lamp intensity** swatch. Enter **100** as the value of the intensity and click **OK** in the **Lamp Intensity** dialog box.

　　Next, you will create a new light diagonally opposite to the first light you added.

6.　Click on the **Create Light** flyout and select **Point**.

7.　Move the cursor to the blank area of the graphics window; the cursor changes to the hand cursor and the point light glyph is attached to it.

8.　Move the cursor over the corner of the handrailing shown in the ellipse in Figure 22. When the hand cursor changes to the circular cursor, click on that location; a new point light is added and the scene is lit using that light. Also, the move gizmo is displayed on the light.

9.　Drag the Blue axis of the move gizmo on the new point light to a location whose **Position Z** value is displayed close to **41000** in the **Geometry** area of the **Lighting** tab of the **Autodesk Rendering** window.

Figure 22 *The ellipse showing the location of the second point light*

10. Click on the **Lamp intensity** swatch. Enter **100** as the value of the intensity and click **OK** in the **Lamp Intensity** dialog box.

Next, you will add a web light. The web light has a location point and a target point. You will use the location of the first point light as the initial location of the web light and the location of the second point light as the target location of the web light. You will then edit the initial location of the web light using the values in the **Autodesk Rendering** window.

11. Click on the **Create Light** flyout and select **Web**.

12. Move the cursor over the handrailing that you used as the location of the first point light. When the hand cursor changes to the circular cursor, click on that location; the light glyph is displayed at that location.

You will now define the target of this light.

13. Move the cursor over the handrailing that you used as the location of the second point light. When the hand cursor changes to the circular cursor, click on that location; a new web light is added.

14. In the **Geometry** area of the **Lighting** tab, enter **29000, -2900, 41000** as the values in the **Position X**, **Y**, and **Z** boxes.

15. Click on the **Lamp intensity** swatch. Enter **100** as the value of the intensity and click **OK** in the **Lamp Intensity** dialog box.

Next, you will change the color of the web light.

16. From the **General** area of the **Lighting** tab, click on the **Lamp color** swatch; the **Lamp Color** dialog box is displayed.

17. From the **Standard colors** list, select **Fluorescent Daylight** and then click **OK** in the dialog box.

    Next, you will add a distant light. The distant light also has a location and a target. You will use the initial location of the second point light as the location of the distant light and the initial position of the first point light as the target of the distant light. You will then edit these values in the **Autodesk Rendering** window.

18. Click on the **Create Light** flyout and select **Distant**.

19. Move the cursor over the handrailing that you used as the location of the second point light. When the hand cursor changes to the circular cursor, click on that location; the light glyph is displayed at that location.

    You will now define the target of this light.

20. Move the cursor over the handrailing that you used as the location of the first point light. When the hand cursor changes to the circular cursor, click on that location; a new distant light is added.

21. In the **Geometry** area of the **Lighting** tab, enter **18300, 5200, 43000** as the values in the **From Vector X**, **Y**, and **Z** boxes.

22. Enter **18775, 6550, 37500** as the values in the **To Vector X**, **Y**, and **Z** boxes.

23. In the **General** area, enter **2** in the **Lamp intensity** edit box.

24. Click in the blank area of the graphics window to deselect the light.

25. From the left pane of the **Lighting** tab, right-click on **Distant Light** at the top of the lights list and select **Delete** from the shortcut menu.

26. Similarly, delete **Distant Light (1)**.

    By default, when you add lights, their glyphs are displayed in the graphics window. These can be turned off using the **Light Glyphs** button on the right of the **Create Light** flyout.

27. Click the **Light Glyphs** button on the right of the **Create Light** flyout in the **Autodesk Rendering** window; all the light glyphs are turned off from the graphics window.

28. Activate the **Overview** viewpoint; the scene looks similar to the one shown in Figure 23.

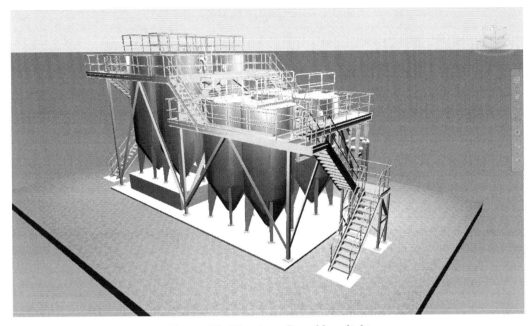

Figure 23 *The view after adding lights*

Section 3: Rendering the Scene using Ray Trace Rendering

In this section, you will render the scene using high quality ray trace rendering.

1. From the **Render** ribbon tab > **Interactive Ray Trace** ribbon panel, click **Ray Trace** flyout > **Coffee Break Rendering**; this rendering preset is selected as the type of rendering.

2. Now, click the **Ray Trace** button in the **Render** ribbon panel; the scene starts to render using high quality ray trace rendering. Note that coffee break rendering process takes 10 minutes to render this scene.

 Note: *If the ray trace rendering is turned on, changing the view using any navigation tool will restart the rendering.*

Figure 24 shows the Autodesk Navisworks scene rendered using high quality ray trace rendering. Notice the shadows displayed in the scene because of various lights.

 Tip: *The settings related to the render presets in the **Ray Trace** flyout can be edited using the **Settings** tab of the **Autodesk Rendering** window. Make sure you select the render preset that you want to edit from the **Current Render Preset** drop-down list before editing the settings.*

Section 4: Exporting the Rendered Image

In this section, you will export the rendered image of the scene.

1. From the **Render** ribbon tab > **Export** ribbon panel, click **Image**; the **Save As** dialog box is displayed.

Figure 24 The scene rendered using the high quality ray trace rendering

2. From the **Save as type** list, select **JPEG (*.jpg)**.

3. Browse to the **Chapter 6 > Exercise Plant** folder and specify the file name as **Sand Filters.jpg**.

4. Click the **Save** button; the image is saved.

5. Open the JPEG file using Windows Explorer and notice the render quality.

6. Close the image file and return to the Autodesk Navisworks window.

Section 5: Rendered in Cloud (Optional)

You can work on this section only if you have an Autodesk 360 account. If not, you can create a free Autodesk 360 account by visiting **https://360.autodesk.com/Login**.

1. From the **Render** ribbon tab > **System** ribbon panel, click **Render in Cloud**.

   If you are not already signed in using your Autodesk 360 account, the **Autodesk - Sign In** dialog box is displayed.

2. Enter your Autodesk 360 credentials and sign in; the **Render in Cloud** dialog box is displayed, as shown in Figure 25.

3. From the **Output Type** list, select **Interactive Panorama**.

4. From the **Render Quality** list, select **Final**. Figure 25 shows the **Render in Cloud** dialog box with these settings configured.

*Figure 25 The **Render in Cloud** dialog box*

Notice that the area below the **Exposure** list shows that this rendering requires 3 cloud credits. This dialog box also informs you that the estimated wait time for this rendering is 1 hour. Generally, it does not take this long to finish the rendering.

5. Select the **Email me when complete** tick box.

6. Click the **Start Rendering** button; the **Render in Cloud** dialog box is displayed informing you that the model is being uploaded to the cloud for rendering.

 Note: *While rendering on the cloud, the scene will be rendered only using the exterior sun or interior sun lighting.*

You can keep a track of the cloud rendering progress using the **Autodesk Cloud Render** gallery.

7. From the **Render** ribbon tab > **System** ribbon panel, click **Render Gallery**; the Web browser window will be opened displaying the **Autodesk A360 Rendering** gallery.

Notice that the **Sand Filters.nwd** file is listed and the progress of the current rendering is shown under this file.

8. When the rendering is finished and the thumbnail image of the rendered image is displayed, move the cursor over the thumbnail image; an arrow is displayed on the lower right corner of the thumbnail image.

9. Click on the arrow and from the shortcut menu and then click **Download Panorama > As HTML Viewer**; the download process will start.

10. Once the file is downloaded, open the HTML file of the rendered image. Remember that the HTML file opens in your default Web browser. Figure 26 shows the rendered image in the Web browser.

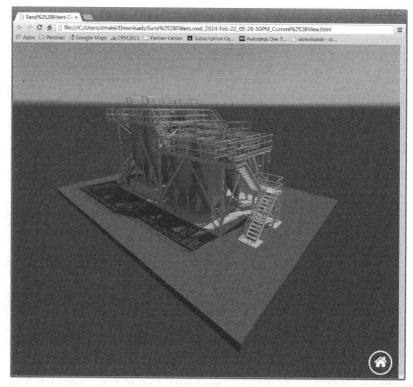

Figure 26 The rendered panoramic image displayed in the Web browser

One of the advantages of the panoramic rendering is that you can drag the image and view its surroundings.

11. Press and hold down the left mouse button in the Web browser window and drag it. Notice how the view changes. However, it still appears as fully rendered.

12. Click the **Home** button on the lower right corner of the Web browser window to restore the original view that you rendered.

13. Close the Web browser window and return to the Autodesk Navisworks window.

14. Start a new file to close the current file. If prompted, save the file.

15. Change the current workspace to **Training**.

Hands-on Exercise (BIM)	*In this exercise, you will complete the following tasks:* *1. Open a model and assign materials to the objects in it using the **Autodesk Rendering** module.* *2. Add lights to the scene.* *3. Render it using the ray trace rendering.* *4. Save the rendered image.* *5. Render the same scene in cloud (optional).*

Section 1: Opening the Autodesk Navisworks File and Assigning Materials to the Objects in the Scene

In this section, you will open the **Office-Building.nwd** file and assign materials to the objects in the scene.

1. From **Chapter 6 > Exercise Building** folder, open the **Office-Building.nwd** file. The building model for this exercise is courtesy **Ankur Mathur, Founder and CEO, SANRACHNA:BIM and Virtual Construction Consultants**. The model looks similar to the one shown in Figure 27.

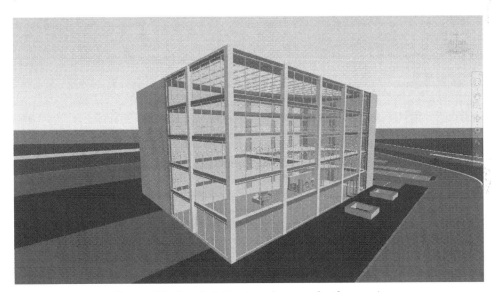

Figure 27 Autodesk Navisworks scene for the exercise

2. From the **Render** ribbon tab > **System** ribbon panel, click **Autodesk Rendering**; the **Autodesk Rendering** window is displayed.

3. Dock this window on the left of the graphics window.

4. Hide the **Selection Tree**, **Properties** and **Saved Viewpoints** windows to make more space for the graphics window.

   For the ease of selection, there are sets created in this file that you can select to assign the materials.

5. Dock the **Sets** window on the left of the graphics window.

6. From the **Sets** window, select the **Exterior Walls** set.

7. In the lower half of the **Materials** tab of the **Autodesk Rendering** window, expand **Autodesk Library > Masonry** in the left pane and then select **Brick**; all the available brick materials are displayed in the right pane.

8. In the right pane, scroll to the **Uniform Running - Yellow** material. Right-click on it and select **Assign to Selection** from the shortcut menu; the material is assigned to the selection set.

 *Note: As you assign the materials to the objects, they are also added to the **Document Materials** area in the upper half of the **Materials** tab.*

9. From the **Sets** window, select the **Interior Walls** set.

10. In the left pane of the **Materials** tab, scroll down and select **Wall Covering**.

11. In the right pane, right-click on **Abstract Light Brown** and select **Assign to Selection** from the shortcut menu; the material is assigned to the interior walls.

12. From the **Sets** window, select the **Floor** set.

13. In the left pane of the **Materials** tab, select **Flooring > Stone**.

14. In the right pane, right-click on **Granite - Brown Mauve-Black** and select **Assign to Selection** from the shortcut menu; the material is assigned to the floors.

15. From the **Sets** window, select the **Glazed Panels** set.

16. In the left pane of the **Materials** tab, select **Glass > Glazing**.

17. In the right pane, right-click on **Light Bronze** and select **Assign to Selection** from the shortcut menu; the material is assigned to the glazed panels.

18. From the **Sets** window, select the **Mullions** set.

19. In the left pane of the **Materials** tab, select **Metal**.

20. In the right pane, right-click on **Bronze - Polished** and select **Assign to Selection** from the shortcut menu; the material is assigned to the mullions.

21. From the **Sets** window, select the **Concrete Columns** set.

22. In the left pane of the **Materials** tab, select **Flooring > Stone**.

23. In the right pane, right-click on **Flagstone** and select **Assign to Selection** from the shortcut menu; the material is assigned to the columns.

24. From the **Sets** window, select the **Door Panels** set.

25. In the left pane of the **Materials** tab, select **Wood**.

26. In the right pane, right-click on **Cherry - Natural Low Gloss** and select **Assign to Selection** from the shortcut menu; the material is assigned to the door panels.

27. From the **Sets** window, select the **Door Frames** set.

28. In the right pane, right-click on **Cocobolo** and select **Assign to Selection** from the shortcut menu; the material is assigned to the door frames.

29. From the **Sets** window, select the **Sofa Base** set.

30. In the left pane of the **Materials** tab, select **Fabric > Leather**.

31. In the right pane, right-click on **Brown** and select **Assign to Selection** from the shortcut menu; the material is assigned to the objects in the set.

32. From the **Sets** window, select the **Sofa Seats** set.

33. In the right pane, right-click on **Pebbled - Light Brown** and select **Assign to Selection** from the shortcut menu; the material is assigned to the objects in the set.

34. From the **Sets** window, select the **Sofa Wood** set.

35. In the left pane of the **Materials** tab, select **Wood**.

36. In the right pane, scroll down and right-click on **Red Oak - Natural Low Gloss** and select **Assign to Selection** from the shortcut menu; the material is assigned to the objects in the set.

 *Tip: Sometimes, the **Sets** window does not show all the sets available in the scene. In this case, you need to refresh this window by turning it off and turning it back on.*

37. From the **Sets** window, select the **Carpet** set.

38. In the left pane of the **Materials** tab, select **Flooring > Carpet**.

39. In the right pane, scroll down and right-click on **Saxony - Flower Pattern Colored** and select **Assign to Selection** from the shortcut menu; the material is assigned to the objects in the set.

40. From the **Sets** window, select the **Railing** set.

41. In the left pane of the **Materials** tab, select **Metal**.

42. In the right pane, right-click on **Copper - Polished** and select **Assign to Selection** from the shortcut menu; the material is assigned to the objects in the set.

43. From the **Sets** window, select the **Reception Back Frame** set.

44. In the left pane of the **Materials** tab, select **Wood**.

45. In the right pane, scroll down and right-click on **White Ash** and select **Assign to Selection** from the shortcut menu; the material is assigned to the objects in the set.

46. From the **Sets** window, select the **Reception Desk** set.

47. In the right pane, scroll up and right-click on **Cherry - Natural Low Gloss** and select **Assign to Selection** from the shortcut menu; the material is assigned to the objects in the set.

48. From the **Sets** window, select the **Revolving Door Frame** set.

49. From the **Document Materials** in the upper half of the **Autodesk Rendering** window, right-click on **Bronze - Polished** and select **Assign to Selection** from the shortcut menu; the material is assigned to the objects in the set.

50. From the **Sets** window, select the **Revolving Door Glass** set.

51. From the **Document Materials** in the upper half of the **Autodesk Rendering** window, right-click on **Light Bronze** and select **Assign to Selection** from the shortcut menu; the material is assigned to the objects in the set.

52. From the **Sets** window, select the **Tiles** set.

53. In the left pane of the **Materials** tab, select **Flooring > Tile**.

54. In the right pane, scroll down and right-click on **Square - Brown** and select **Assign to Selection** from the shortcut menu; the material is assigned to the objects in the set.

55. Activate the **Sofa** viewpoint. Notice various materials assigned to the sofa objects and also to the other objects in the scene. Figure 28 shows this viewpoint with materials assigned to various objects.

56. Activate the **Overview** viewpoint.

Section 2: Adding Lights to the Scene

In this section, you will add various lights to the scene.

1. Hide the **Sets** window.

2. Click on the **Create Light** flyout at the top in the **Autodesk Rendering** window and select **Web**.

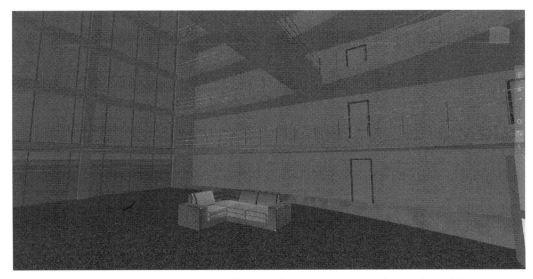

Figure 28 *The **Sofa** viewpoint showing the materials assigned to various objects*

3. Move the cursor over the corner of the building shown in the bigger ellipse in Figure 29. When the hand cursor changes to the circular cursor, click on that location; a new web light is located there. You now need to specify the target point for this light.

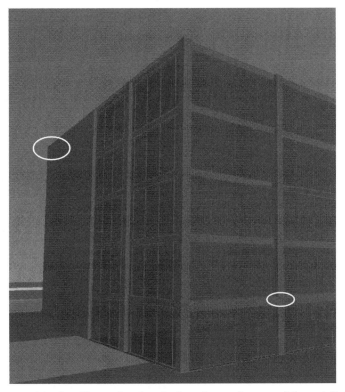

Figure 29 *The ellipses showing the location and target of the web light*

4. Move the cursor over the corner of the column and floor displayed in the smaller ellipse in Figure 29. Click when the hand cursor changes to the target cursor; the scene is lit using this light and the move gizmo is displayed on the light.

When a new light is added, its location and target information is displayed in the **Geometry** area of the **Lighting** tab of the **Autodesk Rendering** window.

5. In the **Geometry** area of the **Lighting** tab, enter **150**, **75**, **50** as the values in the **Position X**, **Y**, and **Z** boxes.

6. Click in the blank area of the graphics window to deselect the light.

By default, all the viewpoints created in this file are configured to display the scene with the scene lights. But as you assign lights to a scene, the lighting style automatically changes to full lights. Therefore, you need to update the viewpoints to display full lights.

7. Right-click on the **Overview** viewpoint and select **Update** from the shortcut menu.

Next, you will add point lights in the **Sofa** and **Reception** viewpoints.

8. Activate the **Reception** viewpoint.

9. Click on the **Create Light** flyout at the top in the **Autodesk Rendering** window and select **Point**.

10. Move the cursor to the bottom face of the floor above reception, as shown in Figure 30.

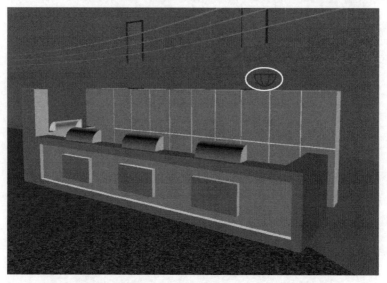

***Figure 30** The ellipse showing the location of the point light*

11. When the hand cursor changes to the target cursor, click to place the light; the scene is lit using this light.

    You will now edit this light.

12. In the **Geometry** area of the **Lighting** tab, enter **55**, **108**, **7.9** as the values in the **Position X**, **Y**, and **Z** boxes.

13. Click on the **Lamp intensity** swatch to display the **Lamp Intensity** dialog box.

14. Enter **150** as the value of intensity and click **OK** in the dialog box.

15. Select any object in the scene to deselect the light and then press ESC to deselect the object.

16. Right-click on the **Reception** viewpoint and select **Update** from the shortcut menu.

    Next, you will activate the **Sofa** viewpoint. However, on doing this, the lights will be set to scene lights.

17. Activate the **Sofa** viewpoint.

18. Click on the **Create Light** flyout at the top in the **Autodesk Rendering** window and select **Point**.

19. Place the light at the bottom face of the floor above the sofa, as shown in Figure 31; the scene is lit using this light.

    You will now edit this light.

20. In the **Geometry** area of the **Lighting** tab, enter **88**, **108**, **17.9** as the values in the **Position X**, **Y**, and **Z** boxes.

21. Click on the **Lamp intensity** swatch to display the **Lamp Intensity** dialog box.

22. Enter **300** as the value of intensity and click **OK** in the dialog box.

23. Select any object in the scene to deselect the light and then press ESC to deselect the object.

24. Right-click on the **Sofa** viewpoint and select **Update** from the shortcut menu.

25. Activate the **Overview** viewpoint.

    When you add lights in the scene, their glyphs are by default turned on. You will now turn off these glyphs.

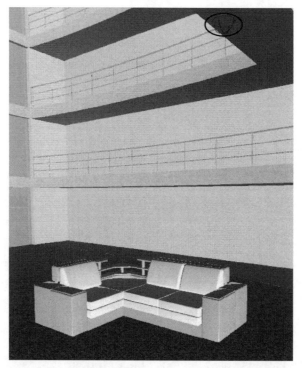

***Figure 31** The ellipse showing the location of the point light*

26. In the **Autodesk Rendering** window, click the **Light Glyphs** button on the right of the **Create Light** flyout to turn off the light glyphs.

Section 3: Rendering the Scene using Ray Trace Rendering

In this section, you will render the scene using the ray trace rendering. Before doing that, you will modify the sun and location settings.

1. Click the **Sun** button at the top in the **Autodesk Rendering** window; the scene will be lit using the sunlight.

2. Click the **Environments** tab, if it is not active.

   By default, the **Relative Lighting** option is selected from the **Sun Angle Calculator** area. You will now change this to the lighting based on geographical location.

3. Select the **Geographical** option from the **Sun Angle Calculator** area.

4. Click the **Settings** button from the left of the **Location** option; the **Geographic Location** dialog box is displayed.

5. Enter **33.86** in the **Latitude** box and select **South** from the list on the right of this box.

6.   Enter **138** in the **Longitude** box and select **East** from the list on the right of this box.

7.   From the **Time Zone** list, select **(UTC + 10.00) Canberra, Melbourne, Sydney**.

8.   Set the **North direction Angle** value to **45**.

9.   Click **OK** in the dialog box.

10. In the **Geographical** area, set the date to February 23, 2015.

11. Set the time to 2:00 PM.

12. From the **Render** ribbon tab > **Interactive Ray Trace** ribbon panel, click **Ray Trace** flyout > **Coffee Break Rendering**; this rendering preset is selected as the type of rendering.

13. Now, click the **Ray Trace** button; the scene starts to render using high quality ray trace rendering. Note that coffee break rendering takes 10 minutes to render the scene.

 Note: *If the ray trace rendering is turned on, changing the view using any navigation tool will restart the rendering.*

Figure 32 shows the Autodesk Navisworks scene rendered using the ray trace rendering preset. Notice the shadows displayed in the scene because of various lights.

Figure 32 The scene rendered using the specified ray trace preset

*Tip: The settings related to the render presets in the **Ray Trace** flyout can be edited using the **Settings** tab of the **Autodesk Rendering** window. Make sure you select the render preset that you want to edit from the **Current Render Preset** drop-down list before editing the settings.*

Section 4: Exporting the Rendered Image

In this section, you will export the rendered image of the scene.

1. From the **Render** ribbon tab > **Export** ribbon panel, click **Image**; the **Save As** dialog box is displayed.

2. From the **Save as type** list, select **JPEG (*.jpg)**.

3. Browse to the **Chapter 6 > Exercise Building** folder and specify the file name as **Office-Building.jpg**.

4. Click the **Save** button; the image is saved.

5. Open the JPEG file using Windows Explorer and notice the render quality.

6. Close the image file and return to the Autodesk Navisworks window.

Section 5: Rendered in Cloud (Optional)

You can work on this section only if you have an Autodesk 360 account. If not, you can create a free Autodesk 360 account by visiting **https://360.autodesk.com/Login**.

1. From the **Render** ribbon tab > **System** ribbon panel, click **Render in Cloud**.

   If you are not already signed in using your Autodesk 360 account, the **Autodesk - Sign In** dialog box is displayed.

2. Enter your Autodesk 360 credentials and sign in; the **Render in Cloud** dialog box is displayed, as shown in Figure 33.

3. From the **Output Type** list, select **Interactive Panorama**.

4. From the **Render Quality** list, select **Final**. Figure 33 shows the **Render in Cloud** dialog box with these settings configured.

   Notice that the area below the **Exposure** list shows that this rendering requires 3 cloud credits. This dialog box also informs you that the estimated wait time for this rendering is 1 hour. Generally, it does not take this long to finish the rendering.

5. Select the **Email me when complete** tick box.

6. Click the **Start Rendering** button; the **Render in Cloud** dialog box is displayed informing you that the model is being uploaded to the cloud for rendering.

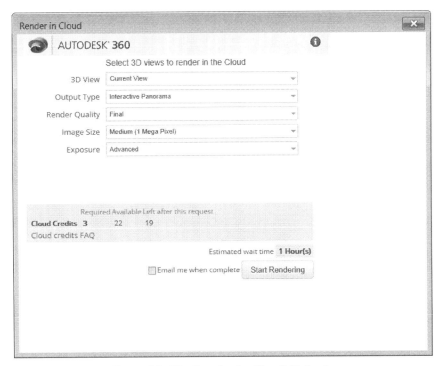

*Figure 33 The **Render in Cloud** dialog box*

 Note: *While rendering on the cloud, the scene will be rendered only using the exterior sun or interior sun lighting.*

You can keep a track of the cloud rendering progress using the **Autodesk Cloud Render** gallery.

7. From the **Render** ribbon tab > **System** ribbon panel, click **Render Gallery**; the Web browser window will be opened displaying the **Autodesk A360 Rendering** gallery.

Notice that the **Office-Building.nwd** file is listed and the progress of the current rendering is shown under this file.

8. When the rendering is finished and the thumbnail image of the rendered image is displayed, move the cursor over the thumbnail image; an arrow is displayed on the lower right corner of the thumbnail image.

9. Click on the arrow and from the shortcut menu, click **Download Panorama > As HTML Viewer**; the download process will start.

10. Once the file is downloaded, open the HTML file of the rendered image. Remember that the HTML file opens in your default Web browser. Figure 34 shows the rendered image in the Web browser.

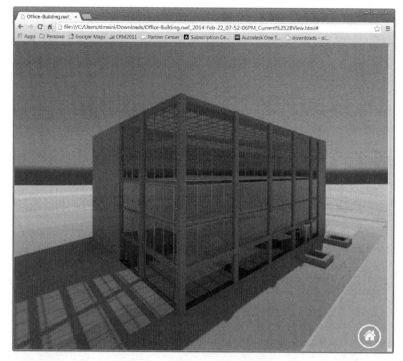

Figure 34 *The rendered panoramic image displayed in the Web browser*

One of the advantages of the panoramic rendering is that you can drag the image and view the surroundings of the image.

11. Press and hold down the left mouse button in the Web browser window and drag it. Notice how the view changes, but it still appears as fully rendered.

12. Click the **Home** button on the lower right corner of the Web browser window to restore the original view that you rendered.

13. Close the Web browser window and return to the Autodesk Navisworks window.

14. Start a new file to close the current file. Save the file, if prompted.

15. Save the file and change the current workspace to **Training**.

Skill Evaluation

Evaluate your skills to see how many questions you can answer correctly. The answers to these questions are given at the end of the book.

1. Autodesk Navisworks 2016 does not allow you to create high quality rendered images. (True/False)

2. The materials assigned to the objects cannot be removed. (True/False)

3. The **Render in Cloud** option requires you to sign in using your Autodesk 360 credentials. (True/False)

4. The **Autodesk Rendering** window allows you to add web lights. (True/False)

5. The lights added to the Autodesk Navisworks scene can be deleted. (True/False)

6. Which of the following is not a type of light available in the **Autodesk Rendering** window?

    (A) Ambient   (B) Distant
    (C) Point   (D) Web

7. Which tool is used to pause the ray trace rendering and restart it??

    (A) **Restart**   (B) **Pause**
    (C) **Stop**   (D) None

8. Which tool is used to render high quality images after assigning materials using the **Autodesk Rendering** window?

    (A) **Ray Trace**   (B) **Ray Form**
    (C) **Render Trace**   (D) **Render Form**

9. Which lights are photometric lights that use nonuniform light distribution information provided by the light manufacturers in .IES format.?

    (A) **Spot**   (B) **Web**
    (C) **Distant**   (D) **Point**

10. Which tab of the **Autodesk Rendering** window allows you to edit the settings related to rendering preset?

    (A) **Materials**   (B) **Assign**
    (C) **Render**   (D) **Settings**

Class Test Questions
Answer the following questions:

1. Explain the steps involved in creating a web light.

2. How to edit the default render presets?

3. If you open an Autodesk Revit file that has some materials assigned to the objects, will those materials be available in Autodesk Navisworks?

4. How will you assign materials to the objects using the **Autodesk Rendering** window?

5. When you assign materials to the objects using the **Autodesk Rendering** window, will those materials be automatically added to the **Document Materials** area?

Chapter 7 – Working with the Animator and Scripter Modules

The objectives of this chapter are to:

√ Introduce you to the **Animator** module of Autodesk Navisworks.
√ Familiarize you with the process of creating animations of moving objects.
√ Explain how to control the visibility of the objects during animation.
√ Teach you how to add a camera animation to the animator scene.
√ Teach you how to add a section plane animation to the animator scene.
√ Introduce you to the **Scripter** module of Autodesk Navisworks.
√ Teach you how to add various types of scripts to the animations.
√ Teach you how to create animations of objects falling from the sky to be linked to the timeliner simulation.

THE ANIMATOR MODULE

> **Home Ribbon Tab > Tools Ribbon Panel > Animator**

In the previous chapters, you learned how to create animations of navigating through the model. However, a number of times you need to display animation of objects moving or rotating in the model. For example, in case of a plant model, you may want show the animation of a skid moving to its assembly position in the design. Similarly, in case of a building model, you may want a truck to bring the load to the construction site and a crane lifting the load from the truck. All these animations can be created using the **Animator** module of Autodesk Navisworks.

The basis of creating an animation in the **Animator** module is the animator scene, which is the holder that contains all your animations. The animator scene can contain the following types of animations:

Animations Based on Animation Sets
Animation set is a selection of objects that will be animated. In this type of animation, you can translate the selected objects, rotate them, scale them, and change their visibility and colors. This is done by capturing keyframes at regular intervals. These keyframes record the changes in the selected objects at the specified intervals.

Camera Animation
To navigate through the model as the objects are getting animated.

Section Plane Animation
To animate the sectioning of a model.

When you invoke the **Animator** module, the **Animator** window will be displayed. This window is divided into four main areas, as shown in Figure 1. The various components of the **Animator** window are discussed next.

Animator Toolbar
The **Animator** toolbar provides various buttons to animate objects in the scene. These buttons are discussed next.

Translate animation set
This button is used to translate the selected objects in the animator scene. When you click this button, the translate gizmo is displayed on the selected object that you can use to specify the translation. You can also enter the translation values in the **Animator** manual entry area shown in Figure 1.

Rotate animation set
This button is used to rotate the selected objects in the animator scene. When you click this button, the rotate gizmo is displayed on the selected object that you can use to specify the rotation. You can also enter the rotation values in the **Animator** manual entry area shown in Figure 1.

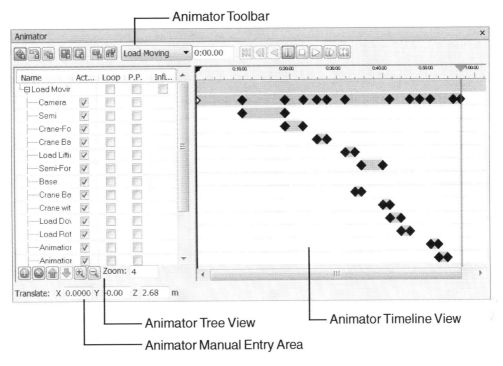

Figure 1 *The various components of the* ***Animator*** *window*

Scale animation set

This button is used to scale the selected objects in the animator scene. When you click this button, the scale gizmo is displayed on the selected object that you can use to specify the scaling. You can also enter the scale factors in the **Animator** manual entry area shown in Figure 1.

Change color of animation set

This button is used to change the color of the objects selected in the animator scene. When you click this button, the **Animator** manual entry area shows **r, g, b** boxes that allow you to enter the Red, Green, and Blue color values of the selected objects. Alternatively, you can click on the **Color** list on the right of these boxes to directly select a color from the color palette.

Change transparency of animation set

This button is used to change the transparency of the objects selected in the animator scene. This is really helpful when you are creating animation sequences of the objects appearing or disappearing in the animator scene. You can enter the transparency value in the **Animator** manual entry area or use the slider in this area to specify the transparency value. A transparency of 0 will mean the objects are fully visible and a transparency of 100 means they are invisible.

Capture keyframe

This button is used to capture the current state of the model and add it to the timeline view. You can double-click on the keyframe in the **Animator** timeline view to edit the time of the captured keyframe and also to edit the translation, rotation, scaling, color, and transparency of the animation set for which the keyframe was added. In Figure 1, the black diamonds are the keyframes that were captured for each animation listed in the **Animator** tree view.

Toggle snapping
While manipulating the animation set using the gizmo, you can use the snapping to snap on to other objects in the scene. This button is used to toggle the snapping on or off.

Scene picker
This list is used to select the scene that you want to manipulate.

Time position
This is where you enter the time at which you want to capture the keyframe for the animation.

Animation Playback Buttons
These are the buttons available on the right of the **Time position** box and are used to playback the animation that you have created.

Animator Tree View
This area lists the animator scenes and the animations contained inside the scenes in the sequence in which they were added. You can right-click in this area to add scenes or you can click the **Add scene** button, which is the Green button with a + symbol, to add a scene. You can right-click on the scene to display a shortcut menu, as shown in Figure 2, to add animations to the scene.

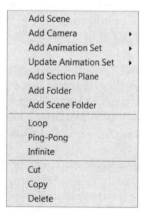

*Figure 2 The **Scene** shortcut menu*

The options in this shortcut menu are discussed next.

Add Scene
This option is used to add a new scene for creating animations.

Add Camera

This option is used to add a camera to the scene. The camera can be a blank camera that you can manipulate using the keyframes or it can be a viewpoint animation that is already saved in the **Saved Viewpoints** window. Note that in an animator scene, there can only be one camera animation.

Add Section Plane

This option is used to create animation of sectioning of the model. When you select this option, a new item called **Section Plane** is added to the scene. The sectioning animation can include sectioning using a single plane or linked planes. Note that an animator scene can only have one section animation. As a result, if section plane is added to a scene, the next time you right-click on that scene, this option will not be available.

Add Folder

This option adds a new folder inside the scene. You can organize the animations in the scene by adding them into this folder.

Add Scene Folder

This option adds a new folder at the scene level. It is generally used when you have a large number of scenes in the **Animator** window. You can add multiple folders and then add relevant scenes to those folders.

Loop

If this option is selected, once the animation ends, it will be replayed in a loop again from start. If you select this option, the **Loop** tick box on the right of the animation or the scene will be shown as selected. You can also turn on or off this option using this tick box.

Ping-Pong

If this option is selected, once the animation will play from start to end and then in reverse from end to start. With this option selected, if the **Loop** tick box is also selected, the animation will play from start to end and then from end to start in continuous loops until you stop the animation.

Infinite

This option is only available for the animator scene and not for the animations and is used to play the scene indefinitely, even past the total time duration of the animation. When you select this option, the **Loop** and **P.P.** tick boxes are disabled.

Active

This option is only available for the animations and not for the animator scene. It is used to specify which animation will be played in the current scene. The animations that are not active will be ignored during the animation playback.

Cut

The **Cut** option from the shortcut menu on an animation is used to cut that animation so that you can paste it in some other scene. However, if you cut a scene, a message box will be displayed that will inform you that it will delete all the content of the animator scene.

Copy

This option is used to copy the animator scene or the animation so that you can paste it again as a new scene or as an animation in a new scene.

Paste

This option will only be available if you have cut or copied an animator scene or animation. It is used to paste the cut or copied content.

Delete

This option is used to delete the selected animation or the animator scene and all its content.

Animator Timeline View

This area shows the animation bar for each animation in the animator scene and also the keyframes that were captured for those animations. As mentioned earlier, you can double-click on the keyframes in this area to edit the time of the keyframe and to manipulate the animation. The animation bars are color coded so you can easily identify the source of the animation. The animation bars of the animation based on the animation sets are light Blue, the animation bar of the section plane animation is Red, and the animation bar of the camera animation is Green.

> ### What I do
> *I generally create selection or search sets of the objects that I want to animate before I start creating the animations. This helps me in selecting the objects to be added as the animation sets. In some cases, I also create a viewpoint animation to navigate through the model in advance and then add it as camera animation to my animator scene.*

PROCEDURE FOR CREATING ANIMATOR ANIMATIONS

The following sections show you how to create various types of animator animations.

Animating the Object Transformation

The following steps show you how to animate the object movements:

a. If the **Animator** window is not already docked on the screen, from the **Home** ribbon tab > **Tools** ribbon panel, click the **Animator** button to display this window.

b. Dock the **Animator** window below the graphics window.

c. Right-click in the **Animator** tree view area and from the shortcut menu, click **Add Scene**; a new animator scene will be added.

d. Rename the animator scene to a relevant name.

e. From the **Selection Tree** or the graphics window, select the objects that you want to animate. You can also click on a saved selection or search set to select the objects.

f. Right-click on the scene that you added earlier and from the shortcut menu, select **Add Animation Set > From current selection** or **From current search/selection set**; a new animation set is added to the scene with the default name of **Animation Set 1**.

g. Rename the newly added animation set to a relevant name.

h. With the animation selected in the animator scene, click the **Translate animation set**, **Rotate animation set**, or **Scale animation set** button from the **Animator** toolbar, depending on whether you want to move, rotate, or scale the selected objects.

i. Press and hold the CTRL key down and drag the transform tool gizmo to the required location on the selected object in the graphics window.

What I do

*While transforming the animation set, especially using the **Rotate animation set** tool, it is very important that the rotate gizmo is properly aligned with the rotation axis even before you capture the start keyframe. In AutoCAD-based programs, I generally draw a line to represent the center of the axis so that I can snap to it while dragging the gizmo.*

---

j. Click the **Capture keyframe** button from the **Animator** toolbar; a keyframe is added at 0 second.

k. In the **Time position** box of the **Animator** toolbar, enter the time duration for which you want to tun this part of the animation. For example, if you want this animation to run for 10 seconds, type 10 in this box and press ENTER.

l. From the **Animator** toolbar, click the **Translate animation set**, **Rotate animation set**, or **Scale animation set** button, depending on whether you want to move, rotate, or scale the selected objects.

m. Using the gizmo or the **Animator** manual entry area, specify the transformation values. If you are rotating the objects, make sure you click on the origin of the gizmo and move it to the proper rotation center. Alternatively, you can use the **cX**, **cY**, and **cZ** boxes in the **Animator** manual entry area to specify the coordinates of the center point of rotation.

 Tip: While transforming the objects, you can navigate around the model to make sure you are making the right selections.

n. Once the object is transformed to the new position, click the **Capture keyframe** button on the **Animator** toolbar; a new keyframe will be added at the specified time.

o. From the **Animator** toolbar, click the **Stop** button to move the timeline back to the start. Also, click the button of the tool that you used to transform the objects to exit that tool and turn off the gizmo from the screen.

p. Press the ESC key to deselect the objects.

q.   From the **Animator** toolbar, click the **Play** button to play the animation.

> **Tip:** *While adding the animation set in step f, if you made a mistake in the object selection, you can reselect the correct objects and right-click on the added animation set and update it using the shortcut menu.*

Controlling the Transparency of the Objects in the Animation Set

As mentioned earlier, while animating objects using the **Animator** window, you can also control the transparency of the objects in the animation set. The following steps show you how to do this.

a.   From the **Animator** tree view, click on the animation set whose objects you want to edit; all the objects in that animation set will be selected.

b.   In the **Time position** box, enter the time in the animation from when you want the object transparency to start changing; the timeline bar will move to that point in the animation.

c.   If there is a keyframe added for the animation already at that point in timeline view, go to the next step. If there is no keyframe, click the **Capture keyframe** button on the **Animator** toolbar to add the keyframe.

d.   In the **Animator** timeline view, double-click on the current keyframe for the selected animation set; the **Edit Key Frame** dialog box will be displayed.

e.   Select the **Transparency** tick box and leave the value to **0**, as shown in Figure 3. Exit the dialog box.

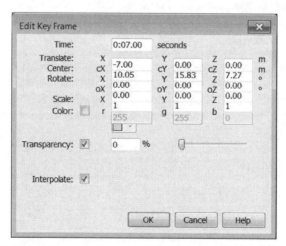

Figure 3 Changing the transparency in the **Edit Key Frame** dialog box

f.   In the **Animator** timeline view, double-click on the last keyframe for the selected animation set where you want to change the transparency; the **Edit Key Frame** dialog box will be displayed.

g.   Select the **Transparency** tick box and set the value to the required value. Note that the value of **0** will turn off the visibility of the objects. Exit the dialog box.

h.   Using the **Animator** toolbar, play the animation. Notice how the transparency changes between the keyframes.

Changing the Color of the Objects in the Animation Set

As mentioned earlier, while animating objects using the **Animator** window, you can also change the color of the objects in the animation set. The following steps show you how to do this.

a.   From the **Animator** tree view, click on the animation set whose objects you want to edit; all the objects in that animation set will be selected.

b.   In the **Time position** box, enter the time in the animation from when you want the object color to start changing; the timeline bar will move to that point in the animation.

c.   If there is a keyframe added for the animation already at that point in timeline view, go to the next step. If there is no keyframe, click the **Capture keyframe** button on the **Animator** toolbar to add the keyframe.

d.   In the **Animator** timeline view, double-click on the current keyframe for the selected animation set; the **Edit Key Frame** dialog box will be displayed.

e.   Select the **Color** tick box and then from the **Color** list, select the desired color of the objects, as shown in Figure 4. Exit the dialog box.

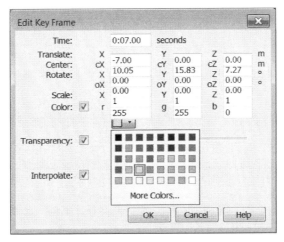

Figure 4 *Changing the color in the **Edit Key Frame** dialog box*

f.   In the **Animator** timeline view, double-click on the last keyframe for the selected animation set where you want to change the color; the **Edit Key Frame** dialog box will be displayed.

g. Select the **Color** tick box and select the required color from the **Color** list.

h. Using the **Animator** toolbar, play the animation. Notice how the color changes between the keyframes.

 Note: *If the animation set has objects to which you have assigned materials using the **Autodesk Rendering** module, their transparency or color cannot be changed while animating.*

Adding a Blank Camera Animation to the Animator Scene

The following steps show you how to add a blank camera animation to the animator scene:

a. Press ESC to make sure nothing is selected.

b. In the **Animator** tree view area, right-click on the animator scene and from the shortcut menu, select **Add Camera > Blank camera**; a new camera animation will be added with the default name of **Camera**.

c. Rename the camera animation to a relevant name.

d. From the **Animator** toolbar, click the **Capture keyframe** button; a keyframe is added at 0 second.

e. In the **Time position** box of the **Animator** toolbar, enter the time duration that you want the camera to take in navigating from the start position to the end position. For example, if you want the camera to take 10 seconds to navigate from the start position to the end position, type 10 in this box and press ENTER.

f. Using any navigation tool, preferably the **Walk** tool, navigate to the area of the design where you want the camera to be at the end of the animation.

g. Click the **Capture keyframe** button on the **Animator** toolbar; a new keyframe will be added at the specified time.

h. From the **Animator** toolbar, click the **Stop** button to move the timeline back to the start.

i. From the **Animator** toolbar, click the **Play** button to play the animation; the camera moves from the start position to the end position during the time that you specified. If there was any other animation created during the same time period, that animation will also play simultaneously with the camera animation.

What I do

In most cases, I add the camera animation at the end. This helps me to make sure that I am navigating through all the important areas of the scene as I know where the objects will be located at various stages of the animation.

Adding a Saved Viewpoint Animation to the Animator Scene

Before adding a saved viewpoint animation to the animator scene, it is important for you to know that the viewpoint animation will be added with original time duration that it was created with. As a result, you need to first edit the time duration of this animation to match the time duration that you want it to play for in the animator scene. If need be, make a copy of this animation before editing it. The following steps show you how to add a saved viewpoint animation to the animator scene.

a. From the **Saved Viewpoints** window, select the animation that you want to add to the animator scene. Make sure its duration is edited to match the duration you want it to run for in the animator scene.

b. In the **Animator** tree view area, right-click on the animator scene and from the shortcut menu, select **Add Camera > From current viewpoint animation**; a new camera animation will be added with the default name of **Camera**.

 *Note: If the viewpoint animation was created using the saved viewpoints, keyframes will be added for each viewpoint in the animation. However, if the viewpoint animation was created by recording the navigation, a keyframe will be added for each frame in the animation. This will make the **Animator** timeline view look messy.*

c. Rename the camera animation to a relevant name.

d. From the **Animator** toolbar, click the **Stop** button to move the timeline back to the start.

e. From the **Animator** toolbar, click the **Play** button to play the animation. If there was any other animation created during the same time period, it will also play simultaneously with the camera animation.

Adding a Section Plane Animation to the Animator Scene

The following steps show you how to add a section plane animation to animate the sectioning of the model:

a. Press ESC to make sure nothing is selected.

b. In the **Animator** tree view area, right-click on the animator scene and from the shortcut menu, select **Add Section Plane**; a new animation called **Section Plane** is added to the scene.

c. From the **View** ribbon tab > **Sectioning** ribbon panel, click **Enable Sectioning**; the **Sectioning Tools** ribbon tab will be displayed.

d. Using the **Current Plane** list in the **Plane Settings** ribbon panel, select the plane that you want to use for sectioning. You can also select two planes and link them, if required.

e. Using the **Move** tool, move the section plane to the start position of sectioning.

f.   In the **Animator** toolbar, click **Capture keyframe**; a keyframe will be added for the section animation.

g.   In the **Time position** box of the **Animator** toolbar, enter the time duration that you want the sectioning to run for. For example, if you want the section plane to take 10 seconds to move from the start position to the end position, type 10 in this box and press ENTER.

h.   In the graphics window, use the **Move** gizmo to move the section plane to the end position.

i.   In the **Animator** toolbar, click **Capture keyframe**; a keyframe will be added for the section animation and the timeline bar will be displayed in Red color.

j.   From the **Sectioning Tools** ribbon tab > **Transform** ribbon panel, turn off the **Move** tool by clicking on it; the section plane visibility will be turned off.

k.   In the **Animator** toolbar, click the **Stop** button to stop the animation; the section plane will disappear and the model will be displayed without sectioning.

l.   Click the **Play** button to play the animation of sectioning of the model.

THE SCRIPTER MODULE

> **Home Ribbon Tab > Tools Ribbon Panel > Scripter**

The **Scripter** module allows you to add interaction to the model by automating certain actions to be performed when something is triggered. For example, in a Remotely Operated Vehicle (ROV) that works in the subsea projects, you can have the ROV arm animate by pressing certain keys on the keyboard. Similarly, while walking into a building, you can have a revolving door to start revolving when the camera or the avatar comes within certain distance from the door. It is important to mention here that after you have added the scripts, you need to enable them to make sure the scripts work. This is discussed later in this chapter. Figure 5 shows the **Scripter** window with a script already added.

The various options in this window are discussed next.

Scripts Area

This area allows you to add scripts and also shows all the existing scripts. The active scripts that you want to run have a tick mark under the **Active** column in this area. To add a new script, click the **Add New Script** button on the lower left corner of this area. Alternatively, right-click in this area and select **Add New Script** from the shortcut menu. You can also add a folder or organize scripts using the **Add New Folder** button on the lower left corner of this area or by using the shortcut menu.

Events Area

The events are the triggers that specify when the script needs to be run. This area will be grayed

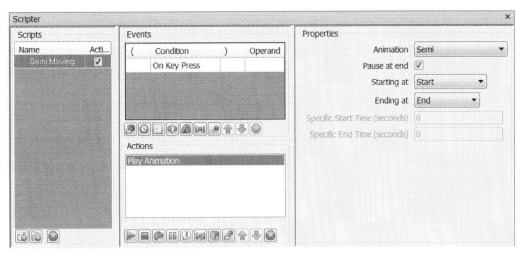

Figure 5 *The **Scripter** window with a script added*

out unless you select a script from the **Scripts** area. The events can be added by using the toolbar at the bottom of this area or by right-clicking in this area and selecting the event from the shortcut menu. Depending on the event that you have added, the **Properties** area on the right of this area will show the options to specify the information about the event. The following are the various types of events that you can add:

On Start
This event is used to trigger the script as soon as you click the **Scripter** button. If this button is already active when you open the file, the script associated with this event will run immediately on file open.

On Timer
This event is used to trigger the script at the specified time intervals. When you select this event, the **Properties** area on the right will display the following options:

Interval (seconds) Box
In this box, you can specify the interval after which you want to run the script.

Regularity List
This list allows you to select how regularly you want to run the script.

On Key Press
This event is used to trigger the script upon pressing a keyboard key. When you select this event, the **Properties** area on the right will display the following two options:

Key Box
In this box, you can specify the keyboard key that you want to use to trigger the event.

Trigger on List

This list allows you to specify whether the script should be triggered on the key down, key up or when you press and hold the key down.

On Collision

This event is used to trigger the script when the camera collides with the predefined objects. When you select this event, the **Properties** area shows the following options.

Select to collide with

The **Set** button in this area is used to define the objects whose collision with the camera will trigger the script. Make sure you select the objects first from the **Selection Tree**, **Sets** window, or from the graphics window. Then click the **Set** button and select the required option from the shortcut menu.

Include the effects of gravity

Selecting this tick box will trigger the script even if the camera or the avatar collides with any object because of the gravity.

On Hotspot

This event is used to trigger the script when the camera or the avatar is within certain distance from some predefined objects or area called the hotspot. When you select this event, the **Properties** area shows the following options:

Hotspot

This list allows you to specify the hotspot to run the script. The hotspot can simply be an area defined by a sphere in the model or a sphere on the selected objects. If you want to set an area in the model as a hotspot, select the **Sphere** option from this list and in the **Hotspot Type** area, specify the location and size of the sphere that will act as the hotspot. If you want the hotspot to be on an object, select **Sphere on selection** from this list. Then select the objects from the **Selection Tree**, **Sets** window, or from the graphics window that you want to act as the hotspot. Next, click the **Set** button in the **Hotspot Type** area and select the appropriate option from the shortcut menu. The **Radius** box allows you to specify the radius of the hotspot.

Trigger when List

This list allows you to specify whether the script should be triggered on entering the hotspot, leaving the hotspot, or when you are within the range of the hotspot.

On Variable

This event is used to trigger the script when a predefined variable meets the specified criteria. When you select this event, the **Properties** area on the right will display the following two options:

Variable Box

In this box, you can specify the name of the variable that you want to use to trigger the script.

Value Box
In this box, you can specify the value of the variable.

Evaluation List
This list is used to specify the criteria that you want the variable and the value to meet to trigger the script.

On Animation

This event is used to trigger the script when a preselected animator animation starts playing or ends playing. When you select this event, the **Properties** area on the right will display the following two options.

Animation
This list shows all the animator animation scenes. You can select the animator scene or an animation inside the scene to trigger the script.

Trigger on List
This list is used to specify whether the script will be triggered when the animator animation starts or ends.

Actions Area

The actions are the operations that will be performed in the Autodesk Navisworks model when a script is triggered. Depending on the action that you have added, the **Properties** area on the right of this area will show the options to specify the information about the action. The following are the various types of actions that you can add:

Play Animation

This action will play an animator animation when the script is triggered. The animator animation that you want to play can be selected from the **Properties** area on the right. This area will show the following options when the **Play Animation** action is selected:

Animation
This list shows all the animator animation scenes. You can select the animator scene or an animation inside the scene to play when the script is triggered.

Pause at end
Selecting this tick box will pause the animation where it ends. If this tick box is cleared, all the objects in the animator animation will move back to the start point of the animation.

Starting at
This is used to specify where you want to start the animator animation from. You can have the animation started at the start, end, current position, or at the specified time. If you select to start it at a specified time, enter the time in the **Specific Start Time (seconds)** box that is available below the **Ending at** list.

Ending at

This is used to specify where you want to end the animator animation. You can have the animation end at the start, end, or at the specified time. If you select to end it at a specified time, enter the time in the **Specific End Time (seconds)** box.

Stop Animation

This action will stop an animator animation when the script is triggered. The animator animation that you want to stop playing can be selected from the **Properties** area on the right. This area will show the following options when the **Play Animation** action is selected:

Animation

This list shows all the animator animation scenes. You can select the animator scene or an animation inside the scene to stop playing when the script is triggered.

Reset to List

This list allows you to specify whether the animator animation should be reset to the default position or left at the current position when it stops playing.

Show Viewpoint

This action will show a saved viewpoint or a saved viewpoint animation when the script is triggered. The viewpoint or the viewpoint animation that you want to show can be selected from the **Viewpoint** list that will be displayed in the **Properties** area when you select this action.

Pause

This action will add a pause between multiple actions that are being triggered in the script. The delay time, in seconds, will be defined in the **Delay (seconds)** box that will be displayed in the **Properties** area when you select this action.

Send Message

This action allows you to write a message in an external file when the script is triggered. The message that you want to be written is specified in the **Message** text box that will be displayed in the **Properties** area when you select this action. The name and the location of this external file can be specified using the **Options Editor** dialog box. In this dialog box, select **Tools > Scripter** from the left pane and specify the location and name of the file using the browse button on the right of the **Path to message file** edit box.

Set Variable

This action will set the value of the preselected variable when the script is triggered. The variable and its value is specified in the **Properties** area. This area will display the following options when the **Set Variable** action is selected.

Variable Name

This box allows you to enter the name of the variable whose value you want to set.

Value

This box allows you to enter the value you want to set for the variable.

Modifier List
This list allows you to select the operand for the value to be assigned to the variable.

Store Property
This action will save the property of the predefined objects in a variable when the script is triggered. The variable to be set and the property to be saved is specified in the **Properties** area. This area will display the following options when the **Set Variable** action is selected.

Selection to get property from
The **Set** button in this area allows you to select the objects whose property you want to save. You need to first select the objects using the **Selection Tree**, **Sets** window or the graphics window. Next, click the **Set** button and select the appropriate option from the shortcut menu.

Variable to set
This box allows you to enter the variable in which you want to save the property of the selected objects.

Property to store
This area allows you to specify the category and the property that you want to save in the specified variable.

Load Model
This action will load a predefined model when the script is triggered. The model to be loaded is defined using the **Browse** button on the right of the **File to load** box that will be displayed in the **Properties** area when you select this action.

ENABLING THE SCRIPTS

Animation Ribbon Tab > **Script Ribbon Panel** > **Enable Scripts**

As mentioned earlier, even though you may have the scripts added to the Autodesk Navisworks model, but they will only work after you enable them. To enable scripts, click the **Enable Scripts** button from the **Animation** ribbon tab > **Script** ribbon panel.

PROCEDURE FOR ADDING INTERACTIVITY TO THE MODEL USING SCRIPTS
The following steps show you how you can add interactivity to the Autodesk Navisworks model using scripts:

a. If the **Scripter** window is not already docked on the screen, from the **Home** ribbon tab > **Tools** ribbon panel, click the **Scripter** button to display this window.

b. Dock the **Scripter** window below the graphics window.

c. From the **Animation** ribbon tab > **Script** ribbon panel, click **Enable Scripts**, if it is not already turned on.

d. In the **Scripter** window, right-click in the **Scripts** area to add a new script. Rename it to the desired name.

e. With the newly added script selected, select the required event to trigger the script from the toolbar at the bottom of the **Events** area. For example, if you want the script to be triggered at the press of a key, click the **On Key Press** button.

f. From the **Properties** area, set the information related to the event that you selected. For example, if you selected the **On Key Press** event, specify the key and its trigger in the **Properties** area.

g. With the event selected, select the action to be performed when the script is triggered from the toolbar in the **Actions** area. For example, if you want to start playing an animation, click the **Play Animation** button.

h. From the **Properties** area, set the information related to the action that you selected. For example, if you selected the **Play Animation** action, specify the animation to play and its related information in the **Properties** area.

i. Repeat steps d to g to add more events and actions to the script.

EXPORTING ANIMATIONS

```
Output Ribbon Tab > Visuals Ribbon Panel > Animation
```

The animations created in the animator scene can be exported as .AVI files to be opened on a machine that does not have Autodesk Navisworks. To do this, click **Output** ribbon tab > **Visuals** ribbon panel > **Animation**; the **Animation Export** dialog box will be displayed, as shown in Figure 6. From the **Source** list, select **Current Animator Scene**. From the **Renderer** list, select the required renderer. Using the **Autodesk Rendering** renderer will assign the material and lighting to the scene. Using the **Viewpoint** renderer will export the animation as it looks in the graphics window without rendering.

From the **Format** list, select **Windows AVI** and then click on the **Options** button on the right of this list to display the **Video Compression** dialog box. Click **Full Frames (Uncompressed)** from the **Compressor** list and click **OK** in the dialog box.

From the **Type** list in the **Size** area, select **Use Aspect Ratio**. Enter **800** in the **Width** edit box; the value in the **Height** edit box will change automatically, depending on your graphics screen size.

In the **FPS** spinner in the **Options** area, enter **12** as the value of frames per second. Remember that bigger the value of frames per second, smoother the animation, but larger will be the resulting AVI file size.

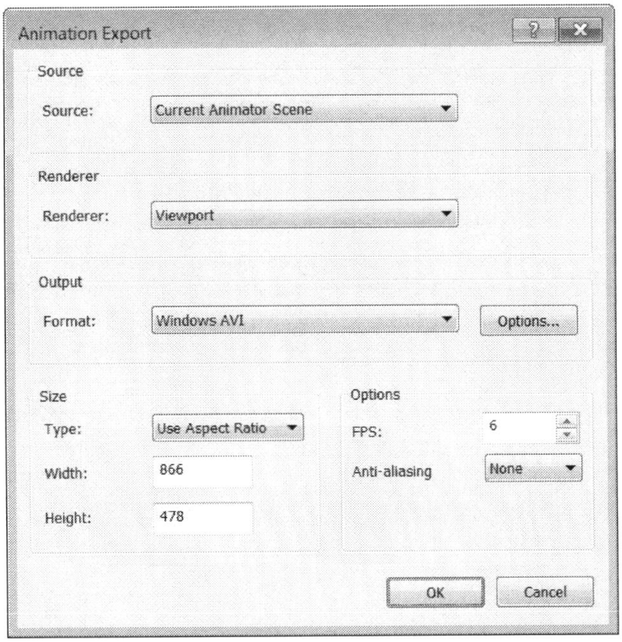

*Figure 6 The **Animation Export** dialog box*

Click **OK** in the **Animation Export** dialog box, the **Save As** dialog box will be displayed that lets you specify the name and location of the AVI file.

HANDS-ON EXERCISES

Next, you will work on hands-on exercises by using the concepts learned in this chapter.

Hands-on Exercise (Plant)	*In this exercise, you will complete the following tasks:* 1. *Open the Autodesk Navisworks file of a Remotely Operated Vehicle (ROV) and add an animator scene to it.* 2. *Add various animations to the animator scene of the ROV.* 3. *Add a script to trigger the animation of the ROV.* 4. *Open the Autodesk Navisworks file of a plant model and add a section plane animation.* 5. *Add script to the plant animation.*

Section 1: Opening the File and Adding an Animator Scene

In this section, you will open a .NWD file of a Remotely Operated Vehicle (ROV) that is used in various subsea operations. You will then add the animator scene to the model.

1. Invoke the **Open** dialog box and from the **Chapter 7 > Exercise Plant** folder, open the **ROV.nwd** file; the model opens and looks similar to the one shown in Figure 7.

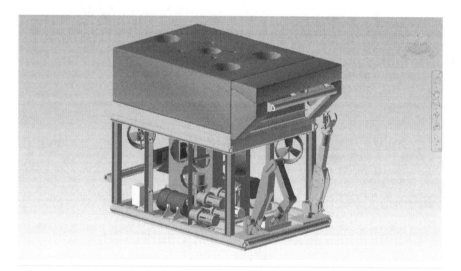

Figure 7 *The model of a Remotely Operated Vehicle (ROV)* **(Model courtesy Scott Gibbs, Senior Subsea Designer, Technip Oceania Pty Ltd)**

2. Click the **Animator** button from the bottom of the graphics window; the **Animator** window is displayed.

3. Dock the **Animator** window below the graphics window.

4. From the lower left corner the **Animator** tree view, click the **Add scene** button and select **Add Scene** from the shortcut menu; a new animator scene is added.

5. Rename the scene to **ROV**.

Section 2: Adding Animations of Moving and Rotating the ROV

In this section, you will add the animation to move the ROV to the other side of the graphics window and rotate it so that it looks like a mirror image of the start orientation. Normally, the ROV moves with the help of the thrusters that are placed around it. But for this exercise, you will not animate the thrusters.

1. From the **Saved Viewpoints** window, activate the **Start** viewpoint.

2. Using the **Options Editor** dialog box, change the display units to **Millimeters**.

3. From the **Selection Tree**, select the **ROV.nwd** file; the entire model is selected and highlighted in the graphics window.

4. In the **Animator** window, right-click on the **ROV** scene and select **Add Animation Set > From current selection** from the shortcut menu; a new animation based on animation set is added.

5. Rename the animation to **ROV Appearing**.

   Next, you will move the ROV to the other side of the graphics window and rotate it so it looks like a mirror image of the start orientation.

6. From the **Animator** toolbar displayed at the top in the **Animator** window, click the **Translate animation set** button; the move gizmo is displayed on the model.

7. From the **Animator** toolbar, click the **Capture keyframe** button; a new keyframe is added at 0 second.

8. In the **Time position** box of the **Animator** toolbar, type **10** and press ENTER; the timeline bar moves to 10 seconds.

   You will now use the move gizmo to move the ROV. It is important for you to make sure you use the correct axis and plane of the gizmo to move the ROV. For your convenience, the colors of the axes and planes are color coded.

9. Move the cursor over the **Blue** plane of the gizmo (horizontal plane); the cursor changes to the hand cursor.

   In the following step, you will move the ROV to the specified location. These values are only for reference. Depending on the size of the monitor you are using, these values can be different. The important thing is to make sure the ROV is visible in the graphics window even after the **Animator** window is turned off.

10. Press and hold down the left mouse button and drag the ROV to the right of the screen. Release the left mouse button at the location whose coordinates are displayed close to **5800, 5200, 0** in the **Translate X, Y, Z** boxes of **Animator** manual entry area at the lower left corner of the **Animator** window. You can also drag the Red and Green axes of the gizmo to change the X and Y values.

Next, you will rotate the ROV so it faces toward the bottom left of the graphics window.

11. From the **Animator** toolbar, click the **Rotate animation set** button; the rotate gizmo is displayed in the graphics window.

    By default, the rotate gizmo is displayed away from the ROV. You first need to move it on the ROV.

12. Move the cursor over the sphere at the origin of the rotate gizmo; the cursor changes to the hand cursor.

13. Press and hold down the left mouse button and drag the rotate gizmo over one of the top holes of the ROV.

    Next, you will use the Blue curved plane on the gizmo to rotate the ROV.

14. Move the cursor over the Blue curved plane of the rotate gizmo; the cursor changes to the hand cursor.

15. Press and hold down the left mouse button and drag it to the left. Release it when the **Rotate Z** box in the **Animator** manual entry area shows a value close to **-80**, refer to Figure 8 below for the orientation of the model.

16. From the **Animator** toolbar, click the **Capture keyframe** button; a new keyframe is added at 10 seconds and a light Blue animation bar is added in the **Animator** timeline view.

17. Click anywhere in the graphics window to deselect the ROV and then click the **Rotate animation set** button again to turn off the rotate gizmo. The model looks similar to the one shown in Figure 8.

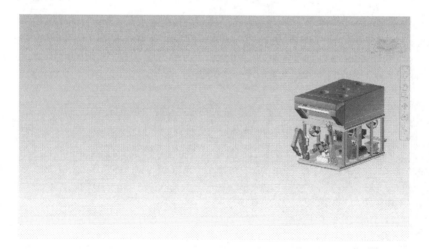

Figure 8 The view after moving and rotating the ROV

It is better to play this animation before proceeding further to make sure it works.

18. In the **Animator** toolbar, click the **Stop** button; the ROV moves back to the start position.

19. In the **Animator** toolbar, click the **Play** button; the animation plays and the ROV moves and rotates from the start position to the end position.

Section 3: Controlling the Color and Transparency of the ROV

In this section, you will change the color and transparency of the ROV. You will start with a transparency of 90% and change the color to light gray. This is to show the effect as if the ROV is moving closer to you in the water.

1. In the **Animator** timeline view, double-click on the keyframe at 0 second; the **Edit Key Frame** dialog box is displayed.

2. In the dialog box, select the **Transparency** tick box and enter **90** as the value.

3. Select the **Color** tick box and change the **r**, **g**, **b** color values to **247, 247, 247**.

4. Click **OK** in the dialog box; the ROV becomes transparent and changes to light gray.

5. In the **Time position** box of the **Animator** toolbar, type **3** and press ENTER; the timeline bar moves to 3 seconds and the ROV is reoriented to match its position and orientation at 3 seconds.

6. From the **Animator** toolbar, click the **Capture keyframe** button; a keyframe is added at 3 seconds.

7. Double-click the keyframe to display the **Edit Key Frame** dialog box.

8. In the dialog box, clear the **Color** tick box and change the transparency value to **75**.

9. Click **OK** in the dialog box; the ROV is changed to the original color and also appears less transparent, as shown in Figure 9.

10. In the **Time position** box of the **Animator** toolbar, type **7** and press ENTER; the timeline bar moves to 7 seconds and the ROV is reoriented to match its position and orientation at 7 seconds.

11. From the **Animator** toolbar, click the **Capture keyframe** button; a keyframe is added at 7 seconds.

12. Double-click the keyframe to display the **Edit Key Frame** dialog box.

13. In the dialog box, change the transparency value to **40**.

14. Click **OK** in the dialog box; the ROV is displayed a lot clearer.

15. In the **Animator** toolbar, click the **Stop** button and then click the **Play** button; the animation plays and shows the effect of change in color and transparency.

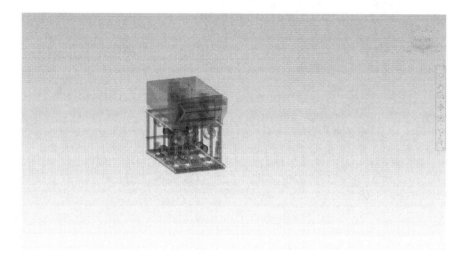

Figure 9 The view after changing the transparency of the ROV

Section 4: Animating the First Arm of the ROV

The ROV has two arms: the first one is named Titian and the second one is named Rigmaster. For your convenience, there are selection sets created that represent various parts of these arms that will be animated.

1. Dock the **Sets** window below the **Selection Tree**.

    Notice the four selection sets already created in the model. These selection sets will be used to create the animations of the arms of the ROV.

2. From the **Sets** window, click the **Titian 1** set; the left arm of the ROV is highlighted in the graphics window.

3. From the **Navigation Bar** on the right side of the graphics window, click **Zoom Window > Zoom Selected**; the view will be zoomed to the selected arm.

4. Enter **10** as the value in the **Time position** box of the **Animator** toolbar to make sure the timeline is at this position.

    Next, you will add an animation set of the selected arm and then rotate it down.

5. With the **Titian 1** set still selected, right-click on the **ROV** scene and click **Add Animation Set > From current search/selection set**; a new animation set is added to the scene.

6. Rename the animation set to **Titian 1 Down**.

7. From the **Animator** toolbar, click the **Rotate animation set** button; the rotate gizmo is displayed in the graphics window.

As you can see, the gizmo is not displayed at the axis that you want to use to rotate the arm. It is important that before you capture the keyframe, this gizmo is moved and aligned with the rotation axis. For your convenience, a line is drawn to represent the axis of rotation, refer to Figure 10.

 Note: *If the line representing the axis is not visible, turn on* **Lines** *from the* **Viewpoints** *ribbon tab >* **Render Style** *ribbon panel.*

8. Move the cursor over the sphere displayed at the origin of the rotate gizmo, shown in the bigger ellipse in Figure 10; the cursor changes to the hand cursor.

9. Press and hold down the left mouse button and drag the rotate gizmo over the axis displayed in the smaller ellipse in Figure 10.

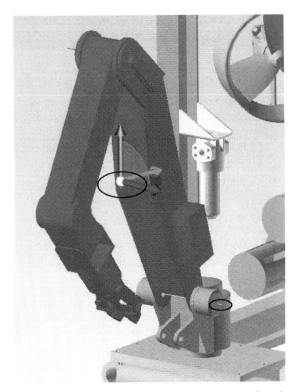

Figure 10 *Figure showing where the rotate gizmo needs to be moved*

10. To make sure the origin of the rotate gizmo is aligned with the axis, zoom close to the axis. If it is not aligned, drag the origin of the rotate gizmo again and drop it on the axis.

After aligning the origin of the rotate gizmo, you will notice that the Red axis of the gizmo is not aligned with the axis of rotation. If the two axes are not aligned, the rotation of the arm will not be correct. So you need to fix this by rotating the gizmo only by pressing and holding the CTRL key down. Note that if you do not hold the CTRL key down, the arm will be rotated.

11. Zoom and orbit the model around so you can see the Blue curved plane of the rotate gizmo.

12. Move the cursor over the Blue curved plane of the rotate gizmo. Now, press and hold down the CTRL key and drag it to the right to a location where the **Rotation oZ** box in the **Animator** manual entry area shows a value of around **11.3**.

13. From the **Animator** toolbar, click the **Capture keyframe** button; a new keyframe is added at 10 seconds for the **Titian 1 Down** animation.

14. In the **Time position** box of the **Animator** toolbar, type **13** and press ENTER; the timeline bar moves to 13 seconds.

15. Zoom and orbit the model so that you can see the Red curved plane of the rotate gizmo.

16. Move the cursor over the Red curved plane of the rotate gizmo; the cursor changes to the hand cursor.

17. Drag the Red curved plane to a position where the **Rotate X** box in the **Animator** manual entry area displays a value close to **25**.

18. In the **Animator** toolbar, click **Capture keyframe**; a new keyframe is added at 13 seconds.

19. Click anywhere in the blank area of the graphics window to deselect everything and then from the **Animator** toolbar, click the **Rotate animation set** button again to turn off the display of the rotate gizmo.

20. In the **Time position** box, enter **10** as the value; the timeline moves back to 10 seconds and the Titian arm moves to the original position.

21. Zoom out to view the complete arm. Now, in the **Animator** toolbar, click the **Play** button; the Titian arm rotates around the specified axis for 3 seconds.

Next, you will animate the **Titian 2** selection set using the same methods described above.

22. From the **Sets** window, click the **Titian 2** animation set; the selected objects are highlighted in the graphics window.

23. From the **Navigation Bar** on the right side of the graphics window, click **Zoom Window > Zoom Selected**; the view will be zoomed to the selected arm.

24. Enter **13** as the value in the **Time position** box of the **Animator** toolbar to make sure the timeline is at this position.

Next, you will add an animation set of the selected arm and then rotate it up.

25. With the **Titian 2** set still selected, right-click on the **ROV** scene and click **Add Animation Set > From current search/selection set**; a new animation set is added to the scene.

26. Rename the animation set to **Titian 2 Up**.

27. From the **Animator** toolbar, click the **Rotate animation set** button; the rotate gizmo is displayed in the graphics window.

    As you can see, the gizmo is not displayed at the axis that you want to use to rotate the arm. It is important that before you capture the keyframe, this gizmo is moved and aligned with the rotation axis. For your convenience, a line is drawn to represent the axis of rotation, refer to Figure 11.

28. Move the cursor over the sphere displayed at the origin of the rotate gizmo, shown in the bigger ellipse in Figure 11; the cursor changes to the hand cursor.

29. Press and hold down the left mouse button and drag the rotate gizmo over the axis displayed in the smaller ellipse in Figure 11.

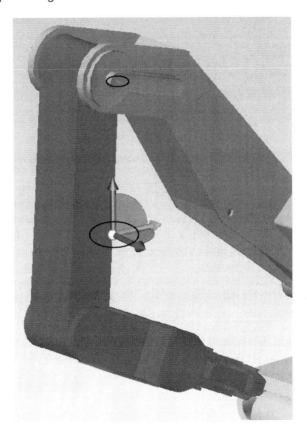

Figure 11 *Figure showing where the rotate gizmo needs to be moved*

30. To make sure the origin of the rotate gizmo is aligned with the axis, zoom close to the axis. If it is not aligned, drag the origin of the rotate gizmo again and drop it on the axis.

Similar to the previous case, this time also you will notice that the Red axis of the gizmo is not aligned with the axis of rotation. As mentioned earlier, if the two axes are not aligned, the rotation of the arm will not be correct. So you need to fix this by rotating the gizmo only by pressing and holding down the CTRL key. Note that if you do not hold the CTRL key down, the arm will be rotated.

31. Zoom and orbit the model around so you can see the Blue curved plane of the rotate gizmo.

32. Move the cursor over the Blue curved plane of the rotate gizmo. Now, press and hold down the CTRL key and drag it to the right to a location where the **Rotation oZ** box in the **Animator** manual entry area shows a value of around **10.5**.

33. From the **Animator** toolbar, click the **Capture keyframe** button; a new keyframe is added at 13 seconds for the **Titian 2 Up** animation.

34. In the **Time position** box of the **Animator** toolbar, type **16** and press ENTER; the timeline bar moves to 16 seconds.

35. Zoom and orbit the model so that you can see the Red curved plane of the rotate gizmo.

36. Move the cursor over the Red curved plane of the rotate gizmo; the cursor changes to the hand cursor.

37. Drag the Red curved plane to a position where the **Rotate X** box in the **Animator** manual entry area displays a value close to **-90**.

38. In the **Animator** toolbar, click **Capture keyframe**; a new keyframe is added at 16 seconds.

39. Click anywhere in the blank area of the graphics window to deselect everything and then from the **Animator** toolbar, click the **Rotate animation set** button again to turn off the display of the rotate gizmo. The Titian arm, after this animation, appears similar to the one shown in Figure 12.

40. In the **Time position** box, enter **0** as the value; the timeline moves back to the start.

41. From the **Saved Viewpoints** window, click the **Start** viewpoint.

42. In the **Animator** window, click the **ROV** scene and then click the **Play** button; the entire animation plays for 16 seconds.

Section 5: Animating the Second Arm of the ROV

In this section, you will animate the Rigmaster arm of the ROV using the selection set that is created for this arm.

1. From the **Sets** window, click the **Rigmaster** set; the left arm of the ROV is highlighted in the graphics window.

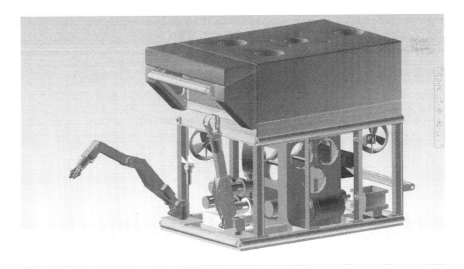

Figure 12 *The Titian arm of the ROV rotated*

2. From the **Navigation Bar** on the right side of the graphics window, click **Zoom Window > Zoom Selected**; the view will be zoomed to the selected arm.

3. Enter **16** as the value in the **Time position** box of the **Animator** toolbar to make sure the timeline is at this position.

   Next, you will add an animation set of the selected arm and then rotate it down.

4. With the **Rigmaster** set still selected, right-click on the **ROV** scene and click **Add Animation Set > From current search/selection set**; a new animation set is added to the scene.

5. Rename the animation set to **Rigmaster**.

6. From the **Animator** toolbar, click the **Rotate animation set** button; the rotate gizmo is displayed in the graphics window.

   As you can see, the gizmo is not displayed at the axis that you want to use to rotate the arm. It is important that before you capture the keyframe, this gizmo is moved and aligned with the rotation axis. For your convenience, a line is drawn to represent the axis of rotation, refer to Figure 13.

7. Move the cursor over the sphere displayed at the origin of the rotate gizmo, shown in the bigger ellipse in Figure 13; the cursor changes to the hand cursor.

8. Press and hold down the left mouse button and drag the rotate gizmo over the axis displayed in the smaller ellipse in Figure 13.

Figure 13 *Figure showing where the rotate gizmo needs to be moved*

9. To make sure the origin of the rotate gizmo is aligned with the axis, zoom close to the axis. If it is not aligned, drag the origin of the rotate gizmo again and drop it on the axis.

    Similar to the previous case, this time also you will notice that the Red axis of the gizmo is not aligned with the axis of rotation. Therefore, you need to rotate the gizmo only by pressing and holding down the CTRL key.

10. Orbit the model around so you can see the Blue curved plane of the rotate gizmo.

11. Move the cursor over the Blue curved plane of the rotate gizmo. Now, press and hold down the CTRL key and drag it to the right to a location where the **Rotation oZ** box in the **Animator** manual entry area shows a value of around **8.7**.

12. From the **Animator** toolbar, click the **Capture keyframe** button; a new keyframe is added at 16 seconds for the **Rigmaster** animation.

13. In the **Time position** box of the **Animator** toolbar, type **20** and press ENTER; the timeline bar moves to 20 seconds.

14. Zoom and orbit the model so that you can see the Red curved plane of the rotate gizmo.

15. Move the cursor over the Red curved plane of the rotate gizmo; the cursor changes to the hand cursor.

16. Drag the Red curved plane to a position where the **Rotate X** box in the **Animator** manual entry area displays a value close to **70**.

17. In the **Animator** toolbar, click **Capture keyframe**; a new keyframe is added at 20 seconds.

18. Click anywhere in the blank area of the graphics window to deselect everything and then from the **Animator** toolbar, click the **Rotate animation set** button again to turn off the display of the rotate gizmo. The zoomed out view of the ROV after rotating the second arm should look similar to the one shown in Figure 14.

Figure 14 Both the arms of the ROV rotated

19. In the **Time position** box, enter **0** as the value; the timeline moves back to the start.

20. From the **Saved Viewpoints** window, click the **Start** viewpoint.

21. In the **Animator** window, click the **ROV** scene and then click the **Play** button; the entire animation plays for 20 seconds.

Section 6: Adding a Camera Animation

You will notice that in the current display, it is hard to see the animation of the two arms of the ROV. The camera needs to move close to the ROV for a better display. To achieve this, you will add a camera animation to the animator scene.

1. In the **Animator** window, right-click on the **ROV** animator scene and select **Add Camera > Blank camera** from the shortcut menu.

2. Press ENTER to accept the default name of the camera animation.

3. Enter **0** as the value in the **Time position** box of the **Animator** toolbar; the animation moves to the start point.

4. With the camera animation highlighted, click the **Capture keyframe** button from the **Animator** toolbar; a keyframe is added at 0 second for the camera animation.

5. Enter **10** as the value in the **Time position** box of the **Animator** toolbar; the animation moves to 10 seconds.

6. Click anywhere in the blank area of the graphics window.

7. Move the cursor over the Titian arm and scroll the wheel mouse button forward to zoom close to this arm of the ROV. Stop scrolling when the view looks similar to the one shown in Figure 15.

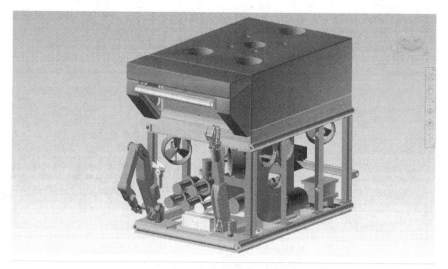

Figure 15 Zooming close to the ROV

8. With the camera animation highlighted, click the **Capture keyframe** button from the **Animator** toolbar; a keyframe is added at 10 seconds for the camera animation.

    Notice that the animation bar of the camera animation is light Green. The color coding allows you to easily identify the source of the animation.

9. Enter **13** as the value in the **Time position** box of the **Animator** toolbar; the animation moves to 13 seconds.

10. Click anywhere in the blank area of the graphics window.

11. Move the cursor over the Titian arm and scroll the wheel mouse button forward to zoom close to this arm of the ROV. If need be, pan the view so that the model looks similar to the one shown in Figure 16.

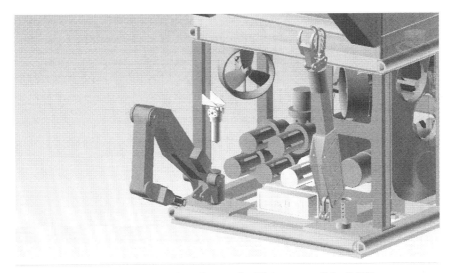

Figure 16 *Zooming close to the Titian arm of the ROV*

12. With the camera animation highlighted, click the **Capture keyframe** button from the **Animator** toolbar; a keyframe is added at 13 seconds for the camera animation.

13. Enter **20** as the value in the **Time position** box of the **Animator** toolbar; the animation moves to end.

14. Click the **Capture keyframe** button from the **Animator** toolbar; a keyframe is added at 20 seconds for the camera animation.

15. Enter **22** as the value in the **Time position** box of the **Animator** toolbar; the animation bar moves to 22 seconds.

16. From the **Navigation Bar** on the right side of the graphics window, click **Zoom All**; the view zooms to the extents of the ROV.

17. Click the **Capture keyframe** button from the **Animator** toolbar; a keyframe is added at 22 seconds for the camera animation.

18. Click the **Stop** button on the **Animator** toolbar; the animation goes to the start.

    Now, you will play the entire animation again.

19. Select the **ROV** scene and then click the **Play** button from the **Animator** toolbar; the animation starts playing. Notice how the camera will change as the animation plays.

20. Click the **Stop** button on the **Animator** toolbar; the animation stops and the ROV moves back to the start position.

21. Hide the **Animator** window.

Section 7: Adding a Script to Animate the ROV

In this section, you will add a script to automate the ROV animation. You will use the keyboard key as the trigger to play the animator scene.

1. From the **Saved Viewpoints** window, click the **Start** viewpoint.

2. Click the **Scripter** button from the bottom of the graphics window; the **Scripter** window is displayed.

3. Dock the **Scripter** window below the graphics window.

4. Right-click in the **Scripts** area and select **Add New Script** from the shortcut menu; a new script is added with the name **New Script**.

5. Rename the script to **ROV**.

6. From the toolbar at the bottom of the **Events** area, click the **On Key Press** button; a new event is added and the **Properties** area is displayed on the right of the **Events** area.

7. In the **Properties** area, click inside the **Key** box and then press the F4 key on the keyboard; the F4 key is assigned as the trigger to the script.

8. From the toolbar at the bottom of the **Actions** area, click the **Play Animation** button; a new action is added and the **Properties** area is displayed on the right.

9. From the **Animation** list in the **Properties** area, double-click **ROV**. The rest of the options will be accepted as they are. Figure 17 shows the **Scripter** window with the required options.

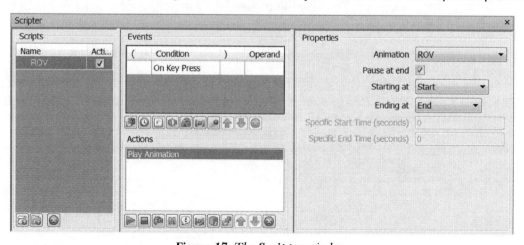

Figure 17 *The Scripter window*

10. Hide the **Scripter** window.

11. From the **Animation** ribbon tab > **Script** ribbon panel, click **Enable Scripts**.

Note: *When the scripts are enabled, the options in the **Scripter** and **Animator** windows will not be selectable.*

12. Press the F11 key to turn on the full screen mode and then press the F4 key; the animator scene is played from start to end.

13. Press the F11 key and then click the **Enable Scripts** button again to disable the scripts.

14. Save the file.

Section 8: Creating a Section Animation

In this section, you will open a plant model and create an animator scene in which you will section the model. You will then create a script to animate the sectioning of this model.

1. Open the **Plant.nwd** file from the **Chapter 7 > Exercise Plant** folder.

2. From the **Viewpoint** ribbon tab > **Render Style** ribbon panel > **Lighting** flyout, click **Scene Lights** to turn on the scene lights.

The plant model looks similar to the one shown in Figure 18.

Figure 18 The plant model for creating section animation

3. Click the **Animator** button below the graphics window to invoke the **Animator** window.

4. Dock this window below the graphics window.

5. Using the **Options Editor** dialog box, set the display units as Meters or Inches.

6. From the **Viewpoint** ribbon tab > **Sectioning** ribbon panel, click **Enable Sectioning**; the **Sectioning Tools** ribbon tab is displayed.

7. From the lower left corner the **Animator** tree view, click the **Add scene** button and select **Add Scene** from the shortcut menu; a new animator scene is added.

8. Rename the animator scene to **Sectioning**.

9. Right-click on the **Sectioning** scene and select **Add Section Plane** from the shortcut menu; a new animation called **Section Plane** is added to the scene.

10. Press ENTER to accept the default name of the section animation.

11. If not already selected, select **Plane 6** from the **Sectioning Tools** ribbon tab > **Plane Settings** ribbon panel > **Current Plane** list.

12. Click the **Move** button from the **Transform** ribbon panel; a new section plane is displayed sectioning the model from the right.

13. Expand the **Transform** ribbon panel and dock it on the screen.

14. With the **Move** tool selected, enter **1100 Inches** or **28 Meters** as the value in the **Position X** box; the plane moves outside the model and no part of the model is sectioned at this stage.

15. In the **Animator** window, click the **Capture keyframe** button from the **Animator** toolbar; a new keyframe is added at 0 second.

16. Type **10** in the **Time position** box of the **Animator** toolbar and press ENTER; the timeline moves to 10 seconds.

    You will now move the section plane using the move gizmo to the left to section the plant.

17. Move the cursor over the Blue axis of the move gizmo; the cursor changes to the hand cursor.

18. Drag the move gizmo to the left and release it when the **Position X** value in the expanded **Transform** ribbon panel is close to **300 Inches** or **7.6 Meters**, the sectioned model looks similar to the one shown in Figure 19.

19. In the **Transform** ribbon panel, click the **Move** tool to turn off the visibility of the section plane.

20. In the **Animator** window, click the **Capture keyframe** button from the **Animator** toolbar; a new keyframe is added at 10 seconds.

    Notice that the color of the section animation bar is Red. As mentioned earlier, the animation bars are color coded so that you can easily identify the source of the animation.

Figure 19 *The plant model sectioned using Plane 6*

21. Right-click on the **Section Plane** animation and select **Ping-Pong** from the shortcut menu; the **P.P.** tick box is selected on the right of the animation.

22. Click the **Stop** button in the **Animator** toolbar.

23. Click the **Enable Sectioning** button in the **Sectioning Tools** ribbon tab > **Enable** ribbon panel to turn off the sectioning.

24. In the **Animator** window, click the **Play** button to play the sectioning animation from start to end and then in reverse from end to start.

25. Click the **Stop** button when the animation stops playing.

26. Close the **Animator** window.

   Next, you will add a script to automatically play this animation. You will use the keyboard key to trigger the script.

27. Click the **Scripter** button below the graphics window to display the **Scripter** window.

28. Dock this window below the graphics window, if it is not already docked.

29. In the **Scripts** area, right-click and select **Add New Script** from the shortcut menu.

30. Rename the script to **Sectioning**.

31. From the toolbar at the bottom of the **Events** area, click **On Key Press**; a new event is added and the **Properties** area is displayed on the right.

32. In the **Properties** area, click inside the **Key** box and press the F4 key.

33. From the toolbar at the bottom of the **Actions** area, click **Play Animation**; a new action is added and the **Properties** area is displayed on the right.

34. In the **Properties** area, click the **Animation** list and double-click **Sectioning**.

35. Accept the rest of the options as they are and close the **Scripter** window.

36. From the **Animation** ribbon tab > **Script** ribbon panel, click **Enable Scripts**.

37. Press the F11 key to activate the full screen mode and then press the F4 key; the sectioning animation plays in auto-reverse mode.

38. Press the F11 key to exit the full screen mode and then click **Enable Scripts** again to disable the scripts.

39. Save the file.

Section 9: Animating Objects to Drop from the Sky

One of the questions that I am regularly asked is how to make objects drop to their location from the sky during the timeliner simulation. It is done by linking the animator animations to the tasks. Therefore, I have added this section in this chapter to show you how to create these animator animations. These animations will then be linked to timeliner tasks in the next chapter.

1. From the **Chapter 7 > Exercise Plant** folder, open the **Object-drop.nwd** file.

    Notice the various sets created in this file. You will animate these sets.

2. Using the **Options Editor** dialog box, set the display units as Meters or Inches.

3. Dock the **Animator** window, if it is not already docked on the screen.

4. From the lower left corner the **Animator** tree view, click the **Add scene** button and select **Add Scene** from the shortcut menu; a new animator scene is added.

5. Rename the animator scene to **Concrete Columns**.

6. From the **Sets** window, click the **Concrete Columns** set; the concrete columns are highlighted in the graphics window.

7. Right-click on the **Concrete Columns** scene and click **Add Animation Set > From current search/selection set**; a new animation set is added to the scene.

8. Rename this animation to **Con-Cols-Drop**.

9. From the **Animator** toolbar, click the **Capture keyframe** button; a new keyframe is added at 0 second for the **Con-Cols-Drop** animation.

10. In the **Time position** box of the **Animator** toolbar, type **5** and press ENTER; the timeline bar moves to 5 seconds.

11. From the **Animator** toolbar, click the **Capture keyframe** button; a new keyframe is added at 5 seconds for the **Con-Cols-Drop** animation.

    So basically you have created a 5 seconds animation in which the concrete columns do not move. This is where you will now go and modify the 0 second keyframe and change the start position of the concrete columns.

12. Double-click on the 0 second keyframe; the **Edit Key Frame** dialog box is displayed.

13. Change the **Translate Z** value in the dialog box to **75 Feet** or **23 Meters**, depending on the units you are using.

14. Close the **Edit Key Frame** dialog box.

15. Click the **Stop** button from the **Animator** toolbar; the animation returns to 0 second.

16. Press ESC to deselect the concrete columns and then click the **Play** button from the **Animator** toolbar; the columns are moved to the defined Z position at the start of the animation and are then dropped at their original position in the animation.

17. Click in the Gray area of the **Animator** tree view to deselect the **Concrete Columns** scene.

18. From the lower left corner the **Animator** tree view, click the **Add scene** button and select **Add Scene** from the shortcut menu; a new animator scene is added.

19. Rename the animator scene to **Steel Columns**.

20. From the **Sets** window, click the **Steel Columns** set; the steel columns are highlighted in the graphics window.

21. Right-click on the **Steel Columns** scene and click **Add Animation Set > From current search/selection set**; a new animation set is added to the scene.

22. Rename this animation to **Steel-Cols-Drop**.

23. From the **Animator** toolbar, click the **Capture keyframe** button; a new keyframe is added at 0 second for the **Steel-Cols-Drop** animation.

24. In the **Time position** box of the **Animator** toolbar, type **5** and press ENTER; the timeline bar moves to 5 seconds.

25. From the **Animator** toolbar, click the **Capture keyframe** button; a new keyframe is added at 5 seconds for the **Steel-Cols-Drop** animation.

26. Double-click on the 0 second keyframe; the **Edit Key Frame** dialog box is displayed.

27. Change the **Translate Z** value in the dialog box to **75 Feet** or **23 Meters**, depending on the units you are using.

28. Close the **Edit Key Frame** dialog box.

29. Similarly, add the animator scenes and animations for the rest of the sets and edit their start position at the 0 second keyframe.

30. Click the **Stop** button from the **Animator** toolbar; the animation returns to 0 second.

31. Press ESC to deselect everything and then click the **Play** button from the **Animator** toolbar; the animation plays from start to end.

    This is how you create the animator animations of objects dropping at their position. These animations can then be linked to the timeliner simulations. You will learn about this in the next chapter.

Hands-on Exercise (BIM)	*In this exercise, you will complete the following tasks:* *1. Open the Autodesk Navisworks file of a building and then create an animator scene.* *2. Add various animations to the animator scene of the building.* *3. Add a script to trigger the animator scene animations.* *4. Open the Autodesk Navisworks file of a building under construction and add animation of crane rotation and a semitrailer movement.* *5. Add script to play the crane and semitrailer animation.* *6. Open a building model and create the animation of sectioning the building.* *7. Add a script to trigger the sectioning of the building.*

Section 1: Opening the File and Adding an Animator Scene

In this section, you will open a .NWD file of a building that already has some viewpoints and a viewpoint animation saved. You will then add the animator scene to the model. The building model for this exercise is **courtesy Ankur Mathur, Founder and CEO, SANRACHNA:BIM and Virtual Construction Consultants**.

1. Open the **Office_Building.nwd** file from the **Chapter 7 > Exercise Building** folder.

2. From the **Viewpoint** ribbon tab > **Render Style** ribbon panel > **Lighting** flyout, click **Scene Lights** to turn the scene lights on.

    The building model looks similar to the one shown in Figure 20. Notice the two vehicles in the scene. These will be animated later in this exercise.

Figure 20 *The building model for the exercise*

3. From the **Home** ribbon tab > **Tools** ribbon panel, click the **Animator** button to display the **Animator** window. Dock this window below the graphics window.

4. From the lower left corner of the **Animator** window, click **Add scene > Add Scene**; a new scene is added.

5. Rename the scene to **Vehicles**.

6. From the **Options Editor** dialog box, select the display units as Inches or Meters.

Section 2: Animating the Vehicles

In this section, you will animate the car to move from left to right in the scene. At the same time, you will move the SUV from right to left in the scene. You will use the **Animator** manual entry area to enter the values of movement in this case.

1. In the **Selection Tree**, expand **Office_Building.nwd** and select the **Car.nwd** file; the Red car is highlighted in the graphics window.

2. In the **Animator** window, right-click on the **Vehicles** scene and select **Add Animation Set > From current selection** from the shortcut menu; a new animation set is added to the scene.

3. Rename the animation set to **Car**.

4. From the **Animator** toolbar, click the **Capture keyframe** button; a new keyframe is added at 0 second.

5. In the **Animator** toolbar, type **10** in the **Time position** box and press ENTER; the timeline bar moves to 10 seconds.

6. From the **Animator** toolbar, click the **Translate animation set** button; the move gizmo is displayed on the car.

   As mentioned earlier, for moving the vehicles, you will use the manual entry area to enter the values instead of using the move gizmo.

7. In the **Animator** manual entry area on the lower left corner of the **Animator** window, enter **-2300 Inches** or **-58.5 Meters** as the values in the **Translate X** box, depending on the units you are using; the car moves to the right side of the scene.

 Tip: You can also use the gizmo to move the car. Dragging any axis of the move gizmo moves the selection set in that direction. Dragging a plane of the gizmo moves the selection set along that plane. Dragging the sphere at the origin of the gizmo moves the selection set along all three axes directions.

8. From the **Animator** toolbar, click the **Capture keyframe** button; a new keyframe is added at 10 seconds and a light Blue animation bar is added in the timeline view. This will animate the car moving from the left of the scene to the right in 10 seconds.

Note: *As mentioned earlier, the animation bars are color coded. The light Blue bar represents the animation of an animation set, the Green bar represents the camera animation, and the Red animation bar represents the animation of the section plane.*

9. Press the ESC to deselect the car.

10. From the **Animator** toolbar, click the **Translate animation set** button to turn off this tool.

   Before proceeding further, it is better to check the animation to make sure it works.

11. From the **Animator** toolbar, click the **Stop** button; the animation timeline goes back to 0 second and the car moves back to the original position.

12. From the **Animator** toolbar, click the **Play** button; the animation plays for 10 seconds in which the car moves from the left of the scene to the right of the scene, as shown in Figure 21.

Figure 21 The car moved to the right of the scene

   Next, you will animate the SUV, which will start moving 8 seconds into the animation. Therefore, you need to move the timeline to 8 seconds.

13. Enter **8** in the **Time position** box to make sure the timeline is at 8 seconds.

14. From the **Selection Tree**, select the **Nissan Xtrail.nwd** file; the SUV is highlighted in the graphics window.

15. In the **Animator** window, right-click on the **Vehicles** scene and select **Add Animation Set > From current selection** from the shortcut menu; a new animation set is added to the scene.

16. Rename the animation set to **SUV**.

17. From the **Animator** toolbar, click the **Capture keyframe** button; a new keyframe is added at 8 seconds.

18. In the **Animator** toolbar, type **16** in the **Time position** box and press ENTER; the timeline bar moves to 16 seconds.

19. From the **Animator** toolbar, click the **Translate animation set** button; the move gizmo is displayed in the graphics window.

20. In the **Animator** manual entry area on the lower left corner of the **Animator** window, enter **1575 Inches** or **40 Meters** as the values in the **Translate X** box, depending on the units you are using; the SUV moves to the left side of the scene.

21. From the **Animator** toolbar, click the **Capture keyframe** button; a new keyframe is added at 16 seconds and a light Blue animation bar is added in the timeline view. This will animate the SUV moving from the right of the scene to the left in 8 seconds.

22. Press the ESC to deselect the SUV.

23. From the **Animator** toolbar, click the **Translate animation set** button to turn off the visibility of the move gizmo.

Before proceeding further, it is better to check the animation to make sure it works.

24. From the **Animator** toolbar, click the **Stop** button; the animation timeline goes back to 0 second and the car moves back to the original position.

25. Activate the **Front** viewpoint.

26. From the **Animator** toolbar, click the **Play** button; the animation plays for 16 seconds in which the two vehicles move in the scene. Figure 22 shows the scene after this animation ends.

Section 3: Animating the Revolving Door

In this section, you will create a new animator scene to animate the revolving door at the entrance of the building. While creating the animation of rotating objects in the scene, it is very important that the gizmo is aligned to the axis of rotation. For your convenience, a selection set, called **Revolving Door**, is created that selects the door. In the case of this door, the rotate gizmo will be automatically aligned with the rotation axis of the door. This may not happen in other files that you will work with. Therefore, it is important to mention here that if the rotate gizmo is not aligned with the axis of rotation, you will have to hold the CTRL key down and drag the gizmo to make sure it aligns with the rotation axis.

 Tip: To have a better understanding of how to rotate the animation sets, it is recommended that you also work on the Plant Exercise of this chapter.

1. Right-click in the **Animator** tree view area and select **Add Scene** from the shortcut menu; a new scene is added.

Figure 22 *The two vehicles moved in the animation*

2. Rename the scene to **Revolving Door**.

3. Select the **Revolving Door** selection set and then hide the unselected objects; only the revolving door is displayed in the graphics window.

4. With the revolving door still selected, right-click on the **Revolving Door** scene in the **Animator** window and select **Add Animation Set > From current search/selection set**; a new animation set is added to the scene.

5. Rename the animation set to **Door**.

6. From the **Animator** toolbar, click the **Rotate animation set** button; the rotate gizmo is displayed on the door in the graphics window.

7. Zoom closer to the door and make sure the Blue axis of the rotate gizmo is aligned with the central axis of the door.

8. From the **Animator** toolbar, click the **Capture keyframe** button; a new keyframe is added at 0 second.

9. In the **Animator** toolbar, type **10** in the **Time position** box and press ENTER; the timeline bar moves to 10 seconds.

10. In the **Animator** manual entry area on the lower left corner of the **Animator** window, enter **180** as the values in the **Rotate Z** box; the door rotates through an angle of 180-degrees.

11. From the **Animator** toolbar, click the **Capture keyframe** button; a new keyframe is added at 10 seconds.

12. Press ESC to deselect the door.

13. From the **Animator** toolbar, click the **Rotate animation set** button to turn off the visibility of the rotate gizmo.

14. From the **Animator** toolbar, click the **Stop** button; the animation timeline goes back to 0 second.

15. Activate the **Entrance** viewpoint; the visibility of the building objects is restored.

16. From the **Animator** toolbar, click the **Play** button; the door revolves through an angle of 180-degrees in 10 seconds.

17. From the **Animator** toolbar, click the **Stop** button; the door moves back to the original position.

18. Hide the **Animator** window.

Section 4: Adding Scripts to Automate the Two Animator Scenes

In this section, you will add two scripts to automatically play the two animator scenes. In the first script, you will animate the vehicle movement using the keyboard key. In the second animation, you will play the animation of revolving door as you walk close to it.

1. From the bottom of the graphics window, click **Scripter** to display the **Scripter** window.

2. Dock this window below the graphics window.

3. In the **Scripter** window, right-click in the **Scripts** area and select **Add New Script** from the shortcut menu; a new script is added.

4. Rename the script to **Vehicles**.

5. From the toolbar at the bottom of the **Events** area, click the **On Key Press** button; a new event is added and the **Properties** area is displayed on the right.

6. Click in the **Key** box of the **Properties** area and press the **F4** key; this key will be assigned as the trigger to the script.

7. From the toolbar at the bottom of the **Actions** area, click the **Play Animation** button; a new action is added and the **Properties** area is displayed on the right.

8. Click in the **Animation** list in the **Properties** area and double-click on **Vehicles** from the list; this animation will now be played when you press the F4 key, provided the scripts are enabled.

Next, you will create a new script to play the animation of the revolving door.

9. In the **Scripter** window, right-click in the **Scripts** area and select **Add New Script** from the shortcut menu; a new script is added.

10. Rename the script to **Door**.

In this script, you will trigger the animation when the camera is within the specified range of the revolving door. This will be done using the **On Hotspot** event.

11. From the toolbar at the bottom of the **Events** area, click the **On Hotspot** button; a new event is added and the **Properties** area is displayed on the right.

12. From the **Hotspot** list in the **Properties** area, select **Sphere on selection**.

13. From the **Trigger when** list, select **In Range**.

14. From the **Sets** window, select the **Revolving Door** selection set.

15. From the **Properties** area of the **Scripter** window, click **Set** > **Set From Current Selection Set**.

16. In the **Radius** box, type **150 Inches** or **3.8 Meters** as the value, depending on the units you are using.

17. Press ESC to deselect the revolving door.

18. From the toolbar at the bottom of the **Actions** area, click the **Play Animation** button; a new action is added and the **Properties** area is displayed on the right.

19. Click in the **Animation** list in the **Properties** area and double-click **Revolving Door** from the list; this animation will now be played when the camera or the avatar is within the specified range from the revolving door, provided the scripts are enabled.

20. Hide the **Scripter** window.

Section 5: Playing the Animations Using the Scripts

In this section, you will use the scripts that you added in the previous section to play the animations. For this, you first need to enable the scripts.

1. From the **Animation** ribbon tab > **Script** ribbon panel, click **Enable Scripts**.

2. Activate the **Front** viewpoint and then click on the sky in the graphics window.

3. Press the F4 key to trigger the script; notice how the two vehicles move in the scene.

4. Orbit, zoom, and pan the view to notice the new position of the two vehicles.

Next, you will animate the revolving door by walking close to it.

5. Activate the **Walk** viewpoint; the avatar is displayed in front of the revolving door, as shown in Figure 23, and the **Walk** tool is active.

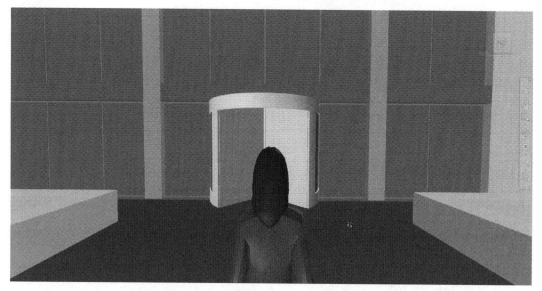

Figure 23 *The avatar in front of the revolving door*

You will now walk towards the revolving door. It is recommended that you walk slowly as the door will start revolving when you are within its specified range.

6. Press the F11 key to activate the full screen mode.

7. Press and hold down the left mouse button and slowly walk towards to the revolving door.

8. Once the door starts revolving, move the avatar along with the door to enter the building.

    Because the camera is behind the avatar, it may appear to be interfering with the door. It is acceptable in this case.

9. Press the F11 key to exit the full screen mode.

10. Activate the **Inside** viewpoint and walk close to the door. Once the door starts revolving, move the avatar along to exit the building.

11. Activate the **Overview** viewpoint.

12. On the **Animation** ribbon tab > **Script** ribbon panel, click the **Enable Scripts** button to disable the scripts; the two vehicles will move to their original position.

13. Save the file.

Section 6: Animating the Crane at a Construction Site

In this section, you will open the Autodesk Navisworks file of a construction site. This file also has a semitrailer and a tower crane. You will create animations of the rotation of the tower crane around the construction site.

1. From the **Chapter 7 > Exercise Building** folder, open the **Construction_Site.nwd** file; the Autodesk Navisworks scene looks similar to the one shown in Figure 24.

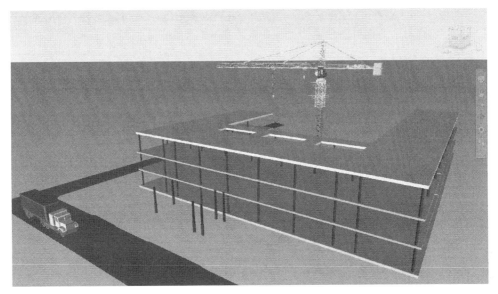

Figure 24 *The Autodesk Navisworks scene to create the crane animation*

2. From the bottom of the graphics window, click **Animator** and make sure the **Animator** window is docked below the graphics window.

   Next, you will create the animator scene to rotate the crane. It will be easier for you to turn off the visibility of everything other than the objects that need to rotate.

3. Select the **Crane Rotate** selection set and then hide the unselected objects; only the upper part of the crane is displayed in the graphics window.

4. Zoom to the selected objects.

5. From the bottom left of the **Animator** window, click **Add scene > Add Scene**; a new scene is added.

6. Rename the scene to **Crane**.

7. With the **Crane Rotate** set still selected, right-click on the **Crane** scene in the **Animator** window and select **Add Animation Set > From current search/selection set**; a new animation set is added to the scene.

8. Rename the animation set to **Rotate**.

9. From the **Animator** toolbar, click the **Rotate animation set** button; the rotate gizmo is displayed in the graphics window.

Notice that the rotate gizmo is not aligned with the axis of rotation. If you create the rotate animation with the first keyframe at this point, the resulting animation will not be correct. Therefore, you first need to align the origin of the rotate gizmo, shown in smaller ellipse in Figure 25, with the rotation axis. For your convenience, there is a line drawn that represents the rotation axis and is shown in the bigger ellipse in Figure 25.

 Note: *If the line representing the axis is not visible, turn on* **Lines** *from the* **Viewpoints** *ribbon tab >* **Render Style** *ribbon panel.*

10. Move the cursor over the sphere displayed at the origin of the rotate gizmo shown inside the smaller ellipse in Figure 25; the cursor changes to the hand cursor.

11. Press and hold down the left mouse button and drag and drop the origin of the rotate gizmo on the rotation axis shown inside the bigger ellipse in Figure 25.

Figure 25 Figure showing the origin that needs to be aligned with the rotation axis

12. Zoom or orbit the model to make sure the Blue axis of the rotate gizmo is aligned with the line representing the rotation axis. If it is not aligned, drag the origin of the gizmo again.

13. From the **Animator** toolbar, click the **Capture keyframe** button; a new keyframe is added at 0 second.

14. In the **Animator** toolbar, type **20** in the **Time position** box and press ENTER; the timeline bar moves to 20 seconds.

15. In the **Animator** manual entry area on the lower left corner of the **Animator** window, enter **180** as the value in the **Rotate Z** box; the crane rotates through an angle of 180-degrees.

16. From the **Animator** toolbar, click the **Capture keyframe** button; a new keyframe is added at 20 seconds.

17. Press ESC to deselect everything and then click the **Rotate animation set** button to turn off the visibility of the rotate gizmo.

18. From the **Animator** toolbar, click the **Stop** button; the crane moves back to the original position.

19. Activate the **Crane** viewpoint.

20. From the **Animator** toolbar, click the **Play** button; the animation plays for 20 seconds. Figure 26 shows the crane position at the end of the animation.

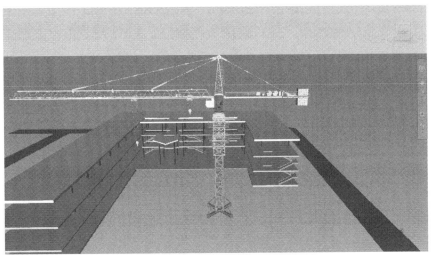

Figure 26 The crane position at the end of the animation

20. From the **Animator** toolbar, click the **Stop** button; the animation stops and the crane moves back to the original position.

21. Save the file.

Section 7: Animating the Semitrailer

In this section, you will animate the semitrailer and move it from the left of the scene to the right. You will also turn off the visibility of the semitrailer in the process.

1. Activate the **Semi** viewpoint.

2. Right-click in the **Animator** tree view area and select **Add Scene** from the shortcut menu; a new scene is added.

3. Rename the scene to **Semi**.

4. Select the **Semi** selection set.

5. Right-click on the **Semi** scene in the **Animator** window and select **Add Animation Set > From current search/selection set**; a new animation set is added to the scene.

6. Rename the animation set to **Move**.

7. From the **Animator** toolbar, click the **Capture keyframe** button; a new keyframe is added at 0 second.

8. From the **Animator** toolbar, click the **Translate animation set** button; the move gizmo is displayed in the scene.

9. In the **Animator** toolbar, type **15** in the **Time position** box and press ENTER; the timeline bar moves to 15 seconds.

10. In the **Animator** manual entry area on the lower left corner of the **Animator** window, enter **-2600 Inches** or **-66 Meters** as the values in the **Translate Y** box, depending on the display units you are using; the semitrailer moves to the right of the scene.

11. From the **Animator** toolbar, click the **Capture keyframe** button; a new keyframe is added at 15 seconds.

12. Press ESC to deselect everything and then click the **Translate animation set** button again to turn off the move gizmo.

13. From the **Animator** toolbar, click the **Stop** button; the semitrailer moves back to the original position.

14. From the **Animator** toolbar, click the **Play** button, the animation plays for 15 seconds. Figure 27 shows the semitrailer moved to the right of the scene.

15. Type **12** in the **Time position** box in the **Animator** toolbar.

16. Click the **Capture keyframe** button to add a keyframe at 12 seconds.

17. Double-click on the keyframe added at 12 seconds to display the **Edit Key Frame** dialog box.

18. Select the **Transparency** tick box in the dialog box and then exit the dialog box with the default transparency value of 0.

19. Double-click on the keyframe at 15 seconds to display the **Edit Key Frame** dialog box.

20. Select the **Transparency** tick box and set the transparency value to **100**.

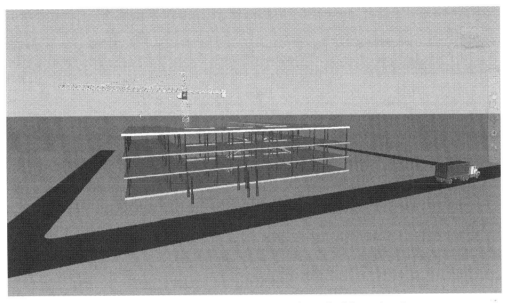

Figure 27 *The semitrailer position at the end of the animation*

21. Click **OK** in the dialog box; the semitrailer is no more displayed in the scene. This is because its visibility is turned off at 15 seconds.

22. From the **Animator** toolbar, click the **Stop** button; the animation moves back to the start and the semitrailer appears in the scene.

23. Click the **Play** button and notice how the semitrailer moves and then disappears at 15 seconds.

24. Stop the animation and then hide the **Animator** window.

Section 8: Adding Scripts to Automate the Two Animator Scenes

In this section, you will add two scripts to automatically play the two animator scenes.

1. From the bottom of the graphics window, click **Scripter** to display the **Scripter** window.

2. Dock this window below the graphics window, if it is not already docked.

3. In the **Scripter** window, right-click in the **Scripts** area and select **Add New Script** from the shortcut menu; a new script is added.

4. Rename the script to **Crane**.

5. From the toolbar at the bottom of the **Events** area, click the **On Key Press** button; a new event is added and the **Properties** area is displayed on the right.

6. Click in the **Key** box of the **Properties** area and press the **C** key; this key will be assigned as the trigger to the script.

7. From the toolbar at the bottom of the **Actions** area, click the **Play Animation** button; a new action is added and the **Properties** area is displayed on the right.

8. Click in the **Animation** list in the **Properties** area and double-click **Crane** from the list; this animation will now be played when you press the C key, provided the scripts are enabled.

    Next, you will create a new script to play the animation of the semitrailer.

9. In the **Scripter** window, right-click in the **Scripts** area and select **Add New Script** from the shortcut menu; a new script is added.

10. Rename the script to **Semi**.

11. From the toolbar at the bottom of the **Events** area, click the **On Key Press** button; a new event is added and the **Properties** area is displayed on the right.

12. Click in the **Key** box of the **Properties** area and press the **S** key; this key will be assigned as the trigger to the script.

13. From the toolbar at the bottom of the **Actions** area, click the **Play Animation** button; a new action is added and the **Properties** area is displayed on the right.

14. Click in the **Animation** list in the **Properties** area and double-click **Semi** from the list; this animation will now be played when you press the S key, provided the scripts are enabled.

15. Hide the **Scripter** window.

Section 9: Playing the Animations Using the Scripts

In this section, you will use the scripts that you added in the previous section to play the animations. For this, you first need to enable the scripts.

1. From the **Animation** ribbon tab > **Script** ribbon panel, click **Enable Scripts**.

2. Activate the **Crane** viewpoint and then click on the sky in the graphics window.

3. Press the F11 key to activate the full screen mode.

4. Click on the sky and then press the C key to trigger the script; notice the crane rotating.

5. Press the F11 key to exit the full screen mode.

6. Activate the **Semi** viewpoint and then press the F11 key to activate the full screen mode.

7. Click anywhere in the blank area of the graphics window. Now, press the S key to animate the semitrailer and then press the C key to animate the crane simultaneously.

8. After the animations end, press the F11 key to exit the full screen mode.

9. On the **Animation** ribbon tab > **Script** ribbon panel, click the **Enable Scripts** button to disable the scripts; the animations are reset to the original position.

10. Save the file.

Section 10: Creating a Section Animation

In this section, you will open a building model and create an animator scene in which you will section the model. This model has some **Presenter** materials assigned, so you may need to open the **Presenter** window to be able to see the effects of these materials. The model for this exercise is courtesy **Ankur Mathur, Founder & CEO, SANRACHNA:***BIM & Virtual Construction Consultants*.

1. Open the **Building_Section.nwd** file from the **Chapter 7 > Exercise Building** folder.

   The model looks similar to the one shown in Figure 28.

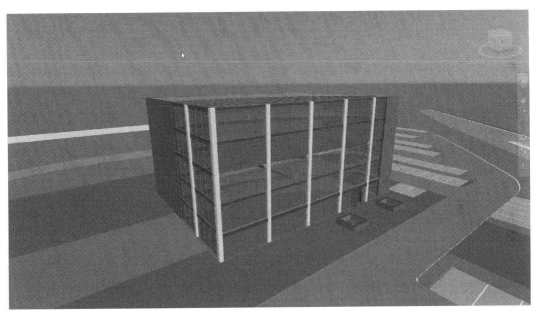

Figure 28 The building model to create the section animation

2. From the bottom of the graphics window, click the **Animator** button to invoke the **Animator** window.

3. Dock this window below the graphics window, if it is not already docked.

4. From the **Viewpoint** ribbon tab > **Sectioning** ribbon panel, click **Enable Sectioning**; the **Sectioning Tools** ribbon tab is displayed.

5. From the bottom left of the **Animator** window, click **Add scene > Add Scene**; a new scene is added.

6. Rename the animator scene to **Sectioning**.

7. Right-click on the **Sectioning** scene and select **Add Section Plane** from the shortcut menu; a new animation called **Section Plane** is added to the scene.

8. Press ENTER to accept the default name of the section animation.

9. Make sure the Yellow light globe icon on the left of **Plane 1** is turned on in the **Sectioning Tools** ribbon tab > **Plane Settings** ribbon panel > **Current Plane** list.

10. Click the **Move** button and expand and dock the **Transform** ribbon panel.

 *Tip: If you do not see the move gizmo on the screen, this means that the **Move** tool is not active. You need to click on the **Move** button to invoke this tool.*

11. With the **Move** tool selected, enter **-7.6 Inches** or **-0.195 Meters** as the value in the **Position Z** box; the plane moves to the bottom of the building and the entire building is sectioned, as shown in Figure 29.

Figure 29 The entire building model sectioned

12. In the **Animator** window, click the **Capture keyframe** button from the **Animator** toolbar; a new keyframe is added at 0 second.

13. Type **15** in the **Time position** box of the **Animator** toolbar and press ENTER; the timeline moves to 15 seconds.

Next, you will move the section plane using the move gizmo so that the sectioning of the building is animated.

14. Move the cursor over the Blue axis of the move gizmo; the cursor changes to the hand cursor.

15. Drag the move gizmo upward and release it when the **Position Z** value in the expanded **Transform** ribbon panel is close to **630 Inches** or **16 Meters**.

16. In the **Transform** ribbon panel, click the **Move** tool to turn off the visibility of the section plane.

17. In the **Animator** window, click the **Capture keyframe** button from the **Animator** toolbar; a new keyframe is added at 15 seconds.

    Notice that the color of the section animation bar is Red. As mentioned earlier, the animation bars are color coded so that you can easily identify the source of the animation.

18. Right-click on the **Section Plane** animation and select **Ping-Pong** from the shortcut menu; the **P.P.** tick box is selected on the right of the animation.

19. Click the **Stop** button in the **Animator** toolbar.

20. Click the **Enable Sectioning** button in the **Sectioning Tools** ribbon tab > **Enable** ribbon panel to turn off the sectioning.

21. In the **Animator** window, click the **Play** button to play the sectioning animation from start to end and then in reverse from end to start.

22. Click the **Stop** button when the animation stops playing.

23. Close the **Animator** window.

    Next, you will add a script to automatically play this animation. You will use the keyboard key to trigger the script.

24. From the bottom of the graphics window, click **Scripter** to display the **Scripter** window.

25. Dock this window below the graphics window, if it is not already docked.

26. In the **Scripts** area, right-click and select **Add New Script** from the shortcut menu.

27. Rename the script to **Sectioning**.

28. From the toolbar at the bottom of the **Events** area, click **On Key Press**; a new event is added and the **Properties** area is displayed on the right.

29. In the **Properties** area, click inside the **Key** box and press the S key.

30. From the toolbar at the bottom of the **Actions** area, click **Play Animation**; a new action is added and the **Properties** area is displayed on the right.

31. In the **Properties** area, click the **Animation** list and double-click **Sectioning**.

32. Accept the rest of the options as they are and close the **Scripter** window.

33. From the **Animation** ribbon tab > **Script** ribbon panel, click **Enable Scripts**.

34. Press the F11 key to activate the full screen mode.

35. Click on the sky in the scene and then press the S key; the sectioning animation plays in auto-reverse mode.

36. Press the F11 key to exit the full screen mode.

37. From the **Animation** ribbon tab > **Script** ribbon panel, click **Enable Scripts** to disable the scripts.

38. Save the file.

Section 11: Animating Objects to Drop from the Sky

One of the questions that I am regularly asked is how to make objects drop to their location from the sky during the timeliner simulation. It is done by linking the animator animations to the tasks. Therefore, I have added this section in this chapter to show you how to create these animator animations. These animations will then be linked to timeliner tasks in the next chapter.

1. From the **Chapter 7 > Exercise Building** folder, open the **Building-Object-Drop.nwd** file.

   Notice the various sets created in this file. You will animate these sets.

2. Using the **Options Editor** dialog box, set the display units as Meters or Inches.

3. Dock the **Animator** window, if it is not already docked on the screen.

4. From the lower left corner the **Animator** tree view, click the **Add scene** button and select **Add Scene** from the shortcut menu; a new animator scene is added.

5. Rename the animator scene to **Structural Foundations**.

6. From the **Sets** window, click the **Structural Foundations** set; the structural foundation objects are highlighted in the graphics window.

7. Right-click on the **Structural Foundations** scene and click **Add Animation Set > From current search/selection set**; a new animation set is added to the scene.

8. Rename this animation to **Foundations-Drop**.

9. From the **Animator** toolbar, click the **Capture keyframe** button; a new keyframe is added at 0 second for the **Foundations-Drop** animation.

10. In the **Time position** box of the **Animator** toolbar, type **5** and press ENTER; the timeline bar moves to 5 seconds.

11. From the **Animator** toolbar, click the **Capture keyframe** button; a new keyframe is added at 5 seconds for the **Foundations-Drop** animation.

    So basically you have created a 5 seconds animation in which the foundation objects do not move. This is where you will now go and modify the 0 second keyframe and change the start position of these objects.

12. Double-click on the 0 second keyframe; the **Edit Key Frame** dialog box is displayed.

13. Change the **Translate Z** value in the dialog box to **115 Feet** or **35 Meters**, depending on the units you are using.

14. Close the **Edit Key Frame** dialog box.

15. Click the **Stop** button from the **Animator** toolbar; the animation returns to 0 second.

16. Press ESC to deselect the concrete columns and then click the **Play** button from the **Animator** toolbar; the columns move to the defined Z position at the start of the animation and are then dropped at their original position in the animation.

    In this case, the foundation objects are dropping through various slabs and columns. However, when this animator animation is linked to the timeliner simulation task, this does not happen. You will learn more about this in the next chapter.

17. Click in the Gray area of the **Animator** tree view to deselect the **Structural Foundations** scene.

18. From the lower left corner the **Animator** tree view, click the **Add scene** button and select **Add Scene** from the shortcut menu; a new animator scene is added.

19. Rename the animator scene to **L1-Structural Columns**.

20. From the **Sets** window, click the **L1-Structural Columns** set; the level 1 columns are highlighted in the graphics window.

21. Right-click on the **L1-Structural Columns** scene and click **Add Animation Set > From current search/selection set**; a new animation set is added to the scene.

22. Rename this animation to **L1-Structural-Drop**.

23. From the **Animator** toolbar, click the **Capture keyframe** button; a new keyframe is added at 0 second for the **L1-Structural-Drop** animation.

24. In the **Time position** box of the **Animator** toolbar, type **5** and press ENTER; the timeline bar moves to 5 seconds.

25. From the **Animator** toolbar, click the **Capture keyframe** button; a new keyframe is added at 5 seconds for the **L1-Structural-Drop** animation.

26. Double-click on the 0 second keyframe; the **Edit Key Frame** dialog box is displayed.

27. Change the **Translate Z** value in the dialog box to **115 Feet** or **35 Meters**, depending on the units you are using.

28. Close the **Edit Key Frame** dialog box.

29. Click the **Stop** button from the **Animator** toolbar; the animation returns to 0 second.

30. Press ESC to deselect everything and then click the **Play** button from the **Animator** toolbar; the animations plays from start to end.

31. Similarly, add the animator scenes and animations for the rest of the sets and edit their start position at the 0 second keyframe.

    This is how you create the animator animations of objects dropping at their position. These animations can then be linked to the timeliner simulations. As mentioned earlier, you will learn about this in the next chapter.

Skill Evaluation

Evaluate your skills to see how many questions you can answer correctly. The answers to these questions are given at the end of the book.

1. You can change the color and transparency of the objects in the animator scene. (True/False)

2. The keyframes once added can be edited. (True/False)

3. The animator scenes cannot be exported as .AVI files. (True/False)

4. A single script can have multiple events and actions. (True/False)

5. The animator animations can be used to create sectioning animations. (True/False)

6. Which tool is used to trigger the automatic playing of the animator animations?

   (A) **Player**   (B) **Section**
   (C) **Presenter**   (D) **Scripter**

7. Which option is used to play an animation from start to end and then again from end to start?

   (A) **Ping-Pong**   (B) **Reverse**
   (C) **Auto-Reverse**   (D) None

8. Which action is used to play an animation as soon as the avatar comes within the specified distance of the object?

   (A) **On Key Press**   (B) **On Collision**
   (C) **On Hotspot**   (D) **On Sectioning**

9. To turn off the visibility of the objects in the animation, their transparency should be set to what value?

   (A) 100   (B) 0
   (C) 50   (D) None

10. Which event is used to trigger the animation when the avatar comes in contact with the ground plane?

   (A) **On Key Press**   (B) **On Collision**
   (C) **On Hotspot**   (D) **On Sectioning**

Class Test Questions

Answer the following questions:

1. Explain the process of adding a blank camera animation to the animator scene.

2. Although you may have scripts added to the scene, they will not be triggered unless which option is turned on?

3. How many section animations can you have in a single animator scene?

4. What are the various colors assigned to the animation bars in the animation scene?

5. Explain how will you change the color of the object in the animator scene.

Chapter 8 – Creating Construction Simulations Using the TimeLiner Module

The objectives of this chapter are to:

√ Introduce you to the **TimeLiner** module of Autodesk Navisworks.
√ Familiarize you with the **TimeLiner** window.
√ Teach you how to automatically create tasks for all sets in Autodesk Navisworks scene.
√ Teach you how to manually create tasks within Autodesk Navisworks.
√ Teach you how to create timeliner schedules from external data source and project files.
√ Teach you how to use rules to link external projects to the objects in the scene.
√ Teach you how to link animator and scripter scenes to the timeline tasks.
√ Teach you how to modify the overlay text in the simulation animation.

THE TIMELINER MODULE

> **Home Ribbon Tab > Tools Ribbon Panel > TimeLiner**

The **TimeLiner** module of Autodesk Navisworks allows you to create construction simulations by attaching the objects in the Autodesk Navisworks scene to the scheduling tasks. These tasks can be manually created within the Autodesk Navisworks file or can be imported from an external scheduling project file. You can also automatically create the tasks based on the sets in the current file. All this is done using the **TimeLiner** window. Figure 1 shows various components of this window. These are discussed next.

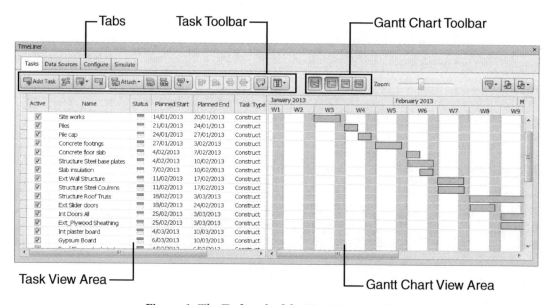

*Figure 1 The **Tasks** tab of the **TimeLiner** window*

Tasks Tab

This tab displays the tasks and their associated Gantt chart and also the tool buttons to manipulate them. All these are discussed next.

Task View Area

This area shows the names of the tasks created in the Autodesk Navisworks file or imported from the external project file and their associated information in various columns. You can add or remove columns from this area by using the **Columns** flyout, which is the last button in the **Task** toolbar.

Task Toolbar

The **Task** toolbar displays various buttons to add and manipulate the timeliner tasks. These buttons are discussed next.

Add Task
This button is used to add a new task to the timeliner. If there are some tasks already created, the new task, by default, is added at the bottom of the list. You can use the **Move Up** or **Move Down** button in the **Task** toolbar to move the new task up or down in the list.

Insert Task
This button is used to add a new task above the highlighted task in the task view.

Auto-Add Tasks
This flyout is used to automatically add tasks. Clicking this flyout will show you three options to automatically create tasks, as shown in Figure 2. Clicking the **For Every Topmost Layer** option adds a task for every topmost layer in every file appended or merged in the current scene. Also, the objects in these layers will be attached to these tasks. If there are duplicate layer names in files, there will be duplicate tasks created for all those layers as well. Clicking the **For Every Topmost Item** option adds a task for every topmost item in the **Selection Tree**. Also, the topmost items are attached to their respective tasks. If the topmost items are appended or merged files, tasks will be created for every file in the scene and these files will be attached to their respective tasks. Clicking the **For Every Set** option adds a task for every selection and search set created in the current scene. These sets are attached to their respective tasks.

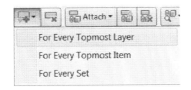

*Figure 2 The **Auto-Add Tasks** flyout*

 Note: *While creating the automatic tasks, the first task is assigned today's date as the planned start date and all the rest of the tasks are assigned the planned dates with an increment of one day.*

 Tip: *It has been noticed that sometimes when you are automatically adding tasks, some options are grayed out in the **Auto-Add Tasks** flyout. In this case, you can right-click in the **Task View** area and create automatic tasks using the shortcut menu.*

Delete Task
This button is used to delete the currently selected tasks. You can hold the CTRL key or the SHIFT key to select multiple tasks to delete.

Attach
This flyout is used to attach selection sets, search sets, or the selected objects to the currently selected task, as shown in Figure 3. The **Append Current Selection** option allows you to attach additional items to the tasks.

Figure 3 The **Attach** *flyout*

Auto-Attach Using Rules

This option allows you to automatically attach the items to the tasks based on some predefined or user-defined rules. When you click this button, the **TimeLiner Rules** dialog box will be displayed, as shown in Figure 4. This dialog box has three rules created by default. You can create your own custom rules by clicking the **New** button in this dialog box. Attaching items automatically using rules is discussed in detail later in this chapter.

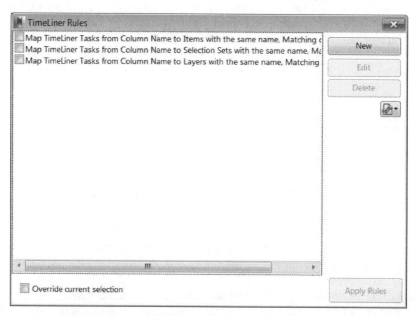

Figure 4 The **TimeLiner** *dialog box to automatically attach objects to the tasks*

 Tip: *You can also attach items to the task by simply selecting and then dragging and dropping them on the tasks.*

Clear Attachment

This button is used to remove the items attached from the tasks.

Find Items

This flyout allows you to find items in the current timeliner schedule based on the option you click from the flyout. The various options available in this flyout are shown in Figure 5. These options are discussed next.

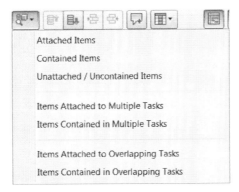

Figure 5 *The **Find Items** flyout*

Attached Items: This option finds and selects all the items attached to all the tasks in the current schedule.

Contained Items: This option finds and selects all the items contained in all the tasks in the current schedule.

Unattached/Uncontained Items: This option finds and selects all the items that are not attached or contained in any task in the current schedule.

Items Attached to Multiple Tasks: This option finds and selects all the items that are attached to multiple tasks in the current schedule.

Items Contained in Multiple Tasks: This option finds and selects all the items that are contained in multiple tasks in the current schedule.

Items Attached to Overlapping Tasks: This option finds and selects all the items that are attached to overlapping tasks in the current schedule.

Items Contained in Overlapping Tasks: This option finds and selects all the items that are contained in overlapping tasks in the current schedule.

Move Up
This button is used to move the selected task up in the task list.

Move Down
This button is used to move the selected task down in the task list.

Indent
This button is used to indent the selected task in the task immediately above in the task list.

Outdent
This button is used to move the selected task out of the task inside which it is indented. This option will only be available when you select an indented task.

Add Comment

This button is used to add comments to the selected task. When you select this button, the **Add Comment** dialog box will be displayed in which you can add the comment. Once added, the comment will be displayed in the **Comments** window when you select this task.

Column Chooser

This flyout shows the options to specify what columns you want to display in the task list area, as shown in Figure 6. Clicking the **Choose Columns** option displays the **Choose TimeLiner Columns** dialog box from where you can select all the columns you want to display and deselect the ones that you do not want to display.

*Figure 6 The **Column Chooser** flyout*

Gantt Chart View Area

This area shows the schedule tasks in the form of bars representing the start and end dates of each task. Moving the cursor over a bar shows you the details of that task, such as the name of the task, the start and end dates, and the duration of the task. This is a quick way to find out if there are any overlapping tasks in the current schedule. Figure 7 shows a Gantt chart view showing the information about a task.

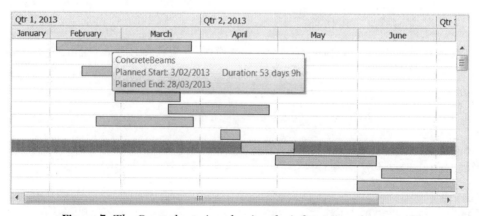

Figure 7 The Gantt chart view showing the information about a task

Gantt Chart Toolbar

The Gantt chart toolbar provides the following tool buttons.

Show or hide the Gantt chart

This button is used to toggle on or off the display of the Gantt chart view in the **TimeLiner** window.

Show Planned Dates

This button is used to display the task bars in the Gantt chart based on the planned dates. If the tasks are not assigned the planned dates, the Gantt chat will be blank when this button is clicked.

Show Actual Dates

This button is used to display the task bars in the Gantt chart based on the actual dates. If the tasks are not assigned the actual dates, the Gantt chat will be blank when this button is clicked.

Show Planned vs Actual Dates

This button is used to display the task bars in the Gantt chart based on the planned as well as actual dates. This is a good way to compare the actual progress of the construction with the planned progress.

Zoom Slider

This slider is located on the right of the Gantt chart toolbar and is used to zoom in or out of the Gantt chart view area.

Filter by Status Flyout

This flyout allows you to filter the timeliner tasks based on the options shown in Figure 8.

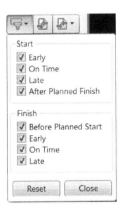

*Figure 8 The **Filter by Status** flyout*

Export to Sets

This button creates the selection sets of objects contained in each timeliner task. The name of the sets will be the same as the name of the timeliner task. Also, after exporting the sets, the **Attached** column in the **Tasks** tab will show the sets attached instead of **Explicit Attachment** that it was showing before you exported the sets. Figure 9 shows the **TimeLiner** window showing various tasks and the sets created for the objects contained in those tasks. Also, notice the **Attached** column now shows sets attached.

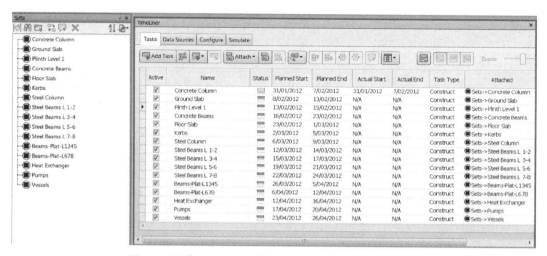

Figure 9   The sets created by exporting the timeliner tasks

Export the schedule Flyout

This flyout allows you to export the current timeliner tasks as schedules in a CSV file or a Microsoft Project XML file. When you click any of the options from the flyout, the **Export** dialog box will be displayed that allows you to specify the name and the location of the exported file.

Data Sources Tab

This tab provides you the option of adding and managing the scheduling files. The various components of this tab are shown in Figure 10. These are discussed next.

Add Flyout

Clicking this flyout shows you all the project scheduling sources that you can link to Autodesk Navisworks, as shown in Figure 11. To add a data source, click on the format of the required source and then specify the information about the source project file. Depending upon the data source you select to add, the **Field Selector** dialog box will be displayed that allows you to map the timeliner columns to the columns in the external data source.

 Note: *The option to link scheduling programs such as Asta Powerproject will only be available in the **Add** flyout if they are installed on the current computer.*

The step by step procedure for adding a project file is discussed later in this chapter.

Delete

This button deletes the data source selected from the data source view area. Note that by default, when you delete a data source, its tasks are not deleted automatically. You need to go the **Tasks** tab and then delete the root data source task at the top of the list.

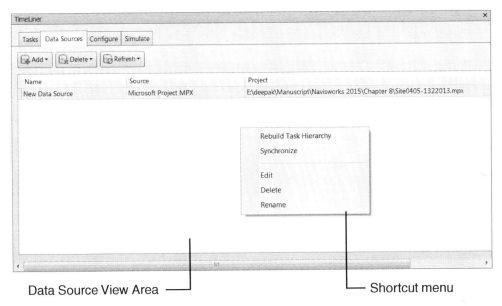

Data Source View Area ——————   —— Shortcut menu

*Figure 10 The **Data Sources** tab of the **TimeLiner** window*

*Figure 11 The **Add** flyout*

Refresh Flyout

Clicking this flyout shows you the options of refreshing the selected data source or all the data sources. When you click either of these options, the **Refresh from Data Source** dialog box will be displayed, as shown in Figure 12. These options allow you to refresh the data source and rebuild the task hierarchy from the data source or only synchronize the data source and still maintain the existing task structure.

Data Source View Area

This area shows all the project data sources that are added to the current Autodesk Navisworks scene.

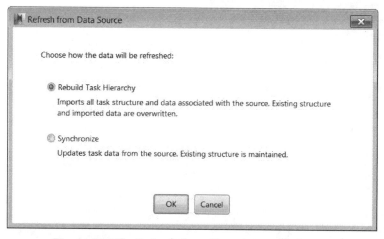

*Figure 12 The **Refresh from Data Source** dialog box*

Shortcut Menu

This menu is displayed when you right-click on an existing data source. The options in this shortcut menu are discussed next.

Rebuild Task Hierarchy

This option rebuilds the task hierarchy from the data source to include any new tasks that were added to the source project file.

Synchronize

This option updates all the tasks so they are still in synchronization with the source project file without altering the existing task structure.

Edit

This option displays the **Field Selector** dialog box that allows you to map the timeliner columns with the fields in the external data source.

Delete

This option deletes the selected data source. Note that the tasks associated with the deleted data source will only be removed when you refresh the data source.

Rename

This option allows you to change the name of the data source that is displayed in the **Name** column of the data source view area.

Configure Tab

This tab provides you the option of specifying how various tasks will be displayed during the simulation. The components of this tab, shown in Figure 13, are discussed next.

Configuration View Area

This area shows various tasks in rows and their associated appearances in various columns. To

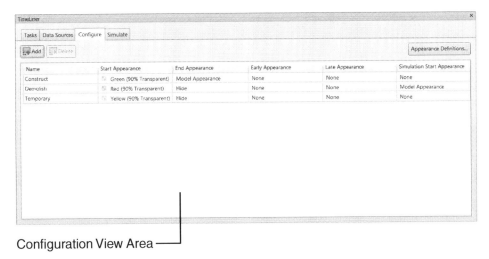

Configuration View Area ⎯⎯⎯⎯

Figure 13 *The* ***Configure*** *tab of the* ***TimeLiner*** *window*

change appearance of a task, double-click on the field under the appearance column you want to change and select a different appearance style.

Add
This button allows you to add a new task type as a row that can then be assigned various appearances.

Delete
This button is used to delete the selected task type.

Appearance Definition
Clicking this button, located near the top right of this tab, displays the **Appearance Definitions** dialog box that shows all the existing appearance definitions and also lets you create a new appearance definition.

Simulate Tab
This tab provides various tools to simulate the animation of the construction tasks. The simulation is played in the graphics window, therefore, you will need to move the **TimeLiner** window, if it is floating on the screen. The various components of this tab, shown in Figure 14, are discussed next.

Simulate Toolbar
This toolbar provides various buttons to playback and export the animations. These buttons are discussed next.

Rewind
This button takes the animation back to the start.

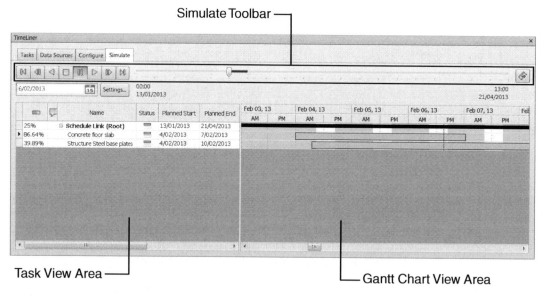

*Figure 14 The **Simulate** tab of the **TimeLiner** window*

Step Back
This button takes the animation one step back. The animation steps are defined using the **Settings** button, which is discussed later in this chapter.

Play Backwards
This button plays the animation backwards.

Stop
This button stops the animation and takes it back to the start.

Pause
This button pauses the animation.

Play
This button is used to play the animation from the current task.

Step Forwards
This button takes the animation one step forward. The animation steps are defined using the **Settings** button, which is discussed later in this chapter.

Forward
This button takes the animation to the end.

Simulation Position Slider
This slider bar represents the length of the animation. You can use this slider bar to drag the animation to any step in the sequence.

Export Animation
This button allows you to export the timeliner simulation as an external AVI file. Clicking this button displays the **Animation Export** dialog box, which is discussed in the earlier chapters of this book.

Calendar Box
This box allows you to select a date and the animation will be moved to that date showing you how the construction will look like on that particular date. You can either type the date or click the button and select the date from the calendar.

Settings
Clicking this button displays the **Simulation Settings** dialog box, as shown in Figure 15. The options in this dialog box are discussed next.

*Figure 15 The **Simulation Settings** dialog box*

Start / End Dates Area
This area displays the start and end dates of the simulation. By default, the **Override Start /**

End Dates tick box is cleared. As a result, the original start and end dates of the tasks are used for simulation. Selecting this tick box allows you to override the start and end dates.

Interval Size Area

This area displays the options to define the step size of the simulation. You can specify the value of the step in the spinner available in this area. From the list on the right of the spinner, you can specify whether the step value relates to the percentage of the total simulation or the number of weeks, days, hours, minutes, or seconds.

Playback Duration (Seconds) Area

This area provides the spinner that allows you to specify the total duration, in seconds, of the simulation.

Overlay Text Area

This area displays the options to specify the text that will be displayed in the graphics window as the simulation is playing. Clicking the **Edit** button displays the **Overlay Text** dialog box in which you can specify the text you want to overlay. The list on the right of the **Edit** button allows you to specify if the text will be displayed or not. This list also provides you the option to display the text at the top or the bottom of the graphics window.

 Note: The process of customizing the overlay text is discussed later in this chapter.

Animation Area

This area provides you the list from where you can select an existing viewpoint animation or an animator camera animation that will be played throughout the timeliner simulation.

View Area

This area allows you to select the view based on which the simulation will be played. You can play the simulation based on planned dates, planned dates with the differences in actual dates, planned against actual dates, actual dates, or actual dates with the differences in planned dates.

What I do

*If I know the planned as well as actual start and end dates of the tasks, I generally run a simulation with **Planned against Actual** to see the difference between the two dates and the issues the actual dates might cause with other planned tasks.*

Task View Area

This area shows the tasks that are currently being simulated in the timeliner simulation on the graphics window.

Gantt Chart View Area

This area shows the Gantt chart bar of the tasks that are currently being simulated in the timeliner simulation on the graphics window.

PROCEDURE FOR AUTOMATICALLY ADDING TASKS

The following are the procedures to automatically add various tasks to the timeliner simulation.

Automatically Adding Tasks for Every Topmost Layer

The following steps show you how to add tasks for every topmost layer in the scene.

a. Open the file in which you want to add the timeliner tasks.

b. If the **TimeLiner** window is not already docked, click the **TimeLiner** button from the **Home** ribbon tab > **Tools** ribbon panel.

c. Dock the **TimeLiner** window below the graphics window.

d. From the **Task** toolbar of the **Tasks** tab, click the **Auto-Add Tasks** flyout and click **For Every Topmost Layer**; a task for every topmost layer will be added and the items in those layers will be automatically attached to those tasks. Figure 16 shows the layers in a building file and the **TimeLiner** window showing the tasks added for all those layers.

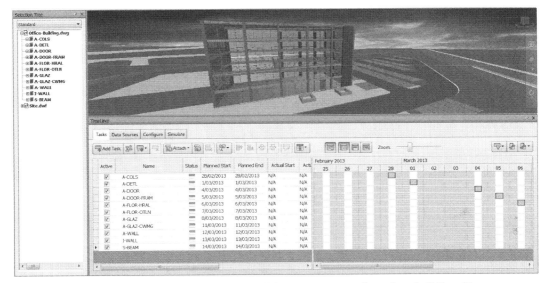

Figure 16 *The timeliner tasks added for every topmost layer in a building file*

By default, the first task is assigned today's date as the planned date and the rest of the tasks have planned dates incremented by one day.

e. If required, click on the **Planned Start** and **Planned End** dates for each of the tasks and modify them.

f. Right-click on any task and click **Find > Unattached/Uncontained Items** from the shortcut menu to make sure no object in the model is unattached or uncontained in the tasks.

Automatically Adding Tasks for Every Topmost Item

The following steps show you how to add tasks for every topmost item in the model.

a. Open the file in which you want to add the timeliner tasks.

b. If the **TimeLiner** window is not already docked, click the **TimeLiner** button from the **Home** ribbon tab > **Tools** ribbon panel.

c. Dock the **TimeLiner** window below the graphics window.

d. From the **Task** toolbar, click the **Auto-Add Tasks** flyout and click **For Every Topmost Item**; a task for every topmost item will be added and those items will be automatically attached to the tasks. Figure 17 shows the topmost items in the Plant.nwd file and the **TimeLiner** window showing the tasks added for all those items.

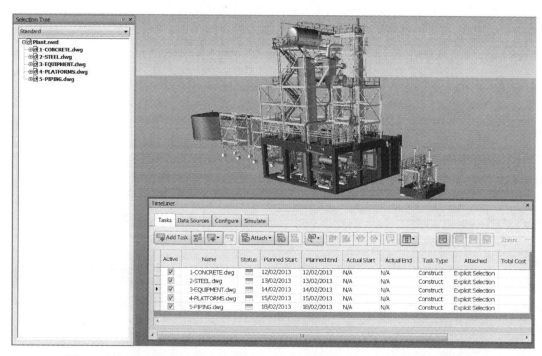

Figure 17 The timeliner tasks added for every topmost item in the Plant.nwd file

e. If required, click on the **Planned Start** and **Planned End** dates for each of the tasks and modify them.

f. Right-click on any task and from the shortcut menu, click **Find > Unattached/Uncontained Items** to make sure no object in the model is unattached or uncontained in the tasks.

Automatically Adding Tasks for Every Set

The following steps show you how to add tasks for every set in the model.

a. Open the model that has all the required sets created.

b. From the **Task** toolbar of the **Tasks** tab of the **TimeLiner** window, click the **Auto-Add Tasks** flyout and click **For Every Set**; a task for every set will be added and those sets will be automatically attached to the tasks. Figure 18 shows all the sets in the building model and the **TimeLiner** window showing the corresponding tasks added for all those sets.

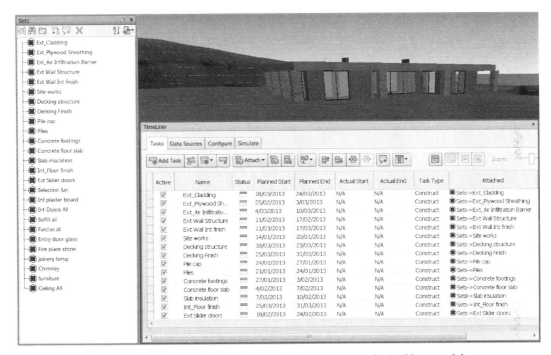

Figure 18   The timeliner tasks added for every set in the building model

Note*: Notice the **Attached** column in Figures 16 and 17 show **Explicit Selection**, but in Figure 18 this column shows the name of the set attached to each task. You can click on any of these attachments to highlight the attached objects in the graphics window and the **Selection Tree**,*

c. If required, click on the **Planned Start** and **Planned End** dates for each of the tasks and modify them.

d. Right-click on any task and from the shortcut menu, click **Find > Unattached/Uncontained Items** to make sure no object in the model is unattached or uncontained in the tasks.

PROCEDURE FOR AUTOMATICALLY ATTACHING ITEMS TO THE TASKS USING RULES

If the scheduling tasks are manually created in the **TimeLiner** window or are created using a linked project file, there are no items attached to those tasks by default. In that case, Autodesk Navisworks allows you to use some existing rules or create your own custom rules to attach the items to those tasks. The following steps show you how to do this.

a.   Create the timeliner tasks manually or link an external project file.

b.   From the **Task** toolbar of the **Tasks** tab of the **TimeLiner** window, click the **Auto-Attach Using Rules** button; the **TimeLiner Rules** dialog box will be displayed, as shown in Figure 19.

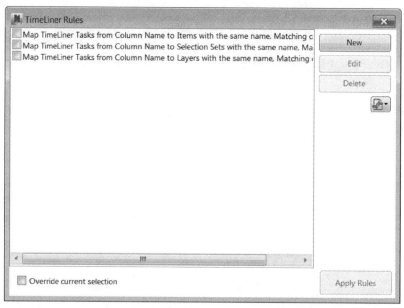

Figure 19 *The **TimeLiner Rules** dialog box to attach objects to the tasks using rules*

c.   If the task names match the names and the case of the items in the model, select the tick box of the first default rule and then click the **Apply Rules** button at the lower right corner of the **TimeLiner Rules** dialog box.

d.   If the tasks names match the names and case of the sets in the model, select the tick box of the second default rule and then click the **Apply Rules** button at the lower right corner of the **TimeLiner Rules** dialog box.

e.   If the tasks names match the names and case of the layers in the model, select the tick box of the third default rule and then click the **Apply Rules** button at the lower right corner of the **TimeLiner Rules** dialog box.

f. If you have the task names matching a combination of items, sets, and layers, select the tick boxes of all the three default rules and then click the **Apply Rules** button.

g. To create your own custom rules, click the **New** button in the **TimeLiner Rules** dialog box; the **Rules Editor** dialog box will be displayed, as shown in Figure 20.

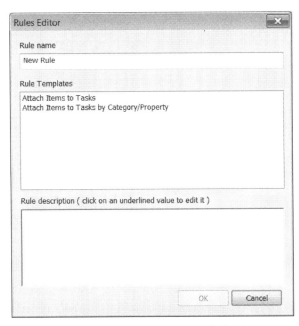

Figure 20 The **Rules Editor** *dialog box*

h. Click on the first rule template in this dialog box to create a new rule that attaches the items, layers, or sets to the tasks with the same name, but ignoring the case.

i. Click on the second rule template to create a new rule that attaches the items with the properties matching the specified criteria to any of the specified columns of the tasks.

j. Rename the new rule to any suitable name and then click **OK** in the dialog box.

k. Select the tick box of the new rule and then click the **Apply Rules** button to attach the items matching the rules criteria to the tasks.

PROCEDURE FOR IMPORTING SCHEDULING TASKS BY LINKING EXTERNAL PROJECT FILES

Autodesk Navisworks allows you to import the scheduling tasks created in external project files or databases to create construction simulations. Autodesk Navisworks supports the following scheduling software or database to be linked:

CSV: *If you do not have a scheduling software installed on your computer, you can have the files exported from them in CSV format and then link the CSV files to timeliner schedules.*

Microsoft Project MPX: *To link this project source, you do not need to have any release of Microsoft Project installed on your computer.*

Microsoft Project 2007 - 2013: *To link this project source, you need to have any release of Microsoft Project 2007 to 2013 installed on your computer.*

Primavera Project Management 6 - 8: *To be able to link Primavera Project Management 6-8, you need to have this program installed on the same computer as Autodesk Navisworks. Additionally, you will need ActiveX Data Objects 2.1 and Primavera Software Development Kit installed on the same computer as well.*

Primavera P6 (Web Services) V6 - V8.2: *While linking Primavera, using Web Service is a better option as the process of synchronizing the timeliner schedules with Primavera schedules is better with Web Services.*

Asta Power Project 11 - 12: *To be able to link Asta Power Project 11 - 12, it has to be installed on your computer. If it is not installed, this option will not be listed while adding the project file.*

The following are the processes to add some of these external project schedules.

Linking CSV Files

The following steps show you how to link a CSV file to the timeliner schedule:

a. On the **Data Sources** tab of the **TimeLiner** window, click the **Add** flyout and then click **CSV Import**; the **Open** dialog box will be displayed.

b. Browse to the CSV file that you want to link and then double-click on the file; the **Field Selector** dialog box will be displayed.

c. If the first row of the CSV file is the header row, click the **Row 1 contains headings** tick box in the **CSV Import Settings** area. Using the other options in this area, you can import the date and time settings from the CSV file or specify your own date and time settings.

d. In the lower half of the dialog box, click on the rows under the **External Field Name** column and select the fields corresponding to the names listed under **Column**. Figure 21 shows the **Field Selector** dialog box with all the fields mapped to the columns in the timeliner schedule.

e. Click **OK** in the **Field Selector** dialog box; the CSV link is displayed in the **Data Source** tab.

f. In the **Data Source** tab, right-click on the data link and click **Rename** from the shortcut menu to rename the data source to the required name.

g. In the **Data Source** tab, right-click on the data link again and click **Rebuild Task Hierarchy** from the shortcut menu; the task hierarchy is created and displayed in the **Tasks** tab with the timeliner columns mapped to the fields you selected in the **Field Selector** dialog box. Figure 22 shows the **Tasks** tab with the tasks built from the CSV file.

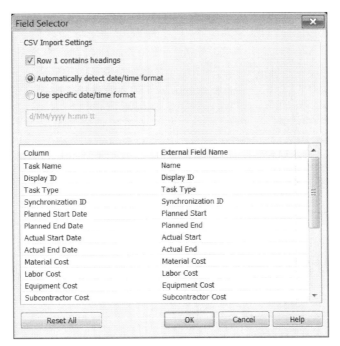

Figure 21 The **Field Selector** *dialog box*

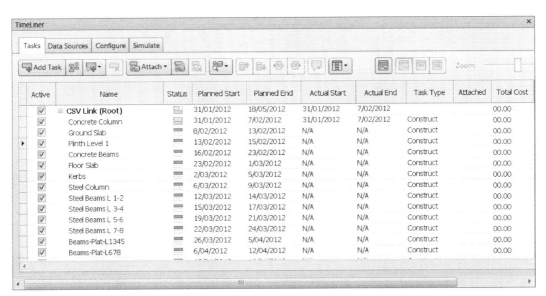

Figure 22 The **Tasks** *tab of the* **TimeLiner** *window showing the tasks built from the CSV file*

h. If the task names match the object names, layer names, or sets in the Autodesk Navisworks model, use the **TimeLiner Rules** dialog box to attach items to the tasks.

i. If the task names do not match, then manually select the objects from the **Selection Tree** or the graphics window.

j.   In the **Tasks** tab, right-click on the task to which you want to attach the selected objects and then click **Attach Current Selection** from the shortcut menu.

Linking Microsoft Project MPX Files

The following steps show you how to link a Microsoft Project MPX file to the timeliner schedule:

a.   On the **Data Sources** tab of the **TimeLiner** window, click the **Add** flyout and then click **Microsoft Project MPX**; the **Open** dialog box will be displayed.

b.   Browse to the MPX file that you want to link and then double-click on the file; the **Field Selector** dialog box will be displayed.

c.   Click on the rows under the **External Field Name** column and select the fields corresponding to the names listed under **Column**.

d.   Click **OK** in the **Field Selector** dialog box; the MPX link is displayed in the **Data Source** tab.

e.   In the **Data Source** tab, right-click on the data link and click **Rename** from the shortcut menu to rename the data source to the required name.

f.   In the **Data Source** tab, right-click on the data link again and click **Rebuild Task Hierarchy** from the shortcut menu; the task hierarchy is created and displayed in the **Tasks** tab with the timeliner columns mapped to the fields you selected in the **Field Selector** dialog box.

g.   If the task names match the object names, layer names, or sets in the Autodesk Navisworks model, use the **TimeLiner Rules** dialog box to attach items to the tasks.

h.   If the task names do not match, then manually select the objects from the **Selection Tree** or from the graphics window.

i.   In the **Tasks** tab, right-click on the task to which you want to attach the selected objects and then click **Attach Current Selection** from the shortcut menu.

Linking Primavera Project Management 6-8 Schedules

Before linking the Primavera Project Management 6-8 schedules, you need to get your computer ready to connect to it. The following steps show you how to do this:

a.   Make sure you have installed Primavera Project Management locally on your computer or the program is remotely accessible.

b.   Use the Primavera Project Management install media to install the Primavera Software Development Kit (SDK), which is listed under **Custom** installation. Make sure you expand **Other Components** during the installation process to view **Software Development Kit**.

c.   After the SDK installation is complete, you will be prompted to configure a database. Generally, Microsoft SQL Server/MSDE database works well in this case.

Once all this is configured, you are ready to link the Primavera Project Management link.

d. On the **Data Sources** tab of the **TimeLiner** window, click the **Add** flyout and then click **Primavera Project Management 6-8**; the **Primavera DSN Data Source Login** dialog box will be displayed.

e. Enter the username and password in the dialog box and click **OK**; the **Select Primavera Project** dialog box will be displayed.

f. Select the project from which you want to import the schedule and click **OK** in the dialog box; the **Field Selector** dialog box will be displayed.

g. Click on the rows under the **External Field Name** column and select the fields corresponding to the names listed under **Column**.

h. Click **OK** in the **Field Selector** dialog box; the MPX link is displayed in the **Data Source** tab.

i. In the **Data Source** tab, right-click on the data link and click **Rename** from the shortcut menu to rename the data source to the required name.

j. In the **Data Source** tab, right-click on the data link again and click **Rebuild Task Hierarchy** from the shortcut menu; the task hierarchy is created and displayed in the **Tasks** tab with the timeliner columns mapped to the fields you selected in the **Field Selector** dialog box.

k. If the task names match the object names, layer names, or sets in the Autodesk Navisworks model, use the **TimeLiner Rules** dialog box to attach items to the tasks.

l. If the task names do not match, then manually select the objects from the **Selection Tree** or from the graphics window.

m. In the **Tasks** tab, right-click on the task to which you want to attach the selected objects and then click **Attach Current Selection** from the shortcut menu.

Linking Primavera P6 (Web Services) V6 - V8.5

Before linking the Primavera P6 (Web Services) V6 - V8.5 schedules, you need to get your computer ready to connect to the P6 Web Services. The following steps show you how to do this:

a. Make sure you have Primavera P6 V6-8.2 Web Services installed within a suitable Web Application Server such as Oracle WebLogic, JBoss, or IBM WebSphere on the same machine as your P6 database.

Once all this is configured, you are ready to link the Primavera Project Management link.

b. On the **Data Sources** tab of the **TimeLiner** window, click the **Add** flyout and then click the required Primavera P6 Webservice that you are using; the **Please Login** dialog box will be displayed.

c. Enter the username, password, server address, and the server port in the dialog box and click **Login**; the **Primavera P6 Database Instance Selection** dialog box will be displayed.

d. Double-click on the database instance ID to select it; the **Primavera Project Selection** dialog box will be displayed.

e. Select the project from which you want to import the schedule and click **OK** in the dialog box; the **Field Selector** dialog box will be displayed.

f. Click on the rows under the **External Field Name** column and select the fields corresponding to the names listed under **Column**.

g. Click **OK** in the **Field Selector** dialog box; the MPX link is displayed in the **Data Source** tab.

h. In the **Data Source** tab, right-click on the data link and click **Rename** from the shortcut menu to rename the data source to the required name.

i. In the **Data Source** tab, right-click on the data link again and click **Rebuild Task Hierarchy** from the shortcut menu; the task hierarchy is created and displayed in the **Tasks** tab with the timeliner columns mapped to the fields you selected in the **Field Selector** dialog box.

j. If the task names match the object names, layer names, or sets in the Autodesk Navisworks model, use the **TimeLiner Rules** dialog box to attach items to the tasks.

k. If the task names do not match, then manually select the objects from the **Selection Tree** or from the graphics window.

l. In the **Tasks** tab, right-click on the task to which you want to attach the selected objects and then click **Attach Current Selection** from the shortcut menu.

PROCEDURE FOR CUSTOMIZING THE SIMULATION OVERLAY TEXT

As mentioned earlier, while playing the construction simulation, you can have the information about the tasks being simulated displayed as overlay text in the graphics window, as shown in Figure 23. You can customize this text and control what information is displayed in the graphics window. The following steps show you how to do this:

a. Click the **Simulate** tab of the **TimeLiner** window.

b. Click the **Settings** button to display the **Simulation Settings** dialog box.

c. From the **Overlay Text** area, click the **Edit** button; the **Overlay Text** dialog box will be displayed.

d. Click at the start of the first line of text to move the cursor there.

e. Click the **Colors** button and specify the color for the first line of text.

Figure 23 *The overlay text displayed during the timeliner simulation*

f. Click at the end of the first line of text and then press CTRL+ENTER to go to the next line.

g. Click the **Colors** button and specify the color for the second line of text.

h. Click the **Cost** button and select the cost you want to display in the overlay text. Note that if the costs are not added in the timeliner tasks, they will be displayed as 0.00 in the overlay text.

i. Click the **Font** button and select the font for the overlay text.

j. Click **OK** in the **Overlay Text** dialog box and then click **OK** in the **Simulation Settings** dialog box; the modified overlay text will be displayed in the graphics window.

PROCEDURE FOR ADDING AN ANIMATOR CAMERA ANIMATION AS A TASK

The **TimeLiner** tool allows you to link the animator camera animation into the timeliner schedule as a task. This means that if the camera animation represents orbiting around the model, that animation will be simulated as a task in the timeliner simulation. The following steps show how to do this.

a. In the **Tasks** tab of the **TimeLiner** window, use the **Add Task** to add the task at the bottom of the list or use **Insert Task** tool to add a task above the selected task.

b. Rename the task to **Animation**.

c. From the **Task** toolbar, click the **Column Chooser** flyout and then click **Choose Columns**; the **Choose TimeLiner Columns** dialog box will be displayed.

d.   From the dialog box, select the tick boxes for the **Animation** and **Animation Behaviour** columns.

e.   Click **OK** in the dialog box; the two columns are added to the task view area.

f.   Specify the start and end date for the **Animation** task.

 ***Tip:** If you want the animator camera animation to run throughout the timeliner simulation, specify the start date of the animation timeliner task as the start date of the simulation and the end date of the task as the end date of the simulation.*

g.   In the task view area, scroll to the right to see the **Animation, Animation Behaviour**, and **Script** columns.

h.   Click on the field in the **Animation** column and select the animator animation.

i.   From the **Animation Behaviour** column, make sure **Scale** is selected.

j.   From the **Script** field, select the script that plays the animation.

What I do

*It has been noticed that if you add a task that links the animator camera animation ending at a view other than the start view of the timeliner simulation, the camera goes back to the original view as soon as that animation task ends. For example, consider a case where you want to display the front half of the building for the first few tasks in the simulation and then want to rotate the view to the back of the building for the rest of the tasks. If you create an animator camera animation that orbits the view to the back of the building and add it as a task, the building will be restored to the original view showing the front of the building as soon as the task ends. I have figured out a little trick to solve this issue. You simply need to create a script that plays the animator camera animation using any event. In the timeliner task, select this script from the **Script** column for the animation task. This will ensure the camera stays at the view where the animator camera animation ended.*

PROCEDURE FOR LINKING A VIEWPOINT ANIMATION OR AN ANIMATOR CAMERA ANIMATION TO THE SIMULATION

Autodesk Navisworks allows you to link a saved viewpoint animation or an animation camera animation to the timeliner schedule such that it plays throughout the timeliner simulation. The following steps show you how to do this:

a.   Click the **Simulate** tab of the **TimeLiner** window.

b.   Click the **Settings** button to display the **Simulation Settings** dialog box.

c.   From the **Animation** area, click on the list and select the animator camera animation or the saved viewpoint animation. This animation will play throughout the timeliner simulation.

HANDS-ON EXERCISES

You will now work on some hands-on exercises using the concepts learned in this chapter.

Hands-on Exercise (Plant)	In this exercise, you will complete the following tasks:

In this exercise, you will complete the following tasks:

1. *Open a plant model and create automatic tasks for all top most items in it.*
2. *Change the dates of the automatic tasks and then play the simulation.*
3. *Add automatic tasks for all the sets in the model.*
4. *Edit the dates of the tasks and play the simulation.*
5. *Create a task for the animator camera animation and then play the simulation.*
6. *Open a third plant model and link an external CSV file to import the construction schedules.*
7. *Use the timeliner rules to link the items in the model to the timeliner tasks imported from the CSV file.*
8. *Simulate the construction sequence of the tasks created using the linked CSV file.*
9. *Link animator animations to the timeliner tasks.*

Section 1: Opening the Plant File and Automatically Adding Tasks

In this section, you will open the **TimeLiner-Plant.nwd** file and then automatically create tasks for every top most item in the **Selection Tree**. You will then change the dates of the tasks and rearrange them based on your requirements.

1. From the **Chapter 8 > Exercise Plant** folder, open the **TimeLiner-Plant.nwd** file.

2. Activate the **Overview** viewpoint. The model looks similar to the one shown in Figure 24.

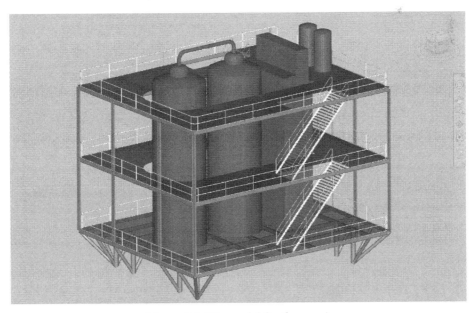

Figure 24 The model for the exercise

3. Expand the **Selection Tree** and notice the hierarchy. This file was created using an Autodesk Inventor model. As a result, there are no layers in this model.

   You will now create the timeliner tasks for all the top most items in the **Selection Tree**.

4. Click **TimeLiner** from the bottom of the graphics window or from the **Home** ribbon tab > **Tools** ribbon panel; the **TimeLiner** window is displayed.

5. Dock the **TimeLiner** window below the graphics window.

6. In the **Tasks** tab, click the **Auto-Add Tasks** flyout > **For Every Topmost Item**; a task is added for every top most item listed in the **Selection Tree** and those items are attached to the tasks.

7. Click the **Show or hide Gantt chart** button to turn off the Gantt chart. You will now be able to see more columns in the task view area.

   If you scroll to the top of the tasks, you will notice that a task called Skeletal:1 is created. In Autodesk Inventor, skeletal models are created for adding frames. You need to delete this task as the frame skeletal is not displayed in the Autodesk Navisworks scene. You will also rearrange some of the tasks in the list.

8. Scroll to the top of the tasks list. Now, right-click on the **Skeletal:1** task and click **Delete Task** from the shortcut menu.

   The tasks are automatically added based on the hierarchy of the items in the **Selection Tree**. You will now rearrange some of these tasks.

9. Click on the **Stairs:1** task and from the **Task** toolbar, click the **Move Down** button.

10. Click the **Stairs1:1** task and from the **Task** toolbar, click the **Move Down** button.

Section 2: Editing the Start and End Dates of the Tasks

The tasks are automatically assigned planned start and planned end dates, starting from today's date. You will now change some of these dates.

1. Scroll to the top of the tasks list and then click in the **Planned End** field of the **Frame0001:1** task.

2. Increment this date by two days so the planned end date of the first task is two days after the planned start days.

3. Right-click on the date field you just changed and from the shortcut menu, click **Copy Date/Time**.

4. Right-click on the **Planned Start** field of the **Platform Base:1** task and click **Paste Date/Time** from the shortcut menu; the start date of this task is the same as the end date of the previous task.

5. Increment the planned end date of this task by one day.

6. Change the duration of the rest of the tasks based on the dates shown in Figure 25. Only the duration of the tasks needs to be based on Figure 25. The day, month, and year should be based on the dates added by default.

Active	Name	Status	Planned Start	Planned End
✓	Frame0001:1		21/01/2014	23/01/2014
✓	Platform Base:1		23/01/2014	24/01/2014
✓	Platform Mid:1		24/01/2014	27/01/2014
✓	Platform Mid:2		27/01/2014	28/01/2014
✓	Handrailing:1		28/01/2014	29/01/2014
✓	Handrailing:2		29/01/2014	30/01/2014
✓	Handrailing:3		30/01/2014	31/01/2014
✓	Stairs:2		31/01/2014	3/02/2014
✓	Stairs:1		3/02/2014	4/02/2014
✓	Stairs1:2		5/02/2014	6/02/2014
✓	Stairs1:1		6/02/2014	7/02/2014
✓	Equipment:1		7/02/2014	10/02/2014
✓	Cylinder:1		10/02/2014	11/02/2014

Figure 25 The planned start and end dates of the tasks

 Note: *Notice the difference between the end and start dates of the* **Platform Mid:1**, **Stairs:2**, *and* **Equipment:1** *tasks. This difference is because the timeliner schedule by default does not include weekends.*

Section 3: Editing and Playing the Simulation

In this section, you will edit the start date of the simulation and also edit the overlay text. You need to note the start date of the first task and the end date of the last task. You will then edit the start and end dates of the simulation based on these dates.

1. Make a note of the planned start date of the first task and the planned end date of the last task. Now, in the **TimeLiner** window, click the **Simulate** tab.

2. Click the **Settings** button to display the **Simulation Settings** dialog box.

3. In the **Start / End Dates** area, click the **Override Start / End Dates** tick box.

4. Override the start date to be a day before the start date of the first task.

5. Override the end date to be a day after the end date of the last task.

6. In the **Overlay Text** area, click the **Edit** button; the **Overlay Text** dialog box is displayed.

7. By default, the overlay text displays **%A %X %x Day=$DAY Week=$WEEK** in the first line of text. If there is any other text displayed, delete it.

This will display the day of the task, the current time in simulation, days since the start of the first task, and the weeks since the start of the first task.

8. Click at the start of the first line of text and then click the **Colors** button and click **Red**; the first line of the overlay text will be displayed in Red while playing the simulation.

9. Click at the end of the first line to move the cursor there. Now, click the **Colors** button and click **Blue**; the text starting from here will be displayed in Blue in the overlay text.

10. Click **Extras > Currently active tasks**. This will ensure that the currently active task is displayed in Blue in the second line of the overlay text during the simulation.

11. Click the **Font** button to display the **Select Overlay Font** dialog box.

12. Select **Arial > Regular > 12** font and then click **OK** in this dialog box.

13. Click **OK** in the **Overlay Text** dialog box and then click **OK** in the **Simulation Settings** dialog box.

14. On the **Simulate** tab, click the **Play** button; the timeliner simulation starts and the overlay text is displayed in the graphics window. Figure 26 shows the graphics window during the simulation.

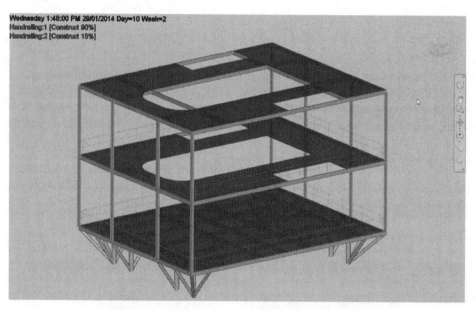

Figure 26 The view from the timeliner simulation

15. After the timeliner simulation ends, click the **Tasks** tab.

 Note: If you do not click the Tasks tab in the TimeLiner window, you will not be allowed to perform certain operations, such as creating or selecting an animator scene.

Section 4: Creating Automatic Tasks Based on Sets

While playing the simulation in the previous section, you would have noticed that the entire structure is created as a single task. This is because this task was created using an item called **Frame0001:1**. Normally, the structure will be broken down into smaller sections, which can then be simulated. This can be done by creating sets that define the smaller sections of the structure. In this section, you will create automatic tasks using the sets that are already created in this file and then simulate them. But first, you will delete the existing tasks.

1. Dock the **Sets** window below the **Selection Tree**.

    Notice the sequence of the sets created in this file. The tasks will be added in this sequence.

2. In the **Tasks** tab of the **TimeLiner** window, scroll to the top and select the first task.

3. Scroll to the bottom and then hold down the SHIFT key and select the last task.

4. Click the **Delete Task** button from the **Task** toolbar; all the tasks are deleted.

5. Right-click in the gray **Tasks View** area and from the shortcut menu, click **Auto-Add Tasks > For Every Set**; timeliner tasks are added for every set in the **Sets** window. Also, all these sets are attached to the tasks, as shown in Figure 27.

Active	Name	Status	Planned Start	Planned End	Task Type	Attached
✓	Structure Foundation		30/03/2015	30/03/2015	Construct	Sets->Structure Foundation
✓	Structure Level 1		31/03/2015	31/03/2015	Construct	Sets->Structure Level 1
✓	Level 1 Platform		1/04/2015	1/04/2015	Construct	Sets->Level 1 Platform
✓	Columns		2/04/2015	2/04/2015	Construct	Sets->Columns
✓	Handrailing Level 1		3/04/2015	3/04/2015	Construct	Sets->Handrailing Level 1
✓	Level 2 Structure		6/04/2015	6/04/2015	Construct	Sets->Level 2 Structure
✓	Level 2 Platform		7/04/2015	7/04/2015	Construct	Sets->Level 2 Platform
✓	Handrailing Level 2		8/04/2015	8/04/2015	Construct	Sets->Handrailing Level 2
✓	Level 1 Stairs 1		9/04/2015	9/04/2015	Construct	Sets->Level 1 Stairs 1
✓	Level 1 Stairs 2		10/04/2015	10/04/2015	Construct	Sets->Level 1 Stairs 2
✓	Level 3 Structure		13/04/2015	13/04/2015	Construct	Sets->Level 3 Structure
✓	Level 3 Platform		14/04/2015	14/04/2015	Construct	Sets->Level 3 Platform
✓	Handrailing Level 3		15/04/2015	15/04/2015	Construct	Sets->Handrailing Level 3
✓	Level 2 Stairs 1		16/04/2015	16/04/2015	Construct	Sets->Level 2 Stairs 1
✓	Level 2 Stairs 2		17/04/2015	17/04/2015	Construct	Sets->Level 2 Stairs 2
✓	Equipment		20/04/2015	20/04/2015	Construct	Sets->Equipment
✓	Cylinders		21/04/2015	21/04/2015	Construct	Sets->Cylinders

Figure 27 Tasks added for every set and the sets attached to those tasks

6. Make a note of the start date of the first task and the end date of the last task. Now, click the **Simulate** tab in the **TimeLiner** window.

7. Click the **Settings** button; the **Simulation Settings** dialog box is displayed.

8. With the **Override Start / End Dates** tick box still selected, override the start date to be a day before the start date of the first task. Also, override the end date to be a day after the end date of the last task.

9. Click **OK** in the dialog box.

10. In the **Simulate** tab, click the **Play** button to play the simulation; the simulation is played showing the construction sequence of the model.

Section 5: Linking a Viewpoint Animation to the TimeLiner Simulation

In the previous sections, the simulations that you played showed the construction of the model from the same viewpoint. In this section, you will link a saved viewpoint animation to the timeliner simulation so that the camera is rotated around the model as it is constructed.

1. With the **Simulate** tab still active, click the **Settings** button to display the **Simulation Settings** dialog box.

2. In the **Animation** area, click the **No Link** list and then select **Saved Viewpoints Animation**; the viewpoint animation is linked to the timeliner simulation.

3. Click **OK** in the dialog box.

4. In the **Saved Viewpoints** window, click the **Fly Around** animation once.

5. In the **Simulate** tab of the **TimeLiner** window, click the **Play** button; notice how the model is orbited as the timeliner simulation is played.

Section 6: Creating a Task for the Animator Camera Animation

In the previous section, the saved viewpoint animation that you linked to the simulation plays throughout the simulation. But some times, you need to orbit the model during the simulation to a particular view and then leave the camera there to view the rest of the simulation from that camera view. This can be done using the animator camera animation, which is what you will do in this section.

1. With the **Simulate** tab still active, click the **Settings** button.

2. In the **Animation** area, click the **Saved Viewpoints Animation** list and select **No Link**; the viewpoint animation is removed from the timeliner simulation.

3. Click **OK** in the dialog box.

4. Click the **Tasks** tab.

5. Scroll down in the tasks list and select the **Level 1 Stairs 2** task.

6. From the **Task** toolbar, click the **Insert Task** button; a new task is added above the **Level 1 Stairs 2** task.

7. Rename the new task to **Animator Camera**.

   Next, you need to change the planned start and end dates of this task. You can manually type the dates or copy and paste them from the other tasks, as discussed below.

8. Right-click on the **Planned End** date of the **Level 1 Stairs 1** task and click **Copy Date/Time** from the shortcut menu.

9. Right-click on the **Planned Start** date of the **Animator Camera** task and click **Paste Date/Time** from the shortcut menu.

10. Right-click on the **Planned Start** date of the **Level 1 Stairs 2** task and click **Copy Date/Time** from the shortcut menu.

11. Right-click on the **Planned End** date of the **Animator Camera** task and click **Paste Date/Time** from the shortcut menu.

    You will now add the **Animation** and **Script** columns, as they are not displayed by default. It will be easier to view all these columns if the visibility of the Gantt chart is turned off.

12. If the visibility of the Gantt chart is turned on, turn it off by clicking the **Show or hide the Gantt chart** button **Gantt Chart** toolbar.

13. From the **Task** toolbar, click the **Columns** flyout and then click **Choose Columns** to display the **Choose TimeLiner Columns** dialog box.

14. Click the tick boxes on the left of the **Script** and **Animation** columns and then click **OK** in the dialog box.

15. For the **Animator Camera** task, click on the field under the **Animation** column and select **Scene 1\Camera** from the list.

    You will now play the simulation to see how the animator camera animation will be played in the timeliner simulation.

16. Click the **Simulate** tab and then click the **Play** button.

    The simulation will play and the animator camera will orbit the model when that task is played. However, the camera view is restored to the original view as soon as the **Animator Camera** task ends. To make sure the camera stays at the view where the animator camera animation stops, you need to add a script to the **Animator Camera** task. This script has an action that plays the same animator camera animation. In this case, the event that triggers the animation action is **On Key Press**. You can use any other event to trigger this script as the events are not considered while playing this animation in timeliner tasks.

17. Click the **Tasks** tab and then scroll to the **Animator Camera** task.

18. Click on the field under the **Script** column and select **Rotate**, which is the name of the script that plays the animator camera animation.

19. Click the **Simulate** tab and then click the **Play** button.

    Notice that after the **Animator Camera** task ends, the camera stays at the new orientation instead of moving back to the original orientation.

20. Click the **Tasks** tab and then save the file.

Section 7: Linking an External Scheduling File to TimeLiner

In this section, you will open the **Plant8.nwd** file and then link a CSV file to the timeliner. The CSV file has the construction schedules of the plant. You will then use the rules to attach the sets to the scheduling tasks.

1. From the **Chapter 8 > Exercise Plant** folder, open the **Plant8.nwd** file.

2. From the **Viewpoint** ribbon tab > **Render Style** ribbon panel, set the lighting to **Scene Lights**.

3. With the **Sets** window still docked, notice the various sets already created in this file.

    You will now add the CSV file to the timeliner schedule.

4. In the **TimeLiner** window, click the **Data Sources** tab.

5. Click the **Add** flyout > **CSV Import**; the **Open** dialog box is displayed.

6. In the **Open** dialog box, browse to **Chapter 8 > Exercise Plant** folder and then double-click on the **Construction Schedule.csv** file; the **Field Selector** dialog box is displayed.

7. Click on the fields under the **External Field Name** column and map them to the fields under **Column**. You only need to map the fields up to the **Subcontractor Cost**, as shown in Figure 28.

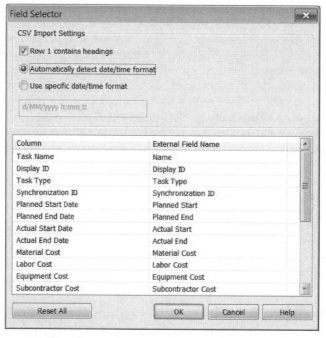

*Figure 28 The **Field Selector** dialog box showing the mapped fields*

8. Click **OK** in the dialog box; the linked file is listed in the **Data Sources** tab.

9. Rename the linked data source to **CSV Link** by right-clicking on it and selecting **Rename** from the shortcut menu.

   If you click on the **Tasks** tab, you will notice there are no tasks created yet. This is because you have not yet built the task hierarchy.

10. In the **Data Sources** tab, right-click on **CSV Link** and click **Rebuilt Task Hierarchy**.

11. If the error message is displayed about the missing synchronization ids and invalid date and time values, click **OK** in the dialog box.

12. Click the **Tasks** tab.

   Notice the task hierarchy automatically created from the linked CSV file. However, the **Task Type** and **Attached** columns for all the tasks are blank. You will first specify the task type to the tasks.

13. For the **Ground Slab** task, click on the field under the **Task Type** column and select **Construct**; this ensures that the current task is a construction task.

14. Scroll down to the last task. Now, hold down the SHIFT key and click on the field under the **Task Type** column of the last task; all the tasks are highlighted.

15. With the tasks highlighted, right-click in the **Task Type** column of the last field and select **Fill Down** from the shortcut menu; all the tasks will be assigned the **Construct** task type.

   Next, you will attach the sets to the task using the timeliner rules.

16. From the **Task** toolbar, click the **Auto-Attach Using Rules** button; the **TimeLiner Rules** dialog box is displayed.

17. Select the tick box on the left of the second rule, if not already selected, and deselect the tick boxes of the remaining two rules. This will attach those sets to the tasks that have matching names and cases.

18. Click the **Apply Rules** button and then close the dialog box; the sets are automatically attached to the tasks that have matching names and cases.

   Scroll down and notice that nothing is attached to the **Pump** and **Vessel** tasks. This is because there are no sets created for pumps or vessels. Therefore, you need to manually attach these objects to the tasks.

19. In the **Selection Tree**, expand **Plant8.nwd > 3-EQUIPMENT.dwg** and then click the **Pumps** layer.

20. For the **Pump** task, right-click in the field under the **Attached** column and click **Attach Current Selection**; the selected layer is attached to the task and is displayed as **Explicit Selection** in the **Attached** field.

21. From the **Selection Tree**, select the **Vessels** layer.

22. For the **Vessel** task, right-click in the field under the **Attached** column and click **Attach Current Selection**; the selected layer is attached to the task and is displayed as **Explicit Selection** in the **Attached** field.

    Next, you will find all the unattached or uncontained objects in the scene.

23. Right-click on any task and click **Find > Unattached/Uncontained Items** from the shortcut menu; notice that there are some 3D solid, pipes, and pipe asset items highlighted in the selection tree.

    You will append these to the **Piping-2** task.

24. Scroll down to the **Piping-2** task.

25. Right-click on this task and from the shortcut menu, click **Append Current Selection**; the field under the **Attached** column changes from **Sets->Piping-2** to **Explicit Selection**.

Section 8: Adding Various Costs to the TimeLiner Tasks

In this section, you will add the material cost, labor cost, equipment cost, and subcontractor cost to the tasks. When all these costs are added, their sum is automatically displayed as the total cost. To add these costs, you first need to display these columns.

1. From the **Task** toolbar, click the **Columns** flyout and then click **Choose Columns**; the **Choose TimeLiner Columns** dialog box is displayed.

2. Clear the tick boxes on the left of the **Actual Start**, **Actual End**, **Animation**, and **Script** columns.

3. Select the tick boxes in the left of the **Total Cost**, **Material Cost**, **Labor Cost**, **Equipment Cost**, **Subcontractor Cost** columns and click **OK** in the dialog box.

    Next, you will enter the costs for each task. Remember that you only have to enter the material, labor, equipment, and subcontractor cost. The total cost information is automatically displayed as the sum of these values.

4. For all the tasks starting from the **Ground Slab** task, enter the cost values, as shown in Figure 29.

 *Note: In Figure 29, the various costs columns were moved next to the **Name** column by dragging and dropping them one by one.*

Active	Name	Total Cost	Material Cost	Labor Cost	Equipment Cost	Subcontractor Cost
☑	▣ CSV Link (Root)	490,500.00	411,000.00	43,100.00	13,000.00	23,400.00
☑	Ground Slab	8,935.00	6,585.00	1,500.00	350.00	500.00
☑	Concrete Column	8,350.00	5,500.00	1,850.00	250.00	750.00
☑	Plinth Level 1	5,550.00	3,500.00	1,250.00	300.00	500.00
☑	Concrete Beams	6,850.00	4,500.00	1,500.00	350.00	500.00
☑	Floor Slab	4,350.00	2,500.00	1,000.00	350.00	500.00
☑	Kerbs	4,050.00	2,250.00	1,000.00	300.00	500.00
☑	Steel Column	27,500.00	22,500.00	2,500.00	750.00	1,750.00
☑	Steel Beams L 1-2	9,850.00	7,500.00	1,500.00	500.00	350.00
☑	Steel Beams L 3-4	9,850.00	7,500.00	1,500.00	500.00	350.00
☑	Steel Beams L 5-6	9,850.00	7,500.00	1,500.00	500.00	350.00
☑	Steel Beams L 7-8	9,850.00	7,500.00	1,500.00	500.00	350.00
☑	Beams-Plat-L1345	9,850.00	7,500.00	1,500.00	500.00	350.00
☑	Beams-Plat-L678	9,850.00	7,500.00	1,500.00	500.00	350.00
☑	Heat Exchanger	143,200.00	128,750.00	5,750.00	1,200.00	7,500.00
☑	Pump	20,225.00	18,875.00	750.00	300.00	300.00
☑	Vessel	87,250.00	75,000.00	7,500.00	1,250.00	3,500.00
☑	Handrails	15,100.00	12,500.00	1,250.00	850.00	500.00
☑	Ladders	11,000.00	8,500.00	1,250.00	750.00	500.00
☑	Piping-1	44,520.00	37,520.00	3,500.00	1,500.00	2,000.00
☑	Piping-2	44,520.00	37,520.00	3,500.00	1,500.00	2,000.00

Figure 29 Figure showing various costs added to the tasks

Section 9: Displaying Costs in the Simulation Overlay Text

Once the costs are added to the tasks, these can also be displayed in the overlay text during the simulation. This will be done in this section.

1. Click the **Simulate** tab in the **TimeLiner** window.

2. Click the **Settings** button to display the **Simulation Settings** dialog box.

3. Click the **Override Start / End Dates** tick box.

4. Change the start date to **January 30 2012**, which is a day before the start date of the first task.

5. Click the **Edit** button in the **Overlay Text** area; the **Overlay Text** dialog box is displayed.

6. By default, **%A %X %x Day=$DAY Week=$WEEK** is displayed in the dialog box. If there is any other text displayed, delete it.

7. Click at the start of the first line of text and then click **Colors > Red**; this will ensure the first line of text is displayed in Red.

8. Click at the end of the first line of text and then press CTRL+ENTER to go to the next line.

9. Click **Colors > Blue** to change the second line of text to blue.

10. Type **MC=** in the second line of text and then click **Cost > Material Cost**.

Next, you need to add the other costs in the same line of text. Each cost needs to be separated by a comma (,) and a space.

11. Type , **LC=** and then click **Cost > Labor Cost**.

12. Type , **Eq.C=** and then click **Cost > Equipment Cost**.

13. Type , **Sub.C=** and then click **Cost > Subcontractor Cost**.

14. With the cursor at the end of the second line, press CTRL+ENTER to go to the third line of text.

15. Click **Colors > Green** to change the color of the third line of text to Green.

16. Type **Total Cost=** and then click **Cost > Total Cost**.

Next, you will change the font of the overlay text.

17. Click the **Font** button and from the **Select Overlay Font** dialog box, select **Arial > Regular > 10** font, if it is not already selected.

18. Click **OK** in the **Select Overlay Font** dialog box and then click **OK** in the **Overlay Text** dialog box.

You will now link the saved viewpoint animation to the timeliner simulation.

19. In the **Animation** area, click the **No Link** list and select **Saved Viewpoints Animation**, if it is not already selected.

20. Click **OK** in the dialog box to return to the Autodesk Navisworks screen.

21. From the **Saved Viewpoints** window, click on the **Flythrough** animation.

22. Click the **Play** button on the **Simulate** tab to play the construction simulation.

Notice the various costs displayed in the overlay text. Figure 30 shows a screen shot from the simulation.

23. Once the simulation ends, click on the **Calendar** list on the left of the **Settings** button and pick any date during the month of April.

Notice the construction progress on that date and also the various costs that are required for the project by that particular date. This helps in budgeting for the project.

24. In the **TimeLiner** window, click the **Tasks** tab.

25. Save the file.

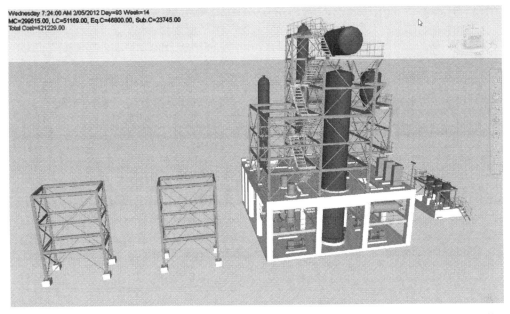

Wednesday 7:24:00 AM 2/05/2012 Day=93 Week=14
MC=299515.00, LC=51169.00, Eq.C=46800.00, Sub.C=23745.00
Total Cost=421229.00

Figure 30 *A screen shot from the simulation*

Section 10: Animating Objects to Drop from the Sky During Simulation

In this section, you will make objects fall from the sky to their respective locations in the timeliner simulation. For this, you will link the animator animations already created in the model to the timeliner simulation.

1. Dock the **Animator** window; various animator scenes created in the file are listed in this window.

2. Select the **Concrete Columns** scene from the **Animator** tree view; the concrete columns move to some location in the sky. This is the position from where you will make these columns drop in the timeline simulation.

3. From the **Animator** toolbar, click the **Stop** button; the columns move back to their original position.

4. Click the **Play** button from the **Animator** toolbar; the columns move back to the position in the sky and are dropped at their original position in the model during animation.

    To know more about how this animator animation was created, refer to **Section 9** of the plant tutorial in Chapter 7.

5. Return to the **TimeLiner** window.

6. If the **Animation** column is not already turned on in the **Tasks** tab, turn it on by clicking **Columns > Choose Columns**.

7. Click on the **Animation** field of the **Concrete Column** task; a list is displayed in the field.

8. From the list, select **Concrete Columns\Columns Drop** animator animation.

9. Click on the **Animation** field of the **Steel Column** task; a list is displayed in the field.

10. From the list, select **Steel Columns\Steel Drop** animator animation.

11. Similarly, use the following table to link the animator animations to their respective tasks:

Task Name	Animator Animation
Steel Beams L 1-2	Steel Beams L 1-2\Beams L 1-2 Drop
Steel Beams L 3-4	Steel Beams L 3-4\Beams L 3-4 Drop
Steel Beams L 5-6	Steel Beams L 5-6\Beams L 5-6 Drop
Steel Beams L 7-8	Steel Beams L 7-8\Beams L 7-8 Drop
Heat Exchanger	Heat Exchanger\Heat Exchanger Drop
Piping-1	Piping-1\Piping-1 Drop
Piping-2	Piping-2\Piping-2 Drop

12. Click the **Simulate** tab.

13. Click the **Settings** button to display the **Simulation Settings** dialog box.

14. From the list in the **Animation** area, select **No Link**.

15. Click **OK** to close the **Simulation Settings** dialog box.

16. Click the **Play** button and then press the F11 key to play the simulation in the full screen mode.

    Notice how the objects fall from the sky to their required location in the simulation.

17. After the animation ends, press F11 to exit the full screen mode.

18. Click the **Tasks** tab in the **TimeLiner** window and then hide this window.

19. Save this file and then start a new file.

Hands-on Exercise (BIM)	In this exercise, you will complete the following tasks: 1. Open a building model and create automatic tasks for all top most items in it. 2. Change the dates of the automatic tasks and then play the simulation. 3. Automatically add tasks for all the sets in the model. 4. Edit the dates of the tasks and play the simulation. 5. Create a task for the animator camera animation and then play the simulation. 6. Open another building model and link an external CSV file to import the construction schedules. 7. Use the timeliner rules to link the items in the model to the timeliner tasks imported from the CSV file. 8. Simulate the construction sequence of the tasks created using the linked CSV file.

Section 1: Opening the Building File and Automatically Adding Tasks

In this section, you will open the **TimeLiner-Building.nwd** file and then automatically create tasks for every top most item in the **Selection Tree**. This model is courtesy **Samuel Macalister Senior Technical Sales Specialist – BIM, Autodesk Inc**. You will then change the dates of the tasks and rearrange them based on your requirements.

1. From the **Chapter 8 > Exercise Building** folder, open the **TimeLiner-Building.nwd** file.

2. Change the lighting style to **Full Lights**. The model looks similar to the one shown in Figure 31.

Figure 31 *The model for the tutorial* (*Courtesy Samuel Macalister – Senior Technical Sales Specialist – BIM, Autodesk Inc.*)

3. Expand the **Selection Tree** and notice the hierarchy. This file was created using an Autodesk Revit model. As a result, the hierarchy is based on that.

 *Tip: If you have the grids and grid location readout displayed in the graphics window, you can turn them off by going to the **View** ribbon tab. The grids are turned off using the **Show Grid** button on the **Grids & Levels** ribbon panel and the grid location readout is turned off by clicking the **HUD** flyout on the **Navigation Aids** ribbon panel.*

You will now create the timeliner tasks for all the top most items in the **Selection Tree**.

4. Click **TimeLiner** from the bottom of the graphics window or from the **Home** ribbon tab > **Tools** ribbon panel; the **TimeLiner** window is displayed.

5. Dock the **TimeLiner** window below the graphics window.

6. In the **Tasks** tab, click the **Auto-Add Tasks** flyout and click **For Every Topmost Item**; a task is added for every top most item listed in the **Selection Tree** and those items are attached to the tasks.

7. Click the **Show or hide Gantt chart** button to turn off the Gantt chart. You will now be able to see more columns in the task view area.

Section 2: Editing the Start and End Dates of the Tasks

The tasks are automatically assigned planned start and planned end dates, starting from today's date. You will now change some of these dates.

1. Scroll to the top of the tasks list and then click in the **Planned End** field of the **<No level>** task.

2. Increment this date by ten days so the planned end date of the first task is ten days after the planned start days.

3. Right-click on the date field you just changed and click **Copy Date/Time** from the shortcut menu.

4. Right-click on the **Planned Start** field of the **FFL** task and click **Paste Date/Time** from the shortcut menu; the start date of this task is the same as the end date of the previous task.

5. Increment the planned end date of this task by ten days.

6. Modify all the remaining tasks such that they start on the date the previous task ends and the duration of each task is ten days, refer to Figure 32.

 Note: By default, Autodesk Navisworks does not include the weekends in the schedule. So if there are dates that are on the weekends, Autodesk Navisworks will assign the date of the following Monday to the task, unless you manually overwrite it.

Active	Name	Status	Planned Start	Planned End	Task Type	Attached
☑	<No level>	▭	30/03/2015	10/04/2015	Construct	Explicit Selection
☑	FFL	▭	10/04/2015	20/04/2015	Construct	Explicit Selection
☑	FRL	▭	20/04/2015	30/04/2015	Construct	Explicit Selection
☑	FSL	▭	30/04/2015	10/05/2015	Construct	Explicit Selection
▶ ☑	FCL	▭	10/05/2015	20/05/2015	Construct	Explicit Selection

Figure 32 The dates assigned to the tasks

Section 3: Editing and Playing the Simulation

In this section, you will edit the start date of the simulation and also the overlay text of the simulation and then play the simulation. Note the start date of the first task and the end date of the last task. You will edit the start and end dates of the simulation based on these dates.

1. Make a note of the start date of the first task and the end date of the last task. Now, in the **TimeLiner** window, click the **Simulate** tab.

2. Click the **Settings** button to display the **Simulation Settings** dialog box.

3. In the **Start / End Dates** area, click the **Override Start / End Dates** tick box.

4. Override the start date to be a day before the start date of the first task.

5. Override the end date to be a day after the end date of the last task.

6. In the **Overlay Text** area, click the **Edit** button; the **Overlay Text** dialog box is displayed.

   By default, the overlay text displays **%A %X %x Day=$DAY Week=$WEEK** in the first line of text. This will display the day of the task, the current time of the task in simulation, the current time in simulation, days since the start of the first task, and the weeks since the start of the first task.

7. Click at the start of the first line of text and then click the **Colors** button and click **Red**; the first line of the overlay text will be displayed in Red while playing the simulation.

8. Click at the end of the first line to move the cursor there. Click the **Colors > Blue**; the text starting from here will be displayed in Blue in the overlay text.

9. Click **Extras > Currently active tasks**. This will ensure that the currently active task is displayed in Blue in the second line of the overlay text during the simulation.

10. Click the **Font** button to display the **Select Overlay Font** dialog box.

11. Select **Arial > Regular > 12** font and then click **OK** in this dialog box.

12. Click **OK** in the **Overlay Text** dialog box and then click **OK** in the **Simulation Settings** dialog box.

13. On the **Simulate** tab, click the **Play** button; the timeliner simulation starts and the overlay text is displayed in the graphics window. Figure 33 shows the graphics window during the simulation.

Figure 33 *A screen shot during the timeliner simulation*

14. After the timeliner simulation ends, click the **Tasks** tab.

 Note: *If you do not click the **Tasks** tab in the **TimeLiner** window, you will not be allowed to perform certain operations, such as creating or selecting an animator scene.*

Section 4: Creating Automatic Tasks Based on Sets

While playing the simulation in the previous section, you would have noticed that construction sequence is not correct. The fascias at the roof and the chimneys are added even before the walls and columns are added. This is because of the layers and items created from the Autodesk Revit model. This issue can be overcome by simply creating the sets of the items in the model and making sure they are organized in the right sequence in the **Sets** window. In this section, you will create automatic tasks using the sets that are already created in this file and then simulate them. But first, you will delete the existing tasks.

1. Dock the **Sets** window below the **Selection Tree**.

   Notice the sequence of the sets created in this file. The tasks will be added in this sequence.

2. In the **Tasks** tab of the **TimeLiner** window, select the first task.

3. Hold down the SHIFT key and select the last task.

4. Click the **Delete Task** button from the **Task** toolbar; all the tasks are deleted.

You will now add tasks for all the sets.

Tip: *In some cases, it is noticed that when you click on the **Auto-Add Tasks** flyout, the **For Every Set** and **For Every Topmost Layer** options are grayed out. In this case, you can right-click in the tasks view area and select these options from the shortcut menu.*

5. Right-click in the Gray **Task View** area and from the shortcut menu, click **Auto-Add Tasks > For Every Set**; timeliner tasks are added for every set in the **Sets** window. Also, all these sets are attached to the tasks, as shown in Figure 34. Note that in this figure, some tasks at the bottom are not displayed due to the size of the window.

Active	Name	Status	Planned Start	Planned End	Task Type	Attached
✓	Site		30/03/2015	30/03/2015	Construct	Sets->Site
✓	Site works		31/03/2015	31/03/2015	Construct	Sets->Site works
✓	Piles		1/04/2015	1/04/2015	Construct	Sets->Piles
✓	Pile cap		2/04/2015	2/04/2015	Construct	Sets->Pile cap
✓	Concrete footings		3/04/2015	3/04/2015	Construct	Sets->Concrete footings
✓	Concrete floor slab		6/04/2015	6/04/2015	Construct	Sets->Concrete floor slab
✓	Structure Steel base plates		7/04/2015	7/04/2015	Construct	Sets->Structure Steel base plates
✓	Slab insulation		8/04/2015	8/04/2015	Construct	Sets->Slab insulation
✓	Ext Wall Structure		9/04/2015	9/04/2015	Construct	Sets->Ext Wall Structure
✓	Structural Steel Column		10/04/2015	10/04/2015	Construct	Sets->Structural Steel Column
✓	Structure Roof Truss		13/04/2015	13/04/2015	Construct	Sets->Structure Roof Truss
✓	Ext Slider doors		14/04/2015	14/04/2015	Construct	Sets->Ext Slider doors
✓	Int Doors All		15/04/2015	15/04/2015	Construct	Sets->Int Doors All
✓	Ext_Plywood Sheathing		16/04/2015	16/04/2015	Construct	Sets->Ext_Plywood Sheathing
✓	Int plaster board		17/04/2015	17/04/2015	Construct	Sets->Int plaster board
✓	Gypsum Board		20/04/2015	20/04/2015	Construct	Sets->Gypsum Board
✓	Roof Plywood substrate		21/04/2015	21/04/2015	Construct	Sets->Roof Plywood substrate
✓	Ext_Air Infiltration Barrier		22/04/2015	22/04/2015	Construct	Sets->Ext_Air Infiltration Barrier
✓	Roof VCL		23/04/2015	23/04/2015	Construct	Sets->Roof VCL
✓	Ceiling All		24/04/2015	24/04/2015	Construct	Sets->Ceiling All
✓	Roof Insulation		27/04/2015	27/04/2015	Construct	Sets->Roof Insulation
✓	Ext Wall Int finish		28/04/2015	28/04/2015	Construct	Sets->Ext Wall Int finish
✓	Roof Finish		29/04/2015	29/04/2015	Construct	Sets->Roof Finish
✓	Soffit all		30/04/2015	30/04/2015	Construct	Sets->Soffit all

Figure 34 The tasks created for all the sets

6. Make a note of the start date of the first task and the end date of the last task. Now, click the **Simulate** tab in the **TimeLiner** window.

7. Click the **Settings** button; the **Simulation Settings** dialog box is displayed.

8. With the **Override Start / End Dates** tick box still selected, make sure the start date is overridden to be a day before the start date of the first task. Also, make sure the end date is overridden to be a day after the end date of the last task.

9. Click **OK** in the dialog box.

10. In the **Simulate** tab, click the **Play** button to play the simulation; the simulation is played showing the construction sequence of the model. Notice that this construction sequence looks more realistic with the tasks broken down into smaller tasks. Figure 35 shows a screen shot during the simulation.

Friday 2:24:00 PM 21/02/2014 Day=34 Week=5

Figure 35 *A screen shot during the timeliner simulation*

Section 5: Linking a Viewpoint Animation to the TimeLiner Simulation

In the previous sections, the simulations that you played showed the construction of the model from the same viewpoint. In this section, you will link a saved viewpoint animation to the timeliner simulation so that the camera is rotated around the model as it is constructed.

1.   With the **Simulate** tab still active, click the **Settings** button to display the **Simulation Settings** dialog box.

2.   In the **Animation** area, click the **No Link** list and then select **Saved Viewpoints Animation**; the viewpoint animation is linked to the timeliner simulation.

3.   Change the duration of the animation in the **Playback Duration (Seconds)** spinner to **30**.

4.   Click **OK** in the dialog box.

5.   Click the **Play** button to play the timeliner simulation.

Notice how the model is orbited as the timeliner simulation is played.

Section 6: Creating a Task for the Animator Camera Animation

In the previous section, the saved viewpoint animation that you linked to the simulation plays throughout the simulation. But some times, you need to orbit the model during the simulation to a particular view and then leave the camera there to view the rest of the simulation from that camera view. This can be done using the animator camera animation, which is what you will do in this section.

1. With the **Simulate** tab still active, click the **Settings** button.

2. In the **Animation** area, click the **Saved Viewpoints Animation** list and select **No Link**; the viewpoint animation is removed from the timeliner simulation.

3. Click **OK** in the dialog box.

4. Click the **Tasks** tab.

5. Scroll up in the tasks list and select the **Ext Wall Structure** task.

6. From the **Task** toolbar, click the **Insert Task** button; a new task is added above the **Ext Wall Structure** task.

7. Rename the new task to **Animator Camera**.

    Next, you need to change the planned start and end dates of this task. You can manually type the dates or copy and paste them from the other tasks, as discussed below.

8. Right-click on the **Planned End** date of the **Slab insulation** task and click **Copy Date/Time** from the shortcut menu.

9. Right-click on the **Planned Start** date of the **Animator Camera** task and click **Paste Date/Time** from the shortcut menu.

10. Right-click on the **Planned Start** date of the **Ext Wall Structure** task and click **Copy Date/Time** from the shortcut menu.

11. Right-click on the **Planned End** date of the **Animator Camera** task and click **Paste Date/Time** from the shortcut menu.

    You will now add the **Animation** and **Script** columns, as they are not displayed by default. It will be easier to view all these columns if the visibility of the Gantt chart is turned off.

12. If the visibility of the Gantt chart is turned on, turn it off by clicking the **Show or hide the Gantt chart** button from the **Gantt chart** toolbar.

13. From the **Task** toolbar, click the **Columns** flyout and then click **Choose Columns** to display the **Choose TimeLiner Columns** dialog box.

14. Click the tick boxes on the left of the **Script** and **Animation** columns and then click **OK** in the dialog box.

15. For the **Animator Camera** task, click on the field under the **Animation** column and select **Rotate\Camera** from the list.

   You will now play the simulation to see how the animator camera animation will be played in the timeliner simulation.

16. Click the **Simulate** tab and then click the **Play** button.

   The simulation will play and the animator camera will orbit the model when that task is played. However, the camera view is restored to the original view as soon as the **Animator Camera** task ends. To make sure the camera stays at the view where the animator camera animation stops, you need to add a script to the **Animator Camera** task. This script has an action that plays the same animator camera animation. In this case, the event that triggers the animation action is **On Key Press**. You can use any other event to trigger this script as the events are not considered while playing this animation in timeliner tasks.

17. Click the **Tasks** tab and then scroll to the **Animator Camera** task.

18. Click on the field under the **Script** column and select **Camera**, which is the name of the script that plays the animator camera animation.

19. Click the **Simulate** tab and then click the **Play** button.

   Notice that after the **Animator Camera** task ends, the camera stays at the new orientation instead of moving back to the original orientation.

20. Save the file.

Section 7: Linking an External Scheduling File to TimeLiner

In this section, you will open the **Link-Building.nwd** file and then link a CSV file to the timeliner. The CSV file has the construction schedules of the building. You will then use the rules to attach the sets to the scheduling tasks.

1. From the **Chapter 8 > Exercise Building** folder, open the **Link-Building.nwd** file.

2. Change the lighting style to **Scene Lights**.

3. With the **Sets** window still docked, notice the various sets already created in this file.

   You will now add the CSV file to the timeliner schedule.

4. In the **TimeLiner** window, click the **Data Sources** tab.

5. Click **Add > CSV Import**; the **Open** dialog box is displayed.

6. In the **Open** dialog box, browse to **Chapter 8 > Exercise Building** folder and then double-click on the **Building_Schedule.csv** file; the **Field Selector** dialog box is displayed.

7. Click on the fields under the **External Field Name** column and map them to the fields under **Column**. You only need to map up to the **Subcontractor Cost** field, as shown in Figure 36.

*Figure 36 The **Field Selector** dialog box showing the mapped fields*

8. Click **OK** in the dialog box; the linked file is listed in the **Data Sources** tab.

9. Rename the linked data source to **CSV Link** by right-clicking on it and selecting **Rename** from the shortcut menu.

    If you click on the **Tasks** tab, you will notice there are no tasks created yet. This is because you have not built the task hierarchy yet.

10. In the **Data Sources** tab, right-click on **CSV Link** and click **Rebuild Task Hierarchy**.

11. If the error message is displayed about the missing synchronization ids and invalid actual start and end date values, click **OK** in the dialog box.

12. Click the **Tasks** tab.

Notice the task hierarchy automatically created from the linked CSV file. However, the **Task Type** and **Attached** columns for all the tasks are blank. You will first specify the task type to the tasks.

13. For the **Site** task, click on the field under the **Task Type** column and select **Construct**; this ensures that this is a construction task.

14. Scroll down to the last task. Now, hold down the SHIFT key and click on the field under the **Task Type** column; all the tasks are highlighted.

15. With the tasks highlighted, right-click in the **Task Type** column of the last field and select **Fill Down** from the shortcut menu; all the tasks will be assigned the **Construct** task type.

    Next, you will attach the sets to the task using the timeliner rules.

16. From the **Task** toolbar, click the **Auto-Attach Using Rules** button; the **TimeLiner Rules** dialog box is displayed.

17. Select the tick box on the left of the second rule, if not already clicked. This will attach the sets to the tasks that have matching names and cases.

18. Click the **Apply Rules** button and then close the dialog box; the sets are automatically attached to the tasks that have matching names and cases.

    Scroll down and notice that nothing is attached to the **Chimney** and **Furniture** tasks. This is because there are no sets created for chimney or furniture. Therefore, you need to manually attach these objects to the tasks.

19. On the **Home** ribbon tab > **Select & Search** ribbon panel, type **Chimney** in the **Quick Find** box and press ENTER; the **Selection Tree** expands and shows **Chimney** and **Chimney1**.

20. From the **Selection Tree**, select **Chimney** and **Chimney1**.

21. For the **Chimney** task, right-click in the field under the **Attached** column and click **Attach Current Selection**; the selected objects are attached to the task and is displayed as **Explicit Selection** in the **Attached** field.

    Next, you need to select the furniture from the **Selection Tree** and attach to the task.

22. From the **Selection Tree**, expand the **<No level>** layer and select **Furniture**.

23. From the **Selection Tree**, expand the **FFL** layer. Hold down the CTRL key and select **Furniture**.

24. For the **Furniture** task, right-click in the field under the **Attached** column and click **Attach Current Selection**; the selected layer is attached to the task and is displayed as **Explicit Selection** in the **Attached** field.

    Next, you will find the unattached or uncontained objects in the scene.

25. Right-click on any task and click **Find > Unattached/Uncontained Items** from the shortcut menu; notice that there are some model lines highlighted in the **Selection Tree**, which can be ignored.

Section 8: Adding Various Costs to the TimeLiner Tasks

In this section, you will add the material cost, labor cost, equipment cost, and subcontractor cost to the tasks. When all these costs are added, their sum is automatically displayed as the total cost. To add these costs, you first need to display these columns.

1. From the **Task** toolbar, click the **Columns** flyout and then click **Choose Columns**; the **Choose TimeLiner Columns** dialog box is displayed.

2. Clear the tick boxes on the left of the **Actual Start**, **Actual End**, **Animation**, and **Script** columns.

3. Select the tick boxes in the left of the **Total Cost**, **Material Cost**, **Labor Cost**, **Equipment Cost**, **Subcontractor Cost** columns and click **OK** in the dialog box.

   Next, you will enter the costs for each task. Remember that you only have to enter the material, labor, equipment, and subcontractor costs. The total cost information is automatically displayed as the sum of these values.

4. For all the tasks starting from the **Site works** task, enter the cost values, as shown in Figure 37. Notice that there is no cost assigned to the **Site** task. This is because the site already exists and will not be built as part of the construction.

 Note: In Figure 37, the various costs columns were moved next to the **Name** column by dragging and dropping them one by one.

Section 9: Displaying Costs in the Simulation Overlay Text

Once the costs are added to the tasks, these can also be displayed in the overlay text during the simulation. This will be done in this section.

1. Click the **Simulate** tab in the **TimeLiner** window.

2. Click the **Settings** button to display the **Simulation Settings** dialog box.

3. Click the **Override Start / End Dates** tick box.

4. Change the start date to **January 14 2013**; this will ensure that the site is not simulated.

5. Make sure the end date is **April 21 2013**.

6. Click the **Edit** button in the **Overlay Text** area; the **Overlay Text** dialog box is displayed.

7. By default, **%A %X %x Day=$DAY Week=$WEEK** is displayed in the dialog box. If there is any other text displayed, delete it.

Active	Name	Total Cost	Material Cost	Labor Cost	Equipment Cost	Subcontractor Cost
✓	⊟ CSV Link (Root)	173,815.00	140,610.00	16,905.00	4,050.00	12,250.00
✓	Site					
✓	Site works	6,350.00	3,850.00	1,000.00	750.00	750.00
✓	Piles	13,350.00	11,500.00	750.00	250.00	850.00
✓	Pile cap	4,500.00	3,750.00	350.00	150.00	250.00
✓	Concrete footings	22,250.00	17,850.00	2,500.00	650.00	1,250.00
✓	Concrete floor slab	14,100.00	10,500.00	1,500.00	350.00	1,750.00
✓	Structure Steel base plates	1,730.00	1,250.00	330.00	00.00	150.00
✓	Slab insulation	1,900.00	1,500.00	250.00	00.00	150.00
✓	Ext Wall Structure	17,250.00	12,500.00	2,500.00	1,000.00	1,250.00
✓	Structure Steel Coulmns	6,000.00	3,500.00	1,100.00	650.00	750.00
✓	Structure Roof Truss	6,300.00	4,550.00	650.00	250.00	850.00
✓	Ext Slider doors	2,825.00	2,500.00	150.00	00.00	175.00
✓	Int Doors All	6,300.00	5,450.00	500.00	00.00	350.00
✓	Ext_Plywood Sheathing	3,950.00	3,250.00	350.00	00.00	350.00
✓	Int plaster board	3,075.00	2,250.00	450.00	00.00	375.00
✓	Gypsum Board	7,750.00	6,500.00	500.00	00.00	750.00
✓	Roof Plywood substrate	4,450.00	3,500.00	350.00	00.00	600.00
✓	Ext_Air Infiltration Barrier	2,650.00	2,500.00	150.00	00.00	00.00
✓	Roof VCL	1,850.00	1,500.00	350.00	00.00	00.00
✓	Roof Insulation	2,100.00	1,750.00	350.00	00.00	00.00
✓	Ext Wall Int finish	3,800.00	3,500.00	150.00	00.00	150.00
✓	Roof Finish	3,850.00	3,250.00	350.00	00.00	250.00
✓	Soffit all	3,925.00	3,350.00	275.00	00.00	300.00
✓	Fascias all	12,700.00	11,750.00	300.00	00.00	650.00
✓	Decking structure	3,750.00	3,500.00	250.00	00.00	00.00
✓	Ext_Cladding	2,725.00	2,550.00	175.00	00.00	00.00
✓	Entry door glass	850.00	750.00	100.00	00.00	00.00
✓	Fire place stone	525.00	375.00	150.00	00.00	00.00
✓	Decking Finish	335.00	185.00	150.00	00.00	00.00
✓	Int_Floor finish	425.00	275.00	150.00	00.00	00.00
✓	Gabion Columns clad	3,450.00	2,850.00	300.00	00.00	300.00
✓	Joinery	1,925.00	1,550.00	375.00	00.00	00.00
✓	Chimney	325.00	225.00	100.00	00.00	00.00
✓	Furniture	6,550.00	6,550.00	00.00	00.00	00.00

Figure 37 The various costs assigned to the tasks

8. Click at the start of the first line of text and then click **Colors > Red**; this will ensure the first line of text is displayed in Red.

9. Click at the end of the first line of text and then press CTRL+ENTER to go to the next line.

10. Click **Colors > Blue** to change the second line of text to blue.

11. Type **MC=** in the second line of text and then click **Cost > Material Cost**.

    Next, you need to add the other costs in the same line of text. Each cost needs to be separated by a comma (,) and a space.

12. Type **, LC=** and then click **Cost > Labor Cost**.

13. Type **, Eq.C=** and then click **Cost > Equipment Cost**.

14. Type , **Sub.C=** and then click **Cost > Subcontractor Cost**.

15. With the cursor at the end of the second line, press CTRL+ENTER to go to the third line of text.

16. Click **Colors > Green** to change the color of the third line of text to Green.

17. Type **Total Cost=** and then click **Cost > Total Cost**.

    Next, you will change the font of the overlay text.

18. Click the **Font** button and from the **Select Overlay Font** dialog box, select **Arial > Regular > 10** font.

19. Click **OK** in the **Select Overlay Font** dialog box and then click **OK** in the **Overlay Text** dialog box.

    You will now link the saved viewpoint animation to the timeliner simulation.

20. In the **Animation** area, click the **No Link** list and select **Saved Viewpoints Animation**, if not already selected.

21. Click **OK** in the dialog box to return to the Autodesk Navisworks screen.

22. Click the **Play** button on the **Simulate** tab to play the construction simulation.

    Notice the various costs displayed in the overlay text. Figure 38 shows a screen shot from the simulation.

23. Once the simulation ends, click on the **Calendar** list on the left of the **Settings** button and pick any date during the month of March.

    Notice the construction progress on that date and also the various costs that are required for the project by that particular date. This helps in budgeting for the project.

24. In the **TimeLiner** window, click the **Tasks** tab.

25. Save the file.

Section 10: Linking Crane Rotation and Semitrailer Animations to the TimeLiner Simulation

In this section, you will create a complex timeliner simulation by linking crane rotation and semitrailer movement animations to it.

1. From the **Chapter 8 > Exercise Building** folder, open the **Construction_Site.nwd** file.

2. Change the lighting style to **Scene Lights**. The model for the tutorial looks similar to the one shown in Figure 39.

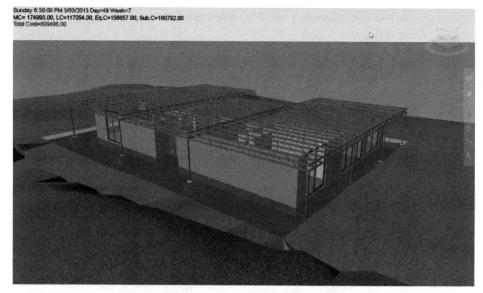

Figure 38 *A screen shot from the simulation*

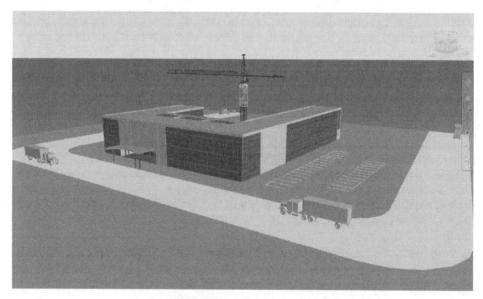

Figure 39 *The model for the tutorial*

This file has scripts already created that animate the crane and the semitrailers in the scene. It is better to view these animations to understand what to expect once you add them to the timeliner simulation.

3. From the **Animation** tab > **Script** ribbon panel, click **Enable Scripts**.

4. Click on the sky in the graphics window and then press the S key and then the C key; the S key plays the Semi animation and the C key plays the Crane animation.

Notice how the semitrailers and crane animate in the scene. These will be added to the timeliner simulation.

5. From the **Animation** tab > **Script** ribbon panel, click **Enable Scripts** again to stop the animations.

6. In the **TimeLiner** window, click the **Data Sources** tab.

7. Click **Add** > **CSV Import** to display the **Open** dialog box.

8. Browse to the **Chapter 8 > Exercise Building** folder and double-click on the **Complete_Construction.csv** file; the **Field Selector** dialog box is displayed with all the fields already mapped correctly.

9. Click **OK** in the dialog box; the CSV file is linked and is displayed in the **Data Sources** tab.

10. Right-click on the linked data source and select **Rebuild Task Hierarchy** from the shortcut menu.

11. Click **OK** in the dialog box that informs you about the missing synchronization id and invalid date and time formats.

12. Click the **Tasks** tab; the task hierarchy is automatically created from the linked data source.

    Notice that the **Task Type** and **Attached** columns are blank. You will now attach the sets to these tasks.

13. From the **Task** toolbar, click the **Auto-Attach Using Rules** button; the **TimeLiner Rules** dialog box is displayed.

14. Select the tick box on the left of the second rule and click **Apply Rules** button in the dialog box, if not already selected. This will attach those sets to the tasks that have matching names and cases.

15. Exit the dialog box.

16. Click on the field under the **Task Type** column for the **Site** task and select **Construct**.

17. Scroll down to the last task. Hold down the SHIFT and select the last task.

18. With all the tasks selected, right-click in the **Task Type** field of the last task and select **Fill Down** from the shortcut menu; all the tasks are now assigned **Construct** task type.

    Next, you will add the tasks to play the Crane and Semi animations. Because there is no camera animator animation, you do not need to add the script to the timeliner simulation.

19. Using the **Columns** button in the **Task** toolbar, display the **Animation** column.

20. On the **Task** toolbar, click the **Add Task** button to add a task at the bottom of the list.

21. Rename the task to **Crane**.

22. Similarly, add another task at the bottom and rename it to **Semi**.

23. Change the planned start dates of both the tasks to **March 18, 2014**.

24. Change the planned end dates of both the tasks to **April 29, 2015**.

 *Tip: It is sometimes noticed that if start date of a task linked to the animator animation is before the start date of the simulation in the **Simulation Settings** dialog box, the animations do not play in the simulation.*

25. For the **Crane** task, click on the field in the **Animation** column and select **Crane**.

26. For the **Semi** task, click on the field in the **Animation** column and select **Semi Movement**.

    You will now change the start date of the simulation to make sure the site, crane and semitrailers are already displayed in the scene with the simulation starts.

27. Click the **Simulate** tab and then click **Settings**; the **Simulation Settings** dialog box is displayed.

28. Click the **Override Start / End Dates** tick box.

29. Change the start date to **March 18, 2014**.

30. Make sure the end date is **April 29, 2015**.

31. Click **Edit** in the **Overlay Text** area to display the **Overlay Text** dialog box.

32. Click at the start of the first line of text and then click **Colors > Red**; the overlay text will be displayed in Red.

33. Click **OK** in both the dialog boxes to return to the Autodesk Navisworks window.

34. Click the **Play** button to play the simulation.

    You will notice that when the simulation ends, all the semitrailers disappear but the crane still remains in the scene. This is because the visibility of the semitrailers in the animator animation was turned off. However, this is not the case with the crane. But because this is the end of the construction, you need to remove the crane also from the scene. This will be done by creating a demolition task for the crane.

35. Click the **Tasks** tab.

36. Click the **Add Task** button from the **Task** toolbar; a new task is added at the bottom of the list.

37. Rename the new task to **Crane Removal**.

38. Change the planned start and planned end dates of this task to **April 28, 2015**.

39. Click on the **Task Type** list for this task and select **Demolish**.

40. From the **Selection Tree**, expand **Construction_Site.nwd** and select the **Crane Base** and **Crane Rotate** layers.

41. Right-click on the **Crane Removal** task and select **Attach Current Selection** from the shortcut menu.

42. Click in the blank area of the graphics window to deselect the crane.

43. Click the **Simulate** tab and play the simulation again. Figure 40 shows a screen shot from this simulation. Notice how the crane is removed from the scene at the end of the simulation.

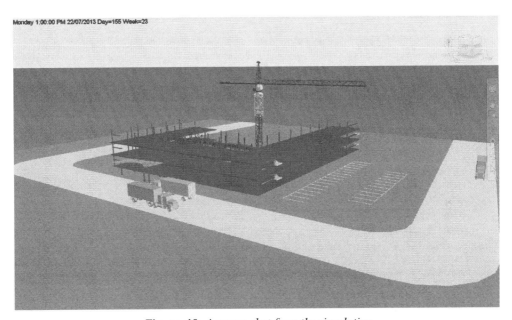

Figure 40 A screen shot from the simulation

44. After the simulation ends, click the **Tasks** tab to stop the simulation and return to the tasks.

Section 11: Animating Objects to Drop from the Sky During Simulation

In this section, you will make objects fall from the sky to their respective locations in the timeliner simulation. For this, you will link the animator animations already created in the model to the timeliner simulation.

1. Dock the **Animator** window; various animator scenes created in the file are listed in this window.

2. Select the **L1-Slab** scene from the **Animator** tree view; the slab moves to some location in the sky. This is the position from where you will make these objects drop in the timeline simulation.

3. From the **Animator** toolbar, click the **Stop** button; the objects move back to their original position.

4. Click the **Play** button from the **Animator** toolbar; the objects move back to the position in the sky and are dropped at their original position in the model during animation.

   To know more about how this animator animation was created, refer to **Section 11** of the building tutorial in Chapter 7.

5. Return to the **TimeLiner** window.

6. If the **Animation** column is not already turned on in the **Tasks** tab, turn it on by clicking **Columns > Choose Columns**.

7. Click on the **Animation** field of the **L1-Slab** task; a list is displayed in the field.

8. From the list, select **L1-Slab\L1-Slab Drop** animator animation.

9. Click on the **Animation** field of the **Columns-L1** task; a list is displayed in the field.

10. From the list, select **Columns-L1\Columns-L1l Drop** animator animation.

11. Similarly, use the following table to link the animator animations to their respective tasks:

Task Name	Animator Animation
L1-Internal Walls	L1-Internal Walls\L1-Internal Walls Drop
L2-Slabs	L2-Slabs\L2-Slabs Drop
Columns-L2	Columns-L2\Columns-L2 Drop
L2-Internal Walls	L2-Internal Walls\L2-Internal Walls Drop
L3-Slabs	L3-Slabs\L3-Slabs Drop
Columns-L3	Columns-L3\Columns-L3 Drop
L3-Internal Walls	L3-Internal Walls\L3-Internal Walls Drop
Roof	Roof\Roof Drop

12. Click the **Simulate** tab.

13. Click the **Play** button and then press the F11 key to play the simulation in the full screen mode. Notice how the objects fall from the sky to their required location in the simulation.

14. After the animation ends, press F11 to exit the full screen mode.

15. Click the **Tasks** tab in the **TimeLiner** window and then hide this window.

16. Save this file and then start a new file.

Skill Evaluation

Evaluate your skills to see how many questions you can answer correctly. The answers to these questions are given at the end of the book.

1. Autodesk Navisworks only allows you to create manual timeliner tasks. (True/False)

2. The tasks created using an external project file can be attached objects using some predefined or custom rules. (True/False)

3. You can link a saved viewpoint animation to the timeliner simulation. (True/False)

4. The animator scenes can also be linked to the timeliner simulation as tasks. (True/False)

5. You can edit the text that is displayed in the graphics window during the timeliner simulation. (True/False)

6. Which option is used to create automatic tasks from the sets?

   (A) **Auto-Add Tasks > For Search Set**   (B) **Auto-Add Tasks > For Selection Set**
   (C) **Auto-Add Tasks > For Every Set**   (D) None

7. Which one of the following costs type is not available to be added?

   (A) Equipment cost   (B) Material cost
   (C) Subcontractor cost   (D) Transportation cost

8. While linking an animation to the timeliner simulation in the **Simulation Settings** dialog box, which type of simulation can be selected?

   (A) Animator camera animation   (B) Saved viewpoint animation
   (C) Both   (D) None

9. Which tab of the **TimeLiner** window is used to add an external data source or a project file to create tasks?

   (A) **Project**   (B) **Simulate**
   (C) **Tasks**   (D) **Data Sources**

10. Which one is not a type of task that can be selected from the **Task Type** column?

    (A) Demolish   (B) Construct
    (C) Temporary   (D) Moving

Class Test Questions

Answer the following questions:

1. Explain the procedure of adding an external data source and creating tasks using it.

2. Explain how you can change the color of the overlay text.

3. While creating automatic tasks, which dates are automatically assigned to the tasks?

4. What does **Explicit Selection** in the **Attached** column mean?

5. What is displayed in the Gantt chart?

Chapter 9 – Introduction to the Quantification Module

The objectives of this chapter are to:

√   *Introduce you to the **Quantification** module.*
√   *Familiarize you with **Quantification Workbook** window.*
√   *Explain item and resource catalogs.*
√   *Explain how to add or edit formulas in the catalogs.*
√   *Teach you how to perform quantity takeoffs on the objects in the scene.*
√   *Teach you how to perform quantity takeoffs on virtual objects that are not present in the scene.*
√   *Teach you how to export the quantity takeoffs data in various formats.*

THE QUANTIFICATION MODULE

The **Quantification** module is used to create a cost estimation of the project by performing quantity takeoff from 3D and 2D objects in the Autodesk Navisworks scene. You can also perform quantity takeoff from virtual objects that are not present in the scene but will be a part of the project. It is important to note that the 2D quantification is only supported with native or non-native DWF files. Any other format 2D files will first have to be published as DWF to be used for 2D quantification. The quantity takeoff can be exported in the format such as Microsoft Excel that can be read by the project members who do not have Autodesk Navisworks.

The following flowchart shows you a brief concept of various steps involved in performing quantity takeoffs.

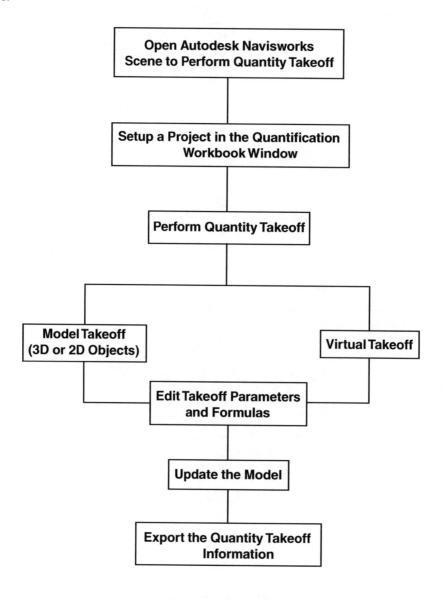

TYPES OF QUANTITY TAKEOFFS

As shown in the flowchart on the previous page, Autodesk Navisworks allows you to perform model quantity takeoffs using 3D model objects or 2D DWF sheets, or using virtual objects. All these types of takeoffs are discussed next.

Model Quantity Takeoff

This type of takeoff is used for an Autodesk Navisworks scene created using the supported native CAD files that bring the model properties into Autodesk Navisworks. The supported CAD files include AutoCAD, AutoCAD Architecture, AutoCAD MEP, Autodesk Civil 3D, AutoCAD Map 3D, Autodesk Inventor, and Autodesk Revit. Alternatively, you can use the DWF files to perform model quantity takeoffs.

 Note: *Remember that you may need the object enablers to be installed to read the object properties for some of these native CAD files. You can use the* **Scene Statistics** *dialog box to find if you need any object enabler to be installed. Refer to Chapter 1 of this textbook to know more about this.*

It is important to mention here that in the native files, the quantity takeoff can only be performed on groups of objects, layers, or objects that have GUID (Globally Unique Identifier) property. If you try to perform quantity takeoff on an object that is not acceptable, an error dialog box will be displayed, as shown in Figure 8. Clicking **Yes** in this dialog box will display a help document informing you about the objects that are allowed to be selected for quantity takeoff.

2D Quantity Takeoff

This is a new feature introduced in Autodesk Navisworks 2015 and is used to support the 2D and 3D integrated workflow from software such as Autodesk Revit. Remember that the 2D takeoff is only supported in DWF drawing sheets. Therefore, to work with the integrated workflow, you will have to export the Autodesk Revit files into the DWF format. You can also publish 2D DWF sheets from other native Autodesk software to perform 2D takeoff in Autodesk Navisworks. However, if you want to use other file formats, such as a PDF file, you need to first convert it into a DWF file using the print driver software available from the Autodesk website.

While working with the integrated 2D and 3D workflow in a DWF file published from Autodesk Revit, you will need to use the **Project Browser** or the multisheet buttons on the status bar below the graphics window to switch between various sheets.

 Note: *The snap to vertex options while drawing the 2D takeoff markups are only available in the DWF files published from the native CAD software.*

Virtual Quantity Takeoff

This type of takeoff is used for objects that do not exist in the model. You can also use this type of takeoff for the objects that do not have any native property defined or their native properties were lost while exporting the files from the native CAD program. The virtual takeoff allows you to create a viewpoint where you want to perform a takeoff. You can then use the measure tools in that viewpoint to measure objects with no properties or add redline markups. For the objects that do not exist, you can edit the formulas to get the required quantity.

THE QUANTIFICATION WORKBOOK

Home Ribbon Tab > Tools Ribbon Panel > Quantification

When you invoke the **Quantification** tool for the first time to perform the quantity takeoff, the **Quantification Workbook** window will be displayed. The first thing you need to do in this window is to set up the project. This involves defining the catalog that you will use for the quantity takeoff and the units that you want to work with. A catalog contains the categories of items in which you will organize the model objects to takeoff the quantity. Because you need to first set up the project, the **Quantification Workbook** window will be blank when you open it and only the **Project Setup** button will be available on the top left corner of this window. When you click this button, the **Quantification Setup Wizard** dialog box will be displayed showing the **Select Catalog** page, as shown in Figure 1.

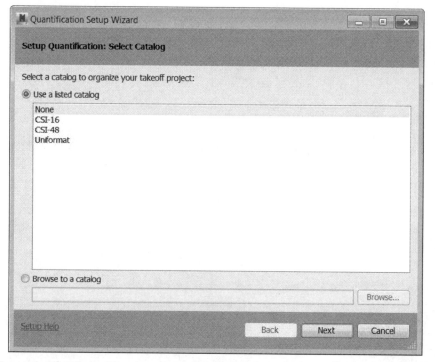

*Figure 1 The **Quantification Setup Wizard** dialog box showing the **Select Catalog** page*

On the **Select Catalog** page, by default, the **Use a listed catalog** radio button is selected that allows you to select one of the listed catalogs in this area. You can also select **None** from this area if you do not want to use your own catalog. If you have your own catalog that you want to use, you can click the **Browse to a catalog** radio button and then browse and select your own catalog. Once you have specified the catalog, click the **Next** button; the **Select Units** page of the wizard will be displayed, as shown in Figure 2.

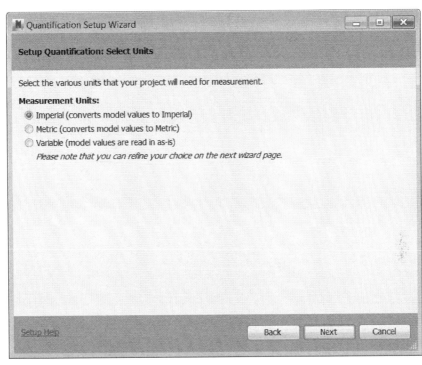

Figure 2 The ***Quantification Setup Wizard*** *dialog box showing the* ***Select Units*** *page*

Select the units of measurements from this page. If you are not sure of the units of the model, select the **Variable (model values are read in as-is)** radio button. As a result, the units will be automatically read from the model that you use for quantity takeoff. Click the **Next** button; the **Select Takeoff Properties** page will be displayed, as shown in Figure 3.

In the **Select Takeoff Properties** page, you can select individual units for general properties such as model length, model width, model area, model volume, and so on. Selecting the **Show Metric and Imperial units for each takeoff property** will allow you to display the units for all the takeoff properties in both Metric and Imperial units.

Click the **Next** button; the **Ready to Create Database** page will be displayed, as shown in Figure 4. Click on the **Finish** button on this page to complete the project set up.

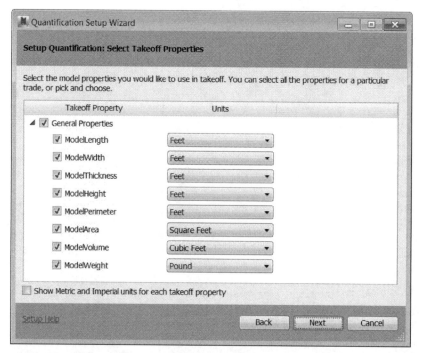

Figure 3 *The **Quantification Setup Wizard** dialog box showing the **Select Takeoff Properties** page*

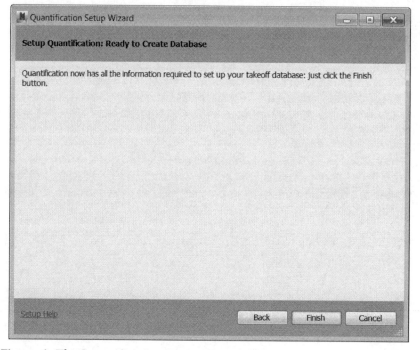

Figure 4 *The **Quantification Setup Wizard** dialog box showing the **Ready to Create Database** page*

Figure 5 shows the **Quantification Workbook** window after adding a catalog using the project set up.

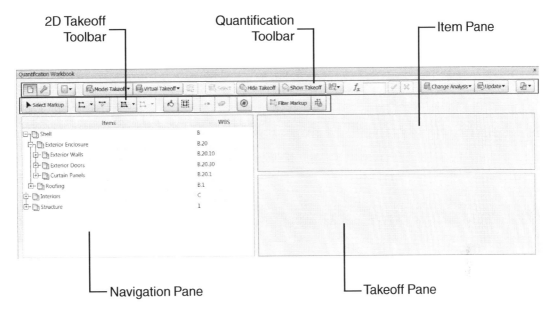

*Figure 5 The **Quantification Workbook** window after adding a catalog*

The various components of the **Quantification Workbook** window are discussed next.

Quantification Toolbar

The **Quantification** toolbar located at the top in the **Quantification Workbook** window shows the following buttons:

Switch to Item View/ Switch to Resource View

These are the first two buttons on the **Quantification** toolbar and are used to switch the view to either the item catalog view or resource catalog view.

Show and hide Item and Resource Catalogs

This flyout is used to display the **Item Catalog** and **Resource Catalog** windows.

Model Takeoff

This flyout is used to perform a model takeoff to the catalog item selected in the left pane of the **Quantification Workbook** window or a new catalog item.

Virtual Takeoff

This flyout is used to perform a virtual takeoff of the nonexisting objects to the catalog item selected in the left pane of the **Quantification Workbook** window or a new catalog item.

Add a viewpoint to the takeoff, or update an existing viewpoint

This button is only available during virtual takeoff. It allows you to create a viewpoint for the virtual takeoff so that you can perform measurements of the objects using that viewpoint. This button can also be used to update the viewpoint that you have previously created for the virtual takeoff.

Select

This button is used to select the objects in the graphics window that correspond to the takeoffs selected in the **Quantification Workbook** window. Alternatively, you can click on the name of the objects in this window to select them in the graphics window.

Hide Takeoff

This button is used to toggle on or off the visibility of the objects corresponding to the takeoff selected in the **Quantification Workbook** window.

Show Takeoff

This button is used to toggle on or off the visibility of all the objects other than the objects corresponding to the takeoff selected in the **Quantification Workbook** window.

Control the appearance of model items

This button is used to specify whether the model objects should be displayed with the quantification appearance or the original model appearance.

 Note: *If the model objects have been assigned materials and the render mode is set to* **Full Render** *in the* **Viewpoint** *ribbon tab >* **Render Style** *ribbon panel, the quantification appearance will not be displayed on the model.*

fx Function

This field displays the information of the field selected for the takeoff object.

Change Analysis

This flyout is used to analyze the model for any changes in the geometry. This is generally used when you perform model take off from a native file and the model is updated in the native file.

Update

This flyout is used to update the takeoff from the changed model. This flyout can also be used to delete the selected takeoff.

Import/Export Catalogs and export Quantities

This flyout is used to import or export the catalogs. You can also use this flyout to export all or selected takeoffs into a Microsoft Excel file.

2D Takeoff Toolbar

This toolbar is located below the **Quantification** toolbar. The tools in this toolbar are used to perform 2D takeoffs from a DWF file. These tools are discussed next.

Select Markup
This button is used to select an existing markup.

Polyline Flyout
This flyout provides the **Polyline** and **Rectangle Polyline** tools to draw a markup by tracing over the objects in the 2D DWF sheets. These markups can be used for length or perimeter takeoffs. If you are using a native 2D DWF sheet, you will be able to snap to the endpoints of the objects while drawing the markups. To create linear markup, use the **Polyline** tool and click on the points to draw the polyline. After specifying all the line segments, right-click to end this tool and accept the takeoff. To create perimeter markup, use the **Rectangle Polyline** tool and specify the two opposite corners.

 Tip: While drawing the polylines, you can hold down the SHIFT key to draw horizontal and vertical lines.

Quick Line
This tool is used to takeoff the lengths and perimeters of the existing objects in the native DWF files by directly selecting them on the sheet. When you select an object, the **Quick Line** toolbar is displayed, as shown in Figure 6. This toolbar allows you to specify whether you want to only select the object on which you clicked, all the connected lines with it, or the entire loop.

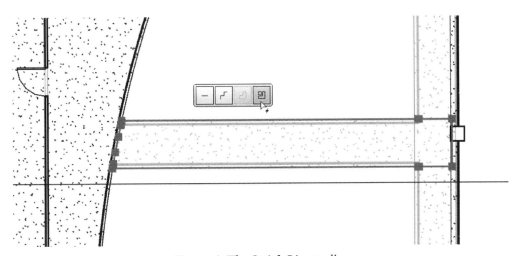

*Figure 6 The **Quick Line** toolbar*

Area Flyout
This flyout provides the **Area** and **Rectangle Area** tools to create a markup for the area takeoffs by tracing over the objects in the 2D DWF sheets. If you are using a native 2D DWF sheet, you will be able to snap to the endpoints of the objects. To create the area takeoff using the **Area** tool, pick all the required points and then right-click to accept the area. To create the area takeoff using the **Rectangle Area** tool, specify the two opposite corners.

Tip: At any point, you can select a markup using the **Select Markup** tool and press the DELETE key on the keyboard to delete the markup and the takeoff values associated with it.

Backout Flyout

This flyout is used to remove a certain region from the existing area takeoff and will only be available when you select an existing area takeoff. You can specify the region to remove using the **Backout** tool that allows you to specify the endpoints of the region you want to remove. Alternatively, you can use the **Rectangle Backout** tool and specify the two opposite corners of the region to remove.

Bucket Fill

This is a smart tool that lets you bucket fill a region and then takeoff the measurement as a length or area. When you invoke this tool, the cursor will change to the bucket cursor. Now, click inside a closed region to highlight the vertices of that region. At this stage if you right-click, the length and perimeter takeoff values will be shown. However, if you want to change this to the area markup, click inside the same closed region again and then right-click to accept. The region will be color filled and the area and perimeter takeoff values will be shown. Figure 7 shows a region selected using the **Bucket Fill** tool to create linear markup and Figure 8 shows the same region changed to the area markup by clicking inside the region again.

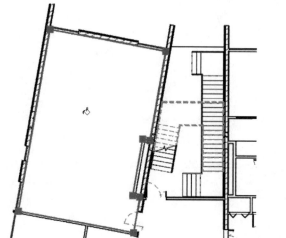
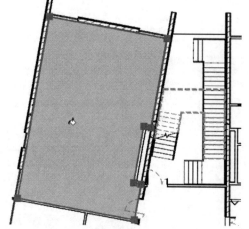

Figure 7 *Linear markup created using the* **Bucket Fill** *tool*

Figure 8 *Area markup created using the* **Bucket Fill** *tool*

Tip: You can toggle between the linear and area markup by repeatedly clicking in the same region. But as you as you right-click, the markup will be accepted and cannot be changed later.

Quick Box

This tool is similar to the **Quick Line** tool and is used to draw an area markup by dragging a box around the region. After dragging the box, right-click to accept the area markup.

Add Vertex

This tool is used to add a new vertex to the existing markup. Once you have added a vertex, you can then drag it to any other location in the sheet.

Erase

This tool is used to erase a selected area or linear takeoff.

 Note: *Remember that depending on the vertex you are deleting, you may lose an entire segment from the markup. In this case, you will have to add a new vertex and then drag and drop it at the location from where you deleted the vertex.*

Count

This tool is used to create a count takeoff by placing a pin on the object. This type of takeoff is generally used to count things such as number of tables, chairs, workstations, and so on.

Filter Markup

This tool is used to select an item or group of items from the **Navigation** pane of the **Quantification Workbook** and only show their associated takeoff geometries. All the rest of takeoff items will be turned off from the current display.

Hide background and annotations

This tool is used to turn off the visibility of the background and annotation objects from the drawing sheet. Figure 9 shows a 2D sheet with the background and annotation objects turned on and Figure 10 shows the same sheet with this information turned off.

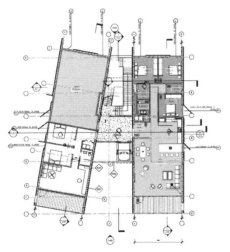

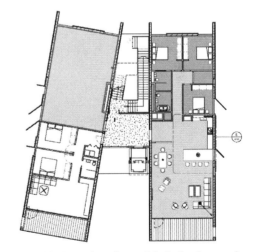

Figure 9 *Drawing sheet with the background and annotation objects turned on*

Figure 10 *Drawing sheet with the background and annotation objects turned off*

Navigation Pane

The navigation pane displays the groups and items of the catalog selected for the project. The group icons are displayed with the double file icon and the item icons are displayed as a single file icon.

Item Pane

The item pane displays the information about the group or item selected from the navigation pane. If you select a group or an item that has objects with quantities taken off, this pane will display the sum quantities of all the objects in the takeoff.

Takeoff Pane

The takeoff pane displays the details of the individual quantities of the objects that were used for the quantity takeoff. If you select an item or a group that does not have any object with the quantity taken off, this pane will be blank.

ITEM AND RESOURCE CATALOGS

Before you proceed any further with the quantity takeoff, it is important for you to understand the **Item Catalog** and **Resource Catalog**. These are discussed next.

Item Catalog

The **Item Catalog** is a database of categories and groups to associate the objects in the Autodesk Navisworks scene to perform quantity takeoff. Figure 11 shows a default **Item Catalog** window.

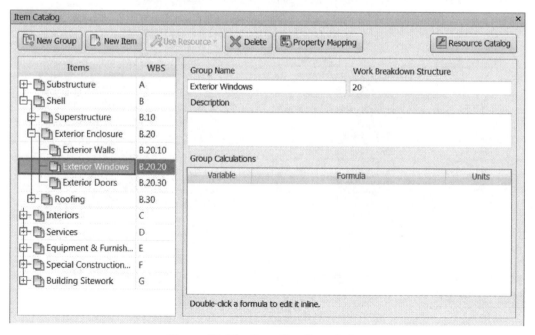

*Figure 11 The **Item Catalog** window*

The left pane of this window shows various categories and groups of items and the Work Breakdown Structure (WBS) of those items. The right pane shows the group information and the formulas for the calculation of these groups.

Resource Catalog

The **Resource Catalog** is a database of resources that you need to perform quantity takeoff against in the current Autodesk Navisworks scene. By default, this catalog is blank. You can add groups and resources to this catalog. Figure 12 shows a **Resource Catalog** window in which a group called **Structural Steel** is created. Inside this group, three resources are created for the steel columns, beams, and bracings. The right pane of this window can be used to create or edit formulas for each of these resources.

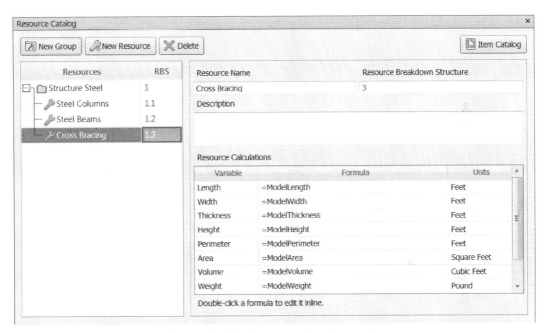

*Figure 12 The **Resource Catalog** window*

TAKEOFF PROPERTY MAPPING

While performing model takeoffs from most native files, the properties embedded in those files are automatically mapped to the items in the selected catalog. However, in some cases, such as AutoCAD Plant 3D files, the properties are not mapped automatically. Therefore, to perform quantity takeoff from such files or from the files in which you want to change this mapping or select new property mapping, you can use the options available in the **Item Catalog** window.

You have an option to map the properties for individual catalog items or globally for all items in the catalog. The new property mapping will be valid for both 2D and 3D takeoffs. The following section explains the procedures of how to do this.

PROCEDURES REQUIRED WHILE WORKING WITH THE QUANTIFICATION MODULE

The following are the various procedures that are required while working with the **Quantification** module.

Procedure for Mapping Properties of Individual Catalog Items

The following is the procedure for mapping properties of individual items:

a. Open the **Item Catalog** window. From the left pane, select the item whose mapping properties you need to change.

b. From the right pane, select the **Item Map Rules** tab.

c. Double-click in the **Category** field of the takeoff property you want to edit and select the required category from the list.

d. Double-click on the **Property** field to display the list of available properties for the selected category. From the list, select the property that you want to map to.

e. Repeat the same process for all the takeoff properties that you want to edit. The takeoffs performed henceforth will use the new mapping.

Figure 13 shows the **Item Catalog** window with the takeoff properties modified for the 310 UB 32.0 item.

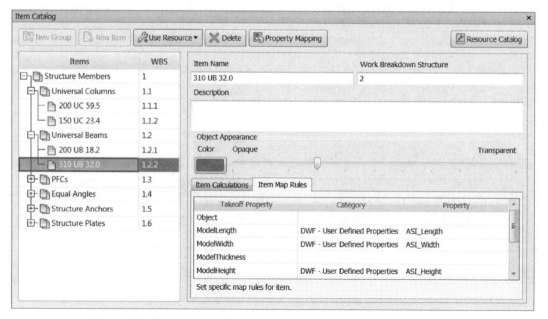

*Figure 13 The **Item Catalog** window with modified property mappings*

Procedure for Globally Mapping Takeoff Properties

The following is the procedure for globally mapping takeoff properties:

a. Open the **Item Catalog** window.

b. From the toolbar at the top, click **Property Mapping**; the **Property Mapping** dialog box will be displayed.

c. Click the **Add Mapping Rule** (**+**) button from the right of this dialog box; a new takeoff property row will be added.

d. Double-click on **Object** in the row recently added and select the takeoff property that you want to edit.

e. Double-click in the **Category** field and select the required category from the list.

f. Double-click on the **Property** field to display the list of available properties for the selected category. From the list, select the property that you want to map to.

g. Repeat the same process for all the takeoff properties that you want to edit. Figure 14 shows the **Property Mapping** dialog box with the modified takeoff properties.

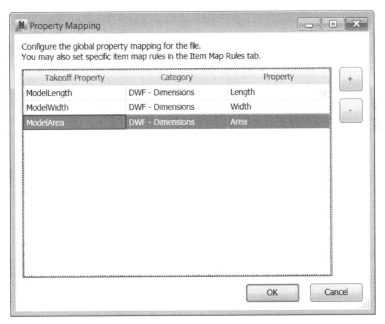

*Figure 14 The **Property Mapping** dialog box with modified properties*

h. Click **OK** in the dialog box. The takeoffs performed henceforth will use the new mapping.

Procedure for Adding Groups and Items to the Item Catalog

The following is the procedure for adding groups and items to the **Item Catalog**.

Adding a New Group to the Item Catalog

The following steps show you how to add a group to the item catalog.

a. Click on **Item Catalog** from the left of the **Selection Tree** and then dock this window.

b. In the left pane, click on the category under which you want to add the new group. If it is a blank catalog, skip to step c.

c. From the toolbar at the top in the **Item Catalog** window, click the **New Group** button; a new group is added in the window.

d. Rename the group to the required name.

e. In the right pane, specify the Work Breakdown Structure (WBS) and the description for the group.

Figure 15 shows the **Item Catalog** window with some groups and subgroups created.

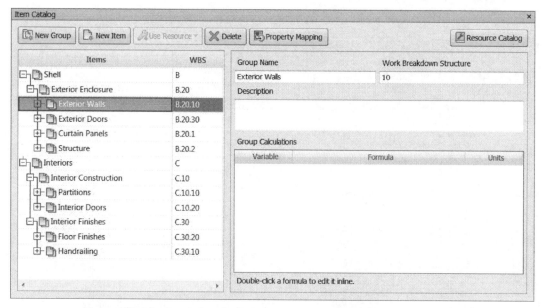

Figure 15 *The **Item Catalog** window with groups and subgroups created*

 Tip: The group icon is displayed as a double file icon in the left pane of the **Item Catalog** window.

Adding a New Item to the Item Catalog

The following steps show you how to add an item to the item catalog.

a. Click on **Item Catalog** from the left of the **Selection Tree** and then dock this window.

b. In the left pane, click on the group category under which you want to add the new item.

c. From the toolbar at the top in the **Item Catalog** window, click the **New Item** button; a new item is added in the window.

d. Rename the item to the required name.

e. In the right pane, specify the Work Breakdown Structure (WBS) for the group and add description of the group.

f. In the **Object Appearance** area of the right pane, specify the color and transparency for the takeoff objects that will be under the item you created.

g. In the **Item Calculations** area, specify the formulas and calculations for the item that you have created.

Figure 16 shows the **Item Catalog** window with various items added to the groups.

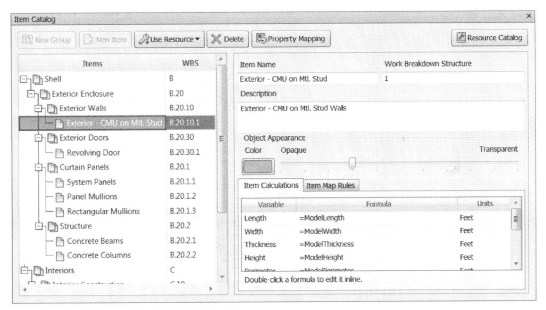

Figure 16 The **Item Catalog** *window showing various items added to the groups*

 Tip: The item icon is displayed as a single file icon in the left pane of the **Item Catalog** window.

Procedure for Exporting Catalogs

If there are some items and categories that you often use during quantity takeoff, you can export the catalog with those items and categories and then use them in your new project or import them in the existing project. The following is the procedure for exporting catalogs:

a.   In the **Item Catalog** window, create the required groups and items.

b.   Return back to the **Quantification Workbook** window.

c.   From the top right corner of the **Quantification Workbook** window, click the **Import/export Catalogs and export Quantities** flyout > **Export Catalog to XML**; the **Export Catalog to XML** dialog box will be displayed.

d.   Browse and select the folder in which you want to save the catalog file.

e.   Specify the name of the catalog and save the file.

Procedure for Selecting a User-defined Catalog in a New Project

The following steps show you how to select a user-defined catalog in a new project.

a.   Open the Autodesk Navisworks scene in which you want to perform quantity takeoff using the user-defined catalog.

b.   From the **Quantification Workbook** window, click the **Project Setup** button; the **Quantification Setup Wizard** dialog box is displayed with the **Select Catalog** page active.

c.   Select the **Browse to a catalog** radio button at the bottom of the dialog box; the **Browse** button is activated.

d.   Click the **Browse** button; the **Open** dialog box is displayed.

e.   Browse and select the XML file of the user-defined catalog that you want to use. Click **Open** in the dialog box to return to the **Quantification Setup Wizard** dialog box.

f.   Click the **Next** button; the **Ready to Create Database** page is displayed.

g.   Click **Finish**; the user-defined catalog is displayed in the **Quantification Workbook** window.

Procedure for Importing a User-defined Catalog in an Existing Project

The following steps show you how to import a user-defined catalog in an existing project.

a.   From the top right corner of the **Quantification Workbook** window of the existing project, click the **Import/export Catalogs and export Quantities** flyout > **Import Catalog**; the **Import Catalog** dialog box will be displayed.

b.   Browse and select the user-defined catalog that you want to import. Click **Open**.

c.   If the catalog you are importing has items with the same name as those in the current project, the **Import Catalog** dialog box will be displayed informing you about the duplicate names. You can click the **Replace** or **Keep** button, depending on whether you want to replace the existing items or not.

Procedure for Performing Model Takeoffs

The following steps show you how to perform model quantity takeoffs.

a. Open the Autodesk Navisworks scene in which you want to perform the model quantity takeoff.

b. Dock the **Quantification Workbook** window.

c. From the left pane of the **Quantification Workbook** window, select the catalog item in which you want to place the takeoffs.

d. Using any selection method, select the model objects that you want to takeoff the quantity from.

e. From the toolbar at the top in the **Quantification Workbook** window, click **Model Takeoff > Takeoff to Selected Catalog Item**; the lower half of the right pane of the **Quantification Workbook** will show all the objects included in the takeoff and their respective values. The upper half of the right pane will show the item category and the sum of all values.

Procedure for Performing 2D Takeoffs

The following steps show you how to perform model quantity takeoffs.

a. Open the Autodesk Navisworks scene in which you want to perform the model quantity takeoff.

b. Using the **Project Browser** or the multisheet buttons on the status bar, go to the 2D sheet on which you want to perform the 2D takeoffs.

c. Dock the **Quantification Workbook** window.

d. From the left pane of the **Quantification Workbook** window, select the catalog item in which you want to place the takeoffs.

e. From the **2D Takeoff** toolbar, select the tool to create the linear or area takeoff markups. Alternatively, select the **Count** button if you are creating the count takeoffs.

f. Draw the required 2D markup. If need be, right-click to accept the markup; the right pane of the **Quantification Workbook** will show the length and perimeter or the area and perimeter values, depending on whether it was a length takeoff or the area takeoff.

Procedure for Performing Virtual Takeoffs

As mentioned earlier, virtual takeoffs can be performed on objects that have geometry but do not have any native properties. It can also be performed on the objects that do not have any geometry. The following are the procedures to perform virtual quantity takeoffs on both these types of objects.

Virtual Quantity Takeoff on the Objects with no Properties

The following steps show you how to perform virtual takeoffs on the objects with no properties.

a. Open the Autodesk Navisworks scene in which you want to perform the virtual quantity takeoff.

b. Dock the **Quantification Workbook** window.

c. From the left pane of the **Quantification Workbook** window, select the catalog item in which you want to place the takeoffs.

d. Zoom to the area that shows the objects that you want to include in the virtual takeoff.

e. Select the objects to be included in the virtual takeoff.

f. From the toolbar at the top in the **Quantification Workbook** window, click **Virtual Takeoff > Takeoff to Selected Catalog Item**; a new row is added in the takeoff pane of the **Quantification Workbook** window and a new viewpoint is added.

g. Use the measure tools to measure the objects in the graphics window.

h. Enter the measurements in the takeoff pane of the **Quantification Workbook** window to get the individual quantities.

i. Edit the formulas in the item pane to get the total quantities.

Virtual Quantity Takeoff for Objects with No Geometry

The following steps show you how to perform virtual takeoffs on the objects with no geometry.

a. Open the Autodesk Navisworks scene in which you want to perform the virtual quantity takeoff.

b. Dock the **Quantification Workbook** window.

c. From the left pane of the **Quantification Workbook** window, select the catalog item in which you want to place the takeoffs.

d. Zoom to the area where you want to perform the virtual takeoff.

e. From the toolbar at the top in the **Quantification Workbook** window, click **Virtual Takeoff > Takeoff to Selected Catalog Item**; a new row is added in the takeoff pane of the **Quantification Workbook** window and a new viewpoint is added.

f.   Enter the measurements of the virtual objects in the takeoff pane of the **Quantification Workbook** window to get the individual quantities.

g.   Edit the formulas in the item pane to get the total quantities.

Procedure for Exporting the Quantities to Microsoft Excel

The following procedures show you how to export all the quantity takeoffs or selected quantity takeoffs to a Microsoft Excel spreadsheet.

Exporting all Quantities to Microsoft Excel

The following steps show you how to export all the quantities to a Microsoft Excel file.

a.   From the top right corner of the **Quantification Workbook** window, click **Import/export Catalogs and export Quantities > Export Quantities to Excel**; the **Export Quantities to Excel** dialog box will be displayed.

b.   Browse and select the folder where you want to save the Microsoft Excel file.

c.   Specify the name of the file and click **Save** in the dialog box.

Exporting Selected Quantities to Microsoft Excel

The following steps show you how to export the selected quantities to a Microsoft Excel file.

a.   In the navigation pane of the **Quantification Workbook** window, hold down the CTRL key or the SHIFT key and select the quantities that you want to export.

b.   From the top right corner of the **Quantification Workbook** window, click **Import/export Catalogs and export Quantities > Export Selected Quantities to Excel**; the **Export Quantities to Excel** dialog box will be displayed.

c.   Browse and select the folder where you want to save the Microsoft Excel file.

d.   Specify the name of the file and click **Save** in the dialog box.

GETTING AUTODESK NAVISWORKS READY TO PERFORM MODEL TAKEOFF FROM the AutoCAD PLANT 3D FILES

As mentioned earlier, while performing model takeoffs, some of the properties embedded inside the AutoCAD Plant 3D files are not automatically mapped to the items in the catalog. Therefore, while working with these files, you will first have to use the **Item Catalog** to map the required properties. The procedure for this was shown in the previous section.

GUID PROPERTY FOR QUANTITY TAKEOFF

It is important to mention here that only the objects that have GUID property listed in the **Item** tab of the **Properties** window can be selected in an AutoCAD Plant 3D file for the quantity takeoff.

HANDS-ON EXERCISE

You will now work on the hands-on exercise using the concepts learned in this chapter.

Hands-on Exercise (Plant)	*In this exercise, you will complete the following tasks:* *1. Open a plant model to perform quantity takeoff.* *2. Set up a new quantification project by selecting a custom catalog.* *3. Map the properties from the Plant 3D files that you will include in the takeoff.* *4. Perform model takeoff on various structure and piping members in the scene.* *5. Export all quantities to a Microsoft Excel file.*

Section 1: Opening the Plant Model and Setting up a New Quantification Project

In this section, you will open the **Quantification-Plant.nwf** file that has AutoCAD Plant 3D structure and piping models. You will then set up a new quantification project using a custom catalog.

1. From **Chapter 9 > Exercise Plant** folder, open the **Quantification-Plant.nwf** file.

    The model opens in the **Overview** viewpoint and looks similar to the one shown in Figure 17.

Figure 17 *The overview of the plant model*

2. Dock the **Sets** window and notice the various search sets available in this window.

Next, you need to dock the **Quantification Workbook** window, if it is not already docked on the screen.

3. From the bottom of the graphics window, click **Quantification Workbook** to display this window.

4. Dock this window at the bottom of the graphics window.

Next, you will set up a new project that will use a custom catalog.

5. From the top left corner of the **Quantification Workbook** window, click **Project Setup**. If you are prompted to view the quantification tutorial, click **Remind Me Later**; the **Quantification Setup Wizard** dialog box is displayed with the **Select Catalog** page active.

6. Select the **Browse to a catalog** radio button close to the bottom left corner of this dialog box.

7. Click the **Browse** button; the **Open** dialog box is displayed.

8. Browse to **Chapter 9 > Exercise Plant** folder and double-click the **MyCatalog-Imperial.xml** or **MyCatalog-Metric.xml** file, depending on the units you are using; the file and its path is displayed in the **Quantification Setup Wizard** dialog box, as shown in Figure 18.

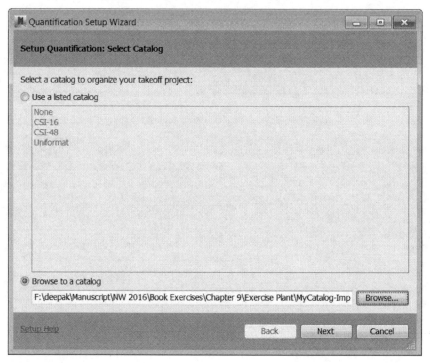

Figure 18 *The custom catalog selected in the* ***Select Catalog*** *page of the* ***Quantification Setup Wizard*** *dialog box*

9. Click the **Next** button to display the **Ready to Create Database** page.

10. Click the **Finish** button; the custom catalog now appears in the navigation pane of the **Quantification Workbook** window. Figure 19 shows the navigation pane of this window with some of the catalog groups expanded.

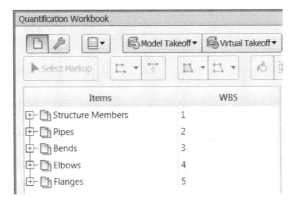

Figure 19 *The navigation pane showing the custom catalog*

 Note: *The AutoCAD Plant 3D objects in this Autodesk Navisworks file were created with Millimeters as their units. However, this does not stop you from using an Imperial catalog to takeoff the properties.*

Section 2: Mapping Takeoff Properties

As mentioned earlier, the properties that are required to be included in the model takeoffs are not automatically mapped for the AutoCAD Plant 3D files. Therefore, you need to manually map these properties. You will do that in this section. But before you start mapping the properties, you will first view them in the **Properties** window.

1. Change the selection resolution to **Geometry**.

2. From the graphics window, select any steel column.

3. In the **Properties** window, activate the **Item** tab, if not already active. Notice the **GUID** property shows a value. It is important to remember that only the items that have GUID properties can be included in the model takeoff.

4. Activate the **AutoCad** tab. Notice the value of the **Size** property. This property will determine the category under which the selected steel member will be included while performing the model takeoff.

5. Notice the **Length** property and its value. This is the property you will have to map for structural members.

6. From the graphics window, select any pipe.

7. Notice the **Length** property in the **AutoCad** tab for the selected pipe.

   This is the property you will have to map for pipes. However, the issue with mapping this property is that it does not show any units. As a result, this property will be mapped as is in whatever units the **Item Catalog** is set in. This means that there will be no automatic unit conversion by applying any formula. To avoid this, if you are using the **MyCatalog-Imperial** catalog, the **Length** variable will automatically use a formula =**ModelLength/304.8**. This formula will convert Millimeter units into Feet.

8. Notice the value of the **Long Description** property. This property will determine that while performing the model takeoff, the selected pipe will be included under which item category.

   You are now ready to map the **Length** property embedded inside the AutoCAD Plant 3D objects to the related takeoff property in the item catalog. Autodesk Navisworks allows you to map individual takeoff properties or map them globally. In this tutorial, you will map them globally so that they are mapped for all the structural members as well as pipes.

9. Click **Item Catalog** near the lower left corner of the **Quantification Workbook** window; the **Item Catalog** becomes the active window.

   Perform steps 10 and 11 only if you selected **MyCatalog-Imperial** while creating the quantification project at the start of this tutorial.

10. In the left pane of the **Item Catalog** window, expand **Structure Members > Universal Columns** and select **200 UC 59.5**.

11. In the right pane, notice the formula for the **Length** variable. As mentioned above, this formula converts the Millimeter units into Feet.

    Similarly, you can expand any structural or pipe item and you will notice the formula for the **Length** variable.

12. Click the **Property Mapping** button; the **Property Mapping** dialog box is displayed.

13. From the right in this dialog box, click the **Add Mapping Rule (+)** button; a new row is added for property mapping.

14. Double-click on the **Object** property under the **Takeoff Property** column and select **ModelLength**.

15. Double-click in the field under the **Category** column and select **AutoCad**.

16. Double-click in the field under the **Property** column and select **Length**; this will globally map the **Length** property of all the objects in the Autodesk Navisworks scene to the **ModelLength** property of the **Item Catalog**.

17. Click **OK** to close the **Property Mapping** dialog box.

18. Click on **Quantification Workbook** near the bottom left corner of the **Item Catalog**; the **Quantification Workbook** window becomes active.

You are now ready to perform model takeoffs.

Section 3: Performing Model Takeoffs of the Structural Members

In this section, you will perform model takeoff on various structural members in the scene. For the ease of selecting objects for the model takeoff, there are search sets created in this file.

1. From the **Sets** window, select the **200 UC 59.5** set; all the structure columns of this size are selected.

2. From the navigation pane of the **Quantification Workbook** window, expand **Structure Members > Universal Columns** and select **200 UC 59.5**.

This is the catalog item to which you will perform the model takeoffs of the selected columns.

3. From the toolbar at the top in the **Quantification Workbook** window, click **Model Takeoff > Take off to: 200 UC 59.5**; the takeoff pane on the right shows the individual columns and their takeoff values while the item pane shows the sum of all these values.

4. Scroll to the right in the **Quantification Workbook** window to view the values of lengths of the columns displayed in the **ModelLength** and **Length** columns in the takeoff pane.

If you are using Imperial catalog, it is important to remember that the value of the **ModelLength** is incorrect as it does consider the formula to convert Millimeters into Feet.

The value in the **Length** column gives the estimators the idea of the total length of this type of steel column to order.

5. Click anywhere in the blank area of the graphics window to deselect the columns.

6. With the takeoff still selected in the **Quantification Workbook** window, click the **Hide Takeoff** button from the toolbar at the top in this window; all the columns that were used for quantity takeoff are hidden in the graphics window.

7. From the toolbar at the top in this window, click **Show Takeoff**; notice that only the columns used for takeoff are displayed in the graphics window and rest everything is turned off.

8. Click the **Show Takeoff** button again to restore the visibility of all the objects.

Note: When you perform a model takeoff, the objects are automatically assigned the quantification appearance. However, these appearances will not be displayed if the model has materials assigned and the Autodesk Navisworks scene is displayed as full render. To view the quantification appearance in this case, you will have to change the scene display setting.

Tip: *You can toggle the appearance of the model between the quantification appearance of the original model appearance using the* **Control the appearance of model items** *flyout from the toolbar in the* **Quantification Workbook** *window.*

9. From the **Sets** window, select the **150 UC 23.4** set; all the structure members of this size are selected.

10. From the navigation pane of the **Quantification Workbook** window > **Structure Members > Universal Columns**, select **150 UC 23.4**.

11. From the toolbar at the top in the **Quantification Workbook** window, click **Model Takeoff > Take off to: 150 UC 23.4**; the **Takeoff Pane** on the right shows the individual columns and their takeoff lengths while the **Item Pane** shows the sum of all these values.

12. From the toolbar at the top in this window, click the **Show Takeoff** button; notice that only the columns used for takeoff are displayed in the graphics window and rest everything is turned off.

13. Click the **Show Takeoff** button again; everything is turned back on.

14. From the **Sets** window, select the **310 UB 32.0** set.

15. From the navigation pane of the **Quantification Workbook** window > **Structure Members > Universal Beams**, select **310 UB 32.0**.

16. Click **Model Takeoff > Take off to: 310 UB 32.0**; the quantities are taken off and are listed in the two right panes of the **Quantification Workbook** window.

17. From the **Sets** window, select the **200 UB 18.2** set.

18. From the navigation pane of the **Quantification Workbook** window > **Structure Members > Universal Beams**, select **200 UB 18.2**.

19. Click **Model Takeoff > Take off to: 200 UB 18.2**; the quantities are taken off and are listed in the two right panes of the **Quantification Workbook** window.

    Next, you will takeoff the quantities of the PFCs in the model.

20. From the **Sets** window, select the **200 PFC** set.

21. From the navigation pane of the **Quantification Workbook** window > **Structure Members > PFCs**, select **200 PFC**.

22. Click **Model Takeoff > Take off to: 200 PFC**; the quantities are taken off and are listed in the two right panes of the **Quantification Workbook** window.

Notice that in the **Sets** window, there are two more sets for PFC. However, in the navigation pane of the **Quantification Workbook** window, there are no items to takeoff the quantities of these sets. In the next section, you will modify the **Item Catalog** to include these.

Next, you will takeoff the quantities of the Equal Angle objects in the structural model.

23. From the **Sets** window, select the **EA 75x75x10** set.

24. From the navigation pane of the **Quantification Workbook** window > **Structure Members > Equal Angles**, select **75x75x10**.

25. Click **Model Takeoff > Take off to: 75x75x10**; the quantities are taken off and are listed in the two right panes of the **Quantification Workbook** window.

26. Save the file.

Section 4: Modifying the Item Catalog and Takingoff the Quantities of the Remaining PFCs

As mentioned earlier, the default **Item Catalog** that you selected while setting up the quantification project did not include the catalog items for some of the PFC members. In this section, you will modify the **Item Catalog** to include those members.

1. From the **View** ribbon tab > **Workspace** ribbon panel > **Windows** flyout, turn on the visibility of the **Item Catalog** window.

2. From the left pane, expand **Structure Members** and click on **PFCs**.

3. From the toolbar at the top in this window, click **New Item**; a new item is added under **PFCs**.

4. Rename this new item to **250 PFC**.

   Perform step 5 only if you are using the **Imperial** catalog.

5. In the right pane, change the formula of the **Length** variable to **=ModelLength/304.8**.

6. In the left pane, click on **PFCs** again add another new item.

7. Rename the new item to **300 PFC**.

   Perform step 8 only if you are using the **Imperial** catalog.

8. In the right pane, change the formula of the **Length** variable to **=ModelLength/304.8**.

9. Close the **Item Catalog** window. Notice the two new items are now listed in the navigation pane of the **Quantification Workbook** window.

   Next, you will perform the model takeoffs of the two PFC items that you recently added.

10. From the **Sets** window, select the **250 PFC** set.

11. From the navigation pane of the **Quantification Workbook** window > **Structure Members** > **PFCs**, select **250 PFC**.

12. Click **Model Takeoff > Take off to: 250 PFC**; the quantities are taken off and are listed in the two right panes of the **Quantification Workbook** window.

13. From the **Sets** window, select the **300 PFC** set.

14. From the navigation pane of the **Quantification Workbook** window > **Structure Members** > **PFCs**, select **300 PFC**.

15. Click **Model Takeoff > Take off to: 300 PFC**; the quantities are taken off and are listed in the two right panes of the **Quantification Workbook** window.

16. Save the file.

Section 5: Performing Model Takeoffs of the Pipe Members

In this section, you will perform model takeoff on various pipe members in the scene.

1. From the **Sets** window, select the **Pipe DIN 2448** set; all the pipes of this category are selected.

2. From the navigation pane of the **Quantification Workbook** window, expand **Pipes** and select **Pipe DIN 2448**.

   This is the catalog item to which you will perform the model takeoffs of the selected pipes.

3. From the toolbar at the top in the **Quantification Workbook** window, click **Model Takeoff > Take off to: Pipe DIN 2448**; the takeoff pane on the right shows the individual columns and their takeoff values while the item pane shows the sum of all these values.

4. Scroll to the right in the **Quantification Workbook** window to view the values of lengths of the pipes displayed in the **ModelLength** and **Length** columns in the takeoff pane. Also, notice the item pane shows a sum of all the lengths.

5. From the **Sets** window, select the **PIPE, PE, ASME B36.10** set.

6. From the navigation pane of the **Quantification Workbook** window > **Pipes**, select **PIPE, PE, ASME B36.10**.

7. Click **Model Takeoff > Take off to: PIPE, PE, ASME B36.10**; the quantities are taken off and are listed in the two right panes of the **Quantification Workbook** window.

8. From the **Sets** window, select the **PIPE, SCH10S, ASME B36.10** set.

9. From the navigation pane of the **Quantification Workbook** window > **Pipes**, select **PIPE, SCH10S, ASME B36.10**.

10. Click **Model Takeoff > Take off to: PIPE, SCH10S, ASME B36.10**; the quantities are taken off and are listed in the two right panes of the **Quantification Workbook** window.

11. From the **Sets** window, select the **PIPE, SCH10S, SEAMLESS** set.

12. From the navigation pane of the **Quantification Workbook** window > **Pipes**, select **PIPE, SCH10S, SEAMLESS**.

13. Click **Model Takeoff > Take off to: PIPE, SCH10S, SEAMLESS**; the quantities are taken off and are listed in the two right panes of the **Quantification Workbook** window.

Section 6: Performing Model Takeoffs of Bends, Elbows, and Flanges

In this section, you will perform model takeoff on various bends, elbows, and flanges. Because you only need the counts of these items, you do not need to map any property.

1. From the **Sets** window, select the **Bend DIN 2605-1-45-2** set.

2. From the navigation pane of the **Quantification Workbook** window > **Bends**, select **Bend DIN 2605-1-45-2**.

3. Click **Model Takeoff > Take off to: Bend DIN 2605-1-45-2**; the quantities are taken off and are listed in the two right panes of the **Quantification Workbook** window.

4. Scroll to the right in the **Quantification Workbook** window and notice that the only value that is displayed is the **Count** in the item pane, which shows there are two of these bends.

5. From the **Sets** window, select the **Bend DIN 2605-1-45-3** set.

6. From the navigation pane of the **Quantification Workbook** window > **Bends**, select **Bend DIN 2605-1-45-3**.

7. Click **Model Takeoff > Take off to: Bend DIN 2605-1-45-3**; the quantities are taken off and are listed in the two right panes of the **Quantification Workbook** window.

8. From the **Sets** window, select the **Bend DIN 2605-1-90-3** set.

9. From the navigation pane of the **Quantification Workbook** window > **Bends**, select **Bend DIN 2605-1-90-3**.

10. Click **Model Takeoff > Take off to: Bend DIN 2605-1-90-3**; the quantities are taken off and are listed in the two right panes of the **Quantification Workbook** window.

11. Similarly, one by one, select the remaining elbow and flange sets and takeoff their quantities in their respect items in the **Quantification Workbook**.

Section 7: Adding Comments in the Structure Members and Pipe Groups

Perform the steps in this section only if you are using the **Imperial** catalog. As mentioned earlier, the **ModelLength** column does not consider the formula to convert Millimeters into Feet. Therefore, you need to inform the people reviewing the quantity takeoff to only look at the lengths in the **Length** columns. This can be done by adding comments to the required groups.

1. From the navigation pane of the **Quantification Workbook** window, select **Structure Members**.

2. In the item pane on the right, right-click on **Structure Members** in the **Name** column and select **Add Comment**; the **Add Comment** dialog box is displayed.

3. In the first line of the comment, type **Actual Length**. Now, press and hold down the CTRL key and press ENTER to go to the next line.

4. Enter the following text in the next line:

   Please refer to the lengths in the Length column and not in the ModelLength columns. The ModelLength column does not consider the formula to convert Millimeter into Feet.

5. Repeat the same process to add comments for the **Pipes** group as well.

Section 8: Exporting All the Quantities to a Microsoft Excel File

In this section, you will export all the taken off quantities into a Microsoft Excel file format.

1. From the top right corner of the **Quantification Workbook** window, click **Import/export Catalogs and export Quantities > Export Quantities to Excel**; the **Export Quantities to Excel** dialog box is displayed, as shown in Figure 20.

2. Browse to **Chapter 9 > Exercise Plant** folder.

3. Specify the name of the file as **Structure-Quantity.xlsx**.

4. Click the **Save** button in the dialog box; you are returned to the **Quantification Workbook** window and the export process starts.

   Once the quantities are exported in the Microsoft Excel file, the **Export Quantities to Excel** dialog box is displayed prompting you to specify if you want to open the Microsoft Excel file.

5. Click **Yes** in the dialog box to open the Microsoft Excel file of the quantities taken off. Figure 21 shows the **All Data** tab of the Microsoft Excel file that was created.

   Notice that the comments you added are displayed at the top of each group.

6. Browse through various tabs of this file to view the information written in those tabs.

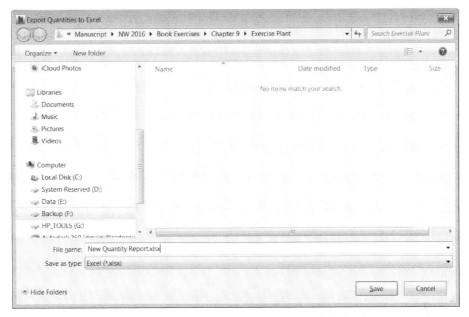

Figure 20 *The **Export Quantities to Excel** dialog box*

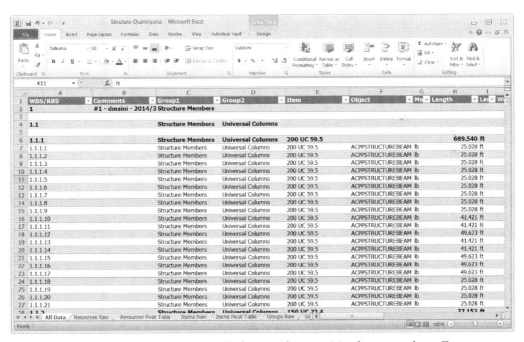

Figure 21 *The **All Data** tab showing the quantities that were taken off*

7. Close the Microsoft Excel file without saving changes and return to the Autodesk Navisworks window.

8. Save the Autodesk Navisworks file and then start a new file to close this file.

Hands-on Exercise (BIM)	*In this exercise, you will complete the following tasks:* 1. *Open an Autodesk Navisworks file that has a DWF file of a 3D model and two drawing sheets of an apartment block.* 2. *Setup a new quantification project by selecting a custom catalog.* 3. *Perform model takeoffs on various objects in the scene.* 4. *Perform 2D takeoff using the 2D sheets.* 5. *Export all quantities to a Microsoft Excel file.*

Section 1: Opening the Building Model and Setting up a New Quantification Project

In this section, you will open the **Quantification-Apartment.nwf** file that has a DWF file exported from Autodesk Revit. This file includes the 3D model and two 2D sheets. You will then set up a new quantification project using a custom catalog.

1. From **Chapter 9 > Exercise Building** folder, open the **Quantification-Apartment.nwf** file. The model opens in the **Overview** viewpoint and looks similar to the one shown in Figure 22. (The model for this exercise is courtesy **Samuel Macalister, Senior Technical Sales Specialist – BIM, Autodesk Inc.**)

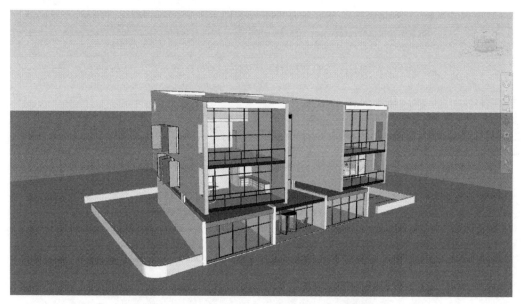

Figure 22 The overview of the building model

2. Dock the **Sets** window and notice the various sets created in this file.

   Next, you need to dock the **Quantification Workbook** window, if it is not already docked on the screen.

3. From the bottom of the graphics window, click **Quantification Workbook** to display this window.

4.   Dock this window at the bottom of the graphics window.

Next, you will set up a new project that will use a custom catalog.

5.   From the top left corner of the **Quantification Workbook** window, click **Project Setup**. If you are prompted to view the quantification tutorial, click **Remind Me Later**; the **Quantification Setup Wizard** dialog box is displayed with the **Select Catalog** page active.

6.   Select the **Browse to a catalog** radio button close to the bottom left corner of this dialog box.

7.   Click the **Browse** button; the **Open** dialog box is displayed.

There are two catalogs provided; Metric and Imperial. You can select the catalog based on the units that you use for quantification.

8.   Browse to **Chapter 9 > Exercise Building** folder and double-click on the Imperial or Metric catalog file, depending on the units you are using; the file and its path are displayed in the **Quantification Setup Wizard** dialog box, as shown in Figure 23.

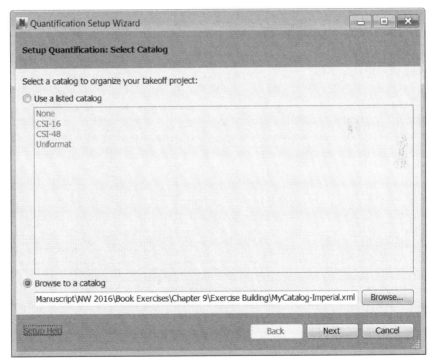

*Figure 23 The custom catalog selected in the **Select Catalog** page of the **Quantification Setup Wizard** dialog box*

9.   Click the **Next** button to display the **Ready to Create Database** page.

10. Click the **Finish** button; the custom catalog now appears in the navigation pane of the **Quantification Workbook** window. Figure 24 shows the navigation pane of this window with some of the catalog groups expanded.

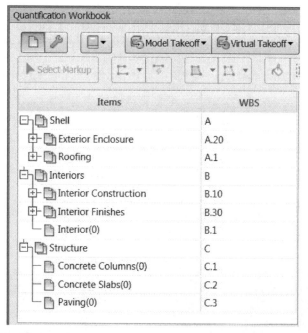

Figure 24 The navigation pane showing the custom catalog

Section 2: Performing Model Takeoffs

In this section, you will perform model takeoff on various objects in the scene. For the ease of selecting objects for model takeoff, there are sets created in this file.

1. From the **Sets** window, select the **Retaining Walls** set; all the retaining walls are selected. These walls are highlighted as **Basic Wall** objects in the **Selection Tree**.

 *Note: Notice the icon on the **Basic Wall** objects in the **Selection Tree**. You need to make sure the objects are selected at this level or they will not be accepted for quantity takeoff. For example, if you expand one of the **Basic Wall** objects and select an item inside it and try to perform model takeoff, you will get an error message that the object cannot be used for the model quantity takeoff.*

2. From the navigation pane of the **Quantification Workbook** window, expand **Shell > Exterior Enclosure > Exterior Walls** and select **Retaining**.

    This is the catalog item to which you will perform the model takeoffs of the external walls.

3. From the toolbar at the top in the **Quantification Workbook** window, click **Model Takeoff > Take off to: Retaining**; the takeoff pane on the right shows the individual external walls and their takeoff values while the item pane shows the sum of all these values.

4. Scroll to the right in the **Quantification Workbook** window to view the values of length, height, area, volume, and so on.

5. Click anywhere in the blank area of the graphics window to deselect the walls.

6. With the takeoff still selected in the **Quantification Workbook** window, click the **Hide Takeoff** button from the toolbar at the top in this window; the walls that were used for quantity takeoff are hidden in the graphics window.

7. From the toolbar at the top in this window, click the **Show Takeoff** button; notice that only the walls used for takeoff are now visible in the scene.

8. Click the **Show Takeoff** button again to restore the visibility of all the objects.

 Note: *When you perform a model takeoff, the objects are automatically assigned the quantification appearance. However, these appearances will not be displayed if the model has materials assigned and the Autodesk Navisworks scene is displayed as full render. To view the quantification appearance in this case, you will have to change the scene display setting to **Shaded**.*

 Tip: *You can toggle the appearance of the model between the quantification appearance of the original model appearance using the **Control the appearance of model items** flyout from the toolbar in the **Quantification Workbook** window.*

9. From the **Sets** window, select the **Timber Clad** set; all the timber clad walls are selected. These walls are also highlighted as **Basic Wall** objects in the **Selection Tree**.

10. From the navigation pane of the **Quantification Workbook** window > **Shell > Exterior Enclosure > Exterior Walls**, select **Timber Clad**.

11. From the toolbar at the top in the **Quantification Workbook** window, click **Model Takeoff > Take off to: Timber Clad**; the takeoff pane on the right shows the individual walls and their takeoff values while the item pane shows the sum of all these values.

12. From the toolbar at the top in this window, click the **Show Takeoff** button; notice that only the retaining walls and timber clad walls are displayed in the graphics window and rest everything is turned off. This is because the quantities of only these two item types have been taken off yet.

13. Click the **Show Takeoff** button again; everything is turned back on.

14. From the **Sets** window, select the **Brick veneer** set.

15. From the navigation pane of the **Quantification Workbook** window > **Shell > Exterior Enclosure > Exterior Walls**, select **Brick Veneer**.

16. Click **Model Takeoff > Take off to: Brick Veneer**; the quantities are taken off and are listed in the two right panes of the **Quantification Workbook** window.

17. Scroll down in the **Sets** window and select the **Exterior Doors** set.

18. From the navigation pane of the **Quantification Workbook** window > **Shell** > **Exterior Enclosure**, select **Exterior Doors**.

    Notice the icon of **Exterior Doors** in the navigation pane. This icon is different from the icon of the items such as **Retaining, Timber Clad**, and so on. This is because **Exterior Doors** is a group and not an item.

19. Click **Model Takeoff > Take off to Selected**.

    Notice that there are items created inside the **Exterior Doors** group and the quantities were taken off inside those items.

20. From the navigation pane of the **Quantification Workbook** window, select **Door - Single Glass - Push plate (AUS)(2)**; the two doors that were taken off in this item are listed in the right pane.

    Remember that for the doors, there are no properties mapped as you only need the description of the door types and their quantities. The description is automatically displayed under the **Name** and **Object** column and the quantity is displayed under the **Count** column.

21. From the **Sets** window, select the **Glazed Panels** set.

22. From the navigation pane of the **Quantification Workbook** window > **Shell** > **Exterior Enclosure** > **Curtain Panels**, select **Glazed Panels**.

23. Click **Model Takeoff > Take off to: Glazed Panels**; the quantities are taken off and are listed in the two right panes of the **Quantification Workbook** window.

24. From the **Sets** window, select the **Mullions** set.

25. From the navigation pane of the **Quantification Workbook** window > **Shell** > **Exterior Enclosure** > **Curtain Panels**, select **Rectangular Mullions**.

26. Click **Model Takeoff > Take off to: Rectangular Mullions**; the quantities are taken off and are listed in the two right panes of the **Quantification Workbook** window.

    For the **Mullions** set, only the length property is mapped. This is because you only need the total length and the count of the mullions.

27. From the **Sets** window, select the **Timber finish black** set.

28. From the navigation pane of the **Quantification Workbook** window > **Shell** > **Roofing**, select **Timber finish black**.

29. Click **Model Takeoff > Take off to: Timber finish black**; the quantities are taken.

Note that for the roofing elements, only the area and volume properties were available for mapping. As a result, only these two values are displayed in the right panes.

30. From the **Sets** window, select the **Steel Truss - Insulation** set.

31. From the navigation pane of the **Quantification Workbook** window > **Shell** > **Roofing**, select **Steel Truss - Insulation**.

32. Click **Model Takeoff > Take off to: Steel Truss - Insulation**; the quantities are taken off and are listed in the two right panes of the **Quantification Workbook** window.

33. From the **Sets** window, select the **Warm Roof - Timber** set.

34. From the navigation pane of the **Quantification Workbook** window > **Shell** > **Roofing**, select **Warm Roof - Timber**.

35. Click **Model Takeoff > Take off to: Warm Roof - Timber**; the quantities are taken off and are listed in the two right panes of the **Quantification Workbook** window.

    Next, you will perform takeoffs of the interior construction items.

36. From the **Sets** window, select the **Interior - Partition** set. Now, press and hold down the CTRL key and select **Interior Timber-150**, **Interior Yellow - 150**, and **Interior - 165 Partition** sets.

37. From the navigation pane of the **Quantification Workbook** window > **Interiors** > **Interior Construction**, select **Partition Walls**.

    Notice that **Partition Walls** is a group and not an item.

38. Click **Model Takeoff > Take off to Selected**; the quantities are taken off and items are created for each of the interior wall types inside the **Partition Walls** group.

39. From the navigation pane, click on **Interior - 165 Partition (1-hr)** and review the properties of the eight walls taken off under this item.

40. From the **Sets** window, select the **Interior Doors** set.

41. From the navigation pane of the **Quantification Workbook** window > **Interiors** > **Interior Construction**, select **Interior Doors**.

    Notice that **Interior Doors** is also a group and not an item.

42. Click **Model Takeoff > Take off to Selected**; the quantities are taken off and items are created for each of the interior door types inside the **Interior Doors** group.

43. From the **Sets** window, select the **Glass shower screen** set.

44. From the navigation pane of the **Quantification Workbook** window > **Interiors** > **Interior Construction**, select **Glass Shower Screen**.

45. Click **Model Takeoff > Take off to: Glass Shower Screen**; the quantities are taken off and are listed in the two right panes of the **Quantification Workbook** window.

    Next, you will perform takeoff on the floor finishes. For these types of objects, only the perimeter, area, and volume properties will be mapped.

46. From the **Sets** window, select the **Finish Wood** set. Now, press and hold down the CTRL key and select **Timber Suspended**, **Finish Tile**, and **Finish Cream Carpet** sets.

47. From the navigation pane of the **Quantification Workbook** window > **Interiors** > **Interior Finishes**, select **Floor Finishes**.

    Notice that **Floor Finishes** is also a group and not an item.

48. Click **Model Takeoff > Take off to Selected**; the quantities are taken off and there are items created for each of the interior floor finish type inside the **Floor Finishes** group.

    Next, you will perform model takeoff on various structural objects in the scene.

49. From the **Sets** window, select the **Concrete Columns** set.

    For this set, only the length and volume properties are mapped.

50. From the navigation pane of the **Quantification Workbook** window > **Structure**, select **Concrete Columns**.

51. Click **Model Takeoff > Take off to: Concrete Columns**.

    The length and volume quantities are taken off and are listed in the two right panes of the **Quantification Workbook** window.

52. From the **Sets** window, select the **Slabs** set.

    For this set, only the area, perimeter, and volume properties are mapped.

53. From the navigation pane of the **Quantification Workbook** window > **Structure**, select **Concrete Slabs**.

54. Click **Model Takeoff > Take off to: Concrete Slabs**.

    The perimeter, area, and volume quantities are taken off and are listed in the two right panes of the **Quantification Workbook** window.

55. From the **Sets** window, select the **Paving** set.

   For this set also, only the area, perimeter, and volume properties are mapped.

56. From the navigation pane of the **Quantification Workbook** window > **Structure**, select **Paving**.

57. Click **Model Takeoff > Take off to: Paving**; the quantities are taken off and are listed in the two right panes of the **Quantification Workbook** window.

Section 3: Performing 2D Takeoffs

While performing the interior floor finish takeoffs on **Timber Suspended** set, only the two floors on level 3 were selected. However, level 2 has floors assigned the same floor finish, which were not included as part of the model takeoff. These two floor areas are shown in the 2D drawing sheet of level 2. You will now perform the 2D takeoff of these two areas.

1. From the status bar near the bottom right of the Autodesk Navisworks window, click the **Sheet Browser** button; the **Sheet Browser** window is displayed, as shown in Figure 25.

*Figure 25 The **Sheet Browser** window showing the 3D model and the two 2D sheets*

2. Double-click on the **Floor Plan: Level 1** sheet; the view in the Autodesk Navisworks window changes to show the 2D sheet.

3. Double-click on the **Floor Plan: Level 2** sheet; the view in the Autodesk Navisworks window changes to show this 2D sheet.

    This is the sheet on which you will perform the 2D takeoff. However, notice all the annotation objects displayed on this sheet. All these annotation objects make this sheet difficult to work with. Therefore, you will first turn off the background and annotation objects. But before that, you will close the **Sheet Browser** window.

4. Close the **Sheet Browser** window.

5. From the **2D Takeoff** toolbar in the **Quantification Workbook** window, click the **Hide background and annotations** button; all the annotation and background objects are hidden from the sheet.

    The 2D sheet after hiding these objects looks similar to the one shown in Figure 26. This figure also shows rectangles around the two floor areas at the front of the building where you will perform the 2D takeoff.

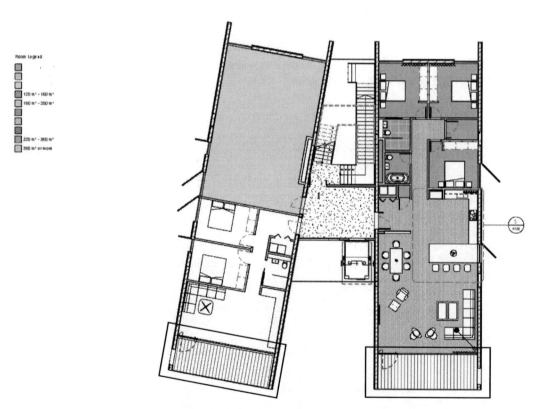

Figure 26 The 2D sheet after hiding the background and annotation objects

6. Zoom close to the floor area enclosed inside the rectangle shown on the left of the building.

While performing 2D takeoff, it is a lot easier to use the **Bucket Fill** tool and click inside a closed area to takeoff. However, in case of the two floors, they have been hatched with line pattern. As a result, if you try to use the **Bucket Fill** tool, it will only select the area inside the small rectangular boxes represented by the hatches. Therefore, you will use the **Area** tool to perform the 2D takeoff.

Before proceeding with drawing the 2D takeoff markup, you need to select the catalog item to which you want to perform the takeoff.

7. From the navigation pane of the **Quantification Workbook** window > **Interiors** > **Interior Finishes** > **Floor Finishes**, select **Timber Suspended Floor**.

8. From the **2D Takeoff** toolbar at the top in the **Quantification Workbook** window, click the **Area** button; the cursor changes to crosshairs and you are prompted to click to create a vertex. This prompt sequence is displayed on the lower left corner of the Autodesk Navisworks window.

9. Move the cursor close to one of the inside corners of the suspended floor. Once the cursor snaps to the corner, a dot is displayed.

10. Using the corner snaps, carefully pick the four inside corners of the suspended floor, as shown in Figure 27.

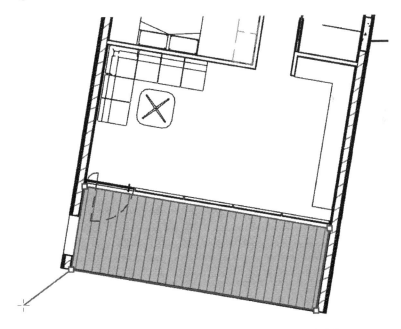

Figure 27 *Selecting the four corners of the suspended floor*

11. Right-click to accept the 2D takeoff; the area and perimeter of this selected area are now listed in the right pane of the **Quantification Workbook** window.

12. Similarly, using the same **Area** tool, draw a 2D takeoff markup on the suspended floor on the right.

Figure 28 shows the **Quantification Workbook** window displaying the two 2D takeoffs, along with the two 3D model takeoffs for the **Timber Suspended Floor** item. Notice that for the two 2D takeoffs, there is no volume property taken off.

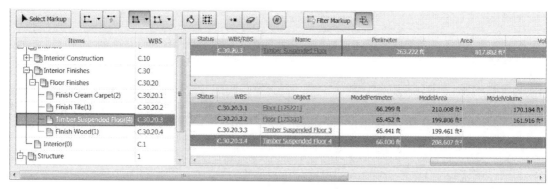

*Figure 28 The two 2D takeoffs listed in the **Timber Suspended Floor** item*

 Tip: *When you are on the 2D sheet, you can directly zoom to the 2D takeoff markup by clicking on the name of the 2D takeoff in the **Object** column in the right pane of the **Quantification Workbook** window.*

13. Using the **Sheet Browser** or the multisheet buttons available near the bottom right corner of the Autodesk Navisworks window, restore the 3D view of the model.

14. Close the **Sheet Browser** window, if it was opened.

Section 4: Exporting All the Quantities to a Microsoft Excel File

In this section, you will export all the taken off quantities into a Microsoft Excel file format.

1. From the top right corner of the **Quantification Workbook** window, click **Import/export Catalogs and export Quantities > Export Quantities to Excel**; the **Export Quantities to Excel** dialog box is displayed, as shown in Figure 29.

2. Browse to **Chapter 9 > Exercise Building** folder.

3. Specify the name of the file as **DWF-Quantity.xlsx**.

4. Click the **Save** button in the dialog box; you are returned to the **Quantification Workbook** window and the export process starts.

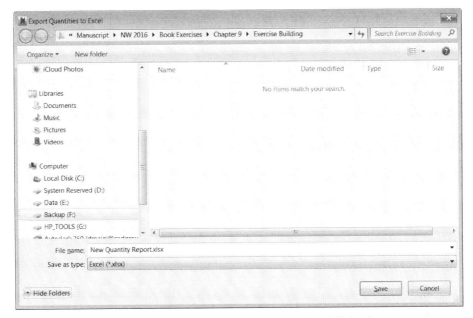

*Figure 29 The **Export Quantities to Excel** dialog box*

Once the quantities are exported in the Microsoft Excel file, the **Export Quantities to Excel** dialog box is displayed prompting you to specify if you want to open the Microsoft Excel file.

5.   Click **Yes** in the dialog box to open the Microsoft Excel file of the quantities taken off. Figure 30 shows the **All Data** tab of the Microsoft Excel file that was created.

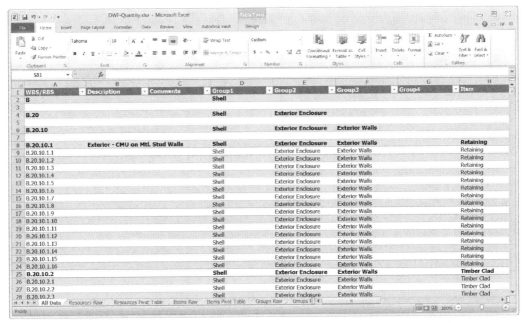

*Figure 30 The **All Data** tab showing the quantities that were taken off*

6. Browse through various tabs of this file to view the information written in those tabs.

7. Close the Microsoft Excel file without saving changes and return to the Autodesk Navisworks window.

8. Save the Autodesk Navisworks file and then start a new file to close this file.

Skill Evaluation

Evaluate your skills to see how many questions you can answer correctly. The answers to these questions are given at the end of the book.

1. The **Quantification** module is only available in Autodesk Navisworks Simulate. (True/False)

2. You can perform 3D as well as 2D takeoffs in the Autodesk Navisworks scene. (True/False)

3. The item catalog that is regularly used can also be exported for future use. (True/False)

4. While exporting the quantities to Microsoft Excel, you can decide to export all the quantities or the selected quantities. (True/False)

5. When you set up a new quantification project, you can only select some predefined catalogs and not the one that you created. (True/False)

6. Which window is used to perform quantity takeoffs?

   (A) **Takeoff**   (B) **Quantity Takeoff**
   (C) **Quantification**   (D) **Quantification Workbook**

7. Which format is the catalog exported in?

   (A) XLS   (B) XLSX
   (C) XML   (D) HTML

8. Which types of quantity takeoffs can be performed in Autodesk Navisworks?

   (A) 3D and Feature Takeoffs   (B) 3D, 2D, and Virtual Takeoffs
   (C) 3D Takeoffs   (D) Model and Feature Takeoffs

9. To start a new quantification project, which tool is used?

   (A) **Project Setup**   (B) **Quantity Takeoff**
   (C) **New Catalog**   (D) **New Project**

10. In which one of the following file formats can you export the taken off quantities?

   (A) PPT   (B) XLS
   (C) DOC   (D) XLSX

Class Test Questions

Answer the following questions:

1. Explain the difference between the model takeoff and the virtual takeoff.

2. Which file types support 3D and 2D takeoffs??

3. Explain in brief how to export a catalog.

4. After performing virtual takeoffs, what needs to be done to find out the values of the virtual objects?

5. What is the use of exporting catalogs?

Chapter 10 – Working with the Clash Detective Module

The objectives of this chapter are to:

√ Introduce you to the **Clash Detective** module of Autodesk Navisworks.
√ Familiarize you with the **Clash Detective** window.
√ Explain various types of clashes that can be performed.
√ Teach you how to view various clash results.
√ Teach you how to fix clashes using the **Switchback** option.
√ Teach you to create the clash report.
√ Teach you how to use rules to ignore certain objects during clash detection.
√ Teach you how to perform clash test with point cloud data.

THE CLASH DETECTIVE MODULE

Home Ribbon Tab > Tools Ribbon Panel > Clash Detective

The **Clash Detective** module available in Autodesk Navisworks Manage is used to perform clashes between various items in the Autodesk Navisworks scene. These clashes can then be reviewed and reported to the concerned stakeholders. This is a very handy tool for the project managers that allows them to avoid any unexpected problems during the construction phase. For example, the project manager can perform clashes between the structural model and the elevator shafts to make sure the shafts do not intersect with any beams or columns in the structure.

Autodesk Navisworks also provides an option called **SwitchBack** that allows you to switch back to the native Autodesk CAD software to resolve the clashes if you are working with native CAD files with the CAD software installed on the same computer. Once the clashes are resolved, the rerunning of the clash test will show those clashes as resolved.

Autodesk Navisworks allows you to perform the following four types of clashes:

Hard: In this type of clash, only the objects that physically intersect will be considered as clashing.

Hard (Conservative): In this type of clash, even though the geometry triangles are not intersecting, the objects will be considered as clashing.

Clearance: In this type of clash, the objects will be considered as clashing if they come within the specified distance of each other.

Duplicates: This type of clash is performed to make sure there are no duplicate overlapping objects in the model.

All these types of clashes are performed using the **Clash Detective** window, which is shown in Figure 1. The various components of this window are discussed next.

Tests Panel

The **Tests** panel shows all the information about all the clash tests available in the current Autodesk Navisworks scene. Note that this panel is blank unless you first add a test using the **Add Test** button on the **Clash** toolbar. Once you have performed the clash test, a brief summary about when the test was last performed and the number of open and closed clashes are displayed on the top left of this panel. The various columns displayed in this panel are discussed next.

Name

This column displays the name of the tests that you have added or performed in the current scene. If the model has altered since the last test was run, an error symbol will be displayed on the left of the name of the clash informing you that the model or the test settings have changed since the last run. In this case, you can rerun the test to update the results to reflect the current state of the model.

Tests Panel —— ——Tabs ——Clash Toolbar

Figure 1 *The **Clash Detective** window*

Status

This column displays the status of the clash test. If the test is performed, this column will display **Done**. If the clash is not yet performed, this column will display **New**.

Clashes

This column displays the total number of clashes found in the test. If the test is not performed yet, this column will display **0**.

New

This column displays the total number of new clashes found when you run the test for the first time or the new clashes found when you rerun the test after modifying the model.

Active

This column displays the total number of the clashes that are found to be still active when you rerun the test after modifying the model.

Reviewed

This column displays the total number of clashes that have been reviewed using the **Status** column of the **Results** tab.

Approved

This column displays the total number of clashes that have been approved using the **Status** column of the **Results** tab.

Resolved

This column displays the total number of clashes that have been resolved by making modifications in the model and rerunning the clash test. You can also use the **Status** column of the **Results** tab to override the display of the clash as resolved.

Clash Toolbar

This toolbar provides the following buttons:

Add Test

This button is used to add clash tests to the **Tests** panel. If there are no clash tests added, the **Tests** panel will be blank and all the options in the **Clash Detective** window will be grayed out.

Reset All

This button resets the status of all the clashes to **New**, which means that the tests are set to a state where they are not yet run.

Compact All

This button removes all the resolved clashes from the **Tests** panel for all the clash tests.

Update All

This button will only be active if there are changes made in the model and the clash tests needs an update or when you reset the clash tests using the **Reset All** button. By clicking the **Update All** button, the tests are rerun to show the results based on the current state of the model.

Import/Export Clash Tests

If you regularly perform clashes by searching objects in the scene or by selecting the objects based on their properties, you can export and import those clash setups using this flyout. Note that only the clash selections based on the search sets or properties of the objects can be exported and imported. When you click the **Export Clash Tests** option in this flyout, the **Export**...

dialog box is displayed that allows you to save the clash test settings as a .XML file. You can specify the name and location of the clash test settings using this dialog box. To import a saved test, click the **Import Clash Tests** option from the flyout and use the **Import...** dialog box to select and import the clash test settings.

 *Tip: You can use the **Collapse** or **Expand** arrows on the top left of the **Tests** panel to hide or show this panel and the **Clash** toolbar.*

Rules Tab

This tab allows you to ignore objects matching the rules criteria from the clash tests. There are some default rules available in this tab, as shown in Figure 1. To ignore objects during clash test using any of these rules, select the tick box on the left of that rule. To create a new rule, click the **New** button in this tab to display the **Rules Editor** dialog box. Figure 2 shows a custom rule created using this dialog box.

*Figure 2 The **Rules Editor** dialog box*

Select Tab

This tab allows you to select the objects between which you want to perform clash tests, as shown in Figure 3. The options available in this tab are discussed next.

Selection A Area

This area provides the options to make the first selection for the clash test. The list at the top in this area allows you to control the display the tree in this area. By default, **Standard** is selected from this list. As a result, the standard tree is displayed that you can expand and select the object in the first selection set. If you want to select saved search or selection sets as your first selection,

*Figure 3 The **Select** tab of the **Clash Detective** window*

from the list at the top in this area, select **Sets**. The toolbar available at the bottom of this area provides the following buttons:

Surfaces
Use this button if the objects in the first selection comprise of surfaces. It is important to mention here that the solid models created in the native CAD software are considered as surface objects in Autodesk Navisworks.

Lines
Use this button if the objects in the first selection are wireframe objects made up of lines, arc, circles, and so on.

Points
Use this button if the objects in the first selection are made up of points. This is generally used when you are performing clashes with the point cloud data.

Self-Intersect
Use this button if you want to perform clash tests of the objects with themselves.

Use Current Selection
Use this button if the objects that you want in the first selection set are already selected in the graphics window. When you click this button, the objects that are selected in the graphics window are also highlighted in the tree in this area.

Select in Scene
This button is used to highlight in the graphics window the objects you have selected from the tree in this area.

Selection B Area
This area provides the options to make the second selection for the clash test. All these options are the same as those discussed in the **Selection A** area.

Settings Area
The options available in this area are discussed next.

Type
This list allows you to select the type of clash test you want to run. As mentioned earlier in this chapter, you can perform **Hard**, **Hard (Conservative)**, **Clearance**, and **Duplicates** test.

Tolerance
This box allows you to enter a tolerance value for the clashes. If the clash is within this tolerance value, it will be ignored.

Link
This list allows you to link a timeliner simulation or an animator scene to the clash test. The timeliner simulation is generally linked when the construction of the new facility begins after the demolition of an existing facility. In the Autodesk Navisworks scene, generally both the models are shown because of which there will be clashes between those two models. However, linking a timeliner animation that includes demolition of the first model before the new model is constructed ensures there will be no clash between them. The animator scenes are generally linked when you have moving objects in the scene and you want to make sure that during their movement, they do not clash with other objects in the scene.

Step
This box allows you to enter the step size of the timeliner simulation. Note that this box will only be available after you have linked a timeliner simulation to the clash test.

Composite Object Clashing
If this tick box is selected, the clashes with composite objects will be considered as a single clash. This will reduce the total number of clashes that are displayed.

Run Test
After you have selected the two sets of objects for clash test and specified the clash settings, click this button to run the test. Once the test run is completed, you will be taken to the **Results** tab and the currently selected clash result will be displayed in the graphics window.

Results Tab
This tab shows you the clash results and various options to interrogate those results, as shown in Figure 4. The options available in this tab are discussed next.

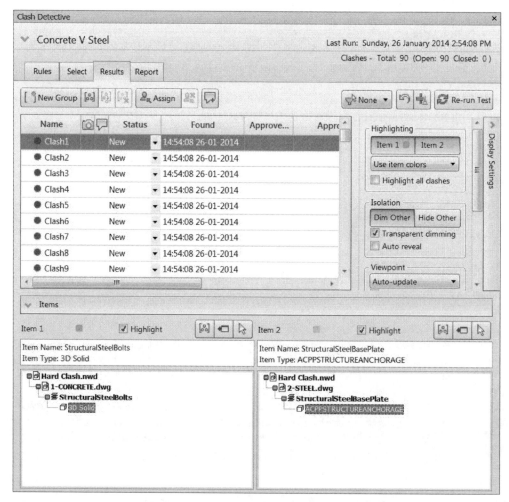

*Figure 4 The **Results** tab of the **Clash Detective** window*

Results Toolbar

The **Results** toolbar is available at the top in the **Results** tab. The buttons available in this toolbar are discussed next.

New Group

If you have a large number of clashes displayed in the results tab, it is recommended to organize them in groups. Clicking this button creates a new group that you can rename to the required name. The clash results can then be dragged and dropped in the new group. You can also drag the groups in the **Results** area to move it up or down in the list.

Group Selected Clashes

This button will only be available when you have clashes selected from the **Results** area. Clicking this button will create a new group and will move the selected clashes in that group. Figure 5 shows the **Results** area with the clashes organized in the **Pipes** and **Supports** groups.

Figure 5 *The **Results** area with the clashes organized in groups*

Remove from Group

This button will only be available when you select a clash result that is placed in a group. Clicking this button will remove the selected clash result from that group.

Explode Group

This button will only be available when you select a group. Clicking this button will delete the selected group and move all the results outside.

Assign

This button is used to assign the responsibility of the selected result to someone in the team. When you click this button, the **Assign Clash** dialog box is displayed in which you can specify the name of the person who will be assigned the responsibility of this clash. You can also enter some notes about this clash in the dialog box, as shown in Figure 6. The name of the person to whom the clash results have been assigned will be displayed in the **Assign To** column in the **Results** area. Also, the **Comments** column will display a number, indicating that there is some information added to the clash result. This information will be displayed in the **Comments** window when you select the clash result.

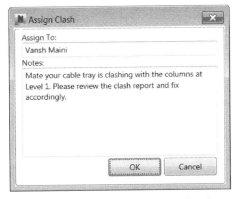

Figure 6 *The **Assign Clash** dialog box*

Unassign

This button is used to unassign the responsibility of the selected result from the person to whom it was assigned earlier. Note that when you select this clash result, the **Comments** window will show two comments. The first one will be about assigning the clash and the second one will be about unassigning it.

Add Comment

Clicking this button displays the **Add Comment** dialog box in which you can enter the comment about the clash. The comment that you add will be displayed in the **Comments** window when you select this clash.

 *Tip: As mentioned in the earlier chapters, to go to the second line of text in the **Comments** dialog box, hold down the CTRL key and then press ENTER.*

Filter by Selection

This flyout allows you to filter the clash results displayed in the **Results** area. By default, **None** is clicked in this flyout. Therefore, the results are not filtered. Click the **Exclusive** option to only show the clash results that involve all the currently selected objects. Click the **Inclusive** option to only show the clash results that involve at least one of the currently selected objects.

Reset

Clicking this button will reset the clash test to **New** and will delete all the clash results. You will have to run the test again to view the clash results.

Compact

Clicking this button will delete all the resolved clashes from the **Results** area.

Re-run Test

Clicking this button will rerun the clash test. This is generally used when you have made changes in the model and you want to update the clash results.

Results Area

The **Results** area displays all the clash results in a tabular format, as shown in Figure 4. The information about the clashes are displayed in various columns in this area. You can click on any clash result in this area to highlight that clash in the graphics window. The clash results in the **Results** area can also be organized in groups for ease of understanding, as shown in Figure 5. Right-clicking on any of the columns in this area displays a shortcut menu from which you can click **Choose Columns** to add or remove columns that are displayed in this area.

Display Settings Area

This is a collapsible area displayed on the right of the **Results** area. This area displays the options to control the visibility of the clashes in the graphics window, see Figure 7. These options are discussed next.

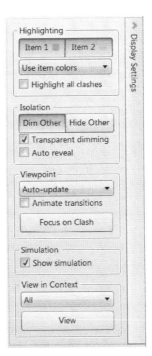

Figure 7 *The **Display Settings** area*

Highlighting Area

This area is used to control the highlighting of the first and second sets of clashing objects. By default, the **Item 1** and **Item 2** buttons in this area are clicked. As a result, both the clashing items are highlighted when you click a clash result. The highlight colors for the two items are defined in the **Options Editor dialog box > Tools > Clash Detective**. The list in this area allows you to specify whether the objects should be highlighted in the graphics window using the item colors specified in the **Options Editor** or using the color of the clash status displayed in the **Results** area. Selecting the **Highlight all clashes** will highlight all the clashes found in the current clash test.

Isolation Area

This area is used to control the visibility of the objects around the clashing objects. By default, the **Dim Other** button is clicked. As a result, all the objects other than the objects participating in the currently selected clash are displayed in gray. Clicking the **Hide Other** button will hide all the objects other than the ones participating in the currently selected clash. The **Transparent dimming** tick box ensures the dimmed objects are also displayed transparent so you can clearly see the clashing objects. Selecting the **Auto reveal** tick box will temporarily turn off the visibility of the objects interfering with your view and the clashing objects. This is generally used when the **Transparent dimming** tick box is not selected.

Viewpoint Area

This area is used to control the viewpoint that displays the clashes in the graphics window. Selecting the **Auto-update** option from the list in this area ensures that if you zoom or pan in the graphics window to view the clash from a different viewpoint, it is saved and restored when you click on the same clash next time. In this case, the **Saved Viewpoint** column in the

Results area will show a viewpoint icon next to the result. Selecting the **Auto-load** option ensures that the changes made in the clash view by zooming or panning are not saved. Selecting the **Manual** option will not automatically take you to a clash view when you click on the clash result. You will have to manually zoom or pan to the clashing objects in the graphics window. The **Animate transition** tick box allows a view to smoothly transition from one clash point to the other instead of an abrupt change in the view. The **Focus on Clash** button is generally used to restore the original clash view if you have changed it by moving or panning.

Simulation Area

This area is used when you have linked a timeliner animation to the clash test. Selecting the **Show simulation** tick box in this area ensures that the timeliner simulation moves to the exact time when the selected clash occurs.

View in Context Area

This area is used to view the clashes on the screen in context of all the objects in the scene, the file containing the clashing objects, or the home view. You can select the option in whose context you want to view the clash and then click the **View** button. The view will zoom out to the selected context and then zoom back into the clash view.

Items Area

This is a collapsible area displayed at the bottom of the **Results** area. This area displays the items that are participating in the current clash. These items, along with their names and types are displayed in the tree view in the **Item 1** and **Item 2** panes, as shown in Figure 8.

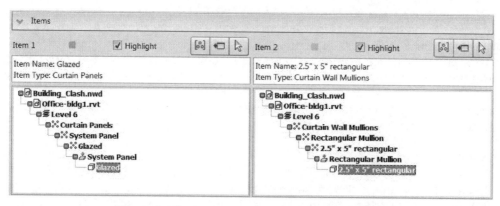

*Figure 8 The **Items** area showing the clashing items*

The options available at the top of the **Item 1** and **Item 2** areas are the same and are discussed next.

Highlight

This tick box is used to highlight the first or second clashing item in the graphics window.

Group Clashes Involving Item

Clicking this button will find all the clashes that the selected item is involved in and will group them together. You can rename the group to any desired name.

SwitchBack

Clicking this button will switch back to the native CAD software to edit the model. The view of the model, when it opens in the native CAD software, will match the view in the Autodesk Navisworks scene. It is important to mention here that the native CAD software has to be installed on the same machine and needs to be ready for switch back. This will be discussed in detail later in this chapter.

Select in Scene

Clicking this button will select and highlight the clashing item in the graphics window.

Report Tab

This options in this tab are used to write a clash report, as shown in Figure 9.

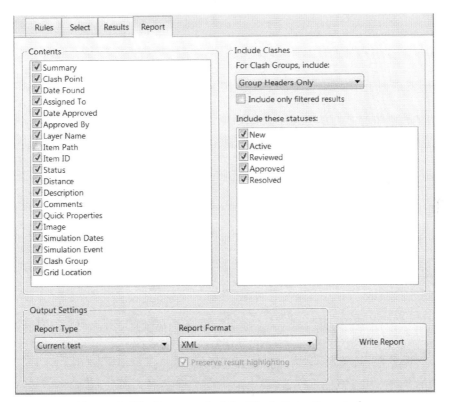

Figure 9 *The **Report** tab of the **Clash Detective** window*

The options available in this tab are discussed next.

Contents Area

This area lets you select the content you want to display in the clash report. You can select the tick boxes on the left of all the items that you want to display in the report.

What I do

*While generating the report of clashes in an Autodesk Revit model, I make sure I select the **Grid Location** tick box from the **Contents** area. This ensures that the grid locations of all the clashes are displayed in the report. As a result, it becomes easy for the person working on resolving the clashes to know the exact clash location.*

Include Clashes Area

This area lets you select the type of clashes to be included in the report. These options are discussed next.

For Clash Groups, include List

This list allows you to select what items you want to include in the report for clash groups. Selecting the **Group Headers Only** option will only include the names of the groups in the report, along with the clashes that are not grouped. The clashes organized inside those groups will not be displayed in the report. Selecting the **Individual Clashes Only** option will include the clashes inside the groups in the report, along with the clashes that are not grouped. In this case, the group names will not be displayed in the clash report. As a result, you will not be able to know if the clashes were grouped. Selecting the **Everything** option will include the group names and the clashes organized in those groups, along with the clashes not grouped in the clash report.

Include only filtered results Tick Box

Selecting this tick box will ensure that only the results that were filtered using the **Filter** flyout on the **Results** tab are displayed in the clash report.

Include these statuses Area

This area shows the status of the various clashes that you can include in the clash report.

Output Settings Area

This area provides various options to specify the clash report output. These options are discussed next.

Report Type List

This list allows you to specify what results need to be included in the report. By default, the **Current test** option is selected. As a result, only the results of the currently selected clash test are included in the report. Selecting the **All tests (combined)** option will include the results of all the clash tests and will combine them together. Selecting the **All tests (separate)** option will write separate reports for all the clash tests. The names of the reports will be the same as the names of the clash tests.

Report Format List

This list allows you to specify what format you want to write the report in. The formats available are **XML**, **HTML**, **HTML (Tabular)**, **Text**, and **As viewpoints**. Remember that selecting the **As viewpoints** option will create viewpoints in the **Saved Viewpoints** window for each clash result. These viewpoints will be organized inside the folder named the same as the clash test. If the clash results were organized inside groups, there will be subfolders in the **Saved Viewpoints** window containing those viewpoints, as shown in Figure 10.

Figure 10 Viewpoints and folders created as clash report

What I do

*I generally generate the reports in the **HTML (Tabular)** format. These reports can be opened in the Microsoft Excel, which makes it very easy to read and manipulate the report. Clicking on the preview of the report viewpoints displays the images in a bigger window.*

Write Report Button

Clicking this button allows you to write the report based on the options selected in the **Report** tab. If you have selected the **Current test** or **All test (combined)** option from the **Report Type** list and you click this button, the **Save As** dialog box is displayed. You can use this dialog box to specify the name and location of the report file. However, if you have selected the **All test (separate)** option from the **Report Type** list, when you click this button, the **Browse For Folder** dialog box will be displayed using which you can specify the location of the report file. The names of the reports will be the same as the names of the clash tests.

PROCEDURES FOR PERFORMING VARIOUS CLASH TEST RELATED ACTIVITIES

The following sections explain procedures for performing various clash test related activities.

Procedure for Performing Hard Clash Tests

The following is the procedure to perform a hard clash test between two sets of objects.

a.   Open, append, or merge the files in which you want to perform clashes.

b.   From the **Home** ribbon tab > **Tools** ribbon panel, click **Clash Detective** to display this window.

c.   Dock the **Clash Detective** window on the left of the graphics window.

d.   From the **Clash** toolbar, click the **Add Test** button to add a new clash test.

e.   Rename the clash test to the desired name.

f.   Click the **Select** tab and from the **Selection A** area, click the first set of objects.

g.   From the **Selection B** area, click the second set of objects.

h.   From the **Selection A** and **Selection B** areas, make sure the **Surfaces** buttons are clicked.

i.   From the **Type** list in the **Settings** area, select **Hard**, if it is not already selected.

j.   In the **Tolerance** edit box, enter the tolerance value up to which the clashes are to be ignored.

k.   Click the **Run Test** button; the clashes will be performed and the results will be displayed in the **Results** tab.

Procedure for Interrogating the Clash Results

Once the clash is performed between two sets of objects, the results are displayed in the **Results** tab. The following is the procedure to interrogate the clash results.

a.   In the **Clash Detective** window, click the **Results** tab, if it is not already active; the first clash will be highlighted and the clashing objects will be displayed in the graphics window.

b.   In the **Results** area, scroll to the right and notice the clash distance and clash point in their respective columns.

c.   From the **Display Settings** area on the left of the **Results** area, click the **Hide Other** button in the **Isolation** area; all the other objects in the view will be hidden.

d.   From the same area, click the **Dim Other** button; the other objects will be displayed as dim.

e.   Clear the **Transparent dimming** tick box from the same area; the other objects will no more be displayed as dim.

f.   Click the **Auto reveal** button; the objects obscuring the clashing objects will be removed from the display.

g.   Select the **Transparent dimming** tick box and then clear the **Auto reveal** tick box.

h.   Scroll down in the **Display Settings** area and make sure **All** is selected from the list in the **View in Context** area.

i.   From the same area, click the **View** button; the camera will zoom out to the extents of all the objects in the scene and will zoom back to the clash, showing you the clash in context of all the objects in the scene.

j.   Perform steps b to k for some other clashes shown in the **Results** area.

Procedure for Writing the Clash Report

The clashes found in the Autodesk Navisworks model can be written in a report. The following steps show you the procedure of writing the clash report.

a.   In the **Clash Detective** window, click the **Report** tab.

b.   From the **Contents** area, select the tick boxes of all the content you want to include in the report.

c.   From the **Include Clashes** area, click the tick boxes of all the statuses you want to include in the report.

d.   From the **Report Type** list in the **Output Settings** area, select the report type that you want to write. If you have multiple clash tests performed, you can select the option to create a combined report for all the tests or separate reports for all the tests.

e.   From the **Report Format** list, select the format in which you want to write the report.

f.   Click the **Write Report** button.

g.   If you selected the report format other than **As viewpoints** from the **Report Format** list and **Current test** or **All tests (combined)** from the **Report Type** list, the **Save As** dialog box will be displayed using which you can specify the name and the location of the report. If you selected **All tests (separate)** from the **Report Type** list, the **Browse For Folder** dialog box will be displayed using which you can specify the folder in which all the test reports will be saved. In this case, the reports will be named the same as the clash names.

h.   If you selected **As viewpoints** from the **Report Format** list, the viewpoints will be saved in the **Saved Viewpoints** window inside a folder with the same name as the clash test.

Procedure for Resolving the Clashes Using the SwitchBack Functionality

As mentioned earlier, the switchback functionality allows you to switchback to the native CAD software from the NWF or NWD files, if you are working with the native files. This is a very useful functionality to modify the CAD model in the native CAD software to resolve clashes. However, for this functionality to work, you need to have the CAD software installed on the same computer as Autodesk Navisworks and also get it ready for switchback.

The following procedures show how to use the switchback functionality to resolve clashes with various CAD software.

Using the Switchback Functionality to Resolve Clashes with AutoCAD or AutoCAD-based Software

Remember that the switchback functionality is only available in AutoCAD 2004 or later versions. The following steps show you how to use the switchback functionality to resolve the clashes in AutoCAD or AutoCAD-based software, such as AutoCAD Plant 3D, AutoCAD Mechanical, and so on.

a.   Start AutoCAD or AutoCAD-based program.

b.   Type a command **NWLOAD** and press ENTER; the command line shows **Navisworks ready**.

> **Note**: *If you regularly work with the switchback functionality, you can add the option to automatically load the Autodesk Navisworks exporter plug-in in AutoCAD. This can be done by adding the required version of the Autodesk Navisworks exporter in the **Startup Suite** of the **Load/Unload Applications** dialog box displayed using the **APPLOAD** command in AutoCAD. The exporter is generally available in the <**Install Drive>:\Program Files\Common Files\Autodesk Shared\Navisworks\20XX\nwexportdbx20XX** folder where XX is the release number.*

> **Tip**: *When you type the **NWLOAD** command and get an error message about the unknown command, this means that Autodesk Navisworks was installed before installing AutoCAD or AutoCAD-based software. This can be resolved by loading the Autodesk Navisworks exporter utility using the **APPLOAD** command. As mentioned earlier, the exporter is generally available in the <**Install Drive>:\Program Files\Common Files\Autodesk Shared\Navisworks\20XX\nwexportdbx20XX** folder where XX is the release number.*

c.   Return to the Autodesk Navisworks window and use switchback on the DWG file; the model will be opened in AutoCAD or AutoCAD-based software zoomed to the same view as that in Autodesk Navisworks.

d.   Make the modification in the model, as required, and then save the file.

e.   Return to the Autodesk Navisworks window and then click the **Refresh** button on the **Quick Access Toolbar**; the changes you made in the DWG file will be reflected in the Autodesk Navisworks scene.

f.   In the **Results** tab of the **Clash Detective** window, click the **Re-run Test** button to rerun the clash test.

Using the Switchback Functionality to Resolve Clashes with Microstation (/J and V8) or Products Based on them

The following steps show you how to use the switchback functionality to resolve the clashes in Microstation /J or V8 or the product based on them.

a.   Start Microstation /J or V8 or the product based on them.

b.   Click **Utilities > Key In** to display the **Key-In** dialog box.

c.   In the dialog box, type MDL LOAD NWEXPORTXX and then exit the dialog box.

 Note: *If you regularly work with the switchback functionality with Microstation, it is better to add NWEXPORTXX to the MDL plug-ins.*

d.   Return to the Autodesk Navisworks window and use switchback on the Microstation file; the model will be loaded in Microstation.

e.   Make the required changes in the model in Microstation and save the file.

f.   Return to the Autodesk Navisworks window and then click the **Refresh** button on the **Quick Access Toolbar**; the changes you made in the Microstation will be reflected in the Autodesk Navisworks scene.

g.   In the **Results** tab of the **Clash Detective** window, click the **Re-run Test** button to rerun the clash test.

Using the Switchback Functionality to Resolve Clashes with Autodesk Revit

Remember that the switchback functionality only works with Autodesk Revit 2012 or later. The following steps show you how to use the switchback functionality to resolve clashes in Autodesk Revit.

a.   Start Autodesk Revit and then start a new project or open an existing one.

b.   Click the **Add-Ins** ribbon tab.

c.   From the **External** ribbon panel, click **External Tools** flyout > **Navisworks Switchback 2016**, as shown in Figure 11.

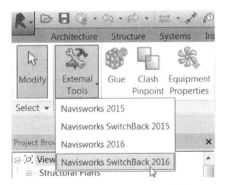

Figure 11 Getting Autodesk Revit ready for switchback

d.   Return to the Autodesk Navisworks window and use switchback on the Autodesk Revit file; the model will be loaded in Autodesk Revit.

e. Make the required changes in the model in Autodesk Revit and save the file.

f. Return to the Autodesk Navisworks window and then click the **Refresh** button on the **Quick Access Toolbar**; the changes you made in the Autodesk Revit will be reflected in the Autodesk Navisworks scene.

g. In the **Results** tab of the **Clash Detective** window, click the **Re-run Test** button to rerun the clash test.

Using the Switchback Functionality to Resolve Clashes with Autodesk Inventor

Autodesk Inventor does not need any special setup to get it ready for switchback. It just needs to be started alongside Autodesk Navisworks. However, it is recommended that the project is changed to the project of the design you are working on in Autodesk Navisworks. The following steps show how to use the switchback functionality to resolve clashes with Autodesk Inventor.

a. Start Autodesk Inventor and change the project to the project of the file opened in Autodesk Navisworks.

b. Return to the Autodesk Navisworks window and use switchback on the Autodesk Inventor file; the model will be loaded in Autodesk Inventor.

c. Make the required changes in the model in Autodesk Inventor and save the file.

d. Return to the Autodesk Navisworks window and then click the **Refresh** button on the **Quick Access Toolbar**; the changes you made in the Autodesk Inventor will be reflected in the Autodesk Navisworks scene.

e. In the **Results** tab of the **Clash Detective** window, click the **Re-run Test** button to rerun the clash test.

Procedure for Linking a TimeLiner Simulation or an Animator Scene to the Clash Test

As mentioned earlier, you can link a timeliner simulation or an animator scene to the clash test. The following are the procedures to do this.

Linking the TimeLiner Simulation to the Clash Test

The following steps show how to link a timeliner simulation to the clash test.

a. In the **Select** tab of the **Clash Detective** window, select the two sets of objects for performing the clash test. Note that these objects need to be included in the timeliner simulation as well.

b. From the **Link** list in the **Settings** area, select the timeliner simulation that you want to link to the clash test.

c. In the **Step (sec)** box, make sure the value is **0.1**.

Tip: It is better to have the time step value to 0.1. The reason is if the value is large, the clashes between the time steps will not be picked during the test.

d. Click **Run Test**; the clash test will be run and the results will be displayed in the **Results** tab.

e. Dock the **TimeLiner** window below the graphics window and then click the **Simulate** tab.

f. In the **Results** tab of the **Clash Detective** window, scroll down in the **Display Settings** area and make sure the **Show simulation** tick box is selected in the **Simulation** area.

g. From the **Results** area, click any clash; the view in the graphics window changes to the clash view and also the simulation bar in the **Simulate** tab of the **TimeLiner** window moves to the date when that clash was detected.

h. Repeat step g for some other clashes and notice how the simulation bar in the **Simulate** tab of the **TimeLiner** window moves to the dates of those clashes.

Linking the Animator Scene to the Clash Test
The following steps show how to link an animator scene to the clash test.

a. In the **Select** tab of the **Clash Detective** window, select the two sets of objects for performing the clash test. Note that these objects need to be included in the animator scene animation as well.

b. From the **Link** list in the **Settings** area, select the animator scene that you want to link to the clash test.

c. In the **Step (sec)** box, make sure the value is **0.1**.

 Tip: It is better to have the time step value to 0.1. The reason is if the value is large, the clashes between the time steps will not be picked during the test.

d. Click **Run Test**; the clash test will be run and the results will be displayed in the **Results** tab.

e. Dock the **Animator** window below the graphics window.

f. In the **Results** tab of the **Clash Detective** window, scroll down in the **Display Settings** area and make sure the **Show simulation** tick box is selected in the **Simulation** area.

g. From the **Results** area, click any clash; the view in the graphics window changes to the clash view and also the simulation bar in the **Animator** window moves to the time duration when that clash was detected.

h. Repeat step g for other clashes and notice how the simulation bar in the **Animator** window moves to the time duration of those clashes.

Procedure for Exporting and Importing Clash Tests

The following procedures show how you can setup a clash test using search sets or using the properties selection and then export it for the use in other files.

Exporting and Importing Clash Tests Based on Search Sets

The following steps show you how to setup a clash test based on search sets and then export and import them.

a. In the **Select** tab of the **Clash Detective** window, select **Sets** from the **Standard** list in the **Selection A** area.

b. Select the first search set to perform the clash test.

c. From the **Standard** list in the **Selection B** area, select **Sets**.

d. Select the second set to perform the clash test.

e. Specify the remaining clash options and click the **Run Test** button; the clash information will be displayed in the **Tests** panel at the top in the **Clash Detective** window.

f. From the **Clash** toolbar, click the **Import/Export Clash Tests** flyout and click **Export Clash Tests**; the **Export...** dialog box will be displayed.

g. Specify the name and location of the clash setup file and then exit the dialog box.

h. Close the current file and then open the file into which you want to import the clash test setup.

i. From the **Clash** toolbar, click **Import Clash Tests** to display the **Import...** dialog box.

j. Browse to the folder where you saved the clash test setup and then double-click on the file; the clash test will be displayed in the **Tests** panel and the objects in the search sets will be selected in the **Select** tab.

k. From the **Select** tab, click **Run Test**; the clash test will be performed based on the imported setup.

Exporting and Importing Clash Tests with the Objects Selected Based on the Properties

The following steps show you how to setup a clash test based on objects selected using their properties and then export and import them.

a. In the **Select** tab of the **Clash Detective** window, select **Properties** from the **Standard** list in the **Selection A** area.

b. Select the properties that you want to have in the first set of objects to perform the clash test.

c. From the **Standard** list in the **Selection B** area, select **Properties**.

d. Select the properties that you want to have in the second set of objects to perform the clash test.

e. Specify the remaining clash options and click the **Run Test** button; the clash information will be displayed in the **Tests** panel at the top in the **Clash Detective** window.

f. From the **Clash** toolbar, click the **Import/Export Clash Tests** flyout and click **Export Clash Tests**; the **Export**... dialog box will be displayed.

g. Specify the name and location of the clash setup file and then exit the dialog box.

h. Close the current file and then open the file that has objects with properties matching the ones you defined in the exported clash setup.

i. From the **Clash** toolbar, click **Import Clash Tests** to display the **Import**... dialog box.

j. Browse to the folder where you saved the clash test setup and then double-click on the file; the clash test will be displayed in the **Tests** panel and the objects in the search sets will be selected in the **Select** tab.

k. From the **Select** tab, click **Run Test**; the clash test will be performed based on the imported setup.

HANDS-ON EXERCISES

You will now work on hands-on exercises by using the concepts learned in this chapter.

Hands-on Exercise (Plant)	*In this exercise, you will complete the following tasks:* 1. *Perform hard clash test between various objects in the Autodesk Navisworks scene.* 2. *Interrogate the clash results.* 3. *Write a report with clash results.* 4. *Export and import clash setups.* 5. *Resolve clashes in the model using various techniques.* 6. *Perform a timeliner simulation based clash.* 7. *Perform clash test with point cloud data.*

Section 1: Performing Hard Clash Test Between Various Objects in the Scene

In this section, you will open the **Hard Clash.nwd** file and then perform hard clashes between various objects in the model.

1. From **Chapter 10 > Exercise Plant** folder, open the **Hard Clash.nwd** file.

2. Change the lighting style to **Full Lights**. The model looks similar to the one shown in Figure 12.

Figure 12 *The model for the exercise*

3. Undock all the windows to make more space for the graphics window.

4. From the left of the graphics window, click **Clash Detective**; the **Clash Detective** window is displayed. Dock this window on the left of the graphics window.

5. From the top right corner of the **Clash Detective** window, click the **Add Test** button; the **Tests** panel is expanded and a new test is added to it with the default name of **Test 1**.

6. Rename the clash test to **Concrete V Pipe**.

7. From the **Selection A** area in the **Select** tab, expand the **Hard Clash.nwd** file and select **1-CONCRETE.dwg**.

8. From the **Selection B** area in the **Select** tab, expand the **Hard Clash.nwd** file and select **5-PIPING.dwg**.

9. In the **Tolerance** edit box, enter **0.04 Inches** or **0.001 Meters** as the value, depending upon your display units.

10. Click the **Run Test** button; the clash test runs and displays 5 clashes found. Also, the results are shown in the **Results** tab and the clashing objects are highlighted in the graphics window, as shown in Figure 13.

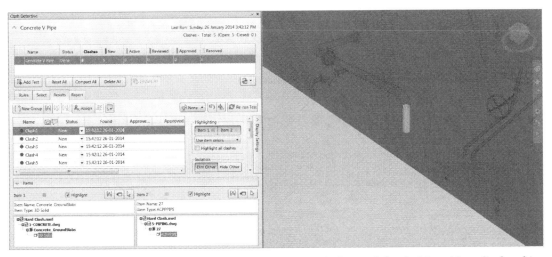

*Figure 13 The clash results shown in the **Clash Detective** window and the clashing objects displayed in the graphics window*

Before interrogating the clash results, you will perform another clash test between structural steel and equipments.

11. From the **Clash** toolbar, click the **Add Test** button; a new test is added to the **Tests** panel.

12. Rename the clash test to **Steel V Equipments**.

13. From the **Selection A** area in the **Select** tab, expand the **Hard Clash.nwd** file and select **2-STEEL.dwg**.

14. From the **Selection B** area in the **Select** tab, expand the **Hard Clash.nwd** file and select **3-EQUIPMENT.dwg**.

15. In the **Tolerance** edit box, enter **0.04 Inches** or **0.001 Meters** as the value, depending upon your display units.

16. Click the **Run Test** button; the clash test runs and displays 6 clashes found. Also, the results will be shown in the **Results** tab.

Section 2: Interrogating the Clash Results

In this section, you will interrogate the results of the clash tests performed in the previous section. With the **Results** tab showing the results of the **Steel V Equipments** test currently, you will view the results of this test.

1. Resize the **Clash Detective** window by dragging it to the right to make sure you can view the **Display Settings** area on the right of the **Results** area, refer to Figure 14.

2. In the **Display Settings** area, scroll down to the **View in Context** area and select **Home** from the **All** list.

3. Click the **View** button; the camera zooms out to the Home view and then zooms back to the clash view.

4. From the **Results** area, click **Clash2**; the clash view is displayed in the graphics window, as shown in Figure 14.

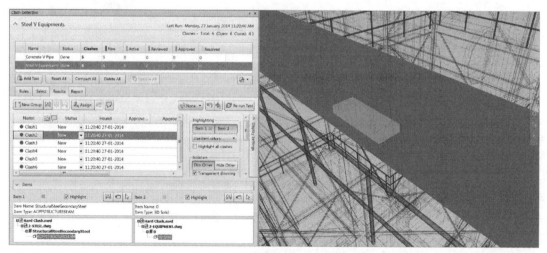

Figure 14 *The clash results shown in the **Clash Detective** window and the clashing objects displayed in the graphics window*

5. In the **Display Settings** area, scroll down to the **View in Context** area and click the **View** button; the camera zooms out to the Home view and then zooms back to the clash view.

6. From the **Results** area, click **Clash6**; the clash view is displayed in the graphics window.

7. In the **Display Settings** area, scroll to the **Isolation** area and clear the **Transparent dimming** tick box. Also, clear the **Auto reveal** tick box, if it is selected; the objects in the graphics window are no more displayed as transparent.

8. From the **Results** area, click **Clash1**; the graphics window turns gray. This is because there are gray objects hiding the clashing objects.

9. In the **Display Settings** area, scroll to the **Isolation** area and click the **Auto reveal** tick box; the gray objects hiding the clashing objects are removed and you can see the clash.

10. In the **Display Settings** area, scroll down to the **View in Context** area and click the **View** button; the camera zooms out to the Home view and then zooms back to the clash view.

11. In the **Display Settings** area, scroll to the **Isolation** area and select the **Transparent dimming** tick box; the objects in the graphics window are again displayed as transparent.

12. From the **Tests** panel at the top in the **Clash Detective** window, select the **Concrete V Pipe** test; the **Results** area shows the results of this clash.

13. Select **Clash1** from the **Results** area. Now, scroll down to the **View in Context** area in the **Display Settings** area and click the **View** button; the camera zooms out to the Home view and then zooms back to the clash view.

14. From the **Results** area, click **Clash4**; the clash view is displayed in the graphics window.

15. In the **Display Settings** area, scroll to the **Isolation** area and clear the **Transparent dimming** tick box; the objects in the graphics window are no more displayed as transparent.

16. In the **Display Settings** area, scroll down to the **View in Context** area and click the **View** button; the camera zooms out to the Home view and then zooms back to the clash view.

17. In the **Display Settings** area, scroll to the **Isolation** area and select the **Transparent dimming** tick box; the objects in the graphics window are again displayed as transparent.

Section 3: Adding Comments to the Clash Results

In this section, you will add comments to various clash results.

1. From the **Results** area, right-click on **Clash1** and click **Add Comment** from the shortcut menu; the **Add Comment** dialog box is displayed.

2. Type the following text in the dialog box:

    Reduce the pipe length based on the clash distance.

3. Click **OK** in the dialog box.

4. Right-click on **Clash4** and click **Add Comment** from the shortcut menu; the **Add Comment** dialog box is displayed.

5. Type the following text in the dialog box:

    Reduce the length of the horizontal pipe based on the clash distance.

6. Click **OK** in the dialog box.

7. From the **Tests** panel at the top in the **Clash Detective** window, select the **Steel V Equipments** test; the **Results** area shows the results of this clash.

8. In the **Results** area, right-click on **Clash1** and click **Add Comment** from the shortcut menu; the **Add Comment** dialog box is displayed.

9. Type the following text in the dialog box:

    Increase the length and width of the support frame of the cyclone based on the clash distances.

10. Click **OK** in the dialog box.

Section 4: Organizing Clashes in Groups

In this section, you will organize the clashes in groups.

1. From the **Tests** panel, select the **Concrete V Pipe** test.

2. From the **Results** area, click **Clash1**; the **Items** area at the bottom in the **Clash Detective** window lists the two clashing objects.

    Notice that the clashing object displayed in the **Item 2** area is ACPPPIPE, which is on layer 27. You will now group all the clashing objects on layer 27 together.

3. From the **Item 2** area on the bottom right of the **Clash Detective** window, select **27** from **5-PIPING.dwg** file.

4. From the toolbar on the right of the **Item 2** area, click the **Group Clashes Involving Item** button; a new group is created and the first three clashes are moved into that group.

5. Rename the new group to **Layer 27 Items**.

    Next, you will repeat this process for the remaining two clashes.

6. From the **Results** area, select **Clash4**.

7. From the **Item 2** area on the bottom right of the **Clash Detective** window, select **301** from the **5-PIPING.dwg** file.

8. From the toolbar on the right of the **Item 2** area, click the **Group Clashes Involving Item** button; a new group is created and the last two clashes are moved into that group.

9. Rename the new group to **Layer 301 Items**. Figure 15 shows the **Results** area with the clashes organized in groups.

Name			Status		Found	Description	Approve...	Assigned To	
◢ Layer 27 Items			New	▾	11:31:35 27-01-2014	Hard			
Clash1	1	New	▾	11:31:35 27-01-2014	Hard				
Clash2		New	▾	11:31:35 27-01-2014	Hard				
Clash3		New	▾	11:31:35 27-01-2014	Hard				
◢ Layer 301 Items			New	▾	11:31:35 27-01-2014	Hard			
Clash4	1	New	▾	11:31:35 27-01-2014	Hard				
Clash5		New	▾	11:31:35 27-01-2014	Hard				

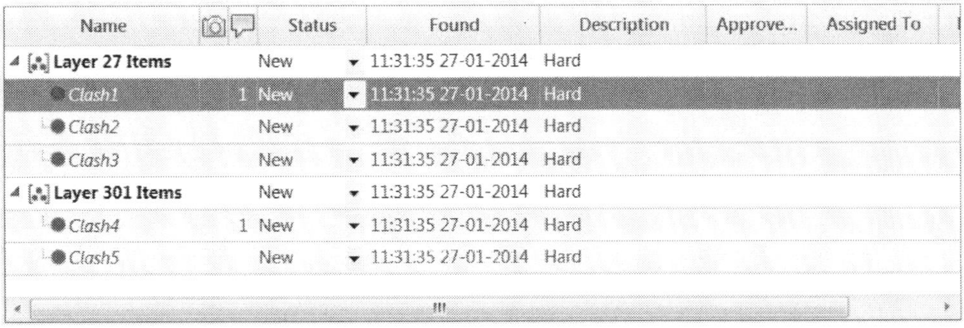

Figure 15 *The clashes organized in groups*

Section 5: Writing the Clash Test Reports

In this section, you will write the reports of the two clash tests that were performed in the earlier sections.

1. In the **Clash Detective** window, click the **Report** tab.

2. From the **Contents** area, make sure all the tick boxes are selected except **Item Path**.

3. From the **For Clash Groups, include** list, select **Everything**.

4. From the **Include these statuses** area, make sure all the tick boxes are selected.

5. From the **Report Type** list in the **Output Settings** area, select **All tests (separate)**; this will ensure separate reports are written for both the tests.

6. From the **Report Format** list, select **HTML (Tabular)**.

7. Click the **Write Report** button; the **Browse For Folder** dialog box is displayed, as shown in Figure 16.

8. Browse to **Chapter 10 > Exercise Plant** folder.

9. Click the **Make New Folder** button from the **Browse For Folder** dialog box and rename the new folder to **Reports**.

10. Click **OK** in the dialog box; the reports will be written and saved in the **Reports** folder.

11. Using Windows Explorer, browse to the **Chapter 10 > Exercise Plant > Reports** folder.

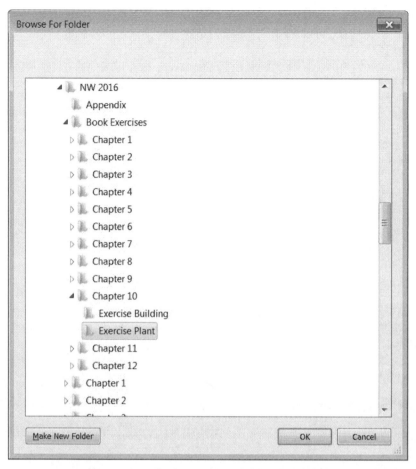

Figure 16 *The **Browse For Folder** dialog box*

Notice the **Concrete V Pipe.html** and **Steel V Equipments.html** files that were created as separate reports for the two tests. Also, notice the **Concrete V Pipe_files** and **Steel V Equipments_files** folders that contain the image files of all the clash views.

12. Double-click on the **Concrete V Pipe.html** file to open it; the clashes are organized in two groups.

    Notice the **Comments** column in the clash report showing the comments that were added earlier in this tutorial.

13. Click on any clash image; a new window is opened and a bigger image of the clash view is displayed.

14. Close the image window and also the clash report to return to the Autodesk Navisworks window.

15. Save the file.

Section 6: Exporting and Importing Clash Test

In this section, you will perform a clash test between two sets of objects based on search sets. You will then export the clash test and import in another file.

1. From the **Clash** toolbar in the **Clash Detective** window, click **Add Test**; a new clash test is added in the **Tests** panel.

2. Rename the clash test to **Con V Struc (Search)**.

3. Click on the **Standard** list in the **Selection A** area of the **Select** tab and select **Sets**; all the selection and search sets are listed in the **Selection A** area.

4. Scroll down and select **Concrete** search set from the list. This is the search set that finds and selects all the objects that contain "concrete" in their item names.

5. Click on the **Standard** list in the **Selection B** area and select **Sets**; all the selection and search sets are listed in the **Selection B** area.

6. Scroll down and select **Structural** search set from the list. This is the search set that finds and selects all the objects that contain "structural" in their item names.

7. Click the **Run Test** button; you will be informed that there are 53 clashes found.

8. From the **Clash** toolbar, click the **Import/Export Clash Tests** flyout and click **Export Clash Tests**; the **Export...** dialog box is displayed.

9. Browse to **Chapter 10 > Exercise Plant** folder and save the clash test settings with the name **Con V Struc (Search)**; the file is saved with .XML as the extension.

    While exporting the clash test, only those tests will be exported that have object selections based on searchable properties or based on search sets. As a result, only the last clash test will be exported out of the three clash tests in the current file.

    Next, you will open the file in which the clash test will be imported. You will not save the changes in the current file.

10. Open the **Clash Import.nwd** file from the **Chapter 10 > Exercise Plant** folder. When prompted to save changes, click **No** in the dialog box.

    The file looks similar to the one that you were working on earlier. However, the **Clash Detective** window is grayed out as there are no clash tests in this file.

11. Click on the **Sets** window and notice that there are only selection sets created but no search sets in the current file.

12. From the top right corner of the **Clash Detective** window, click the **Import Clash Tests** button; the **Import...** dialog box will be displayed.

13. Browse to the **Chapter 10 > Exercise Plant** folder, as shown in Figure 17.

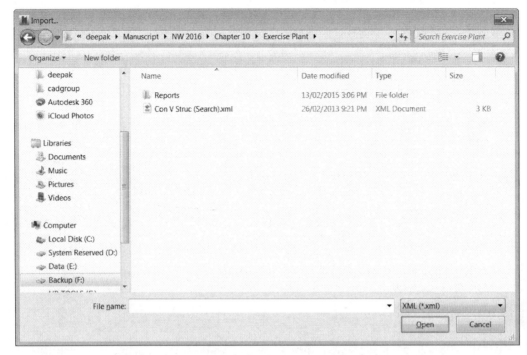

*Figure 17 The **Import**... dialog box to import the clash test settings*

14. Double-click on the **Con V Struc (Search).xml** file; the clash test will be listed in the **Tests** panel.

    Notice the two search sets selected in the **Selection A** and **Selection B** areas of the **Select** tab.

15. From the **Select** tab, click the **Run Test** button; the clash test runs and informs you that there are 53 clashes in this file, as shown in Figure 18.

16. In the **Results** tab, click on various clash results and view the clashes in the graphics window.

17. Start a new file without saving changes in the current file.

Section 7: Resolving the Clashes in the AutoCAD File

In this section, you will perform a clash test between two sets of objects in an AutoCAD file. Depending on the software installed on your computer, you will then use various means to resolve these clashes. If you have AutoCAD or AutoCAD-based software installed on your computer, you will use **Section 7a** to resolve clashes. Else, you will use **Section 7b** to resolve clashes.

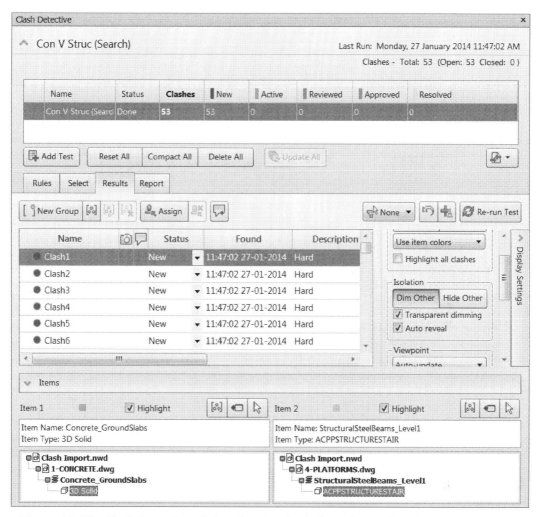

*Figure 18 The **Clash Detective** window showing the clash results based on the imported clash test*

1. From the **Chapter 10 > Exercise Plant** folder, open the **Clash-Switchback.nwf** file; the file looks similar to the one you were working on earlier.

    This NWF file has the native AutoCAD files appended. As a result, you can use the switchback functionality to modify the AutoCAD files at any point of time.

2. From the top right corner of the **Clash Detective** window, click **Add Test**; a new clash test is added to the **Tests** panel.

3. Rename the clash test to **Steel V Pipes**.

4. From the **Selection A** area of the **Select** tab, click on **2-STEEL.dwg**; all the structure steel members are selected as the first set of objects.

5. From the **Selection B** area of the **Select** tab, click on **5-PIPING.dwg**; all the pipes and pipe supports are selected as the second set of objects.

6. Click the **Run Test** button; the clash runs and informs you that there is only one clash found. The clash will also be shown in the graphics window, as shown in Figure 19.

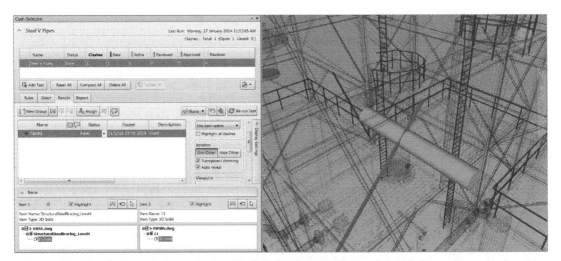

Figure 19 *The clash result shown in the* ***Clash Detective*** *window and the clashing objects displayed in the graphics window*

Next, you will resolve this clash. If you have AutoCAD 2013 or later installed on your computer, go to **Section 7a**. If you do not have AutoCAD 2013 or later installed on your computer, go to **Section 7b**.

Section 7a: Using AutoCAD or AutoCAD-based Software to Resolve the Clash

In this section, you will use the switchback functionality to open the structural steel file in AutoCAD and then modify the steel bracing that is clashing with the pipe.

1. Start AutoCAD 2013 or later or a software based on it installed on your computer.

2. In the command line, type **NWLOAD** and press ENTER.

3. Press the F2 key to open the **AutoCAD Text Window** and make sure the last prompt sequence shows **Navisworks ready**. Close the **AutoCAD Text Window**.

 Note: *If the* ***AutoCAD Text Window*** *shows unknown command, this means that Autodesk Navisworks was installed before installing the AutoCAD-based software on this computer. In this case, refer to the Tip on page 18 of this chapter to resolve this issue.*

4. Return to the Autodesk Navisworks window.

Notice the **Item 1** and **Item 2** areas at the bottom of the **Results** tab of the **Clash Detective** window show the two objects that are clashing. You will use the switchback functionality for the bracing member displayed in the **Item 1** area.

5. From the toolbar displayed in the **Item 1** area, click the **SwitchBack** button; the file is opened in AutoCAD.

6. Activate the AutoCAD window; the bracing member that clashed with the pipe in Autodesk Navisworks is selected in the AutoCAD window.

 *Note: If the bracing member is not selected, return to the Autodesk Navisworks window and click on the **SwitchBack** button again in the **Item 1** area.*

You will now isolate the selected bracing member so that it is easier for you to edit it.

7. With the bracing member selected, right-click in the blank area of the AutoCAD graphics window and from the shortcut menu, click **Isolate > Isolate Objects**; all the other objects are turned off in the graphics window.

To resolve the clash, you need to edit this member. To make it easier for you, a block is created in this file that will be inserted in the position of the current bracing member.

8. Make the **StructuralSteelBracing_New** layer current.

 Tip: You will find it easier to work in AutoCAD if you change the current view from perspective to parallel by right-clicking on the ViewCube in AutoCAD.

9. Using the **Insert** command, insert the **Fixed Bracing** block to overlap the existing bracing member.

10. Turn off the **StructuralSteelBracing_New** layer and delete the original bracing.

11. Turn on the **StructuralSteelBracing_New** layer.

Next, you will restore the visibility of all the steel members.

12. Right-click in the blank area of the AutoCAD graphics window and from the shortcut menu, click **Isolate > End Object Isolation**.

13. Save and close the AutoCAD file.

14. Return to the Autodesk Navisworks window.

15. Click the **Refresh** button on the **Quick Access Toolbar**; the model is refreshed and the **Steel V Pipes** clash test shows an error icon on the left of its name in the **Tests** panel.

16. From the **Clash** toolbar, click the **Update All** button; the clash test is updated and shows the clash as resolved.

17. Save the file and start a new file.

18. Go to **Section 8**.

Section 7b: Resolving the Clash without using AutoCAD

You need to follow the steps in this section only if you do not have AutoCAD 2013 or later or a software based on it installed on your computer and you did not complete **Section 7a**. In this section, you will replace the **2-STEEL.dwg** file with the **2-STEEL-FIXED.dwg** file.

1. Using the Windows Explorer, browse to the **Chapter 10 > Exercise Plant** folder.

2. Rename the **2-STEEL.dwg** file to **2-STEEL-OLD.dwg**.

3. Rename the **2-STEEL-FIXED.dwg** file to **2-STEEL.dwg**.

4. Return back to the Autodesk Navisworks window.

5. On the **Quick Access Toolbar**, click **Refresh**; the model is refreshed to reflect the changes in the **2-STEEL.dwg** file.

   Notice that the **Results** tab of the **Clash Detective** window shows an error informing you that the model or test settings have changes since the test was last run and the results may not reflect the current state of the model.

6. From the **Select** tab of the **Clash Detective** window, click the **Run Test** button; the test runs and the **Result** tab shows the clash as resolved, as shown in Figure 20.

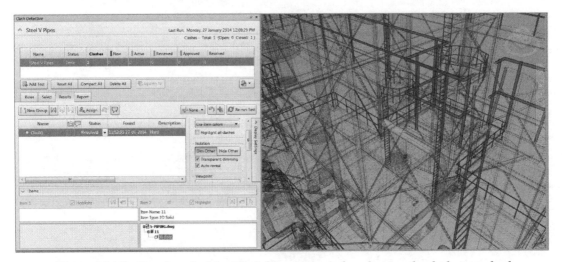

Figure 20 *The* *Results* *tab of the* *Clash Detective* *window showing the clash as resolved*

7. Save the file.

Section 8: Performing a Clash Test Linked to the TimeLiner Simulation

In this section, you will perform a clash test that is linked with the timeliner simulation.

1. From the **Chapter 10 > Exercise Plant** folder, open the **TimeLiner Clash.nwd** file.

   Before you perform the clash test in this file, it is important that you understand how this plant will be constructed by playing the timeliner simulation.

2. Dock the **TimeLiner** window and click the **Simulate** tab.

3. Click the **Play** button to play this simulation.

   Notice that the first task is a demolish task that starts with removing an existing ground slab and then the new slab is constructed followed by the rest of the construction.

4. After the simulation stops, click the **Tasks** tab in the **TimeLiner** window.

5. Undock the **TimeLiner** window.

6. In the **Clash Detective** window, click the **Add Test** button on the top right; a new test is added to the **Tests** panel.

7. Rename the clash test to **TimeLiner Clash**.

8. In the **Selection A** area, expand **TimeLiner Clash.nwd > Plant10.nwd** and select the **1-CONCRETE.dwg** file.

9. In the **Selection B** area, expand **TimeLiner Clash.nwd** and select the **Original Slab.dwg** file.

   You will first run the test without linking the timeliner simulation to see how many clashes are found.

10. Click the **Run Test** button; the clash test runs and you are informed that there are 39 clashes found.

    All these clashes are between the original slab and the new concrete slab that is displayed on top of this at this stage. However, in reality, this is not the case. The new slab will only be constructed after demolishing the old slab, which is represented in the timeliner simulation. Therefore, you will now run the same test by linking with the timeliner simulation.

11. From the **Clash** toolbar, click the **Reset All** button; the clash test is reset as new and there are no clashes displayed.

12. From the **Saved Viewpoints** window, click on the **Flythrough** animation to restore the original view of the plant model.

13. Click the **Select** tab in the **Clash Detective** window.

14. From the **Settings** area, click the **Link** list and select **TimeLiner**.

15. Make sure the **Step (sec)** value is set to **0.1**.

16. Click the **Run Test** button; the **Tests** panel shows the clash status as **Done**, but there are no clashes found in the clash test, refer to Figure 21.

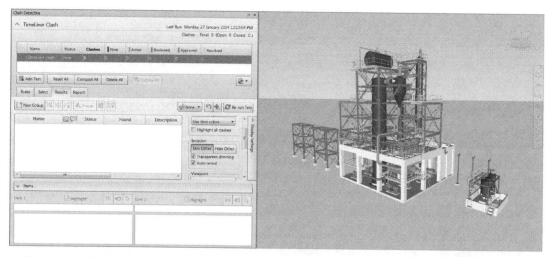

Figure 21 *The* ***Tests*** *panel in the* ***Clash Detective*** *window showing that there are no clashes found*

There are no clashes found because the timeliner simulation ensures that the old slab is demolished before constructing the new slab.

17. Save the file and start a new file.

Section 9: Performing Clash Test with Autodesk ReCap Point Cloud Data

In this section, you will perform clash test between scanned point cloud of an existing plant facility and the new pipework. The scanned point cloud data was indexed in Autodesk ReCap Pro. (The point cloud data of the plant is courtesy **kubit GmBH, www.kubit-software.com**). The point cloud data and new pipework were appended together to create the NWD file that you will use in this section.

What I do

I prefer embedding the point cloud data inside the NWD file by selecting the ***Embed ReCap and Texture data*** *tick box in the* ***Publish*** *dialog box. This ensures that I do not have to provide the linked point cloud file in addition to the NWD file. Also, I prefer to reduce the size of the NWD file by selecting the* ***Compressed*** *option from the* ***On Publish Embed XRefs*** *list. This list is available in the* ***Options Editor*** *dialog box >* ***File Reader*** *>* ***ReCap***. *This is what I did with the file that you are using in this section of the tutorial. The file published with this option selected is around 117 Megabytes. However, the same NWD file published by selecting the* ***Fast Access*** *option from this list has a size of around 192 Megabytes.*

---

1. From the **Chapter 10 > Exercise Plant** folder, open the **Scanned-Plant.nwd** file. The Autodesk Navisworks scene in this file looks similar to the one shown in Figure 22.

*Figure 22 The Autodesk Navisworks scene with the point cloud data of an existing plant and the new pipework (The point cloud data of the plant is courtesy **kubit GmbH, www.kubit-software.com**)*

2. From the top right corner of the **Clash Detective** window, click the **Add Test** button; the **Tests** panel is expanded and a new test is added to it with the default name of **Test 1**.

3. Rename the clash test to **Point Cloud V New Pipes**.

4. From the **Selection A** area in the **Select** tab, expand **Scanned-Plant.nwd** and select **synthetic_plant.rcs**.

5. From the **Selection B** area in the **Select** tab, expand **Scanned-Plant.nwd** and select **Scanned-Plant-Pipework.ipt**.

6. From the toolbar at the bottom of the **Selection A** area, select the **Points** button.

7. From the toolbar at the bottom of the **Selection B** area, select the **Surfaces** button.

8. In the **Tolerance** edit box, enter **0.04 Inches** or **0.001 Meters** as the value, depending upon your display units.

9. Make sure **Hard** is selected from the **Type** list in the **Settings** area.

10. Make sure the **Composite Object Clashing** tick box is not selected.

11. Click the **Run Test** button; the clash test runs and comes up with no clashes.

The reason no clashes were found is because the clashes with the point cloud cannot be considered as hard clashes. These clashes require the type to be changed to **Clearance**.

12. Click the **Select** tab.

13. From the **Type** list in the **Settings** area, select **Clearance**.

14. Click the **Run Test** button; the clash test runs and displays 12 clashes found. Also, the results will be shown in the **Results** tab, as shown in Figure 23.

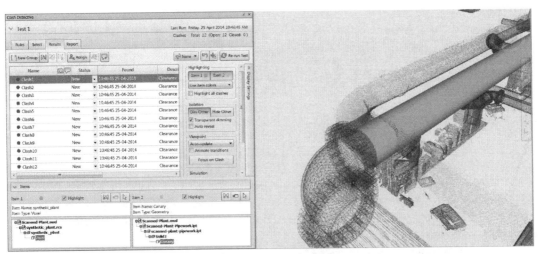

*Figure 23 The **Clash Detective** window and the graphics screen showing the clashes found*

Section 10: Interrogating the Clash Results

In this section, you will interrogate the results of the clash tests performed in the previous section.

1. Resize the **Clash Detective** window by dragging it to the right to make sure you can view the **Display Settings** area on the right of the **Results** area.

2. In the **Display Settings** area, scroll down to the **View in Context** area and select **Home** from the **All** list, if it is not already selected.

3. Click the **View** button; the camera zooms out to the Home view and then zooms back to the first clash view.

4. From the **Results** area, click **Clash2**; the clash view is displayed in the graphics window.

5. In the **Display Settings** area, scroll down to the **View in Context** area and click the **View** button; the camera zooms out to the Home view and then zooms back to the clash view.

6. From the **Results** area, click **Clash3**; the clash view is displayed in the graphics window.

7. In the **Display Settings** area, scroll down to the **View in Context** area and click the **View** button; the camera zooms out to the Home view and then zooms back to the clash view.

8. From the **Results** area, click **Clash4**; you will notice that the clashing pipe and point cloud voxel are highlighted.

9. From the **Results** area, click **Clash7**; you will notice that the clashing pipe and point cloud voxel are highlighted.

10. Zoom out and orbit the model around to view the clash region.

 *Tip: When you orbit the clash view, the new view is automatically saved as the clash view because the **Auto-update** option is selected in the **Viewpoint** area of the **Display Settings**. This is evident by a camera icon that is displayed in the **Saved Viewpoint** column in the **Results** area.*

11. From the **Results** area, click **Clash6**; notice that a camera icon is displayed on the right of **Clash7**.

Section 11: Writing the Clash Test Report

In this section, you will write the reports of the clash test performed in the earlier sections.

1. In the **Clash Detective** window, click the **Report** tab.

2. From the **Contents** area, make sure all the tick boxes are selected except **Item Path**.

3. From the **Include these statuses** area, make sure all the tick boxes are selected.

4. From the **Report Type** list in the **Output Settings** area, select **Current test**.

5. From the **Report Format** list, select **HTML (Tabular)**.

6. Click the **Write Report** button; the **Save As** dialog box is displayed.

7. Browse to the **Chapter 10 > Exercise Plant** folder.

8. Create a new folder and rename it as **Point Cloud Report**.

9. Double-click on this folder and save the report file in this folder with its default name.

10. Using Windows Explorer, browse to the **Point Cloud Report** folder.

    Notice the **Point Cloud V New Pipes.html** file that was created as a report for the test. Also, notice the **Point Cloud V New Pipes_files** folder that contains the image files of the clash views.

11. Double-click on the **Point Cloud V New Pipes.html** file to open it.

12. Click on any clash image; a new window is opened and a bigger image of the clash view is displayed.

13. Close the image window and also the clash report to return to the Autodesk Navisworks window.

14. Start a new file to close the current file. You will not be able to save changes to this file as it is write protected.

15. Restore the **Training** workspace.

Hands-on Exercise (BIM)	In this exercise, you will complete the following tasks: 1. Perform hard clash test between various objects in the Autodesk Navisworks scene. 2. Interrogate the clash results. 3. Write a report with clash results. 4. Export and import clash setups. 5. Resolve clashes in the model. 6. Perform a timeliner simulation based clash. 7. Perform clash test with Autodesk ReCap point cloud data.

Section 1: Performing Hard Clash Test Between Various Objects in the Scene

In this section, you will open the **Building_Clash.nwf** file and then perform hard clashes between various objects in the scene.

1. From **Chapter 10 > Exercise Building** folder, open the **Building_Clash.nwf** file.

2. Activate the **Overview** viewpoint. The model looks similar to the one shown in Figure 24.

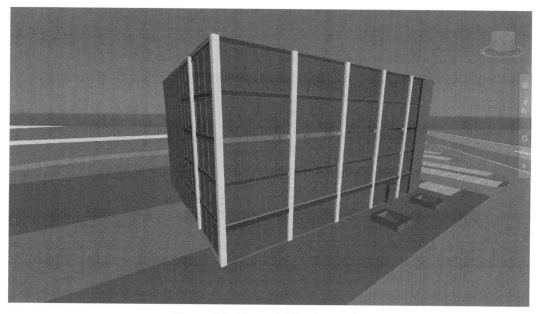

Figure 24 The model for the exercise

3. Undock the **Properties** window, the **Saved Viewpoints** window, and the **Selection Tree** to make more space for the graphics window.

4. From the left of the graphics window, click **Clash Detective**; the **Clash Detective** window is displayed. Dock this window on the left of the graphics window.

The first clash test you will perform is between level 1 curtain panels and structure columns.

5. From the top right corner of the **Clash Detective** window, click the **Add Test** button; the **Tests** panel is expanded and a new test is added to it with the default name of **Test 1**.

6. Rename the clash test to **L1 Cols V Curt Pan**.

7. From the **Selection A** area in the **Select** tab, expand **Office-bldg1.rvt > Level 1** and select **Columns**.

8. From the **Selection B** area in the **Select** tab, expand the **Office-bldg1.rvt > Level 1** and select **Curtain Panels**.

9. Make sure **Hard** is selected in the **Type** list. Now, in the **Tolerance** edit box, enter **0.04 Inches** or **0.001 Meters** as the value, depending upon your display units.

10. Click the **Run Test** button; the clash test runs and displays 10 clashes found. Also, the results are shown in the **Results** tab and the clashing objects are highlighted in the graphics window, as shown in Figure 25.

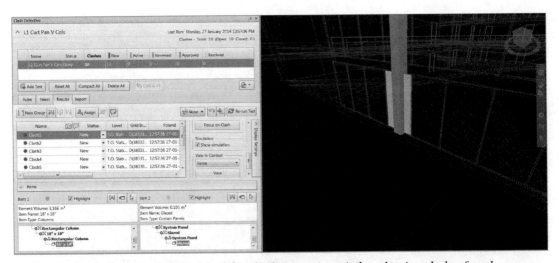

Figure 25 The **Results** tab of the **Clash Detective** window showing clashes found

Before interrogating the clash results, you will perform another clash test between Level 1 mullions and columns.

11. From the **Clash** toolbar, click the **Add Test** button; a new test is added to the **Tests** panel.

12. Rename the clash test to **L1 Mullions V Columns**.

13. From the **Selection A** area in the **Select** tab, expand the **Office-bldg1.rvt > Level 1** and select **Curtain Wall Mullions**.

14. From the **Selection B** area in the **Select** tab, expand **Office-bldg1.rvt > Level 1** and select **Columns**.

15. Make sure **Hard** is selected in the **Type** list. Now, in the **Tolerance** edit box, enter **0.04 Inches** or **0.001 Meters** as the value, depending upon your display units.

16. Click the **Run Test** button; the clash test runs and displays 21 clashes found. Also, the results will be shown in the **Results** tab.

Section 2: Interrogating the Clash Results

In this section, you will interrogate the results of the clash tests performed in the previous section. With the **Results** tab showing the results of the **L1 Mullions V Columns** test currently, you will view the results of this test.

1. Resize the **Clash Detective** window by dragging it to the right to make sure you can view the **Display Settings** area on the right of the **Results** area, refer to Figure 26.

2. In the **Display Settings** area, scroll down to the **View in Context** area and select **Home** from the list, if not already selected. Next, click the **View** button; the camera zooms out to the Home view and then zooms back to the clash view.

3. From the **Results** area, click **Clash2**; the clash view is displayed in the graphics window, as shown in Figure 26.

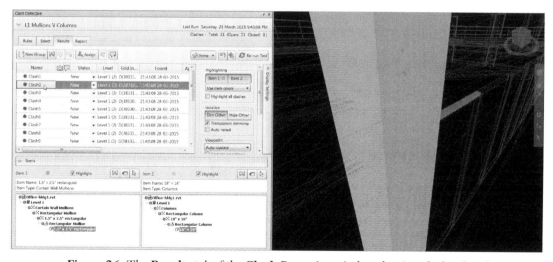

*Figure 26 The **Results** tab of the **Clash Detective** window showing clashes found*

4. In the **Display Settings** area, scroll down to the **View in Context** area and click the **View** button; the camera zooms out to the Home view and then zooms back to the clash view.

5. From the **Results** area, click **Clash6**; the clash view is displayed in the graphics window.

6. In the **Display Settings** area, scroll to the **Isolation** area and clear the **Transparent dimming** tick box; the objects in the graphics window are no more displayed as transparent.

7. From the **Results** area, click **Clash3**; the clashing curtain wall mullion is not fully displayed in this view. Therefore, you need to change the clash view.

8. Move the cursor to the center of the graphics window. Now, press and hold down the SHIFT key and wheel mouse button and drag the view to the right so that you can see the face of the column where the mullion is clashing. You may have to zoom out a little to view the complete clashing mullion.

9. In the **Display Settings** area, click the **Hide Other** button; all other objects are hidden in the scene.

10. Click the **Dim Other** button; all the other objects are turned back on in the scene.

11. Select the **Transparent dimming** tick box; the objects in the graphics window are again displayed as transparent.

12. From the **Tests** panel at the top in the **Clash Detective** window, select the **L1 Cols V Curt Pan** test; the **Results** area shows the results of this clash.

13. Click **Clash1** in the **Results** area.

14. Scroll down to the **View in Context** area in the **Display Settings** area and click the **View** button; the camera zooms out to the Home view and then zooms back to the clash view.

15. From the **Results** area, click **Clash4**; the clash view is displayed in the graphics window.

16. In the **Display Settings** area, scroll to the **Isolation** area and clear the **Transparent dimming** tick box; the objects in the graphics window are no more displayed as transparent.

17. In the **Display Settings** area, scroll down to the **View in Context** area and click the **View** button; the camera zooms out to the Home view and then zooms back to the clash view.

18. In the **Display Settings** area, scroll to the **Isolation** area and select the **Transparent dimming** tick box; the objects in the graphics window are again displayed as transparent.

Section 3: Adding Comments to the Clash Results

In this section, you will add comments to various clash results.

1. From the **Results** area, right-click on **Clash1** and click **Add Comment** from the shortcut menu; the **Add Comment** dialog box is displayed.

2. Type the following text in the dialog box:

    The curtain panels are interfering with the columns throughout. This needs to be modified on all the levels.

3.   Click **OK** in the dialog box.

4.   Right-click on **Clash4** and click **Add Comment** from the shortcut menu; the **Add Comment** dialog box is displayed.

5.   Type the following text in the dialog box:

Better to modify the curtain wall type or the family for resolving all the clashes.

6.   Click **OK** in the dialog box.

7.   From the **Tests** panel at the top in the **Clash Detective** window, select the **L1 Mullions V Columns** test; the **Results** area shows the results of this clash.

8.   In the **Results** area, right-click on **Clash1** and click **Add Comment** from the shortcut menu; the **Add Comment** dialog box is displayed.

9.   Type the following text in the dialog box:

Changing the curtain wall type will also resolve all these clashes.

10. Click **OK** in the dialog box.

Section 4: Organizing Clashes in Groups

In this section, you will organize the clashes in groups.

1.   From the **Results** area, click **Clash1**, if it is not already selected; the clash is highlighted in the graphics window.

2.   In the **Results** area, scroll down to **Clash10**.

3.   Hold down the SHIFT key and click on **Clash10**; the first ten clashes are selected.

4.   From the toolbar above the **Results** area, click the **Group Selected Clashes** button; a new group is created and the selected clashes are moved into that group.

5.   Rename the new group to **Large Clashes**.

Next, you will repeat this process for the remaining clashes.

6.   From the **Results** area, select **Clash11**.

7.   Scroll down to the last clash. Hold down the SHIFT key and select the last clash.

8.   From the toolbar above the **Results** area, click the **Group Selected Clashes** button; a new group is created and the selected clashes are moved into that group.

9. Rename the new group to **Small Clashes**. Figure 27 shows the **Results** area with the clashes organized in groups.

Name	📷💬	Status	Level	Grid In...	Found
▲ [⋮] **Large Clashes**		New ▼	Level 1 (2)	D(38333...	13:00:05 27-01-]
● *Clash1*	1	New ▼	Level 1 (2)	D(38333...	13:00:05 27-01-]
● *Clash2*		New ▼	Level 1 (2)	D(38332...	13:00:05 27-01-]
● *Clash3*	📷	New ▼	Level 1 (2)	D(38331...	13:00:05 27-01-]
● *Clash4*		New ▼	Level 1 (2)	D(38331...	13:00:05 27-01-]
● *Clash5*		New ▼	Level 1 (2)	D(38331...	13:00:05 27-01-]
● *Clash6*		New ▼	Level 1 (2)	D(38331...	13:00:05 27-01-.
● *Clash7*		New ▼	Level 1 (2)	D(38330...	13:00:05 27-01-.
● *Clash8*		New ▼	Level 1 (2)	D(38330...	13:00:05 27-01-.
● *Clash9*		New ▼	Level 1 (2)	D(38333...	13:00:05 27-01-.
● *Clash10*		New ▼	Level 1 (2)	D(38332...	13:00:05 27-01-.
▲ [⋮] **Small Clashes**		New ▼	T.O. Slab...	D(38333...	13:00:05 27-01-]
● *Clash11*		New ▼	T.O. Slab...	D(38333...	13:00:05 27-01-.

Figure 27 The clashes organized in groups

Tip: Clicking a clash group highlights all the clashes in that group in the graphics window. This is a quick technique to find all the clashes in that group.

Section 5: Writing the Clash Test Reports

In this section, you will write the reports of the two clash tests that you performed in the earlier sections.

1. In the **Clash Detective** window, click the **Report** tab.

2. From the **Contents** area, make sure all the tick boxes are selected except **Item Path**.

3. From the **Include these statuses** area, make sure all the tick boxes are selected.

4. From the **Report Type** list in the **Output Settings** area, select **All tests (separate)**; this will ensure separate reports are written for both the tests.

5. From the **Report Format** list, select **HTML (Tabular)**.

6. Click the **Write Report** button; the **Browse For Folder** dialog box is displayed.

7. Browse to **Chapter 10 > Exercise Building** folder, as shown in Figure 28.

8. Click the **Make New Folder** button from the **Browse For Folder** dialog box and rename the new folder to **Reports**.

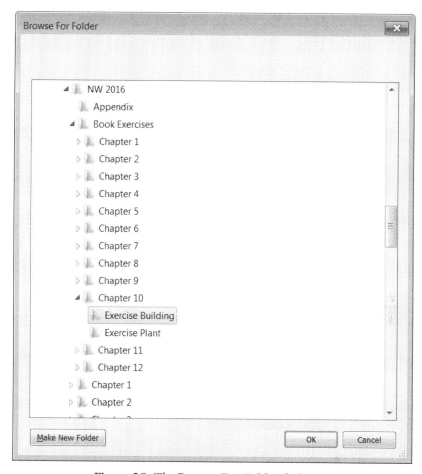

*Figure 28 The **Browse For Folder** dialog box*

9. Click **OK** in the dialog box; the reports will be written and saved in the **Reports** folder.

10. Using Windows Explorer, browse to the **Chapter 10 > Exercise Building > Reports** folder.

    Notice the **L1 Cols V Curt Pan.html** and **L1 Mullions V Columns.html** files that were created as separate reports for the two tests. Also, notice the **L1 Cols V Curt Pan_files** and **L1 Mullions V Columns_files** folders that contain the image files of all the clash views.

11. Double-click on the **L1 Cols V Curt Pan.html** file to open it; the clashes are organized in two groups.

    Notice the **Comments** column in the clash report showing the comments that were added earlier in this tutorial.

12. Click on any clash image; a new window is opened and a bigger image of the clash view is displayed.

13. Close the image window and also the clash report to return to the Autodesk Navisworks window.

   It is important to save the file here as these clash results will be used later in this chapter.

14. Save the file.

Section 6: Exporting and Importing Clash Test

In this section, you will perform a clash test between two sets of objects based on search sets. You will then export the clash test and import in another file.

1. From the **Clash** toolbar in the **Clash Detective** window, click **Add Test**; a new clash test is added in the **Tests** panel.

2. Rename the clash test to **Panels V Mullions (Search)**.

3. Click on the **Standard** list in the **Selection A** area of the **Select** tab and select **Sets**; all the selection and search sets are listed in the **Selection A** area.

4. Select the **Curtain Panels** search set from the list. This is the search set that finds and selects all the objects that contain "curtain panels" in their item names.

5. Click on the **Standard** list in the **Selection B** area and select **Sets**; all the selection and search sets are listed in the **Selection B** area.

6. Select the **Curtain Wall Mullions** search set from the list. This is the search set that finds and selects all the objects that contain "curtain wall mullions" in their item names.

7. Click the **Run Test** button; you will be informed that there are 24 clashes found.

8. From the **Clash** toolbar, click the **Import/Export Clash Tests** flyout and click **Export Clash Tests**; the **Export**... dialog box is displayed.

9. Browse to **Chapter 10 > Exercise Building** folder and save the clash test settings with the name **Panels V Mullions (Search)**; the file is saved with .XML as the extension.

   While exporting the clash test, only those tests will be exported that have object selections based on searchable properties or based on search sets. As a result, only the last clash test will be exported out of the three clash tests in the current file.

   Next, you will open the file into which the clash test will be imported. Note that you will not save these changes in the current file.

10. Open the **Clash_Import.nwd** file from the **Chapter 10 > Exercise Building** folder. When prompted to save the changes, click **No** in the dialog box.

The file looks similar to the one that you were working on earlier. However, the **Clash Detective** window is grayed out as there are no clash tests in this file.

11. Click on the **Sets** window and notice that there are no search sets in the current file.

12. From the top right corner of the **Clash Detective** window, click the **Import Clash Tests** button; the **Import...** dialog box will be displayed.

13. Browse to the **Chapter 10 > Exercise Building** folder, as shown in Figure 29.

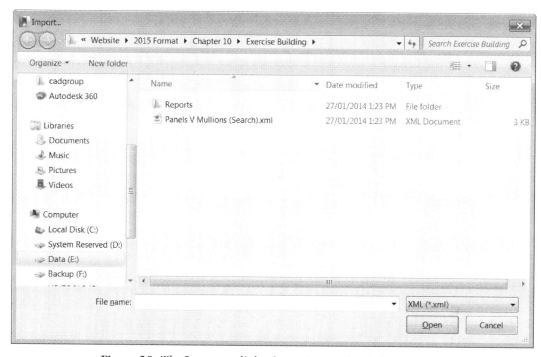

Figure 29 *The **Import...** dialog box to import the clash test settings*

14. Double-click on the **Panels V Mullions (Search).xml** file; the clash test will be listed in the **Tests** panel.

    Note the two search sets selected in the **Selection A** and **Selection B** areas of the **Select** tab. These sets were created upon importing the clash settings.

15. From the **Select** tab, click the **Run Test** button; the clash test runs and informs you that there are 8 clashes in this file, as shown in Figure 30.

16. In the **Results** tab, click on various clash results and view the clashes in the graphics window.

17. Start a new file without saving changes in the current file.

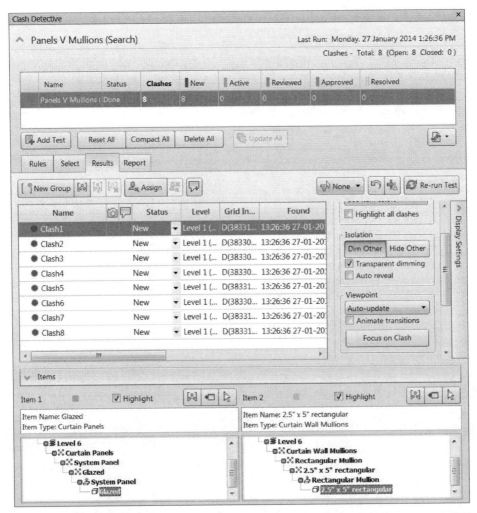

Figure 30 *The **Clash Detective** window showing the clash results based on the imported clash test*

Section 7: Resolving the Clashes

In this section, you will resolve the clash in the **Building_Clash.nwf**. Because the clashes were in the Autodesk Revit file, you will need to modify the geometry in that file. If you have Autodesk Revit installed on your computer and you are an Autodesk Revit expert, follow the steps in **Section 7a** to resolve the clashes. However, it is not expected for everyone to have Autodesk Revit installed on their computer. Therefore, an Autodesk Revit file with the fixed geometry is already made available in the exercise folder for you to use. In this case, follow the steps in **Section 7b** to resolve the clashes.

Section 7a: Using the Switchback Functionality with Autodesk Revit to Resolve the Clash

In this section, you will use the switchback functionality to open the file in Autodesk Revit and then modify the curtain wall to resolve the clashes. Note that if you are not an Autodesk Revit user, it is better for you to follow the steps in **Section 7b** to resolve the clashes even though you may have Autodesk Revit installed on your computer.

1. From the recent files in the **Application Menu**, open the **Building_Clash.nwf** file. From the **Tests** panel in the **Clash Detective** window, select one of the clash tests and then click **Clash1** on the **Results** tab.

2. Start Autodesk Revit 2012 or later installed on your computer.

3. From the **Add-Ins** ribbon tab > **External** ribbon panel > **External Tools** flyout, click **Navisworks SwitchBack 2016**; this will get Autodesk Revit ready for switchback.

4. Return to the Autodesk Navisworks window. Notice the **Item 1** and **Item 2** areas at the bottom of the **Results** tab of the **Clash Detective** window show the two objects that are clashing. Because both the objects are in the same file, you can use the switchback on any of the objects.

5. From the toolbar displayed in the **Item 1** area, click the **SwitchBack** button; the file is opened in Autodesk Revit in a 3D view called **Navisworks SwitchBack**.

6. Use the Autodesk Revit tools to make sure the curtain walls are not interfering with the columns.

7. Save and close the Revit file and return to the Autodesk Navisworks window.

8. Click the **Refresh** button on the **Quick Access Toolbar**; the model is refreshed and the clash tests show error icons on the left of their names in the **Tests** panel.

9. From the **Clash** toolbar, click the **Update All** button; the clash tests are updated and show the clashes as resolved.

10. Save the file and go to **Section 8**.

Section 7b: Resolving the Clash without using Autodesk Revit

You need to follow these steps if you did not complete **Section 7a**. In this section, you will replace the **Office-bldg1.rvt** file with the **Office-bldg1-Fixed.rvt** file.

1. In the Autodesk Navisworks window, open the **Building_Clash.nwf** file from the recent files in the **Application Button**. From the **Tests** panel in the **Clash Detective** window, select one of the clash tests and then click on the **Results** tab.

2. Using the Windows Explorer, browse to the **Chapter 10 > Exercise Building** folder.

3. Rename the **Office-bldg1.rvt** file to **Office-bldg1-OLD.rvt**.

4. Rename the **Office-bldg1-Fixed.rvt** file to **Office-bldg1.rvt**.

5. Return back to the Autodesk Navisworks window.

6. On the **Quick Access Toolbar**, click the **Refresh** button; the model is refreshed to reflect the changes in the modified **Office-bldg1.rvt** file.

    Notice that the **Tests** panel of the **Clash Detective** window show errors on the left of the names of the two clash tests informing you that the model or test settings have changes since the test was last run and the results may not reflect the current state of the model.

7. From the **Clash** toolbar of the **Clash Detective** window, click the **Update All** button; both the tests are rerun and the **Result** tab shows the clashes as resolved, as shown in Figure 31.

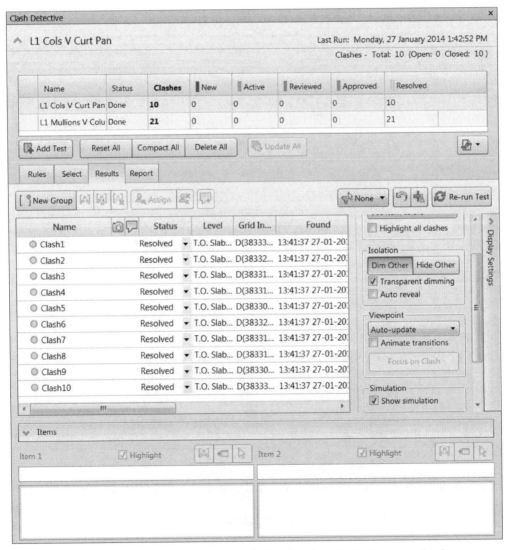

*Figure 31 The **Clash Detective** window showing the clashes as resolved*

8. Save the file.

Section 8: Performing a Clash Test Linked to the TimeLiner Simulation

In this section, you will perform a clash test that is linked with the timeliner simulation.

1. From the **Chapter 10 > Exercise Building** folder, open the **TimeLiner Clash.nwd** file.

    Before you perform the clash test in this file, it is important that you understand how this building will be constructed by playing the timeliner simulation.

2. Activate the **Overview** viewpoint.

3. Dock the **TimeLiner** window and click the **Simulate** tab. Now, click the **Play** button to play this simulation.

    Notice that the first task is a demolish task that starts with removing an existing structure and then the building is constructed.

4. After the simulation stops, click the **Tasks** tab in the **TimeLiner** window.

5. Undock the **TimeLiner** window.

6. In the **Clash Detective** window, click the **Add Test** button on the top right; a new test is added to the **Tests** panel.

7. Rename the clash test to **TimeLiner Clash**.

8. In the **Selection A** area, expand **TimeLiner Clash.nwd** and select the **Office-bldg1.rvt** file.

9. In the **Selection B** area, expand **TimeLiner Clash.nwd** and select the **Old-Building.dwg** file.

    You will first run the test without linking the timeliner simulation to see how many clashes are found.

10. Click the **Run Test** button; the clash test runs and clashes found are displayed in the **Results** tab.

    All these clashes are between the old building and the various objects in the new building. However, in reality, this is not the case. The new building will only be constructed after demolishing the old building, which is represented in the timeliner simulation. Therefore, you will now run the same test by linking with the timeliner simulation.

11. From the **Clash** toolbar, click the **Reset All** button; the clash test is reset as new and there are no clashes displayed.

12. From the **Saved Viewpoints** window, click on the **Overview** viewpoint to restore the original view of the building model.

13. Click the **Select** tab in the **Clash Detective** window.

14. From the **Settings** area, click the **Link** list and select **TimeLiner**.

15. Make sure the **Step (sec)** value is set to **0.1**.

16. Click the **Run Test** button; the **Tests** panel shows the clash status as **Done**, but there are no clashes found in the clash test, refer to Figure 32.

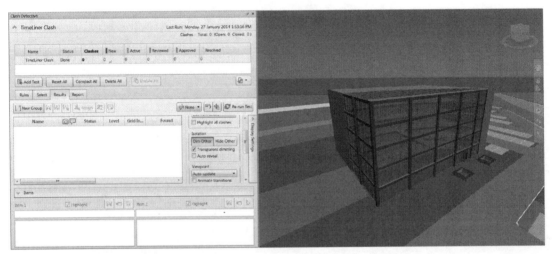

*Figure 32 The **Tests** panel in the **Clash Detective** window showing that there are no clashes found*

There are no clashes found because the timeliner simulation ensures that the old slab is demolished before constructing the new slab.

17. Save the file.

Section 9: Performing Clash Test with Autodesk ReCap Point Cloud Data

In this section, you will perform clash test between scanned point cloud of an existing facility and the new ductwork. The scanned point cloud data was registered and indexed in Autodesk ReCap Pro and the duct work was created in Autodesk Inventor (Autodesk ReCap Pro point cloud data is courtesy **Autodesk - Reality Solutions Group**). Both these files were appended together to create the NWD file that you will use in this section.

1. From the **Chapter 10 > Exercise Building** folder, open the **Scan-Clash.nwd** file; the Autodesk Navisworks file opens with the point cloud data and the ductwork, as shown in Figure 33.

2. Activate the **Overview** viewpoint and then orbit the model to view the point cloud and the ductwork.

3. Dock the **Sets** window and notice the four selection sets created.

Figure 33 *The Autodesk Navisworks scene with the Autodesk ReCap Pro point cloud data and the ductwork (Autodesk ReCap Pro point cloud data is courtesy **Autodesk - Reality Solutions Group**)*

What I do

*I prefer embedding the point cloud data inside the NWD file by selecting the **Embed XRefs** tick box in the **Publish** dialog box. This ensures that I do not have to provide the linked point cloud file in addition to the NWD file. Also, I prefer to reduce the size of the NWD file by selecting the **Compressed** option from the **On Publish Embed XRefs** list. This list is available in the **Options Editor** dialog box > **File Reader** > **ReCap**. This is what I did with the file that you are using in this section of the tutorial. The file published with this option selected is around 164 Megabytes. However, the same NWD file published by selecting the **Fast Access** option from this list has a size of around 288 Megabytes.*

---

4. Activate the **Inside** viewpoint.

5. Click on the **Voxels-Side1** selection set and notice that certain area of the point cloud on the left side of the scanned building is highlighted.

    The reason only a certain area of the point cloud is highlighted is because the entire point cloud is broken down into smaller voxels.

6. Click on the **Voxels-Side2** selection set and notice that certain area of the point cloud on the right side of the scanned building is highlighted.

    You will use these selection sets while performing the clash tests.

7. Press ESC to deselect everything.

8. Restore the **Overview** viewpoint.

9. From the top right corner of the **Clash Detective** window, click the **Add Test** button; the **Tests** panel is expanded and a new test is added to it with the default name of **Test 1**.

10. Rename the clash test to **Duct V Point Cloud**.

11. From the **Selection A** area in the **Select** tab, click on the **Standard** list and select **Sets**; the four sets created in the Autodesk Navisworks scene are displayed.

12. Hold down the CTRL key and select the **Ducts-Side1** and **Ducts-Side2** sets.

13. From the **Selection B** area, click on the **Standard** list and select **Sets**.

14. Hold down the CTRL key and select the **Voxels-Side1** and **Voxels-Side2** sets.

15. From the toolbar at the bottom of the **Selection B** area, click the **Points** button.

16. Make sure **Hard** is selected from the **Type** list in the **Settings** area.

17. In the **Tolerance** edit box, enter **0.04 Inches** or **0.001 Meters** as the value, depending upon your display units.

18. Click the **Run Test** button; the clash test runs and comes up with no clashes.

   The reason no clashes were found is because the clashes with the point cloud cannot be considered as hard clashes. These clashes require the type to be changes to **Clearance**.

19. Click the **Select** tab.

20. From the **Type** list in the **Settings** area, select **Clearance**.

21. Click the **Run Test** button; the clash test runs and now you can see that there are clashes found. The clash results will be shown in the **Results** tab, as shown in Figure 34.

Section 10: Interrogating the Clash Results

In this section, you will interrogate the results of the clash tests performed in the previous section.

1. In the **Display Settings** area, scroll down to the **View in Context** area and click the **View** button; the camera zooms out to the Home view and zooms back into the clash.

2. From the **Results** area, click **Clash2**; the clash view is displayed in the graphics window.

3. In the **Display Settings** area, scroll down to the **View in Context** area and click the **View** button; the camera zooms out to the Home view and then zooms back to the clash view.

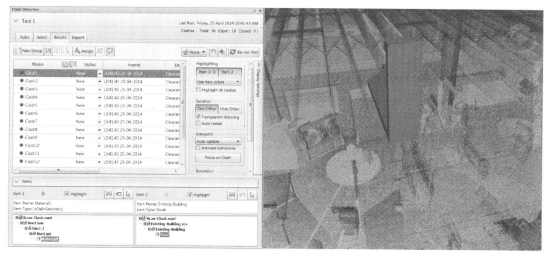

Figure 34 The **Clash Detective** *window and the graphics screen showing the clashes found*

4. From the **Results** area, click **Clash5**; the Red ductwork is displayed, but the point cloud area that is clashing is not clearly displayed. This is because the point cloud is hidden behind the ductwork.

5. Orbit the model around so you can see the highlighted Green point cloud.

 Tip: When you orbit the clash view, the new view is automatically saved as the clash view because the **Auto-update** option is selected in the **Viewpoint** area of the **Display Settings**. This is evident by a camera icon that is displayed in the **Saved Viewpoint** column in the **Results** area.

6. From the **Results** area, click **Clash6**; notice that a camera icon is displayed on the right of **Clash5**.

7. Orbit the model around so you can see the highlighted Green point cloud as well.

8. From the **Results** area, click **Clash7**; notice that a camera icon is displayed on the right of **Clash6**.

9. In the **Display Settings** area, scroll down to the **View in Context** area and click the **View** button; the camera zooms out to the Home view and then zooms back to the clash view.

10. Similarly interrogate other clash results. Orbit the model around as needed to view the clashing point cloud as well.

Section 11: Writing the Clash Test Report

In this section, you will write the reports of the clash test performed in the earlier sections.

1. In the **Clash Detective** window, click the **Report** tab.

2. From the **Contents** area, make sure all the tick boxes are selected except **Item Path**.

3. From the **Include these statuses** area, make sure all the tick boxes are selected.

4. From the **Report Type** list in the **Output Settings** area, select **Current test**.

5. From the **Report Format** list, select **HTML (Tabular)**.

6. Click the **Write Report** button; the **Save As** dialog box is displayed.

7. Browse to the **Chapter 10 > Exercise Building** folder.

8. Create a new folder and rename it as **Point Cloud Report**.

9. Double-click on the folder you just created and save the report file in this folder with the default name.

10. Using Windows Explorer, browse to the **Point Cloud Report** folder.

    Notice the **Duct V Point Cloud.html** file that was created as a report for the test. Also, notice the **Duct V Point Cloud_files** folder that contains the image files of the clash views.

11. Double-click on the **Duct V Point Cloud.html** file to open it.

12. Click on any clash image; a new window is opened and a bigger image of the clash view is displayed.

13. Close the image window and also the clash report to return to the Autodesk Navisworks window.

14. Start a new file to close the current file. You will not be able to save this file as it is write protected.

15. Restore the **Training** workspace.

Skill Evaluation

Evaluate your skills to see how many questions you can answer correctly. The answers to these questions are given at the end of the book.

1. The **Clash Detective** module is only available in Autodesk Navisworks Manage. (True/False)

2. You can only perform hard clashes using the **Clash Detective** window. (True/False)

3. Autodesk Navisworks allows you to link a timeliner simulation to the clash test. (True/False)

4. The switchback functionality only works with Autodesk software. (True/False)

5. The clash tests that are run on searched objects can be exported and then imported in other files. (True/False)

6. Which command is used in AutoCAD to get it ready for switchback?

    (A) **Navisworks**   (B) **NWLOAD**
    (C) **SwitchBack**   (D) **LOAD**

7. What needs to be done in Autodesk Inventor to get it ready for switchback?

    (A) Run a C++ File   (B) Nothing, just start it
    (C) Click on the **SwitchBack** tool   (D) Click on the **SwitchBack** menu

8. Which one of the following formats is not a valid reporting format?

    (A) Microsoft Word   (B) HTML
    (C) XML   (D) Text

9. Which one of the following Autodesk Navisworks modules is not available in Autodesk Navisworks Simulate?

    (A) **Quantification**   (B) **TimeLiner**
    (C) **Animator**   (D) **Clash Detective**

10. Which one of the following clash types is used to perform clashes with a scanned point cloud data?

    (A) **Overlapping**   (B) **Hard**
    (C) **Clearance**   (D) None

Class Test Questions

Answer the following questions:

1. Explain briefly what does the **Duplicates** clash test do.

2. How will you get Autodesk Revit ready for switchback?

3. What does **All tests (combined)** report type do?

4. When will you link the timeliner simulation with a clash test?

5. After modifying the native file to resolve the clashes, what do you need to do to reflect the changes when you return to the Autodesk Navisworks window?

Chapter 11 – Autodesk Navisworks for Autodesk Factory Design Suite

The objectives of this chapter are to:

√ Explain the working of Autodesk Navisworks to the Factory Design Suite users.
√ Familiarize you with various ways of starting Autodesk Navisworks.
√ Explain how to open an AutoCAD, AutoCAD Architecture, AutoCAD Mechanical, or Autodesk Inventor file in Autodesk Navisworks.
√ Teach you how to navigate through the scene in Autodesk Navisworks.
√ Teach you how to create viewpoints and walkthrough animations in the scene.
√ Teach you how to assign material to objects in the scene and create a high quality rendered image.
√ Teach you how to create animations of moving of objects in the scene.
√ Teach you how to create construction simulations in Autodesk Navisworks.
√ Teach you how to perform clashes between various components in Autodesk Navisworks.
√ Teach you how to use the switchback functionality to resolve the clashes between components.

AUTODESK NAVISWORKS FOR THE AUTODESK FACTORY DESIGN SUITE USERS

As mentioned in the earlier chapters of this textbook, Autodesk Navisworks is a 3D design collaboration tool that lets you import models from various design platforms to create an aggregated design for visualization and review. All the tools and modules in Autodesk Navisworks have been discussed earlier in this textbook. This chapter takes a project-based approach of using Autodesk Navisworks with various software that come within the Factory Design Suite bundle. The last section of the project, which talks about the clash detection, is only for the Factory Design Suite Ultimate users. The remaining sections are for Factory Design Suite Premium and Factory Design Suite Ultimate users.

Project	In this project, you will complete the following tasks:

In this project, you will complete the following tasks:
1. *Open a factory building model, which was created in AutoCAD Architecture.*
2. *Append the machine layout created in Autodesk Inventor to the factory building.*
3. *Create a user-defined workspace.*
4. *Use various navigation tools to navigate around the model.*
5. *Create walkthrough and viewpoint-based animations.*
6. *Use various selection resolutions to select components and create selection sets.*
7. *Control the visibility of various components.*
8. *Create search sets by selecting objects based on their properties.*
9. *Add redline markups to the objects in the scene.*
10. *Measure distances between various objects in the scene.*
11. *View properties of various objects in the scene.*
12. *Assign materials to various objects in the scene.*
13. *Create animations of moving forklifts in the factory.*
14. *Create the simulation of the factory construction.*
15. *Perform clashes between various components in the factory.*
16. *Use the switchback functionality to resolve clashes.*

Section 1: Starting Autodesk Navisworks and Opening the Factory Building

In this section, you will start Autodesk Navisworks using the Factory Design Suite dashboard and then open an AutoCAD Architecture file of the factory building.

1. From the desktop of your computer, double-click on the icon of the **Autodesk Factory Design Suite 2016** dashboard; the dashboard is displayed.

You will use the **Workflows** tab of the dashboard to start Autodesk Navisworks. This tab allows you to start a software based on your workflow requirements. Autodesk Navisworks is listed as **Engineering Review** in this tab.

2. From the **Workflows** tab, click on **Engineering Review**; the **Select File** dialog box is displayed using which you can select one or more files to open.

3. Browse to the **Chapter 11 > FDS Project** folder and double-click on the **Factory Building.dwg** file; the file opens in Autodesk Navisworks.

 Note: *If you see the factory building as wireframe, press F12 to display the **Options Editor**. Next, expand **File Readers** from the left pane and click **DWG/DXF**. In the right pane, change the **DWG Loader Version** to **2013**. Now, close Autodesk Navisworks, browse to the **Chapter 11 > FDS Project** folder and delete the .NWC file. Next, start again from step 1.*

4. Move the cursor over the ViewCube displayed on the top right corner of the graphics window and click on the Home icon; the current view is changed to the Home view.

    When running Autodesk Navisworks from Factory Design Suite, by default the display of factory floor is turned on in Autodesk Navisworks. You will now turn off the factory floor.

5. Press the F12 key to display the **Options Editor** dialog box.

6. From the left pane, expand **Factory Layout** and then click on **Grid Floor**; the floor and grid settings are displayed in the right pane.

7. Clear the **Visible** tick boxes in the **Floor Settings** and **Grid Settings** areas.

8. Click **OK** in the dialog box; the floor and grid are turned off in the graphics window.

9. From the **Viewpoint** ribbon tab > **Render Style** ribbon panel > **Mode** flyout, click **Shaded**.

10. On the same ribbon panel, from the **Lighting** flyout, click **Full Lights**.

11. Right-click in the blank area of the graphics window and select **Background** from the shortcut menu; the **Background Settings** dialog box is displayed.

12. From the **Mode** list, select **Horizon**.

13. Click **OK** in the dialog box. Figure 1 shows the factory building.

Section 2: Appending the Autodesk Inventor Machine Layout

In this section, you will append the Autodesk Inventor machine layout that was created as part of the Factory Design Suite workflow.

1. From the **Home** ribbon tab > **Project** ribbon panel, click **Append**; the **Append** dialog box is displayed.

2. From the **Files of type** list in the dialog box, select **Inventor (*.ipt,*.iam,*.ipj)**.

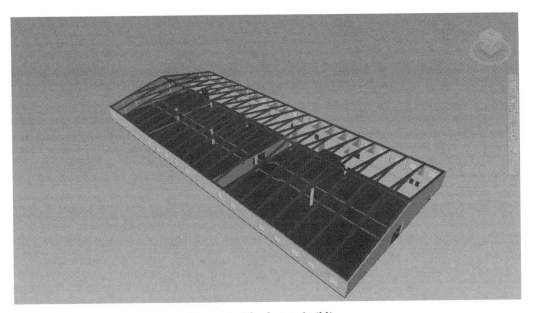

Figure 1 *The factory building*

3. Browse to the **FDS Project > Workspace** folder and double-click on **Factory_Layout.iam** file; the file starts to load in Autodesk Navisworks. If the **Resolve** dialog box is displayed, click **Ignore All** in the dialog box.

    Figure 2 shows the Autodesk Navisworks scene of a factory with the building created in AutoCAD Architecture and the machine layout created in Autodesk Inventor.

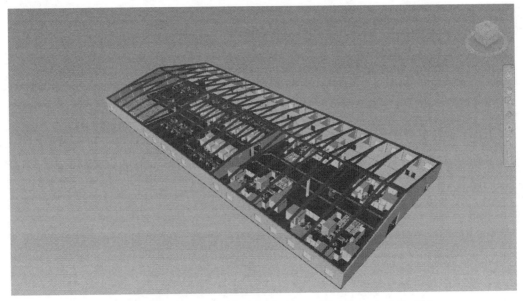

Figure 2 *The factory building with the machine layout appended*

Note: *Depending on the size and content of the native file you are opening in Autodesk Navisworks, it may take a few minutes to open it. However, once the file is opened, Autodesk Navisworks creates a cache file for the native file with .NWC extension. While opening the same native file in Autodesk Navisworks the next time, this cache file will be used to reduce the opening time, if the native file has not changed. If the native file is changed, the .NWC file will be updated for future use.*

Section 3: Creating a User-Defined Workspace

You will now create a user-defined workspace so that all the windows that you regularly need while working with Autodesk Navisworks are available on the screen.

1. From the **View** ribbon tab > **Workspace** ribbon panel > **Load Workspace** flyout, click **Navisworks Extended**; the Autodesk Navisworks session resets to display various windows on the screen.

2. From the left of the graphics window, close the **Plan View** window by clicking on the **Close** button on the top right of this window.

3. Similarly close the **Section View** window.

4. From the right of the graphics window, close the **Tilt Bar**.

5. From the **View** ribbon tab > **Workspace** ribbon panel, click **Save Workspace**.

   By default, the workspaces are saved in the roaming profile of the current user of your computer. The workspaces saved in this folder are automatically displayed under the **Load Workspace** flyout.

6. Type the name of the current workspace as **Factory Workspace** and then click **Save** in the dialog box; the current workspace is saved.

7. From the **Workspace** ribbon panel, click on the **Load Workspace** flyout and notice the workspace you created is listed there, as shown in Figure 3.

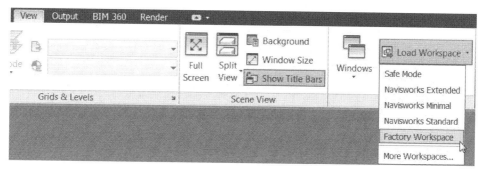

Figure 3 *The newly created listed in the **Load Workspace** flyout*

Section 4: Navigating Through the Model and Saving Viewpoints

In this section, you will use various navigation tools to navigate through the model in the graphics window. You will also save various viewpoints so that you can view the factory from various camera locations.

1. Change the current view to the Home view, if it is not already set.

2. From the navigation bar on the right of the graphics window, click the **Zoom Window** flyout and then click **Zoom All**.

 *Tip: The Page Up key on the keyboard is the shortcut key for the **Zoom All** tool.*

3. In the **Saved Viewpoints** window on the right of the graphics window, right-click and select **Save Viewpoint** from the shortcut menu.

4. Rename the new viewpoint to **Overview 1**.

5. Click the top right corner of the ViewCube to display the factory model from that direction, as shown in Figure 4.

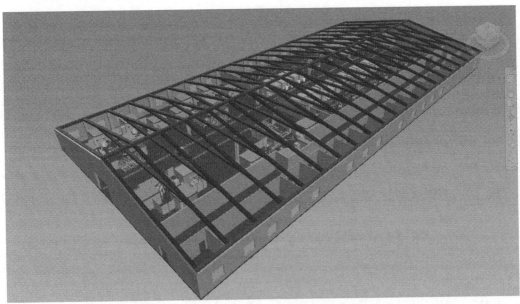

*Figure 4 The Autodesk Navisworks scene for the **Overview 2** viewpoint*

6. Right-click and select **Save Viewpoint** from the shortcut menu.

7. Rename the current viewpoint to **Overview 2**.

8. Similarly, create **Overview 3** and **Overview 4** viewpoints looking at the factory model from the remaining two corners of the ViewCube.

9. Activate the **Overview 1** viewpoint by clicking on it in the **Saved Viewpoints** window.

10. Move the cursor at the center of the graphics window.

11. Press and hold down the SHIFT key and the wheel mouse button and drag the mouse; the model orbits around the default pivot point in the graphics window.

12. Change the current view to Home view.

13. Move the cursor over the top left corner of the factory building and scroll the wheel mouse button once; the pivot point is moved to that corner of the building.

14. Move the cursor at the center of the graphics window and orbit the model using the SHIFT key and the wheel mouse button; the model orbits around the new pivot point at the corner of the factory building.

15. Click on the **Right** face of the ViewCube; the model looks similar to the one shown in Figure 5.

Figure 5 *Viewing the factory from the right view*

16. From the **Navigation Bar** on the right of the graphics window, click the **Walk** tool; the cursor changes to the human feet cursor.

    Before you start walking in the scene, you will pan the left entrance of the factory to the center of the graphics window. This can be done by pressing and holding down the wheel mouse button and dragging the cursor.

17. Press and hold down the wheel button and drag the cursor to the left to pan the view. Stop when the left entrance of the building is at the center of the graphics window.

18. Move the cursor at the center of the left entrance of the building. Now, press and hold down the left mouse button and drag it forward; you will start walking towards the building entrance.

19. Once you are close to the building entrance, press and hold down the wheel mouse button and pan the view vertically and horizontally so that the view is in line with the entrance of the building, refer to Figure 6.

    Depending upon the navigation procedure, sometimes the view that you see in the graphics window is not aligned correctly. Autodesk Navisworks allows you to align the view using the **Align Camera** flyout on the **Viewpoint** ribbon tab > **Camera** ribbon panel.

20. From the **Viewpoint** ribbon tab > **Camera** ribbon panel > **Align Camera** flyout, click **Straighten**; the view looks similar to the one shown in Figure 6.

Figure 6 The view showing the entrance of the building

21. Right-click in the **Saved Viewpoints** window and select **Save Viewpoint** from the shortcut menu.

22. Rename the viewpoint to **Factory Entrance**.

    With the **Walk** tool still active, you will now start walking into the factory.

23. Press and hold down the left mouse button and drag it up to start walking inside the factory.

24. Drag the cursor to the left and stop when the view is just behind the first forklift, as shown in Figure 7.

Figure 7 *The view inside the factory*

25. Right-click in the **Saved Viewpoints** window and select **Save Viewpoint** from the shortcut menu.

26. Rename the viewpoint to **Shopfloor 1**.

27. Press and hold down the left mouse button and drag it up; you will start moving forward.

 *Tip: While walking using the **Walk** tool, you can drag the mouse left or right to walk in that direction. You can also press and hold down the wheel mouse button to pan the view and line it up with the objects in the scene.*

28. Stop when you are just past the wall that divides the factory, as shown in Figure 8.

29. Right-click in the **Saved Viewpoints** window and select **Save Viewpoint** from the shortcut menu. Rename the viewpoint to **Shopfloor 2**.

30. Press and hold down the left mouse button and walk forward.

31. Stop before the second forklift, as shown in Figure 9.

32. Save this view as a viewpoint with the name **Factory Exit**.

33. From the **Saved Viewpoints** window, click on the **Overview 1** viewpoint to activate it.

34. Similarly, click on the other viewpoints in the **Saved Viewpoints** window to view the factory model from these viewpoints.

Figure 8 *The view inside the shopfloor 2*

Figure 9 *The* ***Factory Exit*** *viewpoint*

Section 5: Setting the Display Units

In the coming sections of this project, you will enter various numeric values in the scene. Therefore, it is important for you to specify the correct display units for the scene. This is done using the **Options Editor** dialog box.

1. Press the F12 key to display the **Options Editor** dialog box.

2. From the left pane, expand **Interface** and select **Display Units**; the display units are displayed in the right pane.

3. In the right pane, select the desired display units from the **Linear Units** list. In this project, it is assumed that the display units are either Meters or Inches.

4. Click **OK** in the dialog box.

Section 6: Recording Walkthrough Animation

In this section, you will walk inside the factory. You will also turn on the realism, such as third person and gravity. You will record this walk as an animation so that it can be played again.

1. Activate the **Factory Entrance** viewpoint.

    Before you start walking, you will make a copy of this viewpoint and edit it to turn on the visibility of the avatar.

2. In the **Saved Viewpoints** window, right-click on the **Factory Entrance** viewpoint and select **Add Copy** from the shortcut menu; a new copy of the selected viewpoint is displayed.

3. Drag the new viewpoint to the bottom of the viewpoint list. Next, right-click on it and select **Rename** from the shortcut menu.

4. Change the name of the viewpoint to **Walk Start**.

    You will now edit this viewpoint.

5. Right-click on the **Walk Start** viewpoint and select **Edit** from the shortcut menu; the **Edit Viewpoint - Walk Start** dialog box is displayed.

6. From the **Collision** area at the bottom right, click **Settings**; the **Collision** dialog box is displayed.

7. From the **Third Person** area, select the **Enable** tick box.

8. From the **Avatar** list, select **High Visibility**.

9. Enter the following values for the rest of the options:

    Radius: 11 Inches or 0.3 Meters

    Height: 72 Inches or 1.9 Meters

    Distance: 170 Inches or 4 Meters

10. Click **OK** to exit the **Collision** dialog box and then click **OK** to exit the **Edit Viewpoint - Walk Start** dialog box.

11. If the avatar appears crouching, press and hold down the left mouse button and walk forward.

12. Once the avatar is inside the factory building, click the **Walk** flyout > **Gravity** from the **Navigation Bar** on the right of the graphics window; the gravity is turned on.

13. Press and hold down the left mouse button and walk forward; the avatar comes down to the factory floor level, if it was floating in the air, refer to Figure 10.

 Note: *If the avatar turns red, this means that it is interfering with the factory floor. In this case, press and hold down the wheel mouse button and drag it up.*

14. Right-click on the **Walk Start** viewpoint and select **Update** from the shortcut menu; the viewpoint updates to the current view with the avatar visibility and gravity turned on. Figure 10 shows this viewpoint.

*Figure 10 The **Walk Start** viewpoint showing the avatar on the factory floor*

You will now start walking and recording the walk. This is done using the **Record** tool on the **Animate** ribbon tab > **Create** ribbon panel. You need to remember that if you do not do anything on the screen after clicking the **Record** tool, it will also be recorded in the animation as stationary frames. So it is important that you are ready to start recording the walk before you invoke this tool.

In this walkthrough, you will walk from the current viewpoint all the way to the exit of the factory building at the far end of the building. You can also drag the walk tool to the left or right while walking to view various machines during the walk.

15. From the **Animation** ribbon tab > **Create** ribbon panel, click **Record**; the animation recording starts.

16. Press and hold down the left mouse button and drag it forward to start walking. Go around the first forklift. View the machines on the left and right. Continue walking to the exit of the factory.

17. Stop walking once you go past the second forklift and then click the **Record** button again to stop recording; an animation is added to the **Saved Viewpoints** window.

18. Rename the animation to **Walkthrough**.

    Next, you will edit the duration of this walk.

19. In the **Saved Viewpoints** window, right-click on the **Walkthrough** animation and select **Edit** from the shortcut menu; the **Edit Animation: Walkthrough** dialog box is displayed.

20. Enter **40** as the value in the **Duration** edit box and press **OK** in the dialog box.

    You will now play this animation in the full screen display mode. The full screen display can be turned on and off using the F11 key.

21. From the **Animation** ribbon tab > **Playback** ribbon panel, click the **Play** button and then press the F11 key; the display is set to full screen and the animation starts playing in the full screen mode.

22. Once the animation stops playing, press the F11 key to turn off the full screen display.

23. From the **Animation** ribbon tab > **Playback** ribbon panel, click the **Stop** button to stop the animation.

Section 7: Creating an Animation Based on Saved Viewpoints

In this section, you will create an animation based on saved viewpoints. For this, you will first create a copy of the existing viewpoints.

1. From the **Saved Viewpoints** window, select the **Overview 1** viewpoint.

2. Hold down the SHIFT key and select the **Factory Exit** viewpoint; a total of eight viewpoints are selected. Note that you will not select the **Walk Start** viewpoint.

3. Right-click on one of the selected viewpoints in the **Saved Viewpoint** window and select **Add Copy** from the shortcut menu; copies of all the eight selected viewpoints are added to the **Saved Viewpoints** window with a suffix **(1)**.

4. Rename the **Overview 1 (1)** viewpoint to **1**.

5. Rename the **Overview 2 (1)** viewpoint to **2**.

6. Rename the **Overview 3 (1)** viewpoint to **3**.

7. Rename the **Overview 4 (1)** viewpoint to **4**.

8. Rename the **Factory Entrance (1)** viewpoint to **5**.

9. Rename the **Shopfloor 1 (1)** viewpoint to **6**.

10. Rename the **Shopfloor 2 (1)** viewpoint to **7**.

11. Rename the **Factory Exit (1)** viewpoint to **8**.

12. Right-click in the blank area of the **Saved Viewpoints** window and select **Add Animation** from the shortcut menu; a blank animation is added.

13. Rename the animation to **Viewpoint Based**.

14. In the **Saved Viewpoints** window, select viewpoints **1** to **8**.

15. Press and hold down the left mouse button on the icon of one of the selected viewpoints and drop them on the **Viewpoint Based** animation; the viewpoints are now listed inside the animation.

    Next, you will edit the duration of this animation.

16. Right-click on the **Viewpoint Based** animation and select **Edit** from the shortcut menu; the **Edit Animation: Viewpoint Based** dialog box is displayed.

17. Enter **90** as the value in the **Duration** edit box and then click **OK** in the dialog box.

    Next, you will play this animation in the full screen mode.

18. With the **Viewpoint Based** animation still selected, click the **Play** button from the **Animation** ribbon tab > **Playback** ribbon panel and then press the F11 key; the animation plays in the full screen mode.

19. Once the animation stops playing, press the F11 key to turn off the full screen display.

20. From the **Animation** ribbon tab > **Playback** ribbon panel, click the **Stop** button to stop the animation.

    Notice how the animation goes from the **4** viewpoint to the **5** viewpoint cutting through the roof structure of the factory. To avoid this, you will now create another copy of the **1** viewpoint and add it between viewpoints **4** and **5**.

21. In the expanded **Viewpoint Based** animation, right-click on the **1** viewpoint and select **Add Copy** from the shortcut menu; a new copy of the selected viewpoint is added inside the animation.

22. Press and hold down the left mouse button on the icon of the new viewpoint. Now, drag and drop this viewpoint between viewpoints **4** and **5** in the animation.

You will now edit the viewpoints to reduce the speed of the animation inside the factory.

23. In **Viewpoint Based** animation, right-click on the **5** viewpoint and select **Edit** from the shortcut menu; the **Edit Viewpoint - 5** dialog box is displayed.

24. If you are using Inches as the units, enter **140** as the value in the **Linear Speed** edit box. If you are using Meters as the units, enter **3.5** as the value in the **Linear Speed** edit box.

25. Repeat step 24 for viewpoints **6**, **7**, and **8**.

Next, you need to edit the duration of the animation.

26. In the **Saved Viewpoints** window, right-click on the **Viewpoint Based** animation and select **Edit** from the shortcut menu; the **Edit Animation: Viewpoint Based** dialog box is displayed.

27. Enter **110** as the value in the **Duration** edit box and then click **OK** in the dialog box.

 Note: On changing the overall duration of the animation, the linear speed of the viewpoints is also changed. In this case, the difference is not much and so you will accept whatever the changed values are.

28. Select the **Viewpoint Based** animation.

29. Click the **Play** button from the **Animation** ribbon tab > **Playback** ribbon panel and then press the F11 key; the animation plays in the full screen display.

30. Once the animation stops playing, press the F11 key to turn off the full screen display.

31. Click the **Stop** button from the **Animation** ribbon tab > **Playback** ribbon panel to stop the animation.

Section 8: Saving the File

In this section, you will save the file in the .NWF format. This format has links maintained to the native CAD files. As a result, if anything changes in the native file, you can simply refresh the Autodesk Navisworks scene to reflect the changes.

1. Activate the **Overview 1** viewpoint.

2. From the **Quick Access Toolbar**, click the **Save** button; the **Save As** dialog box is displayed with the **Save as type** list showing **Navisworks File Set (*.nwf)** as the format.

3. Browse to the **Chapter 11 > FDS Project** folder and save the file with the name **Factory.nwf**.

Section 9: Using Various Selection Resolutions to Create Selection Sets

Selecting objects is a task performed frequently in Autodesk Navisworks. However, selecting multiple objects becomes a tedious job, especially if you have to regularly select a large number of objects. To simplify the process, Autodesk Navisworks lets you group the objects that you regularly select in a set so that next time when you need to select the same objects, you can simply click on the set. In this section, you will use various selection resolutions to create selection sets.

1. Click the **Sets** window from the left of the **Selection Tree** and dock it below the **Selection Tree** using the **Auto Hide** button on the top right of this window.

2. From the **Home** ribbon tab, expand the **Select & Search** ribbon panel and dock it on the screen using the push pin icon on the lower left corner of this ribbon panel.

3. From the **Selection Resolution** list in the expanded **Select & Search** ribbon panel, select **Layer**.

   This sets the selection resolution to layer. As a result, when you select any object in the graphics window, the entire layer of that object is selected.

4. From the graphics window, click on one of the beams on the roof structure of the building; the **8S-Beam** layer is selected in the **Selection Tree**, as shown in Figure 11.

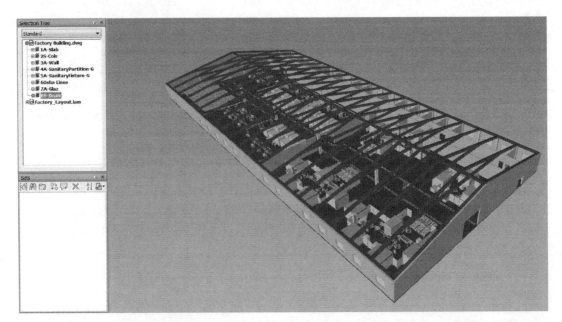

Figure 11 The 8S-Beam layer selected on selecting a beam member from the graphics window

5. From the **Home** ribbon tab > **Visibility** ribbon panel, click the **Hide Unselected** button; all the objects, other than the beams, are hidden.

6. Click on the **Hide Unselected** button again to restore the visibility of all the objects.

7. On the same ribbon panel, click the **Hide** button; the objects on the **S-Beam** layer are hidden.

8. Click on the **Hide** button again to restore the visibility of the beam members.

9. From the toolbar at the top in the **Sets** window, click the **Save Selection** button; a new selection set is added.

10. Rename the set to **Beams**.

11. With all the beam members still selected, click the **Hide** button from the **Visibility** ribbon panel; all the beam members are hidden again.

12. Press ESC to deselect the hidden beam members.

13. Save this view as a viewpoint with the name **Overview-No Beams**.

14. Drag and drop this viewpoint at the top in the **Saved Viewpoints** window.

    Next, you need to edit this viewpoint to ensure that the beam objects are turned off every time you activate this viewpoint.

15. Right-click on the **Overview-No Beams** viewpoint and select **Edit** from the shortcut menu.

16. In the dialog box, select **Hide/Required** from the **Saved Attributes** area.

17. Activate the **Overview 1** viewpoint; the beam members remain turned off. This is because these viewpoints were not saved with the hide/required option turned on. You need to turn this option on now.

18. From the **Home** ribbon tab > **Visibility** ribbon panel, click **Unhide All**; the beams are turned on.

19. Hold down the SHIFT key and select the **Walk Start** viewpoint. Make sure a total of 9 viewpoints are selected.

20. Right-click on one of the selected viewpoints and turn on the **Hide/Required** option from the **Saved Attributes** area of the dialog box. You may need to click on this tick box a couple of times to ensure that the tick box is displayed.

21. Activate the **Overview 1** viewpoint. Because you changed the hide/required option of the viewpoints, the visibility of all objects is turned on in this viewpoint.

22. From the expanded **Select & Search** ribbon panel, expand the **Selection Resolution** list and select **First Object**.

23. From the graphics window, select one of the windows; the **Factory Building.dwg** > **7A-Glaz** layer is expanded and one of the windows in this layer is highlighted in the **Selection Tree**.

24. From the **Select & Search** ribbon panel, click the **Select Same** flyout > **Select Same Window Style**; all the windows in the factory building are selected.

25. From the toolbar at the top in the **Sets** window, click the **Save Selection** button; a new selection set is added.

26. Rename the set to **Windows**.

27. Press the ESC key to deselect all the windows.

28. From the graphics window, select one of the walls of the factory.

29. From the **Select & Search** ribbon panel, click the **Select Same** flyout > **Same Type**; all the walls of the factory building are selected for various layers.

30. From the toolbar at the top in the **Sets** window, click the **Save Selection** button; a new selection set is added.

31. Rename the set to **Walls**.

32. With the **Walls** selection set still selected, hold down the CTRL key and select the **Windows** and **Beams** sets also from the **Sets** window.

33. From the **Home** ribbon tab > **Visibility** ribbon panel, click **Hide**.

34. If an error dialog box appears, click **OK**; all the objects on the selected sets are hidden, as shown in Figure 12.

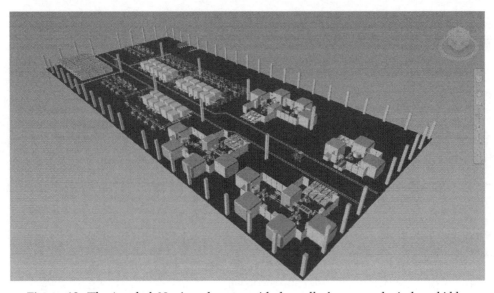

Figure 12 *The Autodesk Navisworks scene with the walls, beams, and windows hidden*

35. Press the ESC key to deselect all the hidden objects.

36. Save this view as a viewpoint with the name **Overview-No Walls** and turn on the **Hide/ Required** option for this viewpoint.

37. Drag and drop this viewpoint at the top in the **Saved Viewpoints** window.

38. Activate the **Overview 1** viewpoint; all the objects are turned on.

39. Click the **Save** button on the **Quick Access Toolbar** to save the current file.

40. Undock the **Select & Search** ribbon panel.

Section 10: Searching Objects Based on their Properties and Creating Search Sets

Search set is a very handy tool that lets you search and select object based on their properties and then save them as a set for future selection. The objects are searched using the **Find Items** window. Therefore, you need to first dock this window below the graphics window.

1. Click **Find Items** near the bottom left corner of the Autodesk Navisworks window to display the **Find Items** window.

2. Dock the **Find Items** window below the graphics window.

3. Click in the first row under the **Category** column in the right pane of the **Find Items** window,

4. From the list, select **Item**.

5. From the list under the **Property** column, select **Name**.

6. From the list under the **Condition** column, select **Contains**.

7. In the **Value** columns, type **CNC**.

8. Click the **Find All** button near the lower left corner of the **Find Items** window; all the machines that have CNC in their names are selected.

9. From the toolbar at the top in the **Sets** window, click the **Save Search** button; a new search set is added.

10. Rename the set to **CNC Machines**.

11. Press ESC to deselect everything.

12. With the search row still displayed in the **Find Items** window, click on **CNC** under the **Value** columns; the field turns blank.

13. Enter **Cylinder Head** as the value and then click the **Find All** button; all the machines with Cylinder Head in their names are selected.

14. From the toolbar at the top in the **Sets** window, click the **Save Search** button; a new search set is added.

15. Rename the set to **Cylinder Head Lines**.

16. Press ESC to deselect everything.

17. With the search row still displayed in the **Find Items** window, click on **Cylinder Head** under the **Value** columns and type **Rack**.

18. Click the **Find All** button; all the racks are selected.

19. From the toolbar at the top in the **Sets** window, click the **Save Search** button; a new search set is added.

20. Rename the set to **Racks**.

21. Press ESC to deselect everything.

22. Undock the **Find Items** window.

23. Save the file.

Section 11: Adding Redline Markups in the Scene

The **Review** ribbon tab provides you a number of tools to add redline markups to the objects in the scene. However, if you use the **Text** tool in the **Redline** ribbon panel to add redline text, you will not be able to search for that text. As a result, it is recommended to use tags to add redline markups. The text added to the tags can be searched in the scene. In this section, you will first add a redline text and then add tags to various other objects in the scene.

1. Activate the **Factory Entrance** viewpoint.

   This viewpoint has the **Walk** tool active.

2. Press and hold down the left mouse button and walk back to a view similar to the one shown in Figure 13.

   The redline markup tools automatically create viewpoints after you finish working with them. Therefore, you do not need a viewpoint to be created first.

3. From the **Review** ribbon tab > **Redline** ribbon panel > **Draw** flyout, click the **Cloud** tool.

4. Click the first point of the cloud near the top left corner of the factory entrance.

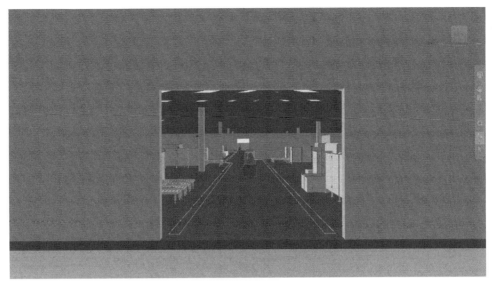

Figure 13 *View for the redline markup*

The cloud is created by specifying the points in the clockwise direction. You can right-click to close the cloud.

5. Start clicking the points in the clockwise direction to create a cloud. Once you come close to the start point of the cloud, right-click to close the cloud, refer to Figure 14; a new viewpoint is automatically created and saved with the name **View**.

6. Rename the viewpoint to **Redline**.

7. From the **Review** ribbon tab > **Redline** ribbon panel, click the **Text** tool.

8. Click anywhere on the left of the cloud to specify the start point of the text.

9. Enter the following text in the dialog box:

   Forceshield Security Shutter.

10. Click **OK** in the dialog box; the redline text is added, as shown in Figure 14.

11. From the **Review** ribbon tab > **Redline** ribbon panel > **Draw** flyout, click the **Arrow** tool.

12. Draw a redline arrow the middle right justification of the redline text to anywhere on the cloud, as shown in Figure 14.

   As mentioned earlier, the drawback of adding a redline text is that you cannot search for this text. Therefore, it is recommended that you add tags in the scene. The tags will also automatically create viewpoints, if they do not exist. The main advantage of adding tags is that the text written as a part of adding a tag can be searched.

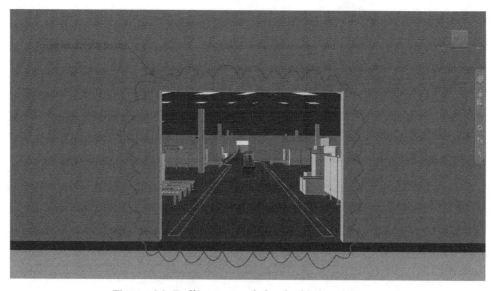

Figure 14 Redline text and cloud added to the scene

13. Activate the **Factory Exit** viewpoint.

14. Using the **Walk** tool, walk past the forklift.

15. From the **Review** ribbon tab > **Tags** ribbon panel, click **Add Tag**; the cursor changes to the pencil cursor.

16. Click anywhere inside the factory exit and then click on the right wall to add a tag, refer to Figure 15; the first tag is added and the **Add Comment** dialog box is displayed. Also, a new viewpoint is added with the name **Tag View 1**.

    In the **Add Comment** dialog box, the first line is generally the header of the comment. The rest of the description is added from the second line onwards.

17. Type **Forceshield Security Shutter** as the first line of text in the **Add Comment** dialog box.

18. Press and hold down the CTRL key and press ENTER; the cursor goes in the second line. Enter the following text in the second line in the **Add Comment** dialog box:

    3.5mm thick high grade aluminium tracks. High security glass nylon reinforced riveted wind lock clips.

19. Click **OK** in the dialog box.

20. Click **Comments** near the bottom left corner of the Autodesk Navisworks window to display the **Comments** window.

21. Dock the **Comments** window below the graphics window. Figure 15 shows the Autodesk Navisworks screen with the tag added in the graphics window and the **Comments** window showing the related comment.

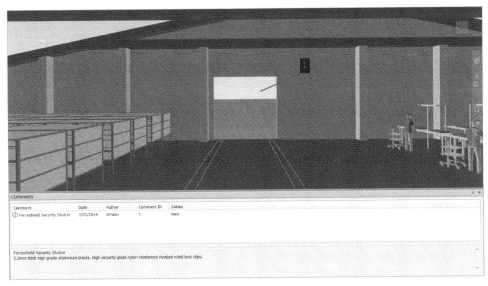

*Figure 15 The view showing the tag and the related comment in the **Comments** window*

22. Activate the **Overview 1** viewpoint; the **Comments** window turns blank as there is no comment added to this viewpoint.

23. From the **Review** ribbon tab > **Comments** ribbon panel, click **Find Comments**; the **Find Comments** dialog box is displayed.

    You will now use this dialog box to find the comments you added earlier. If you know the text you need to search, you can enter it in the **Text** edit box of the dialog box. Alternatively, you can leave everything blank and click the **Find** button. This will search for every comment in the current scene.

24. With nothing specified in the dialog box, click the **Find** button; the comment you added earlier is listed in the lower half of the dialog box.

25. Click on the name of the comment in the lower half of the **Find Comments** dialog box; the **Tag View 1** viewpoint is activated and the comment is displayed in the **Comments** window.

26. Close the **Find Comments** dialog box and undock the **Comments** window.

27. Save the file.

 Note: *To find how to add comments to various other objects in the scene, refer to Chapter 4 of this textbook.*

Section 12: Measuring Distances of the Objects in the Scene

In this section, you will measure distances between various objects in the scene. The tools to perform various measurements in the scene are available on the **Review** ribbon tab > **Measure** ribbon panel. The measured values are displayed in the **Measure Tools** window and also on the graphics window. For this reason, it is recommended that you dock the **Measure Tools** window on the left of the graphics window.

1. Click **Measure Tools** from the left of the left of the graphics window to display the **Measure Tools** window. Dock this window on the left.

2. Hide the **Selection Tree** and the **Sets** window.

   Before you start measuring objects in the scene, it is important to make sure the snapping is turned on in global options.

3. Click the **Options** button from the **Measure Tools** window; the **Options Editor** dialog box is displayed.

4. From the left pane, click **Snapping**; the snap options are displayed in the right pane.

5. Make sure the **Snap to Vertex**, **Snap to Edge**, and **Snap to Line Vertex** tick boxes are selected.

6. Close the dialog box by clicking the **OK** button.

   The **Tag View 1** viewpoint is still active from the previous section. You will measure objects in this viewpoint.

7. From the **Review** ribbon tab > **Measure** ribbon panel > **Measure** flyout, select the **Point to Multiple Points** tool.

   This tool allows you to measure the distance of one point to multiple points. You will use this tool to measure the width and height of the factory exit door.

8. Move the cursor over the top left corner of the factory exit door.

9. When a cross is displayed, click to specify the first point of the measurement; its coordinates are displayed in the **Measure Tools** window.

10. Move the cursor over the top right corner of the factory exit door.

11. When a cross is displayed, click to specify the second point of the measurement; the measurement of the width of the door is displayed in the graphics window and the **Measure Tools** window.

12. Move the cursor over the bottom left corner of the factory exit door.

13. When a cross is displayed, click to specify the second point of the measurement; the measurement of the height of the exit door is displayed in the graphics window and the **Measure Tools** window.

14. Right-click anywhere in the graphics window to clear the measurements.

15. Click the **Select** tool from the **Quick Access Toolbar** to exit the measurement cursor.

    Next, you will measure the shortest distance between the two columns in the current view. You will first make sure that the selection resolution is set to **Last Object**. This can be done using the **Select & Search** ribbon panel, as shown earlier. You can also right-click on any object in the **Selection Tree** to change the selection resolution.

16. Hover the cursor over the hidden **Selection Tree**; it slides out. Right-click on one of the files listed and select **Set Selection Resolution To Last Object** from the shortcut menu.

17. Move the cursor in the graphics window to hide the **Selection Tree**.

18. From the graphics window, click on the column on the left of the exit door.

19. Next, hold down the CTRL key and click on the column on the right of the exit door.

20. From the **Measure** ribbon panel, click the **Shortest Distance** button; the view is zoomed closer to the two columns and the shortest distance between the two is displayed in the graphics window and in the **Measure Tools** window.

    Right-clicking clears all the measured values except for the shortest distance value. To clear this value, you will have to use the **Clear** tool from the **Measure Tools** window.

21. Click the **Clear** button from the **Measure** ribbon panel; the measurement value is cleared from the graphics window.

22. Activate the **Overview 1** viewpoint.

23. From the **View** ribbon tab > **Workspace** ribbon panel > **Load Workspace** flyout, activate the **Factory Workspace** that you created in Section 3 of this project.

24. Save the file.

 Note: *To learn more about the other measurement tools, refer to Chapter 3 of this textbook.*

Section 13: Viewing Properties of Various Objects in the Scene

In this section, you will view the properties of various objects in the scene. These are the properties that were assigned to the objects in the native CAD software. You will also learn to turn on the visibility of the quick properties. This allows you to hover the cursor over the objects and view some of their properties.

1. Dock the **Sets** window and click on the **Beams** selection set in this window; the **8S-Beam** layer is highlighted in the **Selection Tree** and the **Properties** window on the right side of the graphics window shows the properties of this layer.

2. In the **Selection Tree**, expand the **8S-Beam** layer and select any structural member; the **Properties** window shows the properties of the selected beam member, as shown in Figure 16.

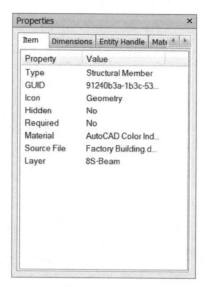

*Figure 16 The **Properties** window showing the properties of the structural beam*

3. Scroll through various tabs of the **Properties** window to look at various properties of the selected beam member.

4. In the **Sets** window, click on the **Windows** selection set; the **Properties** window shows 27 items selected.

5. From the **Selection Tree**, select one of the highlighted windows; the **Properties** window now shows the properties of the selected window.

   Next, you will turn on the visibility of **Quick Properties** that allows you to view some of the properties of the objects when you hover the cursor over it in the graphics window.

6. From the **Home** ribbon tab > **Display** ribbon panel, click **Quick Properties** to turn this option on.

7. Activate the **Walk Start** viewpoint; the avatar is displayed and the cursor changes to the **Walk** cursor.

8. Start walking in the factory and then move the cursor over any object in the scene; the **Last Object** selection resolution is used to display the item name and item type properties of the object.

9. Right-click on any object in the **Selection Tree** and select **Set Selection Resolution To First Object** from the shortcut menu.

10. Now, move the cursor over the same object and notice that the item name and item type properties are displayed based on the **First Object** selection resolution.

11. Continue walking in the factory and hover the cursor over various objects to view their item name and item type properties.

12. From the **Home** ribbon tab > **Display** ribbon panel, turn off the **Quick Properties**.

13. Activate the **Factory Entrance** viewpoint.

14. Save the file.

 Note: *To know more about the quick properties and also to find how to change the properties that are displayed in the graphics window, refer to Chapter 2 of this textbook.*

Section 14: Using the Autodesk Rendering Module to Assign Materials to Various Objects in the Scene

Autodesk Navisworks allows you to create photorealistic views of the factory by assigning materials to the various components in the scene. This can be done using the **Autodesk Rendering** module.

1. From the **Render** ribbon tab > **System** ribbon panel, click **Autodesk Rendering**; the **Autodesk Rendering** window is displayed.

2. Dock this window on the left of the graphics window, if not already docked.

3. From the **Sets** window, select the **Walls** selection set.

4. From the bottom left pane of the **Materials** tab of the **Autodesk Rendering** window, expand **Autodesk Library > Masonry** and click **Brick**; all the standard brick materials are displayed in the right pane.

5. From the right pane, right-click on the **Adobe - Beige** material and select **Assign to Selection**; the material is applied to all the walls.

6. Press ESC to deselect everything. Figure 17 shows the **Factory Entrance** viewpoint with the brick material assigned to the walls.

Next, you will assign a wood material to the beams in the scene.

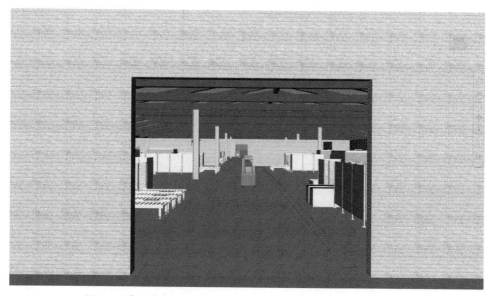

Figure 17 *The view showing the material assigned to the walls*

7. From the left pane, click **Wood**; all the wood materials are displayed in the right pane.

8. From the **Sets** window, select the **Beams** selection set.

9. In the right pane, scroll down to **Red Oak - Natural No Gloss**.

10. Right-click on this material and select **Assign to Selection**; the wood material is applied to all the beams.

    Next, you will apply glass material to all the windows.

11. Activate the **Overview 1** viewpoint.

    This viewpoint is saved with the shade mode set to **Shaded**. Therefore, you will not see the materials you assigned to the objects in this viewpoint. To view the materials, you first need to change this mode to **Full Render**.

12. From the **Viewpoint** ribbon tab > **Render Style** ribbon panel > **Mode** flyout, select **Full Render**; the materials assigned to the objects are now visible.

13. In the **Saved Viewpoints** window, right-click on the **Overview 1** viewpoint and click **Update**; the viewpoint is updated to display the full rendered material.

    Next, you will assign material to the window glass panes. For this, you first need to create a selection set of only glass panels. The **Windows** selection set that you created also includes window frames. So you cannot use that selection set.

14. Right-click on any object in the **Selection Tree** and select **Set Selection Resolution To Geometry** from the shortcut menu.

15. From the graphics window, select any window glass panel; the second **Subentity** inside **Window** is highlighted in the **Selection Tree**.

16. From the **Home** ribbon tab > **Select & Search** ribbon panel > **Select Same** flyout, click **Select Same Material**; all the window panels are selected.

17. Save this selection as a set in the **Sets** window with the name **Window Panels**.

18. From the left pane of the **Materials** tab, expand **Glass** and click on **Glazing**; all the glazing materials are displayed in the right pane.

19. From the right pane, right-click on **Dark Bronze** and select **Assign to Selection**; the glass material is applied to all the window panels.

20. Press ESC to deselect everything.

    Next, you will assign the material to the machines. These materials need to be assigned to some of the objects in the machines. As a result, you cannot use one of the selection sets that you created earlier. You will use the **Select Same** flyout to select objects for this purpose.

21. From the **Selection Tree**, expand **Factory_Layout.iam > Multi_Machine_3_CNC:3 > Multi_Machine_3_CNC > Solid1** object and select **Default**.

22. From the **Home** ribbon tab > **Select & Search** ribbon panel > **Select Same** flyout, click on **Same Name**; all the objects with the name **Default** are selected.

23. From the left pane of the **Materials** tab, click on **Metal**.

24. From the right pane, scroll down to **Copper**. Right-click on this material and select **Assign to Selection**.

25. In the **Selection Tree**, from the expanded **Multi_Machine_3_CNC > Solid1** object, select **Sky Blue Dark**.

26. From the **Home** ribbon tab > **Select & Search** ribbon panel > **Select Same** flyout, click on **Same Name**; all the objects with the name **Sky Blue Dark** are selected.

27. From the left pane of the **Materials** tab, click on **Metal**.

28. From the right pane, scroll down to **Steel - Polished**. Right-click on this material and select **Assign to Selection**.

29. From the expanded **Multi_Machine_3_CNC > Solid1** object, select **Honed - Dark Gray**.

30. From the **Home** ribbon tab > **Select & Search** ribbon panel > **Select Same** flyout, click on **Same Name**; all the objects with the name **Honed - Dark Gray** are selected.

31. From the left pane of the **Materials** tab, select **Metal**. From the right pane, scroll down to **Steel - Polished**. Right-click on this material and select **Assign to Selection**.

    Next, you will create a search set using the **Find Items** window to assign materials.

32. Undock the **Autodesk Rendering** window and then dock the **Find Items** window below the graphics window.

33. If there is any row of search criteria already displayed in the right pane of the **Find Items** window, right-click on it and select **Delete All Conditions**.

34. Click on the first row under **Category** and select **Item**.

35. From the first row under **Property**, select **Name**.

36. From the first row under **Condition**, select **Contains**.

37. Click on the first row under **Value** and type **Fence**.

38. Click **Find All**; all the fence objects are found and selected.

39. In the **Sets** window, save the search as a search set with the name **Safety Fences**.

40. Press ESC to deselect everything.

41. Undock the **Find Items** window and dock the **Autodesk Rendering** window.

42. Activate the **Factory Exit** viewpoint; the racks are displayed on the left in the view.

    Notice how the materials are no more displayed on the objects. To display these materials, you can change the render mode to full render. However, it is automatically done when you assign material to any object.

43. From the **Sets** window, select the **Racks** set that you created earlier in this project.

44. From the left pane of the **Materials** tab, select **Metal**.

45. From the right pane, scroll down to **Steel - Polished**. Right-click on this material and select **Assign to Selection**; the material is assigned to the racks and also the render mode is changed to full render.

46. From the **Sets** window, select the **Safety Fences** set.

47. From the left pane of the **Materials** tab, select **Metallic Paint**.

48. From the right pane, scroll down to **Glossy - Gold**. Right-click on this material and select **Assign to Selection**; the material is assigned to the safety fence objects.

49. Press ESC to deselect everything.

Finally, you will assign concrete material to the floor slab.

50. Activate the **Select** tool from the **Quick Access Toolbar** and then from the graphics window, click on the factory floor.

51. From the left pane of the **Materials** tab, select **Concrete**.

52. From the right pane, scroll down to **Industrial Floor**. Right-click on this material and select **Assign to Selection**; the material is assigned to the factory floor.

53. Activate the **Shopfloor 1** viewpoint.

You will now render this scene using the default lighting style. The quality of rendering needs to be first set. Depending on how much time you have available for rendering, you can select various rendering qualities. For this project, you will select low quality rendering.

54. From the **Render** ribbon tab > **Interactive Ray Trace** ribbon panel > **Ray Trace** flyout, click **Low Quality**.

55. Now, click the **Ray Trace** button; the scene starts to render. This type of rendering will take around 10 minutes to render the scene.

Figure 18 shows a scene rendered using medium quality rendering. This type of rendering takes around 36 minutes to render the scene.

Next, you will export the rendered image.

56. From the **Render** ribbon tab > **Export** ribbon panel, click **Image**; the **Save As** dialog box is displayed.

57. Browse to the **Chapter 11 > FDS Project** folder, if it is not already selected.

58. From the **Save as type** list, select **JPEG (*.jpg)**.

59. Enter **Factory** as the name of the file and click **Save** in the dialog box; the rendered image is saved in the specified folder.

60. Click the **Stop** button **Interactive Ray Trace** ribbon panel to stop the rendering process.

61. Hide the **Autodesk Rendering** window.

 *Note: Refer to Chapter 6 for more details about using the **Autodesk Rendering** module to create photorealistic renderings.*

Figure 18 The rendered scene

Section 15: Using the Animator and Scripter Modules to Animate the Movement of Objects in the Scene

Autodesk Navisworks provides the **Animator** module to animate the movement of the objects in the scene. The **Scripter** module is used to automate these animations created in the **Animator** module. In this section, you will use both these modules to create animations of moving the forklifts in the scene.

1. Activate the **Overview - No Walls** viewpoint.

2. Click **Animator** from the bottom graphics window to display the **Animator** window. Dock this window below the graphics window.

3. Click **Add scene > Add Scene** from the bottom left corner of the **Animator** window; a new animator scene is added.

4. Rename the scene to **Forklifts**.

    You will first animate the right forklift to take it from shopfloor 1 of the factory to shopfloor 2.

5. From the **Selection Tree**, expand **Factory_Layout.iam > Forklifts:1**; the two forklifts are displayed in the **Selection Tree**.

6. Select **Forklift Truck:1**; the first forklift is highlighted in the graphics window.

7. In the **Animator** window, right-click on the **Forklifts** scene that you added earlier and select **Add Animation Set > From current selection**; a new animation set is added to the scene.

8. Rename the animation set to **Forklift1**.

The animator animations work on the concept of keyframes. You first need to capture a keyframe at the initial position of this forklift. You will then move this forklift to its final position and capture the keyframe there.

9. From the toolbar available at the top in the **Animator** window, click **Capture keyframe**; a new keyframe is added at 0 seconds.

10. In the **Time position** box, type **15** and press ENTER; the timeline bar moves to 15 seconds.

11. From the toolbar available at the top in the **Animator** window, click the **Translate animation set** button; the move gizmo is displayed in the graphics window and the **Translate X**, **Y**, and **Z** boxes are displayed at the lower left corner of the **Animator** window.

12. In the **Translate X**, **Y**, and **Z** boxes, enter **-2475, -46, 0** Inches or **-62.9, -1.17, 0** Meters as the values, depending on the units you are using, and press ENTER; the selected forklift moves to this position.

13. From the toolbar available at the top in the **Animator** window, click **Capture keyframe**; a new keyframe is added at 15 seconds and a light Blue animation bar is displayed in the animator timeline window.

14. Press ESC to deselect the forklift and then click the **Translate animation set** button to turn off the move gizmo.

    Next, you will animate the second forklift to move it from shopfloor 2 to shopfloor 1. You will start moving this forklift at 10 seconds.

15. From the **Selection Tree**, select **Forklift Truck:2**; the second forklift is highlighted in the graphics window.

16. In the **Animator** window, right-click on the **Forklifts** scene that you added earlier and select **Add Animation Set > From current selection**; a new animation set is added to the scene.

17. Rename the animation set to **Forklift2**.

18. Type **10** in the **Time position** box and press ENTER; the timeline bar moves to 10 seconds.

19. From the toolbar available at the top in the **Animator** window, click **Capture keyframe**; a new keyframe is added at 10 seconds for the second animation set.

20. Type **20** in the **Time position** box and press ENTER; the timeline bar moves to 20 seconds.

21. From the toolbar available at the top in the **Animator** window, click the **Translate animation set** button; the move gizmo is displayed in the graphics window and the **Translate X**, **Y**, and **Z** boxes are displayed at the lower left corner of the **Animator** window.

22. In the **Translate X** box at the lower left corner of the **Animator** window, enter **2060** Inches or **52.3** Meters as the value, depending on the units you are using, and press ENTER; the selected forklift moves to this position.

23. From the toolbar available at the top in the **Animator** window, click **Capture keyframe**; a new keyframe is added at 20 seconds and a light Blue animation bar is displayed in the animator timeline window.

24. Press ESC to deselect the forklift and then click the **Translate animation set** button to turn off the move gizmo.

25. From the toolbar available at the top in the **Animator** window, click the **Stop** button; both the forklifts move back to their original positions.

Next, you will play this animation and view it from the **Shopfloor 2** viewpoint.

26. Activate the **Shopfloor 2** viewpoint.

27. From the toolbar available at the top in the **Animator** window, click the **Play** button; notice the two forklifts going past the camera view.

28. Once the animation ends, click on the **Stop** button; the two forklifts return to their original position.

 *Tip: If you do not want the two forklifts moving around without a driver, you can go back to Autodesk Inventor and have a human factory asset sitting in the forklift as the driver. Save the file and return to Autodesk Navisworks. Click the **Refresh** button from the **Quick Access Toolbar** to update the view. Remember to select the drivers of the forklifts and then append them to the animation sets by right-clicking on the **Forklift1** and **Forklift2** animation sets.*

 Note: You can also add a camera animation to the animator scene and make the objects such as robots move and rotate during the animation. Refer to Chapter 7 of this textbook for all these types of animations.

You will now use the **Scripter** module to automate the forklift animation.

29. Undock the **Animator** window.

30. From the bottom of the graphics window, click **Scripter** to display the **Scripter** window.

31. Dock this window below the graphics window.

32. From the bottom left corner of the **Scripter** window, click the **Add New Script** button; a new script is added.

33. Rename the script to **Forklift**.

34. From the toolbar displayed below the **Events** area, click the **On Key Press** button; the **Properties** area is displayed on the right of the **Events** area.

35. In the **Properties** area, type **F** in the **Key** box.

36. From the toolbar displayed below the **Actions** area, click the **Play Animation** button; the **Properties** area is displayed on the right of the **Actions** area.

37. In the **Properties** area, click the **Animation** list and double-click on **Forklifts**; this adds the **Forklift** animator scene that will play the animation of moving both the forklifts.

    Although you have added the script to play the animation on pressing the F key, but the animation will not be played until you enable the scripts. This is done using the **Animate** ribbon tab.

38. Undock the **Scripter** window.

39. From the **Animation** ribbon tab > **Script** ribbon panel, click **Enable Scripts**.

40. Make sure the **Shopfloor 2** viewpoint is active. Press the F11 key to activate the full screen display.

41. Click anywhere on the sky in the scene and then press the F key; the forklift animation starts playing.

42. After the animation ends, press the F11 key to exit the full screen display.

43. From the **Animation** ribbon tab > **Script** ribbon panel, click **Enable Scripts** to disable the scripts; the two forklifts will move back to their original position.

44. Save the file.

 ***Note**: Refer to Chapter 7 of this textbook for details of various events and action types that can be added to the scene.*

Section 16: Creating the Simulation of Factory Construction using the TimeLiner Module

In this section, you will create the simulation of a factory construction using the **TimeLiner** module. You will link an external scheduling file to Autodesk Navisworks and then assign objects to the tasks created from the external file. You will then edit the simulation settings and play the construction simulation.

1. Click **TimeLiner** from the bottom of the graphics window to display the **TimeLiner** window.

2. Dock this window below the graphics window.

   You will start with linking the external scheduling file. This is done using the **Data Sources** tab of the **TimeLiner** window.

3. In the **TimeLiner** window, click the **Data Sources** tab.

4. Click **Add > CSV Import**; the **Open** dialog box is displayed.

5. Browse to the **Chapter 11 > FDS Project** folder, if it is not already listed.

6. Double-click on the **Factory Schedule.csv** file; the **Field Selector** dialog box is displayed.

    In this dialog box, the fields under **Column** are the TimeLiner fields and the fields under **External Field Name** are the fields in the CSV file. These fields need to be mapped correctly.

7. Map all the fields under **Column** to the fields under **External Field Name**, as shown in Figure 19. Note that you only need to map the fields up to the **Subcontractor Cost** field.

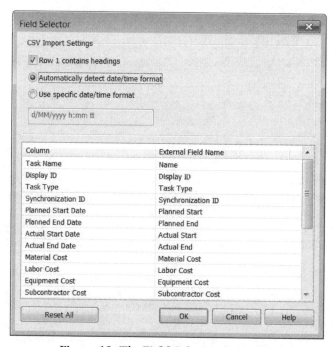

Figure 19 The *Field Selector dialog box*

8. Click **OK** in the dialog box; a new data source is added.

    Although you have added the scheduling file but if you click the **Tasks** tab, you will notice that no task has been added yet. This is because you have not built the task hierarchy yet. This will be done now.

9. Right-click on the data source that you added and select **Rebuild Task Hierarchy**. Click **OK** in the missing synchronization ID error box.

10. Click the **Tasks** tab; notice the task hierarchy is built from the scheduling file.

Because the visibility of the Gantt chart is turned on, you cannot see all the task columns. Therefore, it is recommended that you turn off the visibility of the Gantt chart.

11. From the toolbar available at the top in the **Tasks** tab, click the **Show or hide the Gantt chart** button; the Gantt chart is turned off and you can see all the columns.

Scroll down to the bottom of the tasks list and notice the last task is **8S-Beam**. This task is related to the wooden beams in the factory. Normally, this task has to be completed before installing any machines. The reason this is the last task in this schedule is so that you can view the installation of machines without the beams interfering with your display.

Also, notice that the **Attached** column is blank. This means that no object is assigned to the tasks yet. If you expand the AutoCAD file in the **Selection Tree**, you will notice that the layers have the same name as some of the tasks. Also, if you expand the Autodesk Inventor file, you will notice that the items have the same name as the tasks. Therefore, you will use a couple of predefined rules to attach objects to these tasks.

12. From the toolbar available at the top in the **Tasks** tab, click the **Auto-Attach Using Rules** button; the **TimeLiner Rules** dialog box is displayed.

13. Select the tick box of the first and third rule and clear the tick box of the second rule.

14. Click the **Apply Rules** button and then exit the dialog box.

Notice that the **Attached** column now shows **Explicit Selection**. This means that the objects having the same layer name or the same item name and matching cases are assigned to the tasks.

The **New Data Source (Root)** task at the top of the task list shows the start date of the first task and the end date of the last task. Make a note of these dates as you will now change these dates in the simulation settings.

15. In the **TimeLiner** window, click the **Simulate** tab.

16. Click the **Settings** button; the **Simulation Settings** dialog box is displayed.

17. Click the **Override Start / End Dates** tick box at the top in the dialog box.

18. Click on the **Calendar** on the right of the **Start Date** edit box and change the start date to March 24, 2013.

Next, you will edit the overlay text that appears on the graphics window while playing the simulation.

19. Click the **Edit** button in the **Overlay Text** area; the **Overlay Text** dialog box is displayed.

By default, the dialog box shows **%A %X %x Day=$DAY Week=$WEEK**. This will show the current day, the current time, the current date, the number of days and weeks into the simulation. You will now edit this text and add additional text.

20. Click at the start of the first line of text to move the cursor there. Now, click **Colors > Red**; the first line of the overlay text will now be displayed in Red.

21. Click at the end of the first line of text to move the cursor there.

22. Press and hold down the CTRL key and press ENTER; the cursor moves to the second line.

23. Click **Colors > Blue**; the second line of the overlay text will now be displayed in Blue.

    Next, you will add various costs to the overlay text.

24. With the cursor located on the right of **$COLOR_BLUE**, type **MC=** and then click **Cost > Material Cost**.

    Before adding the next cost, you will add a comma (,) and a space after the material cost.

25. Type **, LC=** and then click **Cost > Labor Cost**.

26. Type **, Eq.C=** and then click **Cost > Equipment Cost**.

27. Type **, Sub.C=** and then click **Cost > Subcontractor Cost**.

28. Press and hold down the CTRL key and press ENTER; the cursor moves to the third line.

29. Click **Colors > Green**; the third line of text will now be displayed in Green.

30. Type **Total Cost=** and then click **Cost > Total Cost**.

    Next, you will change the font of the overlay text.

31. Click the **Font** button; the **Select Overlay Font** dialog box is displayed.

32. Select **Arial** font, **Regular** style with **12** size.

33. Click **OK** in the **Select Overlay Font** dialog box.

34. Click **OK** in the **Overlay Text** dialog box.

35. Click **OK** in the **Simulation Settings** dialog box.

36. Activate the **Overview 1** viewpoint.

37. From the toolbar above the **Settings** button, click the **Play** button; the construction simulation starts playing.

Figure 20 shows a snapshot during the simulation.

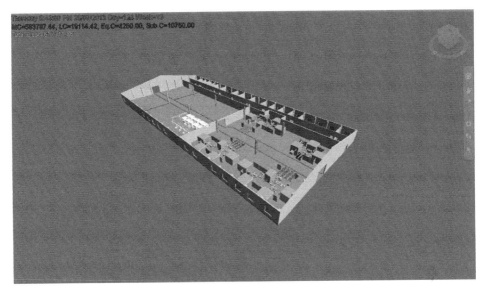

Figure 20 A snapshot during the construction simulation

38. After the simulation ends, click the **Tasks** tab.

 *Tip: If the **TimeLiner** window has the **Simulation** tab active, certain operations such as creating animator and scripter scenes cannot be performed.*

39. Undock the **TimeLiner** window.

40. Save the file.

Section 17: Publishing the NWD File

One of the main advantages of working with Autodesk Navisworks is that you can publish your design in the .NWD format, which can then be opened in the free viewer called Autodesk Navisworks Freedom. The .NWD file that you publish can also be password protected and you can assign an expiry date to this file. In this section, you will publish the .NWD file of the factory.

1. From the **Output** ribbon tab > **Publish** ribbon panel, click **NWD**; the **Publish** dialog box is displayed.

2. In the **Title** edit box, type **My Factory**.

3. In the **Subject** edit box, type **Factory Design Suite**.

4. In the **Author** edit box, type **Deepak Maini**.

5. In the **Publisher** edit box, type your name.

6. In the **Published For** edit box, type **Up and Running with Autodesk Navisworks**.

7. In the **Copyright** edit box, type **Deepak Maini**.

8. In the **Password** edit box, type **1234**.

9. Select the **Expires** tick box and select tomorrow's date as the date on which this file will expire.

10. Make sure the **May be re-saved** tick box is not selected. This will ensure that the changes made to this file cannot be saved.

11. Select the **Display on open** and **Embed ReCap and Texture data** tick boxes.

12. Click **OK** in the dialog box; the **Password** dialog box is displayed, prompting you to confirm the password.

13. Type **1234** in the **Password** dialog box and click **OK**; the **Save As** dialog box is displayed.

14. Browse to the **Chapter 11 > FDS Project** folder, if it is not already listed in the dialog box.

15. Enter **My Factory** as the file name and click **Save**; the file is saved with .NWD extension.

 *Tip: In Autodesk Navisworks Freedom 2016 viewer, you can click **Animation** ribbon tab and use the **Playback** ribbon panel to play the viewpoint or animator animations. To view the timeliner simulation, turn on the visibility of the **TimeLiner Playback** window by clicking **View** ribbon tab > **Workspace** ribbon panel > **Windows** flyout.*

Section 18: Performing a Clash Test Between Factory Building and Machine Layout

This section is only for people using Autodesk Navisworks Manage, which is a part of Autodesk Factory Design Suite Ultimate. If you are using Autodesk Factory Design Suite Premium, you get Autodesk Navisworks Simulate in the suite, which does not have the **Clash Detective** module.

In this section, you will perform hard clash test between the factory building and the machine layout. You will write a report of all the clashes found.

1. From the left of the graphics window, click **Clash Detective**; the **Clash Detective** window is displayed. Dock this window on the left of the graphics window.

 *Tip: To make more space for the graphics window, you can hide the **Selection Tree**, **Sets**, **Properties**, and **Saved Viewpoints** windows.*

2. From the top right corner of the **Clash Detective** window, click **Add Test**; a new clash test is added.

3. Rename the clash test to **Building V Machines**.

4. From the **Selection A** area in the **Select** tab, select **Factory Building.dwg**.

5. From the **Selection B** area, select **Factory_Layout.iam**.

6. From the **Type** list, select **Hard** as the type of clash, if not already selected.

7. Clear the **Composite Object Clashing** tick box.

8. Click the **Run Test** button; the clash test is performed and you are informed there are four clashes found. Also, the **Results** tab of the **Clash Detective** window is activated and the first clash is selected. This clash is also displayed in the graphics window, as shown in Figure 21.

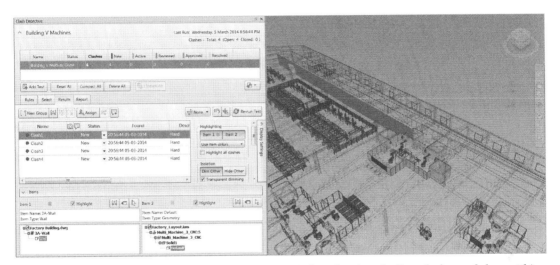

*Figure 21 The **Results** tab of the **Clash Detective** window showing the four clashes and the graphics window highlighting the first clash*

Notice the **Item 1** area at the bottom in the **Results** tab shows the wall that is clashing and the **Item 2** area shows the machine that is clashing.

9. One by one, click on the remaining three clashes from the **Results** tab; the view changes to show you the currently active clash.

You will now write a report of these clashes.

10. In the **Clash Detective** window, click the **Report** tab.

11. From the **Report Type** list, make sure **Current test** is selected.

12. From the **Report Format** list, make sure **HTML (Tabular)** is selected.

13. Click **Write Report**; the **Save As** dialog box is displayed.

14. Browse to the **Chapter 11 > FDS Project** folder.

15. Create a new folder with the name **Report** and double-click on that folder.

16. Save the report file with the name **Building V Machines**. The file is saved with the .HTML format.

17. Using Windows Explorer, browse to the **Chapter 11 > FDS Project > Report** folder.

18. Double-click on the **Building V Machines.html** file to open and view the clash report.

19. Close the clash report and return back to the Autodesk Navisworks window.

Section 19: Resolving Clashes

Next, you will resolve the clash between the wall and the machine. Normally, in a clash like this, you will move the machine to a different location to resolve clashes, as that is easier. However, if you look closely at the clashes, you will notice that there is not enough space in that section of the walls to accommodate the machine. Therefore, you need to move the walls. Because the factory construction has not started yet, it is easier to make the changes at this stage.

If you have AutoCAD Architecture installed on your computer as a part of Autodesk Factory Design Suite Ultimate and you are familiar with AutoCAD Architecture, you can go to **Section 19a** to resolve the clashes. If you do not have AutoCAD Architecture installed on your computer or you are not familiar with this program, go to **Section 19b** to resolve the clashes.

Section 19a: Using the SwitchBack Functionality to Resolve Clashes

Use the steps in this section only if you have AutoCAD Architecture installed on your computer and you are familiar with this software. If not, go to **Section 19b**. In this section, you will switchback to the factory building in AutoCAD Architecture and edit the walls to resolve the clashes. For the switchback functionality to work, you first need to run AutoCAD Architecture and then make it ready for switchback.

1. From the **Application** tab of the **Autodesk Factory Design Suite 2016** dashboard, or from the Start menu, run AutoCAD Architecture.

2. Once the software loads, type **NWLOAD** in the command line and press ENTER; a prompt sequence is displayed showing **Navisworks ready**.

3. Return to the Autodesk Navisworks window.

4. Click on the **Results** tab.

To edit the AutoCAD Architecture file, you need to use the switchback functionality on this file. This is done using the **SwitchBack** button located in the **Item 1** area in the **Results** tab.

5. Click on **Clash4** from the **Results** area; the view changes in the graphics window to show you this clash.

6. Click on the **SwitchBack** button located in the **Item 1** area, as shown in Figure 22; the **Factory Building.dwg** file opens in AutoCAD Architecture.

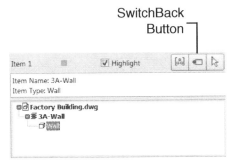

*Figure 22 The **SwitchBack** button*

7. Activate the AutoCAD Architecture window.

    In AutoCAD Architecture, the current view is set to perspective view, which is the same as that in Autodesk Navisworks. As a result, you will not be able to see the wall structure clearly. It is recommended that you first change the view in AutoCAD Architecture to the plan view.

8. Type **PLAN** in the command line and press ENTER twice; the model is displayed from the plan view.

9. Click on the wall highlighted in Figure 23.

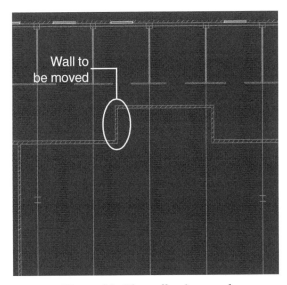

Figure 23 The wall to be moved

10. Use the grip displayed at the midpoint of the wall to move it 4000 to the left.

11. Save and close the AutoCAD Architecture file.

12. Return to the Autodesk Navisworks window.

    Once the changes have been made in the native file, you need to refresh the Autodesk Navisworks scene to reflect those changes.

13. Click the **Refresh** button on the **Quick Access Toolbar**; the Autodesk Navisworks scene refreshes and an error symbol is displayed on the left of the clash test name in the **Clash Detective** window.

    If you move the cursor over this error symbol, it will inform you that the test settings have changed since the test was last run. Therefore, you need to update the test.

14. In the **Clash Detective** window, click the **Update All** button; the clash test updates and all the clashes are now displayed as **Resolved**, as shown in Figure 24.

15. Unhide the **Clash Detective** window.

16. Activate the **Overview 1** viewpoint.

Section 19b: Resolving the Clashes by Renaming the Building File

Use the steps in this section only if you do not have AutoCAD Architecture installed on your computer or if you are not familiar with this software. In the **Chapter 11 > FDS Project** folder, there is a building file with the name **Factory Building - Fixed.dwg** that has the walls modified so that they do not clash with the machines. In this section, you will rename this file so that it is used as the building file in the Autodesk Navisworks scene.

1. Using Windows Explorer, browse to **Chapter 11 > FDS Project** folder.

2. Rename the **Factory Building.dwg** file to **Factory Building - Old.dwg**.

3. Rename the **Factory Building - Fixed.dwg** file to **Factory Building.dwg**.

4. Return back to the Autodesk Navisworks window.

5. Click the **Refresh** button on the **Quick Access Toolbar**; the Autodesk Navisworks scene refreshes and an error symbol is displayed on the left of the clash test name in the **Clash Detective** window.

    If you move the cursor over this error symbol, it will inform you that the test settings have changed since the test was last run. Therefore, you need to update the test.

6. In the **Clash Detective** window, click the **Update All** button; the clash test updates and all the clashes are now displayed as **Resolved**, as shown in Figure 24.

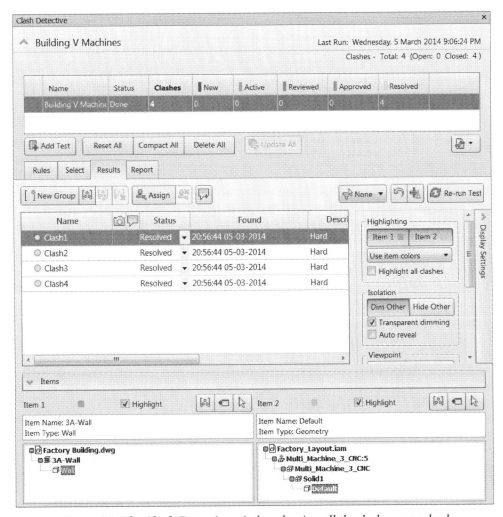

*Figure 24 The **Clash Detective** window showing all the clashes as resolved*

7. Unhide the **Clash Detective** window.

8. Activate the **Overview 1** viewpoint.

9. Save the file.

10. Start a new file to close the current file.

 Note: *Refer to Chapter 10 of this textbook to learn more about the **Clash Detective** module.*

Chapter 12 – BIM Data Collaboration with Autodesk BIM 360 Glue

The objectives of this chapter are to:

√   *Familiarize you with Autodesk BIM 360 Glue environment for Autodesk Navisworks.*
√   *Show you how to create an Autodesk BIM 360 Glue account.*
√   *Explain how to glue Autodesk Navisworks models to Autodesk BIM 360 Glue.*
√   *Explain how to use the Autodesk BIM 360 Glue desktop application.*
√   *Use various tools available in the Autodesk BIM 360 Glue desktop application.*
√   *Open models from Autodesk BIM 360 Glue in Autodesk Navisworks.*
√   *Use the Autodesk BIM 360 Glue iPad app to review the model and create markups.*

Autodesk BIM 360

Before you learn about Autodesk BIM 360 Glue integration with Autodesk Navisworks, it is important for you to understand what is Autodesk BIM 360. It is a cloud-based platform to collaborate, coordinate, and manage your Building Information Modeling (BIM) data from the design and preconstruction phase to field execution phase. The BIM data can be accessed anytime anywhere using computers or iPad devices. Autodesk BIM 360 has the following two components:

BIM 360 Glue: *For BIM data collaboration, coordination, and management*
BIM 360 Field: *For field execution, commissioning, and handover*

Both Autodesk BIM 360 and Autodesk Navisworks share the same core technology for viewing and coordinating large models. Similar to Autodesk Navisworks, Autodesk BIM 360 Glue also lets you work with around 56 different native file formats. For Autodesk products such as Autodesk Revit, AutoCAD, and AutoCAD Civil 3D, you have in-product tab that you can use to glue the models. The files created in other Autodesk products or non-native Autodesk products can be directly uploaded using the Autodesk BIM 360 Glue desktop application.

Starting Autodesk Navisworks 2016, there are major enhancements in the way Autodesk BIM 360 Glue integrates with Autodesk Navisworks. These enhancements allow far better collaboration functionalities between the two products and a lot more integrated workflow for the users.

This chapter takes a project-based approach of using Autodesk BIM 360 Glue for cloud-based BIM data collaboration, coordination and management. This chapter also shows you how to use the Autodesk BIM 360 Glue desktop application and iPad app for design coordination and review.

IMPORTANT INFORMATION

The information provided in this chapter is current as of April 05, 2015. Because Autodesk BIM 360 is a cloud-based technology, the information available in this technology changes regularly. However, the core technology that is discussed in this chapter is not expected to change.

Autodesk BIM 360 Glue Project	*In this project, you will complete the following tasks:* 1. *Create a BIM 360 Glue trial account (only if you do not already have a BIM 360 account).* 2. *Create a new BIM 360 project for tutorial.* 3. *Download and install the Autodesk BIM 360 Glue desktop application.* 4. *Upload NWC files on BIM 360 Glue and then use Autodesk Navisworks to create a merged model.* 5. *Open the Autodesk Navisworks merged model in the Autodesk BIM 360 Glue desktop application.* 5. *Use various tools in the desktop application.* 6. *Notify other members of your team about various activities performed on the glued model.* 7. *Create a merged model using the Autodesk BIM 360 Glue app.* 8. *Open the merged model using Autodesk Navisworks.* 9. *Use the Autodesk BIM 360 Glue iPad app to review the model.*

BEFORE YOU PROCEED

Before proceeding any further in this project, you need to make sure you have an Autodesk 360 account. If you do not have an Autodesk 360 account, go to **https://360.autodesk.com/ Login** and create an account. Once you have created this account, you are ready to proceed with this project.

Section 1: Creating an Autodesk BIM 360 Glue Trial Account

In this section, you will create an Autodesk BIM 360 Glue trial account. Note that this account will only be valid for 30 days. However, if you already have an Autodesk BIM 360 Glue account, you can skip this section.

 Tip: For using Autodesk 360 services, it is recommended to use Google Chrome as your Web browser.

1. Start your Web browser window.

2. Type the following address in the address bar:

   http://www.autodesk.com/products/bim-360-glue/overview

3. From the right side on the **BIM 360 GLUE** page, click on **SIGN UP NOW** under **Try it for free**.

4. On the **Sign up for a free 30-Day Trial** page, enter your Autodesk 360 credentials in the **Autodesk ID** and **Password** fields.

5. In the **Create BIM 360 Glue Site Name** field, enter **Up_and_Running16XX** and replace **XX** with your initials. Note that for this tutorial project, the site is called **Up_and_Running16**, as shown in Figure 1.

Figure 1 *Creating a BIM 360 Glue trial account*

 Note: *If you get an error that the site name is not available, add a number to your initials.*

6. Click **Sign up**.

   Once the sign up process is completed, you will be sent an email with an invitation to get started.

7. Open the email account that you used to create the Autodesk BIM 360 Glue trial account.

8. In the email that you have received from Autodesk BIM 360 Glue, click on the **Get Started** link; a new Web browser window is opened and you are prompted to sign in.

9. Sign in using the same Autodesk 360 credentials that you used to create the BIM 360 Glue trial account.

10. Once you have signed in, you will be informed that you are now a member of the **Up_and_Running16** project, as shown in Figure 2. You will also be prompted to install the BIM 360 Glue desktop application in the same window.

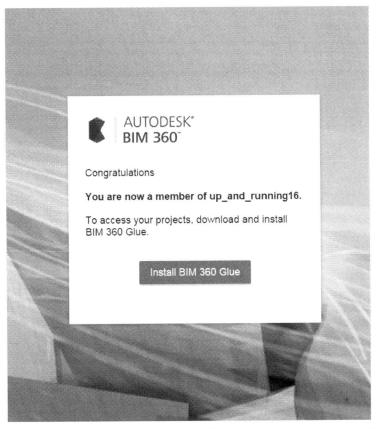

*Figure 2 The information that you have been added to the **Up_and_Running16** project*

11. Click on **Install BIM 360 Glue** and follow the prompt to download and install the desktop application.

 Tip: You can also continue using BIM 360 Glue from your Web browser. However, it is recommended that you download and install the desktop application.

Section 2: Performing Admin Tasks

In this section, you will use the Autodesk BIM 360 Glue desktop application to create a new Autodesk BIM 360 Glue project on the **Up_and_Running16XX** site you created in the previous section. Also, once the project is created and the models are uploaded, you need to make sure all the members in your team have access to the cloud-based model and its activities. Therefore, in this section you will also learn to add users to your project.

Note: *It is assumed that you completed the last step of Section 1 and installed the Autodesk BIM 360 Glue desktop application.*

1. Double-click on the **Autodesk BIM 360 Glue** shortcut icon on the desktop of your computer; because you are using this application for the first time, you are prompted to sign in.

2. Use your Autodesk BIM 360 Glue trial credentials to sign in; the **Up_and_Running16XX** site is opened and the **Sample Project** is listed in the lower half of the Autodesk BIM 360 Glue window, as shown in Figure 3.

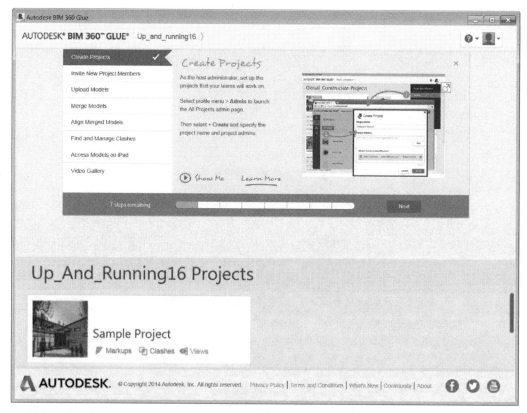

*Figure 3 The **Autodesk BIM 360 Glue** desktop application showing the site and the project*

3. Move the cursor of the avatar icon near the top right corner of this window; a shortcut menu is displayed.

4. From the shortcut menu, click **Admin**, as shown in Figure 4; a new Web browser window is opened with the **Administration** settings of the BIM 360 Glue site.

5. Under the **All Projects** area near the top left of the window, click **+Create**; the **Create Project** window is displayed.

6. Under **Project Name**, type **MyLearning**.

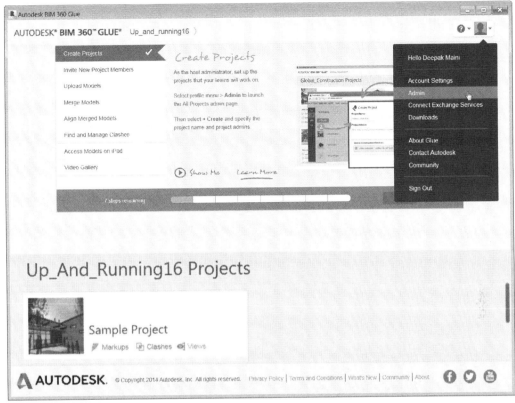

Figure 4 *Activating the **Admin** option to create a new project*

7. Under **Project Value**, type **0**. Since this is a trial project, its value is $0.

8. Under **Project Admins**, start typing your email address and you will see that your name automatically appears in the list.

9. Select your name from the list and click the **Add** button.

10. Similarly, you can add more members to this project by typing their email addresses separated by comma and clicking the **Add** button. If possible, add a few of your colleagues so that you can coordinate with them on this project.

 Note: *If you do not click the **Add** button, the person selected in the **Project Admins** will actually not be added as project members.*

For this project, you will add me as a member to your project.

11. Type **deepak@deepakmaini.com** in the **Project Admins** box and click **Add**.

12. Review the information in the **Create Project** window. It should appear similar to the one shown in Figure 5.

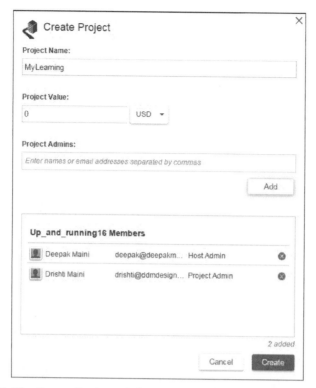

*Figure 5 The **Create Project** window after entering the required information*

13. Click the **Create** button; you are returned to the **Administration** page and the new project is listed there.

14. Close this window and return to the Autodesk BIM 360 Glue desktop application.

    Notice that when you return to the desktop application, the new project you created is not listed there. To display the project, this window needs to be refreshed.

15. From the top of the Autodesk BIM 360 Glue desktop application window, click **Up_and_Running16XX**; the window is refreshed and the new project you created is listed in the lower half of this window, as shown in Figure 6.

Section 3: Uploading the Autodesk Navisworks NWC Files into the MyLearning Project

In this section, you will upload various NWC files into the project you created in the previous section.

1. In the lower half of the Autodesk BIM 360 Glue desktop application window, click on **MyLearning**; the **MyLearning** project page is displayed showing the content and activities of this project, as shown in Figure 6.

Figure 6 *Newly created project listed in the lower half of the **Autodesk BIM 360 Glue** window*

The **MyLearning** page is divided into the following three areas:

Activities: This is the default area that is displayed on the project page. This area shows the list of the activities performed on the current project in the **Activities** area on the left side of this page.

Merged Models: This area shows the models that were merged using BIM 360 Glue. The process of merging the models is similar to appending multiple models in Autodesk Navisworks. You can switch to the expanded **Merged Models** page by clicking on the **Merged Models** button on the right of your project name.

Models: This area shows the models that were glued using the in-application apps such as the BIM 360 Glue app from Autodesk Revit. This area also shows the models that are directly uploaded using the **Upload models** button available on the top right of this area. You can switch to the expanded **Models** page by clicking on the **Models** button on the right of your project name.

2. From the left of the **MyLearning** page, click the **Models** icon; the expanded **Models** page is displayed.

3. From the top right of the **Models** page, click **Add Folder**; a new row for the folder is added under the **MyLearning** project.

4. Rename the new folder to **Glue-Trial** and then press ENTER.

5. With the **Glue-Trial** still highlighted, click **Upload models**; the **Upload Models** window is displayed.

6. Click the **+ Browse** button in this window; the **Open** dialog box is displayed.

7. Browse to the **Chapter 12 > Glue Project** folder and select all the NWC files in this folder.

8. Click the **Open** button; all the selected files are listed in the **Upload Models** window.

9. Click the **Upload** button; the files start to upload and a window is displayed on the lower right corner informing you about the files being uploaded.

10. Once all the files are uploaded, click **Glue-Trial**; the files are listed, as shown in the Autodesk BIM 360 Glue window in Figure 7.

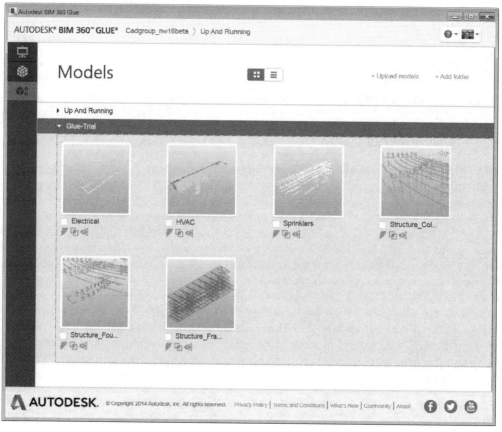

Figure 7 The NWC files uploaded in the project

Section 4: Creating a Federated Model Using Autodesk Navisworks

In this section, you will use Autodesk Navisworks to append all the files uploaded on BIM 360 Glue and create a collaborated model.

1. Start Autodesk Navisworks Manage/Simulate 2016.

   Because you need to create a federated model using the NWC files uploaded on BIM 360 Glue project, you will use the **BIM 360** tab to append the files.

2. From the **BIM 360** tab > **Model** ribbon panel click **Append**; the **Autodesk - Sign In** window is displayed.

3. Use your Autodesk 360 credentials to log in. Once the signing in is complete, the **BIM 360** window is displayed.

4. Click **MyLearning** and then click **Next** in the window.

5. Click the **Models** tab; all the models uploaded are listed in the window, as shown in Figure 8.

Figure 8 *The **Models** tab showing all the models that can be appended*

6. Holding down the SHIFT key, select all the files and then click **Append**; the process of appending all the files from BIM 360 Glue starts.

7. Change the background to horizon and the view to Home. Figure 9 shows the Autodesk Navisworks window after appending all the models from BIM 360 Glue and orbiting the view.

Figure 9   The Autodesk Navisworks window after appending the models from BIM 360 Glue

 Tip: *Once you are logged in to BIM 360 Glue, the Autodesk Navisworks window will show **Connected to BIM 360** on the lower left corner.*

Section 5: Saving the Federated Model

One of the enhancements of Autodesk Navisworks 2016 is that the federated model created by appending the files from BIM 360 Glue can be saved locally or on BIM 360 Glue. In this section, you will save the model on BIM 360 Glue.

1. Click the **Save** button on the **Quick Access** toolbar; the **BIM 360** window is displayed.

 Tip: *If you want to save the federated model locally, you can click the **Save locally as a Navisworks file** option on the lower left corner of this **BIM 360** window.*

2. In the **Name** box, enter **Nav-Federated**.

The default destination of this file is the **Merged Models** folder on BIM 360 Glue. If you want to save the file in a subfolder, you will have to first create it using the Autodesk BIM 360 Glue desktop application window.

3. Click the **Save** button; the model is uploaded on BIM 360 Glue and saved.

4.   Start a new file in Autodesk Navisworks to close the current file.

Section 6: Using the Autodesk BIM 360 Glue Desktop Application to Open the Glued Model

In this section, you will use the Autodesk BIM 360 Glue desktop application to open the model you glued in the previous section.

1.   Restore the Autodesk BIM 360 Glue desktop application window.

The window currently shows all the uploaded models on the **Models** page.

2.   From the left of the **Models** page, click the **Merged Models** icon; the **Merged Models** page is displayed and the federated model you saved from Autodesk Navisworks is listed here.

3.   Click the **Nav-Federated** model thumbnail image; the model is loaded in the BIM 360 Glue window.

4.   Close the **2D View** window. Now, hold down the SHIFT key and the wheel mouse button and orbit the model so that it appears as shown in Figure 10.

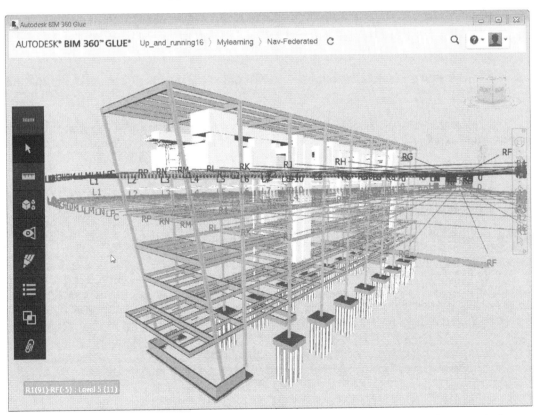

Figure 10 *The federated model opened in Autodesk BIM 360 Glue desktop application window*

Tip: Most of the Autodesk Navisworks shortcut keys work in BIM 360 Glue as well. For example, you can hold down the SHIFT key and wheel mouse button to orbit the model, press the CTRL + T key to turn the third person on, CTRL + G key to turn the gravity on, and CTRL + D to turn the collision on.

 Note: At this stage in the Autodesk BIM 360 Glue desktop application window, you can hover the cursor over the avatar icon on the top right and click the **Admin** option from the shortcut menu. This will open the Web browser window with the administration tools. In this window, you can click **+Add** from the top left to add additional members to the project. While adding these members, you can also set their roles.

Section 7: Turning Off the Grids and Changing the Background

In this section, you will turn off the grids in the model and also change the background to horizon. You will also select the desired display units in this section.

1. Hover the cursor over the avatar icon on the top right corner of the window; the shortcut menu is displayed.

2. In the shortcut menu, click **Options**; the **Options** window is displayed.

 Tip: Notice the **2D View** option is turned off in the **General** tab. This is because you turned off this window in the previous section. If you need to turn this window back on, you can do it from here.

3. On the **General** tab, under **Gridlines**, click **Off**; the gridlines are turned off in the BIM 360 Glue window.

4. Click the **Background** tab and select **Horizon** from the **Plain** list; the background in the BIM 360 Glue window changes to horizon.

5. Click the **Advanced** tab; the advanced options are displayed.

6. From the **Linear Units** list, select your preferred unit system.

7. Click **Save**; your settings are saved and the window is closed.

Section 8: Creating Views

In Autodesk BIM 360 Glue, viewpoints are referred to as views. In this section, you will create a view and save it for further use. You will also notify other members in this project about the views you have created.

1. Move the cursor to the center of the model and then scroll the wheel mouse button forward and backward once; the pivot point is changed to the center of the model.

2. Press and hold down the SHIFT key and wheel mouse button and drag the model to orbit it.

3. Use other navigation tools from the **Navigation Bar** displayed on the right side of the window to navigate through the model.

 Note: *Refer to Chapter 1 of this textbook to learn more about various navigation tools. As mentioned earlier, most of the shortcut keys of the Autodesk Navisworks navigation tools work in BIM 360 Glue as well.*

Next, you will create a viewpoint and save it.

4. Use various navigation tools to display the model similar to that shown in Figure 11.

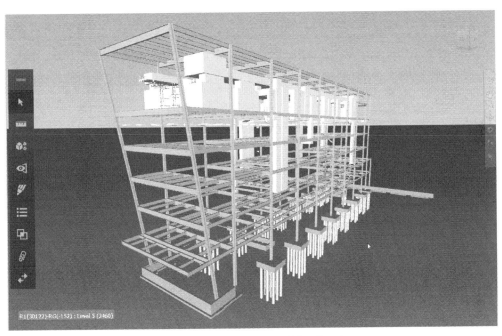

Figure 11 *Model oriented for the view*

5. From the toolbar on the left of the window, click **Views**; the **Views** window is displayed.

6. From the toolbar available on the top of the **Views** window, click **Add view**.

7. Enter **Glue Overview** as the name of this view.

8. Under the **Who has access** area, make sure **Mylearning (Project)** is selected. This ensures that all the members of this project have access to this view.

9. Click **Save** to save the view and return to the **Views** window; the view that you created is now listed in this window.

Next, you will create a new view by turning off the visibility of the curtain walls and exterior walls.

10. Close the **Views** window.

11. Use various navigation tools to display the model similar to that shown in Figure 12.

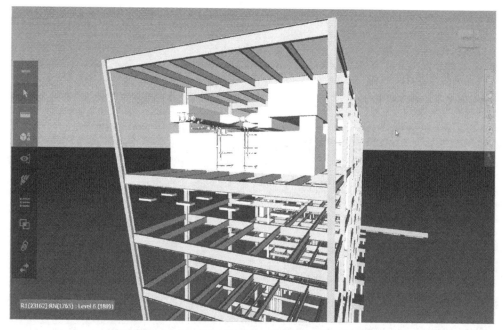

Figure 12 *Model oriented for the viewpoint*

12. Display the **Views** window by clicking on the **Views** button from the toolbar on the left.

13. Click **Add view**.

14. Enter **HVAC** as the name of this view.

15. Click **Save** to save the view and return to the **Views** window; the view that you created is now listed in this window.

16. Click on the **Glue Overview** view; this view is activated.

   Next, you will learn to notify other members of this project about the view you have created.

17. In the **Views** window, select both the views.

   Remember that if you select multiple views to notify your team members, you need to use the **Notify** option available in the **More actions** flyout in the toolbar at the top in the **Views** window. If you use the **Notify** icon on the right of one of the views, the notification will only be sent about that view and not about all the selected views.

18. In the toolbar available at the top in the **Views** window, click **More actions > Notify**; the **Notify Project Members** window is displayed.

19. Select the team members you want to notify.

 Note: *If you want, you can select me (Deepak Maini) to be notified. However, depending on your geographical location and the time zone, I may not have accepted the invitation to this project that was sent to me when you added me to this project in Section 2.*

20. In the **Message** area, type a relevant message and then click **Send**; all the selected team members are sent a notification email.

    When the team members get the notification email, they will be able to click on the link in the email to access this project and the view you notified them about, provided they have the Autodesk BIM 360 Glue access.

21. Once the notification is sent, the **Autodesk BIM 360 Glue** window is displayed informing you about it. Click **OK** in this window.

22. Close the **Views** window.

Section 9: Reviewing Model Components

In this section, you use the **Models** window to review various components of this model. This window is similar to the **Selection Tree** in Autodesk Navisworks.

1. From the toolbar on the left, click **Models**; the **Models** window is displayed with the **Nav-Federated** model. Also, all the files that were appended to create this model are listed, as shown in Figure 13.

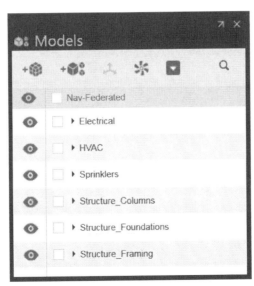

Figure 13 The **Models** *window*

2. Using the **Show/Hide** icon (eye icon) on the left of the model names, turn off the visibilities of various model files and view the results in the graphics window.

Tip: *You can turn off the visibility of certain objects and then create views. The views remember the visibility states of various objects. This is similar to turning on the **Hide/ Required** option in the **Edit Viewpoint** dialog box in Autodesk Navisworks.*

3. Close the **Models** window.

Section 10: Measuring Geometries and Adding Markups

In this section, you will measure the distances between various objects in the model. You will also add markups and then notify your team members about those markups. But before doing that, you will restore the **HVAC** view.

1. From the toolbar on the left, click **Views**; the **Views** window is displayed.

2. Activate the **HVAC** view and then use the wheel mouse button to zoom closer to the HVAC objects.

3. Close the **Views** window.

   Next, you will measure the length of the top horizontal beam in this view.

4. From the toolbar on the left, click **Measure**; the **Measure** window is displayed.

   Using this window, you can measure distances, angles, and areas. The **Clear** button is used to clear the measurement from the graphics window. However, similar to Autodesk Navisworks, you can also right-click to clear the measurements.

5. Click the **Point to Point** tool; the cursor changes to crosshairs.

6. Move the cursor over the top left corner of the horizontal beam.

   You will notice that similar to Autodesk Navisworks, BIM 360 Glue also allows you to pick faces or vertices while measuring objects.

7. Click to select the first point when the cross is displayed.

8. Hover the cursor over various objects and notice how the distance value is dynamically changed in the graphics window.

9. Move the cursor over the top right corner of the horizontal beam. When the cross is displayed, click to select this point.

   Figure 14 shows the length of the beam measured using the two points.

10. Right-click to clear the measured distance value from the graphics window.

11. Similarly, use the **Angle** and **Area** tools to measure these values.

Figure 14 *Measuring distance between two points*

 Note: *Refer to Chapter 3 of this textbook to learn in detail about various measurement tools.*

12. Click the **Clear** button in the **Measure** window to clear all the measurements.

13. Close the **Measure** window.

Next, you will add a markup in the current view.

14. From the toolbar on the left, click **Markups**; the **Markups** window is displayed.

15. In the **Markups** window, click **Add**; the **Markup** toolbar is displayed on top of the graphics window.

16. From the **Select color** flyout in the **Markup** toolbar, change the color to **Red**.

17. Using the **Circle** tool, drag two opposite corners to draw an ellipse around the object, as shown in Figure 15.

18. Click the **Text** tool and then click below the ellipse as the start point of the text, refer to Figure 15.

19. In the **Enter Redline Text** window, type the following text and then press ENTER:

Do we need support here?

Figure 15 *Adding markup to the objects in the view*

20. Click **Save** in the **Markup** toolbar; the markup is saved and is listed in the **Markups** window. Figure 15 shows the view with this markup.

21. Press and hold down the wheel mouse button and pan the view to the level below the current view, refer to Figure 16.

    You will now add another markup in this view. Note that similar to Autodesk Navisworks, you do not need to first save a view to create redline markups in Autodesk BIM 360 Glue.

22. In the **Markups** window, click **Add**; the **Markup** toolbar is displayed on top of the graphics window.

23. From the **Select color** flyout in the **Markup** toolbar, change the color to **Red**.

24. Using the **Freehand** tool, draw a freehand object, as shown in Figure 16.

25. Click the **Text** tool and then click below the ellipse as the start point of the text, refer to Figure 16.

26. In the **Enter Redline Text** window, type the following text and then press ENTER:

    The lighting fixtures need to be based on LOD 300

27. Click **Save** in the **Markup** toolbar; the markup is saved and is listed in the **Markups** window. Figure 16 shows the view with the markup and Figure 17 shows the **Markups** window with the two markups.

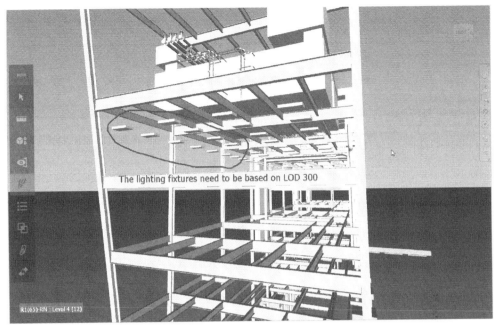

Figure 16 Adding markup for the lighting fixtures

*Figure 17 The **Markups** window showing the two markups*

Next, you will notify your team members about these two markups.

28. Select the two markups in the **Markups** window.

29. Click the **Notify** button (letter icon) from the toolbar available at the top in the **Markups** window; the **Notify Project Members** window is displayed.

30. Select the team members you want to notify.

 Note: *If you want, you can select me (Deepak Maini) to be notified. However, depending on your geographical location and the time zone, I may not have accepted the invitation to this project that was sent to me in Section 2.*

31. In the **Message** area, type a relevant message and then click **Send**; all the selected team members will be sent a notification email.

    When the team members get the notification email, they will be able to click on the link in the email to access this project and the markups you notified them about, provided they have the Autodesk BIM 360 Glue access.

32. Once the notification is sent, the **Autodesk BIM 360 Glue** window is displayed informing you about it. Click **OK** in this window.

33. In the **Markups** window, click on **Markup 1**; the **HVAC** view is activated and the markup added to that view is displayed.

34. In the **Markups** window, click on **Markup 2**; the view is changed to display the second markup.

35. Close the **Markups** window.

 Tip: *At any point of time, you can click on any markup in the **Markups** window to directly go to the markup and its associated view, which is automatically saved with the markup.*

Section 11: Adding Attachments to the Objects in the Model

In this section, you will add attachments to the objects in the model. This is similar to adding links to the objects in Autodesk Navisworks. Before adding the attachments, you will zoom in a little to turn off the visibility of markup from the graphics window.

1. Using the wheel mouse button, scroll forward to zoom closer to the lighting fixtures; the visibility of the markup is turned off.

2. Activate the **Selection** tool from the toolbar on the left and then select the first lighting fixture on the left of the view.

3. Hold down the CTRL key and select the next three lighting fixtures on the left.

4. Right-click anywhere in the graphics window and from the shortcut menu, select **Add attachment > Add link**; the **Autodesk BIM 360 Glue** window is displayed.

5. Type the following Web site address in the **Link** box:

    http://www.westinghouselighting.com/light-fixtures/

6. Click **Add Link**; the window is closed.

Once the link is added, you will be informed that the upload was successful.

7. Click **OK** in the message window.

8. Press ESC to deselect everything.

Next, you will view all the attachments in this model.

9. From the toolbar on the left, click **Attachments**; the **Attachments** window is displayed with four **Electrical** items listed in the **Object** column, as shown in Figure 18. These are the four lighting fixtures that you selected to add attachments.

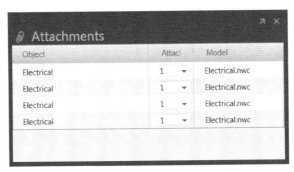

*Figure 18 The **Attachments** window*

10. Drag the **Attachments** window to the right so you can see the four lighting fixtures that were selected to add attachments.

11. Click on the first **Electrical** item in the **Object** column; the **Object Attachments** window is displayed and the first lighting fixture is highlighted in the graphics window.

12. Click on the Web site address in the **Object Attachments** window; the **Version** column shows that the address you added is version 1.

13. Under the **Version** column, click on **Version 1**.

14. Click the flyout available from the toolbar available at the top in the **Object Attachments** window and select **Open**; a new Web browser window will be opened with the Web site address you attached to the lighting fixtures.

15. Close the Web browser window to return to the **Autodesk BIM 360 Glue** window.

16. Close the **Object Attachments** window and then close the **Attachments** window.

17. Click in the blank area of the BIM 360 Glue window to deselect everything.

Section 12: Detecting Clashes Between Various Objects in the Model

Unlike Autodesk Navisworks, where the **Clash Detection** module is only available in Autodesk Navisworks Manage, in Autodesk BIM 360 Glue, all users are able to perform clashes. In this section, you will learn how to do this.

1. From the toolbar on the left, click **Views** and then activate the **Glue Overview** view from the **Views** window.

2. Close the **Views** window.

3. From the toolbar on the left, click **Clashes**; the **Clashes** window is displayed informing you that the clashes have not been analyzed in this model.

4. Click the **Find Clashes** button in the **Clashes** window; the **Clashes** window changes and now shows the **Compare** and **To** areas.

5. From the **Compare** area, select the tick box on the left of **HVAC**.

6. From the **To** area, select the tick boxes on the left of **Structure_Columns** and **Structure_Framing**.

7. In the **Tolerance** box, enter **0ft 0.04in** or **10mm**, depending on the units you are using.

8. In the **Name** box, enter **HVAC Vs Structure**.

9. Click **Find Clashes**; the clash detection process will start. Once the process ends, the **Clashes Overview** window will show that there are 34 clashes found and all of them are listed as open clashes.

10. Scroll down in the **Clashes Overview** window and notice that all the clashes are with the **Structure_Framing** model and there are no clashes with the **Structure_Columns** model.

    This is a good means to check how many clashes are there with each of the models you selected.

11. Close the **Clashes Overview** window.

    In the **Clashes** window, **Ungrouped (34)** is selected from the **Grouped By** list. This ensures that the clash results are not grouped together. Also, notice that the clashes are listed by their clash ID numbers with the last clash being listed at the top.

12. Click on the first clash listed in the **Clashes** window, which is clash **ID 34**; the view in the graphics window is modified to show the clashing items. Also, another window is displayed showing the two individual clashing items, as shown in Figure 19.

13. Similarly, click on other clash results and notice how the views change to show you the selected clash.

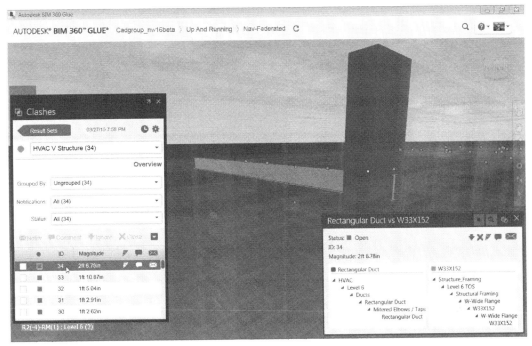

Figure 19 *Showing the clash ID 34 result in the graphics window and the* ***Clashes*** *window*

14. From the **Grouped By** list, select **HVAC > All Models (34)**. This groups various HVAC clashing objects together.

    Notice the first clash item in the **Clashes** window is listed as **Rectangular Duct** and the number in the first column is displayed as **5**. This informs you that this duct is involved in 5 clashes.

15. Click on the first **Rectangular Duct** group; the view in the graphics window changes to show you the 5 structural members clashing with the selected duct, as shown in Figure 20.

    Also, notice that the window on the right shows the rectangular duct and the 5 clashing structural members.

16. Similarly, click on the other clash groups and notice how the view changes to show all the objects involved in the selected clash group.

    Next, you will notify some of your team members about all the clashing ducts.

17. From the **Clashes** window, select all the **Rectangular Duct** clash groups.

18. Click the **Notify** button from the toolbar below the **Status** list; the **Notify Project Members** window is displayed.

19. Select the team members you want to notify and then enter some relevant comment.

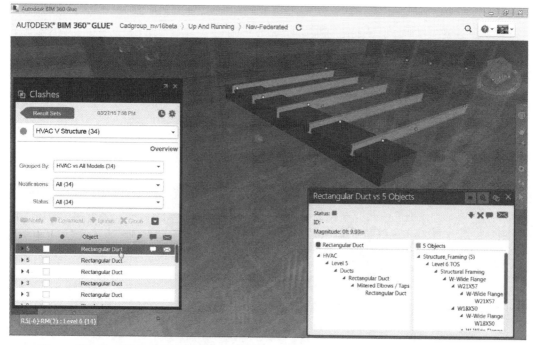

Figure 20 Graphics window showing 5 structural members clashing with the selected duct

20. Click the **Send** button; the notification is sent and you are informed about it in the window.

21. Close the notification window.

22. From the **Clashes** window, click **Result Sets**; the clash visibility is turned off and the model goes back to the normal visibility in the graphics window.

    The **Clashes** window in the current display informs you about the total number of active, open, ignored, closed, and resolved clashes.

 *Tip: You can use the **New** button in the **Clashes** window to perform a new clash test between other groups of items in the model.*

23. Close the **Clashes** window.

24. Using the **Views** window, activate the **Glue Overview** view.

Section 13: Reviewing the Activities of the Model

One of the main advantages of using Autodesk BIM 360 Glue is that you can track the activities that were performed on the selected model. In this section, you will learn how to do this.

1. From the toolbar on the left, click **Activities**; the **Activities** window is displayed, as shown in Figure 21.

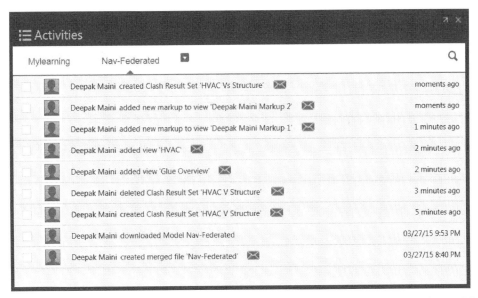

Figure 21 *The* *Activities* *window showing various activities performed on the current model*

2. Scroll through various activities of the model.

3. Close the **Activities** window.

Section 14: Creating Merged Models using BIM 360 Glue

In the previous sections, you learned how to create a federated model from Autodesk Navisworks and then save it on BIM 360 Glue. In this section, you will learn how to create a merged model using the models that you uploaded to your Autodesk BIM 360 Glue project. This workflow is used by the consultants who do not have access to Autodesk Navisworks. Those consultants can directly upload their models on BIM 360 Glue and then create a merged model for coordination and clash detection.

1. From the top bar in the Autodesk BIM 360 Glue window, click **Mylearning**, as shown in the ellipse in Figure 22; you are returned to the activities page of this project.

2. From the right side in the **Merged Models** area, click **New merged model**; the **Create new merged model** window is displayed.

3. From the **Models > Glue-Trial** area, select all the models.

*Figure 22 Returning to the **MyLearning** project activities page*

4.   In the **Name** box, enter **Glue-Merge**, as shown in Figure 23.

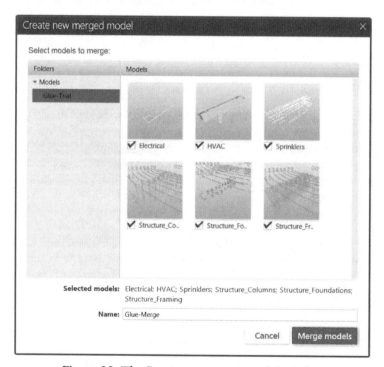

*Figure 23 The **Create new merge model** window*

5.   Click **Merge models**; the process of merging all the models will start.

Once all the files are merged, the merged model will be displayed in the Autodesk BIM 360 Glue window.

6. Hold down the SHIFT key and the wheel mouse button and orbit the model so that it appears as shown in Figure 24.

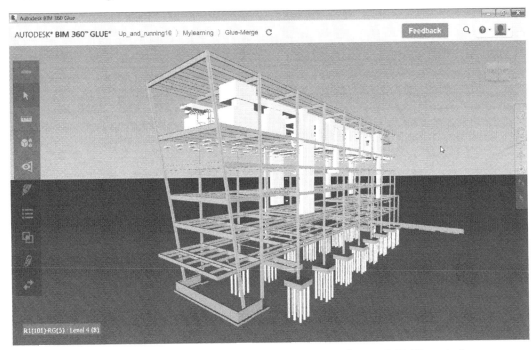

Figure 24 The merged model displayed in the Autodesk BIM 360 Glue window

 Note: *Because you turned off the grid display in Section 7, they will not be displayed in the merged model that you created. If you want to turn on the grids display, refer to Section 7 on how to do that.*

You will now notify all your team members about the merged model that you have created.

7. From the toolbar on the left, click **Activities**; the **Activities** window is displayed.

This window shows an activity that you created a merged model.

8. Click on the **Notify** icon on the right of the activity; the **Notify Project Members** window is displayed.

9. Select the team members you want to notify about the merged models.

 Note: *This is where you select all the contractors and subcontractors that uploaded their individual models and notify them about the merged model that you have created. As a result, everyone from here on will work on the same collaborated model and only exchange notifications about the activities rather than exchanging large size files.*

10. Click **Send** to send the notification to selected team members and then click **OK** in the notification message box.

11. Close the **Activities** window.

12. From the top of the Autodesk BIM 360 Glue window, click **Mylearning** to return to the project page.

Section 15: Opening the Glue-Merged Model in Autodesk Navisworks

In the previous sections, you learned how to create a federated model using the files uploaded on BIM 360 Glue. In this section, you will learn how to use Autodesk Navisworks to open the merged model created in BIM 360 Glue. This is generally done to perform advanced clash tests, such as clearance test or duplicate test. You can also use this model to perform 5D construction simulation. This integrated workflow allows you to work on a model in Autodesk Navisworks that is live streamed from BIM 360 Glue. As a result, when you save the model after making any changes, it is saved back to BIM 360 Glue and not locally on your computer.

1. Minimize the Autodesk BIM 360 Glue window and return to the Autodesk Navisworks window.

2. In the Autodesk Navisworks window, click on the **BIM 360** tab, if it is not already active.

3. Click the **[...]** button on the right of the **Model** list; the **BIM 360** window is displayed, as shown in Figure 25.

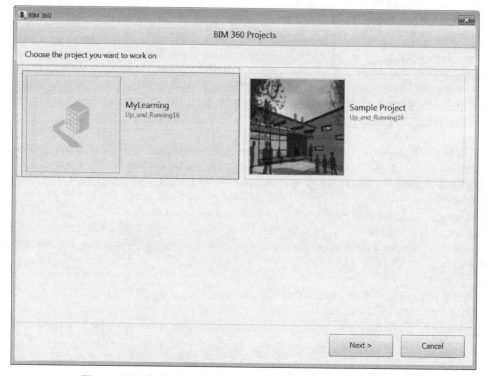

Figure 25 The Select Project window showing various projects

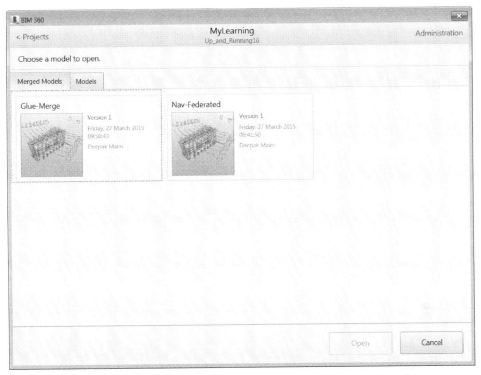

*Figure 26 The **Merged Models** tab displaying all the merged models*

4. Select **MyLearning** and then click **Next**; the **Choose model to open** page is displayed in the **BIM 360** window with the **Merged Models** tab active, as shown in Figure 26. The two merged models created using Autodesk Navisworks and BIM 360 Glue are listed here.

  ***Tip**: If you want to open or append the individual models, click on the **Models** tab; all the individual models will be listed in the window.*

5. Select the **Glue-Merge** model thumbnail and click **Open**; the process to download the model will start.

6. Change the view to Home and the background to horizon. Figure 27 shows the Autodesk Navisworks window with the model opened from the Autodesk BIM 360 Glue site.

    Notice that the files listed in the **Selection Tree** have no extension. Also, notice that the Autodesk Navisworks window titlebar shows the name of the file as **Glue-Merge**. This is because you are working with the model that is live-streamed from BIM 360 Glue. After making changes, if you save this file, it will be saved on BIM 360 Glue. To save this file locally, you can use the **Save As** tool or **Publish** tool.

7. Start a new file in Autodesk Navisworks without saving changes to the current file.

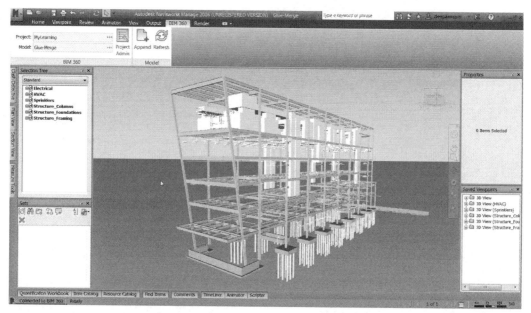

Figure 27 *The Autodesk Navisworks window showing the model opened from the Autodesk BIM 360 Glue*

Section 16: Accessing Autodesk BIM 360 Glue from iPad

As mentioned at the start of this chapter, one of the main advantages of using Autodesk BIM 360 Glue is accessing your BIM data anytime any where. This is because similar to accessing the models from the Autodesk BIM 360 Glue desktop application, you can also access these models and review them using the Autodesk BIM 360 Glue iPad app. You can review the designs by adding markups and measuring distances using this app as well. This section explains how you can download this app and then open the model from the Autodesk BIM 360 Glue project.

1. From the iTunes App Store, download and install the Autodesk BIM 360 Glue app.

2. Start this app and sign in using the Autodesk BIM 360 Glue trial credentials.

    Once you sign in, the **Up_and_Running16XX** site is displayed with the two projects.

3. Tap the **MyLearning** project; your project page is displayed with the merged model.

 Tip: The cloud icon on the top left of the model thumbnail shows that this model has not been downloaded from the cloud. You can tap the cloud icon to download the model and save it in the memory of the iPad.

4. From the top left corner of the projects page, tap the **Models** icon > **Glue-Trial**; all the models are listed, as shown in Figure 28.

    You can click on any model from this area to open and review it. However, in this tutorial, you will open the merged model.

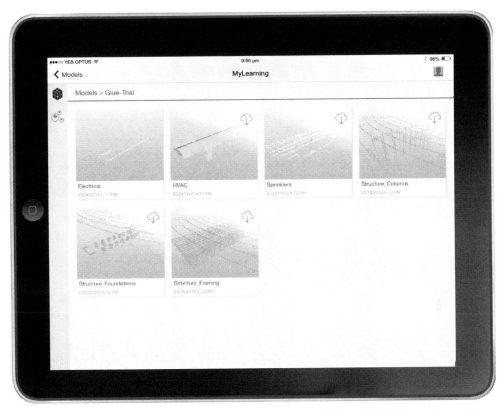

Figure 28 *The **Models** area showing various models available in the **MyLearning** project*

5. From the top left of the projects page, tap the **Merged Models** icon; the **Glue-Merge** and **Nav-Federated** models are listed.

   Because none of these models are currently downloaded, cloud icons are displayed on the top right of the thumbnails of these models.

6. Tap the **Nav-Federated** model; the model is opened in the Autodesk BIM 360 Glue iPad app and looks similar to the one shown in Figure 29.

7. Press and drag one finger on the iPad screen to orbit the model.

8. Press and drag two fingers on the iPad screen to pan the model.

9. Pinch two fingers on the iPad to zoom in or out of the model.

 Tip: Pressing and dragging three fingers lets you undo the last action.

To restore the default start view, tap the Home icon.

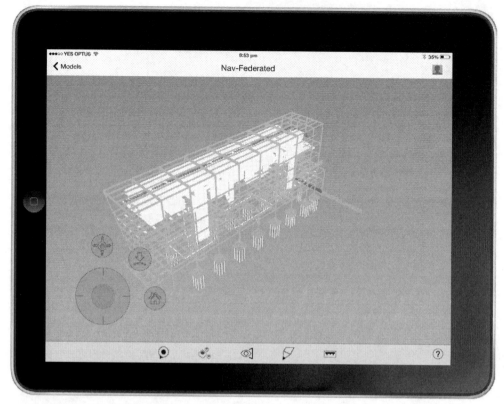

Figure 29 The merged model opened in the Autodesk BIM 360 Glue iPad app

Section 17: Adding Markups using the iPad App

In this section, you will learn to create markups on the model opened in the iPad app and notify your team members about it.

1. Tap the pencil icon on the toolbar at the bottom of the iPad screen to display the **Markups** panel.

    Notice the two markups added using the Autodesk BIM 360 Glue desktop application.

2. Using the one finger orbit or two finger pan and zoom, display the view similar to the one shown in Figure 30.

3. Tap the **Add Markup** icon on the top right of this panel; the markup tools are displayed on the toolbar at the bottom of the iPad screen.

 Note: *While adding markups using the iPad app, you only have the option of drawing freehand objects and writing text.*

4. Tap the color icon and change the color to Red.

5. Tap the **Freehand** tool and draw a freehand circle around the foundation object, as shown in Figure 30.

6. Tap the **Text** tool and tap anywhere close to the freehand circle you drew earlier; the text box is displayed at the top of the screen.

7. Type the following text:

   iPad markup for review only

8. Tap **Done** on the keypad; the text is added next to the freehand circle you drew earlier.

9. Tap **Save** from the top right of the iPad screen; the markup is saved and is listed in the **Markups** panel, as shown in Figure 30.

Figure 30 Markup added using the iPad app

Next, you will notify your team members about this markup.

10. From the top right corner of the **Markups** panel, tap **Notify**; the markup you added recently is automatically selected.

11. Tap **Notify** from the top right corner of the **Markups** panel again; the **Notify** window is displayed.

12. Tap on the **+** icon on the right of the **To** box; all the project members added to your project are listed.

13. Select the project members to notify and then tap on the **To** box; the selected team members are listed in this box.

14. Tap in the message box and type some message.

15. Tap **Send** from the top right of the **Notify** window to send the notification.

16. Similarly, you can continue adding more markups and notify your team members about them.

17. Tap the pencil icon on the toolbar at the bottom of the iPad screen to hide the **Markups** panel.

Section 18: Measuring Distances using the iPad App

In this section, you will learn to measure distances on the model opened in the iPad app. In this app, there are two tools available to measure distances. **Point to Point** and **Shortest Distance**. Both these tools are discussed in this section.

1. Using the one finger orbit or two finger pan and zoom, display the view similar to the one shown in Figure 31.

2. Tap the **Measure** icon, which looks like a ruler, on the toolbar at the bottom of the iPad screen to display the two measurement tools.

    By default, the **Point to Point** tool is active and you are prompted to tap and drag to position the first measurement point. This prompt sequence is displayed at the top of the iPad screen. In the following steps, you will measure the height of the building.

    To help you select accurate points for measuring distances, the iPad app lets you tap and hold your finger to display the magnifying glass.

3. Tap and hold your finger down near the top right corner of the front right column of the building; the magnifying glass is displayed, as shown in Figure 31.

4. Using the magnifying glass, snap to the top right corner; the point is selected and you are prompted to tap and drag to position the second measurement point.

5. Using the pinch to zoom method, zoom out and then zoom into the lower end of the building.

6. Tap and hold your finger down near the bottom right corner, as shown in Figure 32; the magnifying glass is displayed.

Figure 31 *Displaying the magnifying glass to accurately select measurement points*

Figure 32 *Selecting the second measurement point using the magnifying glass*

7. Once you snap to the corner point, lift the finger; the measurement is displayed on the iPad screen, as shown in Figure 33.

Next, you will measure the shortest distance between two objects.

8. Tap the **Shortest Distance** icon, which looks like two boxes, from the toolbar at the bottom of the iPad screen; you are prompted to select the first object.

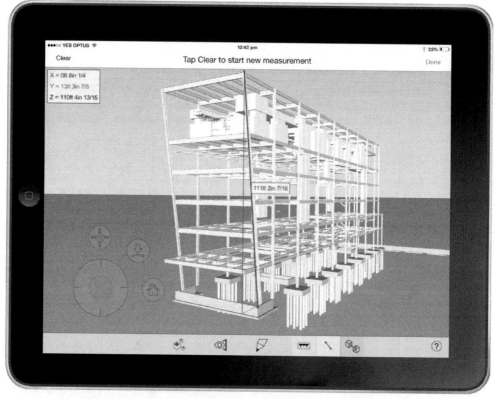

Figure 33 *The measurement values displayed on the iPad screen*

9. Tap on the front left column at the top of the model; you are prompted to select the second object.

10. Tap on the front right column at the top of the model; the view zooms to show you the two selected objects and the shortest distance between those two objects. Also, most other objects in the model are temporarily turned off, as shown in Figure 34.

11. From the top left of the iPad screen, tap **Clear**; the measurement is cleared from the screen and the original visibility of the objects is restored.

12. From the top right of the iPad screen, tap **Done**; the measurement tools are no more active.

Section 19: Working with the Action Menu

The **Action** menu is displayed every time you tap on an object in the model, refer to Figure 35. In this section, you will learn to use the three tools available in this menu.

1. Tap any object in the model; the **Action** menu is displayed, as shown in Figure 35.

    This menu has three tools (from left to right): **Isolate**, **Hide**, and **Properties**.

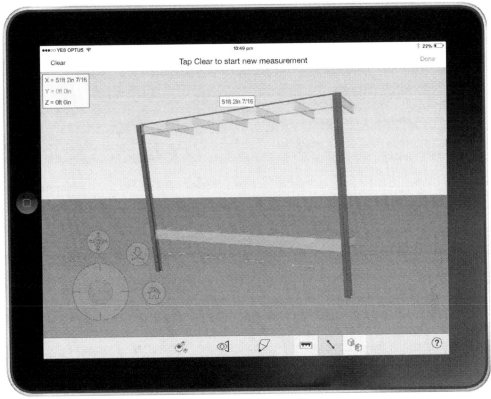

Figure 34 The shortest distance measurement value displayed on the iPad screen

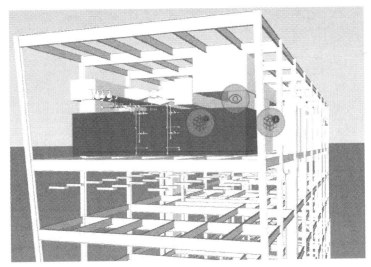

Figure 35 The **Action** menu displayed on tapping an object in the model

2. Tap the **Isolate** tool, which is the first tool on the left; the selected object is magnified and displayed to the extents of the iPad screen. Also, the visibility of other objects is either turned off or they are made transparent.

3. Tap the same object again to display the **Action** menu and tap the **Isolate** tool again to turn off the isolation of the object.

4. Tap any other object to display the **Action** menu.

5. Tap the **Hide** tool, which is the icon at the center; the selected object is turned off.

   Once you hide an object, you will have to use the **Models** tool from the toolbar at the bottom of the iPad screen to turn on the visibility of the hidden object.

6. From the toolbar at the bottom of the iPad screen, tap the **Models** tool, which is the second button on the left; the model selection tree is displayed in the **Models** panel.

   The object that is hidden will have its **Show/Hide** icon displayed in White on the right. Also, the **Show/Hide** icon of the model will be displayed in White.

7. Tap the **Show/Hide** icon of the model on the top right of the **Models** panel; the visibility of all the objects in the scene is restored.

8. Tap the **Models** button from the toolbar at the bottom of the iPad screen to turn off the **Models** panel.

9. Tap any object in the model to display the **Action** menu.

10. Tap the **Properties** tool; the **Properties** panel is displayed with all the properties of the selected object, as shown in Figure 36.

11. Scroll through the various properties of the selected object in the **Properties** panel.

12. Tap the blank area of the iPad screen to turn off the **Properties** panel.

Section 20: Using the Map Tool

One of the recent enhancements in the BIM 360 Glue iPad app is the **Map** tool, which is the first button on the toolbar at the bottom of the iPad screen. This tool allows you to select the level of the building and then place the camera anywhere on that level so that you are navigated to that location in the 3D model. In this section, you will learn to use this tool.

 *Note: The **Map** tool is only available for the models created from Autodesk Revit Files. For other models, this tool will not be displayed in the toolbar.*

1. Tap the **Map** button, which is the first button on the toolbar at the bottom; the view changes to the plan view.

*Figure 36 The **Properties** panel displaying the properties of the selected object*

In this plan view, you will notice that the levels are turned on. Also, at the bottom of the screen, the **Level** list is displayed showing you the level from which you are currently looking.

2. Pinch two fingers on the iPad to display the view similar to Figure 37.

3. Tap the **Level** list at the bottom of the screen and select **Level 4**.

Next, you need to drag the map selector to the area you want to navigate to in the 3D model.

 Note: *If the map selector is not displayed, you may need to pinch two fingers to zoom out of the view.*

4. Tap and drag the map selector, which is displayed as the Orange circle, to a location similar to the one shown in Figure 37.

5. Next, tap and drag the arrow on the map selector and point it towards the direction you want to look at, refer to Figure 37.

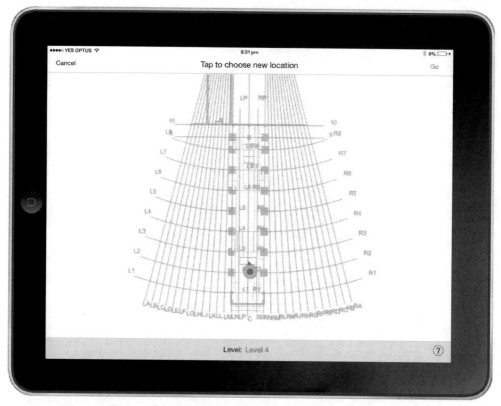

Figure 37 *The plan view displayed using the* **Map** *tool*

6. From the top right corner of the iPad screen, tap **Go**; you are navigated to the selected area on level 4 of the building, as shown in Figure 38.

 Tip: *Instead of tapping* **Go**, *you can also tap and hold down on the map selector to be navigated to that area in the 3D model.*

7. Tap the **Map** tool again to return to the plan view.

8. From the **Level** list, select **Level 1** and then tap **Go**; you are navigated to the same location on level 1 now.

    Similarly, you can tap any level in the plan view to navigate to that level in the 3D model.

    This is the end of this section. Notice that there is no save tool on the iPad app. This is because all the actions performed on the iPad app are automatically saved.

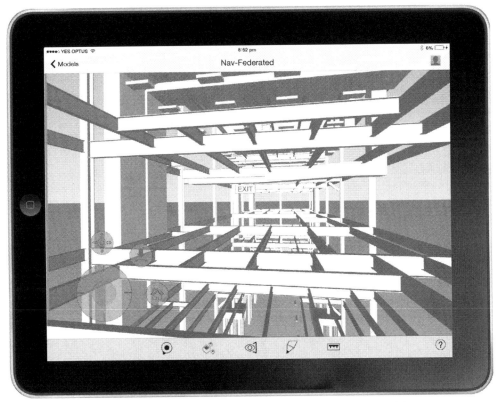

Figure 38 *Navigating to the selected view in the 3D model*

Section 21: Opening the Reviewed Model Using the BIM 360 Glue Desktop Application

In this section, you will open the model (that you reviewed on your iPad) using the desktop application. Because it is the same model that you accessed on the iPad app from BIM 360 Glue, the markups that you added using the iPad app will also be available when you open it using the desktop application.

1. Return to the Autodesk BIM 360 Glue desktop application.

2. Open the **Nav-Federated** model from the **MyLearning** project.

3. Once the model is opened, click **Markups** from the toolbar on the left; the **Markups** window is displayed with a markup.

4. Click on the markup listed in the **Markups** window; the view changes and the markup added using the iPad app is now shown in the graphics window, as shown in Figure 39.

5. Close the Autodesk BIM 360 Glue window.

Figure 39 *The markup added using the iPad app listed in the desktop application*

Index

Answers to Skill Evaluation

Chapter 1
1. F
2. F
3. T
4. T
5. T
6. (C) Autodesk Navisworks Preview
7. (A) NWB
8. (B) Full Orbit
9. (A) Publish
10. (B) 15 minutes

Chapter 2
1. F
2. F
3. T
4. T
5. T
6. (B) Object Set, (D) Transformation Set
7. (A) Quick Properties
8. (B) All Search Sets
9. (B) Item Type, (D) Item Name
10. (A) Find Items

Chapter 3
1. F
2. T
3. F
4. T
5. T
6. (D) Point to Multiple Points
7. (B) Record
8. (A) Convert To Redline
9. (A) Collision
10. (C) CTRL + T

Chapter 4
1. F
2. F
3. T
4. F
5. F
6. (C) Add Tag
7. (A) Find Comments

8. (B) Arrow
9. (D) Fit Selection
10. (C) Link Section Plane

Chapter 5
1. F
2. F
3. T
4. F
5. T
6. (A) File Options
7. (D) F11
8. (C) Both
9. (A) Compare
10. (B) Label, Hyperlink

Chapter 6
1. F
2. F
3. T
4. T
5. T
6. (A) Ambient
7. (B) Pause
8. (A) Ray Trace
9. (B) Web
10. (D) Rules

Chapter 7
1. T
2. T
3. F
4. T
5. T
6. (D) Scripter
7. (A) Ping-Pong
8. (C) On Hotspot
9. (A) 100
10. (B) On Collision

Chapter 8

1. F
2. T
3. T
4. T
5. T
6. (C) Auto-Add Tasks > For Every Set
7. (D) Transportation cost
8. (C) Both
9. (D) Data Sources
10. (D) Moving

Chapter 9

1. F
2. T
3. T
4. T
5. F
6. (D) Quantification Workbook
7. (C) XML
8. (B) 3D, 2D, and Virtual Takeoffs
9. (A) Project Setup
10. (D) XLSX

Chapter 10

1. T
2. F
3. T
4. F
5. T
6. (B) NWLOAD
7. (B) Nothing, just start it
8. (A) Microsoft Word
9. (D) Clash Detective
10. (C) Clearance

APPENDIX

ADD-INS FOR BIM DATA COORDINATION

There are a number of third-party add-ins available for BIM Data Coordination. However, I have picked two add-ins that I find really useful while working with Autodesk Navisworks. These two add-ins are discussed in this appendix.

Disclaimer: The two add-ins discussed in this appendix are not developed by me and I am not involved in the sales/support of any of these add-ins. I do not, in any shape or form, benefit from the sales of these add-ins. For any sales/support related information, please contact the related companies directly. Also, I do not take any responsibility of the working of these add-ins. Please make careful considerations before using these add-ins in your work.

iConstruct™ for Autodesk Navisworks

http://www.iconstruct.com

Contact: Shawn Weir (sales@iconstruct.com)

iConstruct™ software is a powerful information management tool that enables the vast array of information stored in the latest generation of BIM models to be extracted, organized, and used in an efficient and logical way. This program was developed in response to the industry requirement to deliver models from different sources to their clients in a consistent, unified format and with access to the documentation and status of items directly from Navisworks™.

There are 4 broad areas that iConstruct™ covers:

- Efficient Clash Management capability that allows the user to easily filter, group and manage their Clash Data
- Model format unification tools such as ReConstruct™ and Integrator™ whereby models imported from various sources can be made to have a consistent model hierarchy and property set
- Functional tools such as reporting, color coding, centre of gravity, automated marked-up views
- Export tools such as export to DWG and IFC

Some key tools of iConstruct™ are discussed below.

Clash Manager™

Clash Manager™ leverages the data generated by Autodesk Navisworks Clash Detective to allow end users to easily filter, group, and manage their Clash data. Some of the key features of Clash Manager™ are:

- Group clashes by any property, such as grid level, item type, description, and so on
- View any property associated with clashing items in a datagrid view
- Filter clashes by any property
- Push the groups back into Clash Detective window

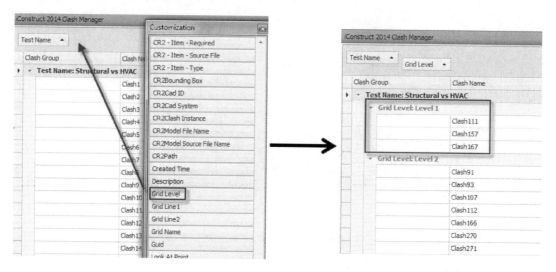

ReConstruct™

ReConstruct™ is a powerful tool that allows the Autodesk Navisworks users to take control of their model hierarchy, optimizing the model, and making it more intuitive for use. It works by extracting all the model geometry with their associated properties and exporting a new NWD file layered and grouped by the model's properties. For example, the Autodesk Revit models can be reorganized layering by category and grouping by family.

ReConstruct™ also introduces options such as hiding data tabs or stripping off the unrequired properties. It can also be configured to export just a crop of a Navisworks model, which is very useful when using models on tablet PCs.

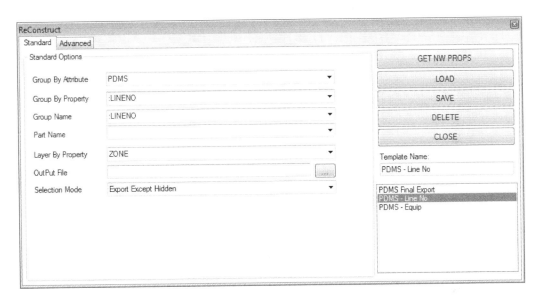

BIMFlow™

This tool uses the intuitive workflow designer that allows for powerful automation of many of iConstruct's modules as well as Navisworks own features. The user can combine various tools to create single-click macros or model conversion templates. Some users harness this power to convert hundreds of models overnight from native format to a federated NWD. The latest release also introduces ReviewTRACK™, a cloud-based model review tool compliant with the open BCF (BIM Collaboration Format).

RTV Xporter PRO for Autodesk Revit
by RTV Tools Limited
http://www.rtvtools.com/rtv-xporter-pro/
Contact: Jason Howden, CEO, RTV Tools Limited (jason@rtvtools.com)
Download a free 30 day trial today from http://www.rtvtools.com/30-day-free-trial/

RTV Xporter PRO software plug-in for Autodesk® Revit® is a powerful and revolutionary tool that enables the batch processing and time-based Scheduling of Autodesk Navisworks NWC files to execute in a fully autonomous mode. The software was developed in response to the increasing demand for BIM file collaboration where BIM managers, consultants, contractors and owners are needing to publish and share their work on daily, weekly and monthly intervals. The RTV Xporter PRO provides a tool where the creation of Navisworks® NWC files can be completed by computers without the need for direct interaction of staff, allowing them to focus on more important tasks.

There are 4 key areas of automation that RTV Xporter PRO provides:

- Digital File creation (PDF, NWC, IFC, FBX, DWG/DXF, DGN, DWF/DWFx, RVZ) with automatic file naming.

- 3D "Export" View creation, including split by levels.

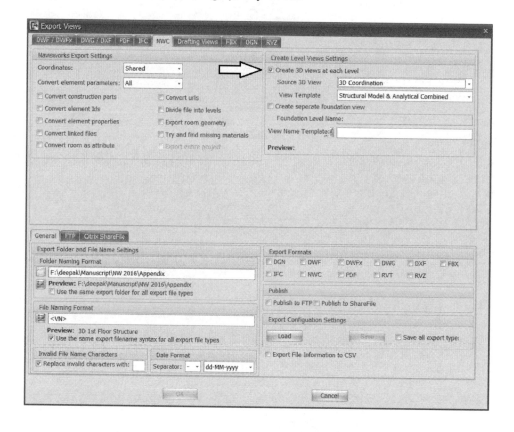

- Uploading and publishing to FTP and Citrix Sharefile sites.

- Scheduled and Batch Task processing, including on a Remote "batch processing" Server.

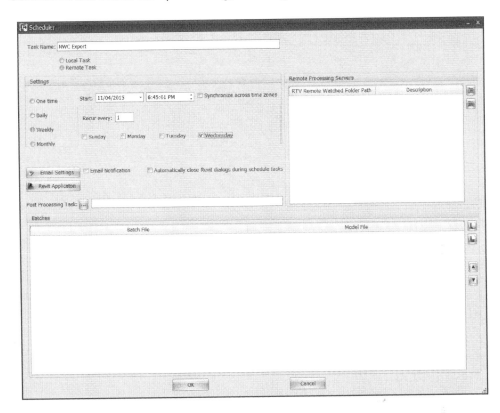

Made in the USA
San Bernardino, CA
22 June 2016